The Evolution of Modern Metaphysics
Making Sense of Things

This book is concerned with the history of metaphysics since Descartes. Taking as its definition of metaphysics 'the most general attempt to make sense of things', it charts the evolution of this enterprise through various competing conceptions of its possibility, scope, and limits. The book is divided into three parts, dealing respectively with the early modern period, the late modern period in the analytic tradition, and the late modern period in various non-analytic traditions. In its unusually wide range, A. W. Moore's study refutes the still prevalent cliché that there is some unbridgeable gulf between analytic philosophy and philosophy of other kinds. It also advances its own distinctive and compelling conception of what metaphysics is and why it matters. Moore explores how metaphysics can help us to cope with continually changing demands on our humanity by making sense of things in ways that are radically new.

A. W. Moore is a Professor of Philosophy at the University of Oxford and Tutorial Fellow of St Hugh's College, Oxford. He is the author of three previous books: *The Infinite* (1990); *Points of View* (1997); and *Noble in Reason, Infinite in Faculty: Themes and Variations in Kant's Moral and Religious Philosophy* (2003). He is also the editor or co-editor of several anthologies, and his articles and reviews have appeared in numerous other scholarly publications.

THE EVOLUTION OF MODERN PHILOSOPHY

General Editors
Paul Guyer and Gary Hatfield (University of Pennsylvania)

Published Books in the Series
Roberto Torretti: *The Philosophy of Physics*
David Depew and Marjorie Greene: *The Philosophy of Biology*
Charles Taliaferro: *Evidence and Faith*
Michael Losonsky: *Linguistic Turns in Modern Philosophy*
W. D. Hart: *The Evolution of Logic*

Forthcoming
Paul Guyer: *Aesthetics*
Stephen Darwall: *Ethics*
William Ewald and Michael J. Hallett: *The Philosophy
of Mathematics*

Why has philosophy evolved in the way that it has? How have its subdisciplines developed, and what impact has this development exerted on the way that the subject is now practiced? Each volume of *The Evolution of Modern Philosophy* will focus on a particular subdiscipline of philosophy and examine how it has evolved into the subject as we now understand it. The volumes will be written from the perspective of a current practitioner in contemporary philosophy whose point of departure will be the question: How did we get from there to here? Cumulatively, the series will constitute a library of modern conceptions of philosophy and will reveal how philosophy does not in fact comprise a set of timeless questions but has rather been shaped by broader intellectual and scientific developments to produce particular fields of inquiry addressing particular issues.

The Evolution of Modern Metaphysics
Making Sense of Things

A. W. MOORE

University of Oxford

CAMBRIDGE
UNIVERSITY PRESS

CAMBRIDGE UNIVERSITY PRESS
Cambridge, New York, Melbourne, Madrid, Cape Town,
Singapore, São Paulo, Delhi, Tokyo, Mexico City

Cambridge University Press
32 Avenue of the Americas, New York, NY 10013-2473, USA

www.cambridge.org
Information on this title: www.cambridge.org/9780521851114

First published 2012

Printed in the United States of America

A catalog record for this publication is available from the British Library.

Library of Congress Cataloging in Publication data
Moore, A. W., 1956–
The evolution of modern metaphysics : making sense
of things / A.W. Moore
p.   cm. – (The evolution of modern philosophy)
Includes bibliographical references and index.
ISBN 978-0-521-85111-4 (hardback) – ISBN 978-0-521-61655-3 (pbk.)
1. Metaphysics – History. 2. Philosophy, Modern. I. Title.
BD111.M66 2011
110.9′03 – dc23   2011023535

ISBN 978-0-521-85111-4 Hardback

In memory of Bernard Williams
(1929–2003)

'William! you've been playing that dreadful game again,' said Mrs Brown despairingly.

William, his suit covered with dust, his tie under one ear, his face begrimed and his knees cut, looked at her in righteous indignation.

'I haven't. I haven't done anything what you said I'd not to. It was "Lions an' Tamers" what you said I'd not to play. Well, I've not played "Lions an' Tamers", not since you said I'd not to. I wouldn't *do* it – not if thousands of people asked me to, not when you said I'd not to. I –'

Mrs Brown interrupted him.

'Well, what *have* you been playing at?' she said wearily.

'It was "Tigers an' Tamers",' said William. 'It's a different game altogether. In "Lions an' Tamers" half of you is lions an' the other half tamers, and the tamers try to tame the lions an' the lions try not to be tamed. That's "Lions an' Tamers". It's all there is to it. It's quite a little game.'

'What do you do in "Tigers and Tamers"?' said Mrs Brown suspiciously.

'Well –'

William considered deeply.

'Well,' he repeated lamely, 'in "*Tigers* an' Tamers" half of you is *tigers* – you see – and the other half –'

'It's exactly the same thing, William,' said Mrs Brown with sudden spirit.

'I don't see how you can call it the same thing,' said William doggedly. 'You can't call a *lion* a *tiger*, can you? It jus' isn't one. They're in quite different cages in the Zoo. "*Tigers* an' Tamers" can't be 'zactly the same as "*Lions* an' Tamers".'

'Well, then,' said Mrs Brown firmly, 'you're never to play "Tigers and Tamers" either...'

(Richmal Crompton, *Just William*, pp. 134–135)

Contents

Preface

The story is familiar, even if it is not true. Some 250 years after the death of Aristotle, Andronicus of Rhodes produced the first complete edition of Aristotle's works. One volume, dealing with nature, was called *Physics*. Immediately after that Andronicus placed a volume of works which became known as '*ta meta ta physica*': the ones after the ones about physics. And so the corresponding discipline acquired its name.

Whether or not the story is true, the name is peculiarly apt. For '*meta*' can also be translated either as 'above' or as 'beyond', and metaphysics is often reckoned to lie at a level of generality above and beyond physics. Come to that, it is often reckoned to be a subject that should be studied 'after' physics.

Aristotle himself described what he was undertaking in that volume as 'first philosophy', or as the search for the first causes and the principles of things, or again as the science of being *qua* being (see, respectively: *Metaphysics*, Bk Γ, Ch. 2, 1004a 2–4; *Metaphysics*, Bk A, Ch. 1, 981b 28–29; and *Metaphysics*, Bk Γ, Ch. 1, 1003a 21). These descriptions variously indicate both the fundamental character of his undertaking and its abstractness. In its approach, the volume was a miscellany. It comprised historical and methodological reflections, a survey of problems and aporiai to be addressed, and a philosophical lexicon, as well as direct treatment of its main topics, which included substance, essence, form, matter, individuality, universality, actuality, potentiality, change, unity, identity, difference, number, and the prime eternal unmoved mover (God).

Plato had earlier dealt with many of the same topics, sometimes at the same high level of abstraction. But he had perhaps shown greater sensitivity than Aristotle towards the relevance of these topics to practical considerations about how one should live. At the same time he had shown less confidence in the power of theory, or even in the power of writing, to convey what needed to be conveyed about them (see e.g. *Phaedrus*, 257ff.). Plato's approach to philosophy was very contextual and open-ended. He wrote in dialogue form, allowing his protagonists, notably Socrates, to respond directly to one another's particular concerns. He also allowed them to probe

xvii

ideas, to toy with them, and to tease out their consequences. For Plato, philosophy was more of an activity than a science. That seems to me an extremely important model for our own understanding of metaphysics.

This book belongs to a series entitled *The Evolution of Modern Philosophy*. The brief of each contributor is to chart the evolution of some branch of philosophy from the beginning of the modern era to the present, my own assignment being metaphysics. To keep the project manageable I shall concentrate on the views of a select group of philosophers whose contribution to this evolutionary history seems to me especially significant. And I shall be more concerned with their views *about* metaphysics than with their views *within* metaphysics – at least insofar as this is a sharp distinction, and insofar as their views about metaphysics can be taken to include views of theirs, perhaps within metaphysics, that have important consequences about metaphysics, or even commitments of theirs, manifest in their practices, that have such consequences. What follows is therefore a kind of history of *meta*-metaphysics.

It is a remarkable history. In particular it contains remarkable cycles. Periods of recession within metaphysics in the glare of hostility from elsewhere in philosophy have alternated with periods of spectacular growth, and these have been marked by striking repetitions. But there has been progress too. 'Evolution' is an apt word. Metaphors of fitness, progeny, and mutation can all be applied in the description of how we have got to where we now are.

What follows belongs, in the useful contrast that Bernard Williams draws in one of his own prefaces, to the history of philosophy rather than the history of ideas (Williams (1978), p. 9). In other words it is in the first instance philosophy, not history. This is reflected in the fact that it is organized by reference neither to periods nor to *milieux* but to individual philosophers, all of whom are reasonably familiar from the canon. I shall do little to challenge the canon. And I shall do little to challenge a relatively orthodox interpretation of each of my protagonists. If I make any distinctive contribution in what follows, then I take it to be a matter of the connections and patterns that I discern and the narrative I tell.

Two points are worth making in connection with this. First, in telling that narrative, I have tried to follow what I take to be a basic precept of the history of philosophy: always, when listening to what philosophers of the past are saying to us, to ask how we can appropriate it. This precept applies even when – perhaps especially when – we cannot hear what they are saying to us as a contribution to any contemporary debate. It signals one of the most important ways in which philosophy differs from science, whose history is always in the first instance history, not science. (I shall have more to say about this in the Conclusion.)

Second, in reflecting on the distinctive contribution that I may have made in what follows, I am very conscious of the fact that I am a philosophical generalist. I do not know whether it will sound hubristic to say this or apologetic, but it is true. To an extent it should sound apologetic. There are very few of my protagonists on whom I would claim to be even a moderate expert. In fact there are only three – or four if the early Wittgenstein and the later Wittgenstein count as two. (I am not going to be any more specific than that lest I give a hostage to fortune!) I am therefore beholden throughout to others. And I owe an apology to all those whose expertise I may have propagated without acknowledgement, or mangled, or worst of all ignored.

Still, whatever apologies may be consonant with my claim to be a generalist, I make no apology for the fact itself. I lament the increased tendency to specialism in philosophy. It is bad enough that there is an increased tendency to specialism in academia, whereby philosophy itself is pursued without due regard to other disciplines. But the narrowness of focus that we see nowadays within philosophy poses a threat to its being pursued at all, in any meaningfully integrated way. We of course need specialists. But – and here I echo Bertrand Russell, in the preface to his *History of Western Philosophy* (Russell (1961), p. 7) – we also need those who are concerned to make sense of the many kinds of sense that the specialists make.

Ought I to apologize, if not for adding a non-specialist book to the market, at any rate for adding a book to the market? It is a real question. As Michael Dummett observes, in yet another preface, 'Every learned book, every learned article, adds to the weight of things for others to read, and thereby reduces the chances of their reading other books or articles. Its publication is therefore not automatically justified by its having some merit: the merit must be great enough to outweigh the disservice done by its being published at all' (Dummett (1991a), p. x). There is huge pressure on academics nowadays to publish, which means that there is a correspondingly huge number of publications. People often complain that the result is a plethora of very poor work. I think the situation is far worse than that. I think the result is a plethora of very good work – work from which there is a great deal to learn, work which cannot comfortably be ignored although there is no prospect of anyone's attending to more than a tiny fraction of it, yet work which could have been distilled into a much smaller, uniformly better, and considerably more manageable bulk. I do therefore need to confront the question, as any author does, of what excuse I have for demanding my readers' attention.

I hope that there is some excuse in the generalism to which I have already referred. Here I should like to single out one particular aspect of this, which I have not yet mentioned. There would, I think, be justification in the publication of this book if it made a significant contribution to overcoming the absurd divisions that still exist between – to use the customary but equally absurd labels – 'analytic' philosophy and 'continental' philosophy. I do not deny that there are important differences between these. Nor do I have any scruples about the fact that I am myself an analytic philosopher. But I unequivocally distance myself from those of my colleagues who disdain all other traditions. The 'continental' philosophers whom I discuss in Part Three of this book are thinkers of great depth and power; they are knowledgeable about philosophy, science, politics, and the arts; their work is rigorous, imaginative, and creative; and it is often brutally honest. I despair of the arrogance that casts them in the role of charlatans. Perhaps, if I were asked to specify my greatest hope for this book, it would be that it should help to combat such narrow-mindedness. Or, if that seemed too vague a hope, then it would be that the book should help to introduce analytic philosophers to the work of one of the most exciting and extraordinary of these 'continental' philosophers: Gilles Deleuze.

I have many acknowledgements. First, I am deeply grateful to the Trustees of the Leverhulme Trust for awarding me a Major Research Fellowship for the academic years 2006–2009, during which I carried out the bulk of the work on this book. I am likewise grateful to the Principal and Fellows of St Hugh's College Oxford, and to the Humanities Divisional Board of the University of Oxford, for granting me special leave of absence for the same period. I am further grateful to the Principal and Fellows of St Hugh's, and to the Philosophy Faculty Board of the University of Oxford, for granting me additional leave of absence for the academic year 2009–2010, during which I finished writing the first draft of the book.

I am very grateful to Paul Guyer and Gary Hatfield for inviting me to write the book. Paul Guyer in particular has provided invaluable help and encouragement throughout the project, not least by supporting my application for a Leverhulme Major Research Fellowship. For similar support I thank David Bell and Alan Montefiore. And I am grateful to Stephanie Sakson for her excellent copyediting and for her additional advice.

Many other people have helped me with the writing of the book. Especial thanks are due to the following: Lilian Alweiss, Pamela Anderson, Anita Avramides, Corine Besson, Kathryn Bevis, Jenny Bunker, Nicholas Bunnin, John Callanan, John Cottingham, Paolo Crivelli, Susan Durber, Naomi Eilan, Sebastian Gardner, Simon Glendinning, Béatrice Han-Pile, Robert Jordan, Gary Kemp, Jane Kneller, Paul Lodge, Denis McManus, Joseph Melia, Peter Millican, Michael Morris, Stephen Mulhall, Sarah Richmond, Gonzalo Rodriguez-Pereyra, Mark Sacks (who died so tragically while I was still writing the book), Joseph Schear, Murray Shanahan, Andrew Stephenson, Robert Stern, Peter Sullivan, Alessandra Tanesini, Paul Trembath, Daniel Whistler, and Patricia Williams. My greatest debt is to Philip Turetzky. His friendship, advice, encouragement, and influence on my work have been inestimable. I especially thank him for directing me to the work of Deleuze. He read an early draft of the entire book and provided detailed critical comments, for which I am extremely grateful.

The influence of Bernard Williams on my thinking will doubtless be apparent even from this Preface. I owe an enormous amount to him. This book is dedicated to his memory.

A.W. Moore

Note on Unaccompanied References: All unaccompanied references in this book to chapters or sections (e.g. Ch. 5, §8) or to notes (e.g. n. 44) are cross-references to material elsewhere in the book. Any other unaccompanied references (e.g. pp. 208–214) are explained in the notes to the chapter in which they occur.

Introduction

1. The Definition of Metaphysics

Metaphysics is the most general attempt to make sense of things. This is my working definition, but I want to make clear from the outset how little, in certain critical respects, I claim on behalf of it. An ideal definition, one might think, would be at once crisp, substantive, and uncontroversial, as well as correct. In fact, of these, I claim only that my definition is crisp. I do not even say that it is 'correct'; not if that means that it is answerable to something other than my own purposes in writing this book. And to have tried to attain substance without controversy would have been foolhardy, because the nature of metaphysics is itself a fiercely contested philosophical issue – indeed, as I see it, a fiercely contested metaphysical issue.

What I aim to do with this definition, first and foremost, is to indicate what my theme is. At the same time I aim to establish early connections between concepts that will be crucial to my project, connections that are intended to elucidate the *definiens* as well as the *definiendum*, though they also commit me on certain matters of dispute as I shall try to explain in the course of this Introduction. I hope that my definition is broadly in accord with standard uses of the word 'metaphysics', at least insofar as these are broadly in accord with one another, and I hope that I am singling out something worthy of the attention that I shall be devoting to it in this book. But if I am wrong in the former hope, then I am prepared to defer to the latter and accept that my definition is revisionary; while if I am wrong in the latter hope, then the fault lies with the book, not with the definition.

How exactly, then, does this definition serve my purposes? What does it provide that is not provided by other pithy definitions of metaphysics that I might have appropriated, say

- the attempt 'to give a general description of the whole of the Universe'
- the attempt 'to describe the most general structural features of reality ... [by] pure reflection'
- the attempt 'to understand how things in the broadest possible sense of the term hang together in the broadest possible sense of the term'

1

- 'a search for the most plausible theory of the whole universe, as it is considered in the light of total science'
- 'the science of things set and held in thoughts ... [that are] able to express the essential reality of things'

or even

- 'the finding of bad reasons for what we believe upon instinct'?[1]

All three of the expressions 'most general, 'attempt', and 'make sense of things' do important work for me. This is as much for what they do not suggest as for what they do. I shall expand on each in turn. I shall also comment on some significant structural features of my definition.

2. 'The Most General ...'

'Most general', or some equivalent, is the expression that is most likely to be shared by any rival definition to mine. I have two observations about its occurrence in my definition that primarily concern what sort of generality is intended, two that are more structural.

The first observation concerning what sort of generality is intended is the obvious one. The generality of metaphysics is in large part the generality of the concepts that it trades in, concepts that subsume a wide range of other concepts and whose application is prevalent, however implicitly, in all our thinking. An unobvious way to appreciate this obvious point is to look at the main section headings of the first part of Roget's *Thesaurus*.[2] They are 'Existence', 'Relation', 'Quantity', 'Order', 'Number', 'Time', 'Change', and 'Causation'. That is almost a syllabus for a standard course in metaphysics.

The second observation concerning what sort of generality is intended, though less obvious, is no less important. Many people take metaphysics to be concerned with what is necessary rather than contingent, typically because they take it to be an *a priori* enterprise and they think that the *a priori* is concerned with what is necessary rather than contingent. Others are unsympathetic to the idea that there is any such necessary/contingent distinction, although this lack of sympathy does not translate into a lack of sympathy for the practice of metaphysics itself. I do not want to beg any questions in this particular dispute. 'Most general' suits both parties, in the

---

[1] These are taken, respectively, from: Moore (1953), p. 1, emphasis removed; Dummett (1992), p. 133; Sellars (1963), p. 1; Smart (1984), p. 138; Hegel (1975a), §24, p. 36, emphasis removed; and Bradley (1930), p. 10. But note that G.E. Moore is giving an account of 'the first and most important part of philosophy' rather than defining metaphysics, while Wilfrid Sellars, similarly, is defining philosophy rather than metaphysics. On the relation between philosophy and metaphysics, see §6 in this chapter.

[2] This part, or 'class' as it is called, is entitled 'Abstract Relations'.

one case because it can be interpreted as extending to all possibilities, not just those that happen to obtain, and in the other case because it need not be interpreted in terms of possibilities at all.[3]

The first of my more structural observations concerns the fact that 'most general' in my definition qualifies 'attempt'. To some ears this will sound strange. 'Most general' will sound better suited to qualify 'sense'. Thus in the other definitions listed in §1 above, 'most general' and its cognates always applied, in the search for some suitable representation of how things are, either to the sought-after representation or to the object of that representation, never to the search itself.

I set no great store by my positioning of this expression. I might just as well have defined metaphysics as the attempt to make the most general sense of things, or indeed as the attempt to make sense of the most general things, provided that in all three cases it was understood to be an open question what ultimately conferred the generality. Whether there is generality in metaphysical dealings with things because of the nature of the dealings or because of the nature of the things, or because of both, or perhaps because of neither, is another matter of dispute about which I do not want to beg any questions. Using 'most general' to qualify 'attempt' strikes me as the best way of registering my neutrality, however clumsy it may be in other respects.

The second of my more structural observations concerns the fact that 'most general' is a superlative. In this context it selects from among all possible attempts to make sense of things whatever is at the highest level of generality. So one immediate consequence of my definition is that *there is no denying the possibility of metaphysics*. (This admittedly presupposes that there is a highest level of generality.[4] But it would not make much difference if the presupposition were rescinded. The definition could be amended in such a way that a pursuit's being a metaphysical pursuit admits of degree: the more general, the more metaphysical. Still there would be no denying the possibility of metaphysics, at least to some degree.) There is room for dispute about whether metaphysics can be pursued in this or that way, or to this or that effect, or in contradistinction to this or that other discipline, but not about whether it can be pursued at all.

That is one controversy on which it suits me to take a stance from the very beginning. Why do I call it a controversy? Because countless philosophers have understood metaphysics in such a way that they have felt able to deny that there can be any such thing: we shall see many examples in what follows. Others, it should be noted, have gone to the other extreme of

---

[3] It even suits those who accept the necessary/contingent distinction but who think that metaphysics is fundamentally concerned with what is contingent: see e.g. Papineau (2009). 'Most general' *can* be interpreted as extending to all possibilities. It need not.

[4] It also of course presupposes the possibility of attempting to make sense of things. On this, see the next section.

insisting that metaphysics is unavoidable. This view is less of an affront than it sounds. It allows for the possibility, if it does not entail it, that the guise in which metaphysics normally appears is one that would not normally count as metaphysical, say the basic exercise of common sense. As Hegel puts it, 'metaphysics is nothing but the range of universal thought-determinations, and as it were the diamond net into which we bring everything to make it intelligible' (Hegel (1970), §246, 'Addition', p. 202); or again, as C.S. Peirce puts it, 'everyone must have conceptions of things in general' (Peirce (1931–1958), Vol. I, p. 229). (This is part of the reason why both Hegel and Peirce, in the same contexts, urge us to be reflective in our metaphysics, lest it has control of us rather than we of it.) But whether or not metaphysics is unavoidable, I want to commit myself from the outset to its being at least possible. For reasons that I hope will emerge, that seems to me the best way of construing much of what those philosophers who have denied the possibility of 'metaphysics' have themselves been engaged in.

3. '… Attempt …'

I now turn to the word 'attempt'. One significant feature of this word is that it would be less likely to play the same role in the definition of a non-philosophical discipline. True, we might define bioecology as the attempt to understand the interrelationship between living organisms and their environment. But it would be at least as natural to define it as the *science* or *study* of the interrelationship between living organisms and their environment. Is there any reason not to adopt something analogous in the case of metaphysics?

There is. An immediate analogue would be to define metaphysics as the most general science of things, or the most general study of things, and there are many who would subscribe to just such a definition. But I want to leave open the possibility that metaphysics is not appropriately regarded as a *science* at all. Indeed I want to leave open the possibility that metaphysics is not appropriately regarded as a *study* of anything either, not even a study of 'things' in whatever liberal sense that already liberal word is taken. (One of the virtues of the expression 'make sense of things', to anticipate some of what I shall say in the next section, is that it can be heard as enjoying a kind of indissolubility that accords with this.)

A second point in connection with the occurrence of the word 'attempt' is that it further ensures the possibility of metaphysics on my definition. Or rather, it insures that possibility – against the impossibility of making sense of things. For, as centuries of attempts to trisect an angle with ruler and compass testify, it is possible to attempt even what is not itself possible.[5]

---

[5] This is less straightforward than I am suggesting; but the main point survives. For discussion of some of the complications, with specific reference to Wittgenstein, see Floyd (2000).

A third and final point. The phrase 'make sense of' may admit of a 'non-success' interpretation whereby it already signifies (mere) endeavour, as in the sentence, 'I spent the entire afternoon making sense of this passage, but in the end I gave up.' I am not sure how natural such an interpretation is. But at any rate I want to exclude it. That is one thing that the word 'attempt' enables me to do. By explicitly referring to endeavour in my definition, I indicate that 'make sense of' is not itself intended to do that work. But this is the only constraint that I want to impose on the interpretation of either 'make sense of' or its concatenation with 'things', as we shall now see.

4. '... to Make Sense of Things'

I turn finally to the expression 'make sense of things'. This is an expression with myriad resonances. They will not all be prominent in the course of this book, but I do want them all to be audible throughout.

The 'sense' in question may be the meaning of something, the purpose of something, or the explanation for something. This is connected to the fact that a near-synonym for 'make sense of' is 'understand' and the range of things that someone might naturally be said to understand (or not) is both vast and very varied. It includes languages, words, phrases, innuendos, theories, proofs, books, people, fashions, patterns of behaviour, suffering, the relativity of simultaneity, and many more. Thus making sense of things can embrace on the one hand finding something that is worth living for, perhaps even finding the meaning of life, and on the other hand discovering how things work, for instance by ascertaining relevant laws of nature. I do not want to draw a veil over *any* of these. The generality of metaphysics will no doubt prevent it from embracing some of them, but that is another matter.[6]

When 'make sense' is used intransitively, there is a further range of associations. It is then equivalent not to 'understand' but to 'be intelligible', 'admit of understanding', perhaps even 'be rational'. I mentioned parenthetically in the previous section that 'make sense of things' can be heard as enjoying a kind of indissolubility. What I had in mind was the way in which the sheer non-specificity of 'things' can put us in mind of simply making sense. As I shall urge shortly, this point must not be exaggerated. 'Make sense of things' does have its own articulation and we must not lose sight of this fact. Nevertheless, I want the many associations of simply making sense, like the many associations of making sense *of*, to inform all that follows.[7]

---

[6] I shall return to this matter at the very end of the enquiry, in the Conclusion, §5.

[7] There is in any case the point that, when someone makes sense of things in a certain way, and thinks and acts accordingly, then others who make sense of things in that same way can make sense in particular of him or her: see further Moore (2003a), p. 124. (The whole of that book is, in a way, a meditation on what is involved in making sense of things. My previous book, Moore (1997a), is likewise deeply concerned with this theme (see e.g. Ch. 10, §1).)

But the phrase 'of things' does make a difference. For one thing, it serves as a check on the temptation, which must surely be resisted, to pursue metaphysics as though it were a form of pure mathematics, to be executed by devising abstract self-contained systems. The phrase may also, despite the non-specificity of 'things', serve to distinguish metaphysics from logic, and from the philosophy of logic, which are arguably concerned with making sense of *sense*. (This is not to deny the relevance of the latter to the former. There will be ample opportunity to witness such relevance in the course of this book.) One other function that 'of things' serves is to reinforce some of the resonances of 'make'. For where simply making sense is a matter of being intelligible, making sense *of* something is a matter of rendering intelligible, with all the associations of productivity that that has. Indeed I want to leave room for the thought, however bizarre it may initially appear, that sense is literally made of things, as bread is made of water, flour, and yeast.

In general, it should be clear that my use of the expression 'make sense of things' is intended to take full advantage of its enormous semantic and syntactic latitude. I want my conception of metaphysics not only to cover as much as possible of what self-styled metaphysicians have been up to, but also to cover a range of practices which seem to me to be profitably classified in the same way even though the practitioners themselves have not conceived what they were doing in these terms.[8] Thus, to take the most notable example, I believe that much of what Aristotle was engaged in, in his *Metaphysics*, would count as metaphysics by my definition (see e.g. the first two chapters of Book Γ). It is worth noting in this connection that the opening sentence of *Metaphysics* is 'All men by nature strive to know,' where the Greek verb translated as 'to know' is '*eidenai*', about which Aristotle elsewhere says that men do not think they do that to something until they have grasped the 'why' of it (*Physics*, Bk II, Ch. 3, 194b 17–19). It would surely not be a strain to construe Aristotle as claiming that all men by nature strive to make sense of things.[9]

Among the many important possibilities left open by the latitude of the expression 'make sense of things' are

- that what issues from a successful pursuit of metaphysics is not knowledge, or, if it is knowledge, it is not knowledge that anything is the case,

---

[8] A word, incidentally, about the beginning of this sentence. Here we see the first explicit reference in this book to a 'conception' of metaphysics. That makes this an apt point at which to comment on my use of the two terms 'concept' and 'conception', each of which will pervade the book. While I do not profess to have a rigorously defined distinction in mind, my intention is roughly to follow John Rawls' usage in Rawls (1971) (see in particular p. 5). On this usage, various relatively determinate 'conceptions' of a thing, such as justice or metaphysics, can all be said to correspond to the same relatively indeterminate 'concept' of that thing.

[9] Cf. Burnyeat (1981); and Lear (1988), Ch. 1.

but rather knowledge *how* to reckon with things, or knowledge *what* it is for things to be the way they are, or something of that sort[10]
- hence that what issues from a successful pursuit of metaphysics is not knowledge which can be expressed by descriptive declarative sentences[11]
- relatedly, that metaphysics is not a search for the truth, still less for the Truth, whatever honour the capitalization might confer
- that the best metaphysics involves creating new concepts

and

- that, on the contrary, the best metaphysics involves being clear about extant concepts and about what it is to make correct judgments with them.

I shall have more to say about some of these possibilities in §6 below (and about all of them in the rest of the book).

Among the many pitfalls that the expression 'make sense of things' signals for the practising metaphysician, there are two that are worthy of special mention. First, trying to make sense of things, or even for that matter successfully making sense of things, can be an unprofitable and even destructive exercise, especially when it involves the analysis of what is already, at some level, understood; jokes, metaphors, and some works of art are particularly vulnerable to this kind of spoiling. As Bas van Fraassen laments, 'metaphysicians interpret what we initially understand into something hardly anyone understands' (van Fraassen (2002), p. 3). The second pitfall is that it simply may not be possible to make (some kinds of) sense of things. We must take very seriously Adorno's question of what the prospects are for metaphysics after Auschwitz.[12]

5. Metaphysics and Self-Conscious Reflection

Many people would say that metaphysics involves a significant element of self-conscious reflection. Ought I to have included some reference to this in my definition?

'Most general' already accounts for it. Or so I claim. To make sense of things at the highest level of generality, I would contend, is to make sense of things in terms of *what it is to make sense of things*; it is to be guided by the sheer nature of the enterprise. To attempt to do that is therefore necessarily to reflect on one's own activity, and to try to make sense, in particular, of the sense that one makes of things.

---

[10] I am presupposing that not all knowledge is knowledge that something is the case; for dissent, see Stanley and Williamson (2001).

[11] Cf. Moore (1997a), Ch. 8.

[12] See Adorno (1973), esp. Pt 3, §III.

If I am right about this, it helps to explain why so much great metaphysics, perhaps all great metaphysics, has included some story about what metaphysics is. By the same token it ensures that, insofar as what follows is a kind of history of meta-metaphysics (as I put it in the Preface), it is at the same time a significant part of the history, simply, of metaphysics.

But even if I am wrong – even if it is not true that whatever satisfies my definition must involve a significant element of self-conscious reflection – the fact is that it *has* done so. There will be examples of this throughout what follows, especially when we come to the various traditions in the late modern period (that is, roughly, the nineteenth and twentieth centuries) where much of the attention is focused on sense itself. But perhaps the most notable example, once again, is supplied by Aristotle, who, in the third chapter of Book Γ of *Metaphysics*, identifies as the most certain principle of reality that nothing can both be and not be, and who does so on the grounds that no making sense of things can include believing something both to be and not to be.[13]

There is however a further pitfall which such self-consciousness creates and which I should mention in this connection. Self-consciousness and self-confidence make notoriously bad bedfellows. It is hard, when we reflect on the sense that we make of things, not to be afflicted by all sorts of doubts about it, as will be evidenced from the very beginning of the historical narrative that I am about to tell.[14] This means that, to whatever extent making sense of things needs a measure of self-confidence, there is a further danger that metaphysics will turn out to be a forlorn endeavour: it will turn out to be an attempt to do something that is subverted by the very methods used in the attempt. And of course, any self-conscious attempt to rectify the problem, like an insomniac's self-conscious attempt to fall asleep, will only make matters worse.

6. Three Questions

My aim in this book is to chart the evolution of metaphysics from the early modern period to the present. Because of its generality, metaphysics is the one branch of philosophy that is not the philosophy of this or that specific area of human thought or experience. It is 'pure' philosophy. That makes its evolution peculiarly difficult to separate from the evolution of philosophy as a whole. One way in which I hope to keep the project manageable is by concentrating more on how metaphysics has been viewed during that time

---

[13] For an interpretation of Aristotle whereby his work serves as an even more striking example, see Lear (1988), Ch. 6, passim, but esp. §3.

[14] For some fascinating insights into the relations between self-consciousness and self-confidence, specifically in relation to ethics, but with relevance to metaphysics too, see Williams (2006o), Chs 8 and 9.

than on how it has been practised, although, for reasons given in the previous section, the two are not cleanly separated.

The story of how metaphysics has been viewed is a story of disagreements about its scope and limits. There are three questions in particular, about what we can aspire to when we practise metaphysics, that have been significant foci of disagreement.

The Transcendence Question: Is there scope for our making sense of 'transcendent' things, or are we limited to making sense of 'immanent' things?

The Novelty Question: Is there scope for our making sense of things in a way that is radically new, or are we limited to making sense of things in broadly the same way as we already do?

The Creativity Question: Is there scope for our being creative in our sense-making, or are we limited to looking for the sense that things themselves already make?[15]

(a) The Transcendence Question

The Transcendence Question in turn raises all manner of further questions. It suggests various contrasts between our making sense of what is 'beyond' and our making sense of what is 'within'. But beyond and within what? Who, for that matter, are 'we'?[16] While it is certainly true that there has been fundamental disagreement about whether our sense-making can take us over this boundary, the divisions between competing conceptions of what the boundary itself comes to may have been even more fundamental. It has variously been viewed as a boundary between:

- what is inaccessible (to us) through experience and what is accessible (to us) through experience
- what is unknowable (by us) and what is knowable (by us)
- what is supernatural and what is natural
- what is atemporal and what is temporal
- what is abstract and what is concrete
- what is infinite and what is finite

[15] There is a muffled echo in these three questions of a tripartite classification that Kant imposes on his philosophical predecessors in the final section of Kant (1998). He classifies them: first, with regard to what they take their subject matter to be (objects of the senses or objects of the understanding); second, with regard to what they take the source of their knowledge to be (experience or pure reason); and third, with regard to what they take their methodology to be (an appeal to common sense or something more scientific and more systematic). It takes only a little strain to hear the echo of these in the Transcendence Question, the Creativity Question, and the Novelty Question, respectively.

[16] This question will come to prominence in Ch. 10, §4, and again in Ch. 21, §7(c).

- what bespeaks unity, totality, and/or identity and what bespeaks plurality, partiality, and/or difference[17]

and even, question-beggingly in the context of the Transcendence Question,

- what we cannot make sense of and what we can.

There is also an important strand in the history in which it has been taken for granted that, if there *is* scope for our making sense of transcendent things, then it is only by operating at the level of generality that is characteristic of metaphysics that we are able to do so, since it is only when we are dealing with the most general features of what is immanent that we are either obliged or indeed able to distinguish it from what is transcendent. The Transcendence Question is then, in effect, the question whether metaphysics has its own peculiar subject matter, radically different in kind from the subject matter of any other enquiry. This possibility also suggests a potential problem for those who think that we are limited to making sense of immanent things, a potential problem whose significance in the history of metaphysics would be hard to exaggerate: there may be no way of registering the thought that our sense-making is limited to what is immanent except by distinguishing what is immanent from what is transcendent, and thus either doing the very thing that is reckoned to be impossible, that is making sense of what is transcendent, or failing to make sense at all. We shall see plenty of manifestations of this aporia in what follows.[18]

(b)   The Novelty Question

The Novelty Question calls to mind P.F. Strawson's famous distinction between 'revisionary' metaphysics and 'descriptive' metaphysics, where 'descriptive metaphysics is content to describe the actual structure of our

---

[17] There is a hint here of what may have been an equally important fourth question: is there scope for our making unified sense of everything, or are we limited to making separate sense of separate things? Cf. the Archilochean distinction between 'the hedgehog', who 'knows one big thing', and 'the fox', who 'knows many things', a distinction developed in Berlin (1978) and further exploited in Hacker (1996), Ch. 5, §1. (In the former Isaiah Berlin argues that Tolstoy was a fox by nature, but a hedgehog by conviction. In the latter P.M.S. Hacker argues that Wittgenstein, by contrast, 'was by nature a hedgehog, but ... transformed himself ... into a paradigmatic fox' (ibid., p. 98). (Hacker is talking about the transition from Wittgenstein's early work to his later work: see Chs 9 and 10, esp. §2 of the latter, in this book.) Another thinker in whom we find a similar contrast between temperament and practice is David Lewis: in Ch. 13, §2, I shall cite a passage which shows him to have been a reluctant hedgehog.)

[18] The first clear manifestation of it will occur in Ch. 5, §8, when I introduce what I there call the Limit Argument.

thought about the world, [while] revisionary metaphysics is concerned to produce a better structure' (Strawson (1959), p. 9).[19] Like the Transcendence Question, but even more pivotally perhaps, the Novelty Question raises the further question of who 'we' are. It is a platitude that people in different cultures, and in different eras, make sense of things in different ways. But the question of who 'we' are cuts deeper than this platitude. P.M.S. Hacker, in an essay on what he calls 'Strawson's rehabilitation of metaphysics', refers to the 'major structural features of our conceptual scheme that lie at the heart of Strawson's investigations' and describes them as 'partly constitutive of our nature as self-conscious human beings, involving concepts and categories that we could not abandon without ceasing to be human' (Hacker (2001b), p. 368). Hacker's intention is to defend a version of the view that metaphysics has to be descriptive. But it is a real question whether 'we' should not be open to just such non-human possibilities, open, that is, to possibilities that involve 'us' in transcending 'our' present humanity.[20]

Why then should anyone think that, as practising metaphysicians, we are limited to making sense of things in broadly the same way as we already do?

Well, the phrase 'as practising metaphysicians' is critical. One view would be the following. Anyone operating at a lower level of generality, attempting to make relatively specific sense of relatively specific things, can have occasion to innovate in all sorts of ways, but the *metaphysician*, responding to nothing but the sheer demand to make sense of things, should be concerned only to protect whatever sense-making is already under way, in particular to protect it from confusion: any innovation not prompted by some specific need merely carries the risk of new confusion. (That is not by any means a crazy view, although it is always in danger of degenerating into a conservative resistance even to *non*-metaphysical innovation – a resistance, more specifically, to any departure, at any level of generality, from 'ordinary language' – which really is crazy.[21]) Another view would be that, at the relevantly high level of generality, there is only one way of making sense of

---

[19] See further ibid., pp. 9–11. See also P.F. Strawson (1992), Ch. 1, where he distinguishes a more negative version of the view that metaphysics has to be descriptive (metaphysics as therapy) from a more positive version (metaphysics as conceptual analysis). And see Davidson (1984a) for scepticism about the idea that there even *are* radically different structures.

Note: in Ch. 17 we shall see reason not to link the Creativity Question too tightly to Strawson's revisionary/descriptive distinction (see n. 75 of that chapter).

[20] I shall return briefly to this possibility in Ch. 21, §7(c).

[21] For a more sensible conservative respect for 'ordinary language', see J.L. Austin (1970), p. 185. At the end of that passage, Austin memorably summarizes his view in the following way: 'Ordinary language is *not* the last word: in principle it can everywhere be supplemented and improved upon and superseded. Only remember, it *is* the *first* word' (emphasis in original). See further Ch. 10, n. 9.

things that is available to us. Strawson himself holds a variant of this view. He claims that descriptive metaphysics aims to 'lay bare the most general features of our conceptual structure,' adding that 'there are categories and concepts [which constitute that structure and] which, in their most fundamental character, [do not] change' (Strawson (1959), pp. 9–10).

That raises the following question. How, if at all, does whatever counts as descriptive metaphysics, on this conception, count as metaphysics on mine? How does the endeavour to 'lay bare the most general features of our conceptual structure' count as a general attempt to make sense of things, as opposed to an anthropological or perhaps even historical exercise in depicting the attempt(s) that we, whoever 'we' are, already make?

Many people, as we shall see, have thought that an exercise of this latter kind is indeed a substantial part of metaphysics, even on roughly my conception – and Collingwood was quite explicit about its being a historical exercise. The point is this. It need not be a detached, 'meta-level' exercise. It can be an engaged, reflexive, self-conscious exercise *in our own sense-making*. The aim of the exercise might be to elucidate that sense-making where it is not clear, or to hone it where it is not sharp, or to reinforce it where it is in danger of disintegrating, or to guard it against distortion and abuse; and its methods might include making explicit what would otherwise be implicit or imposing system where there would otherwise be an assembly of unordered, disconnected parts. Consider the ancient paradoxes of motion, for example, the most famous of which is that of Achilles and the tortoise.

> The Paradox of Achilles and the Tortoise: Achilles, who runs much faster than the tortoise, nevertheless seems unable to overtake it in a race in which it has been given a head start. For each time Achilles reaches a point that the tortoise has already reached, which is something he will always have to do as long as it is still ahead of him, it has moved on.[22]

It would not be implausible to think that these paradoxes result from our having an insecure grasp of our own basic preconceptions about the nature of space, time, and the infinite. And if one did think this, one might respond by using formal mathematical techniques in an effort to give new and clearer expression to those preconceptions. That would certainly count as metaphysics by my definition.

Very well, then, why should anyone give the opposite response to the Novelty Question? Why should anyone think that, as practising metaphysicians, we have license to make sense of things in a way that is radically new?

Because it is not clear that our most general way of making sense of things cannot be radically improved. There is more to be said of course,

---

[22] These paradoxes are generally attributed to Zeno of Elea and are reported by Aristotle in his *Physics*, Bk VI, Ch. 9. We shall return to them briefly in Ch. 16, §6. For discussion, see Moore (2001a), Introduction, §1, and Ch. 4, §3.

but that is the very simple, very basic reason for taking revisionary meta-physics seriously.[23]

Not that it is an entirely straightforward matter what revisionary meta-physics is. There is an issue about how far we count as making sense of things in a way that is radically new if we make judgments that are radically new, but using old familiar concepts.[24] Suppose we are inclined to say one thing and a metaphysician urges us to say the very opposite. Is that revision-ary because the metaphysician is challenging what we think? Or is it non-revisionary because the metaphysician is acceding to the concepts we use?[25] *Is* the metaphysician acceding to the concepts we use? Perhaps saying the very opposite of what we are currently inclined to say would be so revolu-tionary that, if any of us did that, he or she would have to be interpreted as using old words to express new concepts (see further Ch. 7, §7). These are familiar philosophical quandaries. And it is noteworthy, in this connection, how unobvious the classification of metaphysicians as descriptive or revi-sionary can be. Strawson, immediately after introducing his distinction, goes on to classify Aristotle, Descartes, Leibniz, Berkeley, Hume, and Kant. It is an interesting exercise for anyone who is familiar with these six thinkers, but who is unfamiliar with Strawson's classification or who has forgotten it, to see how well they can anticipate his six verdicts! The fact remains that there are some things that would indisputably count as instances of revi-sionary metaphysics, the paradigm being the introduction of highly general concepts enabling us to adopt beliefs that we could not so much as entertain before. And the point is simply this. It is unclear why we should eschew any-thing of that sort. It is unclear why we should think that nothing of that sort could ever be to our advantage.

(c)   The Creativity Question

To turn finally to the Creativity Question, there is a further issue in this case about what is 'scope' and what are 'limits'. In other words, the Creativity Question might be better reversed: is there scope for our discovering the sense that things themselves already make, and thus for being right, or are we limited to inventing the sense that we make of things in a way that admits of no distinction between being right and being wrong?[26] The fact

---

[23] We shall see other reasons in Part Three: see esp. Ch. 15, §6, and Ch. 21, §6.

[24] Cf. Snowdon (2006), pp. 41–43.

[25] Derek Parfit would say the former. He describes his own work, in which he challenges many of our beliefs but retains the concepts we use, as revisionary: see Parfit (1984), p. x.

[26] For a particularly robust defence of the first alternative, see Wright (2002), §9. A simi-larly 'realist' position is defended in Lowe (1998), Ch. 1. The latter alternative is more Wittgensteinian: see Hacker (1986), Ch. VII, and see below, Ch. 10, §3.

Note that, for convenience, I shall sometimes treat this reversal of the original question as presenting the same pair of alternatives, though we should not rule out the possibility

that the Creativity Question is equivocal in this way reflects the fact that we can broach metaphysics with quite different aspirations. If we are limited to inventing the sense that we make of things, then that curbs our more scientific pretensions; if we are limited to looking for the sense that things themselves already make, then that curbs our more artistic pretensions. The equivocality also reflects the fact that the Creativity Question allows for endless variations on a theme. Do we find things intelligible or do we render them intelligible? Does our sense-making inevitably reveal more about us (our sensibilities, our commitments, our values, and suchlike) than it does about the things we make sense of? To what extent can all rational enquirers be expected to make the same sense of things? Can we make sense of things in a way that is completely objective? Does our sense-making have infinite scope? Can our sense-making be, in Edward Craig's terms, a participation in 'the mind of God', or is it a product of 'the works of man'?[27] And of course, underlying all of these, there is the recurring issue of who 'we' are.

Note that, as in the case of the Novelty Question, what is at stake is what we can aspire to *when we practise metaphysics*. It would not be at all outrageous to hold both of the following: that, when we practise physics, we can aspire to complete objectivity, indeed to what Bernard Williams famously calls an 'absolute conception' of reality ([B.] Williams (1978), pp. 65–67), and, in line with what I suggested in the previous section, that our attempting to make sense of things at a higher level of generality involves an unavoidable element of self-consciousness which is in turn incompatible with such objectivity.[28]

(d)   The Significance of the Three Questions

These three questions, then, along with the three[29] pairs of alternatives that they present, have played an important role in shaping disagreement about the scope and limits of metaphysics during the modern period. Those who have accepted any of the more restrained alternatives (whichever that is in the third case) have *ipso facto* repudiated certain activities as 'off-limits'. It is an extremely important fact about the story of metaphysics during

that there is scope *both* for our being creative in our sense-making *and* for our discovering the sense that things themselves already make. Indeed it is clear that, in many projects of *non*-metaphysical sense-making, there are elements of both. That is to say, there are elements both of creation and of discovery: it is less clear whether there are any individual elements that are elements of both. (See further Ch. 16, §6(c), and Ch. 18, §6.)

[27] See Craig (1987). Craig himself would regard the Creativity Question, and the choice that it presents between what he calls 'the Insight Ideal' and 'the Practice Ideal', as pivotal to my historical project: see ibid., passim.

[28] Cf. Williams (2006m).

[29] But see the caveat in n. 26.

this period that, very often, they have also thought of 'metaphysics' as precisely what they were repudiating. This is in part just a fact about their use of the word, which, during the same period, has more often than not served as a derogatory term.[30] But it is not only that. Throughout this period metaphysics has been a source of suspicion, even among those who on my broad conception count as metaphysicians. Time and again metaphysics has been pilloried as something illegitimate by those who, had they been more focused on their own activities and had their own conception been broader, might just as well have championed it, and metaphysics has contracted as a result. Yet each time it has subsequently expanded again. One of my aims is to show that there is something in this recurrent systole and diastole that can properly be regarded as 'the evolution of modern metaphysics', and not just as a wearisome sequence of repeated mistakes.

I shall not make any effort to remain non-partisan. There would be a limit to how well I could achieve the aim just specified if I did. In tandem with telling the evolutionary story that I wish to tell, I shall develop my own stance on these three issues. But I shall do so only incidentally and not very thoroughly; that is not my main concern. For now I shall simply record, without any of the necessary glosses, qualifications, or disclaimers, my own three verdicts.

We are, in practising metaphysics, (a) constrained to make sense of immanent things, (b) free to make sense of things in a way that is radically new, and (c) engaged in a fundamentally creative exercise. Or, to put it glibly and question-beggingly, but also, I hope, suggestively, we are, in practising metaphysics, (a) constrained to make *nothing but* sense of things, (b) free to make *any* sense of things, and (c) attempting, literally, to *make* sense of things.[31]

On this conception there have been real advances in the understanding of what metaphysics is over the past four hundred years, and they have been both liberating and restricting. They have been liberating to the extent that they have revealed the capacity of metaphysics to deepen, broaden, and enrich our understanding of reality (b and c). They have been restricting to the extent that they have revealed the incapacity of metaphysics to carry

---

[30] For some interesting observations on the use of the word as a derogatory term, see Armstrong (1965). See also Locke (1965), Bk III, Ch. X, §2, for an early pejorative use of 'metaphysicians' in the context 'schoolmen and metaphysicians'. Hume famously castigates 'school metaphysics' in the final paragraph of Hume (1975a); for discussion, see Ch. 4, §4 in this book. Kant, in Kant (2002a), 4:258 n., claims to find a much more complimentary reference to 'metaphysics' in Hume: he cites a German translation of Hume (1741–1742), Vol. 2, p. 79. But his quotation contains an ellipsis that somewhat distorts Hume's statement. (Here I am indebted to the editors' n. 6 on p. 473 of Kant (2002a).)

[31] For a similarly glib account of how making sense of things connects with the three 'maxims of the common understanding' which Kant identifies in Kant (2000), 5:294–295, see Moore (2003a), pp. 87–88.

that understanding beyond its inherent finitude or to provide it with any grounding in reality itself (a and, revealing the equivocality of the Creativity Question, c again).

My own combination of answers to these three questions, at least insofar as those answers are conceived as choices between three pairs of alternatives, is one of eight that are possible. I believe that we can find important traces, within this four-hundred-year period, of all eight. This is not to say that we can find eight thinkers who are suitable to act as their representatives. It would be hopelessly simplistic and procrustean to think that we could do that. There are very few thinkers, if any, whom we can straightforwardly categorize in terms of their stance on these three issues, even once the issues have been conceived in binary terms, and even once we have taken into account developments in the thinkers' ideas and the distinction between what they practise and what they preach. Typically, it is more a question of a given thinker wrestling with, and trying to work through, opposed tendencies. For one thing, some combinations of views may be inherently unstable. Thus even if the view that our sense-making is invention rather than discovery is not irreconcilable with the view that we are limited to making sense of things in broadly the same way as we already do, it takes a peculiar kind of philosophy to reconcile them, and a thinker inclined to accept both may decide that subscribing to that kind of philosophy is too costly. The same applies to the pairing of the view that we can make sense of transcendent things with the view that our sense-making involves an element of self-consciousness that precludes complete objectivity. A further complication is that many thinkers have been suspicious, not so much of one of the two rival answers to any given question, but of the idea that there is a genuine focus of disagreement there. And a yet further complication, perhaps the most serious of all, is that only a tiny proportion of the thinkers who can usefully be classified with respect to any of these issues can usefully be classified with respect to all three.

For these and other reasons my references to the issues in what follows will be infrequent and often oblique. Even so, the issues have been a significant factor in my choice of protagonists, and they should be constantly discernible in the background.

7. The Importance of Metaphysics

Metaphysics matters. Making sense of things is an integral part of simply making sense and there is a fundamental nisus in all of us to do that.[32] But to what extent does metaphysics matter for its own sake? Only to a very limited extent, I suggest. In (large) part this reflects my view of metaphysics

---

[32] For defence of this idea, see Moore (2003a), esp. Variations Two.

as a fundamentally creative exercise. If metaphysics were an attempt to find the sense that things themselves already make, then an aphorism of Galileo's might apply to it: 'He who looks the higher is the more highly distinguished, and turning over the great book of nature ... is the way to elevate one's gaze' (Galileo (1967), Dedication, p. 3). But if metaphysics is an attempt to create sense, then it needs to confront the question, 'What is the attempt for?' And if the answer is simply, 'For its own sake,' then it is easy to understand the charge of pointlessness that is so often levelled against metaphysics. I am not denying that there is such a thing as creativity for its own sake. Nor am I denying its importance. But creativity in the context of sense-making incurs special commitments. The most general attempt to make sense of things is part of the overall attempt to make sense of things, in all its diversity and complexity, and with all its myriad specific concerns and its myriad specific purposes. Unless the former subserves the latter, which is as much as to say unless the former *makes a difference*, it will be like a wheel that can be turned though nothing else moves with it.[33] It may have some ornamental value, but it will not perform the function that it purports to perform.[34]

Thus to broach the question of how many angels could dance on the point of a needle, to take the hackneyed example,[35] even if it were part of an attempt to devise suitable conceptual apparatus for relating the incorporeal to the corporeal, would straightway invite the further question, 'Why?' (That is, why bother? What turns on this? In what ways and to what ends do we need to relate the incorporeal to the corporeal?) And it is an obvious point, but still an important point, that this further question would be all the more urgent for anyone who did not believe in angels.[36]

Very well, then, how is metaphysics able to make a difference? One simple way, to which I alluded in the previous section in connection with the Novelty Question, is by combating the confusion to which we are prone when we indulge the urge that we already have to make the most general sense of things. In other words, metaphysics can fulfil the function of rectifying bad metaphysics. Nor should this function be taken lightly. Since we are all, to a greater or lesser extent, natural metaphysicians, and since we are prone to do metaphysics badly, there is a real need for something to counteract the debilitating and damaging effects of our relatively instinctive, relatively primitive efforts. There is a real need, that is, for good metaphysics. On the other hand, the importance of this function should not be exaggerated either. Some philosophers take the view that this is the *only* function

---

[33] Here I echo Wittgenstein (1967a), Pt I, §271.

[34] This view is stoutly defended by F.C.S. Schiller in Schiller (1912), an essay revealingly entitled 'The Ethical Basis of Metaphysics'. See passim, but esp. p. 1, n. 1, and pp. 7–8.

[35] For an account of the history of this question, see Franklin (1993).

[36] Cf. Bernard Williams' comments concerning arguments about God in Williams (2006o), p. 33.

of metaphysics, that we would have no need for metaphysics if we did not have a deleterious attraction to it. But, apart from anything else, that view makes too great a mystery of the attraction itself.

A second way in which metaphysics is able to make a difference is by combining with other endeavours and with other areas of enquiry, including other branches of philosophy, in helping us to make more particular sense of things. Of especial historical significance are the ways in which it has combined with science, ethics, and theology – exemplified respectively in my first three protagonists.[37] There will be plenty of further examples in what follows, but I shall here cite three comparatively simple and much more recent examples to give an indication of what I have in mind. In each case, as we shall see, metaphysics helps that with which it combines to 'make sense', whether in the sense of assisting the latter in its own sense-making or in the sense of helping to render the latter itself intelligible.

Metaphysics Combined with Science: There are various metaphysical quandaries about the existence and nature of properties or universals, such as redness. (Aristotle discusses many of these quandaries in his *Metaphysics*.) David Lewis urges that we do well to acknowledge properties if we conceive them as classes of things, actual or possible, and that we do well to acknowledge universals if we conceive them as properties of a special kind. For a property to be of this special kind, it must 'carve reality at one of its joints'. That is, it must have some relevance to causal laws; the things that instantiate it must thereby genuinely resemble one another; and suchlike. (On this conception, redness, though it is certainly a property, is a poor candidate for being a universal.) It is in these terms, Lewis holds, that we make the best sense of science, and more specifically of physics. For we can see the purpose of physics as being to discover what universals there actually are (Lewis (1999b)).

Metaphysics Combined with Ethics: Another very old metaphysical quandary is whether all propositions concerning the future are (already) true or false. (Aristotle discusses this too, in *On Interpretation*, Ch. 9.) Quine argues that, whatever else might be said in favour of the doctrine that all propositions concerning the future are indeed (already) true or false, that doctrine has serious ethical payoff. His argument runs as follows. Consider the following two principles: first, that conservation of the environment is necessary for the sake of people as yet unborn, and second, that birth control is necessary to combat overpopulation. Both have considerable appeal. But to accede to them both seems inconsistent. For

---

[37] But see Ch. 3, §2, for an important difference between the way in which it is exemplified in the first two and the way in which it is exemplified in the third.

it seems to involve recognizing the interests of those who have not yet been born, while denying some of them the very right to life. If we acknowledge that all propositions concerning the future are (already) true or false, however, then we can dispel the apparent inconsistency. We are free to adopt a tenseless understanding of the phrase 'there are', and then to say that 'there are' people who have not yet been born: their interests must be respected. By contrast, 'there are' no people who have not yet been born and who never will be: birth control denies the right of life to nobody (Quine (1987b)).

Note that the ethical payoff here lies not in the doctrine's helping us to live better, nor yet in its helping us to decide what counts as living better, but in its helping us to think more clearly and more effectively about our reasons for deciding as we do. Note also that, on the view of metaphysics as a creative exercise that admits of no distinction between being right and being wrong, it would be possible *both* to accept Quine's argument *and* to believe that, for other purposes, including other ethical purposes, we do better to deny that all propositions concerning the future are (already) true or false. (Perhaps denying this helps us to think more clearly about our own commitments and responsibilities for example.[38]) This would be a little like choosing to use the Celsius scale for discussing the chemical properties of water, but preferring to use the Fahrenheit scale for discussing the weather.[39]

Metaphysics Combined with Theology: There is a doctrine, which we can call the doctrine of relative identity, whereby it is possible for there to be different things of a certain kind which are nevertheless the *same* thing of some other kind. A case that is often cited is that of a piece of bronze which is formed into a statue s_1, say a statue of a man, then melted down, and then formed into a quite different statue s_2, say a statue of a horse. In this case, an advocate of the doctrine would say, although s_1 is a different statue from s_2, they are nevertheless the same

---

[38] Cf. Cockburn (1997), Ch. 9.

[39] But only a little. For one thing, enormous philosophical work would be required to show that neither of the philosophical doctrines in question had implications whose costs outweighed its ethical benefits. I do not for a moment want to downplay the complexities of these issues, and I trust that my somewhat breezy presentation of this example is not misleading in this regard. For a very illuminating discussion of some of the complexities, see Gibson (2007). For a discussion of another example, in this case a metaphysical doctrine whose ethical payoff is to help us to make sense of ethics itself, see Moore (2007a), esp. §4. (Might a third example be idealism of the sort that Berkeley defends in Berkeley (1962a)? Might that connect better than any realist alternative with our sense of importance, by reducing the starry heavens in whose midst even our planet is a mere speck to tiny packages of information in our own voluminous, teeming minds? It might. But then again it might place intolerable strains on our understanding when we properly think it through.)

piece of bronze. This doctrine is defended by the Catholic philosopher
P.T. Geach, one of whose own examples – surely the example that is
of primary concern to him – is that of the Trinity. The doctrine of relative identity allows Geach to say that, whereas the Father is a different Person from the Son, they are the same God (Geach (1972); and
Anscombe and Geach (1961), pp. 118–119).

A third way in which metaphysics is able to make a difference, and the one
that seems to me the most important and the most exciting, is by providing
us with radically new concepts by which to live. Here I am presupposing that
we have scope, as metaphysicians, to make sense of things in ways that are
radically new. In other words, I am presupposing my stance on the Novelty
Question from the previous section. If I am wrong about this, then metaphysics has far less to offer than I believe – though even then there is scope for it
to be involved in something similar, albeit less radical, namely the protection,
nurturing, adaptation, or rejection of concepts by which we already live.
    When I talk about our 'living by' a concept, I am alluding to the fact that
some concepts are action-guiding in the sense that even to use them is to be
motivated in certain ways. The paradigms are what Bernard Williams calls
'thick' ethical concepts. By a thick ethical concept Williams means a concept
that has both a factual aspect and an ethically evaluative aspect. Thus to
apply a thick ethical concept in a given situation is to say something straightforwardly false if the situation turns out not to be a certain way; but it is also
ethically to appraise the situation. An example is the concept of infidelity. If
I accuse you of being unfaithful, I say something that I am obliged to retract
if it turns out that you have not in fact gone back on any relevant agreement,
but I also thereby register my disapproval of what you have done. Another
example is the concept of a promise, one of whose most striking features is
that its use not only directs us in our living, but creates new possibilities for
our living. You could not so much as make promises, still less confront decisions about whether to keep them or not, still *less* be motivated to keep them,
if you were not part of a community that used the concept of a promise.[40]
    But even someone sympathetic to this idea of an action-guiding concept
might balk at the suggestion that *metaphysics* can provide us with such
things. The worry would be that action-guiding concepts are insufficiently
general for that. There are four points to be made in response to this worry.
First, insofar as the worry is based on the thought that thick ethical concepts are insufficiently general, it is misplaced. For thick ethical concepts are
not the only action-guiding concepts. Indeed, on some ways of construing

---

[40] See Williams (2006o), pp. 140ff.; and Williams (1995a), pp. 205–210. I discuss action-
guiding concepts at greater length in Moore (2003a), esp. Variations One, passim. A helpful discussion is Diamond (1988), of which pp. 276–277 are especially relevant to what I
go on to say in this section.

action-guidingness, *all* concepts are action-guiding.[41] Second, it is anyway not clear that thick ethical concepts are insufficiently general. The concept of freedom and the concept of a person strike me as clear examples of thick ethical concepts.[42] Yet much traditional metaphysics has been concerned with those very concepts. (It is noteworthy that one of the classic metaphysical discussions of the concept of a person, namely Locke's, includes the famous observation that 'person' is a forensic term.[43]) Third, we should not forget a point which was implicit in something I said parenthetically in §2, that whether a concept is a metaphysical concept may admit of degree. This would allow for the possibility that metaphysics can provide us with action-guiding concepts which, though they are less general than some other concepts, are still metaphysical to some degree. Fourth, and most significant, we should in any case not assume that the only concepts that metaphysics can provide us with are metaphysical concepts. The concept of blasphemy strikes me as another clear example of a thick ethical concept. It scarcely counts as metaphysical, yet its very possibility depends on a certain kind of metaphysics. Nor is this an isolated example. Among the most general attempts to make sense of things, those that have had a religious dimension have bequeathed innumerable non-metaphysical concepts by which people have lived.

8.   Prospectus

Finally in this Introduction I want to say something about the structure of this book, and in particular about its division into three parts. The division is partly chronological. The book deals with four centuries. Part One deals, roughly speaking, with the first two. Parts Two and Three each deal, roughly speaking, with the remaining two. It is the division between Parts Two and Three that deserves special comment.

Part Two concerns philosophers belonging to the analytic tradition. The common name for the complement of this tradition, within recent Western philosophy, is 'the continental tradition'. I have already intimated in the Preface my unease both about the name (which makes a particular mockery of the positioning of Frege and Collingwood, for example) and about the normal associations of the name, in particular the implied opposition between two fronts (which, as it happens, is again particularly problematical with respect to Frege and Collingwood, the first because his work connects in important ways with that of Husserl, the second because his work fails to connect in important ways with that of anyone else on the non-analytic

---

[41] See Moore (2003a), Variations One, §2, and p. 42. Cf. Wittgenstein (1967a), Pt I, §§569 and 570.

[42] See Moore (2003a), pp. 83 and 95; and cf. Williams (2006o), pp. 56–57 and 114–115.

[43] Locke (1965), Bk II, Ch. 27, in which the observation occurs at §26.

side). Since I have no quarrel with the idea that there is an analytic tradition, I have reacted to this unease by designating its complement, quite simply, 'non-analytic traditions'. And these are the focus of Part Three.

I hope that my artless title for Part Three does not err in the other direction, by downplaying the many crucial connections and lines of influence between the philosophers whom I discuss there.[44] Certainly, the non-analytic philosophy represented in that part is marked by some distinctive, if broad, features. Two of these are worth emphasizing straight away, because of their considerable importance in what is to come. First, there is a tendency to prioritize difference over identity. This is in contrast to analytic philosophy, where there is the opposite tendency. (Still, even here there is a danger of exaggeration. 'Tendency' is the operative word. Let us not forget that Wittgenstein considered using as a motto for his *Philosophical Investigations* a quotation from *King Lear*: 'I'll teach you differences.'[45]) The second feature, by contrast, does not distinguish the philosophy represented in Part Three from that represented in Part Two. If anything, it distinguishes both of them from the philosophy represented in Part One.[46] I have already mentioned it in §5. I am referring to a tendency, within metaphysics, indeed within sense-making more broadly, to focus attention on sense itself. The impact of this on the nature of metaphysics has been profound. There are times, as we shall see, when it has more or less reoriented the enterprise, turning the most general attempt to make sense of things into something like an attempt to make things of sense.

---

[44] At one stage I toyed with borrowing an idea from Philip Turetzky and, instead of referring to 'the analytic tradition' and 'non-analytic traditions', referring to 'the spear side' and 'the distaff side': see Turetzky (1998), p. 211 and p. 245, n. 1. This would have carried a number of suggestions: principally, that there are links on the non-analytic side, just as much as there are on the analytic side, but less obvious links; perhaps also, given the sexism of the terms, that the distinction was being drawn from one particular, implicated point of view. But the links that exist on the non-analytic side are not in fact less obvious, unless the distinction is drawn from a point of view that is so blinkered as to be of no concern to me. (I intend no criticism of Turetzky here; his use of the metaphor is importantly different.)

[45] This is reported by Maurice Drury: see Rhees (1984), p. 157. The quotation from *King Lear* occurs in Act I, Scene IV, ll. 99–100.

[46] Even that is not quite right. As we shall see in Chs. 4 and 5, it is a vital and signal feature of both Hume's philosophy and Kant's philosophy.

PART ONE

✦

THE EARLY MODERN PERIOD

CHAPTER 1

✦

Descartes

Metaphysics in the Service of Science

1. Introduction

René Descartes (1596–1650) held that some truths are beyond doubt. Among these he held that some are necessary, in a sense robust enough to mean that not even God could have made them false. And he held that metaphysics consists largely in the pursuit of such truths.

You may already be taken aback. Have I not just contradicted two of the best-known facts about Descartes' philosophy? Surely, in his very method of doubt, he showed that there was no truth that he took to be beyond doubt, or no necessary truth.[1] And did he not famously insist that both the truth and the necessity of any necessary truth depend on God's free choice?

I admit that I have opened this chapter in a deliberately provocative way. I do not deny either of these familiar facts, and in due course I must explain how I reconcile my opening claims with them. But I have begun in this way not just to be provocative, but also to highlight what seem to me crucial features of Descartes' conception of metaphysics. Descartes was committed to the pursuit of truth, in the form of the pursuit of scientific knowledge or *scientia*.[2] We might equally say, he was committed to the attempt to make sense of things – on one good interpretation of that phrase. The *most general* attempt to make sense of things is an integral part of this. It involves taking a reflective step back, and enquiring self-consciously into the nature of the

---

[1] Perhaps he took it to be beyond doubt that he existed (see §3), but it is a contingent truth that he existed.

[2] For discussion of how the former pursuit assumes the form of the latter see Williams (1978), Ch. 2. For Descartes' use of the term '*scientia*', see *Replies*, VII: 141, and the translators' n. 2.

Note: throughout this chapter, I use the following abbreviations for Descartes' works: *Correspondence* for Descartes (1991); *Discourse* for Descartes (1985b); *Meditations* for Descartes (1984a), and *First Meditation*, *Second Meditation*, etc. for its separate parts; *Passions* for Descartes (1985d); *Principles* for Descartes (1985c); *Replies* for Descartes (1984b); and *Rules* for Descartes (1985a), and *Rule One*, *Rule Two*, etc. for its separate parts. Page references are to the edition by Adam and Tannery as indicated in the margins

enterprise as a whole, that is into the nature of the very attempt to make sense of things. Its aim might be, and in Descartes' case was, to provide a systematic reconstruction of the methods used in the enterprise, vindicating its claims to succeed in doing what it is an attempt to do. And this requires reflection on what it would be to succeed in that respect, on what it would be, in other words, to make sense of things. Such reflection fulfils its function, in Descartes' view, because it involves careful attention to indubitable truths – if they were not indubitable, metaphysics would stall at the point at which they were being attended to – and because the truths in question are truths about how things must be, in the strongest sense of 'must' – if they were truths only about how things must be in a weaker sense of 'must', they would not be indubitable.[3] Hence my opening claims.

2.   The Nature of the Project: Metaphysics as Providing Science with Foundations

Before I expand on these claims, and on how I propose to reconcile them with the two exegetical facts that are supposed to tell against them, I need to say some more about Descartes' overall project and the context within which it arises.

Descartes is often said to be, among philosophers, the first great modern. That is entirely apt. But there would also be some justice in calling him the last great scholastic. He shares many of the concerns, attitudes, and basic methodological tools of that distinctive combination of Aristotelianism and Christianity which dominated European thought in the previous four centuries. Here are some notable examples, to which we shall return. He retains

- a conviction that knowledge is capable of forming a systematically interrelated whole, in other words a conviction that it is possible to make unified sense of things (e.g. *Rule One*)
- the idea of substance and much of the apparatus that goes with it, including a distinction between corporeal substance and incorporeal substance (e.g. *Sixth Meditation*)

and

- the principle that 'there must be at least as much reality in the efficient and total cause as in the effect of that cause' (*Meditations*, VII: 40).

of these works, with Roman numerals representing volume numbers and Arabic numerals representing page numbers.

[3] See *Replies*, VII: 144–146; and cf. *Meditations*, VII: 69. These remarks should become clearer in §3. Note: I do not claim that *all* the indubitable truths to which Descartes attended were truths about how things must be, in this strong sense. Again (cf. n. 1) there is an issue about his own existence. I claim only that, where the indubitable truths to which he attended were of this kind, their indubitability depended on that fact. (For an especially striking example see *Meditations*, VII: 25, the pair of sentences beginning 'But there is a deceiver…'.)

True, there are issues about the extent to which he merely shares a vocabulary with his predecessors and the extent to which he also shares an understanding of that vocabulary. For instance, he offers his own definition of substance (which we shall consider in §6) and he insists, in opposition to mainstream scholasticism, that God alone is a substance in the strictest sense – though he also recognizes created substances in a less strict sense. But there is no denying that he draws on his heritage in ways that are both crucial in shaping his own philosophical system and, from the perspective of contemporary philosophy, more or less alien.[4]

What earns him the title 'the first great modern' then? Perhaps, more than anything else, a preparedness to reflect critically on his heritage and to ask, using no other resources than are available from that position of critical reflection, what *entitles* him to draw on his heritage in the ways in which he does; a preparedness to question all authority except for that of his own reason, his own faculty for 'clear and evident intuition' and the 'certain deduction' of its consequences (*Rules*, X: 366).[5] One effect of this is an accentuation of epistemology, the study of knowledge, in the overall attempt to make sense of things. Descartes seeks not merely to know, but to know that he knows, and, as a means to that end, to know what it is for him to know. If we find it puzzling that he nevertheless accepts, seemingly uncritically, so much of what we find unacceptable, then we are probably overlooking both the extent to which thinking in general, not just Descartes' thinking, is determined by its historical and cultural context and the extent to which what we find unacceptable is in any case, ironically, a long-term effect of Descartes' own iconoclasm.

Descartes' critical step back leads, as I suggested in §1, to reflection on the very idea of making sense of things and on the means to that end. Since such reflection is itself part of the attempt to make sense of things, we can see Descartes as aspiring to a single self-contained conception that will help to explain how we are able to achieve that very conception. The conception itself is to be pursued largely for its own sake. Descartes' project is, to echo the celebrated subtitle of Bernard Williams' book on him (Williams (1978)), a project of pure enquiry. Not that this flouts any of my reservations, aired in §7 of the Introduction, about pursuing *metaphysics* for its own sake.[6] If those reservations are justified, then metaphysics, the most general attempt to make sense of things, should subserve the overall attempt to make sense

---

[4] For more on the relations between Descartes and his predecessors see Williams (1978), pp. 137–138; Cottingham (1986), pp. 4–6; and Ariew (1992). Husserl, in Husserl (1995), §10, complains about 'how much scholasticism lies hidden, as unclarified prejudice, in Descartes' *Meditations*.' (We shall return to Husserl's criticisms of Descartes in Ch. 17, §3.) Heidegger echoes the complaint in Heidegger (1962a), p. 46/p. 25 in the original German.

[5] For more on Descartes' use of the term 'intuition', see §4.

[6] Such reservations, in any case, have a largely non-Cartesian motivation.

of things; but this leaves open the possibility that the latter can be pursued for its own sake. For Descartes, the former does indeed subserve the latter. Metaphysics plays a *foundational* role in the overall endeavour. In a well-known passage from the Preface to the French edition of his *Principles* he writes:

> The whole of philosophy is like a tree. The roots are metaphysics, the trunk is physics, and the branches emerging from the trunk are all the other sciences. (IXB: 14)[7]

This idea that metaphysics should be in the service of science has recurred in various guises right through to the present day, where it still has many adherents. What is far less common nowadays is the belief that this service should take the form of providing foundations. One currently popular view, deriving from Wittgenstein, is that metaphysics (as I am construing it) is something of an altogether different kind from science, a search for clarity of understanding rather than a search for truth, which is nevertheless capable of assisting science because scientific concepts themselves need to be clearly understood. Another currently popular view, fundamentally opposed to that and associated particularly with Quine, is that metaphysics is entirely of a piece with (the rest of) science, save only for its generality; in particular, it is as much supported by it as supportive of it.[8] In neither case is

---

[7] Just before this passage Descartes gives his own explicit definition of 'metaphysics', which I think conforms well with my own use of the term in application to him. He defines it as 'the first part of philosophy …, which contains the principles of knowledge, including the explanation of the principal attributes of God, the non-material nature of our souls and all the clear and distinct notions which are in us' (ibid.). The rest of this chapter should help to clarify the various elements in this definition.

For the idea that the overall attempt to make sense of things can properly be pursued for its own sake, see Cooper (2002), pp. 59–60. Jonathan Bennett, in Bennett (2003), Ch. 20, attributes an ulterior motive to Descartes, of which he thinks Descartes himself may have an insecure grasp: he sees Descartes as ultimately seeking *peace of mind*, and he thinks that, if there were a pill that would give Descartes this peace of mind, he might just as well take it. There are passages that support this view: see e.g. the passage from *Replies*, VII: 145, quoted in Walker (1989), p. 46. (I mention this quotation by Ralph Walker because he corrects the original translation. He replaces 'alleged "absolute falsity"' by 'absolute falsity'.) Nevertheless, Bennett's view seems to me to downplay Descartes' concern with self-understanding. Insofar as there *are* ulterior motives in Descartes' overall attempt to make sense of things – and it should be noted that such motives do not preclude his making the attempt for its own sake as well – they are motives that he himself occasionally acknowledges, for instance in *Discourse*, VI: 61–62, where he refers to 'a practical philosophy which might replace the speculative philosophy taught in the schools' and says that 'through this philosophy we could … make ourselves, as it were, the lords and masters of nature.'

[8] Both views will receive further discussion: see Ch. 10, §1, and Ch. 12, §6, respectively.

metaphysics reckoned to provide science with foundations. Descartes' view of metaphysics – as a kind of propaedeutic to science, designed to vindicate it and thereby to enable it to be pursued in its own terms, with its own clear rationale, and in good faith – is in that respect decidedly outdated, a lineament, as it now appears, of early modernity.

There is perhaps no clearer indication of Descartes' own deep commitment to this view than his claim that this most general attempt to make sense of things can be made, and should be made, *once for all*. (That sounds very uncongenial to most contemporary ears.) As he says in the opening sentences of his *Meditations*:

> Some years ago I was struck by the large number of falsehoods that I had accepted as true in my childhood, and by the highly doubtful nature of the whole edifice that I had subsequently based on them. I realized that it was necessary, *once in the course of my life*, to demolish everything completely and start again right from the foundations if I wanted to establish anything at all in the sciences that was stable and likely to last. (VII: 17, emphasis added)

3. The Execution of the Project

Something that is 'stable and likely to last' is something that can withstand any sceptical attack. Descartes is preemptive. He assumes the role of archsceptic. He doubts everything. This is precisely in order to see whether there is anything that cannot be doubted, anything that can somehow be used to rebut his own universal doubt. If there is, then it is fit to serve as a foundation for science. For whatever survives his own assault can survive the assault of a genuine sceptic.

But surely Descartes' strategy is self-stultifying? If he doubts everything, then does it not follow, as a matter of simple logic, that there is nothing that cannot be doubted (*ab esse ad posse*)?

It follows only if the antecedent and the consequent here are understood as standing in a suitable relation of '*esse*' and '*posse*' to each other. There are two ways in which Descartes could deny that this is how they are to be understood. First, he could say that 'doubt' means different things in the antecedent and the consequent, for example 'call into question' and 'regard as a genuine candidate for falsity', respectively. This is a less promising response than it looks, however. To be sure, there is a distinction between merely asking whether something might be false and asserting, thinking, or supposing that it might. But Descartes' universal doubt is not purely interrogative. If it is to be characterized as calling everything into question, then calling a thing into question had better involve *some* commitment to the possibility that that thing is false. But how in that case does calling a thing into question fall short of 'regarding' it as 'a genuine candidate' for falsity?

It is not at all clear that there is any relevant substantive distinction to be drawn between these.

More promising, it seems to me, and more in keeping with how Descartes in fact conceives his strategy, is the second available response: to focus on relativization in the notion of possibility.[9] Consider: there is an obvious and clear sense in which somebody's actually moving his rook diagonally in a game of chess is no proof that he can do so, the sense in which the possibility in question is relative to the rules of chess.[10] Likewise, I suggest, in the Cartesian case, where there is relativization to giving full attention to the matter in question. Thus what I can doubt when I prescind from an issue and reflect in general terms on whether I might be mistaken in my beliefs is different from what I can doubt when I give my full attention to the issue. Perhaps, from that position of general reflection, I can doubt that one plus two is three, say on the grounds that I might have been brainwashed into thinking that it is, whereas when I focus on the mathematical issue itself I can no longer doubt (see e.g. *Meditations*, VII: 35–36).[11]

This, incidentally, is how I reconcile my opening claim in this chapter with the first of the two items of common exegetical knowledge. Yes, Descartes adopts a method of doubt which shows that he takes nothing to be beyond doubt[12] from the relevant position of general reflection. No, he does not believe that each thing remains beyond doubt when full attention is given to it.

But does the indubitability of specific beliefs, when full attention is given to them, provide Descartes with the secure foundation that he requires? Surely, their dubitability from the position of general reflection is enough for them to be vulnerable to sceptical attack? From that position a sceptic can always ask, 'Why should the fact that I cannot doubt something, when I give it my full attention, mean that it is true?' Call this question the Reflective Question.

The concern implicit in the Reflective Question bears striking witness to the tension between self-consciousness and self-confidence to which I referred in §5 of the Introduction. Descartes is fully aware of this concern

---

[9] Cf. in this connection Wittgenstein (1967a), Pt I, §183 (although the very last sentence of that section stands in interesting tension with what Descartes says about believing what is true and pursuing what is good (see *Meditations*, VII: 57–58)).

[10] Some people would insist on using the word 'may' in such a context, rather than the word 'can', to emphasize that what is in question is a kind of permissibility. So be it: permissibility itself is still a kind of possibility.

[11] Cf. Williams (2006c), p. 240. Another relativization worth noting is the relativization to effort: there are some things that I can doubt only with a certain degree of effort. Cf. the final paragraph of *First Meditation*; cf. also Hume (1978a), p. 269. But this does not help Descartes, for the simple reason that a genuine sceptic, against whose assault he is trying to protect his edifice, is always liable to apply the requisite effort.

[12] I use 'beyond doubt' and 'indubitable' synonymously.

(e.g. *Meditations*, VII: 36). As part of his response to it he provides his own account of what it is to give something one's full attention. He talks in terms of 'clear and distinct perception'. Roughly, to perceive something clearly is simply to attend to it; to perceive something distinctly is, in addition, to attend to every aspect of it, thereby ensuring that the perception is not confused with any other (*Principles*, Pt One, §§45 and 46).[13] Note that there are two requirements that the notion needs to satisfy if it is to play the foundational rôle that it is supposed to play for Descartes, and if he is to stand any chance of providing a satisfactory answer to the Reflective Question. The first requirement is that it should be possible for whoever clearly and distinctly perceives something to be true to tell this introspectively. In particular, such a person has to be able to tell this without yet being able to tell whether the thing in question is in fact true. This means that 'clearly and distinctly perceives to be true' must not be understood (as 'knows to be true' is understood) in such a way that, by definition, it cannot relate a person to a falsehood (cf. *Discourse*, VI: 38–39 and *Meditations*, VII: 35 and 62[14]). The second requirement is that there should be a normative dimension to the notion. Being convinced that something is true when one is in no fit state to have a view on the matter, for example when one has been drugged or when one is suffering from some kind of delirium, had better not count as clearly and distinctly perceiving it to be true (cf. *Replies*, VII: 461–462). The first requirement is so that clear and distinct perception be *serviceable* in founding science; the second requirement is so that it be *effective* in doing so. The obvious problem, which I here simply note, is that the two requirements are in tension with each other. Be that as it may, the Reflective Question can now be formulated as follows.

> Why should the fact that I cannot doubt something, when I clearly and distinctly perceive it to be true, mean that it is true?

Those who embrace a certain kind of idealism will respond to this question by appeal to a constitutive link between clear and distinct perception and truth. And where metaphysical issues are concerned, this will include those, or at least some of those, whose response to the Creativity Question from §6 of the Introduction is to say that metaphysics is a fundamentally creative exercise. But Descartes has no sympathy for anything of that sort.[15] His own celebrated response to the Reflective Question begins with the one

---

[13] The reference to clarity is thus pleonastic: distinctness entails clarity (ibid.).

[14] In all three of these passages Descartes avers that, but for some guarantee which he believes he can provide (see below), it is an open question whether that which is clearly and distinctly perceived to be true is in fact true. (In the first passage the verb he uses is 'conceive' rather than 'perceive', and he talks of 'ideas' rather than 'perceptions', but the point is the same.)

[15] *Contra* Jonathan Bennett: see Bennett (1998), §VI.

instance of it to which he can see an immediate answer, that in which what is at issue is his own existence. Why should the fact that he cannot doubt that he exists, when he clearly and distinctly perceives it to be true, mean that it is true? Because if it were not true, he would not be in a position clearly and distinctly to perceive anything, nor to doubt anything, nor to be unable to doubt anything. In a word, he would not be in a position to *think*.[16] 'I think,' Descartes famously says, 'therefore I am' (*Discourse*, VI: 32; cf. *Meditations*, VII: 25).

What is distinctive about this case, we now see, is not that it is the one case in which there is an indubitability. For, in the relevant sense of indubitability, there are very many cases in which there is an indubitability. What is distinctive about this case is that it is the one case in which the indubitability, viewed from a position of general reflection, provides its own immediate warrant.

But 'the one case' is the operative phrase. That Descartes has a guarantee of his own existence does not advance his cause very much. How does he proceed from here?

While he is contemplating his own existence he also focuses on various characteristics of himself, including the fact that he has an innate idea of God, an infinite Being whose infinitude, crucially, includes benevolence. Drawing on some of his scholastic heritage, as advertised earlier in §1, and in particular drawing on the principle that 'there must be at least as much reality in the efficient and total cause as in the effect of that cause', he argues that only God could have placed such a grand idea in him, and hence that God must exist (*Meditations*, VII: 49–51).[17] But God, granted His benevolence, would not allow Descartes to be deceived when he is doing all within his powers to discover the truth. So Descartes does after all have a general answer to the Reflective Question: the fact that he cannot doubt something, when he clearly and distinctly perceives it to be true, does mean that it is true because the alternative would be contrary to God's benevolence (*Fourth Meditation*).

Plainly, Descartes could not have made any kind of progress here, even in his own terms, had he not allowed himself to interrupt his general reflection on what he believes by directing his attention, as the need arises, to principles that he clearly and distinctly perceives to be true, principles that he cannot at the same time doubt, and then appropriating those principles. Examples are the principle that his thinking implies his existing, and the scholastic principle just mentioned about cause and effect (see e.g. *Replies*, VII: 135 and 145–146). Before we consider a natural objection to which this

---

[16] For Descartes' very broad conception of 'thinking', see *Principles*, Pt One, §32.

[17] Note that Descartes has another argument for the existence of God: see *Meditations*, VII: 65–67. (In *Replies*, VII: 120, he claims that 'there are only two ways of proving the existence of God.')

gives rise, it is worth pausing to consider what form the indubitability of these principles takes. This will enable me to say how I reconcile the second of my opening claims in this chapter with the second of the two items of common exegetical knowledge.

The fact that we cannot doubt these principles, when we clearly and distinctly perceive them to be true, is of a piece with the fact that we cannot conceive them to be false; that their falsity would, as Descartes puts it, 'conflict with our human concepts' (*Replies*, VII: 150). But for their falsity to conflict with our human concepts, Descartes says in the same context, *just is* for them to be necessary. That is how Descartes understands necessity. Nor is there any suggestion that this is a relativized necessity, of the same sort as the relativized possibilities considered earlier.[18] So it follows that not even God could have made one of these principles false. If it conflicts with our human concepts that somebody should think without existing, or that one plus two should not be three, then it conflicts with our human concepts that God should have made somebody think without existing, or that God should have made one plus two other than three (cf. *Meditations*, VII: 71).

What then of the item of common exegetical knowledge, that both the truth and the necessity of any necessary truth depend on God's free choice (e.g. *Replies*, VII: 432 and 436; cf. 'Letter to Mersenne', dated 15 April 1630, in *Correspondence*, I: 145, and 'Letter to Mersenne', dated 6 May 1630, in *Correspondence*, I: 149)? There is simply no conflict. Dependence here need not be understood in terms of the exclusion of possibilities. That thinking implies existing; and that it is necessary that thinking implies existing, in other words that our human concepts conflict with thinking's failing to imply existing: these can be regarded, for current purposes, as two data. Descartes' view is that, like everything else, they depend on God's free choice. The first holds because of how God has made thinking; the second holds because of how God has made us. But we should not say that, in making thinking thus, God has excluded other possibilities, nor that, in making us thus, He has prevented us from grasping other possibilities. *For there are no other possibilities.* To suggest that there are would simply be to violate the second datum: that it is necessary that thinking implies existing.

(It is only fair for me to add that not everything that Descartes says fits comfortably into this account of his views. Most notably, we find the following in a letter to Antoine Arnauld:

> I do not think we should ever say of anything that it cannot be brought about by God. For since every basis of truth ... depends on his omnipotence, I would not dare to say that God cannot make [it] ... that one and two should not be three. I merely say that he has given me such a

---

[18] We shall return to the relations between relativized modalities and unrelativized modalities in Chs 9 and 10. See §§4 and 3 of those chapters, respectively.

mind that I cannot conceive … an aggregate of one and two which is not
three, and that such [a thing involves] a contradiction in my conception.
('Letter to Arnauld', dated 29 July 1648, in *Correspondence*, V: 224)

It seems to me that Descartes is being over-cautious here. I think he is at perfect liberty, by his own lights, to say what he 'would not dare to say'.[19] There is
admittedly the complication that we might be able to conceive, in the abstract
if not in detail, God's making something true that conflicts with our human
concepts while changing our concepts so as to remove the conflict, or even,
for that matter, God's making something true that conflicts with our human
concepts and allowing the conflict to remain – provided that in the latter
case we prescind from His benevolence. But neither of these, strictly speaking,
precludes our saying, of any particular thing that conflicts with our human
concepts, that God cannot make it true. These considerations about how our
human concepts and their relations with reality might have been different
would in any case have little impact on Descartes' account of modality if that
account were intended, not as an *analysis*, but rather as some version of what
Simon Blackburn calls 'quasi-realism'. On a suitably quasi-realist understanding, 'It is necessary that' is not to be analyzed as (is not equivalent in meaning
to) 'It conflicts with our human concepts that it should not be the case that';
rather, the former serves as an expression of the conflict referred to in the
latter (see Blackburn (1993b)). This certainly allows for the necessity to be
as robust as I am suggesting it is on Descartes' conception. For it allows for
statements of necessity which, because they do not have our human concepts
and what conflicts with them as their subject matter, are not under any direct
threat from considerations about how these might have been different.[20] I do
not however claim that Descartes himself has a quasi-realist understanding
of these matters. Not only would it be anachronistic to do so; it would make
the caution which already causes some exegetical difficulty for me cause even
more. One final point in connection with this caution: when Descartes refuses
to rule out the possibility that God should have made one plus two other than
three, even though such a thing is unintelligible to us, he provides the first hint
in this historical narrative of a general problem to which, or to one version
of which, I referred in §6 of the Introduction, namely that there is no way of
registering the thought that our sense-making is limited in this or that respect
except by transgressing the limit.)

---

[19] In this respect I am less charitable to him than Jonathan Bennett, who tries but fails,
in my view, to justify the circumspection: see Bennett (1998), §VII. In other respects, I
should emphasize, I am greatly indebted to Bennett's excellent essay. (Also very helpful is
James Conant (1991), pp. 115–123, though in various respects I am *more* charitable to
Descartes than Conant is.)

[20] See Moore (2002b). And see Ch. 10, §3, for discussion of a similar idea in the later work
of Wittgenstein.

Descartes allows himself to appropriate these principles which he clearly and distinctly perceives to be true, then. But, as I intimated earlier, this gives rise to a natural objection. The objection is simply that he cannot then claim to be protecting his beliefs against any potential attack from a sceptic. Consider the sceptic who remains at the level of general reflection, where the Reflective Question arises, and who refuses to countenance any reliance on any clear and distinct perception until that question has been given some general answer. Descartes does have a general answer to the Reflective Question, but only because he has already allowed himself to rely on clear and distinct perceptions. (This is in effect the so-called Cartesian Circle.[21]) Does Descartes have a satisfactory reply to this objection?

No, not if a 'satisfactory' reply is a reply that will satisfy the sceptic.[22] But it would be misleading simply to say, without further ado, that Descartes has therefore been defeated in his project by the sceptic. The person we are now calling 'the sceptic' declines to step down from the level of general reflection, in other words declines to give his full attention to anything, until he can be rationally persuaded to do so. But it is obvious that he cannot be rationally persuaded to do *anything* unless he gives his full attention to reasons that are put before him. Furthermore, we *already knew* that at that general level everything can be doubted. It was precisely Descartes' strategy to begin at that level and to doubt everything. And 'everything' here includes his own existence, by the way. He did not find even that indubitable until he eventually turned his attention to the issue (*Meditations*, VII: 24–25). The person we are now calling 'the sceptic' is like one of those tiresome children who, through no desire to learn but simply in order to annoy, persists in asking 'Why?' every time an answer is given to one of his questions. (Here a quotation from William James is pertinent: 'General scepticism is a permanent torpor of the will ... and you can no more kill it off by logic than you can kill off obstinacy or practical joking' (James (1978), pp. 273–274).[23]) So, although we *could* say that Descartes has been defeated in his project by the sceptic, there is at least as much rationale for refusing to dignify this metaphysically uninteresting position with the label 'scepticism'. And then the issue is what to make of the undeniably sturdy structure – by any reasonable standards of sturdiness – which Descartes has built.

---

[21] For excellent discussions of the Cartesian Circle, see Williams (1978), pp. 189–204; Cottingham (1986), pp. 66–70; Loeb (1992); van Cleve (1998); and Bennett (2003), §149.

[22] Cf. Hume (1975a), pp. 149–150.

[23] That James refers to the will here rather than the intellect is noteworthy in the light of Descartes' theory of error (see §4). Cf. Bernard Williams' reference to 'wilful obstinacy' in Williams (2006c), p. 244. Cf. also Spinoza (2002a), ¶77.

4. The Shape of Descartes' System. Its Epistemology

This is a structure in which we, who make sense of things, do so by appeal to data which indicate how things, independently of our sense-making, are. And this applies in particular to our most general sense-making, that which we achieve when we successfully engage in metaphysics. We have seen that Descartes talks in terms of perception where metaphysical matters such as the scholastic principle about cause and effect are concerned. This is perception of a non-sensory kind. He also sometimes uses the word 'intuition' for it (see Rules, X: 368).[24] Henceforth I shall do likewise. But the word 'perception' is entirely apposite. For intuition is in certain fundamental respects just like sensory perception. Whether we intuit that something is so, or sensorily perceive that something is so, there is a more or less metaphorical sense in which we 'see' how things are, and in each case this is something that we are able to do because we have the appropriate mental apparatus which supplies us with data about how things are.[25]

Sensory perception can have its own relative clarity and distinctness. Indeed it can be 'sufficiently clear and distinct' for its own purpose, which is to serve as a rough guide to what benefits us or harms us (Meditations, VII: 83). But it never has the clarity and distinctness of intuition. And there is not the same indubitability in the case of sensory perception as there is in the case of intuition. Nor should there be. For there is not the same reliability either. Sensory perception often inclines us to believe what is not true, for example when a square tower looks round from afar (Meditations, VII: 76). This has two important corollaries for Descartes' overall system. First, Descartes insists that, in order to achieve insight even into the nature of physical objects, we must appeal ultimately to intuition rather than to sensory perception. The essence of a physical object, on Descartes' view, is its sheer spatio-temporality, and this is something that is revealed to us by abstract mathematical reasoning from what we grasp in intuition (see Meditations, XII: 30–31; cf. also Principles, Pt One, §§23ff.).[26] The second important corollary is Descartes' account of error. He certainly needs an account. For he needs an explanation of how, despite God's benevolence, we are not error-proof. Descartes' explanation is that the fault when we err is entirely ours. We judge how things are even where our perceptions do not

---

[24] But intuition is not confined to such metaphysical principles, nor yet to necessities. Descartes includes, among the examples of truths of which he has an intuition, that he exists. Note that he also acknowledges a third kind of perception, which he calls 'imagination' (Principles, Pt One, §32).

[25] Descartes himself emphasizes similarities between intuition and sensory perception in Rules, X: 400–401. Cf. Kurt Gödel's celebrated comparison of mathematical intuition with sensory perception in Gödel (1983), pp. 483–485.

[26] The idea that intuition, rather than sensory perception, reveals the nature of physical reality is a dominant theme of Hatfield (2002). See also Loeb (1990).

have the requisite clarity and distinctness and where it is within our power to withhold our judgment. I see a square tower from a distance, say, and I jump to the conclusion that it is round. (See *Fourth Meditation*.) This does nothing to impugn the assurance that Descartes has given us that, when we do all that is within our power to avoid error, we shall avoid it.

The similarities between intuition and sensory perception are a crucial part of Descartes' overall conception, a conception in whose terms he seeks to explain how we are able to achieve that very conception (see §2). If we set aside any scruples that may still be lingering in connection with the extravagant 'scepticism' considered at the end of the previous section, then the idea that there is some troubling circularity here begins to look baseless. Consider, as an analogy, the physiology of vision. This is concerned with a variant of the Reflective Question: why is the fact that someone takes her environment to be a certain way, when she enjoys a visual experience, symptomatic of the fact that it is that way? The answer consists of a sophisticated story about ocular irradiation, retinas, and suchlike. We would not *think* to doubt such an answer just on the grounds that physiologists themselves make use of their faculty of sight in arriving at it, for example when looking at eyeballs or when looking at the readings on various instruments in their laboratories.[27]

I referred in §2 to the Quinean view that metaphysics is entirely of a piece with (the rest of) science. Part of that view is what Quine himself has famously called 'naturalized epistemology'. This is a conception of epistemology as 'contained in natural science,' so that, in 'studying how the human subject ... projects his physics from his data, ... we appreciate that our position in the world is just like his,' and 'our very epistemological enterprise, therefore, ... is our own ... projection from stimulations like those we were meting out to our epistemological subject' (Quine (1969b), p. 83). As I indicated in §2, Descartes' foundationalism, whereby the scientific story needs to be grounded in an independent metaphysical story, makes him one of Quine's principal targets, if not the principal target (e.g. Quine (1960), pp. 24–25). And yet, ironically, if we prescind from that admittedly profound difference between their conceptions, we see an equally profound similarity in what remains. Descartes too views epistemology as part of his overall conception of the world, a 'projection' from clear and distinct perceptions like those he attributes to his epistemological subject.[28]

---

[27] Cf. in this connection Descartes' pervasive use of the metaphor of light. He often says that what we intuit is manifest to us by 'the natural light' or 'the light of nature' (e.g. *Meditations*, VII: 41), and what is manifest to us by the natural light is supposed to help us see how the natural light makes things manifest to us. For further discussion of Descartes' use of this metaphor, see Derrida (1982d), pp. 266–267, and Ayers (1998), esp. p. 1014.

[28] Cf. van Cleve (1998), §X; and see the reference to Stephen Leeds in his n. 58. Cf. also Quine (1969b), p. 71, where Quine insists that we can understand 'the link between

5.   Analogues of Descartes' Argument for the Existence
of God in Contemporary Analytic Philosophy

That Descartes has built a sturdy structure does not of course entail that he
has built a structure that is invulnerable to attack. Its real weak spot is the
argument for the existence of God. And I shall make no attempt to defend
this argument. Even here, however, it is worth pausing to reflect on analogous arguments that command significant respect in contemporary analytic
philosophy.[29]

These are arguments to the effect that it is impossible to explain the
existence of certain beliefs, perhaps even to understand those beliefs, without oneself sharing them and indeed invoking them, or, relatedly, that it
is impossible to explain the existence of certain concepts, perhaps even to
grasp those concepts, without oneself taking them to have application in
reality and indeed having recourse to that very application; in sum, that it is
impossible to make sense of certain ways of making sense of things without
oneself making sense of things in those ways. This is obviously not in general true. One can explain the widespread belief among children in Father
Christmas even if one does not oneself believe in him, perhaps *only* if one
does not oneself believe in him. But if these arguments are sound, then
such detachment is not always possible. Thus Hilary Putnam has argued
that one could not explain our basic belief in the existence of trees, say,
except with reference to trees, thereby defying a certain scepticism about
'the external world' (Putnam (1981), Ch. 1).[30] And Barry Stroud has argued
that one could not account for our concept of yellowness if, along with
certain physicalists, one subscribed to the view that nothing in the world is
'really' yellow (Stroud (2000)).[31] But the most striking example, in the present context, is supplied by Thomas Nagel. It is the most striking example
because, like Descartes' argument, it involves our idea of infinity, albeit, in
Nagel's case, in a mathematical guise. Nagel reflects on our use of reason –
'a local activity of finite creatures' (Nagel (1997), p. 70) – to arrive at the
idea of infinity. And as against those who think that this both can and must

---

observation and science' by using 'information ... provided by the very science whose link
with observation we are seeking to understand.' If 'observation' is understood as including clear and distinct perception, and if 'science' is understood cognately with '*scientia*'
(see above, n. 2), then Descartes would agree. For a demurral, see Nietzsche (1967c),
§486. And for a profound recoil from any such naturalism, see Ch. 17.

[29] As I remarked in n. 17, Descartes has another argument for the existence of God. That
argument, which is often called 'the ontological argument', has found surprising appeal of
its own among analytic philosophers: see e.g. Russell (1998), p. 60, and Murdoch (1993),
Ch. 13.

[30] Cf. Thomas Baldwin (1988), p. 36, where he explicitly compares this kind of argument
with Descartes' argument.

[31] For an interesting exchange on this argument, see Brewer (2004) and Stroud (2004).

be understood in terms of our finite resources, without appeal to infinity itself, he urges:

> To get [the idea of infinity] we need to be operating with the concept of numbers as the sizes of sets, which can have anything whatever as their elements. What we understand, then, is that the numbers we use to count things ... are merely the first part of a series that never ends.
>
> ... Though our direct acquaintance with and designation of specific numbers is extremely limited, we cannot *make sense* of it except by putting them, and ourselves, in the context of something larger, something whose existence is independent of our fragmentary experience of it.... When we think about the finite activity of counting, we come to realize that it can only be understood as part of something infinite. (Nagel (1997), p. 71, emphasis added)

This is really not so different from what we find in Descartes.[32]

Nevertheless, it is different. And it is different in one crucial respect.[33] Descartes' idea of infinity is not primarily mathematical. That is, it is not primarily a matter of the unending (cf. 'Letter to Clerselier', dated 23 April 1649, in *Correspondence*, V: 356). It is part of his idea of God. And it has, under that more metaphysical guise, an evaluative aspect: it entails God's benevolence. So there is far more room for doubt about whether this style of argument can apply to it. We routinely make sense of evaluative ways of making sense of things without endorsing them, and certainly without taking the values in question to be realized.[34]

There is a related problem for Descartes. Just as his idea's evaluative aspect raises concerns about his argument, so too, ironically, it raises concerns about his perceived need for any such argument. For the significance of this evaluative aspect, in terms of Descartes' overall project, is its relation to his hope that, when he does all that is within his power to avoid error, he shall avoid it. More specifically, Descartes hopes that, when he does all that is within his power to avoid *metaphysical* error, he shall avoid it. And the very fact that this arises for Descartes *as a hope* – the fact that he sees a logical gap between how he takes things to be, when he tries his best

---

[32] For a fuller discussion of the connections between them, with specific reference to Wittgenstein, see Moore (2011).

[33] I do not mean to suggest that it is different only in this respect. Another important difference is that, whereas Descartes argues that he must grant the existence of something infinite if he is to explain how he has his idea, Nagel argues that we must grant the existence of something infinite if we are so much as to characterize our idea. As regards explaining how we have our idea, Nagel takes seriously the possibility that this is something we cannot do (Nagel (1997), p. 76).

[34] Cf. in this connection Bernard Williams on the explanation of people's ethical beliefs in Williams (2006o), Ch. 8.

to make the most general sense of them, and how they really are – must cast doubt on his claim to have made sense of *how he takes things to be*. Consider, for example, the fact that, by his own reckoning, he has a clear and distinct perception that he cannot think without existing. If this perception is answerable to a completely independent reality, and if, granted the perception's high level of generality, such answerability does not involve any direct causal relation between him and that reality, then it is a real question what makes this perception a perception *that he cannot think without existing*. In what relation does this perception stand to the 'fact' that he cannot think without existing, but not to the 'fact' that one plus two is three, say? This concern, which admittedly merits a far fuller and far less schematic discussion than the little I have said here, is part of my own reason for answering the Creativity Question, from §6 of the Introduction, in such a non-Cartesian way, that is, for insisting that metaphysics is a fundamentally creative exercise.[35]

6. 'The Disenchantment of the World'

The logical gap between metaphysical belief and metaphysical reality is not the only logical gap that Descartes acknowledges. He also acknowledges a logical gap between mind and matter. This is in part because, at the point where he first registers the indubitability of his own existence, he takes the existence of material objects to remain in doubt – perhaps he is in the throes of some interminable dream – and concludes that he himself is not a material object (*Meditations*, VII: 26–27). Rather, he is a thinking being, or a mind, and his body, although it is 'very closely joined' to him, is nevertheless independent of him (*Meditations*, VII: 78). This connects with Descartes' views about substance. Substance, on Descartes' definition, is 'a thing which exists in such a way as to depend on no other thing whatsoever' (*Principles*, Pt One, §51). He recognizes three kinds of substance. The first is Divine substance, of which there is only one instance, namely God Himself. As I commented in §2, Descartes takes God to be the only substance in the strictest sense, for everything else is created and sustained by Him and is therefore dependent for its existence on Him. Nonetheless, Descartes also sees an independence among created things, which allows him to recognize two further kinds of substance in a less strict sense. One of these is material substance, or corporeal substance, of which again there is only one instance, an infinite homogeneous fluid that is ultimately no different from

---

[35] Cf. Nietzsche (1967c), §533; and Sullivan (2007), §III passim. We shall return to this issue, more or less directly, in several of the following chapters: see esp. Ch. 2, §5; Ch. 7, §3; Ch. 10, §3; Ch. 15, §6; Ch. 16, §6(c); and Ch. 20, §3. I shall also have a little more to say about my own response to the Creativity Question in the Conclusion, §§3–5.

space (*Principles*, Pt Two, §11). The second is created thinking substance, of which there are milliards of instances, perhaps even infinitely many, including Descartes himself, you, and me.[36]

One consequence of this complicated scheme is that, on at least one reasonable way of construing 'transcendence', Descartes allows us scope, within metaphysics, to make sense of what is transcendent (see the Transcendence Question in §6 of the Introduction). An obvious case in point is when we engage in reflection on God. Note, however, that there is just as much rationale within Descartes' scheme, if not more, for saying that we are making sense of what is transcendent when we engage in geometry or physics. Such is the gap between mind and matter. For this reason among countless others the scheme has had little lasting appeal. In the next two chapters we shall see recoils of particular note on the part of Spinoza and Leibniz.[37]

Nevertheless, the indirect influence of the scheme has been immense. It relates to what is perhaps Descartes' most significant legacy, and what is certainly a highly distinctive feature of the modernity that he helped to inaugurate: a dislocation of the self, or at least of the subjectivity of the self, from the objectivity of its physical surrounds. If this can indeed be said to be Descartes' most significant legacy, then it can be said to be so only *malgré lui*. For, as I have tried to emphasize in this chapter, Descartes' vision is a profoundly synoptic one. The problem is that it is also a profoundly self-conscious one, and self-consciousness is always liable to make the environment appear alien. The self, in Descartes' vision, is autonomous. It is to be conceived independently of its environment, and it directs itself independently of its environment, despite the elaborate story that Descartes tells about how each affects the other and about how the one can know the other (e.g. *Sixth Meditation*).[38] The environment is in turn, and by the same token, to be conceived independently of the self, indeed independently of all intentionality or purpose. The interaction of physical objects – which are parts of the one infinite corporeal substance, and which are distinguished from one another by their relative motion (*Principles*, Pt Two, §23) – is to be explained in a strictly mechanistic way, in terms of the objects' spatio-temporal properties (*Principles*, Pt Four, §200).[39] This is in opposition to the prevailing

---

[36] See Ch. 2, §2, for a brief account of Descartes' considered reason for thinking that minds and matter are separate substances.

[37] Leibniz' recoil, which involves denying the existence of material substance altogether, has a celebrated echo in Berkeley: see Berkeley (1962a). Cf. Lloyd (1994), p. 39.

[38] For more on the idea that the self is to be conceived independently of its environment, and for criticism of the idea, see McDowell (1986), esp. §§5 and 6. For discussion of the essential modernity of the idea, see Burnyeat (1982).

[39] Their *interaction* is to be explained in this way. The same is not true of *all* of their behaviour: Descartes notoriously allows that some of their behaviour is to be explained by the

Aristotelianism of Descartes' day, whereby different sorts of physical object have different 'forms' which explain their interaction teleologically. It is in this revolt against Aristotelianism that we see part of what has come to be known, in a phrase due to Max Weber, as 'the disenchantment of the world' (Weber (1946), p. 155).

Here is the self, then, and there is the 'transcendent' world beyond the self, each independent of the other. And for the former to make sense of the latter, on the full Cartesian conception, is for the former to have clear and distinct perceptions, which answer correctly to how the latter is, and then to deduce their consequences. It is for the former to *represent* the latter.

I have already expressed reservations, at the end of the previous section, about whether we can make sense of this relation of representation at the highest level of generality. Because of the role that God plays in Descartes' system, these must in turn become reservations about whether we can make sense of the relation at any lower level either.[40] A *fortiori* they must become reservations about whether we can actually stand in this relation to anything, let alone knowingly do so, as Descartes requires. It is not just that there is room for suspicion about whether science can be given metaphysical foundations of the sort that Descartes describes, or about whether it needs them. There is room for suspicion of a much deeper kind, about the very idea of (Cartesian) representation.

What alternative is there? One radical alternative is to be found in a vision of physical reality as itself making sense (the 'reenchantment' of the world) and a concomitant vision of us, who aspire to make sense of physical reality, as being ourselves a part of it, as aspiring in effect to become participants in its own sense-making. This makes the relation between us and physical reality akin to the relation between a new member of a linguistic community and the community as a whole. It also replaces the idea that making sense of physical reality consists in representing it by the idea that making sense of physical reality consists in actively expressing the sense that it itself already makes. We shall see many variations on this theme in what is to come. In particular we shall see one very distinctive variation on it in the next protagonist, Spinoza.[41]

Spinoza is a post-Cartesian philosopher.[42] This of course means more than that he succeeds Descartes. It means that many of his problems and

---

actions of the mind (*Passions*, Pt One, §34). For criticism of this idea, see Williams (1978), pp. 287ff.

[40] Cf. Husserl (1995), p. 83.

[41] This reference to *expression* is the first hint of how much I shall be borrowing from Deleuze: see esp. Deleuze (1990a). For a fascinating discussion of the idea and its historical importance, see Taylor (1975), Ch. 1.

[42] Cf. Deleuze (1990a), p. 325.

questions are Cartesian problems and questions, even when his doctrines are not Cartesian doctrines, and that his own philosophy is shaped in ineliminable ways by his borrowing, developing, applying, amending, challenging, and rejecting what Descartes passes on to him. It is a measure of Descartes' greatness that there should be any such thing as post-Cartesian philosophy in this sense.

CHAPTER 2

Spinoza

Metaphysics in the Service of Ethics

1. Introduction

One of the most striking and most significant features of Spinoza's masterpiece *Ethics*[1] is its title. Unless we see this as a work in ethics we do not know the first thing about it. The fact that it is undeniably a work in metaphysics as well tells us something about how Spinoza conceives both ethics and metaphysics, and one of my aims in this chapter is to explain these intertwined conceptions. As we shall see, the attempt to make sense of things, for Spinoza, is itself an ethical enterprise; and the most general attempt to make sense of things, for Spinoza as for Descartes, involves surveying that very enterprise, making sense of making sense of things.[2]

Descartes too had an ethical vision that was tied, in its own way, to his metaphysics. Having acknowledged different grades of freedom, and having equated freedom of the highest grade with determination by reason (Descartes (1984a), AT VII: 56ff.), he urged that our supreme happiness depends on our being so determined, while its chief obstacle depends on our being determined instead by our passions – where the contrast between our being determined by our reason and our being determined by our passions is essentially a contrast between our being active and our being passive (e.g. Descartes (1991), AT IV: 267 and 295, and Descartes (1985d), Pt One, §17).[3] Although Spinoza had no patience for the mind/body dualism

---

[1] Throughout this chapter I use the following abbreviations for Spinoza's works: *Ethics* for Spinoza (2002c); *Letter 1, Letter 2*, etc., for individual letters in Spinoza (2002e); *Political Treatise* for Spinoza (2002d); *Short Treatise* for Spinoza (2002b); and *Treatise* for Spinoza (2002a). All unaccompanied references are to the *Ethics*, for which I adopt the following conventions: 'IIp40s2' names Pt II, Prop. 40, Schol. II, and so forth; 'IVdd1,2' names Pt IV, Definitions 1 and 2, and so forth; 'IVp23+pf' stands for Pt IV, Prop. 23 together with its proof; and 'acc', as in 'IIp29+acc', abbreviates 'all accompanying material'.

[2] For an excellent overview of why the *Ethics* is a work in ethics, see Lloyd (1996), Ch. 5.

[3] For a helpful discussion of these matters, see Cottingham (1986), pp. 152–156. For a discussion pertaining to the seventeenth century more broadly, highlighting its debts to antiquity, see James (1998). In the last paragraph of Descartes (1984a), *Third Meditation*,

in whose terms Descartes expounded this vision, and in whose terms he tried to explain various techniques for mastering our passions,[4] there was much here that aligned them. They were both part of a rationalist tradition that venerates the freedom and power of the mind. But there was a far more carefully worked out and far more compelling development of that tradition in Spinoza than there was in Descartes.[5]

Benedictus de Spinoza (1632–1677) was, in the memorable words of Bertrand Russell, 'the noblest and most lovable of the great philosophers' (Russell (1961), p. 552). He produced work that was both a testament to his nobility and itself ennobling. Deleuze describes Spinoza's philosophical method in the *Ethics* as follows:

> It is opposition to everything that takes pleasure in the powerlessness and distress of men, … everything that breaks men's spirits…. Spinoza did not believe in hope or even in courage; he believed only in joy, and in vision. He let others live provided they let him live. He wanted only to inspire, to waken, to reveal. (Deleuze (1988a), p. 14)

In order to inspire, to waken, and to reveal, Spinoza sought to achieve a general understanding of things which, on the one hand, would conduce to the more particular understanding of things in which the mind's 'highest virtue' consists (Vpp25–28) but which, on the other hand, and in contrast to that more particular understanding of things, could also be communicated to others (see §6). The pursuit of this general understanding of things, which he undertook in the *Ethics*, was a metaphysical pursuit. In what follows I shall try to substantiate these claims.

2. Substance

In §6 of the previous chapter we considered Descartes' complex views about substance, views which first separated God from His creation and then, within that creation, separated freely rational conscious minds from the inert, meaningless, mechanistically regulated material world. At the heart of Spinoza's vision is a profound recoil from this. Spinoza acknowledges

---

he tells us that our 'greatest joy' derives from 'the contemplation of the divine majesty'. This is a related idea which has echoes in what is to come (see §5).

[4] See esp. VPref where, with somewhat uncharacteristic derision, Spinoza makes a series of telling points against Descartes' dualism. See also §2.

[5] One interesting consequence of the differences between them is that, whereas Descartes' dualism, together with his emphasis on 'mastering' our passions, makes his vision something of an anathema to mainstream feminism, Spinoza's vision has attracted significant interest and support among contemporary feminists: see e.g. Lloyd (1994), Gatens (1999), and James (2012). I hope, in the course of this chapter, to cast light on the reasons why.

only one substance. (Descartes acknowledged only one substance 'in the strictest sense'. But in Spinoza there are no concessions.) This substance is 'absolutely infinite'. This means that it must encompass everything, lest there be anything separate from it by which it is limited. Substance is that 'in' which everything that is, is (Ia1,p15). There are no fundamentally different domains of being for Spinoza, no fundamentally different levels of being, no fundamentally different ways of being. To be, even in the case of substance, is to be 'in substance'. Substance is in itself (Id3).[6]

One of the ways in which Descartes distinguished between substances was by means of their attributes, where an attribute of a substance is a property of that substance that constitutes its essential nature (Descartes (1985c), Pt One, §53). In the case of created substances he recognized two attributes: that of thought, which each mind enjoys, and that of extension, which the material world enjoys. And it was because he believed that a substance that enjoys one of these attributes can always be conceived independently of a substance that enjoys the other that he concluded that the one can always exist independently of the other; in other words, that minds and matter are separate substances (Descartes (1984a), AT VII: 78).[7]

Spinoza agrees that a substance that enjoys one of these attributes can in some sense be conceived independently of a substance that enjoys the other. But he does not think it follows that the one can exist independently of the other. For there can be two ways of conceiving the same thing. Thus, to borrow Frege's famous example, it is possible in some sense to conceive the evening star without conceiving the morning star (Frege (1997c), p. 152/p. 27 in the original German).[8] But it does not follow that the evening star can exist without the morning star. Indeed, astronomical investigation has revealed that the evening star *is* the morning star. This one entity can be observed, and can be thought of, in two quite different ways, or from two quite different points of view. So there is no reason, Spinoza insists, why thought and extension should not be two attributes of a single substance (Ip10+acc). And given his understanding of substance as all-encompassing, that is precisely what he thinks they are. 'Thinking substance and extended substance,' he says, anticipating the Fregean analogy, 'are one and the same substance, comprehended now under this attribute, now under that' (IIp7s).[9]

[6] For discussion of how these remarks consist with Spinoza's distinction between '*Natura naturans*' and '*Natura naturata*' (Ip29s), see Deleuze (1990a), pp. 99–104. See further Ch. 21, §2(a).

[7] In Ch. 1, §6, I suggested that Descartes also took a cue from the fact that, when he first registered the indubitability of his own existence, he held the existence of any extended being to be in doubt. For discussion of the relation between that consideration and the argument presented here in the main text, see Williams (1978), Ch. 4, esp. pp. 102–108.

[8] We shall return to this example in Ch. 8, §4. As we shall see, Frege himself would put the point somewhat differently.

[9] For an interesting note of dissent, see Nietzsche (1967c), §523. (We shall return to Nietzsche's view of Spinoza in Ch. 15, §7(a).)

In the created realm, thought and extension were the only two attributes that Descartes recognized. There is a sense in which they are the only two attributes that Spinoza recognizes. They are the only two attributes that he identifies. And he takes them to be the only two of which we are aware. He nevertheless holds that there are infinitely many others, which somehow indicate their existence to us (*Short Treatise*, p. 39, n. 3). What are we to make of Spinoza's commitment to all these further attributes? The first thing that needs to be emphasized is that it plays no role in the *Ethics*. It is true that in the *Ethics* he takes substance to have 'infinite attributes' (Id6,p10s,p11). But in terms of how this relates to the rest of the work he might just as well have taken substance to have all the attributes there are, leaving open how many that is. Indeed, as far as the *Ethics* itself is concerned, he might reasonably be *interpreted* as taking substance to have all the attributes there are: 'infinite', in this context, can be heard as meaning 'unlimited' rather than 'infinitely many'.[10] The conviction that there are infinitely many attributes other than thought and extension, whose existence we can somehow register, is in any case something of an anomaly in Spinoza's overall system, his sole concession to the idea that we can ever make sense of anything transcendent. For, absent that conviction, Spinoza shows absolutely no sympathy for this idea, even on the least demanding conception of what it would be either to make sense of something or for something to be transcendent. Spinoza's metaphysics is very definitely a metaphysics of the immanent.[11]

The notion of a single substance with different attributes of which we are aware may itself suggest an unknowable transcendent reality set apart from different known immanent representations of it. But that is not at all how Spinoza intends the notion. He says that attributes 'express' the very essence of substance, or again, that they express its very existence (Ipp11,20+pf). He also says that a particular body expresses the essence of substance *qua* extended, or, to put it another way, that a particular body is a 'mode' by which substance's extension is expressed, in 'a definite and determinate way' (Ip25c and IId1). And he says the same *mutatis mutandis* in the case of a particular thought (IIp1pf). Some of the terminology here may be bemusing, but the basic point is clear enough. The world with which we are familiar – the

---

[10] Cf. Bennett (2003), pp. 115–116.

Might it not also be heard distributively, as specifying a quality of each attribute, rather than as applying to the whole group? Certainly the language itself allows for that interpretation (the original Latin is '*infinitis attributis*'). And the proof of Ip21, which adverts to Ip11, may even seem to demand it. But the explanation of Id6 and the proof of Ip14 are then problematical.

[11] This is a dominant theme of Yovel (1989). See further nn. 22, 51, and 53. Note: my reference to 'the least demanding conception of what it would be for something to be transcendent' reminds us that there are indeed different conceptions of this (see Introduction, §6). On some conceptions, attributes other than thought and extension would *not* be transcendent. Still, let us not forget that Spinoza is conceding the existence of what is not merely unknown, but unknowable (by us).

world of supernovae, sunshine, and snow, the world of pains, schemes, fears, and dreams – stands in a much more intimate relation to substance than one of representation. This relation is not quite identity for Spinoza, because identifying them would violate his understanding of what it is for us to conceive substance in two ways (and to fail to conceive it in countless other ways).[12] But it is, so to speak, as close to identity as this caveat allows, and certainly close enough for us to be capable not only of knowing the world of snow and pain but of knowing substance (IVp28+pf). Substance itself is both a thinking thing and an extended thing (IIpp1,2). Moreover, the *whole* of substance is both a thinking thing and an extended thing. (Substance does not have parts: Ip13s.[13]) The ways we have of knowing substance may not be all the ways of knowing it. But they are ways of knowing all of it. Whatever is expressed by one attribute is expressed by all of them. It follows that modes of extension and modes of thought must be paired off with one another. To each mode of extension there must correspond some mode of thought that expresses the same thing, albeit differently, and vice versa (IIp7+s and Vp1+pf).[14] In some cases, if not in every case, we may be able to identify the pairing. Thus we may be able to see that some particular headache, say, is paired with some particular activity inside a person's brain. But whatever pairings we may or may not be able to identify, the fact remains that any mode, and in particular any mode of which we are aware, already implicates the whole of substance.[15]

   I have not yet used the word 'God' in this connection. 'God' is Spinoza's name for substance (Id6). But he does not of course use it just as a label. He uses it with every intention of exploiting its normal semantic power. The word has many associations, particularly in the Judæo-Christian context in which Spinoza is writing, that are precisely suited to his purpose: perfection, eternity, necessary existence, wholeness, self-sufficiency, self-explanatoriness; in sum, what I have elsewhere called metaphysical infinitude (Moore (2001a), pp. 1–2), a cluster of ideas that certainly fits Spinoza's conception of substance (Ip11+acc). The word 'God' also calls to mind a being which is not subject to any external standards of assessment and which, in its grandeur and orderliness, is an appropriate object of adoration and awe. This too fits Spinoza's conception and is suited to his purpose (Ip33s2 and Vpp15ff; see §5.).[16]

---

[12] Lloyd (1996), pp. 38–41, is very helpful on this point.

[13] This is another reason why it cannot strictly be said to be identical to the world of snow and pain.

[14] Cf. Quine (1981e), p. 98; and cf. further Ch. 12, §7. In Donald Davidson (2005e), Davidson illuminatingly likens Spinoza's view to his own 'anomalous monism', whereby any event that can be characterized in psychological terms can also be characterized in irreducibly different physical terms.

[15] Cf. Deleuze (1990a), p. 175.

[16] See further Deleuze (1980).

There are nevertheless two utterly fundamental respects in which Spinoza's God differs from the traditional Judæo-Christian God. First, He is not separate from His creation. In particular, even if He has attributes of which we are unaware and is therefore to that extent transcendent, He is in other ways as immanent as the chair on which I am now sitting. Indeed His immanence *is* the immanence of the chair on which I am now sitting – or its is His. Spinoza is a pantheist. He famously refuses to draw any distinction between God and Nature (IVPref and *Letter 6*, p. 776).[17]

The second fundamental respect in which Spinoza's God differs from the traditional Judæo-Christian God is that He is not personal. He has neither hopes nor regrets; He has no purposes; He does not suffer; He does not attend to anything; and He does not strictly speaking love anyone (e.g. Ip18s, Ip33s2, IApp, IIp3s, Vp17c, and *Letter* 23).[18] So to whatever extent we are inclined to think or speak of Spinoza's God in personal terms, we are involved in a basic falsification. In particular, this is true of my deference to convention in using the capitalized masculine singular personal pronoun to refer to 'Him', a deference which is, to say the least, infelicitous – as well as being unwarranted by anything in Spinoza's text.[19] Henceforth I shall revert to 'it'.

Is Spinoza a theist or an atheist then? There cannot be any simple unqualified answer to this question. It is not that Spinoza wavers or is undecided. The one thing that he definitely is not is an agnostic. It is rather that, as we have just seen, he believes in something that deserves to be called 'God' on some reasonable definitions, but not in anything that deserves to be called 'God' on some others. My own view is that, while there is an ineliminable religious strain in Spinoza's thinking, and while there is much to justify Novalis' famous description of him as 'the God-intoxicated man,'[20] there is nonetheless an asymmetry here (very roughly, belief in God is most reasonably construed as belief in something that deserves to be called 'God' on most reasonable definitions) which makes it altogether less misleading to call Spinoza an atheist than to call him a theist. Henceforth, therefore, as well as reverting to 'it' when referring to what Spinoza calls 'God', I shall eschew theological language (unless I am quoting Spinoza) and revert to 'substance'.[21]

---

[17] But see above for why Nature must not then be construed simply as the world with which we are familiar. Henceforth I shall use 'nature' with a lowercase 'n' to refer to the latter.

[18] For the importance of the qualification 'strictly speaking', see Vp36c: God's 'love' is not 'accompanied by the idea of an external cause' (IIIDefEms6). For further opposition to the traditional conception, see Ip15s. Note: some of the features that prevent Spinoza's God from being personal likewise prevent Him from satisfying various other conditions that God is often thought to satisfy, such as susceptibility to petitionary prayer.

[19] Cf. Bennett (1984), p. 34.

[20] Novalis (1892), Vol. 3, p. 318. But note that in the context Novalis appears to be accrediting Spinoza with a kind of atheism.

[21] I have been helped in these deliberations by Bennett (1984), §9, even though he comes down on the opposite side and concludes that 'Spinoza's position is a kind of theism rather than of atheism' (p. 35).

So much, then, for Spinoza's recoil from the Cartesian conception of substance and from all that it entails. In that recoil we find a forthright rejection of Descartes' belief in a transcendent creator God, distinct from His creation, and an equally forthright rejection of Descartes' view of human beings as fractured beings, part minds and part (independent) bodies. The first of these rejections signals a pattern that we shall see repeated many times in this enquiry, whereby a commitment in one philosopher to our being able to make sense of transcendent things is abandoned by later philosophers on the grounds that there is no *sense* there to be made. In Spinoza's case, if we bracket the difficulties about attributes other than thought and extension, it seems fair to say that there is no sense to be made where no sense is expressed, while the only expression there is is expression on the part of immanent attributes and their various immanent modes.[22] The second rejection signals a reintegration of the self, whereby all the power of a person's mind is at the same time power of that person's body (IIIp2s). Both rejections cast us as ourselves participants in the sense-making of whatever we make sense of.[23] And it is on this that Spinoza's ethics turns.

3.   Nature, Human Nature, and the Model of Human Nature

We are part of nature,[24] the very nature that we make sense of. But what does this involve?

For us to be part of nature is for our power to be part of nature's power. What we can do is part of what nature can do. It is part of what substance can do. It is part of the *essence* of substance (Ip35). But the essence of substance, as we saw in the previous section, is what attributes and their modes express. It is the sense that things make. So anything we do is testimony to the sense that things make. In particular this includes our grasping such sense, our making sense of things.[25] It follows that, when we make sense of things, we make sense of ourselves; indeed we ourselves make sense. And to that extent, we are active rather than passive (IIId2). The significance of this, as I intimated in §1 and as I shall now try to show, is that it makes our making sense of things, for Spinoza, an ethical achievement.[26] It also has important implications, as I shall subsequently try to show, for metaphysics.

---

[22] In §5 we shall see an even more basic reason why Spinoza denies that we can make sense of transcendent things, at least insofar as making sense of things involves having knowledge of them.

[23] Cf. IVApp¶¶1–4.

[24] See n. 17.

[25] Cf. *Treatise*, ¶76, n. 2.

[26] It is worth recalling here that 'virtue' can mean the same as 'power'. Spinoza himself uses these words synonymously (IVd8).

It is helpful to begin with the general idea of a body. One of the most fundamental questions that Spinoza raises in the *Ethics*, according to Deleuze in his magnificent commentary, is: what can a body do?[27] The principal context in which this question arises is one in which we find Spinoza arguing for the following thesis: whenever a person's body does anything, there must be a purely physical explanation for what it does (IIIp2+acc). This, Spinoza insists, is true even when there is a conscious decision on the part of the person so to act. It does not follow that the decision is irrelevant to what the person's body does – or, as we would more naturally say, to what the person does. All that follows, in Spinoza's own words, is that

> [the] mental decision on the one hand, and the ... physical state of the
> body on the other hand, are ... one and the same thing which, when con-
> sidered under the attribute of thought and explicated through thought,
> we call decision, and when considered under the attribute of extension
> and deduced from the laws of motion-and-rest, we call a physical state.
> (IIIp2s)[28,29]

Spinoza considers the more intuitively appealing rival view whereby it is sometimes impossible to explain what a person's body does save in terms of the operations of the person's mind. Part of the reason why this rival view is more intuitively appealing than his is that we find it hard, sometimes, to see how a purely physical story, involving nothing about a person but the operations of his or her body, can be adequate to the task of explaining what that body does. Spinoza himself cites the case of someone's painting a picture. It is in response to this that he urges, 'Nobody as yet has learned from experience what the body can do ... solely from the laws of its nature insofar as it is considered as corporeal' (IIIp2s).

Spinoza is making a very particular dialectical point here. But precisely because of the point that he is making, the question of what a body can do takes on a broader significance. And it is to this broader significance that Deleuze alludes. Whenever I ask, 'What can I do?' – and there are, of course, all sorts of ways in which I might ask that – I am in effect asking, 'What can my body do?' (I am also asking, 'What can my mind do?' The various things that my body can do and the various things that my mind can do are the same things, expressed differently in the two cases.[30]) One

---

[27] See Deleuze (1990a), Ch. 14, to which he gives that question as a title.

[28] I have taken the liberty of dropping Samuel Shirley's capitalization of 'Thought' and 'Extension' in his translation, to conform with my own usage in the rest of this chapter. (There is no capitalization in Spinoza's original Latin.)

[29] I referred in n. 14 to Davidson's likening of Spinoza's view to his own anomalous monism. In this passage, taken together with its context (IIIp2+acc), we also see a striking similarity in the routes they take to arrive there. Cf. Davidson (1980).

[30] Genevieve Lloyd draws some interesting conclusions from this with regard to sexual difference: see Lloyd (1994), pp. 160–168. (Cf. n. 5.)

of Spinoza's aims in this passage, and more generally throughout his work, is to remind us that our bodies, and therefore we ourselves, have untold capacities, many of which remain completely unknown to us. This has obvious ethical significance,[31] not least in its implications concerning the benefits and dangers both of scientific research and of various sorts of experimentation. But it has additional ethical significance for Spinoza.

To see why, let us retreat from the question of what a body can do to the yet more fundamental question of what a body is. Spinoza's explicit definition of a body is 'a mode that expresses in a definite and determinate way God's essence insofar as he is considered an extended thing' (IId1). Later he says that bodies are distinguished from one another 'in respect of motion-and-rest' (IIp13lem1) and that

> when a number of bodies ... form close contact with one another through the pressure of other bodies upon them, or if they are moving ... so as to preserve an unvarying relation of movement among themselves, these bodies are said to be united with one another and all together to form one body or individual thing. (IIp13d)

He also makes clear that the identity of the whole in such a case depends on the 'mutual relation of motion-and-rest' rather than on the identity of the parts, which means that, within certain parameters of drasticness, the whole can survive the replacement of its parts, and even the gaining or losing of parts (IIp13lems4–7+acc). In the case of a human body the most obvious natural examples of what he has in mind are breathing, eating, and defecating.

Eating calls to mind what else can happen, apart from the forming of a new, additional body, when two or more bodies meet. Thus a man can eat an orange, say, benefiting himself but thereby destroying the orange; a bullet can enter into the body of a man and rearrange some of his parts, without damaging itself but thereby destroying the man; two pieces of crockery can collide and destroy each other; an egg white can combine with a heap of sugar, each destroying the other but together forming a meringue.[32] However, the case in which none of the original bodies is destroyed and a new body is formed is in many respects the most interesting. It reminds us that not only can bodies be combined, but so too can their powers and capacities. They can do together what they could never do separately. This is true, for instance, of various pieces of wood assembled together to form a chair. Spinoza himself says the following: 'If two individuals of completely

---

[31] Given that these untold capacities are at the same time untold capacities of our minds, it also has significance for whether there can be radical conceptual innovation in metaphysics: see Introduction, §6, the discussion of the Novelty Question. We shall return to this issue in Ch. 21, §6. (See in particular n. 85 of that chapter.)

[32] See further *Letter* 32.

the same nature are combined, they compose an individual twice as powerful as each one singly' (IVp18s). That may be somewhat crude, but the basic point, concerning what bodies or individuals can do when they combine, is clear and relatively uncontroversial.

Nor does this point apply only when some larger body or larger individual is formed. I add this caveat because, despite all that Spinoza says on this subject, it is difficult to decide just what he would count either as a body or as an individual.[33] John, Paul, George, and Ringo are four bodies. Do they together constitute a fifth? Presumably not, in the normal course of events. But what about when they are acting 'in concert', as we might aptly say – that is, when they are coordinating their activities, and in particular when they are keeping time with one another? Are they not then precisely 'moving ... so as to preserve an unvarying relation of movement among themselves'? It is significant in this connection that Spinoza at one point alludes to the possibility that men 'should all be in such harmony in all respects that their minds and bodies should compose, as it were, one mind and one body' (IVp18s). A good deal obviously turns on the force of the qualification 'as it were'. – Or if there is some doubt about whether John, Paul, George, and Ringo ever constitute a fifth body, surely there is no doubt that they sometimes constitute a fifth individual? After all, Spinoza does at one point acknowledge the whole of nature as one individual (IIp13lem17s). – Unfortunately, even this is not clear.[34] The most that seems uncontentious is that the four men sometimes constitute a 'single thing'. Spinoza says:

> If several individuals concur in one act in such a way as to be all together the simultaneous cause of one effect, I consider them all, in that respect, as one single thing. (IId7)[35]

The important point in all of this, however, is the original point: a group of individuals has a collective power that exceeds their powers as individuals. This adds obvious political significance to the obvious ethical significance that we have already noted in the question of what a body can do. Implicated in that question is the question of what a body can do in cooperation with other bodies.[36]

---

[33] See IVp39s for just one of the complications.

[34] For a very interesting discussion, see Barbone (2002). Also helpful is Brandom (2002b), pp. 124–126.

[35] I have taken the liberty of correcting Shirley's translation here. Despite his general reliability he fudges Spinoza's important distinctions in this area. The word that I have rendered as 'individuals' is '*Individua*', and the phrase that I have rendered as 'one single thing' is '*unam rem singularem*'.

[36] Cf. Spinoza's claim in IVp18s that 'nothing is more advantageous to man than men.' For discussion of the political consequences of his views, see *Political Treatise* and IVApp passim.

Now, in order to understand better the additional ethical significance that
the question has for Spinoza, we need first to consider Spinoza's conception
of ethics. Here it is helpful to invoke a contrast that many philosophers
draw between ethics and morality.[37] On one way of drawing that contrast,
ethics is concerned quite generally with what counts as living well, whereas
morality is concerned with what counts as living well only as seen through
the prism of some very particular, very distinctive conceptual tools. Two of
the most basic of these tools are the idea of a moral obligation and the idea
of an act of free will. Morality treats a moral obligation as an inescapable
demand that always takes precedence over a demand of any other kind,
and it equates living well, in the most important sense, with performing
those acts of free will that there is some moral obligation to perform while
refraining from performing those acts of free will that there is some moral
obligation to refrain from performing. In these terms, Spinoza's conception of ethics is decidedly a conception of *ethics*, not of morality. He argues
strenuously that the idea of free will is an illusion, based on our ignorance
of the causes of what we do (Ip32+pf,App, IIpp48+acc,49+acc, and *Letter*
58). Nature leaves no room for us to direct it one way rather than another.
Everything that occurs in nature is governed by laws over which we have no
control, and these laws determine uniquely what will happen at any given
time (Ia3,pp21+pf,22+pf,28+acc,29+acc). Nor, therefore, does the idea of
a moral obligation have any kind of grip on us. Still less does the idea of a
moral obligation impinging on us from some transcendent source, which
is how many of the more religious champions of morality have viewed it.
Spinoza's retreat from the conceptual tools of morality to the broader concerns of ethics is at the same time a retreat from one of the mainstays of a
familiar form of Christianity, dominant in his own time and culture, to a
much more ancient legacy.

What, then, counts as living well? Spinoza adopts a naturalistic and relativistic understanding of good and bad. He denies that these are anything
'positive considered in themselves' (IVPref). Rather, they are ways we have
of thinking of things, according to our desires. Thus, in Spinoza's view, we
judge a thing to be good because we desire it; we do not desire it because
we judge it to be good (IIIp9s). And this, of course, allows for the possibility that different people, with different desires, will accordingly and quite
rightly judge different things to be good (IIIp39s and IVPref). Nevertheless,
because he believes that there is a 'model of human nature that we all set
before ourselves' (IVPref), Spinoza is able to cut through the relativization.
Working from what he takes to be a shared human perspective, from which

---

[37] See e.g. Deleuze (1988a), Ch. 2; Deleuze (1990a), Ch. 16; and Williams (2006o), pp. 6–7
and Ch. 10. An earlier version of the distinction can be found in Hegel (1942), Pts Two
and Three: see further Ch. 7, §6. The distinction is also of prime importance to Nietzsche:
see esp. Nietzsche (1967a), First Essay, and Nietzsche (1973); and see further Ch. 15, §7.

this model is in view as the supreme object of desire, he defines 'good' as 'that which we certainly know to be the means for our approaching nearer to the model' or 'that which we certainly know to be useful to us', and he defines 'bad' as 'that which we certainly know prevents us from reproducing the said model' or 'that which we certainly know to be an obstacle to our attainment of some good' (IVPref,dd1,2).

The question now, therefore, is: what is this model of human nature? Here it helps to return to the general idea of a body. Drawing on some principles of Stoicism, Spinoza argues that each body, indeed each thing, has a conatus which constitutes its very essence and with which it 'endeavours to persist in its own being' (IIIpp6,7).[38] This is as true of men as it is of anything else. Each man, by his very nature, is driven to preserve his own existence, and his happiness consists in his being able to do just that (IVp18s). But existence here is not 'mere' existence, existence of the sort that might be enjoyed by someone in a persistent vegetative state. The conatus is, in a way, a conatus towards *its own* preservation. Each man is driven to preserve his existence *as* a man who is driven to preserve his existence. In a sense, of course, that is a redundant qualification, since it is his very essence to be driven to preserve his existence (and falling into a persistent vegetative state may thus be tantamount to dying[39]). The point, however, is that his drive is a drive to actualize that essence to the greatest possible degree. It is a drive to maximize his activity and to minimize his passivity, to achieve the highest possible preponderance in his life of acting over undergoing (IVpp20ff.). In Spinoza's own terms, it is a drive to maximize, among the things that take place, those 'of which he is the adequate cause' or 'which can be clearly and distinctly understood through his nature alone' and to minimize those 'which take place in him, or follow from his nature, of which he is only the partial cause' (IIId2, subjects and verbs adapted). To have that drive is his very essence, his power, his virtue (IVp20+pf).[40] And this answers our question about the model of human nature in terms of which good and bad are defined. It is a model of maximally active self-preservation. It is a model, we might also say, of *freedom*. For being free, as Spinoza understands it, is not to be confused with exercising free will, the notion that we have already seen him repudiate. A thing is free, on Spinoza's definition, when it 'exists solely from the necessity of its own nature, and is determined to action by itself alone' (Id7).

We can now see why the question of what a body can do has such particular ethical significance for Spinoza. It is what we, or our bodies, can do, and in particular what we can do actively, as opposed to undergo, that determines what counts as our living well. The more we do actively, the better we

---

[38] For a helpful account see Brandom (2002b), pp. 126–129.
[39] See IVp39s.
[40] Cf. n. 26.

live. We can also see the significance of the earlier discussion of cooperation.
Cooperation increases what we can do actively. John can contribute to a
group performance with Paul, George, and Ringo; he cannot do the same
thing on his own. What is not yet clear is the connection that I heralded at
the beginning of this section between our being active (our being free) and
our making sense of things. It is to this connection that I now turn.

4.   Making Sense of Things as an Ethical Achievement

The guiding idea, as we shall see, is familiar from Stoicism and was anticipated by Descartes (see §1).

First, we need to understand two terms of art that Spinoza uses: 'affection' and 'affect'.[41] By an 'affection' of a man, Spinoza means anything that
'takes place' in the man.[42] By an 'affect' of a man he means one of two
things. Sometimes he means any bodily affection of the man whereby his
power to act is increased or decreased, together with the corresponding idea
in the man's mind (IIId3).[43] Sometimes he means just the corresponding
idea (IIIGenDefEms and the sentence immediately preceding it). Either way,
a man's affects can be thought of as his felt transitions from one degree of
power to another.

Now a man's affections can be divided into *passive* and *active*. His passive affections are the ones with causes that lie outside him; his active affections are the ones with causes that lie wholly within him (IIId2). (In these
terms, his life is better the more of his affections are active.) His affects can
likewise be divided into passive and active. The distinction in their case is
derivative. A man's passive affects are the ones whose associated bodily
affections are passive; his active affects are the ones whose associated bodily affections are active (IIId3). And among his passive affects, those that
are felt increases in his power to act are said to be affects of *pleasure* or *joy*,
while those that are felt decreases in his power to act are said to be affects
of *pain* or *sadness* (IIIp11s,DefEms2,3).[44] (In these terms, his life is better

---

[41] The Latin words are '*affectio*' and '*affectus*'. Shirley renders the latter as 'emotion'. But
see Edwin Curley's remarks in Spinoza (1985), p. 625, for why this is unsatisfactory. See
also Deleuze (1988a), pp. 48–51.

[42] I use the phrase 'takes place' in echo of IIId2. For the broadness of Spinoza's use of
'affection', cf. IIIDefEms1e.

[43] By the corresponding idea in the man's mind is simply meant the mode of thought that
corresponds to the mode of extension that is the relevant affection (cf. Ip7+s). ('Idea' is
Spinoza's catch-all term for any mode of thought formed by the mind 'because it is a
thinking thing' (IId3).)

[44] The two Latin words, as Shirley notes in his translation, are '*lætitia*' and '*tristitia*'. Note
that there is not the same distinction to be drawn among his active affects, since a man
never actively decreases his own power to act (IIIpp58+pf,59+pf).

the more of his affects are active, but also the more of his passive affects are joyful.)[45]

Some of a man's affections are bodily, some of them are mental. But even the former, as we have seen, have mental affections corresponding to them, the same things differently expressed. Hence, given that the distinction between the passive and the active is independent of mode of expression, we do no real violence to the scope of that distinction if we concentrate just on a man's mental affections. And what the distinction comes to in their case is this. His passive mental affections are occurrences in his mind for which he sees no reason. It is as if he has unwittingly taken some hallucinogenic drug or, less extravagantly, as if he has been told the conclusion of some piece of reasoning but not the premises (IIp28pf). By contrast, his active mental affections are occurrences in his mind for which he does see a reason and which are sustained precisely *because* he sees this reason. The paradigm is the case in which, through his own initiative, he draws a conclusion from premises that he already knows to be true. When he has a passive mental affection, there is an idea in his mind that is 'fragmentary and confused' (IIIp1pf). It does not fully make sense to him. When he has an active mental affection, there is an idea in his mind that does fully make sense to him. An idea of the former kind Spinoza calls '*inadequate*', and an idea of the latter kind he calls '*adequate*' (IIId4,p1 and IVp23+pf).[46] An adequate idea, we might say, *expresses* its own reason for being true.[47]

But now we begin to discern the familiar Stoic picture. For a man to be passive is for him to be subject to occurrences in the mind, including affects, which he cannot fully understand. These occurrences need not be disagreeable. Nor indeed need they be a threat to his overall activity. They may even enhance it. They may be affects of joy. But still they are passive. Or, as the etymology appropriately invites us to say, they are 'passions'. And these passions do not themselves involve his acting. For him to act, or for him to be active, or again for him to be *free*, is for him to understand what is going on within him – and what is going on around him, insofar as this too impinges on him. It is for him to make sense of things.

We must beware, however, of seeing in this some kind of Manichean struggle between passion and reason. Something of the sort may be a feature of certain forms of Stoicism. But it is not a feature of Spinozism. For Spinoza, reason is not pitted against passion. The free man is not the man whose reason has fought against his passions and destroyed them. For

---

[45] It is important to note that an increase in a man's *power* to act is not the same as an increase in his actual activity. A man's power to act is what he can actively do. But *qua* power this is no different from what he can (simply) do. It is involved no less in his passivity than in his activity: cf. IVp18pf.

[46] See Bennett (2003), §78, for discussion of some complications here.

[47] This way of speaking derives from Deleuze: see Deleuze (1990a), p. 133.

one thing, that would suggest that his passions, which is to say his passive affects, were themselves agents of some sort with a corresponding power of their own.[48] It is rather that a man is free to the extent that (it is important to appreciate that freedom is a matter of degree) he understands his affects and begets them rather than suffers them; they are active rather than passive. Some of his affects may be active because he has come to understand what were previously passive affects. But even if that is so, his reason has not thereby destroyed any of his passive affects: it has not thereby destroyed any of his passions. It has transformed them from *being* passions. He is like someone who has assimilated some piece of reasoning, premises and all, whose conclusion he in any case already accepted, albeit originally without reason (Vp3; cf. IVp66s).[49] As for what it is for him to understand anything, that, given Spinoza's conception of substance, is for him to see it as necessary. It is for him to see both *that* the thing must be and *why* it must be. It is for him to see the thing in relation to substance itself (see IVApp, esp. ¶¶1–5 and 32; cf. also IIp44).

We now have an indication of why it is that, for Spinoza, making sense of things is an ethical achievement. But it remains to be seen what the implications of this are for metaphysics, which is our ultimate concern. This will require consideration of Spinoza's account of knowledge.

5.   The Three Kinds of Knowledge

Spinoza recognizes three kinds of knowledge (IIp40s2[50]).

Knowledge of the first kind is knowledge that is (in the terminology introduced in the previous section) inadequate. To have such knowledge is to have a passive mental affection. Knowledge of this kind is acquired whenever something impinges on somebody from without, as for instance when a man enjoys an ordinary sensory perception or is given a piece of information by somebody else (IIp29c; see also IIp18+s). Such knowledge, though unimpeachable in its own right, can easily lead to error. Thus consider the following example, due to Robert Brandom (Brandom (2002b),

---

[48] What they are, notwithstanding their passivity, are exercises of *his* power, in particular his power to pass from one degree of power to another. (Indeed, in IIIDefEms3e Spinoza says that each one is an 'actuality' – using the Latin word '*actus*', which can also be translated as 'act'.)

[49] Cf. Lloyd (1996), pp. 9–10.

[50] The arithmetical example that he gives in this passage is not altogether happy, inasmuch as it suggests that the three kinds of knowledge are three ways of knowing the same things, which is not his considered view, as we shall see. For interesting discussions of the three kinds of knowledge, see Craig (1987), Ch. 1, §5, and Sprigge (1997). Note: in *Treatise*, ¶¶18–23, there is a related fourfold classification, but Spinoza had not yet fully worked out his ideas when he wrote that: see Deleuze (1990a), pp. 292–293.

pp. 126–127). A man catches a ball. As a result the surface of his hand is modified, with various neural consequences (see IIp13Posts). This is a passive bodily affection, to which there corresponds a passive mental affection: he feels the ball. This in turn constitutes knowledge of the first kind. But this knowledge does not strictly extend further than his hand, whose indentation is compatible with his catching indefinitely many things other than the ball, for instance a hemisphere identical in shape to the half of the ball that actually makes contact with his hand (IIp16c2).[51] Error occurs if, in ignorance of what lies beyond his hand, he proceeds as if he had caught one of these other things instead (IIp17pf,s,p35+acc).

This example also illustrates an ambiguity that arises if we talk about an idea of a mode of extension. An idea is a mode of thought. As such it has its own corresponding mode of extension, the same thing differently expressed. In one sense it is an idea of that very mode of extension. Thus the man's sensation when he catches the ball is an idea of his passive bodily affection (the indentation in his hand and its various neural effects). But in another sense an idea can be an idea of whatever it is that explains, in some suitable sense of explanation,[52] the corresponding bodily affection. In this second sense – which makes the 'idea of' relation a relation of representation – the man's sensation is an idea of, or represents, the impact of the ball itself on his hand. As we might naturally say, he has a sensation of catching the ball. Again, adapting a famous example due to Spinoza himself (IIp17s), when Ringo hears something that reminds him of John, he has an idea which is in one sense an idea of some neurophysiological feature of his own body, but which is in another sense an idea, simply, of John. It is precisely because there are these two things competing for the title of that which his idea is an idea of, or more strictly it is precisely because there are these two senses in which his idea can be said to be an idea of something, that the idea counts as inadequate (IIp25). In the case of an adequate idea, which expresses its own explanation, no such distinction arises.

This is a good cue to turn to knowledge of the second and third kinds. Knowledge of each of these kinds, unlike knowledge of the first kind, is adequate. This means that it is grounded solely in the subject (IIp31), not just in the sense that it lacks a cause external to the subject but also in the sense that it is not *answerable to* anything external to the subject. We could also say: it carries with it its own credentials; it expresses its own reason for being true; it is not in any sense representative of anything else (IIa4+exp).[53]

---

[51] This was part of what I had in mind in n. 22. We see here how Spinoza's account precludes knowledge of the first kind of anything transcendent. See also n. 53.

[52] Much of Brandom (2002b) is concerned with teasing out this sense.

[53] Cf. *Treatise*, ¶¶70–71. And see nn. 22 and 51: here we see how Spinoza's account precludes knowledge of either the second or the third kind of anything transcendent.

In all these respects it differs from Cartesian clear and distinct perception (see §5 of the previous chapter). Descartes came to regard his clear and distinct perceptions as true by reasoning back from them to a story about their origin, a story involving Divine benevolence. This was a kind of inference to the best explanation, where the explanation was at the same time a vindication. Spinoza, by contrast, insists that we attain to adequate knowledge by reasoning, not from effect to cause, as Descartes did, but from cause to effect, or from explicans to explicandum (e.g. *Treatise*, ¶85).[54] Just by carefully attending to one of our adequate ideas, Spinoza believes, we can see it as true, because we can see it as explained by reasons which it itself expresses. The paradigm is the case in which we attend to some mathematical theorem that we have in mind – *as* the conclusion of a piece of mathematical reasoning that we likewise have in mind, the latter implicated in the former.[55]

There is, however, an obvious concern about this account. What about the 'first principles', the axioms and definitions on which the proof of the theorem ultimately rests? In what sense does our acceptance of *them* carry its own credentials with it, if not by enjoying the indubitability of a Cartesian clear and distinct perception?

One possible reply would be that the axioms and definitions are true by stipulation; that it is precisely our acceptance of them that makes them true. Adapted to metaphysics, this reply would chime well with the remarks that I made at the end of §5 of the previous chapter, in opposition to Descartes, concerning my own reasons for regarding metaphysics as a fundamentally creative exercise. It is plain, however, that this reply, at least in any such application, would not be acceptable to Spinoza. In *Letter 9* he makes clear that the grounds of the truth of the axioms and definitions which he himself

---

[54] For criticism of the Cartesian strategy, see *Treatise*, ¶¶19–21, esp. the notes. See further Deleuze (1990a), Ch. 10.

[55] Cf. in this connection Wittgenstein's observation that 'one can often say in mathematics: let the *proof* teach you *what* was being proved' (Wittgenstein (1967a), p. 220, emphasis in original).

Note: both inadequate ideas and adequate ideas have their explanations (IIp36). It is just that, when we have an adequate idea, and only then, we thereby *grasp* the explanation. *The* reason for it is *our* reason for it. There are connections with the notion of unconditionedness which I have tried to develop in various places: see Moore (1997a), pp. 261–262, and Moore (2003a), p. 101.

There are also connections with the notion of ineffability which I have likewise tried to develop in various places: see esp. Moore (1997a), Ch. 8, where I argue that ineffable knowledge is, precisely, knowledge which is not answerable to anything external to the subject. But what then of the thought that such knowledge includes mathematical knowledge? For the beginning of an answer to this question, see Moore (2003b), n. 16. For more on the connections with ineffability, see the next section.

provides in the *Ethics*, and to which the same concern applies, need to be altogether more robust than that (cf. *Treatise*, ¶¶95–98). Another possible reply, more suited to the project in the *Ethics* than to mathematics, is that the axioms and definitions are not, after all, 'first principles', that they are part of a set of interlocking propositions whose truth consists in their mutual support and overall coherence. Spinoza's own reply would surely be (and would need to be) something of this sort.[56]

Be that as it may, we see in mathematical reasoning a model of adequate knowledge. This is knowledge of the second kind. Before we consider what distinguishes knowledge of the third kind from this, let us reflect more generally on the nature and origin of knowledge of the second kind. What enables us to have such knowledge, Spinoza says, is the fact that we have 'common notions', where a common notion is an idea of a common property, and where a common property is in turn 'that which is common to all things ... and is equally in the part as in the whole' (IIp37,p40s2). He gives as examples of common properties the following, shared by all bodies: 'that they involve the conception of one and the same attribute ... and ... that they may move at varying speeds, and may be absolutely in motion or absolutely at rest' (IIp13lem2pf). He then argues that, precisely because these properties are equally in the part as in the whole, our ideas of them, that is to say our common notions, must be adequate. For these notions do not depend on anything beyond us: they carry their own credentials with them (IIpp38,39). We have them, not because of any particular affections of our bodies, but simply because we have bodies, which quite literally incorporate that which is common to all bodies. It is thus that we are able to arrive at knowledge of the second kind, which, we now see, must always be of a highly general character,[57] as for instance our knowledge of the fundamental nature of motion. Relatedly, such knowledge must also be invariant from one context to another. This is in contrast to the knowledge a man has, just as he catches a ball, that his hand *is now* moving, which, were it to be exactly replicated in another context, would nevertheless not survive into that context. There he would have different knowledge, knowledge that his hand *was then* moving, perhaps as a result of his catching a quite different ball, or even half a ball.

---

[56] See Bennett (1984), Ch. 1, §§4–6. See also Walker (1989), Ch. 3, §2. (But even if Spinoza's reply would be of this sort, I think that Walker exaggerates the compass it would have: see esp. p. 53.) Note: whatever Spinoza's reply to this concern would be, he exacerbates it when he suggests that each of his own definitions should '[explicate] a thing as it exists outside the intellect' (*Letter 9*, p. 781).

[57] Or must it? Harking back to Descartes' reflections on his own existence, we might wonder whether each man's knowledge that he himself exists satisfies the criteria for being knowledge of the second kind, despite its particularity. Does that not carry with it its own credentials? For Spinoza's reasons for saying that it does not, see IIp29+acc.

It might appear now that no knowledge can be both adequate and particular.[58] Knowledge of the second kind is adequate; knowledge of the first kind is particular. But the very account of how each is what it is seems to preclude any knowledge's being both. And if it is true that no knowledge can be both, then the prospects for our approaching the model of human nature discussed in §3, which involves our making maximum possible sense of things, look dim. The summit of our aspirations to freedom, it now seems, is proving mathematical theorems, or reflecting on such highly general features of reality as the fundamental nature of motion.

Yet Spinoza sees much brighter prospects for our approaching the model than that. He believes that we have the power to control both our affections and our affects by making sense, among other things, of *them*; by appropriating their explicantia and ensuring that they (the affections and the affects) are active rather than passive; by, as Spinoza himself says, arranging them and associating them with one another (Vp20s; cf. Vp39pf).

The question, therefore, is how this is possible. For precisely what it requires is knowledge that is both adequate and particular: 'adequate knowledge of the essence of things' (IIp40s), where the 'essence' of a thing is as particular as the thing itself (IIIp7). It is in answering this question that Spinoza gives his account of knowledge of the third kind. For what knowledge of the third kind *is* is 'adequate knowledge of the essence of things'.

Spinoza[59] believes that knowledge of the second kind can eventually lead to, and include, an adequate (albeit incomplete) idea of substance: that all-embracing, self-sufficient, unified being whose essence each particular expresses in some way, that integrated being in which all particulars are bound together in relations of necessitation (IIp47 and Vp14).[60] To arrive at knowledge of the third kind, he argues, we must proceed via this adequate idea of substance. We must see all things, ourselves included, in their essential relation to the whole, '*sub specie æternitatis*' as Spinoza famously puts it (Vp29). (To see things in that way combats a solipsistic tendency in knowledge of the first kind, and indeed in some knowledge of the second kind. It brings us to a proper realization that we are part of nature.) Still, no amount of knowledge of the second kind, however necessary it may be for securing knowledge of the third kind, can suffice for doing so. For no amount of knowledge of the second kind can issue in knowledge of the essence of any *particular* (IIp37). For a man to proceed from knowledge of the second kind to knowledge of the third kind, or from an adequate idea of substance to an

---

[58] Cf. IIp31. But, as we shall see, the word 'duration' in this proposition is crucial: see IId5+exp.

[59] I am indebted in what follows to Deleuze (1990a): see esp. pp. 299–301.

[60] Spinoza's own book, of course, testifies to the belief that it is possible for us to attain to such an idea.

adequate knowledge of the essence of any given particular X, he must as it were take a leap in his mind to X.

But how? And how can such knowledge count as adequate? How can it express its own explicans? Why does this 'leap' not mean that whatever idea he has in mind is answerable to something beyond?

No doubt the leap will be facilitated by suitable encounters with X itself, issuing in inadequate knowledge of the first kind. The point, however, is this. The knowledge in question, at which he eventually arrives, does not represent *how* X is. Indeed, it is even impervious to *whether* X is. It is knowledge of *what* X is, in the sense that it is knowledge of *what it is* for X to be.[61] It is knowledge of *what* X *can do*. In principle, if not in practice, the subject could have arrived at such knowledge through creative imagination, even if X had never existed (Vp29+acc). It is in part a kind of practical knowledge: it includes, though it is not exhausted by, knowledge of how to exploit the possibilities that X affords, if ever and whenever the opportunity arises.[62] If the subject himself is X, in other words if the knowledge in question is self-knowledge, then its practical part is, in effect, his knowledge of how to do (some of) what he can do. If X is different from the subject, then the practical part of the knowledge is, in effect, his knowledge of how to do (some of) what he can do in cooperation with X.

Reconsider John, Paul, George, and Ringo. Each of them can arrive at an adequate knowledge of his own essence, whereby he develops his capacity for creativity and performance. But each of them can also, through encounters with the others, arrive at an adequate knowledge of the others' essences, and ultimately at an adequate knowledge of the group's essence. This is what enables them to be creative and to perform *as a group*, achieving not only what none of them could ever have achieved solo but what the four of them could never have achieved as four isolated individuals. And if one of the members of the group dies, or simply leaves the group and forces it to disband, the remaining three retain a capacity, through their knowledge of his essence, to perform, not as the original group, which is no longer possible, but not as 'just another' group either; rather, as a threesome that would not itself have been possible if he and they had not originally functioned together as a foursome.

Such knowledge is a way of making sense of particulars, including particular affections and particular affects. And it is a way of achieving power over those affections and affects (Vp20s,p39pf). When Paul first hears John perform something, he has certain auditory experiences. These are themselves passive mental affections, no doubt accompanied by various passive

---

[61] This explains the significance of the word 'duration' in IIp31 (see n. 58), and, relatedly, the importance of the subject's seeing X *sub specie æternitatis*. (For an interesting account of something closely related, albeit without reference to Spinoza, see Lowe (2008).)

[62] See again Moore (1997a), Ch. 8.

affects, or passions. So are his subsequent memories of them whenever they are triggered (IIp18+acc). But he comes to make sense of these affections, and perhaps also of their attendant passions, in a certain way. He comes to understand why they occur as they do. And thus, to whatever limited extent – Spinoza always acknowledges how severe the limitations are (IIpp3+pf,4+pf and IVApp¶42) – Paul attains to corresponding active affections and affects, through which he is able to make his own creative use of what he has heard John do. In a small way he approaches the model of human nature. (This of course has no implications, pro or contra, for whether he approaches the model in other ways as well, still less for how close he is to it in any of those other ways.)

Knowledge of the third kind, the knowledge which brings us to our highest level of freedom and activity, also brings us to our 'highest conatus' and 'highest virtue' (Vp25). It leads us to what Spinoza calls 'an intellectual love of God' – a kind of joyful affirmation of life[63] – in which both blessedness and virtue consist (Vp36s,p42). In the exhilarating final pages of the *Ethics* Spinoza argues, using resources that unfortunately lie beyond the scope of this chapter, that we also thereby enjoy a kind of eternity (esp. Vpp23+acc,31+acc,39+acc), where by eternity is meant, in Wittgenstein's words, 'not infinite temporal duration, but timelessness' (Wittgenstein (1961), 6.4311).[64] Knowledge of the third kind is the supreme aim of ethics.

6.   Metaphysical Knowledge as Knowledge of the Second Kind

We come at last to the implications of all of this for metaphysics.[65] This final section can be brief. Most of the work has already been done.

Metaphysics is the most general attempt to make sense of things. In Spinoza's terms, it is the most general pursuit of knowledge of the second kind. And this is precisely what we find in the main part of the *Ethics*, where Spinoza tries to convey a system of interrelated metaphysical truths. I refer to the 'main part' of the *Ethics* because, as Deleuze has persuasively argued (Deleuze (1990a), App., and Deleuze (1995e)), something rather different

---

[63] See the definition of 'love' in IIIDefEms6. (Recall that Shirley uses the word 'pleasure' rather than 'joy' to translate the Latin word '*lætitia*': see n. 44.) Also relevant is IIp49+acc.

[64] For discussion, see Deleuze (1990a), Ch.19, and Garrett (2009).

The links between Spinoza and the early Wittgenstein are profound: cf. also Wittgenstein (1961), 6.43–6.45, and Wittgenstein (1979a), pp. 81 and 83–84. In the final section of this chapter I hope to indicate how these links extend to the very structures of their two major works. See further Ch. 9, §8.

[65] For some interesting observations on Spinoza's relation to metaphysics, in the context of a broader discussion of the nature of metaphysics, see Hampshire (1962), Ch. 6.

is to be found in the scholia, where Spinoza's aim is more often to impart knowledge of the first kind. When that is his aim, we find various heuristic props for grasping the metaphysical truths conveyed in the main part of the book, or indications of some of their practical repercussions, or just helpful reformulations of some of them (e.g. IIp8s, IVp37ss1,2, and Vp20s).

In the main part, however, Spinoza tries to impart knowledge of the second kind. But that is not *just* to say, what I have already said, that he tries to convey metaphysical truths. There is more to his trying to impart knowledge of the second kind than that. This is not because there are truths other than metaphysical truths, say general truths about motion, whose knowledge also constitutes knowledge of the second kind, and which he also tries to convey. It is not a question of subject matter at all. (There are *no* truths whose knowledge constitutes knowledge of the second kind, any more than there are truths whose knowledge constitutes having learned something at school. What is known does not dictate how it is known.) The point is this. In trying to convey metaphysical truths, Spinoza might have been content for his readers to accept what he says on trust. Had that been the case, he would have been trying to convey no more than knowledge of the first kind. In fact, of course, it is not the case. Spinoza wants his readers to see the reasons for what he says and to make those reasons their own. He wants his readers to share the knowledge which he himself has. He wants them, like him, to make general sense of things.

Now I talked in §1 about Spinoza's 'communicating' his general understanding of things to others. I had in mind something that was neutral on this question of how his readers may be intended, or may in fact proceed, to assimilate what is communicated. I was referring simply to his putting his understanding into words. Whether his readers bow to his authority and thereby acquire knowledge of the first kind or whether they work through his proofs, come to share his general understanding of things, and thereby acquire knowledge of the second kind – these are questions about the *effects* that his work has.

Here is another effect that his work may have, this time involving knowledge of the third kind. His readers may share his general understanding of things, see the importance of knowledge of the third kind, recognize some of the ways in which knowledge of that kind can be attained, be moved to pursue them, set themselves to do so, and succeed. This, I believe, would be an intended effect. So there is a sense in which Spinoza tries to impart knowledge of the third kind too. But this is not to say that he tries to *communicate* knowledge of the third kind. *Knowledge of the third kind cannot be communicated.* It is, in part, practical knowledge. And the part that is practical cannot be put into words. Or at any rate, it cannot be put into finitely many words, which is as much as I mean when I contend that it cannot be communicated. (I choose the word 'contend' advisedly. I do not claim to be rehearsing anything that Spinoza explicitly says at this point. But I see no other way of making sense of his insistence that knowledge of the third kind is both adequate and yet incapable of issuing from knowledge of the second kind.[66] Note, however, that even if I am wrong about this, the sheer particularity of knowledge of the third kind means that, if ever someone communicated knowledge of the third kind which he or she had, the result would be liable to be of little more than autobiographical interest. It would be some sort of coincidence if the same thing served to communicate knowledge of the third kind which someone else had, or might come to have.) It may yet be possible to communicate a good deal of knowledge *about* knowledge of the third kind. That is certainly something that Spinoza tries to do in the *Ethics*. And his trying to do that is certainly an integral part of his trying to impart knowledge of the third kind (cf. *Treatise*, ¶37) – as of course is his trying to convey the adequate idea of substance on which knowledge of the third kind rests. But these are importantly different from his trying to say what it is that, in having knowledge of the third kind, he or anyone else knows.[67]

What it all comes to, then, is this. Knowledge of the third kind is the supreme aim of ethics. But it cannot be acquired except via knowledge of the second kind. More specifically, it cannot be acquired except via metaphysical knowledge. Metaphysics is therefore in the service of ethics. It helps us to realize the supreme aim of ethics. It also helps us to understand the supreme aim of ethics, to make sense of what it is to make ethical sense. Its own aim is not the same as the supreme aim of ethics. Its own aim is a general understanding of things. Even so, for the reasons given, metaphysics is an integral part of the good life. Such is Spinoza's resplendent vision.

---

[66] See again Moore (1997a), Ch. 8; and on the impartibility of such knowledge see ibid., pp. 208–209. Here I may be departing from Deleuze: see Deleuze (1995e), p. 165.

[67] In n. 64 I referred to links between the *Ethics* and Wittgenstein (1961). In Ch. 9, §8, I shall argue that the latter is likewise an attempt, albeit using very different methods, to impart an ethically important understanding that cannot be put into words.

CHAPTER 3

✦

Leibniz

Metaphysics in the Service of Theodicy

1. The Apotheosis of Making Sense of Things

Both Descartes and Spinoza saw value in metaphysics for its own sake. The ability to make general sense of things was, for each, a mark of humanity, and its execution a mark of human excellence. Nevertheless, there was also, for each, a more fundamental rationale for pursuing metaphysics. This was its service to science in Descartes' case, and its service to ethics in Spinoza's. It was perhaps Leibniz, of the three, who came closest to seeing the value of metaphysics in exclusively non-instrumental terms. Indeed, concerning knowledge 'of the necessary eternal truths, above all those which are the most comprehensive and which have the most relation to the sovereign being,' he wrote that 'this knowledge alone is good in itself,' adding that 'all the rest is mercenary' ('Letter to Von Hessen-Rheinfels', dated November 1686, in 'Correspondence with Arnauld', p. 170[1]).

G.W. Leibniz (1646–1716) took it as something close to a basic datum that things made sense.[2] This was part of the force of a fundamental *a priori* principle of reasoning that he recognized: '*that there is nothing without a reason*' ('Metaphysical Consequences', p. 172, emphasis in original) or

---

[1] Throughout this chapter I use the following abbreviations for Leibniz' works: 'A Specimen' for Leibniz (1973c); 'Correspondence with Arnauld', for Leibniz (1962); *Correspondence with Clarke* for Leibniz and Clarke (1956); 'Discourse' for Leibniz (1998); 'Introduction' for Leibniz (1973a); 'Metaphysical Consequences' for Leibniz (1973j); 'Monadology' for Leibniz (1973k); 'Nature and Grace' for Leibniz (1973l); 'Necessary and Contingent' for Leibniz (1973e); *New Essays* for Leibniz (1996); 'New System' for Leibniz (1973g); 'On Contingency' for Leibniz (1989); 'On Freedom' for Leibniz (1973f); 'Reflections' for Leibniz (1956); 'Résumé' for Leibniz (1973i); *Schriften* for Leibniz (1923–); *Textes Inédits* for Leibniz (1948); *Theodicy* for Leibniz (1985); 'The Ultimate Origination' for Leibniz (1973h); and 'Universal Synthesis' for Leibniz (1973b). All unaccompanied references are to Leibniz (1875–1890), with Roman numerals representing volume numbers and Arabic numerals page numbers.

[2] In this he, like Descartes, showed the influence of his scholastic heritage: see further below.

67

again, that 'nothing unintelligible happens' (*New Essays*, p. 381).[3] This principle, which he called *the principle of sufficient reason*, was one of two fundamental *a priori* principles that he recognized. The other, which he called *the principle of contradiction*, was that 'nothing can at the same time be and not be, but everything either is or is not' ('Introduction', p. 9).[4] Between them, these two principles constituted, for Leibniz, a kind of boundary condition on all attempts to make sense of things. The principle of contradiction precluded success beyond that boundary; the principle of sufficient reason guaranteed success within it. There was never any sense to be made of things beyond the boundary, that is there was never any sense to be made of things in attempts that did not have due regard for consistency, because there was never any *sense* to be made there at all; there was always some sense to be made of things within the boundary, that is there was always some sense to be made of things in attempts that did have due regard for consistency, because things always made sense. And Leibniz held that there was intrinsic value in our striving, as far as possible, to discern this sense (and, thus far, to emulate God, who constantly held this sense in view[5]). In particular, there was intrinsic value in our striving to discern the most general sense that things made. It was a mark of our very humanity that we had the capacity to do this (cf. 'Résumé', §22).

That this was a mark of our humanity held a further significance for Leibniz. It meant that there was something foolhardy in any attempt to discern the most general sense that things made while ignoring the attempts of others. Indeed, in accord with his own most general conception of things (see §3), Leibniz believed that each attempt to discern the most general sense that things made was grounded in a particular point of view from which certain aspects of that general sense were peculiarly perspicuous. We should draw unashamedly on past traditions. Drawing on past traditions would not, in Leibniz' view, spare us the effort of working out why their insights counted as such: metaphysics is a fundamentally *a priori* exercise. But it would at least put us in touch with their insights, which might otherwise elude us. Leibniz was both by nature and by conviction an eclectic.[6]

---

[3] In calling this something close to a basic datum for Leibniz, I am prescinding from some attempts that he made early in his career to prove it (see Mercer (2001), p. 3, and the references given there), attempts which he later abandoned (see Bennett (2003), p. 176, and the references given there). For a fascinating discussion of the principle, in relation to Plato as well as to Leibniz, see Wiggins (1996).

[4] Cf. 'A Specimen', p. 75; 'Monadology', §§31 and 32; and *Correspondence with Clarke*, 'Fifth Paper', ¶10.

[5] Cf. 'Discourse', §35, and 'Letter to De Volder', dated January 1705, in II, 278.

[6] Cf. Christia Mercer (2001), Ch. 1. On p. 471 of ibid., Mercer writes that 'for Leibniz the road to truth was paved with the books of the great philosophers.' Cf. in this connection 'Letter to Remond', dated 10 January 1714, in III.

For his own part, although he was very conscious of the various ancient legacies at his disposal, he tried above all to draw on the more recent scholastic legacy handed down to him in the form of mainstream Christianity.[7] Thus he believed in an omnipotent, omniscient, perfectly good God, whose existence he took to be susceptible to proof (e.g. 'Résumé', §§1–3, and 'Monadology', §§43–45).[8] God, in Leibniz' view, was responsible for all that is contingently the case. And what is contingently the case, in the vivid terminology of 'possible worlds' that he famously introduced, is what is the case in this possible world but not in others ('Monadology', §§53 and 54). But, granted God's nature, this possible world must be the best. For what is the best 'God knows through his wisdom, chooses through his goodness, and produces through his power' ('Monadology', §55). Moreover, 'the best' here was not to be understood in the naturalistic and relativistic way in which Spinoza had understood it (see §3 of the previous chapter). Leibniz explicitly repudiated that conception in favour of a conception whereby the criteria for what is best were firmly engrained in the large-scale structure of reality and were not dependent on the will of anyone, not even on the will of God (e.g. 'Reflections', pp. 911–912 and 916–917; cf. 'Discourse', §2).

Such was Leibniz' own most general attempt to make sense of things, in its broadest outline. If it was a success, then it was as great a success as any such attempt could be. For to show that things are how they are because there is, cosmically, no better way for them to be is a kind of apotheosis of making sense of things.[9] And if that is the prospect afforded by the most general attempt to make sense of things, then this gives further fillip to the idea that there is intrinsic value in its pursuit.

For Leibniz, then, the significance of metaphysics lay not in its subserving some further purpose, nor yet in its providing a solution to any independent problem. Its significance lay, at least in part, in its capacity to achieve, at the highest possible level, the very thing that it was an attempt to achieve. But only in part. There was a price to be paid. And here we come to the real irony of Leibniz' system. For, granted the general sense he made of things, the significance of metaphysics had to be seen as lying also, and in even greater part, not in its providing a solution to any independent problem, certainly, but in its providing a great problem of its own.

2. The Problem of Theodicy

The problem, to put it baldly, is that this does not appear to be the best of all possible worlds.[10] The existence of better possible worlds seems itself to

[7] See Mercer (2001), Ch. 1, §2.
[8] For extensive discussion of Leibniz' proofs of the existence of God, see Adams (1994), Chs 5–8.
[9] Cf. Parfit (2004).
[10] Leibniz' vision was famously satirized by Voltaire in Voltaire (1990).

be a basic datum, impinging on us every bit as forcefully as any principle to the effect that things always make sense – nay, through our various trials and afflictions, altogether more forcefully. To reject that datum is not merely to invite scepticism about whatever reasoning has brought us to do so. It is to invite accusations of intellectualist insensibility. It is to risk making a mockery of our very real, very unmockable suffering. To be sure, the conclusion that this is the best of all possible worlds has scope for profound consolation. For while uncompensated suffering is one thing, suffering with an acknowledged purpose, to avoid what would otherwise be yet worse, is quite different.[11] But the depth of the consolation will be proportional to our ability to understand it. Even if we can dispel the scepticism about whatever reasoning has brought us to the conclusion that this is the best of all possible worlds, such scepticism is liable to give way to scepticism about our capacity to see what the conclusion really means. The consolation will be minimal unless our recognition that things somehow make sense is not itself the limit of our ability to make sense of them; or, if it is the limit, unless we at least have a grip on why it is. One way or another Leibniz needs to confront the problem that his metaphysical story seems to be a repellent lie about what our lives are really like.

This problem is of course a variation on the classic problem that confronts anyone who believes in an omniscient, omnipotent, perfectly good God. It is a harsh fact that such a belief appears incompatible with how the world appears, which is to say, improvable. It is the task of *theodicy* to address this problem.[12] Typically, this task is discharged by rejecting the first of the two appearances, the appearance of incompatibility. Leibniz, however, in insisting that this is the best of all possible worlds, needs to discharge it by rejecting the second of the two appearances, the appearance of improvability. In order to do this he needs to expand on the metaphysical story that he has already told and to provide some account of the illusion. To the extent that he can do this, metaphysics will after all be in the service of some other undertaking for him. It will be in the service of theodicy.

But this is somewhat different from the way in which it was in the service of other undertakings for Descartes and Spinoza. It is different because the very *raison d'être* of theodicy, for Leibniz, is metaphysical. Metaphysics is in the service of an attempt to deal with its own fallout.

I referred in §7 of the Introduction to the way in which good metaphysics can fulfil the function of rectifying bad metaphysics. The function that I am suggesting it has for Leibniz is somewhat different from that too. It is

---

[11] This is something that Nietzsche will later see with especial clarity: see Nietzsche (1967a), Essay II, §7, and Essay III, §28; and see Ch. 15, §6.

[12] It is noteworthy that the only philosophical book that Leibniz published during his lifetime was called *Theodicy*.

the function of addressing a problem created by metaphysics that is itself good, but importantly incomplete. However, this function shares with the function to which I referred in the Introduction that it needs to involve a general attempt to make sense of our original general attempt to make sense of things. We shall see in the development of Leibniz' metaphysical story how clearly he has this need in view.

3. Leibniz' System

The story proceeds as follows. The ultimate constituents of the world are individual substances, what Leibniz calls monads. These are minds, or mind-like. Each of them represents the world in some way. They include God,[13] you, next-door's cat, and countless much less sophisticated monads corresponding to various material features of the world. But none of them is itself, strictly speaking, material.[14] For neither space nor time is an ultimate feature of reality. (The infinite divisibility of space and time means that they have parts whose existence is parasitic on the wholes, which, in Leibniz' view, flouts a basic metaphysical principle of what is real (III, 622).) Rather, space and time are features of how reality appears to certain of these monads. Leibniz is an idealist.[15]

Already we see a striking divergence between the reaction of Spinoza to Descartes' complex pluralism about substance and that of Leibniz. Spinoza reacted by acknowledging only one substance. Leibniz takes the opposite but equally simplifying step of acknowledging an infinity of substances, each of the same basic kind. But despite this divergence, there are important respects in which Spinoza and Leibniz are closer to each other than either is to Descartes. Each of them believes that that which merits the title of 'substance' is without parts – yet also such as to contain within itself all the complexity and diversity of nature. We shall see shortly the form that such containment takes in Leibniz.

Now God, although He is just one monad among infinitely many, is different from all other monads in the following crucial respect. He exists necessarily, whereas they exist contingently. He exists necessarily for reasons

---

[13] It is not entirely uncontroversial that they include God: see Russell (1992a), p. 187. But Russell himself cites passages from Leibniz which imply that God is a monad. He suggests that these are 'slips'. I disagree. Cf. 'Monadology', §§1 and 47.

[14] So to say that monads include you and next-door's cat is to presuppose that you and next-door's cat are independent of your bodies.

[15] Once Descartes separated the self from its environment in the way in which he did (Ch. 1, §6), it was only a question of time before a post-Cartesian philosopher would espouse such idealism: see Heidegger (2003a), pp. 32–33. Note: Leibniz' idealism has much in common with Kant's (see Ch. 5, esp. §4), but, unlike Kant, Leibniz is happy to accept that we can know a good deal about the underlying non-spatio-temporal reality.

made clear by the proofs of His existence. They exist contingently because they depend for their existence on Him, and whatever He creates He could have refrained from creating. Given any non-Divine monad that exists in this world, there are therefore other possible worlds in which it does not exist. And there are other possible worlds in which non-Divine monads exist that do not exist in this world. We might put it like this: God's creative act is to actualize some, but not all, 'possible monads'.[16]

Does this mean that there is nothing more to a possible world than the possible monads it contains, or again, that a possible world just *is* an arbitrary set of possible monads? We might think that there must be more to a possible world than that, namely how the possible monads are 'arranged'. In fact, however, there is plenty in Leibniz to preclude his acknowledging any such notion of 'arrangement'. Indeed, there is plenty to preclude his acknowledging any possible monad's existing in more than one possible world.[17] But if no possible monad exists in more than one possible world, then it immediately follows not only that there is never any more to a possible world than a set of possible monads, but that there is sometimes not that much – by which I mean that some such sets, indeed most such sets, do not correspond to any possible world. This is something to which Leibniz is in any case independently committed, because he recognizes a relation of compossibility among possible monads, a relation whose complement – incompossibility – holds between two possible monads precisely when there is no possible world in which they both exist (III, 572ff.). There are some extraordinarily delicate questions concerning how this and the arguments for it are to be interpreted.[18] I shall have a little more to say about these issues later. Suffice to observe, for the time being, that God's creative act is in an important sense neither more nor less than His actualizing of some possible monads (cf. III, 573).[19]

---

[16] Note: I shall use the phrase 'possible monad' in such a way as to preclude God Himself. A possible monad exists in some *but not all* possible worlds. Note also: although I shall talk of God Himself as existing in all possible worlds, as a way of registering that His existence is necessary, there is at least one respect in which such talk is misleading. Possible worlds themselves depend on God ('Monadology', §43; cf. also n. 23 and the material cited therein).

[17] For an excellent discussion, with references, see Adams (1994), Pt I, esp. Ch. 2, §1.

[18] For two extremely helpful discussions, see Wiggins (1988), esp. §9, and Bennett (2003), §139.

[19] It is a further question, which I here simply note, what exactly this actualizing consists in: what the difference is between a possible monad that exists and one that is 'merely' possible. (For discussion, see Adams (1994), Ch. 6, esp. §§1 and 2.) That such a question should arise, given that it concerns what is, after all, the greatest difference there could be, is indicative of how high the seas of metaphysics are running here. (This is a deliberate echo of both Wittgenstein (1967a), Pt I, §194, and ibid., §304.) P.F. Strawson gives the question a further twist in Strawson (1959), where he discusses the views of 'a

Each monad has two fundamental features for Leibniz. It is 'windowless' ('Monadology', §7) and it 'mirrors' the whole world ('Monadology', §56).

To say that it is *windowless* is to say that 'neither substance nor accident can enter [it] from without' ('Monadology', §7). That is, it is impervious to everything else, or rather, in the case of a created monad, it is impervious to everything else except God. This imperviousness is of a very radical kind. Each monad, Leibniz says, is like a world apart ('Discourse', §14). He also says that 'whatever happens to each [monad] would flow from its nature and its notion even if the rest were supposed to be absent' ('A Specimen', p. 79) and that 'it is as if there were as many different universes [sc. as there are monads]' ('Monadology', §57). In other words, it would *make no difference* to a created monad if 'nothing else existed but only God and itself' ('New System', p. 122). In particular it would make no difference to any of us. It follows that, for Leibniz, just as for Descartes (Ch. 1, §6), unless we can make sense of what is, in a very deep sense, transcendent, we cannot make sense of anything other than ourselves.

But Leibniz would think that it was unacceptably sceptical to deny that we can make sense of what is other than ourselves ('Universal Synthesis', pp. 15–16). He therefore needs, just as Descartes needed, some assurance that we *can* do this and some account of how. His response to this need is very similar to Descartes'. He appeals to God's benevolent guarantee that what is other than us shall conform to the ideas that we form through the proper use of our various faculties of representation.[20] And this connects with the second fundamental feature that each monad has. Each monad *mirrors the whole world*. That is, each monad comprises a full and (because of God's benevolence) accurate representation of the world, which in effect means a full and accurate representation of every other monad. The second fundamental feature therefore serves as a kind of corrective to the first. Here is Leibniz:

> God first created the soul, and every other real unity [i.e. monad], in such a way that everything in it must spring from within itself, by a perfect *spontaneity* with regard to itself, and yet in a perfect *conformity* with things outside.... It follows from this that, since each of these substances exactly represents the whole universe in its own way and from a certain point of view, and since the perceptions or expressions of external

possible philosopher at least very similar to Leibniz in certain doctrinal respects' (p. 117). Strawson asks, in effect, why a possible monad should not be actualized twice.

Note: Deleuze writes that 'in Leibniz ... the world has no existence outside the monads that express it, while yet God brings the world, rather than the monads, into existence' (Deleuze (1990a), p. 334). I am not altogether convinced by his reasons for drawing this distinction, but in any case I intend what I say in the main text to be neutral with respect to any such issue of ontological priority. (I shall return briefly, and parenthetically, to this issue later in this section.)

[20] See 'Discourse', §§23–25, for discussion of what this proper use comes to.

things reach the soul at the proper time by virtue of its own laws..., there
will be a perfect agreement between all these substances, producing the
same effect as would occur if these communicated with one another by
means of a transmission of species or qualities [i.e. the same effect as
would occur if they were not windowless]. ('New System', pp. 122–123,
emphasis in original)

But since, in a sense, there is nothing more to a monad than its representation of the world, there needs to be some difference between any two of
these representations to distinguish the two corresponding monads. This
difference is grounded in the fact that each representation is, as Leibniz puts
it in the quotation above, from a certain point of view.[21] That is to say, each
representation is more distinct either the closer its subject matter is to the
corresponding monad or the larger its subject matter is (in some metaphorical sense of closeness and some metaphorical sense of largeness[22]). This is
why, despite the fact that you carry a full and accurate representation of the
world within you, you cannot always determine the answer to a question
just by elementary introspection. If the question concerns something about
which your representation is very indistinct, then you will need to apply
effort of some appropriate kind to 'reposition' yourself and make it more
distinct. And this may in practice, if not in principle, be beyond you. Leibniz
summarizes these ideas as follows:

The nature of the monad is representative, and consequently nothing can
limit it to representing a part of things only, although it is true that its
representation is confused as regards the detail of the whole universe
and can only be distinct as regards a small part of things; that is to say
as regards those which are either the nearest or the largest in relation to
each of the monads.... In a confused way [all monads] go towards the
infinite, towards the whole; but they are limited and distinguished from
one another by the degrees of their distinct perceptions.... [A] soul can
read in itself only what is distinctly represented there; it is unable to
develop all at once all the things that are folded within it, for they stretch
to infinity. ('Monadology', §§60 and 61)

(Note that Leibniz uses the language of representation in this quotation.
Elsewhere, for example in 'Discourse', §§9 and 35, he uses the language of

---

[21] Cf. II, 251–252.

[22] These senses have to be metaphorical because monads are not literally in space. Quite
what they amount to is not easy to say. For an excellent discussion, see Brandom (2002c).
See also Deleuze (1990b), 24th Series, esp. pp. 171–172. Note: Deleuze distinguishes
Leibniz' views from a perspectivism that we find in Nietzsche. We shall return to the latter
in Ch. 15, §3. One important difference worth noting straight away is that on Leibniz'
view there is one point of view, namely God's, that is privileged (e.g. 'Discourse', §14, and
'Monadology', §60).

expression. This reflects the fact that he is talking about a relation that is in some ways like the representational relation that holds between a Cartesian mind and the radically independent world to which that mind's thinking is answerable, but which is in other ways like the expressive relation that holds between a Spinozist attribute and the reality that finds corresponding articulation in every other attribute.)

At this point there arises a particularly difficult exegetical question. Call the relation that obtains between two possible monads when their representations of the world cohere *harmony*. The question is this: what is the relation between harmony and compossibility?

We might think that they must be different relations. In particular, we might think that there must be instances of compossibility that are not instances of harmony. For, although it is impossible for two conflicting stories both to be true, it is not impossible for two conflicting stories both to be told. There is corroboration for this in Leibniz' definition of the compossible as 'that which, with another, does not imply a contradiction' (*Textes Inédits*, p. 325). For there is surely no contradiction in two monads' failing to be in harmony with each other. Furthermore, unless there were instances of compossibility that were not instances of harmony, either God would not after all be required to ensure that all monads are in harmony with one another, for it would be impossible for them not to be, or God would be required to ensure that the world is so much as possible. Either of these alternatives would be contrary to what Leibniz actually says. The former would be contrary to his insistence that 'it is God alone ... who is the cause of [harmony]' ('Discourse', §14). The latter would be contrary to his denial that 'the eternal truths of metaphysics ... are only the effects of God's will' ('Discourse', §2; cf. IV, 344). (It is surely an eternal truth of metaphysics that the world is possible.)[23]

On the other hand, as against all of that, unless compossibility just *is* harmony, then it is hard to see what else it can be. What else, given the windowlessness of monads, might be thought to explain why not every set of possible monads constitutes a possible world? What, other than disharmony, might be thought to prevent any pair of possible monads from existing in the same possible world, or any one possible monad from existing in two different possible worlds?

---

[23] Could Leibniz say that God *is* required to ensure that the world is possible on the grounds that the world's being possible, although it does not depend on His will, does depend on His understanding (cf. 'Discourse', §2, the clause immediately after that cited in the main text, and 'Monadology', §§43–46)? Perhaps. But this would still not leave room in his system for the view that compossibility entails harmony. This is because he takes the harmony of monads with one another, which on that view would be a consequence of the world's being possible, to depend on God's will, not just on His understanding (e.g. 'New System', pp. 131–132 and *Correspondence with Clarke*, 'Second Paper').

These are genuine questions, not rhetorical questions. I raise them just to signal the exegetical difficulty. We could not accede to the suggestion that compossibility is the same as harmony without dismissing some of the quotations above as aberrations on Leibniz' part. And in any case there are all sorts of further complications that I have not considered. (Here is one. I said earlier that there is surely no contradiction in two monads' failing to be in harmony with each other. But if God necessarily creates everything for the best, and if the best necessarily requires harmony, perhaps disharmony does imply a contradiction? Here is another. It may be a basic error in the first place to think of possible worlds combinatorially. Perhaps each possible monad is just an aspect of some possible world, the worlds being ontologically more fundamental than the monads, so that the question whether a possible monad can exist in more than one possible world trivially receives the answer no.[24] But then, to complicate this complication, how would that consist with the monads' windowlessness?[25]) All that matters for our purposes is that somewhere in the process of determining which of all the arbitrary sets of possible monads is to constitute this world there is a benevolent decree on the part of God that prohibits any whose monads are not in harmony with one another.[26]

But harmony is not the only desideratum. If it were, there would be no reason for God to create anything at all. For in a world with no created monads, it would be vacuously true that every monad was in harmony with every other. So, by the principle of sufficient reason, there must be something else guiding God's creative act ('Nature and Grace', §7; cf. 'Monadology', §53).

What there is, Leibniz urges, is the value of sheer existence. The more that exists, the better. God's own necessary existence serves as a ground for this desideratum, which Leibniz expresses as follows: '*everything possible*

---

[24] Cf. Wiggins (1988), pp. 278–279.

[25] For discussion of these and further complications, see Russell (1992a), §69; D'Agostino (1981); Savile (2000), pp. 15–16; Bennett (2003), §139; and McDonough (2010). And for some further striking suggestions about what compossibility consists in, see Deleuze (1993), 59ff.; Deleuze (1994), pp. 263–264; and Deleuze (1990b), pp. 171–172. (But see also Ch. 21, n. 27, for some concerns about Deleuze's handling of this notion.)

[26] That the possible monads that are actualized should at least form a *set*, where this is understood in such a way that those that are not actualized form the complement of the set, in other words that each possible monad should be either actualized or not but that none should be both, is determined by the principle of contradiction. (I am prescinding from nominalistic concerns about the existence of sets, and also from anachronistic concerns about whether there are too many monads to form a set: see Moore (2001a), Ch. 8, §§3–5.) That they should form *this* set is determined by the principle of sufficient reason. Again, that they should form a set depends on God's understanding; that they should form *this* set, on God's will ('Monadology', §46).

demands existence' ('Résumé', §6, emphasis in original).[27] So God actualizes as much as He can, subject to the constraint that there should still be harmony.

But subject only to that constraint? Or are there yet further desiderata besides these two? Leibniz does sometimes write as though harmony and plenitude were the only two desiderata. Indeed, in one striking passage he combines that suggestion with the suggestion – which, if it were intended, would settle the question we have just been considering about the relation between compossibility and harmony – that compossibility is indeed tantamount to harmony. He writes, 'It does not follow from this [sc. that everything possible demands existence] that all possibles exist; though this would follow if all possibles were compossible' ('Résumé', §7; cf. 'The Ultimate Origination', p. 139). Elsewhere, however, he seems to acknowledge beauty, order, and their perception by intelligent beings as further determinants of creation (e.g. 'Résumé', §§17 and 18). The issue is whether they really are *further* determinants. There is certainly more to beauty and order than harmony. But is there more to them than plenitude? Leibniz glosses plenitude in such a way as to make clear that there is more to *it* than sheer population size. Form and variety also count (e.g. 'Résumé', §12). And indeed he explicitly relates form and variety to beauty and order (ibid., §§13–15). But does he relate them tightly enough to derive the value of the latter from the value of the former? And what about the value of their perception by intelligent beings? Once again, the exegetical waters are deep. Once again, we do not need to wade through them. All that matters for our purposes is that there are, if not two desiderata influencing God's creative act, then two broad categories of desiderata, one essentially quantitative and the other essentially qualitative, and these are in conflict with each other, so that what God needs to achieve in creation is a balance between the two, maximizing

---

[27] Cf. ibid., §§4 and 5. In §5 he expresses it as follows: 'everything possible *has an urge to* existence' (emphasis added). This might put us in mind of Spinoza's notion of conatus (see Ch. 2, §3). But see Deleuze (1990a), pp. 230ff., for why the two should not be assimilated: Spinoza's notion has no application to what is 'merely' possible, a category that Spinoza does not so much as recognize. Indeed, if Leibniz' formulae were understood in too Spinozist a way, for instance in such a way as to entail that each possible thing would exist unless it were prevented from doing so, then we might begin to wonder what need there was for any creative act on God's part (as opposed to acts of prevention): cf. Lovejoy (1964), pp. 177ff., and Neiman (2002), p. 27. See Bennett (2003), p. 181, where he addresses this concern and scotches any such interpretation. See also Blumenfeld (1981) for a very interesting discussion. (I should concede, as both Jonathan Bennett and David Blumenfeld do, that Leibniz sometimes states his view in a way that precisely encourages such an interpretation: see e.g. II, 194, and 'The Ultimate Origination', pp. 137–138. But see also 'A Specimen', pp. 75–76, n. 1, for a more careful statement.)

each to the least detriment of the other.[28] This world is the possible world in which that balance is struck. Or, as Leibniz himself puts it, this world is that which is 'most perfect, that is to say that which is simultaneously simplest in theories and the richest in phenomena' ('Discourse', §6; cf. 'The Ultimate Origination', p. 138, and 'Monadology', §58). In sum, this world is the best of all possible worlds.

4. Leibniz' Various Modal Distinctions

Before we turn to Leibniz' account of how this world appears not to be the best of all possible worlds, we should note an important implication of the story so far concerning the contingency of how things are. If, per impossibile, we had an infinite intellect, and were thereby able to perform the infinitely complex calculations necessary to determine how things must be for the balance referred to at the end of the previous section to be struck, then we would be in a position to determine *a priori* how things in fact are. For in Leibniz' view we have an *a priori* guarantee that there is an omniscient, omnipotent, perfectly good God, who ensures that things are just how they must be for that balance to be struck. That it would be possible in this way to determine *a priori* how things are is not however supposed to impugn our conviction that this world is just one of a range of possible worlds, in other words that it is contingent that things are the way they are.

How comfortable should we be with this? For any positivistically minded philosopher there is a harsh dissonance in the idea of determining *a priori* how, among all the ways things could have been, they are. If things could have been otherwise, such a philosopher will say, then nothing short of experiential contact with things can rule out their actually being otherwise.[29]

Three points can be made straight away, each of which should make Leibniz' idea sound a little easier on the positivist ear. First, there is always *some* sense, if only an epistemic sense indicating a prior ignorance, in which determining *a priori* how things are means ruling out other possibilities. It is not obvious that what would be ruled out in the Leibnizian story need be possible in a sense that would be any more awkward to accommodate, positivistically, than that. (We shall return to this point.) Second, Leibniz' conception of the *a priori* is in any case somewhat different from the positivist conception. It is closer to the original conception, which applied to

---

[28] Not even this is uncontroversial. David Blumenfeld, in Blumenfeld (1995), adduces an impressive variety of textual support for a reading whereby there is just one kind of desideratum. If there is, then some of what I shall say later in this chapter needs to be recast, but I do not think its gist is affected.

[29] See further Ch. 11, esp.§1. See also Ch. 4, §3, for the Humean inspiration behind this conviction. See Kripke (1981), pp. 54–55, for some well-known contemporary (non-Leibnizian) dissent.

reasoning from explicans to explicandum. Roughly, on Leibniz' conception, to determine *a priori* how things are is to determine how they are in a way that explains why they are that way.[30] And third, there is of course the very grossness of the counterpossibility signalled in the phrase *'per impossible'*. Small wonder if the posit that we have an infinite intellect has such strange consequences![31]

This third point can be helpfully reinforced by looking at one familiar aspect of the Leibnizian idea of determining *a priori* how things are. Leibniz writes, 'In every true affirmative proposition, necessary or contingent, universal or particular, the notion of the predicate is in some way contained in the notion of the subject' ('Necessary and Contingent', p. 96).[32] Thus suppose that Adam sins. Then the 'notion' of sinning must be contained in the 'notion' of Adam. This makes it sound as if Adam could not have failed to sin, and indeed, strictly speaking, Leibniz thinks, he could not. For strictly speaking there is only one possible world, namely this world, in which Adam, this actual man, this very monad, so much as exists, and that is a world in which he sins (cf. 'Discourse', §31). But it remains contingent that Adam sins, because it is contingent that Adam exists at all. The point about his notion containing the notion of sinning is just that a full infinite grasp of what it takes to be Adam must include a grasp of all that is involved in the possible world in which he exists, including his sinning. And that grasp would be part of the *a priori* exercise of determining that the world in question was the best, thereby inferring that the world in question was this world, thereby inferring that Adam exists, and thereby inferring that Adam sins (cf. 'Letter to Arnauld', dated 4–14 July 1686, in 'Correspondence with Arnauld').

We, however, have only a partial, finite grasp of what it takes to be Adam. We cannot determine *a priori* that Adam sins. The only truths that *we* can determine *a priori*, which Leibniz calls 'truths of reasoning' ('Monadology', §§33–35), are those whose denial can, by a finite process of analysis, be reduced to absurdity.[33] (A simple example might be that any father who sins

---

[30] There is a nice account, with references, in Adams (1994), pp. 109–110.

[31] God, by contrast, does have an infinite intellect: He 'comprehends the infinite at once ... and can understand *a priori* the perfect reason for [any] contingency' ('Necessary and Contingent', p. 97). And He can infer from this, together with His own perfection, that the contingency in question holds (cf. 'On Freedom', p. 109). But He can also be said to 'sense' the contingency, not in the way in which we might sense it, but in as much as 'it pleases Him' (*Schriften*, Series VI, Vol. III, p. 56).

[32] Leibniz seems to hold that every proposition is of subject-predicate form, though the exegesis is delicate. For discussion, with references, see Ishiguro (1972), Ch. 5.

[33] What counts as absurdity? Running together the ideas in 'Monadology', §§33–35, we can say that absurdity consists in denying a 'primary principle'. And what is a 'primary principle'? According to 'Monadology', §35, it is a proposition whose denial contains an express contradiction. So the upshot of these three sections is that truths of reasoning

is a parent who sins – fathers being by definition male parents.) And the distinction between truths of reasoning and all other truths, the latter of which Leibniz calls 'truths of fact' (ibid.), just is the distinction between what is necessarily true, or true in all possible worlds, and what is contingently true, or true merely in this world ('Necessary and Contingent', esp. pp. 96–98; cf. 'Discourse', §13, and 'On Freedom', pp. 108–109). So once the counterpossible presumption of our infinite intellect has been dropped, Leibniz' view is not so different from what a positivistically minded philosopher might choose to say after all.

That Leibniz talks about the notion of the predicate being contained in the notion of the subject has led some commentators, notably Bertrand Russell, to compare his idea to Kant's idea of analyticity, which he (Kant) defines in a superficially very similar way. Kant calls a judgment analytic when 'the predicate B belongs to the subject A as something that is (covertly) contained in the concept A' (Kant (1998), A6/B10). Having made this comparison, Russell struggles with Leibniz' claim, quoted above, that 'in *every* true affirmative proposition ... the notion of the predicate is in some way contained in the notion of the subject' (emphasis added). For on even a remotely Kantian understanding of this, there is one kind of proposition, namely an existential proposition such as the proposition that Adam exists, which *must* be an exception (ibid., A225/B272–273 and A592–602/B620–630). And Russell, accordingly, does not see how it can fail to be an exception for Leibniz too (Russell (1992a), pp. 9–10).[34] Russell does not see how even a full infinite grasp of what it takes to be Adam can suffice for seeing that anyone actually fills the bill. But in fact, once we realize that Leibniz' idea allows for appeal to what would be visible to an infinite intellect capable of seeing *a priori* how this world qualifies as the best of all possible worlds, and that Kant's idea allows for appeal to nothing save what would be visible to a finite intellect trying to make sense of what is given to it in experience (ibid., B145), so that Kant's idea, if it corresponds to anything in

are those that can be shown, by a finite process of analysis, not to be deniable without violating the principle of contradiction, the second of the two fundamental *a priori* principles of reasoning introduced in §1 (cf. 'Discourse', §13). But that seems to exclude the other one, the principle of sufficient reason, which Leibniz elsewhere suggests should be included (e.g. VII, 301). The fact is that Leibniz' views on these matters are not settled (see n. 3). In what follows I shall make the assumption which seems to me to be in the greatest harmony with the greatest amount of what he says: that the principle of sufficient reason does indeed count as a primary principle, and is therefore itself a truth of reasoning. (One important consequence of this assumption is that, insofar as that principle is needed to prove any given proposition, for instance the proposition that God exists (see e.g. 'Nature and Grace', §8), that is no threat to the proposition's being a truth of reasoning).

[34] Cf. Edward Craig (1987), p. 61, n. 47, where Craig likewise says that this kind of proposition is an exception for Leibniz, but without any reference.

Leibniz, corresponds to Leibniz' idea of a truth of reasoning,[35] then there is no obstacle to our accepting that Leibniz really does mean *every* true affirmative proposition, including the proposition that Adam exists.[36] And if we insist on using the Kantian label 'analytic' for Leibniz' much broader idea, however foreign that may be to Kant's own use of the label, then we can say, with Louis Couturat, that just as part of the purport of the principle of contradiction is that every analytic proposition is true, so too part of the purport of the principle of sufficient reason is that every true proposition is analytic (Couturat (1901), pp. 214–221).

I have been arguing, then, on Leibniz' behalf and in what I hope to be something like Leibniz' own terms, that his conviction that every proposition is analytic *in that broad, non-Kantian sense* does not in any way compromise his conviction that some propositions are contingent. But there is one further concern that we might have about this, which must be addressed. The concern is as follows. On Leibniz' view, it is not only analytic, in that sense, that there is an omniscient, omnipotent, perfectly good God who ensures that everything is for the best; it is also necessary. For it is a truth of reasoning: it is a truth that even we, with our finite intellects, can determine *a priori*. It follows that, in every possible world, there is a God ensuring that everything is for the best.[37] Yet only in one possible world, namely that which in fact qualifies as the best, *is* everything for the best. (On Leibniz' view, of course, that world is this world.) So must not something give (the most obvious candidate being that there is more than one possible world)?

Here is another way of voicing the same concern. Leibniz sometimes calls what is necessary 'metaphysically necessary', and he sometimes calls what is for the best 'morally necessary' (e.g. *Correspondence with Clarke*, 'Fifth Paper', ¶9).[38] In these terms, he holds that some of what is morally necessary – some of what is actually the case, in other words – is not metaphysically necessary. But that seems straightforwardly incompatible with something else that he holds, namely that it is metaphysically necessary that there is an omniscient, omnipotent, perfectly good God who ensures that whatever is morally necessary is true.

Leibniz is well aware of this concern. To meet it, he urges that it is contingent what is for the best, in other words that what is for the best varies from

---

[35] In fact Kant's views are complicated in a way that makes even this comparison questionable: see below, Ch. 5, §3. (This is quite apart from the complication that, for Leibniz, it is a truth of reasoning that God exists, whereas Kant denies that *any* existential truths are analytic.)

[36] See 'Letter to Arnauld', dated 4–14 July 1686, in 'Correspondence with Arnauld'. See also Wiggins (1988), esp. §§IV and V, and Adams (1994), Ch. 1, §2.6, and Ch. 2, §3, for helpful discussions.

[37] 'A' God – but unique, and the same in all possible worlds. (See further n. 16.)

[38] Cf. 'The Ultimate Origin', p. 139, where he calls the latter 'physically necessary'.

one possible world to another ('On Contingency', esp. p. 30).[39] This leaves him free to say that each possible world is the best *by its own lights*. And this in turn leaves him free to accept both of the following, without denying that there is more than one possible world.

(1) In every possible world there is a God ensuring that everything is for the best.

(2) In only one possible world, this one, is there a God ensuring that everything is for the best.

The point is this. Proposition (1) can be understood as a *de dicto* proposition about what is for the best (in every possible world there is a God ensuring that everything is for the best by the lights of that world), while proposition (2) can be understood as a *de re* proposition about what is for the best (given what is in fact for the best, by the lights of this world, this is the only possible world in which there is a God ensuring that that is how everything is).[40]

But surely, someone might object, it is preposterous to say that each possible world is the best by its own lights, and quite antithetical to Leibniz' own non-relativistic conception of what qualifies as the best (see §1). Surely, he should hold that what qualifies as the best, and what guides God in His creative act, is itself necessary, in the most robust sense of necessity – or, if not in the most robust sense, then certainly in a sense robust enough to prevent its being true that, *whatever* form God's creative act had taken, it would have been for the best (proposition (1)).

This objection is confused. We must not be misled by the imagery of possible worlds. Possible worlds are not like foreign countries where they do things differently.[41] Whether or not something is true in all possible worlds, in other words whether or not it is (metaphysically) necessary, *just is* a matter of whether or not it can be shown, by a finite process of analysis, not to be deniable without absurdity. All that Leibniz is saying is something to which we already know him to be committed, which is this: although such a finite process of analysis is enough to show that there is an omniscient, omnipotent, perfectly good God who ensures that everything is for the best, it takes a kind of infinite analysis, based on sensitivity

---

[39] But see Adams (1994), Ch. 1, for a thorough discussion of these matters. Leibniz' response to this concern is less settled than I am suggesting; there are some definite changes of view from one writing to another.

[40] Jonathan Bennett, in Bennett (2003), pp. 177–178, denies that this is a satisfactory way of meeting the concern. He seems to me to miss the import of the *de dicto/de re* distinction. (But note that he, like Robert Adams, cites passages illustrating Leibniz' changes of view: see the previous note.)

[41] This point will be very pertinent again much later in our narrative: see Ch. 13, §3 and esp. §4.

to the balance that needs to be struck, to determine what exactly this requires of Him.

Leibniz is really talking about how different truths are ascertained, then. And since we do not have infinite intellects, we must sometimes use our sensory faculties to determine what is required of God to ensure that everything is for the best. We must see what form His creation has actually taken. Whenever we do that, we are ruling out possibilities concerning how the balance is struck. This connects with something I said in passing earlier: that Leibniz' conception of the possible is in certain respects like an epistemic conception indicating temporary ignorance on our part. I do not want to exaggerate these respects. For instance, it would be straightforwardly false to say that, on Leibniz' conception, 'It is possible that …' is equivalent to 'For all we know, it is true that ….' Apart from anything else, any use of the latter expression is sensitive to who uses it and when, in a way in which no use of the former is. Still, it would be closer to the truth to say this than might be suggested by Leibniz' use of the label 'metaphysically necessary', especially if we have in mind what contemporary analytic philosophers mean when *they* use such phrases as 'metaphysically necessary'.[42] What is possible, on Leibniz' conception, is what cannot be reduced to absurdity by a finite process of analysis. It thus pertains, if not to a temporary lack of knowledge, then certainly to an irremediable lack of finite *a priori* knowledge ('For all we finite creatures *can* know *a priori*, it is true that …') – which finally brings us back to the question of how all of this subserves theodicy.

5. Leibniz' Solution to the Problem of Theodicy. Its Unsatisfactoriness

The original problem was this. Leibniz' metaphysics furnishes a proof that this is the best of all possible worlds – which it appears, pertinaciously, not to be. It is patent what Leibniz needs to do. And it is patent, for that matter, how his metaphysical story equips him to do it. Or at least, these things are patent in outline. He needs to make sense of how we make sense of things in such a way as to subvert the appearances. But the problem is more acute for him than that suggests. For he needs, obviously enough, to subvert the relevant appearances. It will be of no avail to show how we are misled about the world's overall value, by whatever standards make this the best of all possible worlds, if those are not the standards that give us such a powerful impression of the world's improvability.[43] Leibniz' story is perfectly suited

---

[42] Usually, they are signalling the notion of necessity which Saul Kripke discusses in Kripke (1981) and which he there describes as a metaphysical notion (pp. 35ff.).

[43] Cf. Williams (2006a), pp. 49–50. (It would be of avail to do this if Leibniz needed only to defend the *truth* of his account. But the issue is not just whether his account is true; the issue is also whether his account is all that it affects to be.)

to account for the general possibility of a mismatch between how things appear and how they ultimately are. What is less clear, as I shall try to show in this section, is its capacity to apply that possibility to what seems so egregious in the conclusion that this is the best of all possible worlds.

That there may be a mismatch between how things appear and how they ultimately are is an essential feature of our finitude, as it is written into Leibniz' story. We see the world in a limited, perspectival way. The fact that we also, despite that, carry within us a full and accurate representation of the world, albeit a representation that is less distinct the less well positioned we are with respect to what is being represented, perhaps means that, for any particular question about how the world is, we can eventually, in principle, determine the answer to it. But we can never, even in principle, determine the combined answers to all such questions. We can never achieve that infinite insight into the whole which shows how everything is for the best; how there is nowhere a complexity in theories or a poverty in phenomena that is not worth enduring for the sake of a richness in phenomena or a simplicity in theories elsewhere. So while we remain in ignorance about aspects of the whole, we are liable to err, either in the judgments we make ('Discourse', §14) or indeed about whether we are making judgments at all, there always being a danger, when we take ourselves to be reflecting on the grand scheme of things, that what we are really doing is dallying with notions that are incoherent ('Discourse', §25). We may think we see possibilities for improving the world. In fact we are just fastening on isolated 'evils' and failing to grasp fully the implications of their elimination. Here is Leibniz:

> We have knowledge of a tiny part of that eternity which stretches out immeasurably.... And yet out of so little experience we rashly make judgments about the immeasurable and the eternal.... Look at the most lovely picture, and then cover it up, leaving uncovered only a tiny scrap of it. What else will you see there, even if you look as closely as possible, and the more so as you look from nearer and nearer at hand, but a kind of confused medley of colours, without selection, without art! And yet when you remove the covering, and look upon the whole picture from the proper place, you will see that what previously seemed to you to have been aimlessly smeared on the canvas was in fact accomplished with the highest art by the author of the work.... [Similarly, the] great composers frequently mingle discords with harmonious chords so that the listener may be stimulated and pricked as it were, and become, in a way, anxious about the outcome; presently when all is restored to order he feels so much the more content. ('The Ultimate Origination', p. 142; cf. *Theodicy*, p. 248, and 'Résumé', §19)

That may seem to be as much as Leibniz needs to say, in his own terms, to provide for a theodicy. For he seems to have shown adequately how we may think we see possibilities for simpler theories or richer phenomena overall when really all we see are such possibilities in the small. The crucial question, however, is whether that is why we think things could have been better.

In §2 I adverted to the scepticism that we may feel, in the face of Leibniz' argument that this is the best of all possible worlds, about whether we really understand its conclusion. Precisely what I had in mind was the possible objection that Leibniz' argument uses standards of assessment that are foreign to us. As David Wiggins puts it, 'a world could furnish by the simplest means the greatest possible variety of forms yet be brutally indifferent to all human concerns and moral purposes' (Wiggins (1996), p. 126; see further ibid., §11). Almost immediately after the passage quoted above, Leibniz tries to forestall any such objection by urging that his standards take due account of 'the good of individual people' (ibid., p. 143). 'As for [our] afflictions,' he continues, '… [these] are for the time being evil, but in effect good, since they are short cuts to a greater perfection' (ibid., pp. 143–144). But there is at least one form that the objection can take that is completely immune either to this or indeed to any other response at Leibniz' disposal.

It takes this form in the mouth of Ivan Karamazov, in Dostoevsky's novel *The Brothers Karamazov*. Ivan's heart is rent by stories of suffering among innocent children. He proclaims, 'I don't want harmony [whose price this suffering is]. I don't want it, out of the love I bear to mankind…. Too high a price has been placed on [it]' (Dostoevsky (1982), p. 287). The target of his outcry appears to be the value accorded, as he says, to harmony (in whatever way harmony is to be understood in this context – it is not, of course, the notion of harmony introduced in §3). But a more fundamental target is the value accorded to sheer existence. For the protest is really that if *this* is the price that has to be paid to attain the best version of a world such as ours, then it would have been better had there never been a world such as ours; it would have been better had nothing been created at all. It is all very well for Leibniz to reply that this protest ignores the larger picture. But the protest is precisely that no larger picture can be relevant – save insofar as a blank canvas counts as a larger picture.

Leibniz writes:

> There is a perpetual and most free progress of the whole universe towards a consummation of the universal beauty and perfection of the works of God. ('The Ultimate Origination', p. 144)

Ivan says:

> I believe in the underlying order and meaning of life. I believe in the eternal harmony into which we are all supposed to merge one day. I believe in the Word to which the universe is striving and which itself … [is] God…. [But] I refuse to accept this *world* of God's….
>
> We cannot afford to pay so much for admission…. It is not God that I do not accept…. I merely most respectfully return him the ticket. (Dostoevsky (1982), pp. 275 and 287, emphasis added)

Leibniz, in his most general attempt to make sense of things, seemed to achieve the ultimate prize: a way of coming to terms with how things are. But he cannot genuinely be said to have achieved this prize unless his metaphysics engages properly with what we antecedently recognize as coming to terms with how things are. To be sure, he is entitled to disturb or challenge our preconceptions. But if we are to accede to his metaphysics, or even to make sense of it, then there had better be a firmer connection within it than there appears to be between what he says matters in the end and what matters now, to us. Otherwise, although what he says need not be untrue, it will be untruthful.[44]

---

[44] This is an allusion to Williams (2002). But see also Kant (1996d), 8:267. And cf. the parenthetical comment in the previous note. (Bernard Williams' own indictment of what I am suggesting is untruthful in Leibniz is characteristically blunt. 'Like some other … metaphysical geniuses,' Williams writes, '… [Leibniz is] capable of being ethically very crass' (Williams (2006b), p. 184, n. 39).) For further exploration of the idea of confronting the world's suffering truthfully, see Ch. 15, §6.

CHAPTER 4

✦

Hume

Metaphysics Committed to the Flames?

1. Empiricism and Scepticism in Hume

Descartes acknowledged substances of three kinds. These comprised one Divine substance; one extended substance; and many, maybe infinitely many, created thinking substances (Ch. 1, §6). Spinoza held that there was just one substance, which he called 'God', and he took this substance to be both extended and thinking, though he took it to have countless other attributes as well (Ch. 2, §2). Leibniz held that there were infinitely many substances, which included God, and which, despite differing in profound ways, were all of the same basic kind, thinking but not extended (Ch. 3, §3).

It takes only a modicum of scepticism about whether they were engaged in a single shared enquiry to wonder whether they meant the same thing by 'substance', and only a modicum more to wonder whether they meant anything at all, and perhaps not much more than that to wonder whether there could ever be any real enquiry at this level of abstraction. It is scarcely surprising, then, that within a quarter of a century of Leibniz' death Hume had published a book in which he not only referred to 'that unintelligible chimera of substance' (*Treatise*, p. 222[1]) and complained that philosophers literally had no idea what they were talking about when they used the word 'substance' (ibid., I.i.7), but urged them to disembroil themselves from all such pseudo-disputes (ibid., I.iv, esp. 2 and 4).

David Hume (1711–1776) introduced a kind of self-consciousness into metaphysics which, whether under his direct influence or not, would never thereafter go away.[2] Sense itself, in the most general attempt to make sense

---

[1] Throughout this chapter I use the following abbreviations for Hume's works: 'Abstract' for Hume (1978b); *Enquiry* for Hume (1975a); 2nd *Enquiry* for Hume (1975b); *Natural History of Religion* for Hume (1976); and *Treatise* for Hume (1978a). In giving non-page references to the *Treatise* I adopt the convention whereby 'I.iv.2' names Bk I, Pt IV, §II, and so forth.

[2] I do not mean to suggest that Hume's reflections were entirely without precedent. Locke (1965) and Berkeley (1962a) were important precursors.

of things, was to become a principal focus of attention. There would be a concern with the scope and limits of sense-making which, by the twentieth century, was to become almost obsessive. But that concern was already there in Hume. And in keeping with what I said in §5 of the Introduction, such self-consciousness brought with it then, and has continued to bring with it ever since, a crisis of self-confidence in the very practice of metaphysics.

Not that this crisis was confined to the practice of metaphysics. It is important to appreciate that Hume was concerned at least as much with mainstream religious thought.[3] Towards some mainstream religious thought he had the straightforwardly sceptical attitude that it lacked any warrant. This was most famously true of the belief in miracles (*Enquiry*, §X). But towards some – including, as I shall urge in §2, theism itself, in one of its most orthodox guises – his attitude was more radical. He doubted whether it concerned matters of genuine belief at all, matters for which the question of a warrant could even arise. That is, he doubted whether it made sense.[4]

Why? What was his criterion for whether something made sense? Or for whether sense had been made of something?

It was a criterion grounded in empiricism. And what is empiricism? On one standard definition, empiricism is the view that all knowledge derives from sense experience. That strikes me as being, for many purposes, a perfectly acceptable definition, though the devil is obviously in the detail of 'derives from'.[5] For current purposes, however, we do well to adopt a definition that makes the connection with sense-making explicit. Empiricism, I shall say, is the view that all *sense-making* derives from sense experience.[6] Here I am still exploiting the latitude of the phrase 'derives from', to which I shall need to return. But more significantly, I am exploiting the latitude of

---

[3] For a good account, see Williams (2006e). In *Treatise*, p. 272, Hume wrote, 'Generally speaking, the errors in religion are dangerous; those in philosophy only ridiculous.'

[4] We might well expect, in view of the example of substance with which we began, that another case in point would be the doctrine of transubstantiation. In fact, in his *Enquiry*, Hume directed scepticism of the more modest kind at this doctrine, borrowing an argument due to John Tillotson (p. 109). We must however wonder, as so often in reading Hume, whether he was understating his case for various rhetorical and prudential reasons. (Incidentally, to say that religious thought does not concern matters of genuine belief, or does not make sense, is not *obviously* to indict it: cf. Wittgenstein (1980a), pp. 30ff. This is not to deny that it would have counted as a straightforward indictment for Hume.)

[5] Deleuze decries this definition in Deleuze (1991), pp. 107ff. I think I am less at odds with him than I appear to be. For one thing, there is my qualification 'for many purposes'. For another, I accept that his reservations are included in the difficulties that would have to be confronted when it came to examining what is involved in derivation. See Ch. 21, §2(d), for a further brief discussion of this issue.

[6] Cf. Hume's claim in *Treatise*, p. xviii, that no science or art 'can go beyond experience, or establish any principles which are not founded on that authority.'

the phrase 'sense-making' itself. In particular, I am exploiting the fact that this phrase is ambiguous between something broadly epistemic, indicating an understanding or knowledge of what things are like or, more modestly, a reliable and workable conception of what things are like, and something broadly semantic, indicating the production or expression of meaning. I welcome this ambiguity, for the simple reason that we find both elements in Hume – and not always clearly distinguished.[7] This definition therefore amalgamates the two ways in which Hume wanted to check the indiscipline of thought. He denied both that a belief could be warranted, or count as knowledge,[8] unless it stood in a suitable relation to sense experience, and that a belief could be present at all – that an apparent expression of belief could be meaningful – unless there was some suitable provision for it in sense experience.

But there is an important asymmetry. If it is true that Hume subscribed to an empiricism that included both these elements, the epistemic and the semantic, then the latter must have been the more fundamental, in that any failure to make semantic sense would mean that the opportunity to make epistemic sense could not so much as arise. (If I do not even express a belief when I say, 'There are infinitely many substances,' then *a fortiori* I do not express a belief that is warranted.)

This is a good cue for me to signal a fierce debate that has dominated recent exegesis of Hume. In attributing a fundamentally semantic empiricism to him, I am adopting a more or less traditional interpretation. But a new interpretation has recently gained prominence. According to this new interpretation, the semantic element in Hume's empiricism has been seriously exaggerated, if indeed it is there at all; his interests were fundamentally epistemic, and much of what would count as meaningless by the lights of any remotely powerful semantic empiricism he did not regard as meaningless at all.[9]

Unfortunately, I cannot hope to make a serious contribution to this debate in these confines.[10] Having stated my own allegiance, I must, reluctantly,

---

[7] Cf. Pears (1990), p. 10.

[8] I am using 'knowledge' in its customary sense, not the more restricted sense that Hume introduced in *Treatise*, p. 124.

[9] For examples of this new interpretation, see Craig (1987), Ch. 2; and G. Strawson (1992). For debate, see the essays in Read and Richman (2000). For (what seem to me to be) correctives, see Pears (1990); Bennett (2001), §§273–275; Millican (2002), (2007), and (2009).

[10] But nor can I resist a brief comment on the final paragraph of the chapter by Edward Craig cited in the previous note, in which he comments on what he describes as 'an amazing paragraph' from Moritz Schlick (1938). Schlick there argues that one consequence of the semantic empiricism that he and his fellow positivists claim to find in Hume, and that I likewise claim to find there, is that there is nothing we cannot know, at least in principle. Craig objects both to what he perceives as the absurdity of this consequence in its own

proceed as though it were uncontroversial. There is however one brief point that I shall make in this connection. It concerns the relation between Hume's *Treatise* and his *Enquiry*. In the 'Advertisement' to the latter he famously described the former, 'which [he] had projected before he left College, and which he wrote and published not long after,' as 'that juvenile work.' And he went on to say, 'Henceforth, the Author desires, that the following Pieces may alone be regarded as containing his philosophical sentiments and principles' (p. 2). It is only fair for me to concede, therefore, that any attributions to him in what follows that are based on the *Treatise* should be treated with due circumspection. I mention this point here because some defenders of the new interpretation triumphantly appropriate the *Enquiry* as the work that is more conducive to their view. And they insist that we take that as our authoritative source.[11] (Mind you, so do some defenders of a more traditional interpretation![12])

2. The Semantic Element in Hume's Empiricism and the Epistemic Element in Hume's Empiricism

Hume distinguishes between ideas and impressions. These exhaust what he calls 'perceptions of the mind', and they 'are distinguished by their different degrees of force and vivacity' (Enquiry, p. 18). Impressions are the more forceful and the more vivacious. They are what we ordinarily count as items of sense experience, such as a glimpse of a rabbit scurrying by or a stomach ache. Ideas are what we ordinarily count as memories of such items of sense experience, imaginative anticipations of them, and suchlike. Hume draws the distinction in terms of force and vivacity because he wants to appeal to the intrinsic properties and powers of perceptions; he does not want to beg questions about their origin (cf. *Treatise*, p. 84). We might worry that this makes a quantitative distinction out of what should be a qualitative one, so that, for example, it inappropriately likens imagining a vindaloo to tasting a korma.[13] However that may be, these are the terms in which Hume expresses his empiricism.

The critical statement of that empiricism, or at least of its core, is as follows: '*Every idea ... is copied from a similar impression*' (*Enquiry*, p. 19,

right, ridiculing the 'potential omniscience' with which it credits us, and to the idea that there is anything of the sort in Hume, citing a passage from the *Enquiry* in which Hume makes clear that 'our ignorance' is not 'a good reason for rejecting any thing' (pp. 72–73). On the first point Craig confuses there being nothing we cannot know with our being able (simultaneously) to know everything. On the second point he confuses our being unable to know something with our (simply) not knowing it.

[11] E.g. Strawson (2000), §2.
[12] E.g. Millican (2007), §IV.
[13] For an interesting defence of Hume against this kind of worry, see Everson (1988).

emphasis added).[14] We should note straight away, however, that there is an implicit restriction here, which Hume makes explicit in the passage immediately preceding this quotation. It is a restriction to 'simple' ideas. Thus I have an idea of a mermaid even though I have never had any such impression. This is possible because I have had an impression of the upper part of a woman's body and I have had an impression of a fish's tail: I thereby have two ideas that I have joined in my imagination. And even if I had not had those two impressions, it would still have been possible for me to have an idea of a mermaid. For I have had yet simpler impressions with corresponding simpler ideas that I could have combined to form an idea of a mermaid. More generally, the human mind has a faculty for 'compounding, transposing, augmenting, or diminishing the materials afforded [it] by the senses and experience' (*Enquiry*, p. 19). The fundamental point, then, is that 'our thoughts or ideas, however compounded or sublime, ... always ... resolve themselves into such simple ideas as were copied from a precedent [impression]' (ibid.).

Let us not pause to ask the thousands of questions that naturally arise about this doctrine.[15] What matters for our purposes is that it captures the semantic element in Hume's empiricism. This is because Hume thinks of the meaning of a term, roughly, as its capacity to excite an idea of a certain kind in the mind of whoever understands the term. ('Of a certain kind' needs to be interpreted broadly enough to accommodate the fact, learnt by Hume from Berkeley, that all ideas are particular. Thus the word 'triangle' may excite an idea of an isosceles triangle in one person's mind and an idea of a scalene triangle in another's, or one of these ideas in one person's mind on one occasion, the other on another (cf. *Treatise*, I.i.7). However, since Hume also thinks that particular ideas can, through their annexation to terms, be 'general in their representation' (*Treatise*, p. 22), he will sometimes allow himself to talk loosely and construe the meaning of a term as a single corresponding idea.[16]) Hume is now able to say the following: 'When we entertain ... any suspicion that a philosophical term is employed without any meaning or idea ..., we need but enquire, *from what impression is that supposed idea derived?* And if it be impossible to assign any, this will

---

[14] Cf. the famous empiricist formula, '*Nihil est in intellectu quod non prius fuerit in sensu*' ('Nothing is in the intellect that has not first been in the senses,'). For interesting material on the origin of this formula, see Cranefield (1970).

[15] Hume himself, notoriously, cites a counterexample to it: the case of a man who has an idea of a particular shade of blue deriving from the impressions of other shades near it on the scale from darker to lighter. Hume says, 'This instance is so singular, that it is scarcely worth our observing, and does not merit that for it alone we should alter our general maxim' (*Enquiry*, p. 21).

[16] See e.g. *Enquiry*, §IV, revealingly entitled 'On "The" Idea of Necessary Connexion' (double quotation marks added), esp. the first few pages.

serve to confirm our suspicion' (*Enquiry*, p. 22, emphasis in original; cf. 'Abstract', pp. 648–649 and 656–657).

One immediate casualty is the term 'substance' – unless it is understood in a sufficiently modest way to allow for the idea of a substance to be 'nothing but a collection of simple ideas, that are united by the imagination' (*Treatise*, p. 16). Another casualty is the term 'infinity' in some of its mathematical applications (*Treatise*, I.ii, esp. 1, and *Enquiry*, pp. 155ff.). And a third,[17] which is particularly striking, is the term 'God', as understood, for instance and most notably, by Descartes. True, Hume does allow in the *Enquiry* that 'the idea of God, as meaning an infinitely intelligent, wise, and good Being, arises from reflecting on the operations of our own mind, and augmenting, without limit, those qualities of goodness and wisdom' (p. 19). Nevertheless, even if he is being ingenuous when he says this, it does not salvage the Cartesian conception of our idea of God. The very point of the Cartesian conception is that, according to it, our idea of God is an idea that cannot be arrived at by any such means, which is why Descartes thinks that God Himself must have placed the idea in us (see Ch. 1, §3; and cf. Descartes (1984a), AT VII: 46ff.). No idea that we could form by 'compounding, transposing, augmenting, or diminishing the materials afforded us by the senses and experience' – to repeat that Humean formula – could be adequate to our idea of God, as Descartes understands it.[18]

So much, then, for the semantic element in Hume's empiricism. What of the epistemic element? It is related. For just as Hume takes meaning to require a corresponding idea or ideas, so too he takes belief to require a corresponding idea. More specifically, Hume takes a belief to be an idea accompanied by a certain feeling.[19] This feeling, which he describes as a feeling of 'vividness' and 'steadiness', and which distinguishes the ideas to which it attaches from mere flights of fancy, 'gives them more weight and influence; makes them appear of greater importance; enforces them in the mind; and renders them the governing principle of our actions' (*Enquiry*, pp. 49–50). Now, because there is no belief without an idea, belief is subject to precisely the same constraints, as far as its origins are concerned, as meaning. One cannot believe what one cannot conceive by assembling ideas derived from previous impressions. But there is more to Hume's epistemic empiricism than that. His epistemic empiricism concerns not just the conditions for a belief to be formed, but the conditions for it to be warranted or

---

[17] For others, see *Treatise*, I.iv.3.

[18] I am here ignoring the distinction between a term's being used without any corresponding idea and its being used with a corresponding idea that (some of) its uses serve to misdescribe. (No doubt Hume would concede that Descartes has *something* in mind when he uses the term 'God'.) In many cases this distinction is merely terminological.

[19] For a helpful discussion, see Broackes (2002).

to merit the title 'knowledge'. And again Hume will insist on there being a derivation from impressions, or from sense experience.[20]

This time, however, the derivation will need to be more exacting. That much would be obvious if the conditions for a belief to be warranted were thought of as both necessary and sufficient. For in that case, unless the derivation were more exacting, every belief would count as warranted, just by virtue of being formed. But even if the conditions are thought of only as necessary – an issue that we can leave open – any account that deserves to be called a version of epistemic empiricism will require more of the derivation than whatever enables a belief simply to be formed. Hume's account certainly requires more.

But how much more? Here again there is room for exegetical debate.[21] On one extreme view Hume denies that the derivation should use any resources other than those of pure deductive reasoning – from which it would follow that hardly any of our beliefs count as warranted. On that view Hume is fundamentally a sceptic. An apparently polar opposite view is that Hume takes for granted the warrant of most of our beliefs and accordingly allows that the derivation may use other resources, which he sees it as his business to identify. (I say 'apparently' polar opposite. In fact both views share a vital component. On both views Hume denies that the resources of pure deductive reasoning are sufficient to derive most of our beliefs from our impressions. But there can surely be no exegetical dispute about *that*. That is surely one of Hume's most distinctive philosophical tenets, to be acknowledged by all parties to this debate (see *Enquiry*, §IV).)

Fortunately, this is not a debate in which we need to get involved. Given any view about what resources Hume would admit into the derivation, there will be a corresponding set of beliefs on which Hume's epistemic empiricism thereby casts doubt, the fewer the resources, the larger the set. The largest such set will contain any beliefs that cannot be derived from our impressions using only the resources of pure deductive reasoning. But that is not what really matters from our point of view. What matters from our point of view is the smallest such set, the set of beliefs on which *all* parties to the debate will agree that his epistemic empiricism casts doubt. And to determine what that is, we need only determine what the corresponding view about the resources is. In effect, then, our question is this: what is the largest set of resources that anyone could reasonably think Hume would admit into the derivation?

The answer, I suggest, is the set of resources that we *in fact* use, as a matter of basic human nature, when we proceed from our impressions to our

[20] In what follows I shall prescind from the question, a variant of which will be prominent in Ch. 12, §8, of whether impressions, or items of sense experience, are entities of the right *sort* for beliefs to be derived from them;: see McDowell (1996), esp. Lecture II.

[21] For a particularly helpful contribution to this debate, see Millican (2002).

beliefs. If this suggestion is correct, then of course the devil in the detail of
'derives from' is now in the detail of 'as a matter of basic human nature.' (In
particular, there are difficult questions about how natural it is for us to form
religious beliefs of various kinds, questions with which Hume wrestles in his
Natural History of Religion.[22]) But I think this is just what we should expect.
For I take Hume's own primary concern to be precisely with developing a
science of human nature, be the warrants for our beliefs as they may.[23] This
means, among other things, that he wants to explore the various natural
processes whereby human beings arrive at their beliefs. My suggestion is
that any beliefs arrived at by processes that cannot be duly assimilated to
the most basic of these natural processes will not constitute sense-making
for Hume, on any epistemic interpretation of 'sense-making'.[24]

But I also claim, conversely and crucially, that any beliefs arrived at by
processes that *can* be duly assimilated to the most basic of those natural
processes *will* constitute sense-making for Hume, *on at least the most liberal epistemic interpretation of 'sense-making'*. For these are the beliefs
on the strength of which we in fact negotiate our way through the world
and conduct our various affairs, again be the warrants for them as they
may. Certainly, they would constitute, for Hume, 'a reliable and workable
conception of what things are like', to use the phrase that I used in §1.[25]
This further explains the irrelevance to our concerns of the debate above.
Relative to our concerns, that debate is little more than a terminological dispute about how to use the word 'warrant'.[26] It does not significantly affect

---

[22] See also *Treatise*, I.iv, passim, esp. pp. 225–226. There is also of course the issue of how
the natural is defined; see further n. 24.

[23] That this is Hume's primary concern is nowadays relatively uncontroversial. It is a dominant theme of Stroud (1977): see esp. pp. 1–8. Cf. also Craig (1987), pp. 81ff.; and, for
an interesting discussion, Biro (1993).

[24] This suggestion is not meant to preclude artifice in the construction of the concepts in
whose terms the beliefs are framed, a caveat that is particularly significant where beliefs
about justice are concerned; see *Treatise*, III.ii, passim. The artificial is in any case opposed
to the natural only on a narrow definition of the natural; see *Treatise*, p. 484, and *Enquiry*,
pp. 307ff.

[25] See *Enquiry*, pp. 54–55. Also relevant is that famous passage from the *Treatise* in which
Hume, having noted how little help he is afforded by pure deductive reasoning in dispelling various doubts by which he is afflicted, comments, 'Most fortunately it happens
that ... nature herself suffices to that purpose, and cures me of this philosophical melan-
choly and delirium.... I dine, I play a game of back-gammon, I converse, and am merry
with my friends; and when after three or four hours' amusement, I wou'd return to these
speculations, they appear so cold, and strain'd, and ridiculous, that I cannot find it in my
heart to enter into them any further' (p. 269; cf. *Enquiry*, pp. 159–160). Not only are the
processes of pure deductive reasoning unable to do the work done by the natural processes, then, but they are unable to subvert it.

[26] This is not one of Hume's own favoured words. It occurs only once in the *Enquiry*
(p. 122), and not at all in the *Treatise*.

Hume's conception of the scope and limits of sense-making, on the liberal interpretation of 'sense-making' which I am, appropriately enough in this context I take it, adopting.

The question now, therefore, is: what are the relevant natural processes?

3. Relations of Ideas and Matters of Fact

It is far beyond the scope of this chapter to give anything but the merest sketch of an answer to this question. But the crucial point is that these processes are of two fundamentally different kinds, issuing in beliefs of two fundamentally different kinds. Processes of the first kind are those of pure deductive reasoning, in abstraction from any of our particular impressions. The beliefs in which these issue are beliefs about how our ideas are related to one another.[27] Processes of the second kind issue in beliefs about how our ideas and impressions are related to what lies beyond them. Although these too include pure deductive reasoning, at their core is an appeal to causal connections.

Here is Hume:

> All the objects of human reason or enquiry may naturally be divided into two kinds, to wit, *Relations of Ideas*, and *Matters of Fact*. Of the first kind are the sciences of Geometry, Algebra, and Arithmetic; and in short, every affirmation which is either intuitively or demonstratively certain. *That the square of the hypothenuse is equal to the square of the two sides*, is a proposition which expresses a relation between these figures.... Propositions of this kind are discoverable by the mere operation of thought, without dependence on what is anywhere existent in the universe. Though there never were a circle or triangle in nature, the truths demonstrated by Euclid would for ever retain their certainty and evidence.[28]
>
> Matters of fact, which are the second objects of human reason, are not ascertained in the same manner.... The contrary of every matter of fact ... is conceived by the mind with the same facility and distinctness, as if ever so conformable to reality. *That the sun will not rise to-morrow* is no less intelligible a proposition, and implies no more a contradiction, than the affirmation, *that it will rise*....

---

[27] For scepticism about whether there can be a good Humean account of these processes, see Bennett (1971), §52; Stroud (1977), pp. 240ff.; and Bennett (2001), §286. Cf. also Husserl (1962), §20.

[28] Note that the status of geometry is one of the issues on which Hume changes his mind between the *Treatise* and the *Enquiry*. In the former he regards geometry as dealing (inexactly) with matters of fact; see I.ii.4 and pp. 70–72. (But see also p. 69 for something more in keeping with the *Enquiry* view.)

All reasonings concerning matters of fact seem to be founded on the relation of *Cause and Effect*. By means of that relation alone we can go beyond the evidence of our memory and senses. If you were to ask a man, why he believes any matter of fact, which is absent; for instance, that his friend is ... in France; he would give you a reason; and this reason would be some other fact; as a letter received from him.... If we anatomize all the other reasonings of this nature, we shall find that they are founded on the relation of cause and effect.... (*Enquiry*, pp. 25–27, emphasis in original)

This is reminiscent of Leibniz' distinction between truths of reasoning and truths of fact (see §4 of the previous chapter).[29] Like Leibniz' distinction, it is meant to signal a fundamental dichotomy between what we can ascertain by the inspection and analysis of our ideas and what we can ascertain only by appeal to experience and the principles of extrapolation fitted to it. There is no middle ground. Nothing can be known by, say, divine revelation, or by some sort of *a priori* insight into the structure of reality. There can be no sense-making, even on the most liberal epistemic interpretation of 'sense-making', that is not derived in one of these two ways from sense experience.

Hume is typically self-conscious about this. He realizes that his strictures must apply, in particular, to his own attempts to make sense of things. That is why he is keen to emphasize that he himself is using 'the experimental method of reasoning'.[30] He takes himself to be developing a conception of the human mind, and its various operations, by appeal to causal connections that he has discerned between episodes in his own and other people's thinking (e.g. *Enquiry*, §I).[31]

---

[29] But of course, it lacks anything corresponding to Leibniz' idea that an infinite intellect could arrive at truths of the second kind in some quite different way, namely by calculating what is for the best. Jonathan Bennett argues, in Bennett (1971), §23, that it differs from Leibniz' distinction in a yet more profound way. He thinks that relations of ideas include 'present-tense statements about [perceptions]' (p. 247). (In effect, then, he would drop the qualification 'in abstraction from any of our particular impressions' in the definition I gave of processes of the first kind.) I suggest that Bennett has overlooked the fact that Hume, in his account of matters of fact, is concentrating on those that are 'absent', or, as we could also say, on those that are ascertained by reasoning.

[30] This phrase occurs in the subtitle of the *Treatise*, which is 'Being an Attempt to Introduce the Experimental Method of Reasoning into Moral Subjects'.

[31] This makes his cavalier treatment of his own counterexample to the doctrine that all simple ideas are copied from impressions all the more remarkable; see n. 15.

Note: we should not forget that there is, in 'the experimental method of reasoning', still a place for pure deductive reasoning. It is by means of pure deductive reasoning, for instance, that we are able to recognize the powerlessness of pure deductive reasoning itself to derive most of our beliefs from our impressions; cf. *Enquiry*, pp. 29–30.

Similarly, he wants to be sure that he is respecting his semantic empiricism. In particular, he wants to be sure that he is doing this when he makes claims about causation. That is one reason why such a large part of his enquiry is devoted to a search for the impression from which the idea of a (causally) necessary connection derives. He eventually concludes that the relevant impression is the 'customary transition' which is felt in the mind when, 'after a repetition of similar instances, the mind is carried by habit, upon the appearance of one event, to expect its usual attendant' (*Enquiry*, p. 75; cf. *Treatise*, pp. 266–267, and 'Abstract', pp. 656–657). Thus suppose that every time I see the striking of a ball by a bat I immediately thereafter see a deviation of the ball from its previous course. And suppose that my mind is so constituted that, after this has happened a few times, my seeing the striking of a ball by a bat induces in me the expectation that the ball will once again deviate from its previous course. Then the feeling I have of this inducement is the impression from which my idea of a (causally) necessary connection derives.[32]

Hume is reasonably confident, then, that his empiricism has no adverse consequences for his own attempt to make sense of things.[33] But what are its consequences for metaphysics, the most general attempt to make sense of things?

4.   Metaphysics as an Experimental Science of Human Nature

There are some immediate negative consequences that are obvious, and some immediate positive consequences that are only a little less obvious.

On the negative side, metaphysics affords no more prospect than any other enquiry for sense-making that does not derive from sense experience. Or, as we could also say, we have no more scope in metaphysics than we do in any other enquiry for making sense of what is transcendent (see the Transcendence Question from §6 of the Introduction).

As we have seen, this is partly a semantic matter, partly an epistemic matter. Insofar as it is a semantic matter, then it provides another instance of the

---

[32] This is, in effect, a quasi-realist account of causal necessity (see Ch. 1, §3); see Blackburn (2000). One of the many objections that might be levelled against it is the following. If this inducement is itself a causal connection, as it had presumably better be, then I cannot feel it without violating Hume's own insistence that 'there is not, in any single, particular instance of cause and effect, any thing which can suggest the idea of ... necessary connexion' (*Enquiry*, p. 63). On one view, this is just the sort of objection that Hume himself has in mind when he famously writes, in the Appendix to the *Treatise*, 'There are two principles, which I cannot render consistent; nor is it in my power to renounce either of them, viz. *that all our distinct perceptions are distinct existences*, and *that the mind never perceives any real connexion among distinct existences*' (p. 636, emphasis in original).

[33] 'Reasonably' confident – but see the previous note.

pattern noted in Chapter 2, §2. There is, in Hume, a recoil from attempts in earlier philosophers to make sense of what is transcendent, grounded in the conviction that there is no *sense* there to be made. I have already noted some of the casualties; see §2.

Insofar as it is an epistemic matter, then it curbs our aspirations to establish, by reasoning of any kind, that whose 'best and most solid foundation is faith and divine revelation' – as Hume puts it, with what we must surely regard as characteristic irony – for instance 'the existence of a Deity, and the immortality of souls' (*Enquiry*, p. 165, emphasis removed; cf. ibid., §XII, Pt III, passim). For Hume, the word 'metaphysics' sometimes serves as a label for just the sort of thing that is thereby precluded.[34] On that understanding of metaphysics, his work is an assault on the very possibility of metaphysics.

But, as I emphasized in §§2 and 3 of the Introduction, provided that metaphysics is understood as nothing but the most general attempt to make sense of things, then it is not subject to any such assault. There can at most be controversy about how it is to be pursued or what it can achieve.[35] And here we see the positive consequences of Hume's empiricism for metaphysics. To whatever extent his empiricism directs his own attempts to make sense of things, it directs the most general attempt to make sense of things. For, as Hume himself insists, his own attempt to make sense of things is, precisely, an attempt to do so at the highest level of generality. In his introduction to the *Treatise* he writes:

> 'Tis evident that all the sciences have a relation, greater or less, to human nature.... Even *Mathematics, Natural Philosophy, and Natural Religion*, are in some measure dependent on the science of MAN; since they lie under the cognizance of men, and are judged of by their powers and faculties. 'Tis impossible to tell what changes and improvements we might make in these sciences were we thoroughly acquainted with the extent and force of human understanding, and cou'd explain the nature of the ideas we employ, and of the operations we perform in our reasonings....
>
> There is no question of importance, whose decision is not compriz'd in the science of man; and there is none, which can be decided with any certainty, before we become acquainted with that science. In pretending therefore to explain the principles of human nature, we in effect propose a compleat system of the sciences, built on a foundation almost entirely

---

[34] See Introduction, n. 30. But see also the next note.

[35] Cf. *Treatise*, p. xiv, where there is a suggestion that 'metaphysics' is simply an umbrella term for 'every kind of argument, which is in any way abstruse, and requires some attention to be comprehended.' On that understanding too, there can be no objection to metaphysics, as indeed Hume goes on to emphasize (cf. *Enquiry*, pp. 15–16).

new, and the only one upon which they can stand with any security. (pp. xv–xvi, emphasis in original; cf. *Enquiry*, §I)[36]

Metaphysics is entirely acceptable, then, provided that it consists in an experimental science of human nature.

(Notice, incidentally, the deep structural affinity between what Hume aspires to do and what Descartes aspired to do. The project, in each case, is to provide a firm foundation for the sciences by making sense of how we make sense of things. In each case this means arriving at a set of beliefs about how we arrive at our beliefs about the world from our 'perceptions', a set of beliefs that must apply, in particular, to the execution of this very project. (See Ch. 1, §4, and the comparison there with Quine's naturalized epistemology.) But of course, there are vital differences between Hume's execution of the project and Descartes'. Descartes took himself to be trafficking in indubitable *a priori* insights into where we stand in relation to things and how we make sense of them. Hume believes that there is only one route to an understanding of where we stand in relation to things and how we make sense of them: the ever fallible investigation, through observation and experiment, of human nature.)

But can the study of human nature, at any level of generality, really do duty for metaphysics? On my definition, perhaps; but is there not reason now to regard that definition as too gross a departure from ordinary usage?

I do not think so. When Hume explores the processes whereby we acquire our idea of a (causally) necessary connection, and reflects on how much, in our talk of causation, registers our reaction to the regularities that we observe, rather than the regularities themselves, then he is engaged in what would by any reckoning count as the metaphysics of causation. Likewise when he explores the psychological mechanisms that underpin our talk of 'external' objects, or our talk of personal identity (though it should be noted, where these latter topics are concerned, that his discussions are pretty much confined to the *Treatise*, which is a decidedly more metaphysical work than the *Enquiry*).

Very well. There may be good reason to regard some of Hume's investigations into matters of fact as a significant contribution to metaphysics. But unless the same can be said for his investigations into relations of ideas, then must he not be regarded, as he so often is regarded, as eschewing standard traditional metaphysics? For if the distinction between relations of ideas and matters of fact is to be granted at all, then the extreme generality of metaphysics must surely mean that its principal home is the former, where

---

[36] Part of this striking vision, omitted from the quotation above, is that even logic has as its 'sole end' 'to explain the principles and operations of our reasoning faculty, and the nature of our ideas' (p. xv). This is a view that will later be severely criticized by Frege: see e.g. Frege (1997g), pp. 246ff./pp. 157ff. in the original German, and see further Ch. 8, §6.

not only can it issue in results about the sense that we succeed in making of things, as revealed in the way we acquire and marshal our ideas, but it can also issue in results about the sense that things make, as revealed in the ideas themselves. Yet Hume notoriously refuses to allow that there can be any interesting or important relations of ideas beyond the realm of mathematics. It is in this spirit that he famously writes, in the final paragraph of the *Enquiry*:

> When we run over libraries, persuaded of these principles, what havoc must we make? If we take in our hand any volume; of divinity or school metaphysics, for instance; let us ask, *Does it contain any abstract reasoning concerning quantity and number?* No. *Does it contain any experimental reasoning concerning matter of fact and existence?* No. Commit it then to the flames: for it can contain nothing but sophistry and illusion. (p. 165, emphasis in original)

No doubt any sophistry and illusion that we encounter will be due to the fact that someone, at some point, has attempted to make sense of what is transcendent, in one or other of the ways that we have already seen Hume decry. Even so, he is offering, in this paragraph, a new criterion for such sophistry and illusion. He is saying that they reside wherever people try to engage in enquiries that are neither mathematical nor factual (in a suitably Humean sense of 'factual'). And, in the light of that, no amount of fast and loose play with the definition of 'metaphysics' can prevent his work from still appearing to be what it has always appeared to be: an attack, if not on metaphysics *per se*, then at least on metaphysical hubris, an attack on any attempt to make highly general sense of things by establishing substantive *a priori* non-mathematical necessities.

5.   Metaphysics as More Than an Experimental Science of Human Nature

Why does Hume have such a restricted conception of relations of ideas? Mathematics itself testifies to the fact that there can be non-trivial connections between our ideas – indeed, substantive connections, provided that 'substantive' is understood in a sufficiently modest psychological way. If there can be such connections 'concerning quantity and number', then why not concerning causation, or free will, or any of the other items traditionally reckoned to be of metaphysical concern? Indeed, does Hume not do himself a disservice by overlooking some of his own substantive non-factual conclusions about just such topics?[37]

---

[37] See e.g. *Enquiry*, pp. 98–99, 127, and 136ff., for conclusions about relations between, respectively: liberty, praise, and blame; evidence and testimony; and cause and effect.

Here is what Hume says:

> It seems to me, that the only objects of the abstract sciences are quantity and number, and that all attempts to extend this more perfect species of knowledge beyond these bounds are mere sophistry and illusion. As the component parts of quantity and number are entirely similar, their relations become intricate and involved; and nothing can be more curious, as well as useful, than to trace, by a variety of mediums, their equality or inequality through their different appearances. But as all other ideas are clearly distinct and different from each other, we can never advance farther, by our utmost scrutiny, than to observe this diversity, and, by an obvious reflection, pronounce one thing not to be another. Or if there be any difficulty in these decisions, it proceeds entirely from the undeterminate meaning of words, which is corrected by juster definitions. That *the square of the hypothenuse is equal to the squares of the other two sides*, cannot be known, let the terms be ever so exactly defined, without a train of reasoning and enquiry. But to convince us of this proposition, *that where there is no property, there can be no injustice*, it is only necessary to define the terms, and explain injustice to be a violation of property. (*Enquiry*, p. 163, emphasis in original)[38]

In the *Treatise* there is more detail. Hume tells us there that the only relations among our (simple?) ideas that can issue in relations of ideas, other than 'proportions in quantity or number', are 'resemblance', 'contrariety', and 'degrees in quality', and that these are all 'discoverable at first sight' (p. 70; see further the rest of I.iii.1).

Hume's contention, then, is as follows. Outside mathematics, our (simple?) ideas are more or less independent of one another. The only relevant relations that they enter into are relations whose obtaining is always blatant even given such independence, for instance the relation of comparative intensity which obtains between an idea of burning heat and an idea of gentle warmth. Hence there is no scope for our non-mathematical ideas to feature in necessary truths that are interesting, surprising, or in any other sense 'substantive'.

---

[38] See also *Enquiry*, pp. 60–61, where Hume contrasts mathematical ideas and non-mathematical ideas on the grounds that the former have a clarity which the latter (for very good reason and to very good purpose) lack. Jonathan Bennett, in Bennett (1971), p. 243, complains that this conflicts with the passage cited in the main text, where non-mathematical ideas are said to be 'clearly distinct … from each other.' But I suspect that what Hume really means, when he says that non-mathematical ideas lack the clarity of mathematical ones, is something hinted in the passage cited in the main text, namely that non-mathematical *terms* lack the clarity of mathematical ones, in other words that it is unclear, from our use of non-mathematical terms, which of various (clear) ideas are supposed to attach to them.

It is a contention which, within Hume's own framework, can be refuted only by the specification of a counterexample: either some relation that he has overlooked or some unexpected hidden complexity in one of the relations that he has considered. And, I think we must concede, there are no obvious counterexamples. Suppose, for instance, that we were to turn his own work against him in the way suggested above, by invoking some of the connections that he himself has established. He might well reply that all he has done, as in the example concerning injustice, is to define certain key terms – by indicating the meaning already attaching to them, where they already had a clear meaning, and by assigning a meaning to them where they did not – whereafter nothing more was needed to establish these connections than a few trivial steps of logic.[39]

But to concede that there are no obvious counterexamples is not to concede much. Part of the reason why there are no obvious counterexamples is that it is not obvious what would count as a counterexample. It is not obvious *even* within Hume's framework, never mind that every feature of that framework, most notably the very dichotomy between relations of ideas and matters of fact, is itself contestable. Thus reconsider the list of relations that Hume tells us can issue in relations of ideas. That this is an exhaustive list is itself, presumably, supposed to be a matter of (introspectively testable) fact, about the human mind. But we would surely need more guidance in construing these relations before we could be confident that we would recognize a counterexample when we encountered it. Hume tells us, for instance, that 'no two ideas are in themselves contrary, except those of existence and non-existence' (*Treatise*, p. 15). This means, in particular, that the idea of red and the idea of blue are not 'in themselves contrary'. That there may be interesting ways of explicating the relation of contrariety to allow for this I shall not dispute. That the relation *needs* to be explicated is surely beyond dispute.[40] Or again, suppose we found what we took to be some substantive non-mathematical relation of ideas, say that no barber can shave all and only the men in his village who do not shave themselves.[41] It would always be open to Hume either simply to deny that there was any substantiveness there or to attribute the substantiveness to a kind of applied mathematics of concepts.[42]

But be the refutation of Hume's contention as it may, we should consider what motivates it. Our own chief concern is with its implications

---

[39] Cf. the remarks about liberty with which he frames his discussion of that topic, in *Enquiry*, p. 95.

[40] See e.g. the apparently conflicting claim about contrariety in 2nd *Enquiry*, p. 288. Is this a change of view?

[41] See Russell (1992b), p. 261.

[42] The latter, as we shall see in Ch. 11, §3a, is essentially what Carnap does.

concerning metaphysics. But that is not, I suggest, Hume's chief concern. Hume's chief concern, I suggest, is manifest in that famous passage from the *Treatise* in which he expresses his commitment to the 'is'/'ought' distinction:

> In every system of morality, which I have hitherto met with, I have always remark'd, that the author proceeds for some time in the ordinary way of reasoning ...; when of a sudden I am surpriz'd to find, that instead of the usual copulations of propositions, *is*, and *is not*, I meet with no proposition that is not connected with an *ought*, or an *ought not*. This change ... is of the last consequence. For as this *ought*, or *ought not*, expresses some new relation or affirmation, 'tis necessary that it shou'd be observ'd and explain'd; and at the same time that a reason should be given, for what seems altogether inconceivable, how this new relation can be a deduction from others, which are entirely different from it. (*Treatise*, p. 469, emphasis in original)   521 人 Peng

Hume, who is adamant that nothing short of a suitable feeling of approbation or disapprobation in someone could force him or her to subscribe to a prescriptive or evaluative statement, wants to allow no refuge to the idea that 'a train of reasoning and enquiry' could reveal some deep, unexpected connection between how things are and how they ought to be.[43] But if I am right that this is Hume's chief concern, then he must confront the possibility – a possibility on which we shall see Kant fasten tenaciously in the next chapter, albeit with his own different set of concerns – that there is a healthy baby in the bathwater that he has ejected.

This is a comment specifically about what scope there is for making a significant contribution to metaphysics that does not consist in establishing matters of fact, but consists rather in establishing relations of ideas. It leaves out of account the further important question of what scope there is for making a significant contribution to metaphysics that does not consist *either* in establishing matters of fact *or* in establishing relations of ideas – a question that arises even if we grant the Humean dichotomy between these. I have in mind something to which I adverted in §7 of the Introduction: the possibility of reflecting on the concepts that we have at our disposal and creating new ones to meet needs that the former do not.[44] Hume himself is not averse to using familiar concepts to make radically new sense of things. I take it that this is a fair description of what he does when he says, in opposition to what anyone else at the time would say, that '[the] tie, which

---

[43] See esp. 2nd *Enquiry*, Appendix I, and the telling reference to metaphysics on p. 289. Cf. also *Treatise*, III.i.1; and see further Stroud (1977), pp. 173–176.
[44] Cf. Wittgenstein (1978), Pt IV, §29.

connects [cause and effect] together[,] … lies merely in ourselves' (*Treatise*, p. 266). But using radically new concepts to make radically new sense of things is one degree of innovation higher than that. And it is not obvious why it should not be a staple of good metaphysics.[45]

To be sure, if effort is to be expended on the creation of new concepts, then it needs a rationale. But there are all sorts of rationales that would be congenial to Hume. It is instructive in this connection to consider some stories that he himself tells about concept creation, such as the story that he tells about how we come by our concept of a promise. 'In order … to distinguish [interested commerce from disinterested commerce],' Hume writes, 'there is a *certain form of words* invented for the former, by which we bind ourselves to the performance of any action. This form of words constitutes what we call a *promise*' (*Treatise*, pp. 521–522, emphasis in original).[46] The rationale in this case is thoroughly practical. But so too, on Hume's conception, is the rationale for every operation of the human mind whereby we make sense of things.[47] There is certainly nothing in the practicality of concept creation to prevent his acknowledging it as a significant component in any worthwhile attempt to make sense of things at the highest level of generality.

Hume's view does admittedly preclude conceptual innovation of the most radical kind, the kind that is not restricted to working with old material. For the ultimate grounding for any conceptual innovation must, on Hume's view, be the imaginative reconfiguration of extant simple ideas to form new complex ideas. Even so, if the view is correct, then mathematics shows how far such reconfiguration can take us.

In sum, then, it takes neither scepticism about Hume's empiricism nor susceptibility to talk of the transcendent to wonder whether there are, in the libraries, untold volumes of metaphysics – including perhaps volumes in which concepts are created by using the various resonances of the word 'substance' – that should be snatched back from the flames.

Appendix: Scepticism About Human Reasoning

In the *Enquiry* Hume treats the distinction that he draws between relations of ideas and matters of fact as reasonably robust. But we should pause to note some earlier scepticism, which he voices in the *Treatise*, about how robust any such distinction can be, or at least about what form any such robustness can take (I.iv.1). Hume there reminds us that, whenever

---

[45] This of course bears on the Novelty Question which I posed in §6 of the Introduction. It will come especially to the fore again in Ch. 21, §6.

[46] See also ibid., III.ii.2, for a similar story about our concept of justice. And cf. n. 24.

[47] Cf. Deleuze (1991), p. 104.

something is established by a lengthy chain of pure deductive reasoning, as is the case for much of what we accept in mathematics, then our confidence in it must be based, in part, on confidence in various relevant matters of fact about the proper functioning of our associated faculties (p. 180; cf. p. 144). And, as we reflect on this, we cannot but wonder, not just whether our faculties have been functioning properly on this or that occasion, but whether there is any such thing as a proper functioning of our faculties; whether they are faculties for arriving at true beliefs at all. For Hume, this is itself a question about a matter of fact. It is a question about the relation between 'our reason ... considered as a kind of cause' and 'truth[, its] ... natural effect' (p. 180). It is also clearly a variation on Descartes' Reflective Question (see Ch. 1, §3). And Hume, unlike Descartes, sees no hope for meeting such scepticism by redeploying the very faculties whose certification is in question.[48] The more we use our resources to corroborate our resources, the greater, not the less, will be our concern about those resources. Instead, we must appeal to the natural impulses that guide us where our beliefs concerning any other matters of fact are concerned, impulses that lead us to accept that whose acceptance we could never justify by processes of pure deductive reasoning. 'Whoever has taken the pains to refute the cavils of this total scepticism,' Hume comments, 'has ... endeavour'd by arguments to establish a faculty, which nature has antecedently implanted in the mind' (p. 183, emphasis removed).[49]

This is of interest not only in its own right, but also in relation to themes that will dominate subsequent chapters. Wittgenstein, in his later work, is acutely conscious of the 'matters of fact' that make it possible for us to have practices of mathematical calculation and reasoning.[50] Yet he is also very keen to separate mathematical questions from questions concerning any such 'matters of fact'. This is part of what he means when he denies, as he does in his earlier work too, that calculation is a kind of experiment.[51] More than once in his manuscripts, at a point where he denies this, he also adds, as a kind of item of marginalia, 'The limits of empiricism' (Wittgenstein (1967a), pp. 197 and 379).

We should beware, however, of seeing anything in Humean empiricism as a target. Hume still *has* his distinction between relations of ideas – in particular, relations of mathematical ideas – and matters of fact. He is as

---

[48] As I pointed out in Ch. 1, n. 22, this is scepticism that survives into the *Enquiry*; see pp. 149–150.

[49] For an interesting discussion of this section of the *Treatise*, see Bennett (2001), Ch. 38, esp. §§288–290. For some additional complications, see Craig (1987), pp. 88–89.

[50] E.g. Wittgenstein (1967a), Pt I, §240. See further Ch. 10, §3. See also Bennett (2001), p. 320.

[51] E.g., in the later work, Wittgenstein (1978), pp. 194–199 and 379–382; and, in the earlier work, Wittgenstein (1961), 6.2331.

keen as Wittgenstein to ward off any confusion of the former with the latter. And Hume, too – witness both the scepticism to which we have just seen him respond and his response – knows all about 'the limits of empiricism'.[52] Hume's error, I believe, lies not in his failing to see where the limits of empiricism lie, but in his failing to see how much of metaphysics lies within them.

---

[52] Wittgenstein's gloss on this phrase at Wittgenstein (1978), p. 387, is very Humean.

CHAPTER 5

Kant

The Possibility, Scope, and Limits of Metaphysics

1. Introduction

At this point in the narrative something extraordinary happens. What has gone before and what will come after are both largely to be understood in terms of what occurs here. Like the central node in a figure 'X', this point can be seen as a singularity that draws together the various strands above it and issues in those below.

Immanuel Kant (1724–1804) was, like Leibniz, a philosophical eclectic. He made free and creative use of the various attempts at sense-making that other great philosophers had bequeathed to him, including some of the most general attempts that we have observed. But he did so in a way that was highly measured. It needed to be. Much of what had been bequeathed to him was in conflict with much else. The most distinctive feature of his eclecticism was the way in which he took rival systems of thought and rooted out inveterate assumptions that were common to them. On the one hand this enabled him to show that some of the fundamental points of controversy between them were ill-conceived. On the other hand it enabled him to salvage and to reconcile some of their apparently irreconcilable insights. In the process he in turn bequeathed a philosophical system of breathtaking depth and power. At the end of Chapter 1 I outlined a sense in which Spinoza was a post-Cartesian philosopher. In just the same sense, there would never be a great philosopher after this point who was not a post-Kantian philosopher.

Nor was Kant oblivious to the significance of what he was doing. Apart from anything else, he had contracted too much of Hume's self-consciousness for that to be possible. He knew that, in drawing together what he did in the way he did, and in dispelling the impression that it could not be drawn together, he had effected a revolution in our very understanding of what it is to make sense of things. He also thought that this liberated sense-making of the kind which, if the suggestion I made in §5 of the Introduction is correct, depends on just such a reflexive understanding, that is to say sense-making of the very kind that metaphysicians pursue, sense-making at the highest level of generality. He was famously emboldened to say, in the Preface to the first edition of his masterwork, his first *Critique*,[1] that 'there cannot be a single metaphysical problem that has not been solved here, or at least to the solution of which the key has not been provided' (Axiii).[2]

What gave him the courage even to contemplate such a revolution in our understanding of what it is to make sense of things? His commitment to a certain ideal, whose pursuit he took to be the defining characteristic of enlightenment, namely to dare, when attempting to decide ultimate matters of truth and value, and therefore when attempting to make the most general sense of things, to appeal to no other authority than the authority of one's own reason.[3]

But given the self-consciousness of his commitment to this ideal, it was inevitable that he should seek not only to pursue it, but also to justify it, and

---

[1] Throughout this chapter I use the following abbreviations for Kant's works: *Correspondence* for Kant (1999); 2nd *Critique* for Kant (1996c); 3rd *Critique* for Kant (2000); 'Enlightenment' for Kant (1996a); first *Critique* for Kant (1998); *Groundwork* for Kant (1996b); *Lectures* for Kant (1997); 1st 'Logic' for Kant (1992a); 2nd 'Logic' for Kant (1992b); 3rd 'Logic' for Kant (1992c); *Prolegomena* for Kant (2002a); and *Religion* for Kant (1996e). Page references are to the Akademie edition as indicated in the margins of these works, except in the case of the first *Critique*, where page references are to the two original German editions, 'A' representing the first edition and 'B' the second. All unaccompanied references are to the first *Critique*.

[2] It does no great harm to think of Kant as using the term 'metaphysics' and its cognates pretty much in accord with my definition, at least in its extension if not in its intension. He himself defines metaphysics in more than one way (see e.g. n. 44). But on what I take to be his most interesting and most considered definition, metaphysics is 'the investigation of everything that can ever be cognized *a priori* as well as the presentation of that which constitutes a system of pure philosophical cognitions of this kind, but in distinction from all empirical as well as mathematical use of reason' (A841/B869; see also A850–851/ B878–879; and see n. 13 for discussion of Kant's use of the term 'cognition'). He insists that this definition is to be preferred to the Aristotelian definition, whereby metaphysics is 'the science of the first principles of human cognition' (A843/B871), on the grounds that the Aristotelian definition invokes a difference of degree – at what point does a principle cease to be a 'first' principle and become a 'secondary' one? – whereas the difference between metaphysics and any other science is, for Kant, a difference of kind. This presumably means that he would take issue with my definition too ('… most general …'). Nevertheless, what I count as metaphysics can certainly embrace what Kant counts. And even if it can embrace more, this does not affect anything I shall say in this chapter. We can afford to prescind from the differences between Kant's definition and mine.

[3] See 'Enlightenment', *passim*. Whether this ideal, in this form, was a defining characteristic of enlightenment, in each of *its* forms, is debatable. Hume, who was a central figure in the Scottish Enlightenment, would have contested it. 'Reason,' Hume wrote, 'is, and ought only to be the slave of the passions, and can never pretend to any other office than to serve and obey them' (Hume (1978a), p.451); see further §5 of the previous chapter. But the ideal was certainly not Kant's figment. It was another of the bequests that he received. It had several sources. The most notable, from our point of view, was Descartes; see Ch. 1, §2.

should do so, moreover, under its own guidance. Kant put pure reason on trial. And he appointed pure reason itself as both judge and jury. In his own terms he provided a *critique* of pure reason (Axi–xii).[4]

Here we see what is by now a familiar reflexivity. Once again there is a connection with the suggestion I made in the Introduction. Granted my suggestion, such reflexivity is a hallmark of metaphysics. There is good reason to think that, even if Kant had not enjoyed the wider philosophical significance that he did, this critique of his would have been pivotal to our enquiry.[5]

2. Bad Metaphysics and Good Metaphysics

Let us begin with Hume. This is appropriate not just because Hume has been the most recent focus of our attention, but also because Kant himself was greatly exercised by Hume's stirrings, especially by his onslaught against the excesses of traditional metaphysics. In the *Prolegomena* – Kant's own brief summary of the main ideas of his first *Critique* – nobody else's name occurs with anything like the frequency of Hume's. And in one of the best known sentences of that book Kant writes:

> I freely admit that the remembrance of *David Hume* was the very thing that many years ago first interrupted my dogmatic slumber and gave completely different direction to my researches in the field of speculative philosophy. (4:260, emphasis in original; cf. 4:257)[6]

Kant's attitude to Hume, as I intimated in the previous chapter, can usefully be summarized in another metaphor, if a trite one: the metaphor of the baby and the bathwater.[7]

Let us begin with the bathwater. Kant is persuaded that much of what has hitherto passed for good metaphysics is to be thrown out, either on broadly semantic grounds, for failing to make sense, or on broadly epistemic grounds, for failing to have a suitable warrant in experience. Indeed, as we shall see in §6, he goes further than Hume by insisting not only on the

---

[4] Cf. Deleuze (2006a), p. 85.

[5] For three excellent overviews of Kant's relation to metaphysics, each covering much of the territory that I aim to cover in this chapter, see Warnock (1957), pp. 128–136; Gardner (1999), Ch. 1; and Rescher (2000), Ch. 6.

[6] This is not Kant's only use of the 'dogmatic slumber' metaphor. Later in the *Prolegomena*, in §50, and in 'Letter to Garve', dated 21 September 1798, in *Correspondence*, 12:258, he alludes to the antinomies of pure reason – which we shall consider in §6 – in much the same terms. And there is a fourth use of the metaphor, historically the first, at A757/B785.

[7] This attitude is well expressed, albeit without reference to Hume, in 'Letter to Mendelssohn', dated 8 April 1766, in *Correspondence*, 10:70, and in *Lectures*, 29:957–958.

prevalence of such bad metaphysics but also, absent a certain restraint that we need to learn, on its unavoidability. There are certain metaphysical questions and pseudo-questions that we have neither the power to ignore nor the wherewithal to answer (Avii). And until we have properly assimilated this fact, we cannot help trying to answer them. The outcome is bad metaphysics, of the very sort that Hume decried.

Moreover, given that there is no agreed procedure for even *trying* to answer these questions, our various attempts to answer them give rise to endless irresoluble controversy. This is why the history of metaphysics stands in such stark contrast to the history of, say, mathematics. Where the latter has been marked by a steady but spectacular accumulation of universally accepted results, the former constitutes a tiresome sequence of false starts and repeated squabbles.[8] By the latter stages of the eighteenth century the enthusiasm for indulging in metaphysical disputation has begun to give way to weariness and cynicism. This is partly under the influence of Hume. But it is partly a feature of the *Zeitgeist*, which was ripe for Hume's intervention. 'There was a time,' Kant laments, 'when metaphysics was called the *queen* of all sciences.... Now ... the queen proves despised on all sides' (Aviii, emphasis in original).

'Laments' is the operative word, however. We must now consider the baby. Kant is convinced that there can also be good metaphysics – importantly good metaphysics – of a kind for which Hume is entirely unable to account and, worse, which Hume is forced to reject along with its counterfeit.[9] In fact, Kant thinks that Hume's over-zealous strictures also make trouble for much more quotidian, non-metaphysical ways of thinking that are perfectly innocuous and that therefore need to be understood quite differently from how Hume was forced to understand them. The prime example is causal thinking. We saw in §3 of the previous chapter that Hume's semantic empiricism forced him to search for the impression from which his idea of a causally necessary connection derived, and how he was led to conclude that the impression was a habitual transition in his own mind from one kind of perception to another. For Kant, the resultant conception

---

[8] This explains the inferiority complex that metaphysics has long had, as has philosophy more generally, where mathematics is concerned. Ever since the time of Plato, mathematics has been seen as a model for philosophy to aspire to. Plato's own veneration of mathematics is said to have been given celebrated expression in the inscription which he placed over the door of the academy he founded: 'Let no one enter here who is ignorant of geometry.' (The story may however be apocryphal: see Gilbert (1960), p. 88.) Cf. also Hume's urge to privilege mathematics over any other *a priori* endeavour (Ch. 4, §5).

[9] Note that Kant sometimes uses the word 'metaphysics' elliptically for good metaphysics, sometimes elliptically for bad metaphysics, and sometimes neutrally. See respectively A850–851/B878–879, Aviii, and Axii (which is echoed in the title that I have given this chapter) or B21–22. This creates a hazard for anyone quoting him out of context. In context, I think, his intention is always clear.

of causation is manifestly inadequate. It accords to the necessity in a causal relation a kind of subjectivity that Kant thinks does it a gross injustice. As a result, Hume fails to make sense even of such mundane judgments as that the sun has melted the butter (e.g. B5; *Prolegomena*, 4:257ff.; and 2nd *Critique*, 5:50–52). But this failure on Hume's part, as Kant sees it, is still at root a metaphysical failure. This is evidenced by its connection with another failure: the failure properly to secure the metaphysical principle that whatever happens in nature has a cause; call this the Causal Principle. Hume certainly endorsed the Causal Principle (e.g. Hume (1975a), p. 82). But he thought that we arrived at it by natural processes of extrapolation from regularities that we had experienced in the past, whereas for Kant that is another injustice, of a piece with the earlier injustice, this time to the *a priori* necessity of the Causal Principle. Kant is convinced that we have the same kind of assurance that this principle holds as we do that 7 + 5 = 12.

Not that he takes the Causal Principle to be what Hume would call a relation of ideas. Kant is quite happy to accredit Hume with having shown that it is not. There is therefore no alternative, in Kant's view, but radically to rethink Hume's entire empiricist framework and to reassess his reasons for throwing out the dirty water that he has (quite rightly, of course) thrown out.[10]

What we need, Kant believes, is some *principled* way of distinguishing between what is to be rejected and what is to be saved (*Prolegomena*, 4:255ff.). Not that that is any rebuke to Hume, who certainly provided a principle for effecting this distinction – though the principle that he provided was empirical, so that, even by his own lights, it was vulnerable to the possibility that the human mind would one day start operating in some hitherto unknown way. Kant will provide a principle that is *a priori*, thereby revealing once again how much further than Hume he takes the domain of the *a priori* to extend. But more to the point, he will provide a principle that *differs* from Hume's, a principle that will allow for some of what Hume's principle excluded. It will allow for substantive *a priori* necessities in metaphysics, no less than in mathematics. (It will allow, among other things, for itself.) Hence, if Kant's project is successful, we shall be clear about what we can aspire to in metaphysics, we shall be clear about what we cannot aspire to, and we shall be clear about why the line between these is to be drawn where it is. Metaphysics will have been established as a proper, respectable science.

The first step is to reconsider what might count as a 'substantive' *a priori* necessity and to ask whether Hume was right even in his account of mathematics.[11]

---

[10] Kant beautifully and concisely summarizes the task at hand, and his proposed way of meeting it, at *Prolegomena*, 4:360. Cf. also, much more extensively, B Introduction, esp. §§III, VI, and VII, and A758–769/B786–792.

[11] Cf. B20. For a scathing attack on the whole project, see Nietzsche (1967c), §530 (and see further Ch. 15, §2). For a very interesting and instructive account of Kant's relation to Hume, see Stern (2006).

3.   Synthetic *A Priori* Knowledge

Hume held that mathematics consists of relations of ideas. He also held that mathematical relations of ideas can be substantive in a way in which no others can. But this was still only substantiveness of a modest psychological kind. It was due simply to the fact that, granted our limitations, some mathematical relations of ideas are unobvious to us. We cannot acknowledge them except by following a chain of reasoning. And the result of any such chain of reasoning may be quite unexpected.

It is significant that Hume did not exhibit unwavering confidence in this account. It took him a while to come round to the view that it applied, in particular, to geometry.[12] Nor did he give a clear or compelling explanation for why mathematical ideas are peculiarly equipped to issue in such substantiveness. All he ventured was the following:

> As the component parts of quantity and number are entirely similar, their relations become intricate and involved; and nothing can be more curious … than to trace … their equality or inequality through their different appearances. But as all other ideas are clearly distinct … from each other, we can never advance farther … than to observe this diversity.…
> (Hume (1975a), p. 163)

At the very least this requires elucidation. Hume seemed to be struggling.

The fact is, Kant urges, we need to draw some distinctions which have not yet been drawn. Hume offered us a dichotomy between relations of ideas and matters of fact. Leibniz earlier offered us a dichotomy between truths of reasoning and truths of fact. Whatever the relation was between these two dichotomies, neither on its own was able to bear the weight of a satisfactory account of mathematical necessity. For that purpose, Kant believes, there are two dichotomies that need to be recognized, not one. These are in danger of being conflated – if indeed they have not already been conflated, either by Hume or by Leibniz, or by both.

First, there is the dichotomy between truths that can be known *a priori* and truths that cannot.[13] A truth is known *a priori* if it is known 'absolutely

---

[12] See n. 28 of the previous chapter and accompanying text.

[13] Here and throughout this chapter, except when I am directly quoting from Kant, I put in terms of knowledge what Kant himself typically puts in terms of cognition. 'Cognition' is the word used in the Cambridge edition of his works to translate '*Erkenntnis*'. The translators are quite right not to use 'knowledge' for this purpose, as their predecessors did. For, although it is not abundantly clear what Kant means by '*Erkenntnis*' – either from his various uses of the term or indeed from his explicit definitions of it, which are not always consistent with one another – it *is* clear that he does not mean knowledge. He seems to mean what might best be characterized, in his own terms, as 'the conscious representation of an object': see e.g. A320/B376–377 and 2nd 'Logic', 24:702. (There are further questions, of course, about his understanding of 'conscious', 'representation', and 'object'. In a much looser, non-Kantian formulation he seems to mean the having of something in mind, or better a state

independently of all experience and even of all impressions of the senses' (B2–3, two passages combined, emphasis removed).[14] It is a mark of a truth's being knowable *a priori* that it is necessary, for 'experience teaches us … that something is constituted thus and so, but not that it could not be otherwise' (B3). It is likewise a mark of a truth's being knowable *a priori* that it is universal, for 'experience never gives its judgments true or strict... universality' (B3, emphasis removed). (Kant's discussion, here and elsewhere, indicates that he understands these 'marks' to be both necessary conditions and sufficient conditions.) An example of a truth that is knowable *a priori* is that all aunts are female. An example of a truth that is not knowable *a priori* is that some aunts are younger than some of their siblings' children.

Second, there is the dichotomy between truths that are analytic and truths that are synthetic. Kant distinguishes between two kinds of judgment rather than two kinds of truth, but I shall assume that the application of his distinction to truths is unproblematical. (Thus a truth can be said to be analytic if it can be the object of an analytic judgment. Likewise, a truth can be said to be synthetic if it can be the object of a synthetic judgment.)[15] Very well, when is a judgment analytic, and when synthetic? An affirmative judgment of subject-predicate form is analytic 'if the predicate *B* belongs to the subject *A* as something that is (covertly) contained in this concept *A*' (A6/B10); it is synthetic otherwise.[16] As we saw in Chapter 3, §4, Leibniz worked with

---

that centrally involves the having of something in mind.) This excludes some knowledge and it includes some non-knowledge. The knowledge that it excludes is knowledge that is purely conceptual and makes no reference to any object: I shall have more to say about such knowledge in §8. (But note that this is *not* the same as what will shortly be identified in the main text as analytic knowledge: see A151–152/B190–191 and *Prolegomena*, 4:276.) The non-knowledge that it includes is the conscious representation of an object that contains some error: see 1st 'Logic', 24:93–94 and 105, and 3rd 'Logic', 9:53–54. My reason for bracketing cognition and talking in terms of knowledge is that this connects better with my broader concerns. My justification for doing so is that, in all the relevant contexts, the questions that Kant raises about cognition, and the answers that he gives, are equally questions and answers about knowledge. When he asks, for example, how cognition of a certain kind is possible (see e.g. B19ff. and *Prolegomena*, §5, and see further §4 below), the kind of cognition in question is likewise a kind of knowledge. Cf. in this connection Bvii–x and *Prolegomena*, 4:371.

[14] This is intended to allow for the possibility that the knowledge involves concepts 'that can be drawn only from experience' (B3).

[15] Cf. *Prolegomena*, 4:266.

[16] Kant may be presupposing a Leibnizian view whereby every judgment is of subject–predicate form (see Ch. 3, n. 32). Or he may be presupposing that the extension of his definition to judgments of other forms, like its extension to negative judgments, 'is easy' (A6/B10). If the former, then either this is a lapse on his part or some account has to be given of how it consists with what he says at A73–74/B98–99 and B140–141. For an interesting discussion of these matters, see Ian Proops (2005), pp. 592–596. (Proops there argues for a third possibility, namely that Kant does not intend his dichotomy to extend to all judgments. I remain unconvinced.)

a notion that was superficially similar to this notion of an analytic truth, and which he took to embrace *every* truth. But by the time Kant has clarified what he means, in particular by 'containment', and by the time he has given various examples, his own notion looks far closer to Leibniz' notion of a truth of reasoning, which Leibniz took to embrace only some truths of course. Indeed, on what Kant takes to be an equivalent definition of his own notion, an analytic truth is one that can be shown, by a (finite) process of analysis, not to be deniable without violating the principle of contradiction (*Prolegomena*, 4:266–267; cf. A150–153/B189–192 and 3rd *Critique*, 5:197 n.). This is highly reminiscent of Leibniz' definition of a truth of reasoning.[17] It is also reminiscent of what Hume said about relations of ideas. It certainly leaves room for analytic truths that are substantive in the modest psychological sense. (See, for example, Kant's discussion of the conceptual taxonomy that he envisages in *Prolegomena*, 4:325 n.) What really concerns Kant, however, is the much more robust sense in which analytic truths are not substantive. Their discovery never 'amplifies' our knowledge (A8/B12). An example of an analytic truth is that all aunts are female. An example of a synthetic truth is that some aunts are younger than some of their siblings' children.[18]

I have chosen the same two examples as before for the simple reason that the two dichotomies can easily appear to amount to the same thing. It can easily appear that yet another mark of a truth's being knowable *a priori* is that it is analytic. For that matter, it can easily appear that Kant has found two equivalent characterizations of the single dichotomy which both Leibniz and Hume, each in his different way, was also attempting to characterize. But Kant is adamant that it is not so.

He accepts that an analytic truth is always knowable *a priori* (B11–12). What he denies, crucially, is the converse. This is the real trademark of his view. Kant holds that there is synthetic *a priori* knowledge (knowledge of synthetic *a priori* truths).

His primary example is mathematical knowledge. He believes, as would most philosophers who are prepared to think in these terms, that such knowledge is *a priori*. But he also insists, more controversially, that it is synthetic. He writes:

> To be sure, one might initially think that the proposition '7 + 5 = 12' is
> a merely analytic proposition that follows from the concept of a sum of

---

[17] Whether they coincide or not depends on, among other things, whether Leibniz also allowed for truths of reasoning that can be shown, by a finite process of analysis, not to be deniable without violating the principle of sufficient reason: see Ch. 3, n. 33. If he did, they do not.

[18] For helpful discussions of Kant's two dichotomies, see Bennett (1966), §§2–4, and Gardner (1999), pp. 52–55; and for a helpful discussion of the second, see Allison (1983), pp. 73–78. For an excellent discussion of the two dichotomies with particular reference to mathematics, see Potter (2000), Ch. 1.

seven and five in accordance with the principle of contradiction. Yet if one considers it more closely, one finds that the concept of the sum of 7 and 5 contains nothing more than the unification of both numbers in a single one.... The concept of twelve is by no means already thought merely by thinking of that unification of seven and five, and no matter how long I analyze my concept of such a possible sum I will still not find twelve in it. One must go beyond these concepts, seeking assistance in ... one's five fingers, say, or ... five points....

Just as little is any principle of pure geometry analytic. That the straight line between two points is the shortest is a synthetic proposition. For my concept of *the straight* contains nothing of quantity, but only a quality. (B15–16, emphasis in original)

In the geometrical example Kant is interestingly anticipated by Hume, who, in the earlier phase of his thinking, before he came to regard geometry as consisting of relations of ideas, wrote:

'Tis true, mathematicians pretend they give an exact definition of a right [i.e. straight] line, when they say, *it is the shortest way betwixt two points*. But ... this is more properly the discovery of one of the properties of a right line, than a just definition of it. For I ask any one, if upon mention of a right line he thinks not immediately on such a particular appearance, and if 'tis not by accident only that he considers this property? A right line can be comprehended alone; but this defini-tion is unintelligible without a comparison with other lines, which we conceive to be more extended. (Hume (1978a), pp. 49–50, emphasis in original)

Hume concluded that geometry consists of matters of fact, discoverable only by appeal to experience. He did not see any difficulty with this view until later. On a Kantian conception, his problem was precisely that he had not distinguished between the question whether geometrical truths are ana-lytic, which in his earlier work he in effect recognized that they are not, and the question whether they are *a priori*, which in his later work he in effect recognized that they are.

Another of Kant's examples is our knowledge of what I earlier called the Causal Principle, that whatever happens in nature has a cause (A9–10/B13). Hume, who took this to be a matter of fact, did not feel the same discomfort with it. But on a Kantian view he should have done.

As we shall see, most of what Kant is offering here will later be rejected. Some philosophers will reject his very dichotomies.[19] Others will accept the dichotomies but reject his application of them, claiming, for instance, that arithmetical truths are analytic.[20] *Some* of what Kant is offering will

---

[19] Quine is the best known example: see Ch. 12, esp. §4.
[20] Frege is the best known example: see Ch. 8, esp. §§2 and 3.

suffer a fate that is unusual for philosophical ware: it will be decisively refuted (notwithstanding a few brave attempts to salvage it by creative reinterpretation[21]). Thus twentieth-century advances in science will show that some of his purported examples of synthetic *a priori* knowledge, so far from being that, are not even examples of knowledge. Nay, the things that are said to be known are not even *true*. (Between two points there can be more than one straight line.[22] This is a fact about physical space. But let no one deny that it is physical space that Kant is talking about, too (A157/B196 and A163/B204).) Moreover, the fact that these scientific advances will be made partly through experimentation means that not only will those particular examples be discredited, but the *a priority* of other examples will be called into question. Geometry, by the twentieth century, will seem a decidedly empirical discipline.[23]

Fortunately, the importance of Kant's doctrines does not depend on their detailed truth. It does not even depend on their broad truth. Kant may be fundamentally wrong. But if he is, his errors are of that deep sort that can still instruct us, prompt us, stimulate us, and guide us, opening up significant new possibilities for us to explore. If we prescind from the objections to his doctrines, as we *pro tempore* must if we are properly to learn from them, then one significant possibility that they immediately open up is the following: just as mathematics can be seen as the pursuit of synthetic *a priori* knowledge, so too can metaphysics. That is, in the most general attempt to make sense of things, success may accrue from following a method that consists, *contra* Hume, neither in conceptual analysis nor in empirical investigation.

4.   How Synthetic *A Priori* Knowledge Is Possible: Transcendental Idealism

Before we can so much as consider that possibility, however, we need to address the following fundamental Kantian question, on which his entire critique turns: how is synthetic *a priori* knowledge possible (B19)? In raising this question Kant is not having second thoughts about whether it is possible. Throughout his discussion he stands by his various arguments

---

[21] See e.g. Strawson (1966), Pt V, countered by Hopkins (1982).

[22] This explicitly contradicts Kant's example at A157/B196. But it also implicitly contradicts the geometrical example that he has already given, because it means that none of the relevant straight lines is 'the' shortest.

[23] See Einstein (1920), §I and Appendix V. Note: my tone in this paragraph may be a little more cavalier than is strictly warranted. For a different, somewhat fuller account of how Kant is superseded by twentieth-century science, see Ch. 11, §3. For a reversion to something more cavalier, see Ch. 12, §4.

that mathematical knowledge fills the bill. A philosophical sceptic might caution, 'Provided there is such a thing as mathematical knowledge.' But that is not a proviso that Kant ever feels the need to add. He takes it to be a kind of datum that there is such a thing as mathematical knowledge (B20–21 and *Prolegomena*, 4:327).[24] He also takes for granted that any non-trivial knowledge that deserves to be called 'metaphysical' must likewise be both synthetic and *a priori* (B18 and *Prolegomena*, 4:368). His question about the possibility of synthetic *a priori* knowledge is not intended in a sceptical vein then. It is rather intended to serve the following two functions: first, to help us to overcome certain natural assumptions that make synthetic *a priori* knowledge, knowledge that is both substantive in some robust sense and yet independent of experience, seem impossible; and second, concomitantly, to give us a grasp of what the scope and limits of synthetic *a priori* knowledge are, so that we can decide whether such knowledge is possible, in particular, in metaphysics. 'That metaphysics has until now remained in such a vacillating state of uncertainty and contradictions,' Kant observes, 'is to be ascribed solely to the cause that no one has previously thought of this problem.... On the solution of this problem, or on a satisfactory proof that the possibility that it demands to have explained [sc. the possibility of synthetic *a priori* knowledge in metaphysics] does not in fact exist at all, metaphysics now stands or falls' (B19; cf. *Prolegomena*, 4:276).

What are the natural assumptions that make synthetic *a priori* knowledge seem impossible? There are two. The first is that synthetic knowledge must answer to what is independent of it.[25,26] The second is that it can answer to what is independent of it only if it is empirical (where empirical knowledge – which is roughly what Kant means by 'experience' (B147

---

[24] Cf. Carr (1999), p. 62. This goes some way towards countering an objection that Edward Craig voices to the answer that Kant will eventually give to his own question: see Craig (1987), pp. 237–239.

[25] Throughout this chapter I use 'answer to' elliptically for 'answer correctly to.' See also n. 28 for a gloss on how independence is to be understood here.

[26] Cf. Bernard Williams' famous formula that 'knowledge is of what is there *anyway*' (Williams (1978), p. 64, emphasis in original). This is Williams' summary way of putting what he describes as 'a very basic thought,' namely 'that if knowledge is what it claims to be, then it is knowledge of a reality which exists independently of that knowledge, and indeed (except in the special case where the reality known happens itself to be some psychological item) independently of any thought or experience' (ibid.). (We might wonder whether incorrigible knowledge of one's own sensory states is a counterexample – albeit a counterexample that would do nothing to assuage scepticism about the possibility of synthetic *a priori* knowledge. In fact, however, there is good reason not to count anything of that kind as 'knowledge': cf. Wittgenstein (1967a), Pt I, §246. Certainly nothing of that kind is included in what Kant calls 'cognition': see n. 13.)

and 218)[27] – is simply the complement of *a priori* knowledge). More fully and more formally:

> The Independence Assumption: For any item of knowledge k, if k is synthetic, then there is something x such that x is independent of k and such that k answers to x.[28]
>
> The Experience Assumption: For any item of knowledge k and anything x that is independent of k, k answers to x only if k is grounded in some sensory effect of x, hence only if k is empirical.

A Cartesian (among others) would object to the Experience Assumption. An item of *a priori* knowledge, the Cartesian would say, can answer to what is independent of it through God's benevolent guarantee that the former accords with the latter. But Kant, who leans far enough in the direction of empiricism to be sympathetic to the Experience Assumption – it is on the Independence Assumption that he will eventually mount his attack – would reject this Cartesian view on the grounds that it fails to do justice to the necessity that the knowledge must enjoy if it is to qualify as *a priori* (cf. B167–168). It is almost as if the Cartesian is positing a sixth sense which, where the other five are linked to their objects by (psycho-)physical causal relations, is linked to its objects by Divine ordination.[29] But note that, even if the Cartesian were to concede that he had done that (thereby leaving the Experience Assumption unchallenged), he would still owe us an account of how this link between the sixth sense and its objects enables the former to represent the latter, or, equivalently, how the relation between the item of knowledge in question and the independent reality in question enables the former to answer to the latter. Of course, the Cartesian owes us an account of the second of these anyway. This was the issue to which I drew attention at the end of Chapter 1, §5. And although I did not there call for a complementary account of how the (psycho-)physical causal relation enables the other five senses to represent their objects – or equivalently, how relations between items of ordinary empirical knowledge and occurrences in the physical world enable any of the former to answer to any of the latter – in fact there is an issue about that too (cf. *Prolegomena*, §9). We are owed an account of how any purported relation of representation qualifies for that

---

[27] 'Roughly' because he actually defines experience as a kind cognition, not as a kind of knowledge: see n. 13.

[28] By 'x is independent of k' I mean something that requires x to be independent not only of the actual formation of k but also (for instance) of the concepts that k involves. On this understanding, analytic knowledge does not answer to anything independent of it.

[29] Cf. the analogies between Cartesian 'intuition' and sensory perception which I emphasized in Ch. 1, §4. And see Ch. 1, §3, for the rather anaemic sense in which Descartes himself took what was knowable *a priori* to be necessary. For further worries about the Cartesian view, see 'Letter to Herz', dated 21 February 1772, in *Correspondence*, 10:131.

title. So although Kant has the Independence Assumption in his sights, the very fact that his problem helps to bring these issues to our attention means that he cannot rest content with overcoming the Independence Assumption. He must also motivate the Experience Assumption. He must say what it is about experience that equips it, and it alone, to constitute knowledge of an independent reality. The question, 'How is synthetic *a priori* knowledge possible?' thus assumes a much wider significance for Kant. It eventually comes to embrace the question, 'How is knowledge of an independent reality possible?', or, more broadly, 'How is representation possible?'[30]

I can scarcely even begin to go into the details of Kant's extraordinary answers to these questions – or should I say, answer (in the singular)? Part of what is extraordinary about how he addresses the questions is that he has what is in effect a single story to tell in response to all of them. He states a 'clue to the discovery' of this story – to borrow a phrase of his from elsewhere (A66/B91) – in the following very well-known passage from the Preface to the second edition of the first *Critique*:

> Up to now it has been assumed that all our cognition must conform to the objects.... [Let] us once try whether we do not get farther with the problems of metaphysics by assuming that the objects must conform to our cognition.... This would be just like the first thoughts of Copernicus, who, when he did not make good progress in the explanation of the celestial motions if he assumed that the entire celestial host revolves around the observer, tried to see if he might not have greater success if he made the observer revolve and left the stars at rest. (Bxvi)

Very roughly, Kant's story proceeds as follows. When we have knowledge of something that is independent of us, and hence of something that is independent of that knowledge, this is made possible by the fact that we are 'given' the thing in question: it affects us in some way (A19/B33; cf. A635/B663).[31] And the way in which it affects us is sensory (A19–20/B33–34 and B147). So that is why the Experience Assumption holds. But we can be

---

[30] Cf. Brandom (2002a), pp. 22–23, and McDowell (2007b), p. 399. Cf. also what Kant says in a famous passage from the letter to Marcus Herz cited in the previous note, referring to an early version of the first *Critique* for which he had made plans: 'As I thought through the theoretical part, considering its whole scope and the reciprocal relations of all its parts, I noticed that I still lacked something essential, something that in my long metaphysical studies I, as well as others, had failed to consider and which in fact constitutes the key to the whole secret of metaphysics, hitherto still hidden from itself. I asked myself the question: What is the ground of the relation of that in us which we call "representation" to the object?' (*Correspondence*, 10:129–130).

[31] Kant takes it to be a fundamental mark of our finitude that our knowledge involves reception of this kind. An infinite being, Kant holds, could produce what it knew in knowing it (B145). For further discussion of this idea, see Ch. 6, §3, and Ch. 21, §§2(d) and 2(e). And cf. Heidegger (1962b), p. 31.

affected in this way, or we can be given something in this way, only because we have certain capacities for reception. Through these we ourselves make a contribution to the form and structure of our experience. It is as though we have native spectacles through which we view things. And because these spectacles are native, we can have *a priori* knowledge pertaining to them: we can know, *a priori*, how things must appear through them. Such knowledge is synthetic. For it does not accrue from pure conceptual analysis. On the other hand, given that it is knowledge of the appearances of things, and given that it derives solely from our very capacity for such knowledge, neither does it answer to anything that is independent of it. So it falsifies the Independence Assumption. This means that we have an account of how synthetic *a priori* knowledge is possible,[32] which is in turn part of an account of how knowledge of an independent reality is possible, which is in turn part of an account of how representation is possible. It is part of an account of how representation is possible because our receptive capacities ensure that we are not just affected by objects but are given them as being a certain way, and hence as capable of being thought to be a certain way, albeit, granted the 'Copernican revolution', a way that is determined partly by our spectacles: objects are given to us as appearing thus and so through our spectacles.[33]

Moreover, objects are given to us *only* as appearing thus and so through our spectacles. We cannot take our spectacles off. We cannot have (synthetic) knowledge of 'things in themselves'. Kant accordingly classifies his position as a kind of idealism. It is a kind of idealism in the sense that the objects of our knowledge, as they are known to us, have a form that depends on the knowledge itself. In Kant's own words, 'all objects of experience possible for us … are nothing but appearances,… which, as they are represented,… have outside our thoughts no existence grounded in itself' (A490–491/B518–519). But this idealism is not a matter of *what* we know about such objects. It is a matter of *how* we know it. (It is not a matter of what we see through our spectacles. It is a matter of our seeing through spectacles at all. For instance, included in what we know about such objects are both of the following: that the sun is larger than the moon, and that the sun's being larger than the moon *does not depend in any way on our knowing it to be so*. Both of these, however, involve the occupation of space, and, as we are about to see, Kant takes space to constitute part of our spectacles.[34]) Kant accordingly classifies his idealism as 'transcendental', where

---

[32] Kant further insists that it is the only possible account (B41; cf. A92/B124–125).

[33] In the last sentence of this paragraph I am compressing one strain in the notoriously difficult 'Transcendental Deduction', at A84–130 and, differently in the second edition, B116–169. A very helpful and much more accessible account of this material occurs in *Prolegomena*, §§18ff. For a thorough and very interesting discussion of the issues raised in this paragraph, see Guyer (1987), esp. Pt II.

[34] I shall return briefly to this example in §10.

the word 'transcendental' signifies not 'a relation of our cognition to things, but only to the *faculty of cognition*' (*Prolegomena*, 4:293, emphasis in original; cf. A11/B25); not our knowledge of objects, but our knowledge of how we know them.[35] Transcendental idealism will hereafter play a crucial role in our narrative.[36]

To understand better how radical Kant's transcendental idealism is, we need to reflect on the nature of our spectacles. Where Hume distinguished

[35] Kant therefore distinguishes between the 'transcendental' and the 'transcendent' (see A296/B352–353 and *Prolegomena*, 4:373, n.). We could say, in what is admittedly something of a caricature, that whereas immanence belongs to what is inside our sensory bubble, i.e. to objects of our experience, and transcendence belongs to what is outside our sensory bubble, i.e. to things in themselves, transcendentality belongs to the bubble itself, or to its film. (Two caveats. First, there is much talk, mostly in the first edition of the first *Critique*, of 'transcendental objects', where what seems to be intended is something at the level of things in themselves: see e.g. A379–380. This is connected with complications in the system to which we shall return in §§8–10. Second, this caricature completely abstracts from the idea that the immanent is related to the transcendent as appearance to reality.)

[36] There is an issue about Kant's transcendental idealism which I should mention here, though I do not propose to address it. It concerns the contrast between the knowledge of appearances that we can have and the knowledge of things in themselves that we cannot have. That Kant accepts such a contrast is clear. The issue is about what exactly it comes to. One view would be that the two kinds of knowledge are distinguished by their subject matter. The fact that we can have the one and cannot have the other is, on that view, akin to the fact that we can know about events inside our light cone but cannot know about events outside it. (See Matthews (1982) and Allison (1983) for two of the many notable attempts to oppose this view, in apparent opposition to Strawson (1966), though we should beware that they may be as guilty of misrepresenting Strawson as they take him to be of misrepresenting Kant.) A quite different view is that the two kinds of knowledge are two kinds of knowledge about the same things. The fact that we can have the one and cannot have the other is then more like the fact that we can have historical knowledge about events of which we cannot have eyewitness knowledge. Both views cast knowledge of things in themselves as free of any 'human' perspective. But on the first view, unlike the second, this is dictated by the very subject matter of the knowledge. On the second view, the phrase 'things in themselves' should strictly speaking only ever be used syncategorematically, in tandem with some suitable epistemic expression: to say, for instance, that things in themselves are not coloured is an improper way of saying that our knowledge of the colours of things is not knowledge of things in themselves (is not free of 'human' perspective). With the possible exception of the caricature in the previous note, I have presented Kant's transcendental idealism in such a way as to evoke the second view, but I certainly do not take myself to have refuted the first. For material conducive to the first view, see *Prolegomena*, 4:318, and 3rd *Critique*, 5:195. For material conducive to the second view, see Bxviii–xix, n.; A45–46/B62–63; *Prolegomena*, 4:289; and *Groundwork*, 4:450–452. For a third view, to which I cannot hope to do justice but which I should certainly mention, see Bird (2006), esp. Chs 1 and 30. For some remarks relevant to the role that transcendental idealism will play in our narrative, see the Appendix to this chapter.

between impressions and ideas, and saw this as a distinction of degree (see §2 of the previous chapter), Kant has a distinction of kind between *intuitions*,[37] whereby we are directly given objects, and *concepts*, whereby we think about objects, as thus given (A19/B33). Intuitions are products of our pure receptivity; there is something passive about them. Concepts are products of our 'spontaneity'; there is something active about them.[38] Our knowledge, or at any rate our synthetic knowledge, requires both (A50–51/B74–75). And our spectacles involve both. Thus, given that our synthetic *a priori* knowledge includes knowledge of the structure of space and time, Kant concludes that not even these are features of things in themselves, but are rather two *a priori* intuitions that constitute part of our spectacles (A19–49/B33–73).[39] He likewise identifies twelve fundamental *a priori* concepts that he takes to constitute part of our spectacles (A79–80/B105–106).[40] Significantly, in the light of some of the difficulties with which Hume wrestled, these concepts include (pure forms of) both the concept of substance and the concept of causality (A80/B106; cf. *Prolegomena*, §27). These twelve concepts serve as a kind of noetic glue. It is by means of them that our intuitions are combined together so as to ensure that we are not just given objects but are given them as being a certain way.

Our spectacles, to repeat, involve both intuitions and concepts. It is because they involve intuitions that Kant is able to reject the Independence Assumption. For synthetic knowledge must answer to *something*. So given that, *qua* synthetic, it does not answer merely to the concepts involved in it, the only way in which it can fail to answer to what is independent of it is by involving something other than concepts. *A priori* intuitions play just this role. (This is related to the principle, on which Kant again and again insists in the first *Critique*, that synthetic knowledge is never possible

---

[37] Note that this use of the term 'intuition' is very different from Descartes' (see Ch. 1, §4). For an excellent discussion of Kant's use, see Hintikka (1969).

[38] Just as empiricists have missed this distinction by effectively trying to make do with differences of degree among our intuitions, so too, Kant alleges, Leibniz missed it when he spoke of monads representing the world more or less distinctly (see Ch. 3, §3) and effectively tried to make do with differences of degree among our concepts (A44/B61–62 and A270–271/B326–327).

[39] See Ch. 3, n. 15: there is a comparison to be drawn here with Leibniz. But Kant believes that Leibniz' view is vitiated by the error to which I referred in the previous note (A275–276/ B331–332).

[40] That we have the *a priori* intuitions we have and that we have the *a priori* concepts we have are, for Kant, brute facts about us (see e.g. B145–146 and *Prolegomena*, 4: 350–351). To be sure, what Kant says at B148 might be interpreted as meaning that any being that is given objects in intuition must (can? will?) use the same *a priori* concepts as we do to think about those objects. But what Kant surely means is rather that, for any being that is given objects in intuition, *we* must (can? will?) use these concepts to think about those objects.

without intuitions (see e.g. B16, A62/B87, A155–156/B194–195, B288–289, and A238–240/B297–299). This principle will later prove to be critical to his determination of the limits of metaphysics: see §6.)

The fact that our spectacles also involve concepts violates any counterpart of Hume's basic empiricist principle that our simple ideas are copied from our simple impressions. It is nevertheless too soon to conclude that Kant distances himself from any direct equivalent of Hume's semantic empiricism. For it remains to be seen what sort of meaning, if any, he thinks can attach to these concepts when they are disassociated from experience. On the other hand it is not too soon to conclude that Kant distances himself from any direct equivalent of Hume's epistemic empiricism. His sheer commitment to synthetic *a priori* knowledge ensures that he does *that*. The question we must now broach is how far, if at all, we can aspire to such knowledge in the most general attempt to make sense of things, that is in metaphysics.

5. Good Metaphysics: The 'Transcendental Analytic'

Kant believes that this aspiration is, up to a point, perfectly legitimate. He devotes at least a third of his first *Critique*, essentially the part entitled 'Transcendental Analytic', to the pursuit of it. There is a section entitled 'Second Analogy', for example, in which he considers what I called in §2 the Causal Principle, or what he calls 'the principle of temporal sequence according to the law of causality' (B232), and in that section he attempts a proof of this principle. If he succeeds – it is beyond the scope of this chapter to address the issue of how far he does[41] – then the upshot is, precisely, an item of synthetic *a priori* knowledge of a sufficiently high degree of generality to count as metaphysical. In this part of the first *Critique*, then, Kant's project is to establish various metaphysical results, much as a mathematician's project is to establish mathematical results.

(Later in the first *Critique* Kant explicitly compares and contrasts these two disciplines (A712–738/B740–766). There is one crucial feature that they have in common. Because metaphysicians and mathematicians are both in pursuit of synthetic knowledge, they must both appeal to intuitions. But this in turn signals the principal contrast between the two disciplines, which is methodological. Mathematicians appeal to the relevant intuitions by actually exhibiting them (A713/B741). For example, a geometrician might begin a proof by constructing a triangle. Metaphysicians, however, are concerned rather with *experience*, and hence with intuitions at least some of which are empirical. So if they exhibited any relevant intuitions, it would compromise their claim to be engaged in an *a priori* exercise. Their appeal to the relevant intuitions is instead an appeal to the sheer *possibility* of our being given

---

[41] For discussion, see Bennett (1966), Chs 11 and 15; Strawson (1966), Pt Two, Ch. 3; Allison (1983), Ch. 10; and Guyer (1987), Ch. 10.

objects in intuition in the various ways we are (A766/B794). It is thus that metaphysics comes to involve the highly distinctive style of proof that Kant labels 'transcendental proof' (A786/B814ff.). A transcendental proof is a proof whose conclusion concerns the conditions that must obtain, as a matter of *a priori* necessity, in order for us to be given objects in intuition in the ways we are, or in order for us to enjoy experience of the kinds we do.[42])

6.   Bad Metaphysics: The 'Transcendental Dialectic'

The 'Transcendental Analytic' reveals the scope of metaphysics. It is followed in the first Critique by an even larger part, entitled 'Transcendental Dialectic', which reveals its limits. Some of what metaphysicians aspire to do, nay most of what they aspire to do, is not legitimate. This means that their task is twofold: not just to establish metaphysical results, and thereby to attain synthetic *a priori* knowledge, but also to keep in check their own impulses to try to establish metaphysical results where there is no synthetic *a priori* knowledge to be had; that is to say, not just to practise good metaphysics, but to combat bad metaphysics. Both tasks are united in Kant's delightfully memorable *aperçu* concerning philosophy, which he might just as well have applied to metaphysics, that it 'consists precisely in knowing its bounds' (A727/B755).

Metaphysicians attempt to transgress these bounds whenever they attempt to make sense of what is transcendent. In a second, more Kantian formulation, they attempt to transgress these bounds whenever they attempt to attain synthetic *a priori* knowledge without appeal to intuitions. In the first of these formulations – which supplies a direct answer to the Transcendence Question in §6 of the Introduction – I am presupposing a suitably epistemic interpretation of what it is to make sense of something and a suitably experiential interpretation of what it is for something to be transcendent. The two formulations are equivalent because the knowledge that we can attain by appeal to intuitions, whether these be empirical or *a priori*, is the synthetic knowledge that we can attain about objects of a possible experience (for us). Such knowledge pertains to what we are actually given in experience if the intuitions are empirical. It pertains to our spectacles and therefore, indirectly, to what we are capable of being given in experience if the intuitions are *a priori*.

As we have seen, Kant denies that there is any other synthetic knowledge available to us. He is adamant that herein lie the only two epistemic uses to which we can put our spectacles. We can look through them at the world

---

[42] For further discussion, including discussion of other contrasts that Kant recognizes between metaphysics and mathematics, see Moore (2010b), esp. §2. For reservations about the idea that we can determine conditions that must obtain in order for us to enjoy experience of the kind we do, see Ch. 21, §2(e).

and see how the world actually appears through them. Or we can reflect on the spectacles themselves and draw conclusions about how the world *must* appear through them. But there is no other synthetic knowledge that we can attain with their aid (e.g. Bxix, A92–94/B124–127, B147–148, B165–166, A139/B178, A238–240/B297–299, and A702/B730). Nor – Kant is just as adamant about this – can we take them off and look at the world directly.

Yet that is what metaphysicians most deeply aspire to do. They seek, as Kant would put it, synthetic *a priori* knowledge of things in themselves.[43] They want to establish whether or not there is a God sustaining all that we experience and directing its various operations; whether or not, in the multifarious episodes that make up our lives, there are any exercises of pure free will; whether or not we each have a soul, persisting through all the vicissitudes of our physical existence and beyond.[44] (Each of our protagonists so far has had something to say about each of these.) These are the great questions of metaphysics. Kant himself insists that such questions are of vital concern to us. He regards the three concepts of God, freedom, and immortality as the three most important and most potent concepts of mainstream Christianity (e.g. 2nd *Critique*, Pt One, Bk II, Ch. II, §VI). But such questions, at any rate on Kant's understanding of them, are questions about what is transcendent. We cannot hope to answer them.[45]

In the 'Transcendental Dialectic' Kant supplements his general account of what is wrong with attempts to answer such questions, and of why we nevertheless feel the urge to make these attempts, with a case-by-case rebuttal of the various specific attempts that metaphysicians have made, their various forays into transcendent metaphysics, as we might say. Kant himself comments, in the very last sentence of the 'Transcendental Dialectic':

> It was not only necessary to carry out an exhaustive examination of the vain elaborations of speculative reason in their entirety down to its primary sources, but also – since dialectical illusion is here not only

---

[43] Or, as Kant says at one point, they seek the '*unconditioned*, which reason necessarily and with every right demands in things in themselves for everything that is conditioned' (Bxx, emphasis in original).

[44] At B7 Kant says that the 'unavoidable problems of pure reason ... are God, *freedom* and *immortality*,' and adds that 'the science whose final aim in all its preparations is directed properly only to the solution of these problems is called *metaphysics*' (emphasis in original; cf. A798/B826).

[45] There is an issue here about the Causal Principle which Kant takes himself to have proved. Why does that not yield a negative answer to the question about free will, at least given something else that Kant holds, namely that any attempt to reconcile the Causal Principle with our possession of free will by maintaining that our exercises of free will have a distinctive type of cause (any attempt of the kind that Hume made: see Hume (1975a), §VIII) is 'a wretched subterfuge' (2nd *Critique*, 5:96)? We shall return to this issue in the next section.

deceptive for our judgment but ..., owing to the interest we take in these judgments, is also alluring and natural, and so will be present in the future too – it was advisable to draw up an exhaustive dossier, as it were, of these proceedings and store it in the archives of human reason, so as to prevent future errors of a similar kind. (A703–704/B731–732)

Kant divides the misguided efforts of metaphysicians into two broad classes, according to whether their questions are ill-conceived or well-conceived (A740–741/B768–769).[46] There is an echo in this division of a division that Hume would recognize between violations of his semantic empiricism and violations of his epistemic empiricism. To see how Kant understands the division, we need first to see what he means by an 'idea of reason'. By an idea of reason Kant means one of the twelve fundamental *a priori* concepts that constitute part of our spectacles or else a concept that can be defined in terms of these twelve, freed of whatever apparatus allows it to be applied to objects of possible experience (A320/B377 and A408–409/B435). So freed, it can be applied to things in themselves. And Kant believes that the questions addressed by metaphysicians in their misguided efforts to attain synthetic knowledge of what transcends experience always involve some idea of reason. Such a question is ill-conceived if it involves a confused amalgam of an idea of reason with some concept that can be applied only to objects of possible experience. It is well-conceived if it involves ideas of reason without any such distortion. In the former case the question has no answer.[47] In the latter case the question has an answer, but only at the level of things in themselves. The problem with a question of the latter kind, for those metaphysicians trying to answer it, is simply that they (we) lack the resources to do so. The three questions mentioned earlier, concerning God, freedom, and immortality, are of this latter kind. The three concepts of God, freedom, and immortality (suitably understood) are undistorted ideas of reason. We may speculate about whether they are instantiated among things in themselves. But we can never know whether they are.

Not all metaphysical questions are of this kind, however. Many are of the former kind, that is to say ill-conceived. Thus metaphysicians in the past, notably Leibniz and his followers on the one hand and followers of Newton on the other hand,[48] have debated whether the physical universe is either infinitely old or infinitely big. Kant urges that these questions do not so much as arise unless there *is* such a thing as the physical universe, *as a whole*. But on Kant's view there is not. The concept of the physical universe

[46] The terminology is mine, not Kant's.

[47] Or at least, it has no answer *as intended*. Thus if the question is which of two apparent contradictories holds, where each of these apparent contradictories involves the confused concept, then it has the answer: neither. See A503–505/B531–533.

[48] That Kant is particularly concerned with debates between Leibnizians and Newtonians is convincingly argued by Sadik J. Al-Azm in Al-Azm (1972).

as a whole is a confused amalgam of the concept of unconditionedness, which is an idea of reason, with the concept of physical reality. This requires something that is both physical and all-encompassing. But the only physical things that can exist are objects of possible experience. And no object of possible experience can be all-encompassing. That is, no object of possible experience can encompass the whole of physical reality. The source of our mistake, when we conflate these concepts in this way, is a genuine insight: namely, that there must ultimately be something unconditioned corresponding to anything conditioned, and in particular corresponding to any conditioned physical thing (Bxx[49]). What we fail to appreciate, however, is that such unconditionedness must reside in things in themselves, which physical things are not. We naturally assume that some *physical* thing must be unconditioned, in other words, that there must be such a thing as the physical universe as a whole, finite or infinite as the case may be. Once we drop that assumption, we can acquiesce in the conclusion that every physical thing is part of some other physical thing that is older and bigger – as the earth, for instance, is part of the solar system – although there is no one physical thing of which every physical thing is part ('Transcendental Dialectic', Bk II, passim, esp. §§IVff.).

These debates about the age and size of the physical universe are especially significant for Kant, for they illustrate perfectly the 'battlefield of … endless controversies' to which he refers at the beginning of the Preface to the first edition of the first *Critique* (Aviii). He holds that, on the assumption that the physical universe does exist as a whole, there are entirely valid reasons both for denying that it can be temporally or spatially infinite and for denying that it can be temporally or spatially finite. It is hardly surprising, then, that metaphysicians in the past have again and again returned to these issues, (unsuccessfully) defending their own views by (successfully) attacking the views of their opponents, with no prospect of reconciliation while the offending assumption is still in place. Kant lays out their arguments alongside one another (as he does arguments concerning the divisibility of matter, the sovereignty of the laws of nature, and the existence of a necessary being) as a way of displaying the dialectic from his own impartial standpoint.[50] He

---

[49] This is the passage cited in n. 43. Cf. also A307–308/B364–365.

[50] This is the section of the first *Critique* entitled 'The Antithetic of Pure Reason'. These arguments, together with the others mentioned in parentheses, constitute what he calls the four 'antinomies'. The arguments concerning the age and size of the physical universe constitute the first of these. I do not propose to dwell on these arguments here (I have done so elsewhere (Moore (1992) and (2001a), Ch. 6, §3)). There are, however, three points to which I think it is worth drawing attention, because commentators often miss them or even deny them. First, Kant never calls into question the infinitude of time or space themselves, of which he thinks we have synthetic *a priori* knowledge (A25/B39 and A32/B47–48). Indeed, their infinitude is a crucial part of the reason why the physical universe cannot be finite (A427–429/B455–457). The second point is related to the first.

then proceeds to explain how removing the offending assumption can lead to a resolution (see esp. A497/B525ff.).

But it is impossible to remove the offending assumption without disentangling the two elements in the confused concept of the physical universe as a whole, and therefore without distinguishing between physical things and things in themselves; in other words without regarding physical things as mere appearances; or in yet other words without accepting transcendental idealism. Kant accordingly regards this dialectic as providing further support for transcendental idealism. He writes:

> One can ... draw from this antinomy a true utility ..., namely that of ... proving indirectly the transcendental ideality of appearances.... The proof would consist in this dilemma. If the world is a whole existing in itself, then it is either finite or infinite. Now the first as well as the second alternative is false (according to the proof offered above for the antithesis [sc. that the world is infinite] on the one side and the thesis [sc. that the world is finite] on the other). Thus it is also false that the world (the sum total of all appearances) is a whole existing in itself. From which it follows that appearances in general are nothing outside our representations, which is just what we mean by their transcendental ideality. (A506–507/ B534–535; cf. Bxx and *Prolegomena*, 4:341, n.)

Not that removing the offending assumption prevents the arguments in question from continuing to impress themselves upon us. Kant believes that he is dealing with an irresistible illusion which, like an optical illusion, survives our knowledge that that is what it is. And we are all subject to it. It is

In the temporal case at least, and possibly also in the spatial case, there is an asymmetry in the two things that Kant denies, i.e. that the physical universe is infinite and that it is finite. The asymmetry is that the first of these is, so to speak, closer to the truth than the second. (After all, the Causal Principle ensures that whatever happens in nature is preceded by something else, which, in one good sense, requires infinite history.) The point, of course, is that the physical universe does not exist as a (temporally) infinite whole because it does not exist as a whole. Finally, although (as we are about to see) Kant believes that the dialectic here provides further support for transcendental idealism, this should not deter us from reading controversial elements of transcendental idealism into the arguments that he parades. He accepts the arguments (except, of course, for the offending assumption: see *Prolegomena*, 4:340) and it is important for his purposes that we accept them too. But he is not offering them in a spirit of persuasion. He is offering them in a spirit of descriptive rational psychology. He takes them, rightly or wrongly, to be arguments that already force themselves upon us as soon as we think about these issues (e.g. A339/B397 and A464/B490).

For further discussion of the first antinomy, see Strawson (1966), Pt Three, Ch. 3; Bennett (1982); Allison (1983), Ch.3; and Guyer (1987), Ch. 18. (I agree with what P.F. Strawson says at ibid., pp. 203–206: the most fundamental objection to these arguments is an objection to Kant's approach too, namely that questions about the age and size of the physical universe are scientific questions, to be tackled empirically.)

utterly natural.[51] True, Kant's concern is with errors perpetrated by meta-physicians. But we are all, to some extent, metaphysicians (cf. *Prolegomena*, 4:367). Kant writes:

> Transcendental illusion ... does not cease even though it is uncovered and its nullity is clearly seen into by transcendental criticism (e.g. the illusion in the proposition: 'The world must have a beginning in time').... [This is] an *illusion* that cannot be avoided at all, just as little as we can avoid it that the sea appears higher in the middle than at the shores, since we see the former through higher rays of light than the latter, or even better, just as little as the astronomer can prevent the rising moon from appearing larger to him, even when he is not deceived by this illusion. (A297/B353–354, emphasis in original)

There are various senses of irresistibility in which it is irresistible for us to form judgments in response to the well-conceived questions too.[52] Indeed, there is a sense, albeit superficial enough to allow for the many unbelievers who have reflected on these questions, in which we have no choice but to believe that God exists and that we are immortal. (I shall say more about this in the next section.) There is an altogether more profound sense in which we have no choice but to believe that we have free will. 'The will of [a rational] being,' Kant contends, 'cannot be a will of his own except under the idea of freedom' (*Groundwork*, 4:448, emphasis added; cf. 2nd *Critique*, 5:30–31 and 103ff.). It remains the case that we cannot prove any of these things. Kant considers and rejects purported proofs of them, much as he did the arguments concerning the ill-conceived questions.[53] By the end of the 'Transcendental Dialectic' his assault on what he sees as bad metaphysics is complete. And it far exceeds, in destructive power, in diagnostic power, and in systematicity, anything that we saw in Hume.[54]

---

[51] One important difference between Kant and Hume is that the former is altogether warier of what is natural.

[52] It is certainly irresistible for us to *raise* such questions. As Kant says, in the very first sentence of the Preface to the first edition of the first *Critique*, 'Human reason ... is burdened with questions which it cannot dismiss, ... but which it also cannot answer' (Avii).

[53] He deals with attempts to establish the existence of Cartesian souls, or thinking substances capable of surviving the destruction of their bodies, in 'The Paralogisms of Pure Reason'. He deals with proofs for the existence of God in 'The Ideal of Pure Reason'. He deals with attempts to establish our freedom in the context of the third antinomy. For extensive discussion of all of these, see Bennett (1974). For something much pithier, see Copleston (1960), Ch. 13, and Gardner (1999), pp. 225–243. For discussion of the relation between Cartesian souls and our existence as things in themselves, see Ch. 6, §3.

[54] It also reinforces Kant's love of the genuine article. Later in the first *Critique* he reflects on how noble and exalted proper metaphysics is, as against the impression that we might have formed in the 'Transcendental Dialectic' from our encounter with its impostor. 'We will always return to metaphysics,' he observes, 'as to a beloved from whom we have been estranged' (A 850/B 878).

7. The Regulative Use of Concepts

Yet even in the ambitions of bad metaphysics there is something that Kant sees fit to salvage. Moreover, what he sees fit to salvage may yet count, on a relaxed, non-epistemic interpretation of what it is to make sense of something, as bona fide sense-making. Indeed, granted the high level of generality at which Kant is operating, it may yet count, on the broad conception of metaphysics that I have adopted, as good metaphysics.

Kant distinguishes between a *constitutive* use of a concept and a *regulative* use of a concept. A constitutive use of a concept is a use of it in representing things to be a certain way. A regulative use of a concept is a use of it in framing a rule, what Kant would call a 'regulative principle', enjoining us to proceed *as if* things were a certain way. What the 'Transcendental Dialectic' shows is that certain constitutive uses of concepts are illegitimate, either because the concepts conflate ideas of reason with concepts applicable only to objects of possible experience, and the questions being addressed are ill-conceived, or because the concepts are undistorted ideas of reason, and the questions being addressed, though they are well-conceived, are questions that we have no way of answering: we have no way of knowing where, if at all, these concepts are instantiated. It does not follow from the fact that some constitutive use of a concept is illegitimate in either of these two ways – not even the first, where the concept is confused – that the corresponding regulative use is illegitimate. It is Kant's conviction that there are many such regulative uses of concepts that are quite legitimate (A644–645/B672–673 and A669/B697ff.).[55] And these are precisely what he wishes to salvage and to champion.

Thus the concept of the physical universe as a whole has in Kant's view a legitimate regulative use: to enjoin us to proceed as if the physical universe existed as an infinite whole, and thus never to give up in our quest for a deeper and more extensive understanding of nature, no matter how much we have already explored (A508–515/B536–543). He likewise believes that there are legitimate regulative uses of undistorted ideas of reason. Reconsider the three concepts of God, freedom, and immortality. Kant calls the three propositions stating that these concepts are instantiated among things in themselves 'postulates of pure practical reason'. Although we can never know whether these postulates are true, it is Kant's conviction that they can serve as vital regulative principles. That is, each of the three concepts has a vital regulative use: to enjoin us to proceed as if it were indeed instantiated among things in themselves (see e.g. 2nd *Critique*, 5:48–49; 3rd *Critique*, §76; and *Religion*, 6:71 n.).

---

[55] Not that a legitimate regulative use of a concept need correspond to an illegitimate constitutive use of it. Both may be legitimate. An example would be a regulative use of the concept of the unconditioned in framing the principle 'never to assume anything empirical as unconditioned' (A616/B644).

Why should we proceed thus? Why should we make sense of things in *these* highly distinctive, totally unfounded ways? Well, as I remarked in the previous section, there is a sense, for Kant, in which we have no choice but to do so. This sense is profound where our own freedom is concerned. But our freedom carries with it certain demands: demands of rational action; demands, as Kant sees it, of morality. And he believes that, because of our imperfection, we cannot sustain a commitment to these demands without the aid of certain non-rational props. These include certain hopes. They include the hope that, imperfect as we are, we have scope to reform, and, as a corollary, that we enjoy an immortality that will enable us to work out our reformation. They also include the hope that virtue and happiness are somehow ultimately aligned, which in turn requires the hope that God, who alone is able to guarantee such an alignment, exists.[56] We need to make sense of things in these ways if we are to make real, practical sense of freedom itself, along with its various demands. We need to hope that the world is a *home* for such practical sense-making, that the world itself, to that extent, makes sense.[57]

It is precisely because we cherish these hopes, Kant suggests, that metaphysicians have such a keen interest in these issues (*Prolegomena*, §60). In the first *Critique* he proclaims:

All interest of my reason ... is united in the following three questions.

1. *What can I know?*
2. *What should I do?*
3. *What may I hope?*

(A804–805/B832–833, emphasis in original)

Bad, transcendent metaphysics is at root an attempt to provide reassurance concerning the third of these questions (*Prolegomena*, §60). But it is an attempt to do more than that. It is an attempt, ironically, to eliminate the very need for hope, by actually establishing the three propositions in question, the three postulates of pure practical reason. The urge not merely to protect these postulates, but to establish them, is an understandable reaction to the very real and very severe threats they face. These threats emanate most directly from natural science, especially in its Newtonian guise, whereby everything in nature seems to be governed by inexorable mechanical laws, laws that already preclude the hope that gives every other hope its rationale, namely that we are free. If we are not free, morality itself makes

---

[56] I am here condensing a vast and complex discussion: see esp. 'The Canon of Pure Reason' and 2nd *Critique*, passim, esp. Pt One, Bk II, Ch. 2. I treat these issues in greater depth in Moore (2003a), Themes Two and Three. For an outstanding discussion see Wood (1970).

[57] Cf. Engstrom (1996), p. 133.

no sense (A468/B496) and all the props that we use to sustain our commitment to morality are a sad mockery. Moreover, these threats are exacerbated
by Kant's own proof of the Causal Principle – as he is well aware.[58]

Kant is nevertheless able to sidestep these threats. By insisting that our
hopes concern how things are in themselves, and in particular that whether
we are free or not is a matter of how we are in ourselves, he can afford to be
insouciant both about the Causal Principle and about any of the findings of
natural science, whose domain is the physical world, the world of appearances
(Bxxvi–xxx).[59] The fact that our hopes cannot be established therefore begins
to look like a mixed curse. For, by precisely the same token, they cannot be
refuted either (A753/781). The form that Kant gives to the third of his questions – 'What *may* I hope?' – is thus entirely apt. Protection of our hopes is as
much as is available to us: it is also as much as we need. The whole complex
machinery that drives Kant's transcendental idealism, with its curbing of our
attempts to answer the great questions of metaphysics, in fact serves to keep
our most important hopes alive. 'I had to deny *knowledge*,' Kant famously
declares in the Preface to the second edition of the first *Critique*, 'in order
to make room for *faith*' (Bxxx, his emphasis).[60] Of all the great reconciling
projects undertaken both in the first *Critique* and elsewhere in Kant's work
(see §1), that between the demands of Christian morality and the demands of
Newtonian mechanics is the most important, the most profound, and the one
to which Kant is most ardently committed (A797–801/B825–829).[61]

---

[58] See nn. 45 and 53. The apparent conflict between the Causal Principle and our belief that
we are free is at the heart of the third antinomy.

[59] Thus Kant holds that one and the same situation can both exhibit complete (freedom-precluding) causal determination, as it appears, and involve an exercise of freedom, as it is in
itself (A532–558/B560–586 and *Groundwork*, 4:455ff.) The third antinomy arises because
we do not properly separate our idea of freedom from the concept of physical reality.

   Note: it is because the postulate that we are free concerns how we are in ourselves
that its truth cannot be inferred from the fact that we cannot help believing it. Contrast
this with the proposition that the straight line between two points is the shortest. In that
case such an inference is permitted. The fact that we cannot help believing such a thing
is due to what our spectacles are like; and our belief is a belief about how things (must)
appear through our spectacles; so what we believe must be true. This obviously bears on
Descartes' Reflective Question (see Ch. 1, §3). Kant's bipartite approach to this issue illustrates one of the many respects in which he resists easy classification as far as his attitude
to the Creativity Question in §6 of the Introduction is concerned. (Even in the case of the
postulate that we are free, he takes the fact that we cannot help believing it to mean that
we are 'really free in a practical respect' (*Groundwork*, 4: 448).)

[60] Kant defines faith as 'reason's moral way of thinking,' and as 'trust in the attainability of
an aim the promotion of which is a duty but the possibility of the realization of which it
is not possible for us to have any insight into' (3rd *Critique*, 5:471–472).

[61] In 2nd *Critique* Kant goes as far as to proclaim it a matter of great fortune that we cannot
prove God's existence. If we could, he says, 'God and eternity with their awful majesty
would stand unceasingly before our eyes.... Transgressions of the [moral] law would, no

8.   Thick Sense-Making and Thin Sense-Making

In this section I want to reflect on three interrelated questions that arise within Kant's system. What can we know about things in themselves? What can we think about things in themselves? What is the importance of this distinction for Kant's metaphysics? (The importance of the distinction for sustaining our commitment to the demands of our own freedom has been one of the main burdens of the previous section, and I shall take that as read.)

Concerning the question of what we can know about things in themselves, the answer is not nothing. Kant does not deny that we can have analytic knowledge about things in themselves (see e.g. A258–259/B314–315).[62] Hence he does not pick any quarrel with metaphysicians when they apply the laws of logic in their abortive attempts to engage in transcendent metaphysics, whatever other quarrels he might pick, and he himself makes free use of such laws, in application to the transcendent, when rebutting them (see e.g. A502/B530ff. and A571/B599ff.).[63]

It would make for an easy exegetical life if we could say that what Kant denies us is synthetic knowledge about things in themselves. And indeed I have already represented him in just these terms. But there is an issue about the very knowledge that there *are* things in themselves, which Kant seems to grant us, referring at one point to 'the absurd proposition that there is an appearance without anything that appears' (Bxxvi; cf. A696/B724 and *Prolegomena*, 4:350–351).[64] He also seems to grant us knowledge about some of the things

---

doubt, be avoided: what is commanded would be done; but ... [mostly] from fear, only [occasionally] from hope, and [never] at all from duty.... Now, when it is quite otherwise with us ... *then* there can be a truly moral disposition.... Thus what the study of nature and of the human being teaches us sufficiently elsewhere may well be true here also: that the inscrutable wisdom by which we exist is not less worthy of veneration in what it has denied us than in what it has granted us' (5:147–148, emphasis adapted). Cf. in this connection A831/B859.

[62] This is the knowledge to which I was referring in n. 13.

[63] It is true that the laws of logic that we recognize depend on the concepts we possess, which leaves room for the possibility of beings who, because they possess different concepts from ours, use different laws of logic from ours in thinking about things in themselves. But that is no threat to the applicability of *our* laws to things in themselves. 'Different' does not entail 'conflicting'. Cf. in this connection n. 40. And cf. the distinction between rejection and denial drawn below in the Conclusion, §3(b).

[64] Kant is adamant that any truth about what there is is synthetic: see e:g. A225/B272 and A594/B622ff.

Note: the view that the phrase 'things in themselves' should strictly be used only syncategorematically (see n. 36) perhaps mitigates this concern in the following respect: it makes our supposed knowledge that there are things in themselves less obviously knowledge about what there is (as opposed, say, to knowledge that how things appear is *only* how they appear). But the mitigation is limited. For the view in question does not make our

that things in themselves are *not*, notably spatial or temporal, or for that matter knowable (synthetically, by us). For instance, he writes that

- 'space represents no property at all of any things in themselves nor any relation of them to each other' (A26/B42)

that

- '[time] cannot be counted either as subsisting or inhering in the objects in themselves' (A36/B52)

and that

- 'objects in themselves are not known to us at all.' (A30/B45)

Are we not reckoned to know *these* things? Or has there perhaps been some tacit restriction, throughout all Kant's knowledge denials, to knowledge of some privileged and robust kind, knowledge which is not purely existential, say, and which is perhaps positive rather than negative, in some suitable sense of these two terms (cf. B307ff.)?[65] (After all, the restriction to synthetic knowledge is often tacit, as in the third bulleted quotation.) Or is it simply that we are beginning to witness cracks in Kant's edifice? I shall express my own pessimism on that score in the next section.

What, then, does Kant think that we can think about things in themselves? Plenty. (The postulates of pure practical reason are three examples.) This is part of Kant's view, which he proclaims on numerous occasions, that we can think far more than we can know (e.g. Bxxvi n., B146, B166 n., and A771–772/B799–800).[66] However, any thinking that we do about things in themselves must be of an extremely attenuated kind. It must involve us in exercising concepts without intuitions, and Kant famously declares that thoughts in which concepts are exercised without intuitions are 'empty' (A51/B75).[67] Elsewhere he is more forthright. He says of our *a priori* concepts that their 'extension ... beyond our sensible intuition does not get us anywhere' (B148, emphasis removed), that 'our sensible and empirical intuition alone can provide them with sense and significance' (B149, emphasis removed), and that they 'are of none but an empirical use, and ... have no

---

supposed knowledge less obviously knowledge of something synthetic – except insofar as it makes it less obviously knowledge.

[65] We may also need to add '... and which is theoretical rather than practical.' Cf. Bx; Bxxvi n.; 2nd *Critique*, 5:103; and 3rd *Critique*, 5:195.

[66] In Ch. 14, §2, we shall consider a profound recoil from this view.

[67] In the opening section of John McDowell (1996), McDowell comments on this passage as follows: 'For a thought to be empty ... would be for it not really to be a thought at all, and that is surely Kant's point; he is not, absurdly, drawing our attention to a special kind of thoughts, the empty ones' (pp. 3–4). But that is precisely what Kant is doing, or at least what he takes himself to be doing.

sense at all when they are not applied to objects of a possible experience, i.e. to the world of sense' (A696/B724; cf. A679/B707).[68]

One very important consequence of all of this is that whether Kant thinks that we can *make sense of* things in themselves depends on how exactly 'make sense of' is interpreted. On most interpretations, and certainly on any remotely robust epistemic interpretation, he does not think that we can make sense of them. But on an interpretation weak enough to allow for 'empty' thoughts, or to allow for the regulative use of concepts discussed in the previous section, he does think that we can make sense of them – as indeed he had better if his system is not to be a complete sham. In what follows I shall adopt the simplifying assumption that there is a core interpretation of what it is to make sense of something whereby Kant does not think we can make sense of things in themselves, which I shall call the 'thick' interpretation, and that there is a core interpretation whereby he does think we can, which I shall call the 'thin' interpretation. (This immediately raises a question about 'transcendental' sense-making and how it should be classified.[69] But let us not forget that any awkwardness attaching to this question may be an awkwardness, not for the simplifying assumption, but for Kant. We shall return to this issue in the next section.)

It is here that the metaphysical importance of Kant's distinction between what we can know about things in themselves and what we can think about them really lies. To see what this importance is, we must first reflect on the fact that Kant's project seems to involve drawing a limit to what we can make sense of. But that in turn can seem an incoherent enterprise. More specifically, it can seem self-stultifying. More specifically still, it can seem vulnerable to the following argument, which, because of its recurring significance to the rest of this enquiry, I shall give a name: I shall call it *the Limit Argument*.

First Premise: The Limit-Drawing Principle: We cannot properly draw a limit to what we can make sense of unless we can make sense of the limit.

Second Premise: The Division Principle: We cannot make sense of any limit unless we can make sense of what lies on both sides of it.

Conclusion: We cannot properly draw a limit to what we can make sense of.[70]

---

[68] See also A139/B178, A239/B298, A240–241/B300, B308, and *Prolegomena*, §30. (The reference to a 'relation to the object' at A241/B300 is especially telling.)

[69] See again the definition of 'transcendental' given in §4; and cf. n. 35.

[70] Perhaps the most famous version of this argument occurs in the Preface to Wittgenstein (1961), where Wittgenstein writes that 'in order to be able to draw a limit to thought, we should have to find both sides of the limit thinkable (i.e. we should have to be able to think what cannot be thought)' (p. 3); we shall return to this in Ch. 9, §4. Cf. also the

Granted the thick/thin distinction, however, Kant can respond to the Limit Argument as follows. He can accede to the suggestion that his project is a matter of drawing a limit to what we can make sense of *under the thick interpretation*, but he can deny that, under that interpretation, both the premises are true. For instance, he can insist that the Limit-Drawing Principle holds only under the thin interpretation of what it is to make sense of a limit: this gives him license to draw the limit that he wishes to draw without being able to make sense of it under the thick interpretation. Nor is there any reason to suppose that the Limit-Drawing Principle then connects in some other problematical way with the Division Principle. For instance, there is no reason to suppose that making sense of a limit under the thin interpretation requires making sense, under the thick interpretation, of what lies on its 'far' side. The threat of self-stultification is, apparently, averted.[71]

Kant himself has a wonderful analogy to illustrate his project. He likens what we can make sense of, under the thick interpretation, to a surface, which, like the surface of the earth, appears flat, so that, given our restricted acquaintance with it, we cannot know how far it extends, though we can know that it extends further than we have managed to travel: however, like the surface of the earth, it is in fact round, and once we have discovered this we can, even from our restricted acquaintance with it, determine both its extent and its limits (A758–762/B786–790). Here, of course, he relies on the important distinction between what we have in fact made sense of and what we can make sense of. He sometimes draws this distinction in terms of what he calls, in the original German, '*Schranken*' and '*Grenzen*' (translated in the Cambridge edition of his works respectively as 'limits' and 'boundaries' – though it is the latter that corresponds to what I have been calling 'limits').[72] The territory covered by what we have in fact made sense of, which is capable of extending over time into what it currently excludes, is marked by *Schranken*; the territory covered by what we can make sense of, which is of an altogether different kind from what it excludes, is marked by *Grenzen* (A767/B795 and *Prolegomena*, §57).[73]

---

problem to which I adverted in §6 of the Introduction about expressing the idea that our sense-making is limited to what is immanent. And cf., for something structurally analogous, the issue on which Philonous says '[he is] content to put the whole' of his dispute with Hylas in Berkeley (1962b), pp. 183–184.

[71] It is worth adding that, since the threat has to do with making sense of things in themselves, then the view that the phrase 'things in themselves' should strictly be used only syncategorematically (see nn. 36 and 64) may also play, as it did earlier, a mitigating role.

[72] The word translated as 'bounds' in the *aperçu* about philosophy from A727/B755 which I quoted in §6 is '*Grenzen*'. So too is the word translated as 'limits' in the passage from Wittgenstein (1961) which I quoted in n. 70.

[73] See also *Prolegomena*, 4:361, esp. the reference to what Kant calls 'the result of the entire *Critique*.'

But here too some cracks are perhaps beginning to appear. For we can legitimately refer to the limits of a globe only because we have access to a dimension other than the surface's own two. If we ourselves were two-dimensional beings on the surface, and had no access to any third dimension, then, while we might still acknowledge the surface's curvature and indeed its finitude, we would have no reason to think of it as having any *limits* (*Grenzen*) at all.[74] It is therefore a real question whether, in these glimpses of ours beyond the limit of our own thick sense-making – in this empty play of concepts of ours in which there is sense-making only of the very tenuous, thin kind – there is anything remotely like access to a third dimension of space. If not, then we may not have succeeded in making sense of this limit after all, not even under the thin interpretation, which calls into question whether there *is* any such limit, which in turn calls into question the very distinction between appearances and things in themselves.

9. Sense-Making That Is Neither Straightforwardly Thin nor Straightforwardly Thick

Since §4 we have been suspending our misgivings about the fundamental doctrines on which Kant's transcendental idealism rests. Even so, there is plenty, as we have just seen, to give pause. In this section I shall rehearse what seem to me to be, in the context of our enquiry, the most serious concerns about where those doctrines have led us.[75]

I note first that this whole exercise, that is to say the exercise of characterizing synthetic *a priori* knowledge and investigating the possibility, scope, and limits of metaphysics in the light of that characterization, has itself been an exercise in metaphysics. That is, it has itself been a maximally general attempt to make sense of things.[76] In Kant's work we find metaphysics in the service not only of science, ethics, and theology, but also of metaphysics.

---

[74] It is in this sense that contemporary physics allows for the finitude but unboundedness of physical space: see Einstein (1920), Ch. 31. Note: here and subsequently I am drawing on Moore (2010b). I am grateful to the editor and publisher of the volume in which that essay appears for permission to make use of material from it.

[75] We shall see Hegel raising related concerns in Ch. 7, §2.

[76] Here, of course, I am presupposing my own definition of metaphysics. But lest anyone think, *contra* my reassurances in n. 2, that Kant himself would not count this exercise as an exercise in metaphysics – that he would not count meta-metaphysics as part of metaphysics – I refer to the following three passages. First, just before the definition that I cited in n. 2, he expressly says that metaphysics, so defined, includes 'the critique', in other words it includes that part of philosophy 'which investigates the faculty of reason in regard to all pure *a priori* cognition' (A841/B869). Second, in *Prolegomena*, 4:327, he identifies 'the core and the characteristic feature of metaphysics' as 'the preoccupation of reason simply with itself.' Third, in (perhaps a draft of?) a letter to Marcus Herz, written

We can therefore ask of Kant a question which, in §5 of the previous chapter, looked as though it had the potential to embarrass Hume when asked of *him*: does his own work conform to the views advocated in it? Can Kant himself be seen as pursuing synthetic *a priori* knowledge about how things (must) appear, but not about how they are in themselves?[77]

There is a problem that threatens to arise here. It is a variation on the problem that we considered in the previous section. Both problems come together in the following question. Can Kant, when he draws a limit to our thick sense-making, do so from anywhere inside that limit, or must he do so from somewhere outside it?[78] The reply that I ventured in the previous section, on Kant's behalf, was that he must do so from somewhere outside it, but that he is exonerated by the fact that he may nevertheless do so from somewhere inside the limit of thin sense-making. (In effect, then, I was suggesting that transcendental sense-making is thin.) The concern about this reply was whether any exercise of thin sense-making can be equal to the task. That concern is now exacerbated by the thought that this task is itself a metaphysical task, whereas metaphysical sense-making, for Kant, must all be thick.[79]

We can approach the problem that threatens to arise here from a different angle by considering the very judgment that our metaphysical knowledge, like our mathematical knowledge, is synthetic and *a priori*. This must itself, presumably, count as an item of synthetic *a priori* knowledge. And yet, precisely in registering the non-analytic character of the knowledge in question, does it not also have some claim to being, at least to that extent, the very thing that an item of synthetic *a priori* knowledge supposedly cannot be, namely a judgment about things in themselves? For, arguably, there is nothing '*from the human standpoint*' (A26/B42, emphasis added)

after 11 May 1781, he says of the investigation in the first *Critique* that it includes 'the *metaphysics of metaphysics*' (*Correspondence*, 10:269, emphasis in original). (It is only fair for me to add that there is something rather different in *Prolegomena*, 4:260, which suggests that meta-metaphysics is a propaedeutic to metaphysics. Still, I do not claim complete constancy in Kant's conception of metaphysics.) I thus disagree with David Carr when he says, of the first *Critique*, 'That work is indeed *about* metaphysics, but it is not itself a work *of* metaphysics' (Carr (1999), p. 33, emphasis in original). (In fact, the 'Transcendental Analytic' is already a problem for Carr's claim: see §5 above.) I should add that there is much else in Ch. 2 of Carr (1999) that I admire.

[77] Cf. various currents in Strawson (1966), esp. Pt One, §4, and Pt Four.

[78] See Strawson (1966), p. 12. Cf. Wittgenstein (1961), 5.61.

[79] The point can also be put this way, in an adaptation of Kant's globe metaphor. One of the tasks of metaphysics is to map the round surface of metaphysical sense-making in such a way as to indicate not only what lies on the surface, but also, through the determination of the curvature of the surface, *how much* lies on it and what sort of thing lies *beyond* it. But metaphysics cannot indicate what sort of thing lies beyond that surface; precisely not.

to preclude our arriving at our metaphysical knowledge, or our mathematical knowledge, by means of pure conceptual analysis. *From the human standpoint* the various *a priori* conditions of our experience cannot be other than they are. Hence, from the human standpoint, these conditions cannot make a substantial contribution to any of our knowledge. That is to say, they cannot make the kind of contribution that they would not have made if they had been suitably other than they are, the kind that prevents the knowledge in question from answering merely to the concepts involved in it. (Thus even if we need to appeal to intuition to determine that the straight line between two points is the shortest, it is a real question what work this appeal to intuition does that is not likewise done by an appeal to intuition to determine, say, that black is darker than grey, a truth that Kant would presumably count as analytic.) In acknowledging that there *is* a substantial contribution made by the *a priori* conditions of our experience to some of our knowledge, which is what we are doing when we register the non-analytic character of the knowledge, must we not therefore already have taken a step back from the human standpoint? – as indeed Kant all but concedes when he writes:

> The proposition: 'All things are next to one another in space,' is valid under the limitation that these things be taken as objects of our sensible intuition. If I here add the condition to the concept and say 'All things, as outer appearances, are next to one another in space,' then this rule is valid universally and without limitation. (A27/B43)[80,81]

(And note that this concern is aggravated when the knowledge is metaphysical, rather than mathematical, by what we saw Kant argue in §5: that in metaphysics, unlike in mathematics, the appeal to intuition is an appeal to the mere possibility of our being given objects in intuition in the various ways we are, so that the knowledge is knowledge 'from concepts' (A713/B741).)

There is a similar awkwardness in Kant's handling of what he sometimes calls 'the sole fact of pure reason', which I take to be the fact that we can put pure reason to practical use in accord with the demands of our own freedom, as indicated in §7 (see e.g. 2nd *Critique*, 5:6, 31, 42, 43, 55, and 104, and 3rd *Critique*, 5:468). It is unsurprising that, among all the facts that Kant recognizes – where by a fact here is meant a contingency – this is the one that he is prepared to describe as the sole fact of pure reason. For what this fact is, on Kant's conception, is a fact about pure reason's purest

---

[80] I have taken the liberty of correcting Paul Guyer's and Allen W. Wood's translation here. The word that I have rendered 'appearances', which they render 'intuitions', is '*Erscheinungen*'.

[81] Cf. Walsh (1975), p. 253. For further very interesting material relating to this problem, see Bird (2006), Ch. 29, §2.

exercise, which is our freely placing demands of pure rational agency on ourselves and freely submitting to those demands. In effect, then, what Kant is prepared to describe as the sole fact of pure reason, in the sense of the sole fact accessible to pure reason, is something that he would also count as the sole fact of pure reason in another sense, the fact that *there is* such a thing as pure reason, capable of being exercised in the purest way, without the aid of any other faculty.[82] But this is a fact about how things are in themselves. It is more like the fact that we have spectacles than like any fact that can be ascertained by looking through those spectacles. There is therefore a certain tension for Kant in supposing it to be accessible to pure reason. In what way accessible? The tension is close to breaking point when Kant says that this fact 'forces itself upon us of itself as a synthetic *a priori* proposition that is not based on any intuition, either pure [i.e. *a priori*] or empirical' (2nd *Critique*, 5:31).[83]

True, there is nothing here that directly violates any of Kant's principles, provided that such 'forcing' does not issue in knowledge on our part, or, more strictly perhaps, provided that it does not issue in knowledge of the kind to which the discussion hitherto has been tacitly restricted (see the previous section). But in what then does it issue? We might say that it is a variation on the compulsion whereby we believe in our own free will. But let us not pretend that that compulsion is itself completely unmysterious. In all these cases, including the cases of supposed transcendental knowledge that Kant takes himself to propagate in the first *Critique*, Kant is accrediting us with sense-making of a singular kind. On the one hand it is synthetic and *a priori*, which means that we cannot regard it as straightforwardly thin. On the other hand it results from sensitivity to transcendent(al?) features of our own faculties for sense-making, which means that we cannot regard it as straightforwardly thick. The truth is, we do not in the end know how to regard it. We cannot make sense of it.[84]

10. The Unsatisfactoriness of Kant's Metaphysics

Kant's most general attempt to make sense of things is ultimately and profoundly unsatisfactory. In his self-conscious reflections on what it is to make sense of things, he achieves insights of unsurpassed brilliance and gives us greater help than anyone before or since in thinking about what we can and cannot aspire to when we practise metaphysics. But in his attempts

---

[82] Cf. how for Descartes intuition, which was a faculty for knowing metaphysical necessities, was also the faculty whereby he knew of his own contingent existence: see Ch. 1, n. 24. There is also a connection with the discussion at B157–159.

[83] For further discussion, see Beck (1960), Ch. 10; O'Neill (1989), esp. pp. 64–65; and Allison (1990), Ch. 13.

[84] Cf. *Groundwork*, 4:463.

to systematize these insights he appears to violate them and leaves us with something that does not itself, in the end, make sense.

It is as if, even by Kant's own lights, the only *real* sense that we can make of things is whatever sense we can make of them by looking through our spectacles, which means, in particular, that we cannot make real sense of the claim that the only real sense we can make of things is whatever sense we can make of them by looking through our spectacles. Transcendental idealism appears to foreclose its own acknowledgement. (This is illustrated by a characteristically stubborn propensity, on the part of various transcendental claims that Kant wants to make, to be interpreted in the wrong way. Thus, to revert to an example that I used in §4, there is a natural and compelling sense, which Kant is the first to recognize, in which the sun's being larger than the moon is quite independent of us. On the other hand, transcendental idealism requires us to recognize a sense in which it is not. In the first edition of the first *Critique* Kant tries to distinguish these senses by appeal to a deep ambiguity in the use of expressions such as 'independent of us': the sun's being larger than the moon is *empirically* independent of us, that is independent of us in terms of the sense we make of things when we look through our spectacles, but not *transcendentally* independent of us, that is not independent of us in terms of the sense we make of things when we reflect on the spectacles themselves (A373). In the later *Prolegomena* Kant laments the fact that, despite having drawn this distinction, he has been interpreted as denying the former independence (§13, Remark III). In other words, he has been interpreted as espousing what, in a slight deviation from Kant's own usage, is often called empirical idealism.[85] In the second edition of the first *Critique* many of Kant's bolder affirmations of transcendental idealism, along with these efforts to distance it from empirical idealism, are simply excised. It is as if he is engaged in an ongoing struggle to suppress the empirical interpretation of his transcendental claims and, in at least some crucial cases, eventually gives up.)

It is too soon to say where the fault lies. Perhaps Kant has not systematized his insights properly; perhaps they cannot be systematized; perhaps, indeed, they cannot be fully articulated.[86] However that may be, the important questions for us, as practising metaphysicians, are 'How should we react to this?', 'How might we use it?', not 'Do we accept it?' For we surely do not. We need some other way of rescuing the Humean baby.

[85] Kant himself uses the term 'empirical idealism' to designate a more Cartesian position whereby the empirical independence in question is merely called into question (*Prolegomena*, 4: 293, and A490–491/B518–519). He identifies Berkeley as the chief representative of the more extreme position, whereby the empirical independence in question is denied: see B70–71 and B274. Berkeley's position is encapsulated in Berkeley (1962a).

[86] Cf. my remarks on Spinoza's third kind of knowledge in Ch. 2, §6.

Appendix: Transcendental Idealism Broadly Construed

I said in §4 that transcendental idealism will play a crucial role in this narrative. But we shall encounter many different versions of it, sometimes only indirectly related to the specific doctrine about space and time that Kant espouses. I therefore need to give some indication of what I mean when I call a doctrine a version of transcendental idealism. That is the purpose of this brief appendix.

I follow Kant in distinguishing transcendental idealism from another kind of idealism, empirical idealism (see the material in parentheses in §10). And, concomitantly with recognizing versions of transcendental idealism that are only indirectly related to anything that Kant himself has in mind, so too I recognize versions of empirical idealism that are only indirectly related to anything that he has in mind. For my purposes, the crucial distinction between the two kinds of idealism with which Kant himself is concerned – the distinction that I wish to generalize – turns on the following question. Is the dependence of the world of our experience on our experience of it of a piece with, or does it utterly transcend, what we can know about that same world through experience?

To clarify: let s be a kind of sense-making. Then idealism with respect to s may for these purposes be defined as the view that certain essential features of whatever can be made sense of in accord with s depend on features of s itself. Empirical idealism, as I intend it, includes the rider that this dependence can itself be made sense of in accord with s. Transcendental idealism, as I intend it, includes the rider that it cannot.

CHAPTER 6

Fichte

Transcendentalism versus Naturalism

1. German Philosophy in the Immediate Aftermath of Kant

No sooner had Kant presented his critical philosophy[1] to the world, and the world begun to assimilate it, than there was a proliferation of what looked like transcendent metaphysics of the most egregious kind, far more excessive and far more extravagant than anything that either he or Hume had been trying to combat. Within four years of Kant's death Hegel had published a book in whose preface he gave the following outline of his conception of what he called 'the living substance'.

> [The] living substance is being which is in truth *subject*, or ... is ... actual only in so far as it is the movement of positing itself, or is the mediation of its self-othering with itself. This substance is, as subject, pure, *simple negativity*, and is for this very reason the bifurcation of the simple; it is the doubling which sets up opposition, and then again the negation of this indifferent diversity and of its antithesis.... Only this self-*restoring* sameness, or this reflection in otherness within itself ... is the true. It is the process of its own becoming, the circle that presupposes its end as its goal, having its end also as its beginning; and only by being worked out to its end, is it actual. (Hegel (1979), ¶18, emphasis in original, capitalization removed[2])

To an untrained eye this appears to be an unlovely mixture of obscurity, jargon, and barbarism, too far beyond the semantic pale even to admit of epistemic censure, though aspiring (insofar as one can tell) to be pretty far

---

[1] 'Critical philosophy' is a name that Kant himself gave to his system: see Kant (2002a), 4:383, and cf. Kant (1998), A855/B883.

[2] In removing the capitalization I am following G.A. Cohen, who writes, 'The capitals are translators' impertinences. German orthography requires that every noun be capitalized, not just names of grand entities ..., but ... names of very mundane entities, such as "fingernail" and "pig". German philosophers writing in German ... are unable to do what translators represent them as obsessionally doing' (Cohen (1978), p. 5, n. 1).

beyond the normal epistemic pale as well. We can readily imagine the alacrity with which Hume would have committed it to the flames, or the urgency with which Kant would have asked Hegel what he took himself to be doing with this bizarre mishmash of concepts and pseudo-concepts, this unruly concatenation of undistorted and distorted ideas of reason, in which little enough qualifies even for the title of 'empty' thought.

The situation would be altogether less remarkable if the philosophers who produced such material did so either in ignorance of Kant's work or in defiant reaction to it. But they were largely trying to appropriate it, or, if not to appropriate it, to reckon with it. German philosophy around the turn of the eighteenth and nineteenth centuries issued in a mass of metaphysical writing of the very sort just illustrated, whose authors were utterly self-conscious about their position after Kant in the evolution of modern metaphysics, knew that they had to situate their work in relation to his, and were deeply sensitive to his attack on what he saw as bad, transcendent metaphysics. Often they were trying to develop, apply, reorient, or modify his own system. This is true of Schelling, for example, who tried to salvage Kantian insights about the relation between what we can know through experience and what underlies our knowledge – between nature and freedom – while trying to overcome the Kantian opposition between these.[3] And it is true of Schopenhauer, who adopted a version of transcendental idealism in which the opposition remains but our knowledge extends to the latter, in the form of the will, a variation on Kant's own view that there is an experience-transcendent fact of pure reason which forces itself upon us, this fact being, more or less, the fact that we have free will.[4] But even those who were less beholden to Kant were sufficiently immersed in the philosophical milieu that he had created, and were sufficiently aware of the obstacles that he had placed in the way of non-critical metaphysics, for it to remain a puzzle that they could have produced material that would have been such an anathema to him.

A large part of the explanation lies in the internal tensions in Kant's own system which we witnessed towards the end of the previous chapter, whereby it is impossible to make sense, of the sort the system requires, about why the system requires sense of that sort. Many of Kant's successors took themselves to be following the dialectic beyond the point at which it showed the system to be inherently unstable to a point at which the system's instability was absorbed into some more powerful system. They were therefore neither simply rejecting what Kant had bequeathed to them nor simply accepting it, but rather trying to *work it out* (in several of the many senses of that phrase,

---

[3] Schelling (1993).

[4] Schopenhauer (1969a) and (1969b). (But 'variation of' is crucial here. Among the many fundamental differences between Kant and Schopenhauer, mention should be made of Schopenhauer's dissociation of the will from both freedom and rationality.)

including the sense in which they were trying to *make sense of* what Kant had bequeathed to them). It was not to be expected, then, that they would observe all its precepts.

In this chapter and the next we shall consider what are probably the two most significant examples of what I have in mind.[5]

2.   The Choice Between Transcendentalism and Naturalism

We start with J.G. Fichte (1762–1814). For Fichte the most general attempt to make sense of things begins with an essentially unprincipled choice between two paradigms. This choice is unprincipled in the sense that there is no neutral Archimedean point from which it can be made. Moreover, it is, from the very first, a practical exercise: a decision about how to proceed as much as reflection on what to think. And it remains a practical exercise inasmuch as it requires a sustained commitment to the choice made.

The two paradigms are themselves systems of thought, whose main lineaments can be depicted, as we shall see shortly, in Kantian terms. To be committed to either is to be prepared, among other things, to engage in theoretical reflection of the highly general sort that we have seen exemplified in Kant and in all our other protagonists so far. Even so, there is a subordination of the theoretical to the practical here.[6]

This subordination is by no means unprecedented. We have glimpsed something of the sort several times already.[7] Most significantly, there is in Kant a clear and explicit insistence on the primacy of practical reason over theoretical reason (Kant (1996c), Pt One, Bk Two, Ch. II, §III). Kant held that pure reason can be put to practical use. But he also held that, in order for pure reason to be put to practical use *by us*, imperfect as we are, we need to place our trust in certain propositions that outstrip anything that we can establish by a theoretical use of reason (see §7 of the previous chapter). By the primacy of practical reason over theoretical reason Kant meant the

---

[5] For two outstanding overviews of German philosophy in the immediate aftermath of Kant, see Copleston (1963), Ch. 1, and Gardner (1999), pp. 331–341. On p. 341 of the latter, Sebastian Gardner emphasizes another part of the impetus to supersede Kant: not just to overcome the instability in his system but to answer questions that it leaves open, e.g. about the nature of freedom and about why we have the *a priori* intuitions and *a priori* concepts that we have.

[6] Cf. *Vocation*, pp. 88–89; and see further §4.

  Note: throughout this chapter I use the following abbreviations for Fichte's works: *Foundations* for Fichte (1992); *Gesamtausgabe* for Fichte (1964–); *Vocation* for Fichte (1956); and *Wissenschaftslehre* for Fichte (1982). All unaccompanied references are to *Wissenschaftslehre*, and they are given in the form of the pagination in the edition by I.H. Fichte as indicated in the margin of that work.

[7] See e.g. Ch. 1, n. 7; Ch. 2, §6; and the comments about concept creation in Ch. 4, §5.

obligation of theoretical reason to sanction our accepting these propositions, even though there is no theoretical rationale for our doing so. Fichte
then extends this same principle to the basic metaphysical presuppositions
that determine how pure reason is to be put to theoretical use in the first
place. Eventually, this will lead to a new conception of how the theoretical
and the practical are united.

What is the choice between? Roughly, something broadly Kantian and
something which, in the metaphor of the previous chapter, ejects both baby
and bathwater, in other words something which eschews substantive *a priori* metaphysics altogether. A little less roughly, we can either accede to some
variation on Kant's system, and acknowledge a knowing willing subject with
spectacles that variously structure what it knows and regulate what it wills,
or revert to something more akin to what we saw in each of Spinoza and
Hume, and deny that there is any such transcendental conditioning of our
engagement with the world, a world that we know and manipulate simply
by being a part of it. On the first, Kantian alternative, what we are given in
experience are appearances of things, and our making maximally general
sense of these, which we do by reflecting on our spectacles, is a different
kind of exercise from our making the more particular sense of them that
is characteristic of the natural sciences, which we do by looking through
our spectacles. On the second, non-Kantian alternative, what we are given
in experience are things as they are in themselves, and our making maximally general sense of these differs only in degree from our making such
more particular scientific sense of them. On the first alternative objectivity is
grounded in subjectivity: the knowable world has a transcendental structure
determined by the knowing subject, and it (the knowable world) extends
no further than what the subject can be given in experience. On the second
alternative subjectivity is grounded in objectivity: the knowing subject is
itself part of the knowable world. Yet still the knowable world extends no
further than what the subject can be given in experience. Precisely what is
precluded, on both alternatives, is experience-transcendent knowledge. To
think that such a thing is possible is to allow objectivity and subjectivity to
be out of joint with each other. It is, in the recurring metaphor, to retain the
bathwater. That is an option that Descartes took. But it is an option which,
in Fichte's view, Kant's critical philosophy has rendered no longer available to us.

Fichte himself presents the choice as follows:

> A finite rational being has nothing beyond experience; it is this that com-
> prises the entire staple of his thought. The philosopher is in the same
> position....[8]

---

[8] This is in effect the rejection of the third, Cartesian option.

But he is able to abstract.... *The thing*, which must be determined independently of our freedom and to which our knowledge must conform, and *the intelligence*, which must know, are in experience inseparably connected. The philosopher can leave one of the two out of consideration.... If he leaves out the former, he retains an intelligence in itself ... as a basis for explaining experience; if he leaves out the latter, he retains a thing-in-itself ... as a similar basis of explanation. The first method of procedure is called *idealism*, the second *dogmatism*. (I, 425–426, emphasis in original)

Fichte also sometimes calls the first alternative 'the critical system', and the second alternative 'materialism'. I shall add to the nomenclature by sometimes calling the first alternative 'transcendentalism', and the second 'naturalism'.

I choose the label 'transcendentalism' to highlight what Fichte himself highlights with his term 'critical', namely that the first alternative is not just *any* idealism, but a specifically Kantian idealism,[9] whereby 'the intelligence' and 'the thing', the knowing willing subject and the object with which it engages, are on two fundamentally different levels: the subject does not and cannot know either itself or its relation to the object in the same way as it can and does know the object.[10] (This counts as a version of transcendental idealism by the lights of the Appendix to the previous chapter: the object's dependence on the subject cannot be known in the same way as the object itself is known.)

I choose the label 'naturalism' for two reasons. The first is to highlight that 'the thing' to which the second alternative reduces all that we can make sense of is that which we make sense of in the natural sciences.[11] The second reason is to highlight connections with views that we shall consider later.[12] There is also the point that the original term 'dogmatism' is not entirely neutral. It is a term that Fichte borrows from Kant, in however extended a sense,[13] and it is arguably an appropriate term to use in this context only from the standpoint of the first alternative.[14]

---

[9] At I, 438, he remarks that Berkeley's system, which is a paradigm of idealism, is dogmatic.

[10] In Fichte's variation, as we shall see in the next section, the subject is said to be an 'act' rather than an object.

[11] Cf. Martin (1997), Ch. 2, §3, esp. pp. 41–42.

[12] See esp. Ch. 12 on Quine. (But see also the important qualification in n. 5 of that chapter.)

[13] See e.g. Kant (1998), Bxxxv.

[14] 'Arguably', because there are some anti-Kantian writers of the time who cheerfully apply the term (in a more or less Kantian sense) to themselves: cf. the quotation by J.A. Eberhard, from *Philosophisches Magazin*, Vol. 1, which Kant gives in Kant (2002b), 8:187.

That Fichte does often represent the dialectic from the standpoint of the
first alternative is strikingly illustrated by some remarks that he makes concerning Spinoza. As I emphasized in Chapter 2, Spinoza is a champion of the
immanent. But from the standpoint of transcendentalism he has no title to
that claim. From that standpoint, to cast the knowing subject as a mere part
of the knowable world is, if not to eliminate the knowing subject altogether,
then to cast the knowable world at large as essentially independent of it and
ipso facto transcendent. 'In the critical system,' Fichte explains,

> a thing is what is posited in the self; in the dogmatic, it is that wherein the
> self is itself posited: critical philosophy is thus *immanent*, since it posits
> everything in the self; dogmatism is *transcendent*, since it goes beyond the
> self. So far as dogmatism can be consistent, Spinozism is its most logical
> outcome. (I, 120, emphasis in original)

Such bias is very revealing.

The truth is, although Fichte talks in terms of a basic choice here, he
takes only one of the two alternatives to be viable. He sees no way of making naturalistic sense of the knowing willing subject. Fichte takes naturalism
to include what I dubbed in the previous chapter the Causal Principle, the
principle that whatever happens in nature has a cause (*Vocation*, pp. 8–10).
And it is in terms of that principle, Fichte argues, that naturalism 'wishes to
explain [the] constitution of intellect' (I, 436). But this is a task to which he
thinks the principle is quite inadequate.

Why?[15] Suppose we grant Fichte both of these things: that naturalism
includes the Causal Principle and that it seeks to explain the constitution of
intellect in terms of that principle (neither of which is unassailable – unless
simply and unhelpfully written into the very definition of naturalism). Even
so, what prevents it from succeeding? Is Fichte perhaps assuming, with what
the naturalist might regard as undue deference to Kant, that the only causal
laws that naturalism can acknowledge are causal laws of a mechanical kind
that preclude any free rational agency?

Certainly, freedom and rationality are crucial to Fichte's understanding
of this issue. But it is not really a question of what sort of causal laws
are involved. Whether naturalism acknowledges only causal laws that
are mechanical or allows also for beings that 'govern themselves on their
own account and in accordance with the laws of their own nature' (I, 437,
adapted from singular to plural), whether it acknowledges only causal laws
that are highly general or allows also for local laws whose instances can
appear random, whether it sees causal laws as being of a robust Kantian

---

[15] In raising the question 'Why?', I do not mean to impugn the original point that the choice
between the two alternatives is unprincipled. Even on Fichte's own conception there is
nothing in what follows with the suasive power to shift the naturalist. We shall come back
to this point, and its significance, in §4.

kind or of a more anaemic Humean kind, it can never, in Fichte's view, do justice to that primordial exercise of 'absolute, independent self-activity' (*Vocation*, p. 84) which constitutes the subject's freedom and rationality and which is what allows the subject to be presented with objects in such a way that they become objects *for it*. He writes:

> From this absolute spontaneity alone there arises the consciousness of the self. – Not by any law of nature, nor by any consequence of such laws, do we attain to reason; we achieve it by absolute freedom.... – In philosophy, therefore, we must necessarily start from the self.... [The] materialists' project, of deriving the appearance of reason from natural laws, remains forever incapable of achievement. (I, 298; cf. I, 494–495)

But what entitles us to take for granted that we are free and rational in the relevant sense, or even that we have such 'consciousness of the self'? Perhaps these are illusions, just as Spinoza took them to be.[16]

Fichte's response to this objection indicates once again the radical extent to which this whole exercise is, for him, a practical exercise. Just as Kant held that we cannot act 'except under the idea of freedom' (see §6 of the previous chapter), so too Fichte holds that we have no choice, ultimately, but to take for granted our own freedom, our own rationality, and our own selfhood (in the relevant senses). I said earlier that, for Fichte, only the first alternative is viable. That literally means that only the first alternative can live. I might also have said that only the first alternative can properly *be lived*.[17] 'Nothing is more insupportable to me,' insists Fichte, 'than to exist merely by another, for another, and through another' (*Vocation*, p. 84). '*Spinoza*,' he further insists, '... could only *think* his philosophy, not *believe* it, for it stood in the most immediate contradiction to his necessary conviction in daily life, whereby he was bound to regard himself as free and independent' (I, 513, emphasis in original).

Very well; suppose we grant Fichte the unliveability of the second alternative. Now there is a new concern. Why should the first alternative take the form of a Kantian idealism? Kant's own reasons for accepting such an idealism were complex. They involved the synthetic *a priori* character of our knowledge and the inability of pure reason to address certain metaphysical questions without lapsing into contradiction. Does Fichte believe that some

---

[16] Cf. *Vocation*, pp. 18–20. Note that 'in the relevant sense' is an important qualification, since, as we saw in Ch. 2, §3, Spinoza distinguished between what he called 'free will', which he did not believe in, and what he called 'freedom', which he did. Fichte is concerned with something more like the former.

[17] Cf. I, 434, where he says that 'a philosophical system is not a dead piece of furniture that we can reject or accept as we wish; it is rather a thing animated by the soul of the person who holds it.'

version of transcendental idealism can be derived merely from 'consciousness of the self'?

In a way he does. Taking 'the intelligence' as a basic datum, and, more to the point, as the only basic datum, Fichte sees the primary metaphysical task as being to explain our experience and knowledge of other things within that framework. 'The immediate consciousness of myself,' he writes, 'is ... the ... condition of all other consciousness; and I know a thing only in so far as I know that I know it; no element can enter into the latter cognition which is not contained in the former' (*Vocation*, p. 37, transposed from the second person to the first person).[18] But since this involves a fundamental contrast between the immediacy with which the self is known and the mediacy, within the framework of such self-knowledge, with which other things are known, precisely what it is is a kind of transcendental idealism.

There is one particularly interesting illustration of the dialectic here when Fichte, finding himself unable to doubt the Causal Principle (which is not a prerogative of naturalism), concludes that it must be an item of knowledge that derives from his own prescription of 'laws to being and its relations' (*Vocation*, pp. 54–55). In effect, then, he argues from a kind of transcendental idealism to the existence of synthetic *a priori* knowledge, where Kant, of course, argued in the other direction.[19]

The important point, however, is that Fichte adopts a system that is at root thoroughly Kantian. The urgent question, for us, is how this system assumes, in Fichte's hands, a form that seems in so many respects so un-Kantian.

---

[18] Cf. Kant (1998), A129, where Kant writes that 'all objects with which we can occupy ourselves are all in me, i.e., determinations of my identical self.' Cf. also the opening section of Schopenhauer (1969a), in which Schopenhauer identifies as the most certain truth that 'everything that exists for knowledge, and hence the whole of this world, is only object in relation to the subject, perception of the perceiver, in a word, representation' (p. 3).

[19] Not that this more direct route to transcendental idealism is entirely foreign to Kant. Consider the following notable passage from Kant (1996b): 'No subtle reflection is required to make the following remark ...: that all representations which come to us involuntarily (as do those of the senses) enable us to cognize objects only as they affect us and we remain ignorant of what they may be in themselves.... Even as to himself, the human being cannot claim to cognize what he is in himself through the cognizance he has by inner sensation.... [But] a human being ... finds in himself a capacity by which he distinguishes himself from all other things, ... and that is *reason*.... [This indicates] a spontaneity so pure that it thereby goes far beyond anything that sensibility can ever afford it.... Because of this a rational being must regard himself *as intelligence* ... as belonging not to the world of sense but to the world of understanding' (4:450–452, emphasis in original).

3. Fichte's System I: The Subject's Intuition of Itself

The system seems un-Kantian inasmuch as it seems a prime instance of the discredited third option. In Fichte's developed system there is an infinite self, whose infinite activity involves, first, the positing of itself; second, the positing of a finite field of activity distinct from itself in which it is to act; and third, the positing of a finite self set over against and in opposition to this non-self.[20] Be the detailed interpretation of this as it may, it looks like just the sort of transcendent metaphysics that Kant was trying to combat.

In a way the appearances are very misleading. In a way they are not at all misleading.

Before we disentangle these, it will be helpful to reconsider the tensions within Kant's own system that we considered in the previous chapter. These showed Kant, willy-nilly, having to acknowledge some basic substantive truths about things in themselves, truths concerning the knowing willing subject and its spectacles: for instance, that the spectacles make an extra-conceptual contribution to some of the subject's *a priori* knowledge, so that the knowledge counts as synthetic, and that the subject can put pure reason to practical use in accord with the demands of freedom, what Kant called 'the sole fact of pure reason'. There is also of course the very fact that the subject exists. Not only did Kant have to acknowledge this fact; he also had to acknowledge its immediate accessibility to each of us. For it is something of which each of us is directly aware through self-consciousness. Kant felt the tension. In his *Critique of Practical Reason* he conceded that the subject is 'conscious of himself as a thing in itself' (Kant (1996c), 5:97). In his *Critique of Pure Reason* he tried to forestall the threat that this posed to his system, and in particular to his principle that there can be no substantive knowledge of things in themselves, by denying that such self-consciousness involved any intuition of the self, or, therefore, that it delivered substantive knowledge of the self. He wrote, 'I am conscious of myself not as I appear to myself, nor *as* I am in myself, but only *that* I am. This *representation* is a *thinking*, not an *intuiting*' (Kant (1998), B157, emphasis in original).[21] And later in the same work he gave the following succinct explanation for why he had been forced to say this:

> It would be ... the only stumbling block to our entire critique, if it were possible to prove *a priori* that all thinking beings are in themselves

---

[20] There is no *locus classicus* for this. The development occupies pretty much the whole of *Wissenschaftslehre*. I shall have more to say about it in the next section. We shall see in particular that the term 'posit' has to be interpreted in a very distinctive way.

[21] Note that Kant did not deny that I have an intuition of myself in the sense of an intuition of my body: see the rest of the paragraph (esp. the footnote) from which the passage just quoted is taken.

thinking substances, ... *and that they are conscious of their existence as detached from all matter.* For in this way we would have taken a step beyond the sensible world, entering into the field of [things in themselves]. (B409, emphasis added)[22]

The problem is that our self-consciousness, like our awareness of the sole fact of pure reason, seems to be too 'thick' to be dismissed as mere empty thinking, or thinking in which concepts are exercised without intuitions – just as, by Kant's enforced reckoning, it is too 'thin' to merit the title of substantive knowledge.[23] Kant was again accrediting us with a distinctive mode of access to things in themselves which, by his very own lights, makes no real sense to us (see §9 of the previous chapter).

Fichte's reaction to this problem is, in effect, simply to concede that there is self-consciousness (of a sort) which delivers substantive knowledge (of a sort) concerning an ultimate feature of reality.[24] There *is* an intuition of the self, as it is in itself. This intuition provides the very framework for transcendentalism.

That already looks distinctly un-Kantian. But Fichte goes further. He characterizes this intuition as an 'intellectual' intuition. Kant repeatedly insisted that no such thing was available to finite creatures such as us.

By an 'intellectual' intuition Kant meant an intuition such as we might attribute to God, an intuition which does not consist in the passive reception of objects, but consists rather in the active creation of them, and which, even without the aid of concepts to think about its objects, already constitutes knowledge of them.[25] Fichte likewise insists that 'my immediate consciousness that I act,' which is what he is happy to characterize as my intellectual intuition, 'is that whereby I know something because I do it' (I, 463). And he assimilates this to my consciousness of the demands of morality, which dictate how I *ought* to act, thereby further calling to mind Kant's sole fact of pure reason, to which Kant himself, however, denied us any kind of intuitive access. Already, then, we can see important respects in which there is, genuinely, a departure from Kant.

[22] The original has 'noumena' where I have inserted 'things in themselves'. But I do not think that I have done violence to Kant's intentions. See further ibid., B410; and for the relation between noumena and things in themselves see ibid., B306–307.
[23] See §§8 and 9 of the previous chapter for clarification of the 'thick'/'thin' distinction.
[24] The first parenthetical qualification is intended to accommodate the fact that Fichte also sometimes uses the term 'self-consciousness' to refer to a mediated knowledge of the self, more akin to what Kant would call knowledge of the self as it appears; see e.g. I, 277. The second parenthetical qualification is included for reasons that should become clear in due course.
[25] Kant (1998), B71–72. Cf. also ibid., B145, where he talks in terms of 'an understanding that itself intuits'; and Kant (2000), §§76 and 77, where he talks in terms of an 'intuitive understanding' (5:406) and an 'intuitive intellect' (5:409).

But this requires immediate qualification. Fichte, who is adamant that he is being true to the spirit of Kant's critical philosophy if not to the letter of it (e.g. I, 420), insists that his own use of the expression 'intellectual intuition' is different from Kant's. As he explains:

> in the Kantian terminology, all intuition is directed to existence of some kind …; intellectual intuition would thus be the immediate consciousness of a nonsensuous entity; the immediate consciousness of the thing-in-itself…. The intellectual intuition alluded to in [my system] refers, not to existence at all, but rather to action, and simply finds no mention in Kant…. Yet it is nonetheless possible to point out also in the Kantian system the precise point at which it should have been mentioned. Since Kant, we have all heard, surely, of the categorical imperative [i.e. the fundamental precept of all morality]? Now what sort of consciousness is that? … [It] is undoubtedly immediate, but not sensory; hence it is precisely what I call 'intellectual intuition'. (I, 471–472)

Fichte is therefore talking about the subject's consciousness of the principles that direct it in its own purest, primordial agency. That is, he is talking about the subject's consciousness of the conditions of its very essence. For the subject is not to be thought of as an 'object' at all. It is, as Fichte elsewhere puts it, 'an act' rather than 'something subsistent' (I, 440; cf. the rest of 'First Introduction to the Science of Knowledge', §7). Its intellectual intuition is creative, just as Kant took intellectual intuition to be, but it does not create objects. Rather, it creates the conditions for its very own creativity. It creates itself.[26]

Kant was worried that, if we are allowed to accredit the subject with knowledge of itself, as it is in itself, then

> no one could deny that we are entitled to extend ourselves further into [the field of things in themselves], settle in it, and … take possession of it. For … synthetic propositions *a priori* would not … be feasible and accessible merely in relation to objects of possible experience …, but rather they could reach as far as things in general and in themselves, which consequence would put an end to this whole critique and would bid us leave things the same old way they were before. (Kant (1998), B410)

Fichte sees no such danger. Once we have accredited the subject with this highly distinctive knowledge of its own essence, this practical knowledge concerning what it is to act, there is neither need nor possibility to invoke any things in themselves beyond that: no need, because transcendentalism provides for an explanation of the subject's knowledge of other objects within the framework of that distinctive self-knowledge; no possibility,

---

[26] Cf. I, 459.

because transcendentalism precludes reference to anything beyond the subject ('Second Introduction to the Science of Knowledge', §6).

Concerning the first of these, the dispensability of things in themselves beyond the subject, I shall say some more in the next section. Concerning the second, the unavailability of things in themselves beyond the subject, note that Fichte sometimes defends it by appeal to a variation of the Limit Argument, which we considered in §8 of the previous chapter, the argument for the incoherence of our drawing a limit to what we can make sense of. In Fichte's variation, for the subject to be able to 'make sense of' something is simply for the subject to be capable of thought in which that thing occurs, which is in turn for that thing not to transcend the subject, in one sense of the word 'transcend'; and the conclusion of the argument is that there is no such limit to be drawn, hence that nothing does in that sense transcend the subject.[27] In the terminology of §8 of the previous chapter, this is a particularly 'thin' interpretation of sense-making under which, for all that was said there, the argument may succeed.[28] Here is one formulation of it:

> Of any connection *beyond the limits of my consciousness* I cannot speak; … for even in speaking of it, I must … think of it; and this is precisely the same connection which occurs in my ordinary natural consciousness, and no other. I cannot proceed a hair's breadth beyond this consciousness, any more than I can spring out of myself. All attempts to conceive of an absolute connection between things *in themselves* and the I *in itself* are but attempts to ignore our own thought, a strange forgetfulness of the undeniable fact that we can have no thought without having thought it. (*Vocation*, p. 74, emphasis in original)

Here is another:

> [We must be] rid of the thing-in-itself; for … whatever we may think, we are that which thinks therein, and hence … nothing could ever come to exist independently of us, for everything is necessarily related to our thinking. (I, 501)

This feature of Fichte's metaphysics may be its best known. It is often portrayed as an anti-Kantian repudiation of the very idea of a thing in itself. Fichte, for reasons that we have glimpsed, does not see it as anti-Kantian at

---

[27] This trivially answers the Transcendence Question from §6 of the Introduction.

[28] Elsewhere Fichte adverts to a thicker interpretation under which he himself hints that the argument fails, specifically in its second premise: the Division Principle. He writes, 'Reason is enclosed within a necessary circle. I cannot go outside of my reason and still philosophize. I can, in turn, philosophize over this fact, but again, precisely in accordance with the laws of reason, and so on. Reason limits itself' (*Vorlesungen über Logik und Metaphysik*, in *Gesamtausgabe*, Series I, Vol. 3, p. 247, trans. in Breazeale (1994), p. 49).

all. But he does cast it as a repudiation of the very idea of a thing in itself, which he elsewhere describes as 'the uttermost perversion of reason, and a concept perfectly absurd' (I, 472). This is less bizarre than it looks. The argument above rests on such a thin interpretation of sense-making, and thereby places such exigent demands on the notion of a thing in itself, that Kant need have no quarrel with it, except possibly a terminological quarrel. Kant's own idea of a thing in itself was far less exorbitant than Fichte's. What Kant called 'things in themselves' were not beyond the reach of thin sense-making, certainly not sense-making as thin as this. If we adopt a more Kantian way of speaking, and if we recall how little Kant himself was prepared to venture about things in themselves, then we shall surely want to describe Fichte, not as repudiating the very idea of a thing in itself, but rather as giving one particular minimalist account of how things in themselves are. It is an account in which the subject (or subjects) is (or are) the only ultimate reality.

What *now* of the appearance of a departure from Kant? Well, such a minimalist account of how things in themselves are, at least as far as its minimalism goes, is not obviously incompatible with anything in Kant. But that is a matter of its content. There is also the matter of the confidence that we are being invited to place in it. Kant could surely not have tolerated that. Such confidence would be an entitlement only to those who could take their spectacles off. So the real departure from Kant now appears to be just what it initially appeared to be: not a recoil from the notion of things in themselves, but, on the contrary, a professed insight into them.

4.   Fichte's System II: Conditions of the Subject's Intuition of Itself. The System's Self-Vindication

This is not *per se* an objection to Fichte's system. Perhaps Kant was wrong to deny us any such insight into things in themselves, as some of his own struggles with that denial have already suggested. But still, what are the prospects for a Fichtean minimalism, for providing a satisfactory explanation of the subject's knowledge of objects without appeal to any things in themselves beyond the subject?

We cannot hope to address this question without some further reflection on what counts as 'the subject'. For even if the subject's knowledge of objects is not a result of its being given that which is independent of it, there does seem to be a passive element in the knowledge which suggests that, at the very least, the subject is given (does not create) that which is *different* from it – as it may be, some part of itself, some feature of itself, some aspect of itself – such as happens when I literally look through my spectacles at my own hand. But what then *makes* what it is given a part of itself, a feature of itself, or an aspect of itself? Is Fichte simply relying once again on his own

extreme conception of independence whereby the sheer fact that the subject
is given something means that that thing is not independent of it? Or is he
perhaps advocating that the subject is creative in its knowledge of objects,
and is not thereby given anything?

Fichte's system is an attempt, in part, to address and clarify just such
questions. He entitles his system '*Wissenschaftslehre*'. This is a term that is
variously translated as 'science of knowledge', 'theory of knowledge', 'theory of scientific knowledge', 'theory of science', and 'science of science'. The
last of these is in several respects the most appropriate.[29] It signals how,
yet again in this drama of ours, we are dealing with something reflexive.
Fichte is offering us an account of our knowledge which is meant to apply,
in particular, to the very knowledge with which it is meant to furnish us. He
is trying to make sense, at the highest level of generality, of how we make
sense of things, including how we make sense of things at that level of generality.[30] From that point of view we do well to remind ourselves that this
whole exercise is supposed to be a fundamentally practical exercise. That
whereof Fichte is offering us an account must also therefore be, to a significant extent, practical. Seen in this light, both his questions and his answers
assume a new significance.

At the very beginning of the previous section I provided a sketch of
Fichte's system. That sketch gave it the appearance of a wild metaphysical
yarn in which the subject, enjoying a kind of infinitude, does indeed create
all the objects of its knowledge – though only having first created itself, and
prior to creating a second, finite version of itself. This appearance was later
reinforced when I spoke of the subject's intellectual intuition as self-creative.
In fact the appearance is grossly misleading. But it can soon be dispelled. The
verb I applied to the subject was 'posit', not 'create', 'posit' being the standard English translation of '*setzen*', and any connotations that positing has
of creation, a notion that I used in connection with the subject's intellectual
intuition but not in connection with the subject itself, are to be dismissed.

Each person's starting point is himself, as a knowing willing subject, confronted with a practical choice about how to affirm himself, both in his
dealings with the world and in his thinking about the world: whether to
take seriously that starting point, and to accept himself as a free agent with
respect to whose free agency all other questions arise, or to regard himself

---

[29] The first is in several respects the least appropriate. That is why I have stuck with the term
'*Wissenschaftslehre*' as my abbreviation for Fichte (1982), though its English title is '*The
Science of Knowledge*'.

[30] This reflexivity is a focus of both Breazeale (1994) and Rockmore (1994). Cf. also
Foundations, p. 89, where Fichte writes, 'The question concerning the possibility of
philosophy is ... itself a philosophical question. Philosophy provides an answer to the
question concerning its own possibility.' (On the next page he identifies philosophy with
metaphysics.)

as a mere part of nature, buffeted along in accord with freedom-precluding mechanical laws. It is a choice that ultimately disappears, since only the first alternative is genuinely liveable. The second is a pretence. But living that first alternative, in good faith, does involve infinitude of sorts. For the freedom in question, together with the person's commitment to it, is a kind of unconditionedness. It is a freedom from limitations. The person does posit himself, or, in the impersonal formulation that I have been using, the subject posits itself, but this self-positing is to be understood as *self-assertion* or *self-expression*, not self-creation. Where there *is* an element of self-creation is in the person's exercise of his unconditioned freedom, to adopt laws – conditions – for the proper exercise of that freedom. The person's intellectual intuition of himself is his knowing how to act in accord with those freely adopted laws, thus how properly to act, in fact how properly to *be*. For what the person most quintessentially *is* is an agent, or, as Fichte also sometimes goes as far as to say (see the previous section), an act. And as for what it is for him properly to act or properly to be – just as in Kant, that is the same as for him to act morally, or to be dutiful.

None of this makes sense, however, without some field of activity in which to act. There has to be something distinct from the person, constraining him in various ways, presenting him with real concrete choices about how to exercise his freedom.[31] Here is Fichte:

> Our consciousness of a reality external to ourselves is ... not rooted in the operation of supposed external objects, which indeed exist for us ... only in so far as we already know of them; nor is it an empty vision evoked by our own imagination and thought ...; it is rather the necessary faith in our own freedom of power, in our own real activity, and in the definite laws of human action, which lies at the root of all our consciousness of a reality external to ourselves.... We are compelled to believe that we act, and that we ought to act in a certain manner. We are compelled to assume a certain sphere for this action: this sphere is the real, actually present world, such as we find it – and the world is absolutely nothing more than this sphere, and cannot in any way extend beyond it.... We act not because we know, but we know because we are called upon to act. (*Vocation*, p. 98)

The person accordingly posits a distinct reality. But, as before, this is not to be thought of as an act of creation. To say that the person posits a distinct reality, having posited himself, is in a sense merely to say that the person's

---

[31] Here an observation of Bernard Williams is relevant: 'We may think sometimes ... that in a happier world [such constraining] would not be [a] necessary [condition of an agent's being some particular person, of living *a* life at all]. But that is a fantasy (indeed it is *the* fantasy)' (Williams (2006o), p. 57, emphasis in original). Note: included in that which constrains the person in various ways are, crucially, other people.

acknowledging a distinct reality is an indispensable part of his positing (asserting, expressing) himself.

Likewise indeed where the third positing is concerned. A necessary condition of the person's acknowledging a distinct reality which constrains him in various ways is that he should acknowledge that he himself is distinct from something by which he is thus constrained, and is therefore finite. Thus, as well as possessing infinitude in his freedom, indeed as a condition of possessing infinitude in his freedom, he must also possess, and must recognize that he possesses, finitude in other respects. His practical use of reason, in the exercise of his infinite freedom, becomes an effort to impose his will on a resistant, recalcitrant world which he must learn to negotiate, in particular by investigating its contours through a theoretical use of reason.[32]

I have already remarked on the reflexivity in the execution of this project. There is also an important reflexivity in its outcome. Though the original espousal of transcendentalism is based on an unprincipled choice, anyone who has made this choice, and who has thought through its implications, can see it as the right choice. In particular, he can see it as the only choice that involves his properly confronting the demands of his own freedom, by doing his duty. 'Transcendental idealism,' Fichte proclaims, '... appears ... as the only dutiful mode of thought in philosophy' (I, 467). Again: 'Wissenschaftslehre is the only kind of philosophical thinking that accords with duty' (Gesamtausgabe, Series I, Vol. 4, p. 219). But of course, no one can acknowledge that this choice is the only dutiful one unless he accepts that there is such a thing as duty and hence, by Fichte's account, unless he has already made this very choice – this unprincipled choice. There is nothing here with which to win over naturalists. (That is precisely what it is for the choice to be unprincipled.) These reflections, as Fichte himself puts it, lie 'altogether beyond [the purview of naturalists] ... and hence this whole statement [sc. the statement of the superiority of transcendentalism over naturalism], which is necessarily beyond them, is made, not for their benefit, but for the sake of others who are attentive and awake' (I, 510).

There remains the worry that transcendentalism is based on an illusion. Someone who has made this choice in favour of transcendentalism can always take a critical step back and ask a version of Descartes' Reflective Question (see Ch. 1, §3). That is, he can always ask himself why the sheer

---

[32] Here we see again (one aspect of) the subordination of theoretical reason to practical reason. For the idea that a Kantian critique of the former is also thereby subordinated to a Kantian critique of the latter, see Copleston (1963), p. 5, and Gardner (1999), pp. 334–335. Cf. also Zöller (2007). For further discussions of the relations between Kant and Fichte, see Ameriks (2000) and Pippin (2000).

fact that he could not help making this choice, and hence cannot now help regarding it as the right choice, should mean that it really is the right choice. Fichte would be the first to acknowledge the force of this question. He would see the dialectical situation in Kantian terms. We can none of us help thinking of ourselves as free. Nor, therefore, can we ultimately help making this corresponding sense of things, even if what we are really thereby doing is using concepts (which may indeed be confused concepts) merely regulatively. The fact remains that, within the security of our unprincipled choice, everything makes sense. And that is as much as we can expect from any attempt, at this level of generality, to make sense of things. Here, in conclusion, is Fichte again:

> If even a single person is completely convinced of his philosophy, and at all hours alike; if he is utterly at one with himself about it; if his free judgment in philosophizing, and what life obtrudes upon him, are perfectly in accord; then in this person philosophy has completed its circuit and attained its goal. (I, 512)

Appendix: Shades of Fichte in Kant

I have tried to give some indication of how Fichte's transcendentalism arises out of Kant's. I also mentioned Fichte's own conviction that the former is true to the spirit of the latter. But what did Kant himself think?

We do not need to speculate. Kant was famously prompted by a reviewer of a book on transcendental philosophy to answer this very question. The reviewer wrote:

> Fichte has realized what the *Critique* proposed, carrying out systematically the transcendental idealism which Kant projected. How natural therefore is the public's desire that the originator of the *Critique* declare openly his opinion of the work of his worthy pupil! (quoted in Kant (1999), p. 560, n. 1, emphasis removed)

In an open letter, Kant responded as follows:

> In response to the solemn challenge made to me …, I hereby declare that I regard Fichte's *Wissenschaftslehre* as a totally indefensible system…. I am so opposed to metaphysics, as defined according to *Fichtean* principles, that I have advised him, in a letter, to turn his fine literary gifts to the problem of applying the *Critique of Pure Reason* rather than squander them in cultivating fruitless sophistries….
>
> There is an Italian proverb: May God protect us especially from our friends, for we shall manage to watch out for our enemies ourselves. ('Declaration Concerning Fichte's *Wissenschaftslehre*', dated 7

August 1799, in Kant (1999), 12:370–371, emphasis in original, some
emphasis removed)

That is pretty unequivocal.

Nonetheless, it is not difficult to find passages in Kant's writings that
testify to Fichte's sense of his own discipleship. There are frequent uses of
strikingly Fichtean language[33] – albeit these are often of relatively superficial significance, since closer inspection often reveals that, although Kant is
using Fichtean language, he is using it in a non-Fichtean way.[34] More significant are passages in which Kant adumbrates Fichte's system by signalling
goals which Fichte later pursued and which for Kant remained goals only.
For example, in his *Critique of Practical Reason* Kant spoke of 'the expectation of perhaps being able some day to attain insight into the unity of the
whole pure rational faculty (theoretical as well as practical) and to derive
everything from one principle' (Kant (1996c), 5:91), the very expectation
that Fichte took himself to have realized. Most significant of all, however,
are notes that Kant left behind after his death.[35] These notes were for a
book on which he had been working for the last decade of his life and
which he himself described as his *chef d'oeuvre*. They show him to have
been engaged in an absorbing combination of reassessment and development of his own most fundamental ideas, but also, more to the point, to
have been drawn closer and closer to Fichte's vision of a self-positing, other-
positing subject.[36]

Kant argued in these notes that the subject's self-consciousness, which
is consciousness of itself *as free*, requires that it appear to itself in a certain way, or, more specifically, that it 'constitute itself' as an empirical
object. The subject does this by, among other things, constituting space
and time, along with various conditions of their occupation. Kant also
came to regard the concept of a thing in itself as an idea of reason that
the subject uses to represent its own fundamental nature and its own fundamental activity. Likewise, for that matter, the concept of God. The subject constitutes itself as a free agent, capable of putting pure reason to
practical use by doing its duty. But it also constitutes itself as an animal,
with countervailing inclinations. And it makes sense of the obligation to
suppress these countervailing inclinations by casting its duty as that which
God commands. It also comes to regard itself, *qua* human being, as uniting
God and the world. For, inasmuch as the human being is an animal, he is

---

[33] E.g. Kant (1998), B157 n.
[34] The example given in the previous note is a case in point (as indicated in n. 21).
[35] These are published as Kant (1993).
[36] They also show him to have shared increasingly in Fichte's opposition to Spinoza: see
e.g. Kant (1993), 21:19 and p. 225, whose use of the word 'enthusiastic' is subsequently
explained at 21:26 and p. 231. (I am indebted here to Guyer (2000), p. 50.)

located in the world; inasmuch as he is free, God is located in him. In one pithy sentence towards the end of his notes Kant summarized his entire train of thought as follows:

> Transcendental philosophy is the act of consciousness whereby the subject becomes the originator of itself and, thereby, of the whole object of technical-practical and moral-practical reason in one system – ordering all things in God. (Kant (1993), 21:78 and p. 245)

Kant looked more Fichtean, in some of his writings, than Fichte.[37]

---

[37] The material alluded to in this paragraph is scattered throughout Kant (1993), but see esp. pp. 179ff. For contrasting views about how much of a departure there was from Kant's earlier, published work, see Guyer (2000), §V, and Edwards (2000).

CHAPTER 7

✦

Hegel

Transcendentalism-cum-Naturalism;
or, Absolute Idealism

1. Preliminaries

At the beginning of the previous chapter, I quoted a passage from the
Phenomenology of G.W.F. Hegel (1770–1831).[1] This passage appeared to
be both linguistically deranged and, once one had somehow reckoned with
the derangement, committed to precisely the sort of transcendent metaphysics that Kant had striven so hard to eliminate. Nor was the passage unrepresentative. There is scarcely a paragraph in Hegel's vast philosophical corpus
that would not have given the same impression.

I hope that this chapter will go some way towards dispelling the impression, in both its aspects. Thus I hope it will give some indication of Hegel's
reasons for wrenching language and for neologizing in the way he did.[2]
And, more important, I hope it will show that his own philosophy was as
much an attempt to eschew transcendent metaphysics as Kant's, nay more
so; also, relatedly, that his system, like Fichte's, departed from Kant's not

[1] Throughout this chapter I use the following abbreviations for Hegel's works: *Encyclopedia
I* for Hegel (1975a); *Encyclopedia II* for Hegel (1970); *Encyclopedia III* for Hegel (1971);
Faith and Knowledge for Hegel (1977b); *Fichte and Schelling* for Hegel (1977a); *Medieval
and Modern Philosophy* for Hegel (1995); *Phenomenology* for Hegel (1979); *Philosophy
of Right* for Hegel (1942); *Reason in History* for Hegel (1975b); *Science of Logic* for
Hegel (1969); *The Concept of Religion* for Hegel (1984); and *The Consummate Religion*
for Hegel (1988). The use of a 'Z' in references to *Encyclopedia I* and II stands for '*Zusatz*'
and indicates one of the supplementary passages based on students' notes: I shall quote
from these passages as though from Hegel himself, though attributions based on these
quotations must be treated with due circumspection. In giving non-page references to the
Science of Logic I adopt the convention whereby 'l.i.ii.2C(a)' names Vol. One, Bk One,
§Two, Ch. 2C(a) and so forth. Note: in my quotations from these works I remove the capitalization in accord with G.A. Cohen's policy, as cited in Ch. 6, n. 2.

[2] I am sure I cannot be alone in having more than once had the following experience: initially finding some turn of phrase in Hegel obscure; eventually satisfying myself that I have
some understanding of it; then struggling to find some less obscure paraphrase; eventually
satisfying myself that I have a perfect candidate; and finally turning back to the original in
order to compare the two, only to find that they are the same.

so much by reverting to what Kant had been fighting against as by trying to extend Kantian principles in such a way as to overcome tensions and oppositions in Kant's own abortive use of them. As far as the second of these is concerned, there is a quintessentially Hegelian term, '*Aufhebung*', which will occur sporadically throughout this chapter and whose use is already irresistible.[3] This term precisely captures the overall relation in which Hegel took his own philosophy to stand to Kant's. For, as Hegel explains (*Science of Logic*, I.i.i.1C3, Remark, and *Encyclopedia* I, §96), in standard German '*Aufhebung*' can mean both 'annulment' and 'preservation', two seemingly incompatible ideas that nevertheless come together in certain transitions from a lower stage of development to a higher stage of development, transitions in which the lower stage, which is both a necessary condition and a sufficient condition of the higher stage, is able in some sense to live on in the higher stage, but only by being superseded. (The relation between a baby and the grown man that he becomes serves as a model.)[4]

A few caveats before I proceed. All philosophy is difficult: this is something that Hegel himself never tires of reminding us (e.g. *Phenomenology*, Preface, ¶¶3 and 67, and *Encyclopedia* I, §5; cf. also *Phenomenology*, Preface, ¶¶29, 63, and 70–71). But there are some special reasons why Hegel's philosophy is difficult. One is its sheer breadth. If it is true, as I suggested in §2 of the Introduction, that the main section headings in the first part of Roget's *Thesaurus* pretty much constitute a syllabus for a standard course in metaphysics, then the main section headings in all six parts of the book, from 'Existence' to 'Religion', pretty much constitute a syllabus for a standard course on the philosophy of Hegel. And although our own focus in this chapter will be specifically on Hegel's metaphysics, and on his conception of metaphysics, there is a holistic interdependence between the various aspects of his philosophy that means that the rest of that philosophy will never be completely outside our field of vision. It also means that there is no natural starting point for any investigation of the kind that follows. Wherever we choose to start, we shall be dealing with material that presupposes ideas of which we cannot make sense until we have progressed from there.[5]

---

[3] '*Aufhebung*' is a noun. I shall also make use of its corresponding verb '*aufheben*' – not only in this its infinitive form, but also in its third-person singular form '*aufhebt*' and in its past participial form '*aufgehoben*'.

[4] Cf. *Phenomenology*, IV.A, ¶188, where Hegel says of a certain kind of negation that concerns him that it 'supersedes in such a way as to preserve and maintain what is superseded, and consequently survives its own supersession.' That Hegel's philosophy stands in this kind of relation to Kant's is evidenced, in the small, by some passages in Kant that look strikingly Hegelian, that certainly anticipate Hegel, but that do not admit of a full Hegelian interpretation: see e.g. Kant (1998), A834–835/B862–863.

[5] In Charles Taylor (1975), pp. 122–124, Taylor identifies three starting points that Hegel himself adopts: one in *Phenomenology*, one in the *Science of Logic* and *Encyclopedia* I, and one in *Encyclopedia* II and III.

If we eventually think not only that we have some understanding of Hegel's system, but that we have sufficient understanding of it to know that we want to *reject* it, then we shall face another very special difficulty. The most direct way of rejecting a philosophical system is to controvert some particular idea or set of ideas within it. But one cardinal feature of Hegel's system, as we shall see in §4, is its emphasis on the power of ideas to provoke just such opposition (opposition which is in turn opposed in an advance to a higher stage of development of the sort described earlier). Any attempt to reject Hegel's system therefore runs the risk of corroborating it.[6] This is one of the many reasons why Hegel's philosophy is so hard to resist. And this in turn is one of the many reasons why it is so hard to resist in the more colloquial sense of being enormously seductive.

2.   Hegel's Recoil from Kant's Transcendental Idealism

One starting point that is as good as any is Hegel's recoil from Kant's transcendental idealism.[7]

In Chapter 5, §8, we considered an argument for the impossibility of drawing a limit to sense-making which I called the Limit Argument: roughly, any attempt to do such a thing confronts the seemingly damning question, 'What sense is to be made of the limit?' But we also saw how Kant, in his own effort to draw a limit to sense-making, attempted to evade the Limit Argument. He distinguished between the 'thick' sense-making whose limit he sought to draw and the 'thin' sense-making whereby he sought to draw it. Later, Fichte invoked a variation on the Limit Argument to show that at any rate it is impossible to draw a limit to sense-making of the thin kind, provided that it is as thin and as inclusive as it can be, for, if it is, there is nowhere analogous to retreat in order to answer the seemingly damning question; there is no sense-making that is thinner still. (See Ch. 6, §3.)

Hegel, suspicious of whether a suitable distinction can be drawn between the thick and the thin,[8] in effect applies his own variation on the Limit Argument to Kant's own original project. He concludes that Kant was unable to draw the limit that he sought to draw. And he accordingly rejects Kant's transcendental idealism.

Here is a passage that neatly captures Hegel's train of thought. (I have interpolated some phrases to indicate how it can be seen as a variation on the Limit Argument.)

> It argues an utter want of consistency to say, on the one hand, that the understanding only knows phenomena [to draw this limit to sense-making]

---

[6] Michael Hardt makes this point in Hardt (1993), p. xi. See also Foucault (1982), p. 74.

[7] For an overview of Hegel's attitude to Kant's transcendental idealism, see *Encyclopedia* I, IV.II.

[8] Cf. *Encyclopedia* I, §65.

and, on the other hand, to assert the absolute character of this knowledge [to assert that *this* exercise in sense-making lies beyond that limit], by such statements as 'Cognition can go no further'; 'Here is the natural and absolute limit of human knowledge.'... No one knows, or even feels, that anything is a limit [no one can make sense of a limit] ... until he is at the same time above and beyond it [until he can make sense of what lies on both sides of it].... A very little consideration might show that to call a thing ... limited proves by implication the very presence of the ... unlimited, and that our knowledge of a limit [our making sense of a limit] can only be when the unlimited is *on this side* in consciousness [can only be when our sense-making is not itself subject to that limit, nor therefore to any other limit of which we can make sense]. (*Encyclopedia* I, §60, emphasis in original, some emphasis removed, translation very slightly adapted)

In rejecting Kant's transcendental idealism, Hegel rejects the fundamental Kantian distinction between how things knowably appear and how they unknowably are in themselves. This distinction is an anathema to Hegel. Not only does he see no satisfactory way of drawing it; he feels no compulsion to draw it. For Hegel, how things knowably appear is how they manifestly are. Reality is not opposed to appearance; it is discerned in appearance. Insofar as there is any distinction to be drawn, it is a distinction of the kind that we saw in the previous section between different stages of development, whereby how things are 'in themselves' is *aufgehoben*[9] in how they ultimately appear. But not even that makes how things are in themselves unknowable. How things are in themselves can be known in its lower stage of development, as an abstraction (*Encyclopedia* I, §44); and it can be known in its higher stage of development, precisely through its manifestation in how things ultimately appear (ibid., §124; cf. *Phenomenology*, III, ¶160).

This is altogether more radical than Fichte's recoil from the same Kantian distinction.[10] As I argued in §3 of the previous chapter, Fichte still retained a broadly Kantian conception of things as they are in themselves. He departed from Kant only in claiming knowledge of such things, testified by a particular minimalist account that he was prepared to give of them. He also retained a distinction of sorts between things as they are in themselves and things as they (merely) appear. For our knowledge of things as they are in themselves, attained through self-conscious reflection on the infinitude of our own freedom and rationality, was to be contrasted with the knowledge available to us in our finitude, attained through our engagement with what we are given in experience. Finitude, for Fichte, just as for Kant, was opposed to infinitude. And, insofar as we ourselves are finite, this means that there is something that in principle eludes us, something from which

---

[9] See n. 3.
[10] For Hegel's reaction to Fichte's work, see *Fichte and Schelling*.

we are in principle cut off. It means that there is something that is, for us, *transcendent*. The Cartesian separation of the finite self from an infinite reality beyond it still persists. Hegel wants to overcome that separation.[11]

He also wants to repudiate transcendent metaphysics. Indeed, as I intimated in the previous section, he is even more vehement in his repudiation of transcendent metaphysics than Kant. And we can now see why. It is not just that he thinks that there is no making sense of what is transcendent. He thinks that there is no transcendent.[12] Or more strictly, he wants to abnegate the very opposition between the transcendent and the immanent. That, for Hegel, is of a piece with the opposition between the real and the merely apparent.[13]

Transcendental idealism promotes these oppositions. That, indeed, is its great irony. It is designed to suppress our aspirations to make sense of what is transcendent, on the grounds that such a thing is impossible. Yet precisely in drawing our attention to what is transcendent, and signalling it as that whereof we should not try to make sense, it entices us to do the very thing that it is designed to stop us from trying to do; and, worse still, it requires that we do that very thing in order to assimilate it (transcendental idealism) in the first place.

It must be dismantled. Hegel is convinced of that. But its dismantling will necessitate, among other things, a radical rethinking of finitude and infinitude. For it is true that we are finite. So we need to understand that fact in such a way that it does not, itself, already issue in just such idealism. We need to understand it in such a way that it does not cleave us from the infinite source of what, in our finitude, we can know.

Hegel has a twin conception of finitude and infinitude that precisely meets this need. His conception is roughly as follows. For something to be finite is for it to be limited and to be set apart from an 'other'. Its other both defines it and negates it. It determines both what the thing is and what the thing is not. But that other must in turn be finite. Nothing can be set apart from the infinite. For nothing can fail to be a part of, or an aspect of, the infinite. If the infinite did not embrace everything, then it too would have an other that served to define it, and negate it, and thereby render it finite. The infinite is not *opposed to* the finite. It embraces the finite. It holds together opposing strains of finitude in the unity of the whole, that is in itself.[14]

---

[11] See *Phenomenology*, Introduction; and *Encyclopedia* I, §42. See also Taylor (1975), pp. 29–41.

[12] Cf. Beiser (1993), p. 8

[13] Thus consider the Transcendence Question from §6 of the Introduction. Hegel would not answer this question by denying that there is scope for us to make sense of what of transcendent: he would reject the question altogether. See further §9.

[14] See *Science of Logic*, I.i.i.2 and I.ii.2.C, and *Encyclopedia* I, §§28Z and 94–95. For discussion, see Taylor (1975), pp. 114–115; Moore (2001a), Ch. 7, §1; and, in much greater detail, Inwood (1983), Chs 6 and 7.

Now this would be all very well, as indeed would the dismantling of Kant's idealism, if we could simply revert to what I called in the previous chapter 'naturalism': a view, à la Spinoza or Hume, whereby each of us knows whatever he or she knows about the world by virtue of being a finite part of it. In fact, however, Hegel sees Kant not only as having changed the course of metaphysics, but as having advanced it along that course, in such a way that there neither can now nor should now be any turning back. Hegel wants to depart from Kant, certainly, but he wants to do so without sacrificing Kant's vital insights. He wants to *aufheben*[15] Kant. To understand better the challenge that he thereby faces, we must consider the balance that he needs to strike. He must, if he is to maintain the evolutionary process, not only reject enough in Kant to advance, but also retain enough not to regress.

3. 'What is rational is actual, and what is actual is rational'

Hegel believes, just as Fichte believed, that a bald naturalism cannot do justice to the phenomenon of subjectivity. For subjectivity cannot be understood merely as an epiphenomenon of objectivity, certainly not of the objectivity of the natural world. Rather, as Kant's Copernican revolution has taught us, the objectivity of the natural world must itself be understood as grounded in subjectivity – if only as one half of a mutual grounding of each in the other. The natural world is itself constituted, in part, by the concepts that we use in thinking about it. To deny this would in Hegel's view be retrograde.[16]

This certainly makes him an idealist, by my definition (see the Appendix to Ch. 5). The question is how he can avoid being the transcendental idealist that he is so determined not to be. Granted my definition, along with its clauses concerning the different species of idealism, the answer is clear enough: he needs to say that the constitution of the natural world by concepts that we use to think about it can itself be thought about by means of those same concepts. And indeed he does say this, as we shall see. (This makes him, again by my definition, an empirical idealist, though his empirical idealism is of an altogether different kind from Berkeley's.[17]) The question, however, is what title he has to say this. How can he accede to as much of Kant's Copernican revolution as he does and not be committed to Kant's principal conclusion, namely that the natural world is a world of

---

[15] See n. 3. (Purists may object to my use of 'to' alongside an infinitive, but 'He wants *aufheben* ...' sounds precious to my ear.)

[16] Since Hegel also shares Kant's view that the concepts in question, and the constitution of the natural world by them, are in some sense *a priori*, he likewise endorses Kant's critique of Humean empiricism; see *Encyclopedia* I, IV.1.

[17] See again Berkeley (1962a). The differences should be clearer by the end of the chapter. For two helpful discussions, see Wartenberg (1993) and Stern (2009).

appearances as opposed to a world of things in themselves, a conclusion that cannot itself be understood in terms of the concepts that we use to think about the natural world?[18]

The answer is that the constituting of the natural world by concepts that we use to think about it is not just a feature of how it is given to us. In other words, it does not depend on our intuitions. There is no analogue of Kant's synthetic *a priori* knowledge.[19] The subjectivity in which objectivity is grounded is not, for Hegel, the subjectivity of something finite and particular, to whom reality thereby appears a certain way. It is the subjectivity of something that is infinite and universal (*The Concept of Religion*, p. 410).

But what does this mean? And how does it help?

It means, in part, that the objectivity of the natural world is grounded not just in the engagement that each of us has with it, at any given time, but in our collective and cumulative engagement with it.[20] But there is considerably more to it than that, as indeed there had better be if transcendental idealism is to be avoided. For if the community has *a priori* concepts that structure what it is given, in some kind of plural diachronic analogue of Kantian intuition, then still there will be a broadly Kantian distinction between how things appear (to the community, over time) and how they are in themselves.

The crucial point is that the subjectivity in question is the subjectivity of something *infinite*. What this means (see the previous section) is that there is no opposition between knower and known. Hegel has in mind a way in which *reality comes to know itself*. It comes to know itself through a process of which the acquisition of knowledge by us, both individually and collectively, is (but) an aspect. The subjectivity in question is the subjectivity of the whole, *qua* knower, which is at the same time its objectivity, *qua* known.

---

[18] Robert Pippin, in Pippin (1989), presents the question of how Hegel manages to keep his distance from Kant very differently: see the useful summary at pp. 9–10. But I hope and believe that he and I are approaching the same issue from two different directions. I have learned much from Pippin's discussion.

[19] In fact, Hegel is unsympathetic to Kant's distinction between intuitions and concepts. See *Faith and Knowledge*, p. 87; *Phenomenology*, I and II; and *Science of Logic*, II, 'The Notion in General', pp. 585ff. For discussion, see Solomon (1985), §I, and Stern (2002), pp. 43–59. For some comments specifically targeted at Kant's 'straight line' example of synthetic *a priori* knowledge, see *Encyclopedia* II, §256Z.

[20] It is tempting at this point to see a connection with what Foucault calls 'the historical *a priori*', which he characterizes as 'an *a priori* that is not a condition of validity for judgements, but a condition of reality for statements,' and which he says 'has to take account of the fact that discourse has not only a meaning or a truth, but a history' (Foucault (1972), p. 127; see further ibid., Ch. 5, passim). In fact, however, what Foucault has in mind – something that he takes to be discernible in any given historically situated, unified set of linguistic practices, characterizing their unity – is far more reminiscent of what we shall see later in Wittgenstein and Collingwood (see Chs 10 and 19, respectively) than it is of anything in Hegel.

The knower is not in any sense cut off from how things are in themselves; precisely not. To accede to this we must obviously be prepared to think of such concepts as knowledge, rationality, and truth as applying not just to finite beings in the midst of reality, along with their various representations of that reality, but to reality itself, as a whole. Reality, for Hegel, *makes sense*. But it does so not just in the intransitive sense that it is understandable. It does so also in the transitive sense that it understands. And, since what it understands is itself, it does each of these *by* doing the other. It is in this vein that Hegel famously declares, 'What is rational is actual, and what is actual is rational' (*Philosophy of Right*, Preface, p. 10, emphasis removed; see also *Encyclopedia* I, §6).

This does not mean that every single part of reality is rational, regarded in isolation. It means that the 'sum of being' – that which 'in itself really deserves the name of actuality' (*Encyclopedia* I, §6, p. 8) – is rational. But the process whereby reality manifests its rationality, that is to say the process whereby it comes to make sense (of itself), is itself reality (*Phenomenology*, Preface, ¶55). So everything that has just been said about reality applies equally to sense-making too, as indeed it does to knowledge, rationality, and truth.[21] We must be prepared to think of these themselves as likewise making sense, having knowledge, being rational, and possessing truth. Above all, we must be prepared to think of each of them as a subject. As Hegel himself puts it, 'everything turns on grasping the true, not merely as *substance*, but equally as *subject*' (*Phenomenology*, Preface, ¶17, emphasis in original).[22] And, as he goes on to explain in that passage which I quoted at the beginning of the previous chapter, by a subject he means not just something that is capable of making sense, having knowledge, being rational, or possessing truth, but something with a biography, something with purposes that it is striving to fulfil, something that acts out its life in accord with concepts, something that, *à la* Fichte, both posits itself and thereby posits that which is finite and distinct from itself (albeit, on Hegel's conception, a part of itself) through which it comes to make sense of itself.[23]

4. Hegel's Logic and the Absolute Idea

Kant's insights about the efficacy of concepts and their role in structuring the natural world are retained, then, after a fashion – but after an utterly non-Kantian fashion. No longer is it a question of how things merely appear,

---

[21] This is truth in the broad sense appropriated by Hegel: see e.g. *Phenomenology*, Preface, ¶55, and *Encyclopedia* I, §213Z.

[22] This is our first indication of how non-Spinozist this otherwise Spinozist vision is: see Ch. 2, §2, and see further §6.

[23] See also *Phenomenology*, Preface, ¶¶22 and 25. For discussion of Hegel's conception of a subject, see Taylor (1975), Ch. 3, §§2 and 3.

from some point of view within reality, still less of how they merely and peculiarly appear from some point of view within reality. It is a question of, as Hegel himself puts it, the 'characteristics of objects' (*Encyclopedia* I, §42Z, p. 70), by which he simply means how things are in themselves.

On the other hand, we and our point of view are not irrelevant to this either. We too make sense (of things), have knowledge, are rational, and have some grasp of the truth. Where many of Hegel's immediate predecessors and contemporaries, notably Jacobi, argue that in our finite discursive thinking we are completely cut off from the infinite, Hegel, keen as ever to overcome any such opposition, argues that our finite discursive thinking is part of the process whereby the infinite, which is to say reality, comes to make sense of itself and comes to know itself. It is part of the development of the infinite's own *self-consciousness* (*Phenomenology*, Preface, ¶54, and VIII, ¶¶801–808; and *Encyclopedia* I, §62).[24] 'To him who looks at the world rationally,' Hegel insists, 'the world looks rationally back; the two exist in reciprocal relationship' (*Reason in History*, p. 29, translation adapted in Stern (2002), p. 11).

What form does the development of reality's self-consciousness take, then? It is a play of reason. It is a process in which concepts are put to use in the grasp of new concepts, in relation to which they are themselves better grasped and in combination with which they are put to use in the grasp of yet new concepts, and so on, until all these concepts and the interrelations between them make maximum possible sense. The result is that sense-making comes to make sense of sense-making, and knowledge comes to know knowledge.[25]

Hegel makes frequent reference to something that he calls 'the' concept, or, in its 'pure form' (*Encyclopedia* I, §237, p. 292) – by which he means in its fully developed form – 'the absolute idea'. And he says of the absolute idea that '[it] alone is *being*, imperishable *life*, *self-knowing truth*, and is *all truth*' – having previously castigated 'all else' as 'error, confusion, opinion, endeavour, caprice and transitoriness' (*Science of Logic*, II.iii.3, p. 824, emphasis in original).[26] We can think of the absolute idea, very roughly, as follows. It is the entire infinite system of interrelated concepts, in their indissoluble unity, as exercised in the self-consciousness towards which the

---

[24] See further Inwood (1983), pp. 193ff. The work by Jacobi that Hegel principally has in mind is Jacobi (1995).

[25] Hegel is well aware of the Aristotelian connotations that this has. Aristotle held God to be thought thinking itself (*Metaphysics*, Bk Λ, Ch. 9), and Hegel explicitly likens his own conception to Aristotle's at *Encyclopedia* I, §236.

[26] See further *Science of Logic*, I, Introduction, 'General Division of Logic'; II.i.1 and II.iii.3; and *Encyclopedia* I, §§15, 16, and 236ff. Note that the German word that I have rendered as 'concept', namely '*Begriff*', is translated by both A.V. Miller and William Wallace as 'notion', which each of them also sometimes capitalizes.

process that I have just been describing leads. It is therefore the *telos* of the process. It should not however be thought of merely as a static end-state, but rather as including the process, of which it is the culmination. It is the *telos* of the process in something like the way in which the *telos* of a musical performance is the entire performance, not just the playing of the last note.[27]

Still, it is possible at the end of the process[28] to do something that it is not possible to do at any earlier stage, namely to grasp how all the concepts that constitute the absolute idea do so, in other words to grasp them in their interrelated entirety. And Hegel, who takes himself to have realized this very possibility, gives an elaborate account of what it is that he takes himself thereby to have grasped. He calls this undertaking 'logic' (e.g. *Encyclopedia* I, §19). But he also identifies logic, on this conception, with metaphysics (*Encyclopedia* I, §24, p. 36). On my conception – of metaphysics, that is – such an identification is entirely apt. For if anything deserves the title of the most general attempt to make sense of things, this does.

I shall shortly sketch the crucial opening moves in Hegel's logic. But first a comment on this use of the word 'moves'.[29] Hegel describes the system of concepts in dynamic terms. He talks of how one concept passes over into another, which in turn combines with the first to pass over into a third, and so on until every concept has its place in the whole. In one respect the use of such temporal language is misleading. It is misleading inasmuch as he is talking about atemporal conceptual relations that are of a piece, at least in their atemporality, with the relation of containment that obtains between the concept of being an aunt and the concept of being female. (In particular, he is talking about an atemporal version of *Aufhebung*.) But the use of temporal language is in another respect very appropriate, inasmuch as Hegel also believes, as we have seen, that reality has to achieve self-consciousness by a literally temporal process, a process that indeed reflects in various ways these atemporal relations.

Very well; what are the moves with which Hegel begins his logic? He starts with the concept of being, that is to say pure undetermined being. This is the appropriate concept with which to start, not only because it is the one concept that must apply to everything, but also because any other proposed starting point, say the concept of the self, would involve something determinate, as it may be the idea of that whose existence cannot be doubted, and would therefore presuppose other concepts which should have preceded it (*Encyclopedia* I, §86).

---

[27] Cf. *Phenomenology*, Preface, ¶20, and *Encyclopedia* I, §§215 and 237Z.

[28] Let us for the time being waive any anxieties that we might have about why there should be any such thing as the end of the process. We shall return to this issue in the next section.

[29] Cf. Hegel's own use of the word 'movement' in *Science of Logic*, I.i.i.1.C.1, p. 83.

But pure undetermined being, as such, without the modification of any other concept, is nothing, where by nothing is meant 'complete emptiness, absence of all determination and content – undifferentiatedness in itself' (*Science of Logic*, I.i.i.1.B, p. 82). The concept of being thus passes over into the concept of nothing, to which, on the one hand, it is opposed and with which, on the other hand, it is to be identified. The same is true in reverse: the concept of nothing likewise passes over into the concept of being, to which it is opposed and with which it is to be identified. This is because, if there is *nothing*, then *there is* nothing: that is then the nature of being. Nothing can be 'thought of, imagined, spoken of, and therefore it *is*' (*Science of Logic*, I.i.i.1.C.1, Remark 3, p. 101, emphasis in original). Each concept issues in and gives way to the other, then. That is, each concept 'vanishes in its opposite' (*Science of Logic*, I.i.i.1.C.1, p. 83, emphasis removed).

But this means that, in order for being to make sense, the opposition between it and nothing must somehow be resolved. It is resolved by being *aufgehoben*. And this in turn is achieved by the two concepts themselves being *aufgehoben* in passing over into a third, that of becoming. In becoming, both being and nothing are both preserved and annulled, each passing over into the other, being in ceasing-to-be and nothing in coming-to-be (*Science of Logic*, I.i.i.1.C.2, p. 106).

Is Hegel saying that it is a matter of conceptual necessity that there is such a thing as time, then? No. Becoming is not the same as time. Time is one form of becoming. Time is becoming as given in a certain way. In time, 'contradictories are held asunder in juxtaposition and temporal succession and so come before consciousness without reciprocal contact' (*Science of Logic*, II.iii.3, p. 835). The *Aufhebung* of the opposition between being and nothing, with respect to light, say, is given in the fact that there *was no* light but there *is now* light. That is, the absence or non-being of light and the presence or being of light, though opposed to each other, are united in the coming-to-be of light by being placed alongside each other in time.[30] It does not follow that such coming-to-be could not have taken some other form.[31]

It is worth adding in this connection that it is compatible with everything that has been said so far that the existence of becoming is itself a deep contingency, a feature of reality which, however pervasive it may be, admits, at some level, of alternatives.[32] It is just that, if it is, then there must also be a

---

[30] For an extensive discussion of time, see *Encyclopedia* II, §§257–259. For a superb account of Hegel's conception of time, see Turetzky (1998), Ch. 8, §1.

[31] Consider, for example, how it is also possible for there to be light *here* but *not there*. (But see also Heidegger (1962a), ¶82, for a discussion that emphasizes the extent to which the existence of time *is* ineluctable for Hegel.)

[32] As to its pervasiveness, see *Science of Logic*, I.i.i.1.C.1, Remark 4, p. 105, where Hegel urges that '*there is nothing which is not in an intermediate state between being and*

contingency further up in Hegel's account, say in the very idea that there are concepts, or in the idea that the opposition between being and nothing is resolved in the way it is, or even in the idea that it is resolved at all, that being does indeed *make sense*. (An alternative in each case would be for there to be nothing. Quite what this would involve, in Hegelian terms, would depend on where the contingency lay. Perhaps it would involve being's and nothing's acquiescing in their mutual opposition. Perhaps it would involve being's failing to make sense.) If there *is* such a contingency further up in Hegel's account, then the contingency of becoming can be thought of as a manifestation of it, the means whereby the opposition in question is resolved.

Still, be any of that as it may, and be the exegesis of Hegel as it may – I pass no judgment on whether he does think it a contingency that there is such a thing as becoming[33] – he certainly thinks that it is through becoming that the opposition in question is resolved. And that is what matters for current purposes. These, in essence, are the opening moves in his logic.[34]

The dialectical structure here, whereby one thing passes over into its opposite and the two together then pass over into a third thing in which their opposition is *aufgehoben*, is not just a feature of the interrelation of concepts in the absolute idea. It is a structure which Hegel claims to be 'the law of things', instantiated 'wherever there is movement, wherever there is life, wherever anything is carried into effect in the natural world' (*Encyclopedia* I, §81Z, p. 116). It is often described in terms of thesis, antithesis, and synthesis – though this is not a Hegelian way of speaking.[35] Hegel himself sometimes describes it in terms of negation and negation of the negation (e.g. *Science of Logic*, I.i.i.2.C(*c*), pp. 148–150, and *Encyclopedia* I, §95; cf. *Encyclopedia* I, §93). These two ways of speaking are not so very different,

---

nothing' (emphasis in original). Cf. the Heraclitean doctrine that everything is in a constant state of flux, to which Hegel refers in *Encyclopedia* I, §88Z: see Barnes (1987), pp. 116–117.

[33] But I note that *Encyclopedia* I, §88, lends some support to the view that he does. (And he definitely allows for *some* contingency in nature, contrary to an impression that he sometimes gives: see e.g. *Encyclopedia* I, §16, and *Encyclopedia* II, §250.) For further discussion, see Hartmann (1972). See also Stern (2002), pp. 18ff. where he argues that Hegel's aim is 'to show how the various categories of thought are dialectically interrelated, in such a way that the conceptual oppositions responsible for our perplexities [i.e. our various philosophical perplexities] can be resolved, once we rethink these fundamental notions' (p. 18).

[34] General references for these opening moves are *Science of Logic*, I.i, 'With What Must the Science Begin?', and I.i.i.1; and *Encyclopedia* I, §§84–88. For discussion, see Taylor (1975), Ch. 11 and pp. 232–233; Pinkard (1985); Burbidge (1993); and, in much greater detail, Houlgate (2006).

[35] Walter Kaufmann, in Kaufmann (1960), p. 166, informs us that this triad of terms occurs only once in Hegel's entire corpus, in a reference to Kant. The occurrence is in *Medieval and Modern Philosophy*, pp. 477–478.

however. For the negation that Hegel intends here is the negation that is characteristic of *Aufhebung*. It is the negation in which the original lives on in a superseded form (see e.g. *Encyclopedia* I, §§91 and 119). In the negation of the negation the original still lives on, but doubly transformed. And likewise for any further iteration.[36]

This living on in negation is highly pertinent to Hegel's logic. The starting point of his logic, as we have seen, is the concept of being. The end point is the entire infinite system of interrelated concepts, the absolute idea. But each of these is implicated in the other. Each, in a sense, *is* the other. For the starting point leads inexorably to the end point, and lives on in it. (The child becomes the man.) And only in the light of the end point, that is only in the context of the absolute idea, can the starting point, that is the concept of being, properly be grasped. Only in the context of the absolute idea can *any* of its concepts properly be grasped. Only at the end does anything make sense. (See *Science of Logic*, I.i, 'With What Must the Science Begin?', pp. 71–72, and II.iii.3; and *Encyclopedia* I, §§236ff.) This is part of what Hegel means by his famous remark that 'the owl of Minerva spreads its wings only with the falling of the dusk' (*Philosophy of Right*, Preface, p. 13).[37]

5. Three Concerns

Hegel believes that the process whereby reality achieves full self-consciousness has reached its final stage, then, and that this is manifest in the fact that he himself has grasped the system of concepts that constitute the absolute idea. Even someone broadly sympathetic to his vision is liable to have

---

[36] Note that, although we are dealing here with something importantly original in Hegel's thinking, ideas of broadly the same kind were already in the air. The following very Hegelian-sounding passage occurs in some of Goethe's lecture notes, written in 1805, before the publication of any of Hegel's major works: 'What appears must put itself asunder, just in order to appear. That which is asunder searches for itself, and it can find itself again and unite.... But the unification can ... take place in a ... sense ... in which what has been separated first intensifies itself and by the combination of the two intensified sides brings forth a third thing, new, higher, unexpected' (Goethe (1893), §II, Vol. 11, p. 166, trans. in Craig (1987), p. 157). The fact that such ideas were already in the air, and sometimes applied in a rather mechanical way, helps to explain Hegel's admonishment against the temptation to reduce the dialectical structure to 'a lifeless schema' (*Phenomenology*, Preface, ¶50). We must, Hegel urges, recover 'the self-moving soul of the realized content [of that dialectical structure]' (ibid., ¶53).

[37] The owl of Minerva was the owl that accompanied Minerva, goddess of wisdom, in Roman mythology; it is seen as a symbol of wisdom. Shortly before the sentence quoted, Hegel amplifies as follows: 'The teaching of the concept, which is also history's inescapable lesson, is that it is only when actuality is mature that the ideal first appears over against the real and that the ideal apprehends this same real world in its substance and builds it up for itself into the shape of an intellectual realm.'

concerns about these specific conceits. There are three questions in particular that seem pressing. Why think that the process in question *has* a final
stage? Why think that, even if it has, there is scope for a finite individual
such as Hegel, never mind for the time being what credentials Hegel himself has, to grasp how all those concepts are interrelated – as opposed to
contributing in some unwitting way to reality's grasp of how they are? And
why think that, even if there is scope for a finite individual to do this, Hegel
himself has done it?[38]

There is a sense in which a satisfactory answer to the third question
would obviate the other two. Hegel, if confronted with these three questions, could always present his logic and say, 'See for yourselves.' But even
those impressed by what they saw might still seek reassurances concerning
the other two questions, to remove lingering doubts about what they were
looking at.

Consider the first question. The concern here is reinforced by the thought
that the entire system of concepts is after all supposed to be infinite. Perhaps
the most that we can expect is an endless progression toward grasp of it,
a progression whereby reality, which is to say the infinite, becomes more
and more self-conscious but never reaches that limit of self-consciousness in
which knower and known completely coincide.

But this, Hegel will say, is to cast the truly infinite in a role more suited
to what he would call the spuriously infinite (*Encyclopedia* I, §94);[39] or
rather, it is at best to do that; at worst, it is to confuse the two. The truly
infinite is the infinite as characterized in §2: the complete self-contained
unified whole, which is not opposed to the finite but embraces it. The spuriously infinite, by contrast, is the infinite as it tends to be characterized in
mathematics. It is the infinite which finds paradigmatic expression in the
sequence of positive integers 1, 2, 3, ... The spuriously infinite is a mere succession of finite elements, each succeeded by another, never complete, never
self-contained, never unified. It is a pale inadequate reflection of the truly
infinite. And, unlike the truly infinite, it *is* opposed to the finite. This is precisely what propels it along from one element to the next, in its never-ending
attempt to escape the finite.[40] In Hegel's view it would be unthinkable for
insight into the truly infinite, the prerogative of the truly infinite itself, to be
some asymptotic ideal that is only ever approached by a spuriously infinite
progression of successively better approximations.[41]

---

[38] Versions of these questions are raised and addressed in Kierkegaard (1941), Bk One,
Pt One, Ch. 2, §4.

[39] 'Spurious' is a common translation of '*schlechte*' in the Hegelian phrase '*schlechte
Unendlichkeit*'. Also common is the more literal 'bad'. Wallace opts for 'wrong'.

[40] It is interesting to observe that, in contrasting the truly infinite with the spuriously infinite
in this way, Hegel is adopting a position that is diametrically opposed to that of Aristotle:
see Aristotle's *Physics*, Bk III, Ch. 6, 206a 27–29, 207a 1, and 207a 7–9.

[41] Cf. *Encyclopedia* I, §234.

There is in any case a further important strain in Hegel's thinking, which I shall mention but to which I cannot begin to do justice, whereby reality, or the infinite, must not only exist

- 'in itself', that is as a self-identical but as yet undeveloped concept,[42]

but also

- 'for itself', that is by being projected in a succession of natural events in which it maintains a progression towards self-knowledge,

and also

- *'in and for itself'*, that is through its eventual attainment of that self-knowledge. (*Phenomenology*, Preface, ¶¶20–25)[43]

To develop the musical analogy that I used in the previous section, a piece of music, if it is to achieve full being, must not only exist

- in conception, that is as an idea in the composer's mind,

but also

- in performance, that is by being projected in a succession of sounds in which the composer's idea is realized,

and also

- *in consummation*, that is through the eventual completion of the performance.

If its performance went on for ever, it would scarcely count as 'a piece of music', but would be some kind of license for endless improvisation or else a blueprint for endless repetition.[44]

But now the second question is urgent. Even if reality must eventually achieve full self-consciousness, and has in fact already done so, and even if human beings are the principal vehicle whereby it has managed to do so,[45] why should this involve any one human being's grasping the entire system

---

[42] Cf. the way in which the absolute idea exists in the concept of pure undetermined being.

[43] Cf. *Encyclopedia* I, §§213 and 235, and *Encyclopedia* III, §§575–577. For a helpful discussion, see Taylor (1975), pp. 111–112. Also helpful is the entry on 'in, for, and in and for, itself, himself, etc.' in Inwood (1992), pp. 133–136.

[44] But note the last three sentences of *Encyclopedia* I, §234Z. Hegel does not believe that, just because reality has already achieved full self-consciousness, we can now rest on our laurels; for, as he puts it, 'the final end of the world ... has being ... only while it constantly produces itself.' The suggestion seems to be that, for as long as nature persists, reality must maintain its self-knowledge through a kind of continual recapitulation.

[45] Cf. *Phenomenology*, Preface, ¶26.

of concepts? Why not, to continue with the musical analogy, an orchestrated effort?[46] This question is exacerbated by Hegel's own insistence that much in the process has happened without direction from any individual.[47] Even those 'world-historical individuals' who were *en route* to this final stage, 'who had an insight into the requirements of the time – *what was right for development* ... [– who knew] the necessary, directly sequent step in progress, which their world was to take; [and who] must, therefore, be recognized as its clear-sighted ones ...': even these 'had no consciousness of the general idea they were unfolding' and 'when their object [was] attained they [fell] off like empty hulls from the kernel' (*Reason in History*, pp. 29–31, emphasis in original).[48]

It seems to me that Hegel has no satisfactory answer to the second question beyond whatever answer he may have to the third. In other words, I think his only reason for holding that there is scope for an individual human being to grasp the entire system of concepts is that he takes himself to have done so. And that *is* largely a matter of his having a logic of which he is prepared to say, 'See for yourselves.'[49] Seeing for ourselves, if he is right, means not only making sense of all the moves in his logic, but also realizing, at a higher level of reflection, that we could not make such sense of them, nay that such sense would not be available to be made, unless the logic were complete. For – again, if Hegel is right – it is only in the context of the whole that any of the moves can have the particular significance that now, in retrospect, we can see them as having (cf. *Phenomenology*, Preface, ¶1, and Introduction, ¶89; and *Encyclopedia* I, §§14 and 17). So we must simply look and see, and try to decide whether Hegel is indeed right.

6.   Shades of Spinoza in Hegel?

It is hard not to be struck by deep affinities between Hegel and Spinoza, especially by their shared vision of reality as a single infinite substance of which we and all the episodes that constitute our lives are but an aspect. Hegel himself comments:

> When one begins to philosophize one must be first a Spinozist. The soul must bathe itself in the aether of this single substance, in which everything one has held for true is submerged. (*Medieval and Modern Philosophy*, p. 165, translation adapted in Beiser (1993), p. 5)

[46] Cf. Popper (1972).
[47] Cf. *Encyclopedia* I, §238Z, and *Encyclopedia* III, §551.
[48] This is what Hegel has in mind when he famously refers to 'the cunning of reason': see *Reason in History*, p. 33.
[49] Cf. in this connection *Phenomenology*, Preface, ¶3. There is a hint of a more substantial answer to the third question in *Phenomenology*, VIII, ¶802, but it is unlikely to allay any real concerns.

Moreover, for both Spinoza and Hegel, our own involvement in the life of substance, including our making sense of substance, is a matter of our participating in its own sense-making. To revert to an analogy that I used in Chapter 1, §6: the relation between us and substance, as we come to make sense of it, is akin to the relation between a member of a linguistic community and the community as a whole. This in turn connects with something else that the two thinkers crucially share: a repudiation of morality in favour of ethics, or at any rate, in Hegel's case, a commitment to the *Aufhebung* of the moral life by the ethical life (*Philosophy of Right*, §141). One Hegelian way of drawing the contrast between these would be to say that morality, grounded as it is in the fact that we are free individuals, is concerned with which unrealized possibilities we ought to realize, whereas ethics, grounded as it is in the fact that we together constitute a community, is more concerned with how we are to develop something that is already real.[50]

All of this is indeed striking. But there are differences between Spinoza and Hegel that are just as striking, and in my view deeper. We can broach these differences by reflecting on the theological dimension of the two systems.

Spinoza named his substance 'God'. But then he treated of it in such a way as to make it far from clear that his position really merited the title of theism. In particular, his substance differed from the traditional Judæo-Christian God in two fundamental respects. It was not transcendent, and it was not personal. In Chapter 2, §2, I concluded that it is altogether less misleading to call Spinoza an atheist than to call him a theist.

Hegel too names his substance 'God' (*The Consummate Religion*, pp. 368–369; cf. *Encyclopedia* I, §1). He too treats of what he names 'God' in such a way as to resist straightforward classification as a theist. Indeed, my inclination is to draw much the same conclusion as I drew in the case of Spinoza, that it is on the whole less misleading to call him an atheist than to call him a theist (though we are of course under no compulsion to call him either, certainly not without the myriad qualifications that would be required in each case). Nevertheless, Hegel is closer to traditional Judæo-Christian theism than Spinoza is. For Hegel's substance differs from the traditional Judæo-Christian God only in the first of the two specified respects: it is not transcendent. It is, however – unlike Spinoza's substance – personal.[51] And this indeed marks the principal difference between the two thinkers – as

---

[50] See *Philosophy of Right*, Pts Two and Three. For a helpful discussion, see Taylor (1975), pp. 376ff.

   Note that there are nevertheless disparities between the two thinkers' conceptions of the ethical life, which in Hegel's case is understood to embrace religion in a way in which it is not in Spinoza's: see *Phenomenology*, VII, passim. This connects with what comes next in the main text.

[51] On the non-transcendence of God, see *Encyclopedia* I, §38. On the personhood of God, see ibid., §151Z. For a helpful discussion, see Taylor (1975), Ch. 3, §5.

Hegel well knows, for it also marks the principal reproach that he levels against Spinoza. He says:

> It is true that God ... is the absolute thing: he is however no less the absolute person. That he is the absolute person however is a point which the philosophy of Spinoza never reached: and on that side it falls short of the true notion of God which forms the content of religious consciousness in Christianity. (*Encyclopedia* I, §151Z, p. 214)[52]

The personhood of substance, for Hegel, is of a piece with the subjecthood of substance, whose importance I emphasized in §3. Hegel's substance has a meaningful biography; it has purposes; it acts out its life in accord with concepts. None of this is true of Spinoza's substance. Moreover, the way in which the life of substance is played out, namely through processes of negation whereby finite elements of that life are *aufgehoben*, is radically non-Spinozist. In ¶19 of the Preface to his *Phenomenology*, Hegel refers to 'the labour of the negative'. He means by this these very processes, the processes that bring substance to 'what it truly is' (ibid., ¶20), in other words the processes through which substance exists for itself. Substance's 'power to move,' Hegel writes, '... is being-for-self or pure negativity' (ibid., ¶22, emphasis removed). This stands in stark contrast to what we find in Spinoza.[53] Spinoza takes his substance to be 'an absolutely infinite being' and glosses this by saying, 'If a thing is absolutely infinite, there belongs to its essence whatever expresses essence and does not involve negation' (Spinoza (2002c), Pt I, Def. 6 and Expl., translation slightly adapted, emphasis added).

It is true that, for Hegel too, substance is absolutely infinite. Indeed, as we have seen, he actually calls it the infinite – just as he variously calls it the absolute, the true, or God.[54] These are all, for Hegel, characterizations of the same ultimate reality. And to be sure, every one of them, as ordinarily construed, might be thought to exclude negation. But Hegel has his own distinctive way of construing them. Thus consider the characterization

---

[52] Two things about the section from which this quotation is taken are worth noting. The first is that Hegel cautions against blankly identifying substance with the absolute idea: it is rather 'the idea under the still limited form of necessity' (p. 214). To *that* extent, Hegel further suggests, there is room also for a distinction between substance and God (cf. *Phenomenology*, Preface, ¶23). But I am prescinding from that subtlety throughout this section. The second thing worth noting is that Hegel insists that Spinoza, despite having failed to appreciate God's personhood, was a genuine theist (cf. also *Encyclopedia* I, §50). Given that he also sees himself as a theist, that goes *some* way – not far, I grant – towards reinforcing my own inclination to co-classify them.

[53] Cf. Deleuze (1988a), p. 13. See also Deleuze (2006a), 'Conclusion', for why it also stands in stark contrast to what we find in Nietzsche, who, so to speak, fights back. See further Ch. 15, §7(b), and Ch. 21, §2(b).

[54] Subject to various qualifications from which I am prescinding: see n. 52.

of substance as the true. By 'truth' Hegel means truth of a philosophical sort: that which ultimately makes sense.[55] And, in accord with this, he not only identifies substance with the true, or with truth; he also holds that there is no truth that does not exhaust it. That is, there is no truth – genuine, unadulterated truth – that falls short of the whole truth.[56] (So truth is not like gold, say. There is certainly gold that does not exhaust all the gold there is – the gold in the crown jewels, for example.) This is because nothing less than the unified whole ultimately makes sense. What then of the false? Well, the false plays the finite to the true's infinite. Recall that, for Hegel, the infinite is not opposed to the finite; it embraces it. (See §2.) So too the true is not opposed to the false; it embraces it. The false is a precondition of the true. This is not to say that the false is *part* of the true in the way in which hydrogen is part of water, nor that particular instances of the false are part of the true in the way in which individual bricks are part of Paddington Station. The point is rather this. The true 'is not a minted coin that can be pocketed ready made' (*Phenomenology*, Preface, ¶39). It must be *arrived at* through the very processes of *Aufhebung* referred to in the previous paragraph. These processes involve moments of falsehood and finitude, which are annulled and preserved in further moments of falsehood and finitude, and so on, until everything eventually makes indissoluble sense.[57] And *that* is the labour of the negative. So although Hegel's various characterizations of substance might appear to bespeak pure Spinozist positivity, his understanding of those characterizations in fact involves something very different.[58]

This is why Hegel is moved to proclaim, in opposition to 'rational theology' – by which he means the attempt to make sense of God using the resources of ordinary human understanding[59] – that

> it resulted in a notion of God which was what we may call the abstract of positivity or reality, to the exclusion of all negation. God was accordingly defined to be the most real of all beings. Anyone can see however that this most real of all beings, in which negation forms no part, is the very opposite of what it ought to be and of what understanding supposes it to be. Instead of being rich and full above all measure, it is so narrowly conceived that it is, on the contrary, extremely poor and altogether empty.... Without definite feature, that is, without negation, contained in the notion, there can only be an abstraction. (*Encyclopedia* I, §36Z, pp. 57–58)

---

[55] See n. 21.
[56] Cf. *Phenomenology*, Preface, ¶40.
[57] Cf. *Phenomenology*. Preface, ¶47.
[58] Cf. *Science of Logic*, I.ii.i.2C, Remark 1.
[59] For more on Hegel's conception of understanding, see the next section.

It is also why he is moved to proclaim, in opposition to Spinoza:

> As intuitively accepted by Spinoza without a previous mediation by dialectic, substance ... is as it were a dark shapeless abyss which engulfs all definite content as radically null, and produces from itself nothing that has a positive substance of its own. (*Encyclopedia* I, §151Z, p. 215)[60]

There is a profound difference, then, between Spinoza's conception of substance, as that self-subsistent whole in which all particulars are bound together, and Hegel's conception of substance, as an organic unity of opposed elements of finitude, whose oppositions are resolved in processes of *Aufhebung*.[61] This difference in turn occasions many others. Where Spinoza believed that each part of nature positively expresses the essence of substance, Hegel believes that nature is substance's 'other', the forum in which these processes of *Aufhebung* are played out so that substance can exist for itself, a forum which, in this very otherness, must itself be *aufgehoben* so that substance can exist in and for itself.[62] (In one remarkable passage in *Encyclopedia* I Hegel says, 'God, who is the truth, is known by us in His truth, that is, as absolute spirit, only in so far as we at the same time recognize that the world which He created, nature and the finite spirit, are, in their difference from God, untrue' (§83Z).) Again, where Spinoza found a paradigm of sense-making in the adequate knowledge of particular essences, Hegel holds that there is no sense ultimately to be made save in the integrated whole. Or, to put it another way, where Spinoza found a paradigm of sense-making in our ideas of what particular things can do, ideas that positively express their own reasons for being true, Hegel finds only moments of falsehood that need to be *aufgehoben* in order for the truth to be fully and properly realized. Or, to put it yet a third way, where Spinoza found, in the various differences and oppositions that we confront, an invitation to extend our knowledge by making sense of them, Hegel holds that the various differences and oppositions that we confront need to be overcome for true knowledge, that is substance's knowledge of itself, to be possible at all. Where Spinoza had no truck with the negative, Hegel talks of our 'looking the negative in the face, and tarrying with it ... [and converting] it into being' (*Phenomenology*, Preface, ¶32). These two thinkers, in countless ways, are worlds apart.[63]

---

[60] Note: the phrase that occurs in the ellipsis here is 'as the universal negative power'. This may look like an exegetical blunder on Hegel's part. In fact we can read him as invoking his own conception of substance.

[61] Hegel would deny that there is anything to bind the Spinozist particulars together; Spinoza, that there are any Hegelian oppositions to be resolved.

[62] The Fichtean echoes here should be very clear.

[63] Hegel at one point appropriates Spinoza as an ally, citing what he calls 'the proposition of Spinoza' that '*omnis determinatio est negatio*': all determination is negation (*Science of*

7.   Contradiction, Reason, and Understanding

I remarked in §1 on the liberties that Hegel takes with language. We have since seen some of his terms of art. 'Absolute idea' is one. Consider also the triad 'in itself', 'for itself', and 'in and for itself'. Not that there is anything especially remarkable about a philosopher's devising new words or phrases to meet particular needs that he or she has. New ideas can obviously require the exercise of new concepts, which can in turn require the use of new terms to express them.

Altogether more striking, if not altogether more shocking, is Hegel's apparent violation of certain basic linguistic rules, both syntactic and semantic. In his argument that the concept of nothing passes over into the concept of being, for instance, he all but insists that if there is nothing, then there is something, namely nothing. This seems to be almost Carrollesque in its combination of solecism and logical punning.[64] Worse, he proceeds to tell us, first, that 'pure being and pure nothing are … the same,' and then that, 'on the contrary, they are not the same, … they are absolutely distinct' (*Science of Logic*, I.i.i.1C, pp. 82–83), a contradiction that is scarcely made any the more palatable when glossed as 'the identity of identity and non-identity' (ibid., I.i, 'With What Must the Science Begin?', p. 74).

Nor is his toleration of contradiction confined to these abstract concepts. We saw in Chapter 5, §6, how Kant, confronted with arguments for the finitude of the physical universe and arguments for its infinitude, reacted by denying that there is any such thing – any such unconditioned whole – as the physical universe. This enabled him to attribute the apparent contradiction to a natural mistake of (human) reason, namely the mistake of assuming that there *must* be such a thing. Hegel, despite being less impressed than Kant by these arguments, likewise acknowledges that there are grounds both for regarding the physical universe as finite and for regarding it as infinite (i.e. spuriously infinite). But he cannot avail himself of the same solution. This is for two reasons. First, the Kantian solution requires a Kantian distinc-tion, of the very sort that Hegel repudiates, between appearance and reality. Second, since Hegel takes the operations of reason to be the operations of reality itself, whatever problem there is with the physical universe's being both finite and infinite must on his view be no less a problem with our being

---

Logic, I.i.i.2A(*b*), Remark, p. 113). But it is far from clear, in what he goes on to say about Spinoza, that he is being faithful to him. (The quotation itself is slightly inaccurate: the nearest approximation is in *Letter 50* in Spinoza (2002e), p. 892, where Spinoza writes, 'and determination is negation,' a translation of '*et determinatio est negatio.*') For an illu-minating discussion, see Duffy (2006), pp. 18–19.

[64] Cf. Carroll (1982), in which the following well-known passage occurs: '"I see nobody on the road," said Alice. – "I only wish *I* had such eyes," the King remarked…. "To be able to see Nobody! … Why, it's as much as *I* can do to see real people…"' (pp. 189–190, emphasis in original).

led to believe, by operations of reason, both that it is finite and that it is infinite. Hegel's own solution is to deny that there is a problem with *either* of these. *He accepts the contradiction.* The truly infinite, for Hegel, embraces a co-existence of opposed aspects, and the relevant arguments concerning the extent of the physical universe simply highlight some of these. Like all such opposed aspects, they are to be *aufgehoben* in the infinite's progress towards self-knowledge. (See *Science of Logic*, I.i.ii.2C(*b*), Remark 2, pp. 234–238, and *Encyclopedia* I, §§28 and 48.)

Now whenever we are confronted with a philosopher who departs from common sense in this way, with evidently serious intent, we seem to have a choice: either to accredit the philosopher in question with a non-standard view of things or to accredit him with a non-standard way of talking. I myself am attracted to the idea that, when the philosopher goes as far as to accept a contradiction, then strictly speaking only the second alternative makes sense; for unless the philosopher in question has his own idiolect, he is violating certain basic linguistic rules (as I said earlier Hegel appears to be doing) and is not strictly speaking saying anything at all.[65] Nevertheless, I am far from suggesting that, in order to interpret Hegel, we must simply forget the standard meanings of (some of) his words and seek suitable ways of translating them back into the vernacular. Even if it is true that what he says does not, strictly speaking, count as part of standard linguistic practice, 'strictly speaking' is the operative phrase. What he says is sufficiently closely related to standard linguistic practice, in sufficiently relevant ways, to gain its own admittance on a looser way of speaking. (An analogy: we may be quite happy to describe two people as playing chess even though they are oblivious to the rule that precludes castling through check and even though they often violate that rule, indeed even if they are aware of the rule and have agreed to ignore it; but *strictly* speaking, they are not playing chess.) *Strictly* speaking, when Hegel says that pure being and pure nothing are the same and are not the same, he is violating rules that govern the workings of some of the words he is using: he is not using those words with their standard meanings. But this is not to deny that he may have discovered compelling reasons for changing the rules; nor to deny that, if he has, saying this thing in the context of everything else he says may be the best way of getting the rest of us to acknowledge these reasons; nor to deny that, if the rules are accordingly changed, the words in question may retain their meanings on a looser way of speaking. (Another analogy: it was when the pawn was first

---

[65] For a forthright expression of this idea, see Quine (1970), p. 81. For discussion of Quine's views of these matters – of which the quoted passage is unrepresentative – see Ch. 12, §4. They are matters that will be intermittently of concern throughout Part Two.

Note: in §5 of the Introduction I mentioned Aristotle's closely related idea that it is impossible to believe a contradiction. For a forthright expression of *this* idea, from a much more recent source, see Davidson (2005a), pp. 44–45.

allowed to move forward two squares, some time in the fifteenth century, that chess strictly speaking came into existence, although on a looser way of speaking chess had already existed for a long time and merely underwent a change then.) So given that I do *not* say that a strict way of speaking is the only correct way of speaking, I am happy to grant that Hegel's toleration of this contradiction, and of others, is more than just a linguistic quirk. It is a genuine heterodoxy, couched in this way because the difficulty and unfamiliarity of the ideas require an assault on our standard ways of thinking, or on our standard ways of making sense of things.[66]

Such deliberate breaking of linguistic rules, to let a concept evolve into something previously beyond the expressive power of the language, is a device that I think we see frequently at work, not only in philosophy but also in the natural sciences. (A prime example, I would argue, is the rejection of basic principles of Euclidean geometry to allow for the development of the non-Euclidean concepts needed to describe physical space.[67]) However that may be, it is precisely the sort of device which, on a Hegelian conception, should be expected to mark transitions in our sense-making from lower stages of development to higher stages of development. For precisely what it does is to bring about the *Aufhebung* of previous forms of sense-making, the eruption of new conceptual resources from old, exhibiting both change and continuity. It is through such metamorphoses that reality eventually attains to the full infinite system of concepts required for its own ultimate sense-making.[68]

Hegel is in any case well aware that he is challenging standard ways of thinking. Of course he is.[69] This is part of what he has in mind when he distinguishes, as he frequently does, between reason and understanding.[70] The processes of conceptual development described above are processes of *reason*. Indeed, 'reason' can be thought of as yet another name for reality, the infinite, the absolute, the true. But *understanding* is the faculty at work in standard ways of thinking, or in standard ways of making sense of things. Its power, which is 'the most astonishing and mightiest of powers, ... the tremendous power of the negative' (*Phenomenology*, Preface, ¶32), is a power

---

[66] Cf. Findlay (1958), Ch. 3, §iii.

[67] But the correct description of this case is a matter of controversy. For some contributions to the controversy, see Ch. 11, §3, and Ch. 12, §4.

[68] It is also, of course, through such metamorphoses that reality keeps track of developments in that of which it makes sense: itself, undergoing those very metamorphoses.

[69] See esp. *Encyclopedia* I, §88. And cf. §1 above: if we react adversely to what he says, then that is exactly as he would predict, which means that we inadvertently corroborate what he says.

[70] See *Encyclopedia* I, VI, where he further distinguishes between negative and positive reason; I shall ignore that further distinction.

of analysis. Understanding breaks its objects up into component parts. It treats of them in isolation from all else and without regard to the whole. It arrives at 'thoughts which are ... familiar, fixed, and inert determinations' (ibid., emphasis removed). This is why it cannot tolerate contradiction, whose resolution is always part of the active processes of reason at work in the whole and is *ipso facto* beyond its purview. It cannot make sense of contradiction. Nor can it make sense of *Aufhebung*. It must, as it were, yield to *Aufhebung*. That is, it must itself be *aufgehoben*. (This is not to deny that understanding has all sorts of practical uses, nor even that it has all sorts of theoretical uses, for instance in mathematics (*Encyclopedia* I, §80Z). But in *metaphysics*, the most general attempt to make sense of things, it must be *aufgehoben*.[71])

Reason, unlike understanding, does tolerate contradiction.[72] But, as I have been urging, tolerating contradiction in this context is not the same as acceding to the possibility that a proposition and its negation should both be true, on a standard conception of what a proposition is, of what negation is, and of what truth is.[73] On a standard conception of these matters, nothing of the sort *can* be acceded to. The point is rather that the standard conception must itself be *aufgehoben*. 'The abstract "either-or"' of understanding (*Encyclopedia* I, §80Z, p. 115) must be overcome. And make no mistake: this is a restless and bloody matter. As Hegel puts it, 'the battle of reason is the struggle to break up the rigidity to which the understanding has reduced everything' (ibid., §32Z, p. 53).

These remarks go some way towards answering a question that naturally arises, at least from the point of view of understanding, about Hegel's dialectic. If reason, or reality, tolerates contradiction, why must contradiction be resolved? Why should it not survive, in all its raw primitive inconsistency, into the final synthesis of the absolute idea?[74] To ask this question is to miss the point that *what* reason tolerates just is something that must be resolved. Or, to put the point in a suitably contradictory way, what reason tolerates is something that cannot be tolerated. 'The so-called world,' Hegel insists, '... is never and nowhere without contradiction' (*Science of Logic*, I.i.ii.2C(*b*), Remark 2, p. 238). 'But,' he straightway adds, 'it is unable to endure it' (ibid.; cf. *Encyclopedia* I, §11). Contradiction is the motor force of change. By its very nature it propels reality to a higher stage of development in which it is *aufgehoben*. Without it, there would be no

[71] Cf. Copleston (1963), pp. 174–175.
[72] Cf. *Encyclopedia* I, §11.
[73] Here I think I part company with Graham Priest, in Priest (1995), Ch. 7, passim. For accounts that are closer to mine, see Hanna (1996) and Pippin (1996).
[74] Cf. Taylor (1975), p. 105; and Inwood (1983), Ch. 10, §§12–15, esp. pp. 459–460.

movement, no activity, no purpose, nothing (see *Science of Logic*, I.ii.2C, Remark 3, p. 439).[75]

One of the best ways to make sense of all of this is in terms of the relation between the finite and the infinite. For a thing to be finite, recall, is for it to be negated by an 'other'. That is as much as to say that, by its very nature, the finite invokes its own negation. And that in turn means that the finite has an inherently contradictory nature. *This* is why there is contradiction everywhere. For there is finitude everywhere. The finite invokes its own negation, not only in thought, but also, *eo ipso*, in reality, since thought and reality are ultimately one on Hegel's conception. For a finite thing to invoke its own negation, however, is for it to bring about its own end in such a way as simultaneously to be true to itself. In a word, then – in the word that Hegel himself unsurprisingly uses – the finite *aufhebt*[76] itself (*Encyclopedia* I §81, p. 116). As Hegel proceeds to explain,

> everything finite, instead of being stable and ultimate, is rather change-able and transient; and this is exactly what we mean by that dialectic of the finite, by which the finite, as implicitly other than what it is, is forced beyond its own immediate or natural being to turn suddenly into its oppo-site.... All things ... – that is, the finite world as such – are doomed....
> (*Encyclopedia* I, §81Z, p. 118; cf. ibid., §§28Z and 214)

But such *Aufhebung* is the resolution of the contradiction. And the infinite, as I have repeatedly said, is not opposed to such finitude; it embraces it, in all its contradictoriness, and along with its nisus towards the resolution of that contradictoriness. The infinite, or reality, is the integrated whole in which this resolution is played out: 'the living unity of the manifold,' as Frederick Copleston puts it (Copleston (1963), p. 165), or 'the Bacchanalian revel in which no member is not drunk,' in Hegel's own evocative image (*Phenomenology*, Preface, ¶47).

All of this is beyond the grasp of understanding.[77] That is why it has the air of the mystical. But, Hegel insists, there is mystery here '*only* ... for the understanding' (*Encyclopedia* I, §82Z, p. 121, emphasis added). This 'mys-tical' is 'the concrete unity of those propositions which understanding only accepts in their separation and opposition.... [It] may be styled mystical – not however because thought cannot both reach and comprehend it, but merely because it lies beyond the compass of understanding' (ibid.). It lies beyond the compass of *understanding*. It does not, on the broad conception of metaphysics with which I am operating, lie beyond the compass of meta-physics. See further §9 below.

---

[75] Cf. Copleston (1963), pp. 176–177; and Taylor (1975), p. 107.

[76] See n. 3.

[77] There is even a hint in *Encyclopedia* I, §88, p. 131, that it is beyond the expressive power of language.

8.   Hegel *Contra* Kant Again. Absolute Idealism

We began this account of Hegel's system with his rejection of Kant's transcendental idealism (§2). It will be instructive, in the light of what has emerged since, to reflect on other more specific parts of Kant's philosophy with which Hegel both must and does take issue.

First, although Kant drew a distinction of his own between understanding and reason, it was but a faint adumbration of the distinction that Hegel urges on us. For Kant, understanding was the faculty of concepts whereby we think about objects of experience. In particular, it was the source of the twelve fundamental *a priori* concepts whereby we do so (Kant (1998), A19/B33 and A79–80/B105–106). Reason was a higher faculty, a faculty that on the one hand enables us to recognize systematic interconnections between the deliverances of understanding (ibid., A130–131/B169–170 and A302/B359) and on the other hand frees the concepts of understanding from their restricted application to objects of possible experience, thereby enabling us to think about things in themselves and indeed to determine fundamental principles of morality (e.g. ibid., §II, Ch. 2, passim). Reason was thus a faculty that we can use to step back from understanding and to make sense of, around, and beyond understanding in ways that understanding itself could never equip us to do. And it was motivated by the demand for the unconditioned. As Kant put it, 'reason is driven by a propensity of its nature to go beyond its use in experience … and to find peace only in the completion of its circle in a self-subsisting systematic whole' (ibid., A797/B825).

That last clause might have been written by Hegel. But there is much else here that is an anathema to Hegel. For one thing, the principal contrast that Kant recognized between understanding and reason made no sense without the further Kantian distinction between appearance and reality which Hegel abjures. Furthermore, Kant cast reason as just another faculty. In fact it was the faculty that we use, plunged as we are in the midst of things, to make sense of that very distinction, the distinction between appearance and reality. For Hegel, reason *is* reality. Again, Kant took reason to be no less bound by principles of standard logic than understanding – which is why, when reason's demand for the unconditioned issued in arguments both for the finitude of the physical universe and for its infinitude, Kant concluded that there had been a malfunctioning of some sort, specifically a failure to draw that same distinction between appearance and reality. For Hegel, Kant's very presumption that something had gone wrong showed that he was assimilating reason to what he (Hegel) calls understanding (*Encyclopedia* I, §45Z; cf. *Science of Logic*, Introduction, 'General Notion of Logic', p. 46).

On Hegel's conception, we can *both* reject the distinction between appearance and reality *and* acknowledge that this leaves us with a rational demand for the unconditioned that is unmeetable without contradiction, simply by acquiescing in the contradiction. Kant would have found this unintelligible.[78] Relatedly, on Hegel's conception, we can regard as constitutive various uses of concepts, such as the use of the concept of the complete physical universe in cosmology, that Kant would have regarded, on pain of contradiction, as regulative. For Hegel there is no such pain; or better, perhaps, there is such pain, but it is to be endured for its corresponding gain.

To return to the twelve fundamental *a priori* concepts that Kant recognized: for Kant these were tools that we use, from our vantage point within reality, to make our own distinctive sense of reality. To revert to the familiar metaphor, they were part of our spectacles. For Hegel fundamental concepts of this sort are at work in reality itself (*Encyclopedia* I, §42Z, p. 70). True, they can be used to make sense of reality. But this is because they are used by reality to make sense (of itself). They are constitutive of reality. Nor should we treat them as simply given. For Kant it was a brute fact that we use these twelve concepts. Hegel, as we saw in §4, seeks to *work out* what the concepts are – what they must be. He seeks to make sense *of* them, not just with them. (Cf. *Encyclopedia* I, §41.) Relatedly, although Kant divided his twelve concepts into four groups of three, in each of which the third 'arises from the combination of the first two' (Kant (1998), B110), and although he subsequently made much of that structure in the architectonic that he imposed on his system,[79] Hegel sees an arbitrariness and an incompleteness in Kant's taxonomy which is for him (Hegel) indicative of the fact that the full infinite system of concepts, while not infinite in the spurious sense of containing infinitely many, nevertheless contains many more than those twelve.[80]

Another objection that Hegel has to Kant's enterprise is that it is impossible to provide a critique of our various epistemic faculties without presupposing them. He writes:

> A main line of argument in the Critical Philosophy bids us pause before proceeding to inquire into God or into the true being of things, and tells us first of all to examine the faculty of cognition and see whether it is equal to such an effort. We ought, says Kant, to become acquainted with the instrument, before we undertake the work for which it is to be employed; for if the instrument be insufficient, all our trouble will be spent in vain.... [Now in] the case of other instruments, we can try to criticize them in other ways than by setting about the special work for which they are destined. But the examination of knowledge can only be carried out by an act

---

[78] Not, as I emphasized in the previous section, that acquiescing in the contradiction means accepting that some proposition and its negation are both true, at any rate not on a standard understanding of these matters. But then what Kant would have found unintelligible is the suggestion that there is a relevant non-standard understanding of these matters.

[79] For one example among many, see Kant (1998), A161–162/B200–201. For further reflections on how the set of concepts is structured, see ibid., B109ff.

[80] Cf. *Encyclopedia* I, §60Z.

of knowledge.... [And] to seek to know before we know is as absurd as the wise resolution of Scholasticus, not to venture into the water until he had learned to swim. (*Encyclopedia* I, §10, p. 14, translation very slightly adapted; cf. *Phenomenology*, Introduction, ¶73, and *Science of Logic*, I.i, 'With What Must the Science Begin?', p. 68)

Kant might reply that this objection misfires when the enterprise takes the form of using one faculty to provide a critique of another, say reason to provide a critique of understanding – which accords with the two-level view of these two faculties sketched above. But

- Kant did also use reason to provide a critique of reason
- Hegel would in any case reject such a two-level view, not because he would deny that understanding is in some sense inferior to reason, but because he would see its inferiority as the inferiority of that which is preserved in its superior, through *Aufhebung*

and anyway,

- not even Kant held understanding and reason to work independently of each other, or at least not independently enough to address Hegel's objection (see e.g. Kant (1998), A298–302/B355–359 and A657–659/ B685–687).

It is important, however, to realize that Hegel's objection is not to the very project of using our epistemic faculties to provide their own critique, only to any pretensions of non-circularity in doing so.[81] He later voices the same objection and adds:

True, ... the forms of thought should be subjected to a scrutiny before they are used: yet what is this scrutiny but *ipso facto* a cognition? So that what we want is to combine in our process of inquiry the actions of the forms of thought with a criticism of them. The forms of thought ... are at once the object of research and the action of that object. (*Encyclopedia* I, §41Z, p. 66)

Here we see another instance of a pattern which I have already noted in both Descartes (Ch. 1, §4) and Hume (Ch. 4, §4), and which I have further identified as a feature of Quine's naturalized epistemology, namely the pattern in which the faculties that we use to make sense of our own sense-making are precisely what we are thereby making sense of.[82]

This is significant for two related reasons. The first has to do with the relative assessment of Kant and Hegel. It is easy to see Kant as the more

---

[81] It is of course a further question to what extent Kant had any such pretensions.

[82] Recall the analogy of the physiologists using their faculty of sight to investigate the faculty of sight (Ch. 1, §4).

level-headed of the two, and Hegel as the wild if systematic visionary. Yet when Hegel insists that we cannot make sense of our own most basic sense-making save from a point of immersion in it, we are reminded that it was Kant who tried to take a critical step back from that sense-making; who accorded it a transcendental structure which he took to be at the same time the structure of what we make sense of; who was then forced to draw a radical distinction between appearance and reality; who was obliged to count even space and time as features (merely) of appearance; who by contrast counted our freedom, which he could not bring himself to disavow, as a feature of reality; who accordingly held the originary exercise of our freedom to be an unlocated, timeless exercise of purely rational self-legislation; who grounded the demands of morality in this self-legislation; and who thus severed those demands, at least to that extent, from the concrete practicalities of our shared life together. At times he makes Hegel look like a model of sobriety.[83]

The second reason why it is significant that Hegel does not raise any objection to our using faculties of sense-making in order to make sense of those same faculties has to do with the Fichtean choice paraded in the previous chapter. This was between, in my terminology, transcendentalism and naturalism. There is a sense in which Hegel adopts naturalism. For he holds that we make sense of things by being in the midst of them: we are ourselves among the things we make sense of. Nevertheless, the sense in which Hegel adopts naturalism is tenuous. There is also a sense, certainly no more tenuous, in which he adopts transcendentalism. For he also holds, as we saw in §3, that the things we make sense of are transcendentally conditioned by concepts that we use in making sense of them. What Hegel really does, of course, is to challenge the dichotomy. It is another instance of 'the abstract "either-or"' of understanding. We could say that he adopts 'transcendentalism-cum-naturalism'.[84]

Hegel's own term for his position is 'absolute idealism' (*Encyclopedia* I, §45Z, p. 73, and §160Z, p. 223). He chooses this term to distinguish his position from Kant's, which he calls 'subjective idealism' (ibid., §45Z, p. 73).[85] His position is in many respects more radical than Kant's, inasmuch as it draws no ultimate distinction between sense-making and reality. Things are as they are because of the sense-making at work in them, a sense-making whose object is ultimately itself, making sense. This is 'absolute' sense-making. But, for reasons that I have just tried to indicate, Hegel's position is also in many respects more restrained than Kant's. Though it has

[83] For Hegel's attempt to represent himself as a thinker of common sense, see e.g. *Encyclopedia* I, §81Z, p. 118.

[84] For a summary account, see *Phenomenology*, V, ¶¶231–239.

[85] As I mentioned parenthetically in §3, Hegel's idealism is by my definition an empirical idealism, though of a highly idiosyncratic kind.

commerce with the absolute, it has no commerce with the transcendent. 'The absolute is ... directly before us, so present that so long as we think, we must ... always carry it with us and always use it' (*Encyclopedia* I, §24 Z, p. 40). 'Absolute idealism' is an entirely appropriate label.[86]

9. The Implications for Metaphysics

What, finally, are the implications of all of this for metaphysics?

I have already pointed out (§4) that Hegel's logic is a paradigm of metaphysics on my definition. I also subsequently alluded to the closely related fact (§7) that the resolution of contradiction in the infinite whole is itself a metaphysical exercise of sorts. This is because it is a way of making sense of contradiction – something that reason does but understanding cannot do – at what must be, in the nature of the case, the highest level of generality.

On my conception of metaphysics, then, Hegel is as great a champion of metaphysics as there could be. Metaphysics is at the heart of his system. Reason, the ground of maximally general sense-making, *is* reality. To paraphrase a quotation from §4: to him who makes maximally general sense of things, things make maximally general sense.

But even on Hegel's own conception (which is in any case not so very different from mine) there is a glorious ineluctability about metaphysics. 'Metaphysics,' he tells us, '[is] the science of things set and held in thoughts – thoughts accredited able to express the essential reality of things' (*Encyclopedia* I, §24, p. 36, emphasis removed). He later adds that 'metaphysics is nothing but the range of universal thought-determinations, and as it were the diamond-net into which we bring everything in order to make it intelligible' (*Encyclopedia* II, §246, Addition, p. 62). And he says:

> Newton gave physics an express warning to beware of metaphysics ...; but, to his honour be it said, he did not by any means obey his own warning. The only mere physicists are the animals: they alone do not think: while man is a thinking being and a born metaphysician. The real question is not whether we shall apply metaphysics, but whether our metaphysics [is] of the right kind: in other words, whether we are not ... adopting one-sided forms of thought, rigidly fixed by understanding, and making these the basis of our theoretical as well as our practical work. (*Encyclopedia* I, §98Z, p. 144)[87]

With metaphysics conceived in this way, and standing in this relation to his system as a whole, Hegel is inevitably concerned as much with the

---

[86] Cf. Copleston (1963), p. 171; Taylor (1975), pp. 109–110; and Stern (2002), pp. 100–101.

[87] Cf. *Encyclopedia* I, §38, p. 62. For an onslaught against the wrong kind of metaphysics, modelled on that of Kant in his 'Transcendental Dialectic', see *Encyclopedia* I, III.

nature of metaphysics as with any question that arises within metaphysics. Not that that is an especially Hegelian way of putting the matter. For this very distinction is yet another that he would renounce. It is here, more than anywhere else in the historical story that I am telling, that any attempt to disentangle the metaphysical from the meta-metaphysical is futile. To make sense of reality, at the highest level of generality, is on Hegel's conception to make sense of how reality makes sense of reality at the highest level of generality (*Phenomenology*, Introduction, ¶88, and *Encyclopedia* I, §17).

Hegel's impatience with such distinctions is further evidenced in his relation to the three questions that I posed in §6 of the Introduction, about the scope and limits of metaphysics. In all three cases Hegel would challenge the contrast presupposed in the question. This is so even in the case of the Novelty Question, where there is greatest temptation to accredit him with a simple and unequivocal answer. In his own sacrifice of the commonplaces of understanding, to make way for the extravagances of reason, he may appear to be a paradigmatically 'revisionary' metaphysician, with a corresponding commitment to the possibility of radically new forms of sense-making. In a way he is. But his commitment is not to radically new forms of sense-making *as opposed to* standard forms: the former must evolve out of the latter, which must in turn be preserved in the former, in the way that is characteristic of *Aufhebung*. As Hegel himself puts it:

> Philosophic thought ... possesses, in addition to the common forms, some forms of its own ... [but] speculative logic [i.e. the logic of these philosophic forms of thought] contains all previous logic and metaphysics: it preserves the same forms of thought, the same laws and objects – while at the same time remodelling and expanding them with wider categories. (*Encyclopedia* I, §9, p. 13, capitalization altered to suit the new division into sentences)

The early modern period draws to a close, then, with a profoundly self-conscious assault on a number of popular conceptions about the scope and limits of metaphysics and about how these are affected by the geometry of sense-making. This is a continuation of the process that we saw initiated in Hume and Kant, of reflecting on what sense can be made of things, at the highest level of generality, by reflecting on what sense can be made of things at all. It heralds a period in the history of (meta-)metaphysics of unprecedented preoccupation, and, it must be said, uneasy preoccupation, with sense itself.

PART TWO

✦

THE LATE MODERN PERIOD I
THE ANALYTIC TRADITION

CHAPTER 8

Frege

Sense Under Scrutiny

1. What Is Frege Doing Here?

Gottlob Frege (1848–1925) was by common consent the greatest logician of all time. He founded the discipline of formal logic, in its contemporary guise.[1] In this he made the first and most significant advance in the study of logic since Aristotle, an advance that was certainly significant enough to belie Kant's famous declaration that 'since the time of Aristotle' logic 'has … been unable to take a single step forward, and therefore seems to all appearance to be finished and complete' (Kant (1998), B viii). Frege was also a brilliant philosopher of mathematics. But he was not a metaphysician, not really.[2] Nor was he a meta-metaphysician: he had no special interest in the nature, scope, or limits of metaphysics. I need to begin this chapter by saying something about why it is included at all.

Part Two of this book is concerned with the analytic tradition in philosophy. There is no clear agreement about how to characterize this tradition. But since on any account one of its principal aims is clarity of understanding and one of the principal means whereby it pursues this

---

[1] See *Begriffsschrift*. Note: throughout this chapter I use the following abbreviations for Frege's works: *Begriffsschrift* for Frege (1967); 'Comments' for Frege (1997d); 'Concept and Object' for Frege (1997e); 'Diary Entries' for Frege (1979); 'Formal Theories' for Frege (1984a); *Foundations* for Frege (1980); 'Foundations of Geometry' for Frege (1984c); 'Function and Concept' for Frege (1997a); 'Insights' for Frege (1997k); 'Knowledge of Mathematics' for Frege (1997n); 'Letter to Husserl' for Frege (1997b); 'Letter to Jourdain' for Frege (1997j); 'Letter to Russell' for Frege (1997h); 'Logic' for Frege (1997g); 'Notes' for Frege (1997m); 'Numbers' for Frege (1997o); 'Review' for Frege (1997f); 'Sense and Bedeutung' for Frege (1997c); *The Basic Laws* for Frege (1964); and 'Thought' for Frege (1997l). Page references for all but *Begriffsschrift*, 'Diary Entries', *Foundations*, and *The Basic Laws* are in duplicate, first to the translations themselves and then to the original German sources as indicated in their margins. All unaccompanied references are to the *Foundations*.

[2] He dissociated his work from what he called metaphysics in *The Basic Laws*, Introduction, p. 18. See also Dummett (1981b), pp. 428ff.

aim is the analysis of language,[3] Frege cannot fail to count as a supremely important contributor both to its inception and to its propagation. This is not least because contemporary formal logic provides the single most powerful set of tools that analytic philosophers use in undertaking such analysis. But furthermore it was Frege who demonstrated how this kind of close attention to language could play a crucial role in addressing philosophical problems.[4]

I say a 'crucial' role. Some commentators would go further and say a 'foundational' role. In their view Frege was the main instigator, or one of the main instigators, of the 'linguistic turn' in philosophy.[5] Michael Dummett is the staunchest and best-known proponent of this view. He characterizes the revolution that he sees Frege as having effected in the following terms:

> Before Descartes, it can hardly be said that any part of philosophy was recognized as being ... fundamental to all the rest: the Cartesian revolution consisted in giving this role to the theory of knowledge ...[, which] was accepted as the starting point for more than two centuries.
>
> Frege's basic achievement lay in the fact that he totally ignored the Cartesian tradition, and was able, posthumously, to impose his different perspective on other philosophers of the analytic tradition....
>
> For Frege the first task, in any philosophical enquiry, is the analysis of meanings. (Dummett (1981a), pp. 666–667).

Dummett later adds:

> [Frege] effected a revolution in philosophy as great as the similar revolution previously effected by Descartes.... We can, therefore, date a whole epoch in philosophy as beginning with the work of Frege, just as we can do with Descartes. (Ibid., p. 669; cf. Dummett (1993a), p. 5)

Dummett accordingly characterizes analytic philosophy as 'post-Fregean philosophy' (Dummett (1978m), p. 441).[6]

I shall not try to arbitrate on whether Frege deserves such an accolade. It is moot whether analytic philosophers do take the study of language to be foundational in this way; moot, for that matter, whether Frege did; moot, therefore, whether there has been any such revolution; and moot whether,

---

[3] See e.g. Williamson (2007), Ch. 1.

[4] Perhaps I should say, 'who demonstrated afresh ...'. For what he demonstrated, at least in broad terms, was hardly unknown to medieval thinkers.

[5] The phrase 'linguistic turn' seems to be due to Gustav Bergmann, in Bergmann (1964), p. 3. See again Williamson (2007), pp. 10ff.

[6] Cf. my comments about post-Cartesian philosophy and post-Kantian philosophy in Ch. 2, §6, and Ch. 5, §1, respectively. For a further indication of Dummett's views on this matter, see Dummett (1993a), esp. Chs 2, 13, and 14. For further discussion of these views, see Ch. 14, esp. §1.

even if there has, Frege can take so much credit for it.[7] What is not moot is that Frege is of colossal significance to the analytic tradition, both historically and philosophically, which is all that matters in the current context. There is much in the next six chapters that will make little or no sense except in relation to his work.[8] That is reason enough for me to have included this chapter.

Even so, what I have said so far does not convey the full force of the reason, nor, perhaps, its most important aspect.

Even within the shared commitment that analytic philosophers have to the study of language – whatever precise form that commitment takes – there is considerable latitude. In particular, what sort of language? Natural language? There is a broad division between those analytic philosophers who see themselves as dealing with language as it is and those who see themselves as dealing with language as it ought to be – but very often is not, absent the imposition of various kinds of reform on our ordinary ways of speaking. Frege himself certainly belonged to the second of these camps. He was largely contemptuous of natural language, which he held to suffer from all sorts of defects that hamper clear thinking. It was in this vein that he invented his own formal language, designed to enable him to address the questions in the philosophy of mathematics that particularly exercised him.[9]

Were Frege's attitude to be extended to the practice of metaphysics, this might appear to involve him in a clear and direct answer to the Novelty Question which I posed in §6 of the Introduction, the question whether there is scope for us, when we practise metaphysics, to make sense of things in ways that are radically new. It might appear that Frege would have been bound to say that there is, and bound indeed to say that we had better do so. In fact, however, there is something profoundly non-revisionary about Frege's own use of his formal language. It was not intended to bring about radical changes in our sense-making. It was intended to exploit, nurture, and consolidate sense-making of ours that is already under way (cf. *Begriffsschrift*, Preface, pp. 6–7, and *Foundations*, §2). In saying this, I do not mean to suggest that Frege had no concern to bring about *any* changes

---

[7] For especially fierce opposition, see Baker and Hacker (1984). For an interesting and compelling attempt to provide a corrective, see Skorupski (1984), §II.

   It is also of course moot whether, if there has been such a revolution, it has pointed philosophy in the right direction. Dummett, who believes that it has, frankly admits that all he has to offer to anyone who is sceptical about this is 'the banal reply which any prophet has to make to any sceptic: time will tell' (Dummett (1978m), p. 458).

[8] There is much in Part Three that makes better sense in relation to it: see e.g. Ch. 17, §4; Ch. 20, §3; and Ch. 21, §4.

[9] See *Begriffsschrift*, Preface, pp. 5–6, and 'Insights', pp. 323–324/p. 272. (Inventing this formal language was a principal component in his founding contemporary formal logic: see *Begriffsschrift*, Preface, p. 7.)

in connection with our sense-making. On the contrary, one thing that he wanted to do with his formal language, as part of the process of consolidation, was to bring about reform in those cases – those many cases – where, because of the imperfections of natural language, we merely *think* that we are making sense and we need the help of some such regimentation either to start making sense of the kind we think we are making or else to see that in fact there is no such sense to be made.[10] But when it came to introducing new concepts, Frege only ever showed an interest in drawing new boundaries in familiar regions of conceptual space, not in entering new regions; an interest, as we might say, in conceptual innovation but not in radical conceptual innovation (cf. §§64 and 88).[11]

None of this is enough to show that Frege would have given a conservative answer to the Novelty Question, had he addressed it. That he himself was not interested in radical changes in our sense-making does not mean that he would have denied the possibility of such a thing, either in metaphysics or in any other discipline. What primarily mattered for Frege was not whether we were making new sense or old sense, but simply whether we were making sense. And this at last brings us back to my reason for including him in my historical narrative. One of Frege's greatest achievements was the way in which he made (linguistic) sense an object of philosophical scrutiny in its own right. Philosophers had certainly reflected on sense before. (See e.g. Ch. 4, §2, where we considered some of Hume's ruminations on it.) There had even been attempts to subject different aspects of sense to close methodical investigation.[12] But these had been relatively piecemeal. Nobody previously, or at least nobody previously in the modern period,

---

[10] Cf. Diamond (1991a), §IV; (1991b); and (1991d).

[11] In distinguishing between non-radical conceptual innovation and radical conceptual innovation I only mean to register a distinction of degree; the spatial metaphor should not be taken to indicate otherwise. Roughly, the degree in question is the degree of independence that the new concepts enjoy with respect to old concepts. The least radical conceptual innovation consists merely in combining old concepts to form new ones. As Frege emphasized in §88, he was interested in conceptual innovation that was more radical than *that*, for he was interested in conceptual innovation that was 'fruitful', in a way in which the combining of old concepts never could be. Nevertheless, to revert to my spatial metaphor, what he was interested in still involved drawing boundaries over, around, and within those that had already been drawn. It did not involve drawing boundaries in new regions altogether. For further discussion, see Moore (2003a), pp. 121–124. (I there introduce a shift of metaphor, to one of fineness of grain. In many ways this is a more appropriate metaphor, though it infelicitously downplays the difference between the conceptual innovation that Frege was interested in and that which I am now calling radical; see p. 123.)

[12] Particularly noteworthy is Arnauld and Nicol (1996), which is commonly known as the *Port-Royal Logic* and which was written during the seventeenth century. This was a logic textbook that incorporated a good deal of semantics.

had attempted to produce a *theory* of sense: a rigorous systematic comprehensive account of what sense is and how it functions. Frege did. I use the word 'attempted' advisedly. It is by no means uncontroversial that he succeeded. It is not even uncontroversial that what he attempted to do was something that could be done. We shall see scepticism of various kinds later in Part Two.[13] The fact remains that Frege helped to provide a new focus in philosophy. Because he wanted to make sense of how we make mathematical sense, he was led to address some very general questions about sense itself. And, linguistic turn or no linguistic turn, he thereby helped to inaugurate a phase in my narrative in which due attention to sense came to be seen as an indispensable tool in the quest to *make* sense. Despite his lack of engagement with metaphysics, he is of immediate and obvious relevance to the story I have to tell.

2.   The Project: Arithmetic as a Branch of Logic

Frege's philosophical project is to show, *contra* Kant, that the truths of arithmetic are analytic. More specifically, it is to show that they are laws of logic (§87). 'More specifically', because a law of logic is a truth that is not only analytic but also composed (exclusively) of logical concepts. It may be analytic that all aunts are female, but it is not a law of logic. Neither the concept of an aunt nor the concept of being female is a logical concept.

Can Frege realize his project *just* by showing that the truths of arithmetic are composed of logical concepts? An analytic truth need not be composed of logical concepts; but is the converse perhaps true? Is a truth that is composed of logical concepts guaranteed to be analytic? No. A putative counterexample is that there are infinitely many non-logical objects[14] (if that is a truth; if it is not, then a putative counterexample is that there are only finitely many non-logical objects).[15]

Frege's task is twofold, then: to show that the truths of arithmetic are analytic, and to show that they are composed of logical concepts. It hardly appears that way to Frege, however. This is because, in Frege's view, there is hardly anything, in the second case, to show. His notion of a logical concept is a concept that can be exercised in thought about any subject matter.[16]

---

[13] See esp. Ch. 10, §2, and Ch. 12, §§4 and 5.

[14] A non-logical object is anything whose existence is not guaranteed by logic alone. What would be an example of the opposite, a logical object? If Frege is right (see below), any of the natural numbers $0, 1, 2, \ldots$.

[15] Why putative? Well, for this to be a genuine example requires, among other things, that the concept of being logical be a logical concept. It is not obvious that it is, though I think Frege would have said it is; see further below.

[16] In the terms of Ch. 5, §8, we could also say that it is a concept that can be exercised in sense-making of the thinnest kind.

This is connected to the fact that he takes logical laws to govern thought (as such), not any of the more specific things that thought may be about ('Thought', p. 323/p. 58; cf. again §87, and cf. 'Foundations of Geometry', p. 338/pp. 427–428). And he takes it to be clear already that arithmetical concepts satisfy this condition; for *whatever* specific things we may think about, they can be counted (see e.g. 'Formal Theories', p. 112/pp. 94–95).[17]

Insofar as it *is* clear already that arithmetical concepts are logical concepts, is it not likewise clear already that arithmetical truths are logical truths, that is laws of logic? If even Kantian things in themselves can be counted, for example, then must it not be the case that seven things in themselves, of some kind, and five things in themselves, of some disjoint kind, together constitute twelve things in themselves? Must not the truths of arithmetic extend as far as the concepts of arithmetic, which, if that is as far as coherent thought, straight away marks them out as laws of logic?

That is too quick. There is an equivocation here. 'To extend as far as coherent thought' may mean to extend to all that actually exists and can be an object of coherent thought, which is as much as is secured for the truths of arithmetic by the fact that its concepts are logical. Or it may mean to extend to all that can coherently be thought to exist, which is what is required of the truths of arithmetic for them to count as laws of logic. Even if the truths of arithmetic extend as far as coherent thought in the former, weaker sense, they may still depend, like the truth concerning how many non-logical objects there are, on some logical contingency about what actually exists. That is, they may fail to extend as far as coherent thought in the latter, stronger sense.

Even so, once we have got as far as agreeing that arithmetical concepts are logical concepts, which, however uncontentious it may seem to Frege, *already sets us apart from Kant,*[18] we have overcome what is probably the main obstacle to viewing the truths of arithmetic as laws of logic. And indeed there is a passage very early in the *Foundations* in which Frege all but gives the quick argument above for his thesis. Having indicated his agreement with Kant that the truths of geometry hold only of what can be given in spatial intuition,[19] he writes:

> Conceptual thought alone can after a fashion shake off this yoke.... For purposes of conceptual thought we can always assume the contrary of some one or other of the geometrical axioms, without involving ourselves in any self-contradictions when we proceed to our deductions, despite the

[17] Cf. Aristotle, *Metaphysics*, Bk Γ, Ch. 3. 1005a19–24.

[18] See Kant (1998), A242/B300, and Kant (2002a), §10.

[19] Frege likewise agrees with Kant that the truths of geometry can be known *a priori*. It is a further matter, however, whether he sees this combination of features in quite the same way as Kant, and in particular whether he sees it as supplying grounds for transcendental idealism; for extensive discussion, see Dummett (1991f), esp. §7.

conflict between our assumptions and our intuition. The fact that this is possible shows that the axioms of geometry are independent ... of the primitive laws of logic, and consequently are synthetic. Can the same be said of the fundamental propositions of the science of number [i.e. arithmetic]? Here, we have only to try denying any one of them, and complete confusion ensues. Even to think at all seems no longer possible. The basis of arithmetic lies deeper, it seems, ... than that of geometry. The truths of arithmetic govern all that is numerable. This is the widest domain of all; for to it belongs not only the actual, not only the intuitable, but everything thinkable. Should not the laws of number, then, be connected very intimately with the laws of thought [i.e. logical laws]? (§14)

It *looks* as if Frege is already where he wants to be. But no; he sees these considerations merely as lending plausibility to his thesis. He takes that thesis still to stand in need of proof.[20] In particular, of course, he thinks he still needs to show that the truths of arithmetic are analytic. That is his great project.

Now although Frege intends nothing other by analyticity than what Kant intended (§3, n. 1), one of his chief services to philosophy is to provide a far clearer characterization of the notion than Kant ever did.[21] Frege's characterization, in application to mathematics, is as follows:

> When a proposition is called ... analytic ..., [this] is a judgement about the ultimate ground upon which rests the justification for holding it to be true.
>
> This means that the question is ... assigned, if the truth concerned is a mathematical one, to the sphere of mathematics. The problem becomes, in fact, that of finding the proof of the proposition, and of following it up right back to the primitive truths. If, in carrying out this process, we come only on general logical laws and on definitions, then the truth is an analytic one, bearing in mind that we must take account also of all propositions upon which the admissibility of any of the definitions depends. (§3)

To show that the truths of arithmetic are analytic, then, Frege needs to supply a set of suitable definitions and a set of 'primitive' logical laws, by which is presumably meant logical laws whose truth is beyond dispute and indeed – if questions are not to be begged – whose status as logical laws is beyond dispute, and then to demonstrate that the truths of arithmetic can be derived from the latter with the aid of the former. (This is reminiscent

[20] Cf. Dummett (1991a), pp. 45–46. I am greatly indebted to Dummett's discussion of these matters: see esp. ibid., Chs 3 and 4.

[21] In §88 he notes some obscurities and other infelicities in what Kant himself proffered: see Ch. 5, §3, esp. n. 16.

of a procedure that Kant implicitly counted as sufficient for establishing that a truth is analytic, and that Leibniz explicitly counted as sufficient for establishing that a truth is a truth of reasoning: namely, to demonstrate that the denial of the truth can, by a finite process of analysis, be reduced to absurdity.[22]) How then does Frege proceed?

3. The Execution of the Project

It is far beyond the scope of this chapter to supply a full answer to this question. But there are some features of Frege's procedure that are especially worth noting in the context of our enquiry.

Despite his wariness of natural language, and despite his knowing full well that, in natural language, numerals sometimes have an adjectival use, Frege takes at face value their *nominal* use there, which is apparently to refer to particular objects: an example is the use of the numeral 'four' in the sentence, 'The number of symphonies written by Schumann is the same as the number of gospels, namely four' (§57). This certainly connects with the role played by numerals in arithmetic itself, where they likewise seem to function as names, used to refer to particular objects. The sentence '7 > 4' has the same surface grammar as the sentence 'Mount Everest is higher than Mount McKinley.' Both sentences seem to relate one object to another. A crucial part of the project is therefore to say what exactly the objects referred to in arithmetic *are* – what numbers are (Introduction, pp. i ff.).

Frege insists, again *contra* Kant, that they are not anything given in intuition (§12). But here already there is a complication. On Kant's definition, intuition is simply 'that through which [cognition] relates immediately to [objects]' (Kant (1998), A19/B33). It is that whereby objects are immediately given to us. And Frege does not deny that numbers are given to us in some way. So does it not follow trivially that they are given to us in intuition?

In fact, granted what Kant goes on to say about intuition, and granted, for that matter, the reference to immediacy in his definition, it is clear that he means something that Frege is quite right to dissociate from his own conception of how numbers are given to us.[23] What Kant means, as Frege

---

[22] The two procedures are in effect the same if (1) analysis is just a matter of applying suitable definitions, (2) absurdity is the violation of a primitive logical law, and (3) a truth can be proved by *reductio ad absurdum*. Concerning (1), see §88. Concerning (2), see Ch. 3, n. 33, and Ch. 5, §3, esp. n. 17. (Leibniz may in fact have had a broader notion of absurdity than this, and Kant, for whom the only absurdity was contradiction, a narrower one.) Concerning (3), see Ch. 14, §§2 and 3, esp. n. 47.

[23] There is also an issue about whether Frege understands the term 'object' in the same way as Kant (see §89; and see Potter (2000), pp. 65–66). Frege understands the term in a way that is extremely broad; see further §7. Kant, arguably, understands it in a way that is much narrower; see e.g. Kant (1998), B137.

himself points out (§12), is a product of the faculty that he (Kant) calls sensibility. Sensibility is a faculty of pure passive receptivity. And it is to be contrasted with the faculty that Kant calls understanding, a faculty of spontaneity, whereby we actively think about what we passively receive. It is understanding which issues in concepts. (See Ch. 5, §4.)[24] For Frege the practice of arithmetic does indeed require only something of the latter kind. Arithmetic is purely conceptual, in a sense in which even Kant would agree that logic is purely conceptual (Kant (1998), A52–53/B76–77).[25] Otherwise, of course, its truths would be synthetic.

How, then, are numbers given to us, if not in intuition? To address this question Frege invokes his famous 'context principle'. This is the principle that it is only in the context of a sentence that words have any meaning (Introduction, p. x, and §62). In particular, it is only in the context of a sentence that any singular noun phrase, such as 'the number of gospels', 'the cube root of 27', or 'five', stands for a number. The question becomes, for Frege: how are we to understand sentences containing such phrases? If we can answer this question, without circularity, we shall have said all that we either can say or need to say not only about how numbers are given to us, but also about what numbers are. And we shall have taken the first crucial step towards showing that all the *relevant* sentences containing such phrases, namely those that occur in arithmetic, express analytic truths.[26]

Of especial concern to Frege are statements of identity, such as the sentence 'The number of symphonies written by Schumann is the same as the number of gospels.' This is because the main reason why we refer to numbers at all is to assign them to properties[27] as a measurement of how 'numerous'

---

[24] Frege reflects on this contrast in §§12 and 89, and in various other places. For discussion, see Dummett (1991f), esp. §5.

[25] Note that Kant's own term for logic is 'general logic'. He contrasts this with 'transcendental logic', the study of how our *a priori* concepts relate to intuition (Kant (1998), A57/B81–82 and A154/B193ff.).

[26] It is in this change of focus, from how we perceive things to how we talk about them, that Michael Dummett thinks we see the very first example of the linguistic turn in philosophy (see §1). He describes the short paragraph in which Frege explains his strategy, i.e. §62, as 'arguably the most pregnant philosophical paragraph ever written' (Dummett (1991a), p. 111). Here, as before, there is an issue about whether Dummett is guilty of overstatement. Here, as before, there is something of undeniable significance to which he is nonetheless drawing our attention.

[27] Beware a significant terminological complication. I talk about 'properties' where Frege, though he also sometimes talks about 'properties' (e.g. §53 and 'Concept and Object', pp. 189–190/pp. 201–202), typically talks about 'concepts'. I avoid the latter term because I have already been using it in a very different, essentially Kantian way to mean something more like an instrument of thought. To anticipate material from §§4 and 7 below, what I call 'concepts' are sense-like; what I, and Frege sometimes, call 'properties', and what Frege typically calls 'concepts', are the *Bedeutungen* of predicates. This means that the

the properties are: to say how many things have the properties (§46). Not that it is always clear from the surface grammar of what we say that this is what we are doing (one of the many defects of natural language). To assign the number four to the property of being a symphony written by Schumann, or to the property of being a gospel, we are unlikely to refer to the number explicitly; we are more likely to use the numeral 'four' adjectivally and say, 'Schumann wrote four symphonies,' or 'There are four gospels.' But still, on a Fregean conception, we are assigning numbers to properties when we say such things. And this makes the statements of identity especially important because we need to be clear about what it takes for two properties to be assigned *the same* number, in other words for there to be just as many things that satisfy the one property as satisfy the other.

Frege explains carefully how such statements of identity are to be understood. On his definition, for two properties to be assigned the same number is for there to be a one-to-one correlation between the things that satisfy the one property and the things that satisfy the other (§§63 and 70–73). He does the same for other sentences that we might naturally use in talking, either explicitly or implicitly, about numbers. But he also feels bound to consider sentences that we would never dream of using, such as 'The number of symphonies written by Schumann is Julius Caesar.' The reason we would never dream of using such sentences is not that they are obviously false. (We would never dream of using their negations either.) It is rather that they appear to be only just this side of gibberish. No doubt, if pressed, we would say that this particular sentence is false, that Julius Caesar is not a number. But only if pressed. And that is not good enough for Frege. He thinks that we do not have a properly clear idea of what we are talking about until we have said *exactly* what numbers are and settled all such matters in advance (§§56 and 63–67).[28]

I said earlier that Frege was not a metaphysician. Here, however, he seems to have got involved in an issue that is 'metaphysical' in the most pejorative sense, that is, in the colloquial sense in which 'metaphysics' connotes utter futility. He seems to be seeking an account of the quintessence of numbers that completely transcends our normal commerce with them. Surely, his own insight, that there is nothing more to numbers than what is required to understand sentences about them, need only ever have extended

latter are very coarsely individuated. If whatever has a heart also has a kidney, and vice versa, then the property of having a heart is the same as the property of having a kidney. For discussion, see Diamond (1991d), p. 118. For a profound problem afflicting this use of 'property', from which for the time being I shall prescind, see §7(b).

[28] For an argument that we need say no more than Frege has said already, see Wright (1983), pp. 113–117. For a rejoinder, see Dummett (1991a), pp. 159–162.

Note: in Cartesian terms, Frege's demand is not just for a clear idea of what we are talking about; it is for a (clear and) *distinct* idea of what we are talking about (see Ch. 1, §3).

to sentences that anyone would dream of using? Or perhaps even, granted his specific project, to sentences of arithmetic?[29] However that may be, Frege gets over the 'Julius Caesar' problem by stipulating that numbers are sets of a certain kind. More specifically, he stipulates that each number is the set of properties to which it is assigned. Four is the set of properties that have four instances, for instance. (See §68.[30])

This stipulation has three remarkable features. First, there is the very fact that it is a stipulation. If it is a legitimate question what exactly numbers are, in this (literally) extraordinary sense, then with what right does Frege settle the matter just by *deciding* what they are? Frege is quite open about the arbitrariness of his stipulation. He writes:

> This way of getting over [the 'Julius Caesar' problem] cannot be expected to meet with universal approval, and many will prefer other methods of removing the doubt in question. I attach no decisive importance even to bringing in [sets] at all. (§107)

Frege's rationale for settling the matter by stipulation seems to be that, since the aim of the exercise at this stage is to show that the truths of arithmetic are analytic, not that they are composed of logical concepts, all he need do is to define numbers in such a way as to allow for the derivation of truths about them from primitive logical laws (cf. §70, p. 81), taking care in particular not to presuppose anything synthetic in the definitions he gives. But this raises a further question. Granted that defining numbers (in the sense of identifying them with things of some independently recognizable kind) is not a prerequisite of realizing this aim, why define them at all? Why not do something that would be just as effective as far as the 'Julius Caesar' problem is concerned, namely accept that numbers are *sui generis*? After all, if any two definitions that satisfy the relevant desiderata are as good as each other, then they are as bad as each other. Why opt for any of them?[31]

---

[29] I believe that this reflects his own attitude later in his career when he is confronted with a similar problem; see Moore and Rein (1986), esp. n. 19. It is true that if we confine attention to sentences of arithmetic, there is a danger that we shall make it harder for ourselves, if not impossible, to explain the applicability of arithmetic. But that is not part of the current project. A much more serious danger, as far as the current project is concerned, is that we shall invoke definitions that depend on synthetic truths not expressible in arithmetical language.

[30] Beware the terminological discrepancies. As I have already noted (n. 27) Frege typically talks of 'concepts' where I talk of 'properties'. But he also talks of 'extensions of concepts' where I talk of 'sets'.

[31] Cf. Benacerraf (1983). These remarks perhaps do insufficient justice to a certain intuitive appeal that Frege's definition has. It is noteworthy, for instance, that Bertrand Russell independently arrived at something very similar (Russell (1992c)). But other definitions have some intuitive appeal too. See e.g. David Lewis (1991), §§4.5 and 4.6, where Lewis motivates an identification of numbers with quite different sets. Cf. also Quine (1960), p. 263.

The second remarkable feature of Frege's stipulation is his insouciance concerning what sets are. 'I assume it is known,' he says, 'what [a set] is' (§68, n. 1; cf. §107). But insofar as we are exercised about whether Julius Caesar is a number, ought we not to be exercised about whether Julius Caesar is a set?[32] This question reinforces the thought that we might just as well accept that numbers are *sui generis*. Sooner or later, it seems, we have to accept that *something* is.

The third remarkable feature of Frege's stipulation is the fact that it does not make him reconsider whether arithmetical truths are composed (exclusively) of logical concepts. By drawing our attention so forcibly to the question of what exactly the subject matter of arithmetic is, does not this discussion likewise impress upon us that arithmetic does after all *have* a subject matter, in other words that there are objects with which it is peculiarly concerned? If a logical concept is a concept that can be exercised in thought about any subject matter, ought it not to be tied to no special subject matter of its own? Frege might reply that properties of all kinds have a numerosity, and that this is enough for the concept of a number to qualify as logical. But properties of all kinds can be thought about in the bath. Does that make the concept of a bath a logical concept?

All three of these features indicate concerns that we might reasonably have about Frege's stipulation. But they are also symptomatic of concerns that we might reasonably have about *all* his definitions, most notably those that take at face value the nominal use of numerals and cast numbers as objects that measure how numerous properties are. What makes such definitions correct? Or 'admissible', to use Frege's own word (§3), a word that the stipulative character of at least some of his definitions suggests is more appropriate? One natural thought would be that a definition is admissible if anyone who already understands the terms in it can in principle be brought to accept it. But 'in principle'? How much latitude does this allow? What background knowledge can be presupposed? Certainly not knowledge of anything synthetic, to echo a point that I made a little earlier. But, given that what we are now grappling with is an idea that plays a crucial role in the very drawing of the distinction between the analytic and the synthetic, this observation scarcely helps.[33] Frege himself, in the *Foundations*, which is the work in which he first proposes these definitions, contributes surprisingly little to this discussion.[34] In later work, however, he provides material that is very pertinent to it, as we shall now see.

---

[32] Cf. Dummett (1991a), p. 159.

[33] See Williamson (2007), Ch. 4, for further problems with this natural thought.

[34] Cf. Dummett (1991a), pp. 33–35. For Dummett's own contribution to the discussion, see ibid., Ch. 12, esp. pp. 152–153, where he provides a suggestion about what makes a definition admissible. See also David Wiggins' fascinating contribution to the discussion in Wiggins (2007).

4. Sense and *Bedeutung*

Frege introduces a distinction between what he calls sense and what he calls, in the original German, '*Bedeutung*'.[35] He holds that linguistic expressions of all types have both a sense and a *Bedeutung*.[36] But he first introduces the distinction specifically in terms of singular noun phrases, which he groups together and calls *names*.[37] It is clearest to start with that case.[38]

By a name's *Bedeutung* Frege means whatever thing the name is used to refer to. Thus the *Bedeutung* of the name 'Plato' is the person Plato; the *Bedeutung* of the name 'the number of symphonies written by Schumann' is the number four. (To be sure, someone may use the latter name without realizing that he or she is referring to the number four. Such a person may even be under a misapprehension and intend to refer to the number five. But – in fact – what that name is used to refer to is the number four because – in fact – Schumann wrote four symphonies.) The *Bedeutung* of a name is all that is directly relevant to the truth or falsity of any declarative sentence in which the name occurs.

Nevertheless, knowing what the *Bedeutung* of a name is is not the same as understanding it. Neither suffices for the other. Someone who has it on good authority that the *Bedeutung* of a particular name in Urdu is the number four does not thereby understand the name. Conversely, someone who does understand both 'the number of symphonies written by Schumann' and 'the number of gospels' cannot tell, without extra knowledge, that they have the same *Bedeutung*. It is in cases of this latter kind that identity statements manage to be both true and informative. An identity statement such as 'The number of symphonies written by Schumann is the same as the number of gospels,' or, to borrow Frege's own celebrated example which we considered in Chapter 2, §2, 'The evening star is the same as the morning star,'

---

[35] '*Bedeutung*' is usually translated as 'meaning'. But Frege is using the word in a technical way. Translators often register this by translating it as 'reference'. I have decided to leave the word untranslated.

[36] Or rather, more strictly, he holds this for expressions of all logically significant types, where by a logically significant type is meant roughly a type that needs to be recognized in the characterization of what follows logically from what else. This excludes words or expressions used syncategorematically, such as 'of' in '16 is the square of 4,' or 'the weather' in 'She is under the weather.' Here and hereafter in this chapter I shall restrict attention to expressions of logically significant types.

[37] Sometimes he calls them *proper names*. But, once again, he is using language in a technical way, and 'proper name', even more than 'name', suggests a category much narrower than he has in mind.

[38] The material that follows draws especially on 'Sense and *Bedeutung*', 'Letter to Jourdain', and 'Thought'.

expresses a substantial truth: it does not simply state, of some particular thing, that that thing is self-identical.[39]

This is where Frege introduces senses. A name's sense is said to be what someone *grasps* when he or she understands the name. The name is said to *express* its sense. And the sense is said to *determine* the name's *Bedeutung*. The sense determines the name's *Bedeutung* in the following respect: although two names with the same *Bedeutung* can have different senses, two names with the same sense (synonyms) cannot have different *Bedeutungen*.[40]

But there is more to the claim that the name's sense determines its *Bedeutung* than that. A name's sense, Frege says, contains the 'mode of presentation' of its *Bedeutung* ('Sense and *Bedeutung*', p. 152/p. 26). In grasping the sense, a person thinks of the *Bedeutung* in a certain way. As a corollary, the sense fixes what the name's *Bedeutung* would have been in any other possible circumstances (so long as the name had had the same sense). If Schumann had written five symphonies, the *Bedeutung* of 'the number of symphonies written by Schumann' would have been the number five.[41]

The whole apparatus is then extended to linguistic expressions of other types. It is admittedly strained to say, of some of these, that they are used to 'refer' to anything. It is even strained to suggest that they have extralinguistic correlates. (Consider a connective like 'unless'.) Still, each of them does have a feature that is directly relevant to the truth or falsity of any declarative sentence in which it occurs. (In the case of 'unless' this feature is that it connects two declarative sentences to form a third declarative sentence that is true if and only if at least one of the original pair is true.) And that provides enough of an analogy to sustain talk of its *Bedeutung*, and, therewith,

---

[39] Nor, as Frege once thought (*Begriffsschrift*, §8), does it state a truth about the two names involved. Frege begins 'Sense and *Bedeutung*' by retracting this view. However, he fails to note one of the most serious objections to the view, namely that it creates an infinite regress. For *what* truth is stated about the two names involved, on this view? That they are used to refer to *the same thing*. (For further discussion of Frege's retraction of this view, somewhat opposed to what I have just said, see Makin (2000), Ch. 4, §IV.)

[40] '*Bedeutungen*' is the plural of '*Bedeutung*'.

[41] That a name's sense contains the mode of presentation of its *Bedeutung* has led to an interesting exegetical debate. Some commentators claim that it follows from this that a name can never have a sense without also having a *Bedeutung*, and they cite textual evidence that this is Frege's own view. Other commentators claim that no such thing follows, and they cite textual evidence that it is *not* Frege's own view. See e.g. respectively Evans (1982), Ch. 1, §6, and Dummett (1981a), Ch. 6, §4. One thing seems clear and is acknowledged on all sides: Frege thinks that something is awry when a name lacks a *Bedeutung*, as e.g. 'Father Christmas' does, and that such a thing cannot be tolerated in a formal language constructed for scientific or mathematical purposes (its happening at all is another defect of natural language). See e.g. 'Function and Concept', p. 141/pp. 19–20; 'Letter to Husserl', p. 150/p. 98; 'Sense and *Bedeutung*', pp. 163–164/pp. 40–41; and 'Comments', p. 178/pp. 133–134.

talk of its sense. In the case of a full declarative sentence what this amounts to is the following: its *Bedeutung* is its truth value (truth or falsity as the case may be), and its sense is the thought it expresses (that things are such and such a way, the way they have to be for the sentence to be true).

As for what manner of things the senses of expressions are, Frege is adamant that they are not subjective ideas that people privately associate with the expressions. If they were, ordinary linguistic communication would be impossible. For it is only when two people grasp the same sense, and know that they do, that they are able to understand an expression in the same way and thereby use it to convey their thoughts to each other. Whatever else senses are, they are objective features of how expressions are used and understood.[42]

5.   The Admissibility of Definitions

With senses now available, an obvious account is ready to hand of when a definition is admissible, namely when the *definiendum* and the *definiens* have the same sense. Call this the Simple Account.[43] On the Simple Account the reason why 'sister' can be defined as 'female sibling' is (simply) that they have the same sense. By application of this definition, and others, the following sentence can be derived from primitive logical laws: 'If you have no sisters, and that man's mother is your father's daughter, then that man is your son.' On Frege's conception, this means that the truth in question is analytic, despite its unobviousness – which is just what he wants to say about the truths of arithmetic.

But can we accept the Simple Account? Even if we grant that the notion of sense is as clear as it should be,[44] there are grounds for doubting this account. For one thing, it seems not to apply to Frege's own definitions. It seems not to apply to the definition of numerical identity in terms of the existence of a one-to-one correlation since the *definiendum* in that case involves reference to an object, a number, that might just as well not exist as far as the *definiens* is concerned.[45] And it seems not to apply to the definition of numbers as sets since that definition, *qua* stipulation, precisely does not seek only to capture what someone grasps who understands the word 'number'. True, any discrepancy between the Simple Account and Frege's own definitions may tell against them rather than against it. To understand Frege's project is not to endorse it. But the Simple Account seems not to apply to what we

---

[42] For extremely helpful accounts of Frege's distinction, and discussion of it, see Dummett (1981a), esp. Chs 5 and 6; Evans (1982), Ch. 1; and Bell (1984).

[43] For a defence of the view that this is Frege's own settled account, see Beaney (1996).

[44] For scepticism about the notion, see esp. Ch. 12, §4.

[45] This is not the pedantry that it may appear to be, as Frege will later learn to his cost; see §7(a).

find in standard dictionaries either. These make liberal use of extrasemantic empirical information. *Perhaps* they do this only when they forget that they are dictionaries and start acting the encyclopedia. But something else that we find in standard dictionaries, for which there should surely be provision, are ampliative definitions resting on non-empirical insights that go beyond whatever is grasped in ordinary understanding – for example the definition of a circle as a plane figure bounded by a line every point on which is equidistant from a given point. (And then of course there is the question of how far these insights in turn rest, as they might be thought to in this case, on Kantian intuition.)

All of that said, the Simple Account is very compelling. If the *definiendum* and the *definiens* in a definition do *not* have the same sense, how can the definition be admissible *as a definition*? Is not the very purpose of a definition to convey what must be grasped in order to understand its *definiendum*?

The tension between the intuitive appeal of the Simple Account and the grounds given above for doubting it lies at the basis of what is often called the paradox of analysis.[46] I cannot hope in these confines to give a full response to this paradox. As it happens I believe that the Simple Account is wrong, on the grounds that there are many purposes that definitions can fulfil other than to convey the senses of their *definienda*.[47] One such purpose, notable from mathematical contexts, is to demonstrate that truths of one kind are mimicked by truths of some other kind, a purpose that can be fulfilled by identifying the subject matter of the former with the subject matter of the latter. This is what Frege does when he identifies numbers with sets, though it remains moot whether that is as much as he himself wants from the identification. (For a non-mathematical application of this technique, see Ch. 12, §7.) It is important to appreciate, however, that even when the purpose of a definition *is* to convey the sense of its *definiendum*, it is not obvious that it can fulfil this purpose only if its *definiens* shares that sense. Suppose it is possible to carve a complex sense somewhere other than at its original joints, thereby creating new parts constituting a new sense. (*Necessarily* constituting a new sense? Yes, if senses are individuated finely enough for their identity to be sensitive to any such change of parts.[48]) Given

---

[46] Frege discusses this paradox in 'Review', and there gives the manifestly inadequate response that in order for a definition to be admissible, at least in mathematics, all that is required is that the *definiendum* and the *definiens* have the same *Bedeutung*. For discussion, see Dummett (1991c) and (2010), Ch. 12. The paradox is related to what is often called the paradox of enquiry, which goes back at least as far as Plato: see *Meno*, 80e.

[47] Cf. Wiggins (2007).

[48] Are they? Frege does not appear to have a settled view on the matter. Sometimes he suggests that they are (e.g. *Basic Laws*, §32, and 'Notes', pp. 364–365/p. 275); sometimes he suggests that they are not (e.g. 'Concept and Object', p. 188/pp. 199–200).

two senses related in this way, the intimacy of the relation makes it an immediate conceptual necessity that they determine the same *Bedeutung*. Suppose next that a complex expression having one of these senses is defined by a complex expression having the other. Then the twin constraints set by the syntactic structure of the *definiendum*, on the one hand, and the intimate relation between its sense and that of the *definiens*, on the other, can ensure that the definition does indeed convey the sense of the *definiendum*. And *this*, arguably, is what we find in Frege's definition of numerical identity in terms of the existence of a one-to-one correlation.[49]

I say 'arguably'. Whether we really do find this depends, of course, on whether such 'contraconstituent' carving is possible, and, even if it is, on whether Frege's definition provides a legitimate case in point.[50] There is ample room for doubt. A similar definition that Frege gives of the identity of what he calls 'courses-of-values' (*Basic Laws*, §3), of which sets are a type, is demonstrably wrong, for reasons that we shall see in §7(a).[51] However that may be, Frege's introduction of senses, which are themselves possible objects of manipulation, reconfiguration, and investigation, has certainly created possibilities for an appealing account of when a definition is admissible, an account that is far more robust, and far more congenial to Frege's project, than the Simple Account.

But at what price?

6. The Objectivity of Sense. The Domain of Logic

There are several grounds for concern. One is that Fregean senses are in danger of forming a veil between us and the *Bedeutungen* that they determine, somewhat like the veil of perception that Descartes was forced to acknowledge between each of us and the material world (Ch. 1, §6).[52] Another ground for concern has to do with Frege's very characterization of a name's sense as containing the mode of presentation of its *Bedeutung*. Does this not stand in some tension with his context principle, which, whether understood as a principle about sense or as a principle about *Bedeutung* – Frege formulated it before distinguishing between these – suggests that a name's *Bedeutung* may have no 'name-sized' mode of presentation at all, no mode

---

[49] Cf. Wright (2001), esp. pp. 277–278. Cf. also Dummett's related discussion of pattern recognition in Dummett (1991a), pp. 36ff.; (1991c); and (1991j), §2. In the light of that discussion it is unclear why Dummett is as hostile as he is in Dummett (1981a), pp. 633–634, to the idea of an equivalence relation among linguistic expressions that is intermediate between sharing a sense and sharing a *Bedeutung*.

[50] For discussion of this and related issues, see Potter and Smiley (2001) and Hale (2001).

[51] This relates back to the point that I made in n. 45.

[52] Bertrand Russell voices this concern in Russell (1980b), p. 169.

of presentation short of whatever is involved in understanding whole sentences that contain the name?[53] If so, so much the worse for senses. For the
context principle surely embodies a genuine insight which, depending on
how great the tension in question is, Frege's introduction of senses has either
obscured or, worse, violated. These two grounds for concern are related.
Fregean senses seem to obtrude. The root problem seems to be that Frege
has construed our making senses of things as a tripartite affair in which we
are directly related to sense and sense is directly related to things, but we are
related to things only indirectly, via this link.

Such concerns are real enough. The notion of sense has to be handled
with great care to assuage them. On the other hand, it is not obvious that
it cannot be. We can think of the sense of an expression as, in David Bell's
words, 'the condition which anything must meet in order to be [the expression's *Bedeutung*]' (Bell (1984), p. 184).[54] And we can think of grasping the
sense, not as confronting some representation of the *Bedeutung*, but rather
as knowing what this condition is, where such knowledge is, in Michael
Dummett's words, 'manifested in a range of interconnected abilities'
(Dummett (1991c), p. 51). There is then no need to regard senses as opaque
intermediaries between us and the *Bedeutungen* that we use language to talk
about and with which our interests, at least in scientific and mathematical
contexts, typically lie. We are nevertheless at liberty to treat senses, along
with the *Bedeutungen* that they determine, as thoroughly objective, just as
Frege wants us to do.

That said, there is room for doubt about whether Frege himself is always
as circumspect and as restrained in his handling of senses as he should be.
The objectivity that he accords them is not just thorough; it is Platonic.[55] He
sees senses as abstract entities whose existence is completely independent of
us (see e.g. 'Thought'). But surely, if senses are to be acknowledged at all,
the objectivity accredited to them needs to be less extreme than that. While
they may be independent of each of us, and in particular of each individual
mind, they are surely not independent of *all* of us, and in particular of the
meeting of our minds in communication. The former, less extreme objectivity is objectivity enough. Certainly, it stands opposed to the subjectivity of
whatever ideas individuals privately associate with linguistic expressions,
which is Frege's principal requirement (see §4).[56]

---

[53] Cf. Dummett (1981b), pp. 425–426, and (1991a), pp. 192ff.

[54] Cf. Dummett (1993d), p. 227. Note: Bell's formulation can be effortlessly applied to the
case, if such there be, in which an expression has a sense but no *Bedeutung*; see n. 41.

[55] For what is intended by the label 'Platonic' here, see Plato's *Republic*, esp. Bks V–VII.

[56] See Dummett (1991a), pp. 77–78, and (1991e), pp. 117–118: Dummett gives this less
extreme objectivity the very appropriate label 'intersubjectivity'. (See also Dummett
(1991h). And see Dummett (2007c) – a response to Dejnožka (2007) – for a retraction
on his part concerning the question of whether senses even qualify as objects on Frege's
broad conception of an object. (We shall consider this conception in §7(b).))

The latter, more extreme objectivity which Frege accords senses – the Platonic variety – is curiously reminiscent of the objectivity that Hegel accorded concepts. For both philosophers, the stuff of thinking stands over against us, no less amenable to scientific investigation than the stuff of nature.[57] Both undertake such an investigation. Both call their investigation 'logic'. The fundamental difference between them is that, for Frege, the stuff of thinking is sharply separated from the stuff of nature ('Thought', pp. 336–337/p. 69); for Hegel, it constitutes the stuff of nature, as indeed it needs to in order to achieve its own full being (see §5 of the previous chapter). For Frege, logic is an attempt to make sense of something transcendent. For Hegel, the very distinction between the transcendent and the immanent is to be overcome.[58]

The fact that the subject matter of logic is transcendent for Frege does not of course mean that he takes it to be irrelevant to the natural world, still less that he takes it to be irrelevant to our thinking about the natural world. Frege expresses very clearly the relation that he sees between these in the following passage from the *Foundations*. (He couches the relation specifically in terms of 'the laws of number', but he would say the same about the laws of logic more generally.)

> The laws of number [do] not ... need to stand up to practical tests if they are to be applicable to the external [i.e. natural] world; for in the external world, in the whole of space and all that therein is, there are no concepts, no properties of concepts, no numbers. The laws of number, therefore, are not really applicable to external things; they are not laws of nature. They are, however, applicable to judgements holding good of things in the external world: they are laws of the laws of nature. They assert not connexions between phenomena, but connexions between judgements; and among judgements are included the laws of nature. (§87)

Elsewhere he clarifies what he means by a 'law' here, emphasizing, in radical opposition to Hume (see Ch. 4, §4), that he is not talking about regularities in how we, human beings, happen to think. Logic, for Frege, is emphatically

---

[57] See respectively 'Logic', p. 250/p.160, and Hegel (1975a), §IX passim.

[58] That distinction is accentuated in Frege. This is a crucial part of his recoil from Hegelian idealism. Dummett is surely right to insist, as he does in the very last sentence of Dummett (1981a), that Frege 'had for idealism not an iota of sympathy', but surely wrong to claim, as he does on the previous page, that Frege's work was instrumental in the overthrow of Hegelian idealism. Dummett subsequently retracts this claim. But he does so on the grounds that 'Hegelianism had little influence at the time when Frege's creative work began' (Dummett (1981b), p. 497). Others would reject it on diametrically opposed grounds. They would say that Hegelianism had then, and still has, great influence. For further discussion of Frege's relation to idealism, see Dummett (1991d), (1991e), and (1991f).

not 'dependent on the science of MAN' (Hume (1978a), Introduction, p. xv).
Frege writes:

> Logic has much the same relation to truth as physics has to weight or
> heat.... [It] falls to logic to discern the laws of truth. The word 'law'
> is used in two senses. When we speak of moral or civil laws we mean
> *prescriptions*.... Laws of nature are general features of what happens in
> nature.... It is ... in this [latter, descriptive] sense that I speak of laws of
> truth.... [But from] the laws of truth there follow prescriptions about
> asserting, thinking, judging, inferring. And we may very well speak of
> laws of thought in this way too. But there is at once a danger here of
> confusing different things. People may very well interpret the expression
> 'law of thought' by analogy with 'law of nature' and then have in mind
> general features of thinking as a mental occurrence. A law of thought
> in this sense would be a psychological law.... That would be misunder-
> standing the task of logic.... I assign to logic the task of discovering the
> laws of truth, not the [descriptive] laws of *taking* things to be true or of
> thinking [as a mental occurrence].... ('Thought', pp. 325–326/pp. 58–59,
> emphasis added; cf. *Basic Laws*, Introduction, pp. 12ff., and 'Logic',
> pp. 246ff./pp. 157ff.)[59]

The realm of sense, which is set over against the realm of 'actual' things
in space and time,[60] has its own laws, then, and occurrences in our mind
had *better* conform to those laws if they are properly to count as thinking, if
we are properly to make sense of things. Hence, although Frege is far from
endorsing the Hegelian tenet that the rational is actual and the actual rational, he does believe that we cannot properly make sense of what is actual
except by doing so rationally. Indeed, he is prompted to ask, rhetorically,
'What are things independent of reason?' (§26, translation slightly adapted).
And although his question is rhetorical, he adds a comment which shows
that he takes rationality to be a prerequisite not only of proper thinking,
or of proper sense-making, but of thinking at all, or of making any kind
of sense; that is, he takes there to be no doing these things except properly
doing them. 'To answer that,' he says, in other words to answer his own rhetorical question, or in yet other words to make sense of things beyond the
limits of rational sense-making, 'would be as much as to judge without judg-
ing' (ibid.). Here there is an echo of Hegel's variation on the Limit Argument
(Ch. 7, §?), in which there was in turn an echo of Fichte's variation on the
Limit Argument (Ch. 6, §3). The conclusion in all three cases is that there is

---

[59] For something strikingly similar, see Kant (1992c), Introduction, §I.
[60] For Frege's notion of actuality, see *Foundations*, §§26 and 85, and *Basic Laws*,
Introduction, p. 16. He gives a slightly more relaxed account of the notion in 'Thought',
pp. 344–345/pp. 76–77. For discussion, see Rein (1982).

no limit to that of which (thin, rational) sense can be made: there is nothing which, by its very nature, fails to make (thin, rational) sense.[61]

But now: I have said that Frege is not a metaphysician. Why not, on my conception of metaphysics? If logic is 'the science of the most general laws of truth' ('Logic', p. 228/p. 139), then why is the pursuit of logic not a maximally general attempt to make sense of things?

This relates back to the fundamental difference between Frege and Hegel. (On Hegel's conception of logic, logic *can* be identified with metaphysics: see §4 of the previous chapter.) The pursuit of logic, for Frege, is a maximally general attempt to make sense not of things, but of sense. I have suggested that metaphysics is bound to be informed by this pursuit (Introduction, §5). But unless everything is constituted by sense – as indeed Hegel, in his own way, thought it was – then the pursuit does not itself have a wide enough scope to be identified with metaphysics.[62,63]

Frege attempts to make sense of sense, then. And what he achieves is remarkable. Much of his work is a model of clarity and depth, a paradigm of how to trade in the very sense with which it is concerned. Here again there is room for a comparison with Hegel, at least in this element of reflexivity. Both, insofar as they are successful in their endeavours, make sense of sense not just in what they say about it but in how they display it.[64] Nevertheless, the two philosophers can easily seem worlds apart. Frege's supporters and Hegel's detractors might well cite the clarity and depth to which I just referred as evidence that they are. There is certainly a great deal

---

[61] Cf. Diamond (1991a), §IV, and Conant (1991), pp. 134–137. (For clarification of this use of 'thin', see Ch. 5, §8.)

[62] In Ch. 14 we shall see how Dummett nevertheless tries to relate them.

[63] This reflects an interesting difference, not only between Frege and Hegel, but also between Frege and most contemporary logicians (in the analytic tradition). For Frege, laws of logic are truths about truth. He would exclude the proposition that, if there is life on Mars, then either there is life on Mars or there is life on Jupiter, on the grounds that that is a proposition about life, Mars, and Jupiter (it is not composed exclusively of logical concepts). That proposition is at most the result of *applying* a law of logic. Logicians nowadays do not typically see laws of logic as truths at all, or, if they do, they do not see them as truths with their own distinctive subject matter. They see them as (schematic) principles determining which combinations of truth, about whatsoever subject matter, are possible. This gives them back a certain scope that they lack in Frege's eyes. The proposition that, if there is life on Mars, then either there is life on Mars or there is life on Jupiter may not count for these logicians as a logical *law*, but it does count as a logical *truth*, arrived at not by application of a logical law, as on Frege's view, but by interpretation or instantiation of one. The difference is clearly marked when Frege says that 'logic is not concerned with how thoughts, regardless of truth value, follow from thoughts' ('Comments', p. 178/p. 133). A contemporary logician would be inclined to say that that is precisely what logic is concerned with. (Cf. Hacker (2001a), pp. 200–201.)

[64] Cf. Diamond (1991d), p. 118.

in Hegel that, from Frege's perspective, will seem not to make any sense at all. The contention, all but explicit in Hegel, that if there is nothing then there is something, namely nothing – if indeed it can be called a contention – seems to rest on precisely the kind of confusion that Frege's work is designed to eradicate. And the doctrine that we should accept certain contradictions, and can do so provided that we allow what is properly called reason to break the stranglehold of our understanding, would surely elicit from Frege his celebrated cry of censure: 'Here we have a hitherto unknown type of madness' (*Basic Laws*, Introduction, p. 14, translation slightly adapted). I tried to show in §7 of the previous chapter that there is more to Hegel's extravagances than meets the literalistically schooled eye. The fact remains that there is plenty in what meets the literalistically schooled eye to arouse deep aversion.

Still, as we shall see in the next section, not everything in Frege is exactly easy on that eye.

7.   Two Problems

In §5 of the Introduction I remarked on the way in which self-consciousness can militate against self-confidence. In this section we shall see two spectacular examples of this, following on from Frege's attempts to make sense of sense, specifically mathematical sense. One of these examples afflicts the very making of mathematical sense. The other afflicts the attempt to make sense of the making of mathematical sense. The sheer clarity and rigour with which Frege imbues his project are part of the problem. The standards are that much higher; failures to meet them are set in that much sharper relief. By his own lights Frege ends up talking nonsense.[65]

(a)   The Set of Sets That Do Not Belong to Themselves

The first example is very well known. Frege, as we have seen, makes pivotal use of the concept of a set in his project. He understands this concept in such a way that sets correspond one-to-one with properties. To each property there corresponds the set of things that have that property; to each set, the property of belonging to that set.[66] Sets, on this conception, do not typically belong to themselves: the set of planets, for example, is not itself a planet. But they do sometimes belong to themselves: the set of sets and the

---

[65] The two examples are not isolated. In 'Insights' Frege similarly struggles with the concept of truth, the subject matter of logic. (Cf. Wittgenstein (1961), 4.063. Cf. also 'Thought', pp. 333–334/p. 66, n. D.)

[66] Recall that properties are very coarsely individuated (see n. 27). The property of being a gospel *is* the property of belonging to the set {Matthew, Mark, Luke, John}.

set of things mentioned in this book are two examples. The problem concerns the set of sets of the former kind, the set of 'typical' sets. It is easy to see that this set belongs to itself if and only if it does not, which is a blatant contradiction.[67]

This contradiction is Frege's, but it is not his alone. Frege's conception of a set is an utterly intuitive one. The discovery of this problem was a blow to the entire mathematical community, and mathematical practice, since then, has never quite regained its lost nerve. Though contemporary mathematicians are relatively comfortable once again about using the concept of a set, which of course they now understand differently, they have had to overcome serious uncertainties to get to where they are, and the effect of these uncertainties is still felt.

The contradiction is also a striking instance of how Frege comes to be embroiled in his own conceptual machinery. Still, when he becomes aware of the contradiction, he at least recognizes the need to eradicate it.[68] He does not, as Hegel might have done, acquiesce in it. From this point of view the second example is even more striking.

(b)   The Property of Being a Horse

To understand the second example we need to reflect a little more on Frege's semantics. We have already witnessed two linguistic categories that are crucial to this semantics: that of a name; and that of a declarative sentence.[69] The category of a name is very broad. It includes any singular noun phrase. And Frege calls whatever a name can be used to refer to an 'object'. The category of an object is therefore likewise very broad. Frege would count all of the following as objects: my desk, Plato, Bucephalus, the number of

---

[67] This problem was communicated to Frege by Bertrand Russell (Russell (1980a)) shortly after Frege had published the first volume of his *Basic Laws* and while the second volume was in press. (*Basic Laws* was the book in which Frege attempted a detailed formal execution of his project. There was also originally intended to be a third volume. – The problem is clearly related, incidentally, to the result that no barber can shave all and only the men in his village who do not shave themselves, likewise due to Russell, which I mentioned in Ch. 4, §5.) Frege was devastated: see 'Letter to Russell'. He struggled unsuccessfully to find a solution to the problem. Eventually, he concluded, 'My efforts to become clear about what is meant by number have resulted in failure' (entry for 23.3.1924 in 'Diary Entries', p. 263). He resorted to the Kantian view that arithmetical truths are synthetic *a priori*: see 'Knowledge of Mathematics' and 'Numbers'.

   Note: the similarity between the way in which Frege takes sets to be assigned to properties and the way in which he takes numbers to be assigned to properties explains my remark in n. 45.

[68] See the material in the previous note.

[69] In *Basic Laws* he counts declarative sentences themselves as a kind of name (§26). But that is immaterial for current purposes.

gospels, the expression 'the number of gospels', the grammatical structure of the expression 'the number of gospels',[70] the Big Bang, transcendental idealism, and joy.[71]

When a name is removed from a declarative sentence what results is a predicate. For example, when the name 'Bucephalus' is removed from the declarative sentence 'Bucephalus is a horse', what results is the predicate '... is a horse'. Now predicates, like any other linguistic expressions, have *Bedeutungen*. And the *Bedeutungen* of predicates are what we have been calling properties. Thus the *Bedeutung* of '... is a horse' is the property of being a horse.

Or so it would seem. But what *exactly* are properties?[72] They had better be something of a fundamentally different kind from objects, Frege insists. Otherwise, declarative sentences would in effect just be lists, like 'Bucephalus, Plato.' That would mean that they could not be used to express thoughts. They could not be true or false.[73] However, given how broad the category of an object is, it seems impossible to resist the conclusion that properties, so far from being fundamentally different in kind from objects, are themselves objects. For both 'the property' of being a horse' and, for that matter, 'the *Bedeutung* of "... is a horse"' are names. Frege concedes this last point. And indeed, in accord with that, he concedes that the property of being a horse is an object. But he continues to insist that properties and objects are utterly heterogeneous. The only way he can see of accommodating this apparent contradiction is to deny that the property of being a horse is a property ('Concept and Object', esp. p. 184/p. 195).

Anyone who thinks that Frege is completely immune to Hegelian excess should pause to reflect on this. The truth is that, by his own high standards, he has got into a hopeless muddle. Indeed, he all but concedes as much. He writes:

> I admit that there is a quite peculiar obstacle in the way of an understanding with my reader. By a kind of necessity of language, my expressions, taken literally, sometimes miss my thought; I mention an object, when what I intend is a [property]. I fully realize that in such cases

---

[70] But not, given Dummett's retraction mentioned in parentheses in n. 56, the sense of the expression 'the number of gospels'. If not, then that seems to me to be yet another problem for Frege.

[71] It is interesting to note that Husserl likewise uses the term 'object' ('*Gegenstand*' in the original German) in this very broad way: see Husserl (1981a), p. 13.

[72] Frege takes them to be functions whose values are always truth values (see e.g. 'Function and Concept', pp. 138–139/pp. 15–16). But that merely postpones the question, at least as intended here; for what *exactly* are functions?

[73] This is a point that is as old as Plato: see his *Sophist*, 261c6–262e2. See also Plutarch (1976), Question X, esp. 1011c. – Note that the previous problem concerning the set

I was relying upon a reader who would be ready to meet me half-way – who does not begrudge a pinch of salt. ('Concept and Object', p. 192/p. 204)

But the problem lies far deeper than this suggests. There is, in a Fregean context, something fundamentally awry with all talk of properties and with all talk of the *Bedeutungen* of predicates – at least pending some explicit account of how not to take such talk at face value.[74]

Nor is this problem just an inconsequential self-inflicted minutia of one particular semantic theory. Within a generation of Frege's stumbling into it, Wittgenstein, as we shall see in the next chapter, relates it in a quite extraordinary way to what he calls 'the problem of life' and its meaning.[75] There are also, for that matter, direct connections with Kant's transcendental project.[76] The fact is, it is a problem that has to do with the very essence of sense-making, the very essence of thought. More particularly, it has to do with what holds the elements of thought together. In Kantian terms (see Ch. 5, §4), it has to do with how representation is possible.

At one point Frege himself comments, of a distinction that is relevantly similar to the distinction that he wants to draw between objects and properties, that 'it is not made arbitrarily, but founded deep in the nature of things' ('Function and Concept', p. 148/p. 31). This suggests that his problem has to do not only with the essence of thought, but with the essence of reality. In a way it does. It is after all couched in terms of the *Bedeutungen* of expressions, in terms of that which determines the truth or falsity of the claims we make, using those expressions, about reality. In another way the suggestion is misleading. What is at stake here is not how thought manages to be, in Cora Diamond's words, 'in agreement ... with some external thing' but how it manages to be in agreement 'with itself' (Diamond (1991a), p. 29). The categories that Frege invokes are intended to reflect requirements that must be met for there to be thought at all. A thought can never be expressed by a mere list of names because there is nothing in a mere list of names to allow for assessment with respect to truth or falsity. And

---

of non-self-membered sets in fact provides another reason why properties had better not be objects: if they were, they would behave just as sets do on Frege's inconsistent conception.

[74] Elsewhere Frege seems to have a better grasp of the muddle, though he by no means completely extricates himself from it: see 'Comments', esp. pp. 174ff./pp. 130ff. For discussion, see Dummett (1981a), pp. 211ff.; Wiggins (1984); and Wright (1998).

Note that the problems afflicting talk of properties arise not only when the predicate '... is a property' is used overtly, but also when it is used covertly, as in the name 'the property of being a horse'. If the property of being a horse is not a property, what business do we have calling it 'the *property* of being a horse'?

[75] See e.g. Wittgenstein (1961), 4.12–4.1213 and 6.5–7. And see §8 of the next chapter.

[76] See e.g. Kant (1998), A129–130 and B141–142. Cf. Bell (2001).

when Frege attempts to say what holds the elements of thought together and finds himself using expressions which precisely fail to fulfil the function that they are intended to fulfil, he does not express unintended false thoughts about reality; he fails to express any thoughts at all. He fails to make sense.[77] Until he says more, and indeed until he retracts some of what he has already said, the predicate '... is a property', as it occurs in his work, simply does not have any authentic meaning. The problem, of course, is that there is no combination of additions and subtractions that will satisfy him. It is as if there are insights that he has achieved into the unity of thought, insights into what it is to make sense of things, which somehow, by their very nature, resist expression; and this too is very pertinent to what will happen in the next chapter.[78]

8. The Implications for Metaphysics

Ever since Hume helped to demonstrate the importance of reflection on sense, in any attempt to make general sense of things, it was only a question of time before metaphysics would have to reckon with an attempt, of the sort we find in Frege, to provide a decent theory of sense. The rest of Part Two will be in large measure a story of how metaphysics in the analytic tradition and, more especially, meta-metaphysics in the analytic tradition come to terms with what Frege bequeaths, both his insights and his aporiae, both his triumphs and his crises.

It is not an easy assimilation. Given the degree of self-consciousness involved, it cannot be. And the aporiae and the crises obviously add to the difficulty. We must wonder whether any attempt to make sense of sense, and therefore, derivatively, any attempt to make sense of how we make sense of things, will, if it has serious theoretical pretensions, merely add to the confusion that it is intended to eliminate. If so, and if there is truth in the recurring suggestion that we cannot make maximally general sense of things without making sense of how we make sense of things, then metaphysics is under renewed threat.

I say 'under renewed threat', not 'doomed'. The qualification 'if it has serious theoretical pretensions', in the previous paragraph, was crucial. Perhaps we can make sense of how we make sense of things in a piecemeal, non-systematic way. Perhaps our making sense of how we make sense of things can be a *practical* exercise. (This would make it akin to improving how we

---

[77] Cf. his comment in 'Comments', p. 175/p. 130: '[Properties] cannot stand in the same relation as objects. It would not be false, but impossible to think of them as doing so.'

[78] Cf. the very last paragraph of 'Concept and Object'. Cf. also the suggestion about Spinoza's third kind of knowledge in Ch. 2, §6; and about Kant's insights into what it is to make sense of things in Ch. 5, §10. I am indebted in this paragraph to Diamond: see Diamond (1991a), §IV; (1991b); and (1991d).

make sense of things, in that it would be manifest *in* how we make sense of things rather than in anything we explicitly say about how we do so.) Perhaps, to echo the point that I made at the end of the previous section, we can achieve insights into how we make sense of things to which we are nevertheless incapable of giving voice. These are all ideas that will resurface at various points throughout Part Two. But they will be especially prominent in the next two chapters on Wittgenstein.[79]

---

[79] Before we leave Frege it is worth considering how his work bears on the three questions that I posed in §6 of the Introduction. It does not bear on them directly of course; Frege is not a meta-metaphysician. But we have seen, in Frege, elements of transcendence-friendliness (§6), conservatism (§1), and Platonism (§6), which mean that it would be at least Fregean in spirit to return the following three answers: we are, in practising metaphysics, (1) free to make sense of transcendent things, (2) constrained to make sense of things in broadly the same way as we already do (notwithstanding my disclaimer in §1), and (3) engaged in an exercise that is fundamentally one of discovery. In other words, it would be at least Fregean in spirit to give precisely the opposite of my own three verdicts.

CHAPTER 9

✦

The Early Wittgenstein

The Possibility, Scope, and Limits of Sense; or, Sense, Senselessness, and Nonsense

1. Why Two Wittgensteins?

Ludwig Wittgenstein (1889–1951) famously produced two masterpieces, both enormously influential, but strikingly different from each other in style, approach, and even, it seems, doctrine: first the *Tractatus*,[1] in his youth, and later the *Investigations*, towards the end of his life, having in the interim been through a long period of philosophical inactivity. It is commonplace, in fact, to refer to 'the early Wittgenstein' and 'the later Wittgenstein' as if to two different thinkers. It is something I myself shall do, and I shall accord a separate chapter to each.

But it would be grotesque to do so without issuing some caveats at the outset. First, there were profound continuities between Wittgenstein's earlier thinking and his later thinking. Some commentators would say that these were far more profound than the discontinuities.[2] Second, and as it may appear conversely – though this is arguably the same point in another guise – if one is going to divide his work into phases at all, there are grounds for not stopping at two. Thus people often refer to his 'intermediate' or 'transitional' work, meaning by this various remarks that he dictated and notes that he produced after his return to philosophy, while he was still struggling with his earlier ideas and while his later ideas were beginning to take shape.[3] There has even recently been a call to acknowledge a 'third Wittgenstein', responsible, among other things, for the drafts that he wrote

---

[1] Throughout this chapter I use the following abbreviations for Wittgenstein's works: *Culture* for Wittgenstein (1980a); 'Ethics' for Wittgenstein (1965); *Investigations* for Wittgenstein (1967a); *Lectures* for Wittgenstein (1980b); *Letters* for Wittgenstein (1995); 'Letter to Ficker', for Wittgenstein (1967b); *Notebooks* for Wittgenstein (1979a); *On Certainty* for Wittgenstein (1974b); *Philosophical Grammar* for Wittgenstein (1974a); *Philosophical Remarks* for Wittgenstein (1975); and *Tractatus* for Wittgenstein (1961). Section-numbered references to the *Investigations* are to Part I of that work. All unaccompanied references are to the *Tractatus*.

[2] Cf. n. 49.

[3] E.g. *Philosophical Remarks*.

222

in the last year and a half of his life that were published posthumously as
On Certainty.[4]

I should also say something at the outset about why, having decided that
it is appropriate to accord Wittgenstein two chapters, I have not reached the
same decision for any of the rest of my protagonists. For Wittgenstein was
not alone among them in giving significant new direction to his work in the
course of his philosophical career.[5] The point is simply this. In both his early
work and his later work Wittgenstein provided insights into what it is to
make sense of things that are of the greatest relevance to my project, but he
did so in ways which, however profound the continuities in his thinking, call
for significantly different treatment. This is not true, or not true to anything
like the same extent, of any of the rest of my protagonists.

2. Wittgenstein's Conception of Philosophy

The 4.11s in the *Tractatus*, along with some scattered remarks elsewhere
(notably p. 3, 4.0031, 6.211, and 6.53), present a very distinctive conception of philosophy.[6] On this conception philosophy is completely different in kind from any of the natural sciences. Its aim is not to discover
truths but to promote clarity of thought. It 'is not a body of doctrine but an
activity' (4.112).[7]

Wittgenstein shares with Frege the idea that whatever we can think at
all we can think clearly (4.116; cf. p. 3 and cf. §6 of the previous chapter).

---

[4] See Moyal-Sharrock (2004).

[5] The same is true of Derrida, for example, whose later work, even if it did not repudiate
his earlier work, exhibited markedly different interests and concerns. (How far it is also
true of Heidegger is an interesting bone of exegetical contention. For two contributions,
see Krell (1986) and Jordan (2004). I shall presuppose relative constancy in Heidegger's
thinking in Ch. 18.)

[6] Distinctive, but by no means completely unprecedented: the conception bears deep affinities with that of Socrates for example (cf. the opening exchanges in Plato's *Meno* and cf.
Davidson (2005d), pp. 249–250).

[7] Cf. P.M.S. Hacker's remark, in Hacker (1996), p. 110: 'If one had to choose one single
fundamental insight from the whole corpus of Wittgenstein's later work, it might well be
argued that it should be the insight that philosophy contributes not to human knowledge,
but to human understanding.' (For elaboration of this conception of philosophy, *in propria persona*, see Hacker (2009).) It is certainly in Wittgenstein's conception of philosophy
that there is most clearly a continuity between the early work and the later work: see further §1 of the next chapter.

Note: in neither the early work nor the later work is philosophy expected to advance
without its practitioners making claims about reality. It is just that, when they do, their
claims will not typically be to inform anyone of anything, but to illustrate the workings
of the concepts involved. Cf. 3.263 and *Investigations*, §128, respectively; and cf. Winch
(1987), pp. 10–11.

Indeed, there is a sense in which, for both of them, our thinking is always clear: unless we are thinking clearly we are not thinking at all.[8] Nonetheless, because of infelicities in natural language, such clarity is not always manifest in the 'outward form' of what we say when we express our thoughts (4.002). So there is another sense in which, for both of them, our thinking is *not* always clear and needs to be made clear. Such is the business of philosophy.[9]

Why? What is wrong with unclear thinking?

Wittgenstein has an antipathy to unclear thinking which, as we shall see in §8, is positively moralistic. But we do not need to share all his scruples to appreciate the problems to which unclear thinking can give rise. There is one kind of problem in particular that exercises Wittgenstein. It is associated with superficial patterns in the various combinations of words that we use to express our thoughts. It arises when we notice the patterns, extrapolate, and suppose that other combinations of words are likewise used to express thoughts, though in fact they are not. We *think* we are thinking, but we are not. This leads us to pose pseudo-questions which, in the nature of the case, we do not know how to address, certainly not in a way that will satisfy us. And this in turn can be frustrating, distracting, time-wasting, sometimes even tormenting.

Here is a simple example. Albert looks out of his window. The traffic passes. The time passes. Albert reflects on these two facts. And he is struck by the superficial similarity between the English sentences used to express them. Realizing that it is perfectly proper to ask, 'At what speed does the traffic pass?', he is led to pose the apparently parallel pseudo-question, 'At what speed does the time pass?'[10] Various pseudo-responses suggest themselves, such as, 'The time passes at one second per second.' But Albert cannot reconcile these pseudo-responses and their various apparent consequences with all sorts of other things that he wants to say, for example that the speed at which anything passes must admit of alternatives. (On occasions in the past, when he has been enjoying himself, the time has seemed to pass more quickly. But it cannot really have done so – can it?) He gets more and more confused, more and more agitated. He fails to see that these pseudo-responses do not express any thoughts at all, that they cannot be proper responses to any question, that there is no proper question there in the first place. It may seem a trivial and unrealistic example,[11] but it illustrates the kind of difficulties that we fall into.

---

[8] Cf. 3.2ff. and 5.5563. (The latter shows that Wittgenstein lacks some of Frege's contempt for natural language. But see the very next point in the main text.)

[9] Cf. Hacker (2001a), p. 202; Diamond (2004), p. 160; and McGinn (2006), Ch. 1, *passim*.

[10] Cf. 6.3611.

[11] In fact it is based, as they say, on real life: see Prior (1993), pp. 36ff., and, for a much more recent contribution to the discussion, Olson (2009). But I must emphasize how

Wittgenstein characterizes these difficulties in terms of a distinction that he draws between 'signs' and 'symbols'. Signs are the written marks or noises that we use to communicate (cf. *Lectures*, p. 26). They are what we ordinarily think of as words. Symbols are signs together with their logico-syntactic use. (Logical syntax is akin to ordinary grammar but deeper. Thus ordinary grammar associates the use of the verb 'are' in 'Humans are animals' with the use of the verb 'eat' in 'Humans eat animals.' Logical syntax recognizes differences between these, reflected in the fact that it makes sense to add to the latter sentence, but not to the former, 'including themselves'.)[12] Wittgenstein expresses the relation between these as follows: 'A sign is what can be perceived of a symbol' (3.32). And he points out that 'one and the same sign ... can be common to two different symbols' (3.321). Thus the word 'round' is sometimes used as a noun to denote a slice of bread, sometimes as an adjective to indicate circularity: one sign, two symbols.

The relevance of this to the difficulties discussed above is twofold. First, the use of a single sign in two contexts, as two different symbols, is a common source of the confusions to which we are prone. Because the word 'passes' is used both in the sentence 'The traffic passes' and in the sentence 'The time passes', it is easy to take for granted that there is some deep common element in what the traffic does and what the time does, and then to agonize about how to understand this common element. We do not pause to ask whether the similarity between these two sentences is the relatively superficial similarity that attends the use of one sign as two symbols. Second, and related, because a sign is used in one context as a certain symbol, with a certain meaning, we naturally assume that this guarantees it a use as that same symbol, with that same meaning, in any other context that is superficially similar. Thus because we know what 'speed' means in the phrase 'the speed at which the traffic passes', we naturally assume that it can retain that meaning in the phrase 'the speed at which the time passes'.[13] But in fact, if what I have been suggesting about this example is correct, this second use

---

much, in examples of this kind, depends on context (cf. Conant and Diamond (2004), p. 76). Albert's confusion has its source in one particular attempt to construe the question 'At what speed does the time pass?' There may yet be decent ways of construing the question, and indeed of construing the proposed answer, that 'fit' other things we want to say – though the issue of what is meant by 'fit' here is a philosophical minefield in its own right, involving issues about the nature and workings of metaphor that I cannot hope to address in these confines. Cf. *Investigations*, §§139 and 537.

[12] It is often said that symbols are signs together with their *meanings* (e.g. Black (1964), p. 130). That this is wrong is well argued by Colin Johnston in Johnston (2007).

Note also: signs are to be construed here as 'sign-types', not 'sign-tokens', i.e. in such a way that the following list – 'tiger', 'lion', 'tiger' – contains two signs, not three, albeit in one case repeated (cf. 3.203). (We shall return to the distinction between sign-types and sign-tokens in Ch. 20, §3.)

[13] Cf. *Investigations*, §§350 and 351.

of the word 'speed' cannot be a use of the same sign with the same meaning. So unless and until some other meaning is conferred on the word 'speed', no sentence or pseudo-sentence that contains the phrase 'the speed at which the time passes' can be used to express any thought at all.[14]

Now Wittgenstein, to repeat, holds that the aim of philosophy is to combat confusion of precisely this kind. But just as Kant distinguishes between good metaphysics and bad metaphysics (Ch. 5, §2), so too Wittgenstein distinguishes between good philosophy and bad philosophy.[15] And he holds that the mark of *bad* philosophy is just such confusion (3.324–3.325 and 4.003). The aim of good philosophy, then, is to combat bad philosophy. (And this is its sole aim. If there were no bad philosophy, there would be no need for good philosophy. This is where the analogy with Kant breaks down.) Moreover, the one use of the term 'metaphysical' in the *Tractatus*, apart from a couple of references to something that Wittgenstein calls 'the metaphysical subject' (5.633 and 5.641), indicates that he equates metaphysics with bad philosophy.[16] Thus he writes:

> The correct method in philosophy would really be the following: to say nothing except what can be said … – i.e. something that has nothing to do with philosophy – and then, whenever someone else wanted to say something metaphysical, to demonstrate to him that he had failed to give a meaning to certain signs in his propositions. Although it would not be satisfying to the other person – he would not have the feeling that we were teaching him philosophy – *this* method would be the only strictly correct one. (6.53, emphasis in original)[17]

It is a further question what the implications of this view are for metaphysics on my conception of metaphysics as the most general attempt to make sense of things. If making sense of things is understood as arriving at truths about the world, then metaphysics is simply the most general of the natural sciences (4.11), which is arguably physics.[18] If making sense of things is understood as introducing the kind of clarity into our thinking that will enable us to arrive at truths about the world without the distractions

---

[14] But cf. n. 11: this is *not* to deny that it is possible to confer such a meaning, nor that such a meaning may already have been conferred, nor indeed that, if it has, the meaning in question may 'fit' the original meaning.

[15] This calls for a caveat similar to that issued in Ch. 5, n. 9. Wittgenstein is not always explicit – in fact he is never explicit – about which he is referring to. The use of 'philosophy' in 4.112, for example, stands elliptically for good philosophy; that in 3.324, for bad philosophy.

[16] There is what appears to be an unrelated use of 'metaphysics' in the *Notebooks*, at p. 106. I shall not try to interpret that use.

[17] For an interesting discussion of this passage, see Conant and Diamond (2004), pp. 76ff.

[18] Cf. 6.3751.

of bad philosophy, then metaphysics is simply good philosophy, in its most general reaches.[19] Either way, we see that the accidents of definition allow for an interpretation of the *Tractatus* whereby it is entirely metaphysics-friendly. Nevertheless, this accords neither with the letter of the text nor with what most self-styled metaphysicians would say about what they were engaged in. Here, just as in Hume (Ch. 4, §4), the fact that it is possible to characterize what we have before us as a celebration of proper metaphysics sits alongside the more blatant fact that, given how metaphysics has traditionally been conceived, and given how it has in fact been practised, what we have before us is an assault on the very enterprise.[20]

And Wittgenstein, in echo of Kant (Ch. 5, §2), is emboldened to say, in the Preface to the *Tractatus*, '[This] book deals with the problems of philosophy [i.e. the problems occasioned by bad philosophy, what Wittgenstein means by metaphysics].... I ... believe myself to have found, on all essential points, the final solution of [these] problems' (pp. 3–4).[21] But there is an ironical twist. He immediately adds, 'If I am not mistaken in this belief, then ... [part of] the value of this work ... is that it shows how little is achieved when these problems are solved' (p. 4).

3.   The Vision of the *Tractatus*

In the light of all of that, the *Tractatus* presents a quite unexpected initial appearance. Where we might have anticipated a series of examples of the confusions that bad philosophy engenders, together with more or less piecemeal attempts to eradicate them and perhaps also to offer some diagnosis – the kind of thing, in other words, that we find in Kant's 'Transcendental Dialectic' – what we actually find, from the very outset, is what looks for all the world like hard-core traditional metaphysics, in the same vein as the great metaphysical systems of Descartes, Spinoza, and Leibniz. 'The world is all that is the case,' Wittgenstein tells us in the opening sentence (1). The world is 'the totality of facts' (1.1) and not the totality of

---

[19] In §8 I shall highlight a third, broader conception of making sense of things, the one that I take to be most significant in the context of the *Tractatus*, on which metaphysics assumes yet another guise.

[20] But the similarity with Hume is structural only. There is nothing in the *Tractatus* that directly corresponds to Hume's repudiation of sense-making that does not derive from sense experience. Cf. Anscombe (1971), pp. 25ff., and Diamond (1993), Lecture One, §IV.

[21] Graham Bird makes the nice point that, just as Wittgenstein's boldness occurs in the Preface to his first book, and is not reflected in the Preface to his later book, so too Kant's boldness occurs in the Preface to the first edition of his masterwork and contrasts with the somewhat more guarded, more pessimistic tone of the Preface to its second edition; see Bird (2006), Ch. 24, n. 18. (We find a similar boldness in Ayer (1971). This is A.J. Ayer's very youthful defence of the logical positivism that we shall encounter in Ch. 11. Its last chapter is entitled 'Solutions of Outstanding Philosophical Disputes'.)

objects.[22] A little later he expands on this with a series of remarks about 'objects' and their relation to 'substance': 'Objects are simple.... [They] make up the substance of the world.... Substance is what subsists independently of what is the case' (2.02ff.). And so it goes on until we reach the climax of the book, where we are told that 'the sense of the world [lies] outside the world' (6.41); that 'God does not reveal himself *in* the world' (6.432, emphasis in original); and finally, in the very last sentence, that 'what we cannot speak about we must pass over in silence' (7). Heady, transcendent, abstract stuff! Or so it seems.

A fuller account of how this is supposed to consist with Wittgenstein's explicit view of philosophy, and his admonishments against the bad variety, must wait until later (§7). But already it is possible to say something to mitigate the impression that he is presenting a grand metaphysical vision of reality that is simply impervious to those admonishments. He is presenting a vision, all right, but a vision that subserves a Fregean project, to make sense, not of things, but of sense, its possibility, its scope, and its limits – where sense is understood to be sense of the kind that can be expressed in propositions.[23] Even the material towards the very end of the book, about what is and what is not 'in the world', is proffered as part of that same vision, the connection being that propositions can only express how things are 'in the world', as opposed to what is 'higher' (6.42). We may still have concerns about whether Wittgenstein's pronouncements can escape his own philosophical censure, but at least this gives some indication of why they might be thought to be relevant to it.

The project, then, is to make sense of propositional sense. And this involves saying what is required of things for such sense to be made of them. Wittgenstein's vision is a result of his execution of this project. The details of the vision need not concern us. Its outline is as follows.[24]

Propositional sense can be made of things because *there are ways those things are.* There are facts. The world is the totality of facts. Facts are determined by states of affairs. States of affairs are configurations of objects. Objects constitute the unanalyzable, inalterable, ungenerable, indestructible substance of the world. These would have existed however the facts had been. If the facts had been different, it would have been because the objects had been configured differently, not because there had been different objects. Propositional sense-making itself consists of facts. Indeed, propositions are facts, determined by configurations of signs. In the most elementary case the signs stand for objects – they are what Wittgenstein calls *names* – and

---

[22] 1.1 mentions 'things' rather than 'objects', but 2.01 suggests that these terms are interchangeable.

[23] We shall see the importance of this qualification in §8.

[24] For two superb compendia, see McGuiness (1990), Ch. 9, and Sullivan (2004). For an excellent, much fuller account, see Morris (2008).

the fact that they are configured in the way they are expresses that the corresponding objects are configured in that same way, in other words that the corresponding state of affairs exists. If it does, the proposition is true. If it does not, the proposition is false. In a less elementary case the conventions of language determine that the proposition is true provided that some suitable selection of states of affairs from a given range exists, false otherwise. For example, suppose that s_1 and s_2 are two states of affairs. Then it is possible to construct a proposition that is true if s_1 and s_2 both exist or if they both fail to exist, and false if just one of them exists. Equivalently, if p_1 and p_2 are the two corresponding elementary propositions, then it is possible to construct a proposition that is true if and only if p_1 and p_2 have the same truth value. At the limit it is possible to construct a proposition that is true whatever the circumstances, and a proposition that is false whatever the circumstances. An example of the former would be a proposition that was true if and only if p_1 and p_2 either had the same truth value or had different truth values. An example of the latter would be a proposition that was true if and only if p_1 and p_2 were both true and both false. But Wittgenstein dissociates such unconditionally true or unconditionally false propositions from sense-making. He explicitly says that they are senseless. This is not to deny that they are bona fide propositions, that the true ones really are true and the false ones really are false.[25] In the contrast that Wittgenstein draws, though they are senseless, they are not nonsensical. They are meaningful signs configured in such a way as to be true or false – the true ones being what he understands by logical truths, the false ones being what he understands by logical falsehoods. The point, however, is that they do not express *thoughts*. To have a thought about how things are, or to make propositional sense of things, is, for Wittgenstein, to represent things as being one of the ways that they could be but also one of the ways that they could fail to be. A true thought manages to *be* a true thought only because it runs the risk, so to speak, of being a false thought.[26]

---

[25] See 4.46ff. It is surprisingly common for commentators to say that it *is* to deny these things: see e.g. McGuiness (1990), p. 312, and Floyd (2000), p. 241. Admittedly, there is material in the 4.06s that may appear to confirm their view. But 4.064 states that 'every proposition must … have a sense,' and this suggests that the 4.06s are tacitly concerned only with those propositions that are not senseless.

[26] The material in this paragraph draws especially on the 1s, the 2s, the early 3s, and the mid 4s. Question: does Wittgenstein retain anything like Frege's sense/*Bedeutung* distinction? Answer: not except on an extremely generous interpretation of 'anything like'. He holds that the only expressions that have senses are propositions, and that propositions do not stand to anything in a relation akin to that in which names stand to objects. Ironically, one of the places where Wittgenstein most clearly registers this departure from Frege is 3.3, where he also, at the same time, commits himself to a version of Frege's context principle. (See further Carruthers (1989), Ch. 3.)

Let us relate this vision back to the confusions that bad philosophy engenders. On Wittgenstein's view, such confusions manifest themselves in the production of pseudo-propositions, such as 'Time passes at one second per second,' or, to adapt one of his own examples, 'The good is more identical than the beautiful' (4.003). And here we are not dealing with senselessness. We are dealing with nonsense, downright nonsense. But still, 'downright nonsense' of a distinctive *kind* – what might be called violations of logical syntax – no? No. A cardinal point of the sign/symbol distinction is precisely to ward us off saying that. Imagine a sign whose sole use hitherto has been as a noun. Suppose it is now used as a verb. We must not say that the original symbol has been put to an improper use. *There is now a new symbol.* Whether any meaning attaches to it or not depends on the circumstances. If no meaning attaches to it, then that is *all there is* to the nonsensicality of the pseudo-proposition in which it occurs. Its nonsensicality really is brute, like the nonsensicality of 'Frumptiliously quirxaceous phlimps keed'. It is due, as nonsensicality always is due, to sheer lack of meaning, not to possession of inappropriate meaning. Here is Wittgenstein:

> The reason why 'Socrates is identical' means nothing is that there is no property called 'identical'. The proposition is nonsensical because we have failed to make an arbitrary determination, and not because the symbol, in itself, would be illegitimate....
> ... [The proposition] says nothing ... [because] we have not given *any adjectival* meaning to the word 'identical'. For when it appears as a sign for identity, it symbolizes in an entirely different way ... therefore the symbols also are entirely different in the two cases. (5.473–5.4733, emphasis in original)

The vision outlined above, whereby propositional sense-making consists in facts, and propositions themselves are facts, reinforces these ideas. Imagine someone who is confused, whose attempts at sense-making misfire, and who produces nonsense as a result. Still this is all a matter of the obtaining of facts. Nothing in what this person says or does can consist in the obtaining of some 'pseudo-fact', as it may be an object's satisfying another object rather than satisfying a property. For nothing of that sort ever does obtain or ever could obtain. So the *only* way in which this person can have produced nonsense is by using signs to which, as so used, 'he has failed to give a meaning' (6.53). Insofar as he is being illogical, this can at most be a matter of his not attending to the symbols in his signs. Neither he nor his thinking processes can actually violate any logical laws, any more than anything else can. To quote G.E.M. Anscombe, 'an *impossible* thought is an impossible *thought*' (Anscombe (1971), p. 163, emphasis in original). Or to quote Wittgenstein himself, 'thought can never be of anything illogical, since, if it were, we should have to think illogically' (3.03). Again: 'In a certain sense, we cannot make mistakes in logic' (5.4731).[27]

4.   Logic. Wittgenstein *Contra* Frege and Kant

Logic, for Wittgenstein – as we have just seen – is the province of that which is true (or false) irrespective of which states of affairs exist. This means – again as we have just seen – that a logical truth, such as the truth that it is either raining or not raining, can never, on Wittgenstein's conception of thinking, be thought.[28] It has no content (cf. 4 and 6.11–6.111). Admittedly, we can prescind from the meanings of our symbols and have genuinely contentful thoughts about logical propositions *qua* combinations of signs, but that is a different matter. We can also, if we so choose, extend the use of the word 'thought' to embrace the vacuous relation in which we stand to logical truths, but that is just a question of how we define our terms. The important point, on Wittgenstein's view, is that logical truths are of a completely different *kind* from non-logical truths. A logically true proposition earns its title of truth by dint of its construction as a proposition, and by dint of that alone, not by dint of any relation in which it stands to reality.

There is a persistent temptation, whose force is felt as keenly by Wittgenstein as by anyone (see §7), to treat logical truth as though it differed only in degree from non-logical truth, as though it were just a matter of utmost generality. Frege can be seen as having succumbed to this

---

[27] I am greatly indebted to Cora Diamond in this paragraph. See e.g. Diamond (1991a), pp. 30–31, and (1991c), pp. 106–107, the latter including quotations from Wittgenstein's later work. (For dissent, see Hacker (2000), pp. 365ff.) Diamond traces many of Wittgenstein's ideas back to Frege. The reference above to an object's not being able to satisfy another object should certainly have rung Fregean bells; see §7 of the previous chapter. But we should pause to note an important corollary of this. Just as there is a problem, for Frege, about the *Bedeutungen* of predicates, so too there is a problem, for Wittgenstein – indeed there is a related problem for Frege – about predicates themselves. If a proposition is a fact, if a name is an object (and hence something that can itself be named), and if a predicate is what results when a name is removed from a proposition, then a predicate is not an object (it is not something that can be named). So just as there is something untoward about the predicate '... is a property', so too there is something untoward about the predicate '... is a predicate'. See further §5.

[28] It can be *known*. But to know that it is either raining or not raining is not to know anything about reality (4.461), and to accredit someone with the knowledge is not to say anything about reality (5.1362). (I cannot however resist reproducing an excellent joke in this connection from Brian McGuiness (1990). McGuiness himself quotes 4.461: 'I know nothing about the weather when I know that it is either raining or not raining.' He then adds a footnote in which he comments laconically, '[Wittgenstein] had been out of England for some time when he wrote this' (Ch. 9, n. 21).)

temptation. Although he distinguished carefully between the jurisdiction of the laws of logic, which he took to be truth, and the jurisdiction of the laws of nature, which he took to be what occurs in space and time (see §6 of the previous chapter), still he saw the two jurisdictions as broadly analogous. And when he contrasted the domain of what is thinkable and therefore subject to the former laws with the domain of what is actual and therefore subject to the latter laws – as indeed he did both of these with the domain of what is intuitable and therefore subject to the laws of geometry – he did so by treating them simply as wider or narrower domains and by calling the first 'the widest domain of all' (Frege (1980), §14). Thus just as physicists study the function that is represented in English by the expression 'the resultant of' – a function which, when applied to two forces as input, yields a force as output – so too, on Frege's view, logicians study the function that is represented in English by the conjunct 'unless' – a function which, when applied to two truth values as input, yields a truth value as output.

Wittgenstein recoils from all of this.[29] Here are three pertinent quotations:

> [When a] logical proposition acquires all the characteristics of a proposition of natural science ... this is a sure sign that it has been construed wrongly. (6.111)

> The mark of a logical proposition is *not* general validity.
>   To be general means no more than to be accidentally valid for all things. (6.1231, emphasis in original)

> My fundamental idea is that the 'logical constants' [such as 'unless'] are not representatives; that there can be no representatives of the *logic* of facts. (4.0312, emphasis in original; cf. 5.4–5.42)[30]

One way to grasp Wittgenstein's conception of these matters is as follows. We can recognize various different kinds of possibility, some strictly subsumed by others. Thus whatever is economically possible is technologically possible, but not vice versa; whatever is technologically possible is physically possible, but not vice versa; and similarly in other cases. These different kinds of possibility can be pictured as a series of concentric circles, in which larger circles include possibilities that smaller circles exclude. It is in these terms, very often, that we indicate what a given kind of possibility excludes, or at least some of what it excludes: we say that certain things are not possibilities of that kind, by first identifying them as possibilities

---

[29] For very helpful overviews, see Conant (1991), pp. 137ff., and Hacker (2001a), §5.

[30] Thus a disjunction of two propositions p_1 and p_2 does not depend for its truth on the behaviour of some function of the sort described above, at work in the world. It depends solely on the truth of p_1 and p_2. And 'unless' is just a sign that enables us to produce the disjunction of any two propositions. It does not designate anything in reality.

of some more inclusive kind. Thus a politician may say, adverting to what is technologically possible, 'There are *some* ways of improving the safety of our railways that are unaffordable.' A botanist may say, adverting to what is physically possible, 'There are *some* temperatures below which plant life is unsustainable.' (The politician is not vindicated by the technological impossibility of a completely fail-safe automated signalling system, nor the botanist by the impossibility of any temperature below absolute zero.) Now logical possibility subsumes all the rest.[31] But this means that it differs from the others in a way that is very radical indeed. It is not just another circle in the space we are considering. We cannot say, except as a kind of joke, that logical possibility excludes possibilities of such and such another kind, such as the 'illogical' possibility that it is neither raining nor not raining. To repeat, logical possibility is not just another circle in the space we are considering. It *is* the space we are considering.[32]

This is not to deny that, even in the case of logical possibility, there are relevant divisions that we can recognize. For instance, and most notably, we can step up a level, talk about language, and distinguish between those combinations of signs that do represent logical possibilities and those combinations of signs that do not (cf. p. 3). But that of course is still not to say that logical possibility excludes any other possibilities.[33]

It follows from all of this that there is a good sense in which logical possibility is the *only* possibility (see the 6.3s, esp. 6.37 and 6.375). It is the only absolute possibility. The others are relative. They are parasitic on it. Thus what is physically possible is what is logically compatible with the laws of physics, where these are just highly general truths about how the world happens, logically, to be.

Does it also follow from all of this that logic sets no limits to reality? That depends on how 'limits' are understood. Logic precisely does set limits to reality in the sense that it displays reality's *essential features*: it displays

---

[31] What about epistemic possibility? Cannot imperfections in our understanding render that which is logically impossible epistemically possible? Not on Wittgenstein's view. Cf. §2: imperfect understanding, for Wittgenstein, is not understanding at all. In fact, in a quite trivial sense, anyone who understands anything knows that any given logical impossibility is false: see n. 28.

[32] Cf. 6.123. And cf. Diamond (1993), Lecture One, §IV.

[33] Cf. Sullivan (2003), esp. pp. 209–211, and (2004), p. 34. And cf. certain currents of thought in Wittgenstein's later work. E.g. at one point in *Philosophical Grammar*, commenting on the infinitude of the sequence of cardinal numbers, Wittgenstein insists that we should not say, 'There is no largest cardinal number' – as though we were excluding some possibility – but should rather say, 'The expression "last cardinal number" makes no sense' (p. 465). And in the *Investigations*, having remarked that '*essence* is expressed by grammar', he says of a puzzle that he is wrestling with there, 'The great difficulty is not to represent the matter as if *there were something* one *couldn't* do' (§§371 and 374, first and third emphasis in original, second emphasis added).

how reality must be. It does not set limits to reality in the sense of imposing *limitations* on reality.[34] Logical possibility excludes nothing. For it excludes nothing that can be thought, nothing of which propositional sense can be made. And we cannot regard what can be *thought* as excluding anything, for reasons encapsulated in the Limit Argument. Wittgenstein gives a version of this argument in the Preface to his book. He writes:

> In order to be able to draw a limit to thought [understood as a *limitation* of thought], we should have to find both sides of the limit thinkable (i.e. we should have to be able to think what cannot be thought). (p. 3)

Provided that thought is understood in a suitably thin way (cf. Ch 5, §8), this argument is surely unassailable.

But does Wittgenstein understand thought in a suitably thin way? After all, the very starting point of this discussion was his insistence that logical propositions do not express thoughts. Is there perhaps scope, in Wittgenstein's own terms, for resisting his version of the Limit Argument? Consider the expanded form of that argument, as set out in Chapter 5, §8. In producing propositions about how things must be, do we not falsify the first premise, the Limit-Drawing Principle? For do we not draw a limit to what we can make sense of without expressing any thoughts about that limit, and hence without making sense of it?

We do not do this in any sense that disrupts the Limit Argument. The point is exactly the same as it was before. We draw a limit to what we can make sense of *only* in the sense that we indicate essential features of what we can make sense of.[35] We do not indicate any limitations of it. There is no inside and outside here, no immanent and transcendent. Logical truth does not *transcend* non-logical truth; it pervades it.[36] It is revealing that the adjective that Wittgenstein uses to describe logic, in what is a clear echo of Kant – almost as if to emphasize that he does not take it to be transcendent – is 'transcendental' (6.13).

In other respects, however, this conception is radically un-Kantian. Wittgenstein is utterly hostile to the idea of the synthetic *a priori*. The synthetic admits of alternatives (cf. 6.11). But the *a priori* does not. It attaches only to absolute, logical necessity; only to the truth of that whose truth can be ascertained without reference to reality (see e.g. 2.225, 3.05, 5.4731, 5.634, 6.31, and 6.3211; and cf. 4.0412). To acknowledge the synthetic *a priori* is, in effect, to acknowledge limits that are limits in both senses of the term – essential features *and* limitations – precisely what Wittgenstein abjures. And, as Peter Sullivan well notes, the 6s in the *Tractatus* consist largely of a case-by-case rejection of Kant's examples of synthetic *a priori*

---

[34] Aristotle recognized such a distinction: see his *Metaphysics*, Bk Δ, Ch. 17.
[35] Cf. 6.12 and 6.124.
[36] Cf. 5.61.

truth.[37] It is thus that Wittgenstein answers what he calls at one point in his *Notebooks* 'the great problem round which everything that I write turns' (p. 53). The question is: 'Is there an order of the world *a priori*, and if so what does it consist in?' (ibid.). The answer, which he gives at 5.634, is: 'There is no *a priori* order of things.'[38]

5. 'Anyone who understands me eventually recognizes my propositions as nonsensical'

Wittgenstein recoils from both a Fregean conception of the *a priori* and a Kantian conception of the *a priori* then. But this does not prevent him from inheriting some of the problems that afflict each of these. In this section we shall consider problems that he inherits from Frege. In §7 we shall consider problems that he inherits from Kant.

In §7 of the previous chapter I mentioned two problems that befell Frege. For reasons that need not detain us Wittgenstein takes himself to be immune to the first of these, the problem about the set of sets that do not belong to themselves (3.333; see also 6.031). But he certainly confronts an analogue of the second problem, the problem about the *Bedeutungen* of predicates.[39] The relation between his semantics and Frege's is too oblique for us to be able to say that he confronts exactly the same problem. But he does hold:

- that there is something in an elementary proposition that enables it to be more than a mere list of names
- that this corresponds to something in reality that enables objects to be combined together in states of affairs

---

[37] Sullivan (1996), pp. 197–198. See in particular the wonderful n. 9 (p. 213) in which he makes clear how the organization of the 6s reflects topics that are of central concern to Kant. See Sullivan (1996) more generally, and Sullivan (2002), esp. §3.3, for his detailed defence of this reading.

Note that, although Wittgenstein aligns himself with Frege in rejecting the view that arithmetic consists of synthetic *a priori* truths, his conception of arithmetic is nevertheless very different from Frege's. While conceding that mathematics is 'a logical method' (6.2), he regards mathematical propositions as strictly nonsensical, hence not even as senseless (6.2 again; and cf. 4.241ff. and 5.53ff.; see also Potter (2000), Ch. 6). This is a useful corrective, very pertinent to what will come later, to the idea that Wittgenstein sees 'nonsensical' as a term of unmitigated opprobrium. In *this* case, at least, Wittgenstein is well aware of the use to which nonsense can be put: see 6.211. (Note that I part company in some of these comments with Conant and Diamond (2004), n. 59, where they deny that Wittgenstein regards mathematical propositions as nonsensical; but I am not sure what their alternative is.)

[38] But see McGinn (2006), pp. 269–270, for a somewhat different reading of this.

[39] Cf. Geach (1976).

- that the something in each case is the same, an abstract unity that he calls 'logical form' (this is the rationale for his holding that elementary propositions are facts)

and

- that logical form can never itself be the subject matter of any proposition, since propositions only ever say how *objects* are

or again,

- that logical form can never be the subject matter of any proposition since a proposition would need to transcend logical form, which is to say it would need to transcend reality, in order to say how, among the ways logical form might be, it is (see the 2.1s, 3.14–3.221, and the 4.12s).

Wittgenstein further holds that propositions 'show' logical form, where what can be shown cannot be said (4.121 and 4.1212).[40] But this appeal to what propositions show cannot hide what in fact it serves only to emphasize, namely that Wittgenstein's own numerous remarks about logical form, like Frege's frequent references to properties, cannot be interpreted in a way that is consonant with his own views and must therefore, by his own lights, be regarded as nonsense.

Nor is this aporia the incidental aporia for Wittgenstein that it was for Frege. There is scarcely a sentence in the *Tractatus* that *can* be interpreted in a way that is consonant with his own views, or at least there is scarcely a sentence in the *Tractatus* that can clearly be so interpreted. Thus consider all the sortal noun phrases in the work that appear to have as one of their uses to indicate 'internal properties', where an internal property is a property such that whatever has it has it of necessity (see 4.122ff.). Examples are 'object' – nothing just *happens* to have the property of being an object – 'state of affairs', 'sense', 'logical form', and indeed 'internal property'. The 4.12s foreclose any such use. (This is related to the principle that the only necessity is logical necessity.) There are related problems for any sortal noun phrase that is defined in terms of any of these, such as 'fact', 'world', 'proposition', or 'thought'. Each occurrence of each of these noun phrases must therefore give pause. I put it no more strongly than that because of how much, in the interpretation of a term, depends on context.[41] Thus when Wittgenstein writes, 'The whole modern conception of the world is founded on the illusion that the so-called laws of nature are the explanations of natural phenomena' (6.371), it is not at all clear that what he writes is vitiated by its mere inclusion of the sortal noun 'world'. (Here it is

---

[40] We shall return to the idea of what can be shown in the next section.
[41] Cf. n. 11.

worth remembering that, insofar as Wittgenstein specifies conditions that a combination of signs must meet in order to be a meaningful proposition, and insofar as we accept what he says, we are at just as much liberty to take what we believe to be a meaningful proposition and conclude by *modus ponens* that it must be a combination of signs meeting those conditions as we are to take what we believe to be a combination of signs failing to meet those conditions and conclude by *modus tollens* that it cannot be a meaningful proposition.[42]) The fact remains that the 4.12s must make us wary of all of these noun phrases. And there is the further complication that each of them, with the exception of 'object', may suffer from a direct analogue of the problem afflicting the Fregean term 'property', namely that when it *is* being used to indicate an internal property, or is supposedly being used to do that, syntax demands that it is a property of objects and semantics demands that it is not.[43,44] Wittgenstein, like Hume and Kant before him, appears to be under serious threat from the challenge of applying his own principles to his own work.

However, unlike either of them, but like Frege, he is pre-emptive. He acknowledges that his book consists mainly of nonsense. In the famous penultimate remark of the book he writes:

> My propositions serve as elucidations in the following way: anyone who understands me eventually recognizes them as nonsensical, when he has used them – as steps – to climb up beyond them. (He must, so to speak, throw away the ladder after he has climbed it.) …
>
> He must transcend these propositions, and then he will see the world aright. (6.54)

Frege asked his reader not to begrudge him a pinch of salt (Frege (1997e), p. 192/p. 204 in the original German). Even a reader ready to grant Frege his wish might think twice about showing Wittgenstein the same indulgence. It is one thing to stumble into nonsense in trying to articulate one component

---

[42] Cf. the parenthetical sentence in 3.328, the last sentence of 4.002, and the first sentence of 5.5563.

[43] I say it 'may' suffer from an analogue of the Fregean problem because, even where nonsense is concerned, 'the outward form of the clothing is not designed to reveal the form of the body' (4.002).

[44] Cf. Peter Sullivan's discussion of Wittgenstein's associated problem with logical category distinctions in Sullivan (2003), pp. 217ff. For Wittgenstein, the logical category to which anything belongs is determined by the quantifier within whose range it lies. But this means that the very use of the word 'anything' in this formulation of the doctrine – 'the logical category to which *anything* belongs' – cannot have its intended generality. It is impossible to generalize about things of different logical categories (as indeed this very admonishment purports to do).

There is a related problem for Frege when he claims in Frege (1997a), p. 140/p. 18 in the original German, that 'an object is *anything* that is not a function' (emphasis added).

of a larger, otherwise coherent theory. It is another thing to produce non-sense at almost every turn throughout an entire book.[45]

To be sure, the fact that a book consists mostly of nonsense is not itself a ground for indictment. Books are written for all sorts of purposes. Some of these might well be served by nonsense. An obvious example is enter-tainment. Another is parody. Another is to ward the reader off engaging in a certain intellectual activity, a purpose that could be served by exhibit-ing the deleterious effects of doing so. But none of these seems to hold out much hope as far as exonerating the *Tractatus* is concerned. *Its* propositions appear to be attempts to convey genuine insights, insights into what it is to make propositional sense of things and into the ways in which bad philoso-phy hinders us in our efforts to do so. It looks as though we are supposed to share these insights by, as one would like to say, 'understanding' the non-sense. What is going on here?

6.   Two Approaches to the *Tractatus*. A Rapprochement?

Recent exegesis of the *Tractatus* has involved two broad approaches. I shall adopt the simplifying assumption that there is enough unity in these approaches to warrant talk of two readings: what I shall call 'the traditional reading' and 'the new reading'.

Advocates of the traditional reading take the *Tractatus* at face value, as an attempt to convey something. But they also take seriously the claim at 6.522 that 'there are … things that cannot be put into words', things that, in the terminology introduced in the previous section, can be shown though they cannot be said. They hold that what the *Tractatus* is an attempt to con-vey are things of just this sort.

> The Traditional Reading: The *Tractatus* is an attempt to convey things that are ineffable.[46] The means that Wittgenstein uses to convey these things is language that he himself recognizes as nonsense. But it is non-sense of a special kind, what might be called 'illuminating' nonsense.[47] It

---

[45] 'Almost' every turn? What are the exceptions? This question is far from straightforward. For one thing the answer may be relative to the reader (cf. Conant and Diamond (2004), n. 102). But on any account of the matter the exceptions are liable to be few, isolated, and miscellaneous. Putative examples, to supplement the sentence from 6.371 already cited, are the remark about notation at 5.531, the parenthetical comment about the ways of seeing the diagram in 5.5423, the reference to Frege in the first sentence of 6.232, the historical remark in the first sentence of 6.372, and the claims about philosophical meth-odology in 6.53. (Note: it is not uncontroversial that there *are* any exceptions. For an argument that there are not, see Morris (2008), pp. 343ff.)

[46] I use 'ineffable' to mean 'incapable of being expressed in words'. This leaves open the possibility of something ineffable's being expressed in some other way, say in actions or in music. We shall see the significance of this possibility in the next section.

[47] This is P.M.S. Hacker's term: see Hacker (1986), p. 18.

enables us to grasp what he is trying to convey. And this in turn enables us, like him, to recognize it (the nonsense) as nonsense.[48]

Advocates of the new reading are prepared *not* to take the *Tractatus* at face value. They adopt a version of the suggestion that Wittgenstein is exhibiting the deleterious effects of engaging in a certain malpractice, namely bad philosophy. This brings the *Tractatus* more into line with what I said earlier we might have expected of it: a catalogue of examples of what not to do, presented in such a way as to enable the reader to see how and why not to do it.[49]

The New Reading: There is nothing that cannot be put into words. There is only the temptation to see sense where it is lacking. Wittgenstein's aim in the *Tractatus* is therapeutic. The reason why the book consists mainly of nonsense is that he is trying, by indulging the temptation, to eliminate it; by producing nonsense that appears to make sense, and then testing the appearance, to get the reader to acknowledge the illusion, so that the temptation disappears, and the reader is left realizing that the nonsense is precisely that: sheer lack of sense. It is an assemblage of signs to which, as used here, no meanings have been assigned. It conveys nothing whatsoever.[50]

These readings look as if they could scarcely be further apart. But two points should be made straight away. First, it is quite compatible with the traditional reading that the nonsense is 'an assemblage of signs to which, as used here, no meanings have been assigned'. And second, conversely, it is quite compatible with the new reading that the nonsense is edifying nonsense. Indeed, advocates of the new reading would be among the first to insist that the nonsense is indeed edifying nonsense, in its own unusual and indirect way. But even apart from these two points there is a crucial and much deeper reason for thinking that the two readings may not be all that far apart.[51]

---

[48] For examples of something more or less traditional, see Anscombe (1971); Hacker (1986), Chs 1–4; and Pears (1987), Pt II.

[49] And it makes Wittgenstein's project in the *Tractatus* not only much more like Kant's in the 'Transcendental Dialectic', but also much more like his own in his later work: see esp. §2 of the next chapter. See also the essays in Part II of Crary and Read (2000), entitled 'The *Tractatus* as Forerunner of Wittgenstein's Later Writings'.

[50] For examples of something more or less new, see Conant (1989); Diamond (1991e); and Kremer (2001). For a powerful recoil in favour of a traditional reading, see Hacker (2000). Poised somewhere in between are Reid (1998); McGinn (1999); Proops (2001); Sullivan (2002); Morris (2008), Ch. 7, §E; and Morris and Dodd (2009). Marie McGinn develops her ideas at much greater length in McGinn (2006). For a quite different reading, see Moyal-Sharrock (2007). For an excellent discussion, see Costello (2004).

[51] What follows summarizes the argument of Moore (2003b), from which I have borrowed some material.

Consider: what does someone mean who claims that there are things that cannot be put into words, or who claims that, on the contrary, there are no such things? What does the term 'things' range over here? If it ranges too widely, there is no interest in either claim. For it is plain that most things, on even a moderately broad construal, cannot be put into words. A brick, for example, cannot. It can be described, certainly. But it cannot be put into words. Nor, come to that, can the opening bar of Beethoven's Fifth Symphony, which gives the (literalistic) lie to the famous quip that F.P. Ramsey directed at the *Tractatus*, that 'what we can't say we can't say, and we can't whistle it either' (Ramsey (1931), p. 238).[52]

On the most natural interpretation of these two claims, an interpretation whereby it is a substantive issue which of them is correct, the term 'things' ranges over truths. And on that interpretation Wittgenstein's view is surely in line with the counterclaim (that there is nothing that cannot be put into words). The idea of an ineffable truth is, surely, an anathema to him, even given whatever distinction we are forced to recognize between what he would say in an authentic mode and what he would say in his assumed role as the producer of this text. For, either way, he would balk at the notion of something that is the case yet cannot be said to be the case (see e.g. the first sentence of 4.002, 4.063, 4.5, and 6.5–6.51).

However, this is by no means the only way of construing the term 'things' that confers interest on the two claims. Consider states of understanding. It is clear that many states of understanding can be put into words; an example would be a solicitor's understanding of some legal nicety that she has to explain to one of her clients. But it is far from clear that all states of understanding can be put into words. (Reconsider the variety of potential objects of understanding to which I drew attention in §4 of the Introduction.) So if the term 'things' ranges over states of understanding, then there is scope, once again, for a substantive debate about which of these two claims is correct. But there is scope too, I suggest, for a substantive debate about what Wittgenstein's own verdict would be.

In the penultimate remark of the *Tractatus*, which I quoted in the previous section, Wittgenstein notably says, 'Anyone who *understands me* eventually recognizes [my propositions] as nonsensical' (emphasis added). 'Anyone who understand me', not 'anyone who understands my propositions'. This allows us to take the remark in just the way in which it asks to be taken – as a remark made *in propria persona* – without saddling Wittgenstein with the paradox of intelligible nonsense.[53] But if there is such a state as

---

[52] Ramsey did direct this quip at the *Tractatus*, but there is an issue about whether he himself (as opposed to the countless people who have subsequently appropriated his quip) intended to direct it specifically at the idea that there are things that cannot be put into words; see Diamond (2011).

[53] Cf. Conant (1991), p. 159; (2000), p. 198; and Diamond (2000), pp. 150–151.

understanding Wittgenstein – if there is such a state as seeing what he is up to in this extraordinary work – then it is a real question whether *that* can be put into words, just as it is a real question whether Wittgenstein thinks it can, just as it is a real question, for that matter, whether the various other states of understanding that Wittgenstein mentions in the *Tractatus* – understanding a proposition (4.024), understanding the constituents of a proposition (ibid.), understanding logic (5.552), and understanding language (5.62) – can be put into words, or whether he thinks they can.[54]

Once we have taken account of all of this, there are ways of construing the two readings of the *Tractatus* whereby, to borrow a wonderful phrase of David Wiggins' from a different context, 'suddenly it seems that what makes the difference between [them] has the width of a knife edge' (Wiggins (1995), pp. 327–328). Where advocates of the traditional reading hold that there are 'things' that cannot be put into words, and that the *Tractatus* conveys 'things' of that sort, we can construe the 'things' in question as states of understanding, including the state of understanding Wittgenstein. Where advocates of the new reading hold that there is 'nothing' that cannot be put into words, and that the *Tractatus* conveys 'nothing' whatsoever, we can construe the 'things' in question as truths. We can then look back at the accounts of the two readings proffered above and see each as entirely consonant with the other.[55]

7. Transcendental Idealism in the *Tractatus*

There is space, then, for an approach to the *Tractatus* that merges the two readings. But what is to be said in favour of any such approach?

I think we can see in outline how a combined reading might help us to make sense of why Wittgenstein has produced this nonsense. Thus:

> The Combined Reading: The nonsense in the *Tractatus* has been carefully crafted both to have the appearance of sense and, in quite

---

[54] See further §8.

[55] I should emphasize that I offer this as much in a spirit of reconstruction as by way of serious exegesis of the exegesis. Indeed, I think that there is need for a corrective on both sides of the debate, precisely because of a shared tendency to overlook the possibility that there are things other than truths that are non-trivially ineffable: see e.g. Conant (1991), p. 160; (2004), p. 171; and Hacker (2000), p. 368. (Among those who show awareness of this possibility are Michael Kremer, in Kremer (2001), §IX, and Peter Sullivan, in Sullivan (2002), §2.4.)

Note: if the idea of ineffable understanding is to be divorced from the idea of ineffable truth, then clearly there must be understanding which is not understanding of any truth. Here there is an echo of a suggestion that first surfaced in Ch. 2, §6, that there is ineffable knowledge which is not knowledge of any truth but rather practical knowledge. It is a particularly loud echo if, as I believe, ineffable states of understanding are themselves states of practical knowledge; see Moore (1997a), pp. 161 and 183ff.

particular ways, to militate against that appearance. We come to appreciate it as nonsense when we find that we cannot in the end make full and integrated sense of it. In Peter Sullivan's excellent metaphor, adapted in turn from a phrase used by Warren Goldfarb, it falls apart in our hands (Sullivan (2004), p. 40; Goldfarb (1997), p. 71). This brings us to an appreciation of the forces that give this nonsense the appearance of sense in the first place, and of what it takes to resist those forces. The understanding that Wittgenstein imparts is a practical understanding. It has, as one of its most significant aspects, an insight into how not to be seduced into thinking that his book is the network of truth-evaluable propositions that it presents itself as being. But there is more to it than that. There had better be more to it than that; otherwise the *Tractatus* will be like the notorious plinth whose sole purpose is to support a sign reading 'Mind the plinth'. The understanding that Wittgenstein imparts has a second, broader aspect: an insight, more generally, into how not to be seduced into thinking that the nonsense that accrues from bad philosophy is what it presents itself as being.[56] This makes the *Tractatus* a significant contribution to good philosophy, albeit an indirect one. It is indirect because Wittgenstein does not so much practise good philosophy in this book as indicate, by assuming the role of the bad philosopher, why, how, and where good philosophy needs to be practised. But that is enough for us to be able to identify a third, still broader aspect to the understanding that he imparts. This understanding has as much to do with sense as it does with nonsense. In particular, it has to do with propositional sense. The *Tractatus* helps us to make sense of propositional sense. But the sense that it helps us to make of propositional sense *is not itself propositional*. The understanding that Wittgenstein imparts has to be expressed, not in words, but in good philosophy, where good philosophy, recall, is an activity, not a body of doctrine (4.112). This activity involves both the clarification of propositional sense and the resisting of illusions of propositional sense. The understanding, of which good philosophy is an expression, is ineffable.

I think we can even see how such a reading would work at a more detailed level; and why the nonsense that Wittgenstein produces (what I called in §3 his 'vision') takes the superficial form of an explicit account of what it is to make propositional sense of things. Here we can take Frege's struggle with the *Bedeutungen* of predicates as our guide. Frege helped us to

---

[56] Cf. McGinn (1999), pp. 502ff. On the power of the seduction, cf. Hacker (1996), pp. 112–113, and Diamond (1991c), pp. 106–107, both of which reference pertinent material elsewhere in Wittgenstein.

an understanding of the semantics of predicates by making pseudo-claims, ostensibly about the semantics of predicates, which the understanding itself exposed as nonsense. An analogue in the *Tractatus*, as we saw in §5, is Wittgenstein's treatment of logical form. It is one of many analogues.[57]

Such a reading would also connect well with something else that I think we can readily see: how the recognition of apparent sense as nonsense is liable to resist verbal expression. For when we attempt to put such a recognition into words, our natural urge will always be to redeploy the nonsense, using some such formula as, 'It does not make sense to say that ....' But if we do that, then clearly we shall have said something that is itself nonsensical. No more sense attaches to 'It does not make sense to say that frumptiliously quirxaceous phlimps keed', if taken at face value, than to 'Frumptiliously quirxaceous phlimps keed.' To be sure, there are various subtleties and complications that I am ignoring here, having to do with the fact that the first of these sentences need *not* be taken at face value. It may be taken as a metalinguistic claim about the last four words in it. But that seems not to extend satisfactorily to a case where there really is an illusion of sense, as when I say, 'It does not make sense to say that time passes at one second per second.' (Think what a monolingual Francophile would say in such a case: certainly not anything about any words of English.)[58] Be all of that as it may, here too we have an indication of why the understanding of what it is to make propositional sense of things, and correlatively of what it is merely to appear to make propositional sense of things, may not admit of verbal expression, either in general or in application to a particular case.

None of this, however, quite does justice to the way in which the nonsense in the *Tractatus* serves to undermine itself; nor indeed to the sense, however tenuous, in which that nonsense is as much the 'content' of the book as its 'target'. (These two things are of course related.) We can begin to do justice to these if we return to the discussion of logic in §4.

As we saw, one of Wittgenstein's primary objectives, where the understanding of logic is concerned, is to counteract the temptation to misconstrue limits, in the sense of essential features, as limitations. This temptation is extremely strong. We easily hear the claim that it is either raining or not raining, for example, not as repudiating the possibility of its doing neither, but as presupposing that possibility, and then excluding it; in other words, not as denying that the possibility exists, but as denying merely that it is realized. That it is either raining or not raining seems to be something that is 'worth saying', something that can genuinely be thought, something that might, at some level, have been otherwise (cf. 6.111). For Wittgenstein, these are deep illusions.

---

[57] See n. 44.

[58] For a much fuller discussion, see Moore (2003b), esp. §VIII. Cf. also the *Investigations*, §58, the paragraph straddling pp. 28–29.

But like the illusion of sense attaching to the sentence 'Time passes at one second per second,' they are illusions whose exposure is most naturally reported in a way that is under their very sway. We naturally say, 'Thought can only be of what is logically contingent; there is no such thing as thinking that it is either raining or not raining.' But this is of a piece with, 'Speed can only be assigned to a process that occurs in time; there is no such thing as the speed at which time passes.' This is an attempted expression of the recognition that 'the speed at which time passes' is nonsense, just as the other sentence is an attempted expression of the recognition that 'thinks that it is either raining or not raining' is nonsense. But the attempt is self-stultifying. The very thing that it is an attempt to express precludes its success.

It is the same when we consider the apparent restriction of reality, not only to what is logically possible, but to the kind of thing that can be represented in propositional sense-making – which excludes, for example, objects. We are liable to say, 'Reality consists of how objects are, not of the objects themselves,' or, as Wittgenstein himself famously does say, 'The world is the totality of facts, not of things' (1.1). And if asked to amplify on these claims, we are liable to say something like the following: 'That grass is green is part of reality, because there is such a thing as thinking or saying that grass is green; greenness itself is not part of reality, because there is no such thing as thinking or saying greenness.' But here we confront the same problem. If 'thinks greenness' is nonsense, then so too is 'There is no such thing as thinking greenness.' To put the point in a way that is itself no doubt under the sway of the illusion: if there is no such thing as either thinking or saying something, then there is no such thing as either thinking or saying that there is no such thing as either thinking or saying that thing.

It is anyway clear that something is awry with 1.1 ('The world is the totality of facts, not of things') when we pit it against the second sentence of 5.61: 'We cannot say in logic, "The world has this in it, and this, but not that."'[59] And what is awry with it is precisely that it casts the world's limits as limitations, as 5.61 goes on to make clear:

> For that [sc. saying in logic 'The world has this in it, and this, but not that'] would appear to presuppose that we were excluding certain possibilities, and this cannot be the case, since it would require that logic

---

[59] *Is* it clear? What about the following riposte? Somebody might say that Wittgenstein is using the word 'world' differently in these two contexts, in the former case to refer to the realm of the actual, and in the latter case to refer to the realm of the possible.

I incline to the view that he uses it to refer to the realm of the actual throughout the *Tractatus*, and that what enables him to refer to the realm of the possible in 5.61 is his use of other words and phrases, notably 'in logic' and 'limits'. But even if I am wrong about that – even if Wittgenstein's use of 'world' is ambiguous in the way mooted – what he says in 1.1, with its clearly implied application to any other possible world, is still surely offensive to the spirit of what he says in 5.61.

should go beyond the limits of the world; for only in that way could it view those limits from the other side as well.

This remark from 5.61 is a reformulation of the Limit Argument, in the version that has already occurred in the Preface and that we considered in §4.

The problem, in a nutshell, is this. Among the sources of the temptation to construe the world's limits as limitations, one of the most significant is the very desire to counteract the temptation. At some level we recognize the incoherence of construing the world's limits as limitations. In recognizing this incoherence we are tempted to forbid any reference to the possibilities that the world's limits exclude, in such a way that we ourselves make reference to the possibilities that the world's limits exclude, and hence in such a way that we ourselves construe its limits as limitations.[60] Wittgenstein has himself, if not succumbed to the temptation, indulged it. (That is one of the lessons of the new reading.) He did so even in his account of good philosophy when he wrote:

> [Philosophy] must set limits to what can be thought; and, in so doing, to what cannot be thought.
>
> It must set limits to what cannot be thought by working outwards through what can be thought.
>
> It will signify what cannot be said, by presenting clearly what can be said. (4.114–4.115)

Better, surely, just to have written:

> Philosophy must set limits to what can be thought.[61] It must present clearly what can be said.[62]

What Wittgenstein produces, again and again in the *Tractatus*, is nonsense designed to prevent the production of just such nonsense. (That too is a lesson of the new reading, but seen now in a different light, whereby what Wittgenstein produces is not just a sequence of strategically chosen instances of what he wants to put us on our guard against, but an abortive attempt to explain why he wants to put us on our guard against it.) This is reminiscent of the celebrated remark that Karl Kraus is reputed to have made: 'Psychoanalysis is that mental illness for which it regards itself as therapy.'[63]

---

[60] Cf. the problem to which I drew attention in the Introduction, §6, in connection with the Transcendence Question: anyone who thinks that we are limited to making sense of what is immanent is liable to register this thought by distinguishing between what is immanent and what is transcendent, and thereby either doing the very thing that they think is impossible or else ceasing to make sense. Cf. also Sullivan (2003), p. 219.

[61] I.e. it must display the essential features of what can be thought.

[62] This does not preclude its exposing some of the nonsense that results from bad philosophy: cf. 6.53, and cf. Sullivan (2002), p. 35.

[63] Cf. Bernard Williams' application of the same remark to Wittgenstein's later philosophy in Williams (2006n), p. 208. Cf. also my earlier example of the sign reading 'Mind the plinth'.

Because Wittgenstein's concern is with the kind of thing that can be represented in propositional sense-making; because the nonsense he produces purports to restrict reality to precisely that, in other words to the kind of thing that can be represented in propositional sense-making; and because this restriction is, even within the 'terms' of the nonsense, not itself the kind of thing that can be represented in propositional sense-making, the nonsense takes what is by now, for us, a familiar form. *It is a species of transcendental idealism.*[64] Wittgenstein's recoil from Kant notwithstanding, the *Tractatus* is in many ways a thoroughly Kantian book, with a thoroughly Kantian problematic.[65]

Here is an excerpt from the *Tractatus* in which the transcendental idealism is more or less explicit. (It is cast using the first-person singular. This is perhaps more reminiscent of Fichte than it is of Kant.[66] It raises some large questions.[67] For our current purposes, however, these lie at something of a tangent. What matters is the idea that reality is limited by propositional sense-making, that the world is limited by language.)

> *The limits of my language* mean the limits of my world.
>
> … [What] the solipsist *means* is quite correct; only it cannot be *said*, but makes itself manifest.
>
> The world is *my* world: this is manifest in the fact that the limits of *language* (of that language which alone I understand) mean the limits of *my* world. (5.6–5.62, emphasis in original)

Does this mean that Wittgenstein – how to put it? – *is* a transcendental idealist? Patently not, in any straightforward sense. The *Tractatus*, as is clear by now, works in far too oblique a way for us to be able to draw any such conclusion from the mere presence of transcendental idealism in the text.

But can we at least say that transcendental idealism is part of the 'vision' that Wittgenstein presents in his book? In other words, can we say that, *to whatever extent he can be said to hold that propositions share logical form with reality* (4.12) – to pick one cardinal example – he can also be said to be

---

[64] Cf. Sullivan (2002), pp. 42–43.

[65] Two noteworthy attempts to portray the *Tractatus* as Kantian are Stenius (1964), Ch. XI, and Hacker (1986), Ch. 4. Not that Kant had much direct influence on Wittgenstein. Wittgenstein is said to have claimed 'that he could get only occasional glimpses of understanding' from Spinoza, Hume, and Kant (von Wright (1958), p. 20). Nevertheless, as both Erik Stenius and P.M.S. Hacker point out, Kant did have a significant indirect influence on Wittgenstein, through Schopenhauer. Schopenhauer made a strong impression on Wittgenstein (ibid., p. 9; see also Janik and Toulmin (1973), passim). The main conduit was a set of ideas concerning ethics and the will to which we shall turn in the next section.

[66] But see again the material from Kant (1998), A129, quoted in Ch. 6, n. 18.

[67] See e.g. Sullivan (1996).

a transcendental idealist? Arguably, not even that. We must not just assume that everything in the text is to be taken in the same way, nor even that it is to be taken in one of two ways, either as part of a single self-consciously nonsensical 'vision' that Wittgenstein is presenting or as something that he is saying, meaningfully, and in a more authentic mode, about how we are to deal with that 'vision' and with related nonsense (e.g. 6.54). This is a *multifarious* text, a text in which ideas are variously developed and suppressed, temptations are variously indulged and dispelled.[68]

One view would be this. The statements of transcendental idealism are quite different from the remarks about logical form. The latter are nonsense that we should regard as resulting from a knowingly unsuccessful attempt to express the understanding that they impart, an understanding that includes the very capacity to recognize them as nonsense. But where the statements of transcendental idealism are concerned, there is a greater critical distance between the author and the doctrine. It is there as if in scare quotes. Wittgenstein's aim is to dissociate himself from it *entirely*, even to the extent of denying it a role as an attempted expression of our understanding of its sources.[69]

That would be one view. And the combined reading does not rule it out. The combined reading is non-committal about how the nonsense in the *Tractatus* enables Wittgenstein to impart whatever understanding he does. Nevertheless, the view in question is not my own view, as is no doubt evident from what I have already said.[70] I do take the statements of transcendental idealism to be of a piece with the remarks about logical form, and therefore part of the 'vision' that Wittgenstein presents in this book. I am prepared to say, with all the myriad qualifications that would likewise be needed with respect to the remarks about logical form, that Wittgenstein is a transcendental idealist. Transcendental idealism is nonsense that he does regard as the result of an attempt to express, in words, understanding that cannot be expressed in words; understanding of what it is to make propositional sense of things; understanding which, on the one hand, is fostered by our seeing that this nonsense is the result of an attempt to put it into words and which, on the other hand, fosters our seeing that this nonsense is nonsense.[71]

---

[68] Apart from anything else there is the complication that the transcendental idealism, here as in Kant, sustains an 'empirical realism' (a denial of empirical idealism, as defined in the Appendix to Ch. 5) to which, however, unlike in Kant, it eventually yields (5.64).

[69] This is Peter Sullivan's view: see Sullivan (1996), esp. §IV; (2002), pp. 59–60; and (2003), §IV.

[70] This has been a matter of exegetical debate between Peter Sullivan and me: see Moore (2003b); Sullivan (2003); Moore (forthcoming); and Sullivan (forthcoming).

[71] I talk about ineffable understanding, and about Wittgenstein's attempts to express it in words. But what about the concept of showing, to which I have made hardly any appeal since first mentioning it in §5? In what sense, for example, are we 'shown' that the world

But I need to say more, both to substantiate my view, and indeed to bring the discussion back to the matter that principally concerns us, which is where the *Tractatus* ultimately stands in relation to metaphysics. I shall try to discharge both tasks in the next and final section. This will involve an attempt to take due account of what seems to me to be in many respects the most significant fact about the appearance of transcendental idealism in the *Tractatus*, a fact which has been completely absent from the discussion so far.

8.   Metaphysics in the Service of Ethics

The *Tractatus*, I have said, is in many ways thoroughly Kantian. Kant tried to acknowledge a limitation to sense-making. As a crucial part of that operation he distinguished between the thick sense-making whose limitation he tried to acknowledge and the thin sense-making whereby he tried to acknowledge it (Ch. 5, §8). Wittgenstein affects to acknowledge a limitation to sense-making too, or at least to propositional sense-making. But the propositional sense-making whose limitation he affects to acknowledge is of the thinnest kind. So he cannot likewise claim that the means whereby he does so is propositional sense-making that is yet thinner. Instead, he claims that it is nonsense. That is why 'affects' is the operative word. Wittgenstein, unlike Kant, wants us in the end to see the whole operation as a charade. The fact remains that, structurally, it is a profoundly Kantian operation.

My aim in this section is to show that it is profoundly Kantian in other ways too. In particular, it is profoundly Kantian in motivation.[72]

Consider: *why* was Kant so keen to distinguish two kinds of sense-making? Not just to sanction his limit-drawing. For the real question is why he was so keen to draw the limit, *as a limitation*, in the first place. And a significant part of the answer, as we saw in Chapter 5, is that he needed 'to deny *knowledge* in order to make room for *faith*' (Kant (1998), Bxxx, emphasis in original). Faith, which he defined as 'reason's moral way of thinking' (Kant (2000), 5: 471), was directed at our freedom, at our capacity to exercise our wills either by obeying the commands of morality or by disobeying them, at our immortality, at the existence of God, and, quite generally, at whatever was ultimately of value, all of which Kant saw as

is the totality of facts, not of things? In one sense, I suggest, and in one sense only: we have ineffable understanding such that, if an attempt were made to express it in words, the result would be: 'The world is the totality of facts, not of things' (see Moore (1997a), Chs 7–9). I.e. the appeal to the concept of showing does nothing, really, to advance the discussion beyond where it already is.

[72] What follows draws on material in Moore (forthcoming) which is in turn taken from Moore (2007b). I am grateful to the editors and publisher of the volume in which the latter essay appears for permission to make use of this material.

lying beyond the reach of our thick sense-making, that is beyond the reach of the kind of sense-making that could take the form of robust discursive knowledge. Freedom, the good or bad exercise of the will, the commands of morality, immortality, God, value: these cannot but ring extremely loud bells for any student of the *Tractatus*. They also provide me with a good cue to reveal what I had in mind when I referred at the end of the previous section to what seems to me to be in many respects the most significant fact about the appearance of transcendental idealism in the *Tractatus*. I had in mind the fact that it appears, not only in the 5.6s, but just as blatantly, if not more so, in the 6.4s, where Wittgenstein treats of each of these topics in the light of it.[73]

What we have so far is an isomorphism, albeit a rough one, between, on the one hand, the Kantian distinction between thick sense-making and thin sense-making and, on the other hand, the Wittgensteinian distinction between genuine thinking and certain kinds of pseudo-thinking involving the production of nonsense.[74]

	Left-hand side	Right-hand side
Kant	Thick sense-making	Thin sense-making
Wittgenstein	Thinking (= propositional sense-making)	Certain pseudo-thinking involving nonsense

Transcendental idealism, for Wittgenstein just as for Kant, can help us to an appreciation of what lies on the right-hand side, including, perhaps, the very endorsement of transcendental idealism.[75] What the 6.4s indicate is that, again for Wittgenstein just as for Kant, this is an appreciation of what lies on the right-hand side in both senses of the phrase: an appreciation *that* it lies there; and an appreciation *of it*, of the forces at work when we engage in it, of the possibilities they reveal to us, of the possibilities they open up for us.

---

[73] See also material shortly before and shortly after the 6.4s: 6.373–6.374 and 6.52–6.522. Cf. n. 37 and the reference there to Sullivan (1996), n. 9.

[74] I caution that this isomorphism is rough for all sorts of reasons. One is that the right-hand side of the Kantian distinction, which involves the bona fide exercise of concepts, does not purport to be anything that it is not. Another is that, whereas it is clear that the endorsement of transcendental idealism lies on the right-hand side of the Wittgensteinian distinction, it is altogether less clear on which side of the Kantian distinction it lies, if indeed it lies on either (Ch. 5, §9).

A further caveat: analytic knowledge occurs on both sides of the Kantian distinction (Ch. 5, §8) but on neither side of the Wittgensteinian distinction (4.461–4.4611 and 6.1–6.11; see further §3).

[75] 'Perhaps', because of the second point made in the previous note, which complicates matters in Kant's case.

Neither Kant nor Wittgenstein thinks that our rational engagement with things – that part of our engagement with things that is made possible by the fact that we are rational beings, what can be called, in the broadest sense of the phrase, *our making sense of things* – is exhausted by whatever lies on the left-hand side. It obviously includes whatever lies on the left-hand side, which for both Kant and Wittgenstein has as its paradigm the kind of knowledge embodied in the natural sciences (cf. 4.11 and 6.53). But for Kant it also includes each of the following:

- faith
- hope
- the practical use of reason
- the regulative use of concepts
- aesthetic judgments

and

- thought about things in themselves;[76]

while for Wittgenstein, I suggest, it includes each of the following:

- the various kinds of understanding mentioned in §6 (including understanding of Wittgenstein)
- the practice of philosophy (§2)
- logical inference (5.13–5.133 and 6.12–6.1201)
- the practice of mathematics (6.2–6.211 and 6.233–6.2341)

and much of what comes under the head of

- evaluation,

including feeling the world as a whole, experiencing its beauty, coming to grips with the problem of life and its meaning, exercising the will, and being happy or unhappy (6.421, 6.43, 6.45, and 6.521).

What, then, is the relation between our making these kinds of sense of things and what lies on the right-hand side? In Kant's case the former always at least finds partial expression in the latter, even if it extends beyond it. (Whether it does extend beyond it raises delicate exegetical questions which it would be impossible to address without further clarifying the notion of thin sense-making. In the present context we can afford to bypass these questions.) In Wittgenstein's case, though the former certainly extends beyond the latter, it sometimes finds apparent or attempted expression there: what we could call, echoing the fact that the right-hand side consists of pseudo-thinking, pseudo-expression.

---

[76] Mention was made of all but the penultimate of these in Ch. 5. For discussion of aesthetic judgment, see Kant (2000), Pt I.

The crucial point, however, is that Wittgenstein is as keen as Kant to acknowledge sense-making beyond that which lies on the left-hand side. It is just as important for him as it is for Kant. And it commands just as much respect.

This is what we see most clearly in the 6.4s. '*The book's point*,' he famously wrote in a letter to Ludwig von Ficker, '*is an ethical one*' ('Letter to Ficker', p. 143, emphasis in original).[77] Part of that point – part of the enterprise of doing justice to sense-making of this non-propositional kind, in particular evaluation – is to uphold a fundamental separation of fact and value.[78] And this is where transcendental idealism has a part to play. For it is largely in trying to come to terms with this separation that we construe the world as the totality of facts, *to the exclusion of* value (6.41), that is to say to the exclusion of what can be affected by acts of will (6.43). There are, for Wittgenstein, genuine insights that lead us to construe the world's limits as limitations in this way, genuine insights that lead us to endorse this version of transcendental idealism. They are ineffable insights into what it is to think, into what it is to exercise the will, and into what separates these.

Wittgenstein does not say a great deal in the 6.4s about how these relate to each other, about how that which is conceived as lying outside the world affects that which is conceived as lying inside it. But the little he does say, exploiting as it does the nonsense inherent in the idea of limits that are at the same time limitations, is highly suggestive. Most strikingly, we find the following:

> The sense of the world must lie outside the world. In the world every-thing is as it is, and everything happens as it does happen: *in* it no value exists – and if it did exist, it would have no value.

[77] Cf. also the letter to Bertrand Russell, dated 19 August 1919, in which he wrote, 'The main point is the theory of what can be expressed by propositions … (and, which comes to the same thing, what can be *thought*) and what cannot be expressed by propositions, but only shown; which, I believe, is the cardinal problem of philosophy' (*Letters*, p. 124, emphasis in original).

[78] This is also, more explicitly, the main point of 'Ethics'. Wittgenstein there gives two further examples of the kind of evaluation I have in mind: wonder at the existence of the world, and the feeling of absolute safety (p. 8). And he later remarks that 'the verbal expression that we give to these experiences is nonsense!' (ibid.). He concludes with some highly per-tinent reflections on how, in ethics, we 'run against the boundaries of language,' adding, '[Ethics] is a document of a tendency in the human mind which I personally cannot help respecting deeply and I would not for my life ridicule it' (pp. 11–12). The *Notebooks* also contain highly pertinent reflections: see e.g. pp. 76–89. (Particularly noteworthy is his com-ment on p. 80: 'The thinking subject is mere illusion. But the willing subject exists.') For discussion, see Janik and Toulmin (1973), esp. Ch. 6; Hacker (1986), esp. Ch. 4; Diamond (2000); Wiggins (2004); McManus (2006), Chs 13 and 14; and Mulhall (2007).

If there is any value that does have value, it must lie outside the whole sphere of what happens and is the case. For all that happens and is the case is accidental.

... If the good or bad exercise of the will does alter the world, it can alter only the limits of the world, not the facts – not what can be expressed by means of language.

In short the effect must be that it becomes an altogether different world. It must, so to speak, wax and wane as a whole.

The world of the happy man is a different one from that of the unhappy man. (6.41–6.43, emphasis in original)[79]

Part of the force of these remarks is that, in acknowledging the various facts that constitute the world, we are free to adopt different attitudes towards those facts. We are free to adopt different attitudes towards the world 'as a whole – a limited whole' (6.45).[80] One way to think of this is that we are free to see the whole in each of its parts. We are free to reflect on the possibilities that each thing affords, and to see how these are related one to another and each to all. The more we manage to do this, the more sense we make of things; the more meaning the world might to said to possess; the greater value it might be said to have; the more it might be said to wax; the better we exercise our wills; the 'happier' we are.[81]

I have been emphasizing affinities between Wittgenstein and Kant. But in the light of the quotation above, together with some of Wittgenstein's subsequent remarks – notably his remarks on eternal life as a kind of time-lessness belonging 'to those who live in the present' (6.4311) and his identi-fication of viewing the world as a limited whole with viewing it '*sub specie aeterni*' (6.45) – and in the light also of some of his glosses on this material in the *Notebooks*,[82] it is hard not to be equally struck by affinities between

---

[79] Robert Fogelin, commenting sceptically on the last sentence in this quotation, remarks, 'A competing sage might say that the world of the happy man is no different from that of the unhappy man (and this too has a ring of profundity)' (Fogelin (1987), p. 103). But if Wittgenstein's sentence is an abortive attempt to put into words what cannot be put into words, then any unclarity about what makes it better suited to this role than its denial, indeed any intimation that it is no better suited to this role than its denial, need occasion neither suspicion nor surprise. Who knows but that both Wittgenstein's sentence and Fogelin's reversal of it, each in a suitable context, may be apt to engage our attention in broadly the same way and thereby to have the same broad effect? (It is worth thinking in this connection about the creative use of contradiction in mystical and religious writing. Examples abound. They can be found in the writings of Plato, the Psalmists, Lao Tze, Nicholas of Cusa, Kierkegaard, and countless others.)

[80] Cf. Murdoch (1993), p. 1.

[81] Cf. *Notebooks*, pp. 72–89 passim. Cf. also Costello (2004), pp. 114–116.

[82] See esp. the entry for 13 August 1916 on p. 81 and the entry for 7 October 1916 on p. 83, the latter of which includes the comments that 'each thing modifies the whole logical

Wittgenstein and Spinoza. I am thinking especially of Spinoza's third kind of knowledge, a sort of seeing of the infinite in the finite, which Spinoza believed brought us to our highest level of freedom and our highest virtue (Ch. 2, §5).

This reference to Spinoza also provides me with a way of saying, finally, where the *Tractatus* stands in relation to metaphysics, on my conception of metaphysics. I argued in Chapter 2, §6, that the design of Spinoza's *Ethics* is to help us in the first instance to make maximally general sense of things, but also thereby to make ethical sense of things, partly indeed by making sense of what it is to make ethical sense of things. In other words, Spinoza tries to impart metaphysical understanding in such a way as to impart also, thereby, ethical understanding.[83] I believe that the same is true of Wittgenstein, provided – it is a crucial proviso[84] – that making sense of things is understood broadly enough to include the non-propositional variety to which I have been urging he is committed. The important difference is that, whereas in Spinoza's case only the ethical understanding is ineffable, which is why it has to be imparted indirectly, in Wittgenstein's case both the ethical understanding and the metaphysical understanding are ineffable (that is, of the non-propositional kind).[85] So the metaphysical understanding too, in his case, has to be imparted indirectly. It is imparted by means of what we are supposed eventually to recognize as sheer nonsense. But, be that difference as it may, for Wittgenstein just as for Spinoza, metaphysics is in the service of ethics. Metaphysical understanding, which is to say maximally general understanding, is itself part of the ethical life.

In Wittgenstein's case there is an additional reason for this. Metaphysical understanding incorporates an understanding of what it is to make propositional sense of things. This in turn enables us to avoid the confusions of bad philosophy. And to avoid such confusions is, for Wittgenstein, another ethical requirement. Consider the famous last sentence of the *Tractatus*:

> What we cannot speak about we must pass over in silence. (7)

There are myriad ways of taking this, even in a sense of 'taking' loose enough to allow for the nonsensicality of the sentence.[86] This is partly because of the different ways of taking the word 'must'. No doubt we are intended to hear

---

world,' and that 'the thing seen *sub specie æternitatis* is the thing seen together with the whole logical space.'

[83] What I am characterizing as 'ethical understanding' here is just Spinoza's third kind of knowledge.

[84] Cf. n. 19 and the accompanying text.

[85] Different standards of effability may also be involved. In Spinoza's case the understanding in question may be ineffable merely in that it cannot be put into finitely many words (Ch. 2, §6). In Wittgenstein's case something more radical is afoot.

[86] Cf. n. 45.

its logical overtones. But we are also surely intended to hear its deontological overtones. In a later remark Wittgenstein says that every philosophical error is the mark of a character failing.[87] To be confused is to lack a certain integrity. It is to fail to be true to oneself. (It is, in a mixture of Spinozist and Wittgensteinian terms, to be subject to sad passions caused by a failure to see the symbols in one's own signs, a failure to 'see the world aright' (6.54).) Where confusion resides in the very desire to say something, the 'happy man' will have no such desire.[88]

In conclusion: the *Tractatus* is, on my conception of metaphysics, a profoundly metaphysical work, if a highly unusual one. It is designed to help us make maximally general sense of things. But since the sense that it is designed to help us make is non-propositional, the means that it uses are indirect. It works through a creative use of nonsense. It is more like a work of art than like a work of science.[89] In this respect, among many others, it is a significant departure from anything we have seen hitherto.

[87] Unfortunately, I have been unable to find a reference. The remark is attributed to Wittgenstein by P.M.S. Hacker in Hacker (1996), p. 112.

[88] Here a famous anecdote from Bertrand Russell's autobiography is relevant: '[Wittgenstein] used to come to see me every evening at midnight, and pace up and down my room like a wild beast for three hours in agitated silence. Once I said to him: "Are you thinking about logic or about your sins?" "Both," he replied, and continued his pacing' (Russell (1998), p. 330). Cf. also Wittgenstein's assertion, 'For me … clarity, perspicuity are valuable in themselves' (*Culture*, p. 7).

For more on Wittgenstein's understanding of the relations between intellectual failure and moral failure, see McManus (2006), Ch. 13, esp. §13.1. For the influence of Karl Kraus on this understanding, see Janik and Toulmin (1973), esp. Chs 6 and 7.

[89] In a letter to Wittgenstein dated 16 September 1919 (Frege (2003)), Frege suggested that the *Tractatus* was 'more an artistic achievement than a scientific achievement,' though he was alluding specifically to what followed from the idea, mooted in the very first sentence of the Preface, that '[the] book will be understood only by someone who has himself already had the thoughts that are expressed in it' (p. 3). This sentence raises several awkward questions for any exegete of the *Tractatus*, not least of course the question of how uncomfortable we should be about the reference to 'the thoughts that are expressed in it'. I shall not attempt to address these questions here.

CHAPTER 10

✦

The Later Wittgenstein

Bringing Words Back from Their Metaphysical to Their Everyday Use

1. Wittgenstein's Conception of Philosophy: A Reprise

Sections 89–133 of Wittgenstein's *Investigations*[1] present a conception of philosophy that is to all intents and purposes the same as that presented in the *Tractatus* (see §2 of the previous chapter[2]). Again philosophy is paraded as an activity, rather than a body of doctrine. Again its aim is said to be the promotion of clear thinking. Again this aim is conceived as a therapeutic one: philosophy is an antidote to unclear thinking, and specifically to the ill effects of our misunderstanding the logical syntax of our own language, or the 'grammar' of our own language as the later Wittgenstein is prone to call it (cf. §90). Notable among these effects, again, are reckoned to be various pseudo-questions posing as deep problems and tantalizing us with their unanswerability.[3] Again the example concerning the passage of time in §2 of the previous chapter could serve as a paradigm. Or consider the case of someone who is grappling with the following conundrum: 'Why can nobody else know with the certainty I do that I have been hurt?' If we attend to the way in which sentences like 'I have been hurt' are actually used, or at least if we do so under the direction of various suggestions that Wittgenstein

---

[1] Throughout this chapter I use the following abbreviations for Wittgenstein's works: *Blue Book* for Wittgenstein (1969); *Culture* for Wittgenstein (1980a); *Investigations* for Wittgenstein (1967a); 'Logical Form' for Wittgenstein (1929); *Notebooks* for Wittgenstein (1979a); *On Certainty* for Wittgenstein (1974b); *Philosophical Grammar* for Wittgenstein (1974a); *Philosophical Remarks* for Wittgenstein (1975); 'Philosophy' for Wittgenstein (2006); *Remarks* for Wittgenstein (1978); *Tractatus* for Wittgenstein (1961); *Vienna Circle* for Wittgenstein (1979b); and *Zettel* for Wittgenstein (1967c). All unaccompanied references are to the *Investigations*, and, where they are section-numbered, to Part I of the *Investigations*. (We do well to remember, incidentally, that only the *Tractatus*, 'Logical Form', and Part I of the *Investigations* were written for publication, and, in the case of the last of these, Wittgenstein would no doubt have changed some of it if he had lived to see it published.)

[2] And note in particular n. 7 of that section.

[3] In Wittgenstein's own metaphor, language, in such cases, 'goes on holiday' (§38).

255

himself makes, then this will appear akin to someone's grappling with the gibberish: 'Why can nobody else know with the certainty I do that *ouch!*?' (See e.g. §§244–246 and 317.) Philosophy can be used to show that there is no real problem here, relieving this person of the urge to find an answer.[4] In sum, then: here, as in the *Tractatus*, it is not the point of philosophy to discover and state truths about reality, but to get into sharp focus various concepts, in particular concepts that bemuse us in certain distinctive ways, which are themselves used in discovering and stating truths about reality. If, in the course of practising philosophy, we make any claims about reality, then this will typically be by way of demonstrating how the concepts in question work. The claims we make will as likely as not be platitudes, or items of common empirical knowledge, not contentions to be debated.[5]

There is also some taxonomical-cum-terminological overlap with the *Tractatus*. The later Wittgenstein, just like the early Wittgenstein, distinguishes between good philosophy, which is what we have just been considering, and bad philosophy, which is the home of the very confusions against which good philosophy is pitted. And he uses the word 'philosophy' sometimes elliptically for the one and sometimes elliptically for the other.[6] Moreover, in the *Investigations*, just as in the *Tractatus*, the only clearly pertinent use of the term 'metaphysical' indicates that he identifies metaphysics with bad philosophy. 'What *we* do,' he says, with a characteristically allusive use of the first-person plural,[7] 'is to bring words back from their metaphysical to their everyday use' (§116, emphasis in original). That is, what 'we' do is to rescue words from their abuse in the hands of bad philosophers – who no doubt, very often, include 'us'.[8,9]

---

[4] This is not to deny, incidentally, that there are circumstances in which it would be appropriate for someone to say, 'I know that I have been hurt.' (Section 278 is relevant here. Cf. also nn. 11 and 14 of the previous chapter.)

[5] Cf., in the case of the *Tractatus*, 3.263 and 4.112. And in the case of the *Investigations*, see esp. §128.

[6] For examples of the former use, see §§126–128. For examples of the latter use, see §§303, 348, 436, 520, 593, and 598. And cf. n. 15 of the previous chapter.

[7] See further §4 below. For remarks on the importance of the italicization of the pronoun, see Baker (2004b), p. 93, and (2004e), p. 242.

[8] There are further uses of 'metaphysical' and its cognates in the *Blue Book*. They accord with this usage, though they also signal a broader conception of the form that bad philosophy can take: see pp. 18, 35, 46, 49, 55, and 66. For discussion, including discussion of Wittgenstein's use of the term 'everyday', see Baker (2004b). This is also very pertinent to the issue raised in the next note.

[9] Is Wittgenstein an 'ordinary language' philosopher, then? (Cf. §§108 and 402.) It depends, of course, on what is meant by ordinary language philosophy. On one fairly standard characterization, ordinary language philosophy certainly shares the Wittgensteinian conviction that philosophical puzzles are a result of our mishandling our own language. But it involves a second conviction too: that we mishandle our own language whenever we

The *Investigations* does however go into greater and more explicit detail than the *Tractatus* about the form that good philosophy can be expected to take. Wittgenstein makes clear that the enterprise must do as much as is required to combat confusion and no more. So it must be purely observational, as opposed to explanatory; it must simply lay bare the grammar of our language and not conjecture about why it is the way it is; it must, in an important sense, highlight what is already open to view. Similarly, it must surrender any pretensions it has to systematicity or generality and be content to apply specific correctives to specific confusions as the need arises. It must, like any therapeutic exercise, have as its end its own end; as its aim, that is, its own termination. ('The real discovery,' Wittgenstein remarks, 'is the one that makes me capable of stopping doing philosophy when I want to' (§133).) In sum, it must be descriptive, piecemeal, contextual, and restorative.[10]

2. Differences Between the Early Work and the Later Work

Granted this fundamental continuity between the early work and the later work – this shared conception of philosophy – perhaps the most striking difference between the two is that in the later work Wittgenstein straightforwardly practises what he preaches. Whatever the reasons for the indirection of the *Tractatus*, they have no counterpart here. The procedure that Wittgenstein adopts in the *Investigations* is utterly different from that

use it in any other than an 'ordinary' way. That second conviction, insofar as it is clear what counts as ordinary, is not Wittgensteinian (see e.g. §132). In fact, as I pointed out in §6 of the Introduction, it is crazy. It is crazy even when attention is confined to language that *has* an ordinary use. Thus physicists do not mishandle language when they confer a technical sense on 'force' or 'work'. Using language in an ordinary way is not a necessary condition of using it properly. Nor indeed is it a sufficient condition. There is no guarantee that the ordinary use of any given expression is free of the confusions of bad philosophy. (This relates to problems to which we shall return in §5.) That said, I am not at all sure that this characterization of ordinary language philosophy, however standard it may be, is fair to those who are typically classified as ordinary language philosophers. It is certainly not fair to J.L. Austin, who is perhaps the arch-example. See again the quotation in n. 21 of the Introduction, in which he captures well the extent of his own deference to the ordinary. For sympathetic treatments of ordinary language philosophy, from a distinctly Wittgensteinian perspective, see Cavell (2002) and Hacker (1996), Ch. 8, §1 – the former illuminatingly discussed in Mulhall (1994), Introduction. For an interesting remark on Wittgenstein's relation to ordinary language, see Quine (1960), p. 261. For discussion of some of the issues that arise here, particularly concerning the extent of Wittgenstein's conservatism, see below, §6.

[10] For three very helpful accounts of Wittgenstein's conception of philosophy, see Hacker (1986), Ch. 6; Pears (1971), Ch. 6; and McGinn (1997), Ch. 1. Also of very great interest are Baker (2004b) and (2004c).

which he adopts in the *Tractatus*. The *Investigations* consists of a succession of examples of philosophical confusion together with Wittgenstein's own efforts at rectification. This is more Kant's 'Transcendental Dialectic' than Leibniz' 'Monadology'.

To be sure, Wittgenstein retains a deep concern with what it is to make linguistic sense of things; and he is as keen as he was in the *Tractatus* to make sense, in particular, of that, so as to be able not just to fight bad philosophy with good philosophy but to understand what he is fighting with what. He is every bit as self-conscious about what he is doing, then, as he was before. But there is also an important respect in which he is keen to be clear about what he is doing simply because what he is doing is one more thing, beset by philosophical confusion, that he is keen to be clear about. (See §121.) And even here he is true to his own methodological scruples. He does not argue for a particular view of the nature of linguistic sense-making. Rather, by a careful interlacing of hints, suggestions, and commonplaces, he gets us to explore the view that we already have.[11] At the same time he tames what he sees as our ill-conceived urge to go beyond that view and to provide something more like a scientific theory of sense (of the kind that we find in Frege and, indeed, that we seem to find in the *Tractatus*).

His concern not merely to effect cures but to provide diagnoses is again reminiscent of Kant's 'Transcendental Dialectic'.[12] So too is something that attends this concern and that we find throughout his work: a very acute sense of the power and the allure of what he is fighting against. Wittgenstein speaks of the problems with which he is grappling as 'deep disquietudes ... [whose] roots are as deep in us as the forms of our language and [whose] significance is as great as the importance of our language' (§111). And he insists that the prejudices that stand in the way of our seeing how words function 'are not *stupid* prejudices' (§340, emphasis in original, adapted from singular to plural).[13] Sometimes when he is reflecting on the forces at work here, the results are very moving. This from *The Big Typescript*:

> Philosophy does not call on me for any sacrifice, because I am not denying
> myself the saying of anything but simply giving up a certain combination

---

[11] See e.g. §§1–88, 143–242, and 525–546. (The idea that this is the view we already have provides a clear echo of Plato's *Meno*, 81ff.)

[12] Is it consistent with his insistence that philosophy must be descriptive, not explanatory? Yes, because the diagnoses themselves need not involve extrapolation beyond what is visible in the circumstances of our confusion.

[13] Cf. Kant (1998), A297/B353–354 and A642/B670. There is even a hint that Wittgenstein is prepared to give a Kantian diagnosis of many of our ills, namely our craving for unity and completeness in the sense we make of things: see, in Kant, ibid., A307–309/B364–366, and, in Wittgenstein, §§97–108 and 183, and *Blue Book*, pp. 17–19. For further comparisons between Kant and Wittgenstein, see Bird (2006), Ch. 24, §2. (Especially noteworthy is the comparison between A485–486/B513–514 and §133.)

of words as senseless.[14] In a different sense, however, philosophy does demand a renunciation, but a renunciation of feeling, not of understanding. Perhaps that is what makes it so hard for many people. It can be as hard to refrain from using an expression as it is to hold back tears, or hold in anger....

The job to be done in philosophy ... is really more a job on oneself. ('Philosophy', p. 46)

Furthermore, by practising philosophy in his later work, as opposed just to providing an account of it, Wittgenstein is able to reveal his sense of the power of bad philosophy not only in what he says about it but also in his very real, very palpable struggles with it. He uses an interlocutor who is able to give resounding voice to the confusions at stake, to make nonsense look for all the world like sense, to say just what we all have an urge to say, Wittgenstein very evidently included.[15] (Wittgenstein's struggles, it has to be said, contrast markedly with the calm assurance and the bullying dogmatism of many of those purporting to follow him.)

As I have stressed, the way in which Wittgenstein proceeds in the *Investigations* is quite different from the way in which he proceeds in the *Tractatus*. But to what extent are there also doctrinal differences?

This issue is utterly unstraightforward. It is unstraightforward partly because of the problem of how far any 'doctrines' advanced in the *Tractatus* can be said to be advanced *in propria persona* and partly because, in the *Investigations*, Wittgenstein can be said not to be in the business of advancing doctrines at all (§128). Nevertheless, I think we may say, subject to all the necessary qualifications, that he comes to make sense of linguistic sense-making in some importantly different ways. It is well known, for example, that there is an explicit *volte-face* in his only lifetime publication apart from the *Tractatus*, namely the article 'Logical Form', published seven years after the *Tractatus*, in which he recoils from his earlier conception of elementary propositions as logically independent of one another.[16]

---

[14] Note that the distinction drawn in the *Tractatus* between senselessness and nonsense is no longer operative (see §3 of the previous chapter). Wittgenstein is referring to that which straightforwardly lacks meaning: that which is to be 'excluded from the language' (§500).

[15] The comparison with Kant, particularly with 'The Antithetic of Pure Reason' in Kant (1998), where Kant presents as forcefully as he can arguments that he takes to have universal appeal but that he wants eventually to expose, continues to impress itself. Note that, the contrast with the *Tractatus* notwithstanding, there is at least *this* much indirection in the *Investigations* (to the extent, in fact, that it is by no means always obvious when Wittgenstein is playing the interlocutor and when he is speaking in his own voice). Note also that the clarity that Wittgenstein seeks, combined with the struggle that he has to attain it, forces him to recognize a deep distinction between what is *simple* and what is *easy*: cf. *Philosophical Remarks*, §2, and *Zettel*, §452.

[16] For discussion, see Hacker (1986), Ch. 5, §1, and Marion (1998), Ch. 5, §1.

There is also a later shift from a commitment to the determinacy of sense. Earlier, he would have been prepared to say that a proposition has no sense unless it not only is true or false, but would have been true or false whatever the circumstances.[17] Later he is happy to sanction the kind of vagueness of sense whereby that which is true or false, say an utterance of 'She is still only a child', would have failed to count as either true or false in suitably borderline circumstances (had she been fourteen years old, say: cf. §§69–71, 79, 80, and 99–107);[18] or the kind of context-dependence of sense whereby that which is true or false, say an utterance of 'That thing is in pain', would have failed to count as either true or false if various conditions for the very application of one of the concepts had not been met (had that thing not been a living creature but a pot full of boiling water, say: cf. §§117, 281, and 282).[19]

Particularly noteworthy is the much livelier appreciation evinced in the *Investigations* than in the *Tractatus* of the varieties of things we can do with words. The early Wittgenstein was not of course oblivious to the fact that there are meaningful linguistic moves that we can make other than asserting something true or false, such as asking a question (cf. *Notebooks*, p. 107). Nor was he oblivious to the fact that there are radically different ways even of asserting something true or false: that was after all the burden of his account of logic (see §4 of the previous chapter). Nor indeed was he oblivious to the possibility of feigning to say something true or false as a way of conveying non-propositional sense-making, or not if what I argued in §8 of the previous chapter is correct: if what I argued there is correct, this is what he took himself to be doing in the bulk of his first book. But the project was to make sense of propositional sense-making. And within that parameter he showed little concern for drawing finer distinctions, while beyond that parameter he showed little concern for drawing distinctions other than with producing senseless logical propositions

---

[17] Cf. *Tractatus*, 2.0211–2.0212, 3.23, and 4.023.

[18] I shall return to this issue in the Conclusion, §3, Interlude.

[19] Bernard Williams writes, in a different connection: 'It may be said that it does not make sense to assert or deny greenness of a prime number. But there is something unsatisfactory about such formulations: they express a doctrine which should surely be about sense, in terms of reference.... [What] we should more accurately say is not that "green" cannot sensibly be ascribed to a prime number, but that "green and a prime number" cannot sensibly be ascribed to anything, because it does not make sense' (Williams (1973b), p. 67). As far as the alleged unsatisfactoriness of formulating such doctrines in terms of reference is concerned, I think Wittgenstein would disagree. I think he would say that, if you are thinking of the number seven, and if you utter the sentence, 'What I am thinking of is green,' then your use of the word 'green' is as infelicitous as it would have been if you had uttered the sentence, 'Seven is green.' But in fact the early Wittgenstein would have reason to say this too. The difference between them is a difference about how much, in a successful attempt to say something true or false, is part of what is said.

or producing nonsensical pseudo-propositions.[20] By contrast the later Wittgenstein reminds us of the 'countless different kinds of use of what we call "symbols", "words", "sentences"' (§23).[21] He puts this in terms of the many different 'language-games' we play (§§7 and 23).[22] Given the point that I made in the previous section about the restricted role that making claims about reality can be expected to have in philosophy, this is significant not least as a way of evoking the many language-games, apart from making claims about reality, that philosophers themselves can be expected to play, such as announcing their problems, raising questions, making suggestions, stating grammatical rules, giving examples, telling stories, expounding their methodology, rehearsing their own and other people's confusions, and transforming pieces of disguised nonsense into patent nonsense.[23] It is also significant in suggesting that, had the early Wittgenstein shown similar sensitivity to the variety of language-games we play, he might have worked with a broader conception of meaningfulness and, correspondingly, of what can be put into words, and he might then have counted the propositions of the *Tractatus* as themselves meaningful expressions of the understanding he was trying to convey.[24]

At any rate there is in the later work a more nuanced, more variegated, less theoretically committed depiction of linguistic sense-making, based more on an investigation of how language is actually used than on any attempt to meet requirements imposed *a priori* (see §§65, 66, 107, and 340).[25]

3.   Metaphysics, Necessity, and Grammar

All of this leaves room, in a curious way, for something like Cartesian metaphysics. Or rather, in one respect it leaves room for something like Cartesian

---

[20] Even such interest as he showed in asking questions was very much parasitic on his interest in providing their answers: see e.g. 5.551 and 6.5–6.52.

[21] And he reminds us of the variety that there is even within what we count as saying something true or false: cf. §136 and *Remarks*, Pt I, App. III, §§1–4.

[22] In §23 he revealingly says, 'It is interesting to compare the multiplicity of the tools in language and of the ways they are used, the multiplicity of kinds of word and sentence, with what logicians have said about the structure of language. (Including the author of the *Tractatus Logico-Philosophicus*.)' This is one of several points at which he targets his earlier self: see also §§59ff., 97ff., 114, and 134ff. The fact that many of these sections occur within the very stretch already identified as harbouring a fundamental continuity between the early work and the later work will seem paradoxical only when we forget the peculiar nature of the early work.

[23] For a reference to the last of these, see §464.

[24] See further Moore (2003b), §VI.

[25] Cf. Pears (1971), pp. 106ff.; Diamond (1991a), §§II and IV; Kuusela (2005); and McGinn (2006), Ch. 12.

metaphysics. In almost every other respect there could scarcely be a more profound or more resolute rejection of Cartesian metaphysics.[26]

Descartes held that metaphysics consists largely in the pursuit of indubitable necessary truths, truths of which we can have clear and distinct perception, truths whose falsity we cannot so much as entertain (Ch. 1, §§1 and 3). Wittgenstein holds that, to combat philosophical confusion, we must 'command a clear view of the use of our words' (§122, emphasis removed), which means, among other things, that we must acknowledge necessary truths involving these words, truths whose falsity we cannot so much as entertain. So far, so Cartesian.[27]

But remember, for Wittgenstein there are truths and there are truths.[28] Acknowledging a necessary truth is fundamentally different from acknowledging a contingent truth. (In this, as we have noted, he is faithful to his earlier view.) *Asserting* a necessary truth and asserting a contingent truth involve different language-games. To assert that aunts are female, for example, is to enunciate a rule rather than to make a claim about reality. Thus we must not count somebody as an aunt unless we are also prepared to count that person as female. Alternatively, we are not allowed to apply the description 'is an aunt but is not female' to anybody: that combination of words has no sense. We cannot (do not, will not) entertain the possibility of a non-female aunt.[29]

So what Descartes conceived as metaphysics is, on Wittgenstein's conception, 'the shadow of grammar', to borrow P.M.S. Hacker's apt phrase (Hacker (1986), Ch. 7[30]). Here is Wittgenstein:

> *Essence* is expressed by grammar.
>
> Consider: 'The only correlate in language to an intrinsic necessity is an arbitrary rule. It is the only thing which one can milk out of this intrinsic necessity into a proposition.'
>
> Grammar tells us what kind of object anything is. (§§371–373, emphasis in original)[31]

---

[26] I am in any case talking about the nature of the enterprise, as Descartes conceived it, not about the views he arrived at, to which, again, there could scarcely be a fiercer opponent than Wittgenstein. (For Wittgenstein's assault on Descartes' mind/body dualism, see §§243–317 and 398–421; and *Blue Book*, pp. 46–74.)

[27] Not that either Cartesian metaphysics or Wittgensteinian clarification of concepts consists exclusively in the pursuit of such truths. A linchpin of the former is the recognition on the part of each metaphysician of his or her own existence, which, though indubitable, is contingent. And Wittgenstein too is much exercised by propositions that are both exempt from doubt and yet contingent: see e.g. *On Certainty*, §§340–344. (I shall have more to say about such propositions in Ch. 19, §3(d).)

[28] Cf. n. 21.

[29] Cf. *Remarks*, p. 238.

[30] This chapter in Hacker (1986), esp. §3, is generally very helpful for the present section. See also Garver (1994), Ch. 14, and Garver (1996).

[31] Intriguingly, and suggestively, Wittgenstein adds in parenthesis, 'Theology as grammar.'

Recall the conflicting accounts of substance advanced by Descartes (Ch. 1, §6), Spinoza (Ch. 2, §2), and Leibniz (Ch. 3, §3). And recall Hume's consequent impatience with the notion (Ch. 4, §1). Recall finally its rehabilitation on the part of Hegel (Ch. 7, §6) and on the part of the early Wittgenstein (Ch. 9, §3). What the later Wittgenstein proffers is this:

> When philosophy is asked 'What is ... substance?' the request is for a rule, a universal rule which holds for the word 'substance'. ('Philosophy', p. 51)

No more, no less.

What Wittgenstein has left room for, then, though it resembles Cartesian metaphysics inasmuch as it consists in the pursuit of necessary truths, is to be conceived in a radically non-Cartesian way. It is not of a piece with science. It does not provide science with foundations (though it may provide us with a more secure grasp of certain scientific concepts). Above all it does not *answer* to anything. Wittgenstein entirely repudiates Descartes' perceptual model of what it is to accept a necessary truth (Ch. 1, §4).[32]

On that model, when we accept a necessary truth, this is both explained and justified, at least in part, by the nature of reality, by its *being* a truth. We preclude talk of male aunts, for example, because we are sensitive to the fact that there are no male aunts. This fact is quite independent of us. It is something that we have *discerned*, like the fact that there are no cubic planets.

For Wittgenstein this model is utterly confused. Nothing explains and justifies our accepting the necessary truths we do. That is to say, nothing explains and justifies our having the grammatical rules we have. Or at any rate nothing explains and justifies these things in the sense intended in the model. We might be justified in the sense that our rules fulfil some important function in our lives, and this too might explain why we have them. But that is not the sense intended in the model. For we have not thereby got anything 'right'. Our rules do not correctly *represent* anything. As Wittgenstein memorably says, in §371 of *Zettel*, after posing the question whether the rules governing our number words and our colour words reside in our nature or in the nature of things: 'How are we to put it? – *Not* in the nature of numbers or colours' (emphasis in original).

Does this mean that Wittgenstein embraces some form of idealism? For if it is not because we have noticed the impossibility of male aunts that we preclude talk of such a thing, then must it not be because we preclude talk of such a thing that it is impossible? More generally, if, as Wittgenstein claims, 'essence is expressed by grammar', and if grammar does not answer to essence, then does it not follow that essence answers to grammar?

---

[32] This in turn enables him to sidestep any equivalent of Descartes' Reflective Question with respect to such a truth (Ch. 1, §3).

Not at all. There is no need to acknowledge an answerability in either direction. True, in saying that there are no male aunts, we are giving voice to one of our grammatical rules. And, as with any of our rules, it is a rule that we might not have had. This is not however to say that, but for us, there might have been male aunts. It is rather to say that we might not have thought and spoken in these terms; we might not have made sense of things in this way; we might not have had the concept of an aunt. We have not *made* aunts female. That aunts are female is a necessity. If it has any explanation, it has a conceptual explanation – say, that an aunt is a sister of a parent, and that sisters have to be female. The point is simply this. *For something to be* a necessity *is* for our stating it to be an enunciation of one of our grammatical rules.

Here, at least, there is another interesting parallel with Descartes. In Chapter 1, §3, I argued that the Cartesian view, whereby for something to be a necessity is for its falsity to conflict with our concepts, does not prevent the necessity from being absolute. Structurally, exactly the same holds here. There is a sense in which both Descartes and Wittgenstein see a contingent grounding for necessity in features of how we make sense of things. But in neither case does this compromise the necessity. In neither case, to invoke the contrast that I drew in §4 of the previous chapter, does it cast limits as limitations.

Not that Wittgenstein is completely nonchalant about this. On the contrary, he is acutely aware, just as he was when he wrote the *Tractatus*, not only of the temptation to cast limits as limitations but of the way in which his own work can exacerbate that temptation. Part of the problem is that he is not only interested in indicating a contingent grounding for necessity. He digs ferociously beneath the surface of our sense-making to show just how deep the contingency lies. He wants to dispel any impression that how *we* make sense of things is 'the' way to make sense of things. Thus he draws attention to what he calls our 'forms of life', something that he in turn describes as 'what has to be accepted' or as 'the given' (p. 226). He is referring to the basic biological realities, the customs and practices, the complex of animal instincts and cultural sensibilities, that dispose us to notice various connections between things, to be struck by certain similarities and differences, to find some things natural foci of attention, to value certain things, to take some things for granted, to defer to certain authorities, and so forth. If it were not for these, we would not be able to make shared sense of things in the way we do. We would not have the concepts we have. We would not have the rules we have. As Wittgenstein graphically reminds us: 'Disputes do not break out ... over the question whether a rule has been obeyed or not. People don't come to blows over it' (§240).[33] He is not especially concerned

---

[33] Actually, where sophisticated and politically sensitive rules are concerned, this is just false, though the context makes plain that Wittgenstein has in mind something more elemental.

with how, among the ways in which any given features of our situation might affect our sense-making, they actually affect it. He is not much concerned, for that matter, with the *fact* that they affect it. His concern is with its very affectability, with the depth of its contingency. He writes:

> I am not saying: if such-and-such facts of nature were different people would have different concepts (in the sense of a hypothesis). But: if anyone believes that certain concepts are absolutely the correct ones, and that having different ones would mean not realizing something that we realize – then let him imagine certain very general facts of nature to be different from what we are used to, and the formation of concepts different from the usual ones will become intelligible to him. (Pt II, §xii)[34]

And Wittgenstein is indeed self-conscious about the threat that this grounding of necessity in contingency poses to the necessity, just as he is about the idealism that is lurking. 'This seems to abolish logic,' he writes in §242 – having in the previous section allowed his interlocutor to comment, 'So you are saying that human agreement decide what is true and what is false?' His response is as follows. (I have interpolated some phrases to connect this response with my own gloss on these issues.)

> It is what human beings *say* that is true and false; and they agree in the *language* they use. That is not agreement in opinions but in form of life.
> If language is to be a means of communication there must be agreement not only in definitions but also (queer as this may sound) in judgments.... This ... does not [abolish logic]. – It is one thing to describe methods of measurement [to describe ways of making sense of things], and another to obtain and state results of measurement [actually to make sense of things]. But what we call 'measuring' ['making sense of things'] is partly determined by a certain constancy in results of measurement [in the sense of things that is actually made]. (§§241 and 242, emphasis in original; cf. §§108 and 520)

The upshot of all of this is a radically new conception of necessary truth and our grasp of it, unlike anything that we have seen hitherto.[35] Kant too, of course, indicated a contingent grounding for necessity, or for some necessity, and effected a philosophical revolution in the process, but only

---

To what extent the existence of contested rule-following of a less elemental kind is a threat to him is a matter for debate; I shall not pursue it here.

[34] For an interesting case in point, see *Zettel*, §309.

[35] Hilary Putnam adverts to Wittgenstein's conception, specifically in application to mathematics, and comments, 'If [it] is right, then it is the greatest philosophical discovery of all time' (Putnam (1983), p. 117). Unfortunately, just prior to this, he characterizes the conception in the very way that I have been resisting, as the view that 'it is human nature and forms of life that *explain* mathematical truth and necessity' (ibid., emphasis in original).

by conceding that the necessity in question, the necessity of the synthetic *a priori*, was not absolute. He was dealing with limitations, not true limits. Wittgenstein's conception concerns the latter. It concerns what Kant would have counted as analytic.[36]

But the novelty of the Wittgensteinian conception is even more radical than the discussion so far suggests. For, unlike Kant's analytic truths – or Leibniz' truths of reasoning, or Hume's relations of ideas, or Frege's analytic truths, or the logical truths of the *Tractatus* – necessities as Wittgenstein conceives them can cease to have that status. (Or rather, more strictly, the propositions whereby we express them can cease to play that role, while still in some loose but important sense retaining their identity as propositions. The significance of this way of putting it should become clearer shortly.) Our rules can change. This may seem to controvert the point I emphasized earlier, that Wittgenstein's conception does nothing to prevent the necessity of that which is necessary from being absolute. But there is no conflict. The necessity of that which is necessary is absolute *for as long as it is necessary*. To say this is not, contrary to appearances, to take away with one hand what one has given with the other. Imagine a board game whose rules change, so that a move that was once obligatory becomes merely optional. And suppose that, even so, players of the game still routinely make this move. Then the proposition that this is how players move was once used to state a rule and is now used to describe a general practice. But *when* it was used to state a rule, it expressed an essential feature of the-game-as-it-was-then. (Recall in this connection the discussion in Ch. 7, §7, of Hegel's deliberate flouting of grammatical rules to allow concepts to evolve; and the distinction drawn there between a strict way of describing such cases and a loose way of describing them.[37]) The important point is the point I made earlier: necessity as Wittgenstein conceives it corresponds to a particular way of using a proposition. This accounts *both* for the absoluteness of necessity, which is secured whenever a proposition is used in that way, *and* for its provisional character, which is a feature of the fact that a proposition used in that way may yet be used in other ways.[38]

Let us return to the issue of where Wittgenstein stands in relation to metaphysics. I have been considering the implications of his views for

[36] But note that Wittgenstein is no longer hostile, as he was when he wrote the *Tractatus*, to the idea of the synthetic *a priori* (though he perhaps has his own idiosyncratic understanding of the idea): see *Philosophical Grammar*, p. 404, and *Remarks*, Pt IV, §43.

[37] And cf. §79, the final sentence in parenthesis; *Blue Book*, pp. 24–25; and *On Certainty*, §§95–99.

[38] For some extremely helpful material on the ideas in this paragraph, based on comparisons between Wittgenstein and Quine, see Hacker (1996), Ch. 7, and Hookway (1996). For Quine's own views, see Ch. 12, §4.

metaphysics on a Cartesian conception. But what are their implications for metaphysics on my conception? What room do they leave for metaphysics if metaphysics is the most general attempt to make sense of things?

It all depends, just as it did when we considered the same question in connection with the early Wittgenstein (see §2 of the previous chapter), on what is meant by making sense of things. If making sense of things is understood as arriving at truths about the world, then we can say now, just as we said then, that by Wittgenstein's lights metaphysics is simply the most general of the natural sciences, and therefore something quite distinct from philosophy.[39] If making sense of things is understood as introducing clarity into our thinking, then we can likewise say now, just as we said then, that by Wittgenstein's lights metaphysics is simply good philosophy in its most general reaches. (But the generality here has to be understood as the generality of the concepts involved.[40] As we observed in §1, Wittgenstein repudiates any pretensions that philosophy may have to methodological generality.) If making sense of things is construed broadly enough to include understanding of a non-propositional kind (see §8 of the previous chapter), then there may also be scope to say now, just as we said before, that by Wittgenstein's lights metaphysical understanding is a way of seeing the world aright, fostered by his own work – though there no longer seems to be any residue of the idea that such understanding could be fostered by trying to express it and making play with whatever nonsense accrues.[41] There are various ways, then, of seeing the later Wittgenstein, just like the early Wittgenstein, as metaphysics-friendly, on my conception of metaphysics.

Of all my protagonists it is the later Wittgenstein whose views I find most compelling. I lament the fact that the little I have been able to convey does them such scant justice. That said, in the remaining sections of this chapter I shall build up to what I take to be the most fundamental objection to them.[42]

---

[39] Wittgenstein's attitude to natural science is a complex matter. Bernard Williams has suggested that Wittgenstein's undoubted 'hatred of the cockiness of natural science ... [is] not easy ... to distinguish from a hatred of natural science' (Williams (2006k), p. 375). That is surely an exaggeration. We nevertheless see something of what Williams has in mind when we read such passages as *Zettel*, §§607–613. Be that as it may, there is nothing in Wittgenstein to impugn whatever claim natural science has to be an attempt to arrive at truths about the world.

[40] Cf. Hacker (1986), p. 204.

[41] For a much more modest role that nonsense may play in fostering such understanding, see again §464, cited in n. 23.

[42] I should note in advance that the underlying exegesis is by no means uncontroversial. For an approach to Wittgenstein that does much to forestall the objection, see the various essays in Baker (2004a), esp. those in Parts IA and IIA. For a rejoinder, see Hacker (2007).

4.   Transcendental Idealism in the Later Work?

In the previous section I considered reasons for thinking that Wittgenstein is committed to some kind of idealism and I applauded his efforts to rebut them. But there are further, subtler reasons that we need to address for thinking the same thing. They are reasons, more specifically, for thinking that he is committed to some variation on the transcendental idealism that we found in the *Tractatus*. If they are sound, the *form* of the commitment must nevertheless be contrasted with that of the *Tractatus*, in terms both of motivation and of the latter's obliqueness, which on the one hand furnishes us with more or less explicit statements of transcendental idealism, something that is quite contrary to the spirit of the later work, and which on the other hand prevents us from regarding these as straightforward affirmations of what Wittgenstein himself thinks, a sort of dissembling that is equally contrary to the spirit of the later work. My own view is that the reasons in question, the reasons for finding a commitment to transcendental idealism in the later work, are not sound. But I think we have to travel a long way to see why not.[43]

Very well; what are these reasons?[44]

We saw in §1 how Wittgenstein dissociates philosophy from science. Among the many profound differences that he sees between them, one of the most important is that philosophy can have no pretensions to *detachment*. We might have thought that the descriptions of the grammar of our language that we need to provide in philosophy should in principle be graspable by those who do not already understand the language. Nothing less, we might have thought, could have any purchase on those who *mis*understand it. For Wittgenstein, however, such detachment is neither necessary nor possible. To engage with those who misunderstand the language (typically ourselves

---

[43] Insofar as he would be prepared to venture any explicit statement *about* transcendental idealism, then no doubt he would say, just as his former self would have said, or at least just as the ingenuous version of his former self would have said, that it is a piece of metaphysical nonsense. Not that I mean to suggest that it is no longer even on his radar. Much of §§90ff., for example, where he is engaging with his former self, is an attempt to counteract what once made it, for him, such enticing nonsense. Some of what he says in the course of this discussion may itself sound transcendentally idealistic: see e.g. §§103, 104, and 114. In fact, however, he is merely emphasizing the contingency of our sense-making. To hear what he says in these sections as *already* transcendentally idealistic – to hear it as already making limitations out of essential features – is to commit the very error that he is trying to guard against: see e.g. §108.

[44] They are advanced most famously in Williams (2006k). They are considered sympathetically in Lear (1984), (1986), Garver (1994), and Forster (2004). They are explored in Anscombe (1981) and Sacks (2000), Ch. 6. They are attacked in Bolton (1982), Malcolm (1982), and, less directly, McDowell (1993). What follows draws on Moore (1997a), Ch. 6, §3, and Ch. 7, §4, where I also discuss them.

in another guise) we must give them the same kind of exposure to it as we give infants, not so much telling them what it is like as showing them what it is like. Thus even when we describe it, and in particular when we describe its grammar – making conceptual connections explicit, distinguishing between different forms of speech, exposing pieces of nonsense, and suchlike – we must do so in terms that are unintelligible except to those who understand.[45] The process is a reflective, reflexive, self-conscious process: a moving to and fro in which the aim is to maintain our linguistic balance while all the time 'commanding a clear view'[46] of what we are doing.

But what *are* we doing? Well, we are exercising our language. But what exactly is 'our language'?

It is certainly not English. It is not any system of expressions of that kind. The example about aunts being female might have looked like an example concerning English. But if it were, there would be no reason to think that the relevant grammatical rules could not be described except to those who already understand the language. There is no impediment to describing the use of the English words 'aunt' and 'female' in, say, French. No, the relevant grammatical rule is: not to count somebody as an aunt without also being prepared to count that person as female. And this is a rule that can be observed, or violated, by monolingual speakers of French, through their use of the expressions *'tante'* and *'le sexe féminin'*.

Our language is something more like the range of conceptual resources that we use to make sense of things, then.[47] Certainly, this helps to explain why anyone should think it impossible to describe our language without using it. But now a second question arises. Who exactly are 'we'?

There are various ways of answering this question, depending on how certain matters are resolved, though nothing of much importance in what has been said so far hinges on their resolution. The matters in question include: whether being one of 'us' means sharing particular forms of life, or merely having the potential to share them; if the latter, in what sense of 'potential'; and, either way, which forms of life. However these matters are resolved, 'we' are not just English speakers. On some ways of resolving them, 'we' are a certain group of human beings. On others, 'we' are all human beings. On others again, 'we' include any beings, actual or imaginable, with whom humans can communicate,[48] or any beings whom humans can recognize as making conceptual sense of things.

So far there is not a hint of any transcendental idealism. But now comes the twist. It is extremely difficult to stop at this point.[49] It is extremely difficult

---

[45] Cf. *Tractatus*, 3.263.

[46] §122.

[47] Cf. §108.

[48] This excludes (for instance) lions: see p. 223.

[49] Cf. *Zettel*, §§313 and 314.

not to envisage the 'we' expanding as it were to infinity. Once we have considered the various possibilities above, we find it hard ultimately not to think of 'ourselves' as all *possible* makers of conceptual sense. One of two things can then happen. First, the contingency of our conceptual sense-making can disappear. 'Our language' comes to admit of no alternative. Any use of language is a use of our language.[50] This possibility would obviously be unacceptable to Wittgenstein, for reasons given in the previous section. The second thing that can happen is that the contingency remains. 'Our language' does admit of alternatives. But by definition these cannot be used to make conceptual sense of anything. Conceptual sense can be made of things only by means of our language. So the limits of our language determine the limits of what can be made conceptual sense of, that is to say the limits of *the world*. They do so, moreover, by excluding what cannot be made conceptual sense of, hence in a way that cannot itself be made sense of by means of our language.[51] This is transcendental idealism. We can now see, therefore, why Wittgenstein might be thought to be committed to such a thing.

But this second possibility is patently no more acceptable to Wittgenstein than the first. It is incoherent. It acknowledges alternatives to our language which it nevertheless does not acknowledge as having any of the marks of alternatives to our language. It sees contingency where it accepts that there is only necessity. (It casts as limits, in the sense of limitations, what it recognizes as limits in the sense of essential features.) True, this need not be a rebuke to the exegesis. It may be a rebuke to Wittgenstein. Whether it is or not depends on what it takes to resist the urge to see the 'we' expanding in this way. The problem for Wittgenstein, which is at the same time an advantage for the exegesis, is that there are forces in his own work that make that urge almost irresistible. Indulging in the kind of self-conscious reflection that Wittgenstein advocates, we cannot help asking such questions as this: 'What, ultimately, does being an aunt *consist in?*' For we cannot help wondering about the quintessence of all that we make sense of, that which gives our language its point and helps to make it possible. We know that aunts have to be female; and we know that females have to have a certain biological constitution. Such are our rules.[52] But what does it *take*, ultimately, for things to be configured in such a way that somebody is an aunt? On a Wittgensteinian view, there is nothing we can summon in response to such a question that is clearly demarcated from the language itself. Someone who wants to know what being an aunt consists in must see how we exercise our

---

[50] Cf. §207 and Davidson (1984a). Cf. also Lear (1984).

[51] Here I am appealing to the Division Principle which features in the Limit Argument (see Ch. 5, §8), with sense-making understood in a suitably thin way.

[52] Or at any rate such, for current purposes, we may treat as our rules. For discussion of how much this glosses over – itself interestingly relevant to what is to come – see Fausto-Sterling (2000).

concept of an aunt, see what role that concept plays in our lives, see how we use it to make sense of things. Such a person must come to share, or already share, our form of life. They must come to be, or already be, one of us. So we cannot answer the question except by acknowledging that what it takes for somebody to be an aunt is determined, at least in part, by us and by how we make sense of things. And the only way to prevent this from being a rather crazy empirical idealism,[53] whereby if human beings had never had the concept of an aunt there could never have been any aunts, is to let the 'we' expand to infinity.

What Wittgenstein must do, then, but what I think he is at perfect liberty to do, is to disallow the questions that lead us to this point. We must not ask, 'What does being an aunt consist in?' Or at least, we must not ask it with a certain philosophical intent. (It may be a perfectly good conceptual question, to be answered by saying that an aunt is a sister of a parent. It might even be a perfectly good scientific question, to be answered in terms of gametes and the mechanics of propagation.) We must see such questions, when they are asked in the wrong way, as pseudo-questions, symptoms of an illness that itself awaits Wittgensteinian therapy.[54] This shows, I think, how Wittgenstein can avoid the charge of being a transcendental idealist.[55]

5. Distinguishing Between the 'Everyday' and the 'Metaphysical'

If it is indeed possible to exonerate Wittgenstein in this way, it is nevertheless possible only at a price. The price is to signal another problem that he must confront. There is a distinctive crisis of confidence to which his work gives rise, having to do with the fact that there is no Archimedean point from

---

[53] See Ch. 5, Appendix, for the definition of empirical idealism.

[54] Cf. Wittgenstein's impatience at §§380 and 381 with the question, 'How do I know that this colour is red?', asked with inappropriate philosophical intent.

[55] I do not claim, however, that he never himself feels the force of the temptation first to raise such pseudo-questions and then to follow where they lead. See e.g. pp. 226–227, where he shows some discomfort with simply saying, 'Even though everybody believed that twice two was five it would still be four.' His discomfort seems to me unwarranted. The situation is analogous to that which I identified parenthetically in Ch. 1, §3, where Descartes, over-cautiously in my view, refused to rule out the possibility of God's making one plus two unequal to three. I would further contend, and have tried to argue elsewhere, that the temptation to raise such pseudo-questions, and eventually to embrace some version of transcendental idealism, is in part a temptation to try to express inexpressible understanding of ours, such as our understanding of what being an aunt consists in: see Moore (1997a), Chs 7–9. If I am right, this reinforces the connections between the early work and the later work. (On the idea that there can be such a thing as understanding what being an aunt consists in, even though there is no such thing as saying what being an aunt consists in, cf. §78.)

which to tell what makes sense. It is impossible, in particular, to tell what makes sense *to us* except in *our* terms and from *our* point of view.

We have noted several times in this enquiry how self-consciousness about our sense-making can militate against self-confidence in it. This is a problem that afflicts philosophy of any broadly analytic kind. But philosophy of the kind that Wittgenstein advocates actually aggravates the problem. For the self-consciousness that is required of good philosophy, on Wittgenstein's conception, involves just the same experimenting with our concepts, just the same prodding and stretching of them, just the same investigation of how they function, that can give rise to bad philosophy. The reflection on our language that is needed to understand its grammar is of a piece with the reflection on our language that can all too easily lead to a misunderstanding of its grammar. There is a sense in which, had we only ever exercised the language and not reflected philosophically on what we were doing (for instance, had Albert, in §2 of the previous chapter, simply mused that the time had been passing, and not wondered how this thought related to the thought that the traffic had been passing), all would have been well. This is part of what Wittgenstein is getting at in his use of the term 'everyday'.[56] But once self-consciousness wreaks its damage, self-consciousness itself must help to rectify the damage. The problem is how to tell when it is doing the latter, as opposed to continuing to do the former; how to distinguish between bringing words back from their metaphysical to their everyday use and subjecting them to further metaphysical use; how to distinguish between good philosophy and bad philosophy.[57]

Perhaps it is obvious that, once we have got as far as counting the same thing both necessary and contingent, something has gone wrong. But what about positing a contingent grounding for necessity? Or denying that our number system 'resides in the nature of numbers' (*Zettel*, §357)? Or, for that matter, insisting that our number system does reside in the nature of numbers?[58] Wittgenstein claims that '3 + 3 = 6' is a rule as to the way in which we are going to talk (quoted by G.E. Moore in Moore (1959), p. 279). The celebrated mathematician G.H. Hardy says that, on the contrary, '[the] truth or falsity [of mathematical theorems] is absolute and independent of our knowledge of them,' and that 'in *some* sense, mathematical truth is part of objective reality' (Hardy (1929), p. 4, emphasis in original).[59] Wittgenstein replies that 'what a mathematician is inclined to say about the objectivity

---

[56] See again nn. 8 and 9.

[57] There are deep connections between this problem and a problem that I signalled for Descartes in Chapter 1, §3: that we need to be able to tell introspectively when we have a clear and distinct perception, and that having a clear and distinct perception is to be understood normatively.

[58] Cf. the hesitancy voiced in both that section of *Zettel* and the next.

[59] Cf. Frege's view, outlined in Ch. 8, §6.

and reality of mathematical facts … is … something for philosophical *treatment*' (§254, emphasis in original). Hardy then turns his attention to 'transfinite mathematics' – the formal mathematical theory of the infinite – and rails against the kind of opposition to such mathematics that he sees encapsulated in the slogan 'The finite cannot understand the infinite' (ibid., p. 5). Wittgenstein concedes that this slogan is 'inept' but denies that it 'is … all that nonsensical' and urges that it serves as a corrective against a misunderstanding of how the relevant mathematics works, a misunderstanding of which he thinks Hardy and others are guilty (*Zettel*, §273). How are we to arbitrate? How are we to tell which of these claims are contributions to good philosophy and which are pieces of bad philosophy needing treatment by means of the former?

Here is another way to view the problem. Wittgenstein's conception of philosophy rests on a fundamental distinction between successful attempts at sense-making, in accord with the grammar of our language, and unsuccessful attempts at sense-making, resulting from a misunderstanding of that grammar. How do we distinguish between these? There seems to be a circularity: to be sensitive to any such distinction we must have a clear understanding of the grammar; to have a clear understanding of the grammar we must discern it in our linguistic activity; to discern it in our linguistic activity we must recognize which parts of our linguistic activity are in accord with it; and to recognize which parts of our linguistic activity are in accord with it we must be sensitive to the original distinction.

I do not claim that this apparent circularity is vicious. I do not even claim that it is real. (Each step in this sequence can be disputed.) Perhaps there is a distinctive discomfort occasioned by attempts at sense-making that are not in accord with the grammar of our language.[60] *Perhaps* there is – though even then, of course, 'distinctive' is the operative word, with its own threat of circularity. (Mathematicians can feel plenty of discomfort when they are wrestling with bona fide mathematical problems.) The point, however, is that whether the circularity is real or not, the distinction needs to be drawn; and it needs to be drawn in practice, not just in theory, so the mere threat of such circularity cannot but dent our confidence, first in our own ability to draw the distinction, and then, *eo ipso*, in our attempts to make self-conscious sense of things. It cannot but issue in doubts about whether various difficulties that we face are the difficulties of trying to answer pseudo-questions or the difficulties of trying to answer genuine questions that just happen to be difficult.

Let us return to the example of transfinite mathematics. Wittgenstein insists that 'philosophy may in no way interfere with the actual use of language,' and, in particular, that 'it … leaves mathematics as it is' (§124).[61]

---

[60] Cf. §§54, 123, and 133, and *Culture*, pp. 86–87.

[61] In fact, just before this remark about mathematics, he says that philosophy, by which he means good philosophy, 'leaves *everything* as it is' (emphasis added). Everything? Well,

Yet we have also seen him prepared to challenge what mathematicians say. This of course reflects the very point that we have just been considering. Wittgenstein is prepared to challenge what mathematicians say because he sees a distinction between what they say *when making mathematical sense* and what they say otherwise. What they say otherwise, in other words what they say when they are not engaged in legitimate mathematics, is not in any sense sacrosanct. Mathematicians are no more immune to the confusions of bad philosophy than anyone else. Moreover – and this again reflects the point that we have just been considering – they may very well import their confusions back into their discipline. Consider, for example, early work on the calculus.[62] Some revisionists would even cite their (mathematicians') use of classical logic as an example.[63] Wittgenstein himself would cite transfinite mathematics.

On what grounds? Well, on several. Most notably, there is the fact that transfinite mathematics involves drawing distinctions of size between infinite sets. In particular, the set of real numbers is said to be bigger than the set of natural numbers – though how much bigger is in turn said to be an unsolved problem.[64] Wittgenstein is deeply suspicious, if not of the results themselves, then of how they are couched and of how they are presented.[65] He thinks they are couched and presented in such a way as to encourage a 'realist' model of mathematics, that is to say a model of the sort that I dubbed in §3 'perceptual' and that we have seen him abjure. Thus in saying that the set of real numbers is bigger than the set of natural numbers, we make 'the determination of a concept – concept formation – look like a fact of nature' (*Remarks*, Pt II, §19; cf. *Philosophical Grammar*, p. 287). We talk about these two sets as though we were talking about Mount Everest and Mount McKinley.

But now: Wittgenstein faces the very problem that I have been highlighting. He needs to be clear that what he is castigating are perversions of the relevant mathematical thinking, which have clouded its exposition, and not the mathematical thinking itself, which he knows he has no business as a philosopher castigating. And there is reason to think that he does not manage it. He writes, 'One pretends to compare the "set" of real numbers in magnitude with that of [natural] numbers.... I believe, and hope, that a

everything untainted by bad philosophy. And here, of course, the threat of circularity is again manifest.

[62] See Moore (2001a), Ch. 4, §§1 and 2.

[63] Wittgenstein himself has reservations about this: see esp. *Remarks*, Pt V. We shall return to this issue in Ch. 14, §§2 and 3.

[64] See Moore (2001a), Ch. 8, §3, and Ch. 10, §§3 and 4. (A 'real' number is a number that can be expressed using an infinite decimal expansion, a 'natural' number a non-negative whole number.)

[65] Cf. the distinction that he draws between the 'calculus' and the 'prose' in mathematical discourse, in *Vienna Circle*, p. 149.

future generation will laugh at this hocus pocus' (*Remarks*, Pt II, §22). But this invites precisely the same impatient retort as he himself might give if misplaced philosophical scruples cast doubt on a more homespun measuring technique: 'One *pretends* no such thing. One does it.' 'Comparing sets in size' may or may not be the most felicitous description of what mathematicians do,[66] but that *is* what they do, and that *is*, for better or worse, its description. Both here and elsewhere there is something almost paranoiac about Wittgenstein's horror of what he finds on the pens and in the mouths of mathematicians; and often, in spite of himself, he allows this to become a horror of the mathematics. The upshot is that he treats as 'metaphysical' what can surely, quite properly, be treated as 'everyday'.[67]

6. Taking Words Away from Their Everyday to a Metaphysical Use?

This problem, though serious for Wittgenstein, still does not bring us to what I take to be the most fundamental objection to his views. As a preliminary to seeing what that objection is, let us reflect on the conservatism that attends philosophy as he conceives it.

This conservatism is perfectly illustrated in what we have just been witnessing. When mathematicians extend the concept of one thing's being bigger than another, to embrace what they have established concerning infinite sets, Wittgenstein recoils. And when they introduce a new concept, that of an infinite cardinal, designed to measure how big any given infinite set is and thereby to effect relevant comparisons of size, again Wittgenstein recoils. He sees here just the kind of meddling with our concepts that is ripe for, if not constitutive of, philosophical confusion. Such is the conservatism that I have in mind.

The problem identified in the previous section is the problem of knowing when such conservatism is misplaced. Philosophers should have no quarrel with conceptual innovation that subserves sense-making. Their only quarrel should be with conceptual innovation that thwarts it. One thing that surely follows from this is that there can be little or no room for conceptual innovation *in philosophy itself*. Philosophy is an antidote to the confusions that arise from our mishandling our own concepts. Conceptual innovation – the introduction of new concepts, the extension of old concepts to new cases, the fashioning of new links between concepts, whether old or new – can

---

[66] I myself see nothing wrong with it. This is related to nn. 11 and 14 of the previous chapter. See also n. 4 above. And see Friedrich Waismann (1959), p. 359, where Waismann discusses the same example in a broadly Wittgensteinian framework, but with what seems to me an altogether cooler head than Wittgenstein.

[67] For a fuller discussion of this example, see Moore (2011). For a superb discussion of the more general issues raised in both this section and the next, see Williams (2006n), §4.

only ever bring with it the risk of new confusions. Philosophers should be looking to minimize that risk.

I say that there can be *little or* no room for conceptual innovation in philosophy itself. I do not think that it is to be ruled out completely, on Wittgenstein's conception. Philosophers do after all need to present the grammar of our language as perspicuously as possible, as indeed they need to reflect on what they themselves are doing, and they may find new conceptual resources helpful for these purposes. (Perhaps the concept of a language-game and the concept of a form of life are two cases in point: see §§2 and 4, respectively.) The fact remains that their business is primarily to protect whatever sense-making is already under way, not to indulge in sense-making of their own (i.e. peculiarly of their own). The conservatism identified above may be a natural concomitant of philosophy on this conception. But *philosophical* conservatism is not merely a natural concomitant of it. It is an integral part of it.

One consequence of this is that, if sense-making is construed in such a way that metaphysics is simply good philosophy of the most general kind (see §3), then we have in Wittgenstein an extremely clear answer to the Novelty Question which I posed in §6 of the Introduction, much clearer than that provided by any of the rest of my protagonists: there is *no* scope for us, as practising metaphysicians, to make sense of things in ways that are radically new.[68] But this brings us to the objection. *Why not?* Even if our aim is solely to promote our conceptual health, why think, as Wittgenstein seems to think, that the only way in which we can do this is to cure ourselves of conceptual diseases? Perhaps we can also take conceptual exercise. This remark is not as flippant as it sounds. There is a serious point underlying it. And the seriousness of the point extends to the broader issue of what it is that forces us to identify philosophy with the promotion of conceptual health in the first place. In sum: why should we accept Wittgenstein's conception of philosophy?

We must of course beware of becoming embroiled in a tiresome quibble about how to use the word 'philosophy'. But there is a point of substance here. It has to do with Wittgenstein's own celebrated notion of a 'family-resemblance' concept, illustrated most famously by the concept of a game. It is remarkable that the same person who writes this:

> Consider for example the proceedings that we call 'games'.... What is common to them all? ... *Look and see* whether there is anything common to all.... To repeat: don't think, but look! ...

---

[68] For the record, there are also clear answers to the Transcendence Question and the Creativity Question, suitably construed. For there is a clear sense in which Wittgenstein will deny that metaphysicians can make sense of what is transcendent (§126), and a clear sense in which he will deny that their enterprise is one of discovery (§3).

… The result of this examination is: we see a complicated network of similarities overlapping and criss-crossing: sometimes overall similarities, sometimes similarities of detail.

I can think of no better expression to characterize these similarities than 'family resemblances'; for the various resemblances between members of a family: build, features, colour of eyes, gait, temperament, etc. etc. overlap and criss-cross in the same way. (§§66 and 67, emphasis in original)

should also write each of these:

Philosophy really *is* 'purely descriptive'. (*Blue Book*, p. 18, emphasis in original)

Philosophy isn't anything except philosophical problems, the particular individual worries that we call 'philosophical problems'. (*Philosophical Grammar*, p. 193)

Philosophy may in no way interfere with the actual use of language; it can in the end only describe it.…
It leaves everything as it is. (§124)

Philosophy simply puts everything before us, and neither explains nor deduces anything. (§126)

The work of the philosopher consists in assembling reminders for particular purposes. (§127)

Some philosophy is like that. But all of it? Has Wittgenstein looked and seen?

Admittedly, Wittgenstein has his distinction between good philosophy and bad philosophy. He might say that he has indeed looked and seen. He has looked at what gets classified as philosophy and he has seen that, apart from what he himself endorses, there is only the bad variety. But Wittgenstein's conception of bad philosophy is as restrictive as his conception of good philosophy.[69] We can agree that what he conceives as bad philosophy is bad, and still wonder how much of what gets classified as philosophy is like that. (In particular, we can wonder how much of what we have been looking at in this enquiry is like that.) Wittgenstein is surely in danger of doing what Kant so clearly saw Hume doing: throwing the baby out with the bathwater, to revert once more to that tired old metaphor (Ch. 4, §5, and Ch. 5, §2).

In my discussion of the Novelty Question in §6 of the Introduction I alluded to the alternative that Wittgenstein so signally fails to countenance: attempting, in philosophical mode, to make maximally general sense of things by supplementing, amending, or replacing the various ways in which

---

[69] See above, §1. And see in particular n. 6 for references to his pejorative uses of 'philosophy'.

we currently make sense of things, and doing so, moreover, in favour of something radically new. And who is to deny that part of this process might even be to wrench words away from their 'everyday' use to new, metaphysical uses, somewhat as mathematicians do with the word 'bigger', or as indeed Hegel did with virtually all of the key terms that he used in the presentation of his dialectic (see esp. Ch. 7, §7)? Wittgenstein is clearly concerned that we should be in control of our concepts, not they of us. This makes him especially sensitive to the confusions we risk when we start bending our own conceptual rules and allowing our concepts to evolve in this way. But let us not forget that being confused by our own concepts is only one way of being in their thrall. Being uncritically closed to new ways of making sense of things is another.

There is in any case the question: what is wrong with not being in control of our own concepts? What is wrong with being confused? Obviously, confusion can have bad consequences, dire consequences even. But is it intrinsically bad? Do we have to share Wittgenstein's abhorrence of it, which, as we saw in §8 of the previous chapter, assumes the form, almost, of an ethical axiom?[70] One thing that must certainly be conceded is that, however bad the potential consequences of confusion are, and whatever the status of its own badness is, it can also be a means to valuable ends, as any teacher knows. (I include Wittgenstein: cf. §464.) Perhaps it can be a means to ends that are not only valuable but quite extraordinary, so extraordinary that their value is currently beyond our comprehension. This again relates to my discussion of the Novelty Question, where I alluded to the possibility of our abandoning concepts at the price of our very humanity, a possibility that is all the more significant in view of the reflections in §4 above about who 'we' are.

This flurry of questions-cum-suggestions points forwards to ideas that we shall encounter in Part Three.[71] They are not themselves objections to anything in Wittgenstein, although, as I have tried to show, they flow from what I do take to be such an objection, indeed the principal such objection. I think it is in fact a measure of Wittgenstein's greatness that they do so, and that his work provokes reflection at such a deep level. My aim in the last three sections of this chapter has been to ask questions of Wittgenstein's work, to challenge it in various ways, and to pit it against alternatives. My aim has precisely *not* been to denigrate it; obviously not. I have wanted to honour it, not to dishonour it.

---

[70] See in particular n. 88 of that section.
[71] See in particular Ch. 21, §§6 and 7(c). See also Conclusion, §5.

CHAPTER 11

✦

Carnap

The Elimination of Metaphysics?

1. Logical Positivism

Here is a cartoon sketch. Hume was appalled by the metaphysical excesses of his predecessors. He opposed them with a radical empiricism. But Kant thought that Hume's empiricism was too radical. On Hume's account, earlier metaphysicians had not only professed to know what they could not know, they had professed to know what they could not even think. Kant believed that they were very often guilty as charged in the first of these respects, much less often in the second. He opposed them with something more subtle. But the subtleties of Kant's view, combined with its own uneasy relation to itself, meant that many of his successors felt that they now had license to try to make sense of things in ways that Hume would have regarded as far more egregious than anything he had been trying to combat in the first place. And so it was that, in the twentieth century, within the analytic tradition, there was a neo-Humean backlash, a reversion to a radical empiricism that could be used to mount a full-scale semantic attack on these new excesses, reducing them to the status of literal meaninglessness. This was the movement known as logical positivism.[1]

That this movement should have arisen in analytic philosophy is hardly surprising. The Humean attention to sense that it demanded was very much of a piece with the attention to sense that had come to be one of the defining features, if not the defining feature, of analytic philosophy. By the same token logical positivists were able to make use of various analytic tools, in executing their Humean project, that had not been available to Hume himself, most notably the tools of the new formal logic that Frege had established.

---

[1] The term 'logical positivism' was introduced by Albert Blumberg and Herbert Feigl in Blumberg and Feigl (1931). 'Positivism' on its own, or 'positive philosophy', had earlier been used by Auguste Comte to designate his loosely related system, e.g. in the very title of his masterwork, Comte (1988). But I use the expression 'loosely related' advisedly. Comte's use of the term 'positivism' and this subsequent use are best regarded as homonymous.

279

In sum – and remember, this is a cartoon sketch – logical positivism was Humeanism made analytic.[2,3]

As a species of Humeanism it involved a descendant of Hume's distinction between relations of ideas and matters of fact. As an analytic movement it involved a version of Frege's distinction between analytic truths and synthetic truths. Indeed, the one was the other. But how *could* the one be the other, without important questions being begged against Kant? Frege, when he introduced his distinction between analytic truths and synthetic truths, claimed that he was merely appropriating Kant's distinction (Ch. 8, §2). And Kant, when he first introduced that same distinction, introduced it as one of a pair of distinctions, the other being the distinction between truths that are knowable *a priori* and truths that are not, his very point being that Hume's single distinction had been unequal to the task of accounting for every kind of truth (Ch. 5, §3). 'What,' Kant would have asked – as for that matter would Frege, who likewise introduced his distinction alongside this second one – 'about the synthetic *a priori*?'

It is unfair, however, to suggest that the logical positivists simply begged this question. They addressed it; and they gave it a non-Kantian answer. They strenuously denied that there *is* any such category.[4] This was precisely one of the hallmarks of their reversion to Hume. The single contrast between that which is analytically true, and therefore knowable *a priori*, and that which is knowable only by suitable appeal to sense experience, and therefore synthetically true, was as much as they thought was needed.

And it gave logical positivism its distinctive stamp. Logical positivists insisted that unless a given statement expressed a truth that could in principle be known in one or other of these two ways, or a falsehood whose negation could in principle be known in one or other of these two ways, it did not express a truth or a falsehood at all and lacked any literal meaning.[5]

---

[2] Another way to put it, equally caricatural, would be to say that logical positivism was Humeanism transposed from a psychological to a logical key.

[3] It is only fair for me to add a reminder that the interpretation of Hume that I am presupposing in this sketch is contested: see Ch. 4, §1. Edward Craig, who reads Hume very differently from how I do, concludes the chapter on Hume in Craig (1987) with a section entitled 'Hume's Heirs?' in which he argues that logical positivists' 'claim to be Hume's twentieth-century heirs is ... in a certain very important respect ... the exact reverse of the truth' (p. 128). The final sentence of Craig's chapter captures well both its tone and its content: 'Hume's heirs indeed!' (p. 130).

[4] See e.g. Ayer (1971), Ch. 4. In this they were in line with the early Wittgenstein (Ch. 9, §4). But the matter is less straightforward than it seems: see further §3(d) below.

[5] For discussion of some of the complications that this glides over, see Ayer (1971), Introduction. Note that Ayer talks in terms of (non-conclusively) verifying a truth rather than knowing it (see e.g. p. 179). But on a suitably undemanding conception of knowledge these can be regarded as equivalent.

This so-called verification theory of meaning arguably entailed that each of the following statements lacked any literal meaning:

Pure being and pure nothing are the same.
The good is more identical than the beautiful.
Time passes at one second per second.
God moves in mysterious ways.
Bananas look purple when they are not being observed.
No human being is ever justified in killing another.

This miscellany of examples should both ring bells from previous chapters and, particularly in the case of the last few, indicate how destructive the view was capable of being. To be sure, it is important not to exaggerate the destructiveness. Logical positivists were denying that certain statements had a certain kind of meaning, what I have followed them in calling 'literal' meaning. That is, they were denying that these statements expressed truths or falsehoods. But this left open the possibility that some of them expressed something else, hence that they had meaning of some other kind. In particular it left open the possibility that some of them expressed feelings, prescriptions, or proscriptions – any of which the last statement in particular might be thought to express.[6] It left open the possibility that, on some reasonable conception of what it is to make sense of things, some of these statements could contribute to doing just that. Nonetheless, it is clear how logical positivists took their view to inflict the damage on earlier metaphysical excesses that they wanted it to inflict.

2. Carnap's Version of Logical Positivism.
Linguistic Frameworks

Rudolf Carnap (1891–1970) was the arch logical positivist.[7] His own brand of logical positivism is however quite distinctive. It is also highly sophisticated. It has, in addition to the features sketched in the previous section, one other crucial feature. Carnap holds that the most fundamental of all the distinctions with which logical positivists are concerned, the distinction between the true and the false, is only ever operative within a linguistic

---

[6] Cf. Ayer (1971), Ch. 6.

[7] Carnap was one of the foremost members of the group with which logical positivism was particularly associated, the Vienna Circle. This was a group of between thirty and forty thinkers, from a range of disciplines, who met regularly in Vienna between the wars to discuss philosophy. The group was united by the aim to make philosophy scientific, in a sense of 'scientific' broad enough to embrace formal logic. Many members of the group thought that a commitment to logical positivism was indispensable to the realization of that aim. Carnap certainly did.

framework, where a linguistic framework is understood to be a systematic way of speaking about entities of a given kind and where a systematic way of speaking is in turn understood to be a set of 'rules for forming statements and for testing, accepting or rejecting them' ('Ontology', p. 208).[8] A paradigm would be the set of syntactic and arithmetical rules that allow us to speak about positive integers. The decision whether or not to adopt any given framework is not itself a matter of truth or falsity. It is a matter of the advantages and disadvantages of doing so.

By way of illustration, suppose we ask whether there is any positive integer whose square is exactly twice that of another. Then we are asking a question *within* a particular framework, what Carnap would call an 'internal' question ('Ontology', p. 206). As it happens the answer is no. And this answer can be determined independently of sense experience: it is an analytic truth, determined by the rules of the framework, that there are no such integers. Now suppose we ask whether we are right to accept the existence of positive integers in the first place. This time we are asking what Carnap would call an 'external' question (ibid.). It is a question *about* the relevant framework, whether we are right to adopt it or not. And it takes us beyond the realm of the true and the false. (Not that this makes it an illegitimate question. It is a perfectly legitimate question about how to speak. There may be no *truth* of the matter, but there are important practical issues about the costs and benefits of speaking in this way.)

In summary, Carnap holds the following package of ideas:[9]

- a linguistic framework comprises rules for speaking about entities of a certain kind
- within the framework there are truths and falsehoods about these entities
- among the truths there are some, the analytic ones, whose truth depends solely on the rules of the framework, and these can be known *a priori*
- the rest, the synthetic ones, can be known by suitable appeal to sense experience, and *only* by suitable appeal to sense experience
- the decision whether or not to adopt the framework is a practical one (it is not itself a matter of truth or falsity).

---

[8] See 'Ontology' more generally, esp. §2, for discussion of the idea of a linguistic framework.

Note: throughout this chapter I use the following abbreviations for Carnap's works: *Aufbau* for Carnap (1967a); 'Autobiography' for Carnap (1963a); *Der Raum* for Carnap (1922); 'Elimination' for Carnap (1959); 'Goodman' for Carnap (1963b); 'Introduction' for Carnap (1958); *Logical Syntax* for Carnap (1937); *Meaning and Necessity* for Carnap (1956a); 'Ontology' for Carnap (1956b); *Philosophy* for Carnap (1935); and *Pseudoproblems* for Carnap (1967b).

[9] See esp. 'Ontology' and *Pseudoproblems*, Pt II.

3.   A First (Themed) Retrospective

One way to see Carnap's place in the evolution of modern metaphysics is by explicitly comparing this package of ideas and its implications for metaphysics with views that we have encountered previously and with views that we shall encounter subsequently. Necessarily, at this stage, I am limited in what I can do by way of the latter. In the next section I shall nevertheless glance ahead. In this section I shall look back. And, in keeping with my cartoon sketch, I shall focus on some of the ways in which Carnap embraces what he can and rejects what he must in order to create a suitably robust, analytically respectable Humeanism.[10]

(a)   Hume

The essential point of comparison with Hume himself is already clear. In the famous final paragraph of his first *Enquiry* (Hume (1975a)) Hume urged us to commit to the flames any volume that contains neither 'abstract reasoning concerning quantity and number' nor 'experimental reasoning concerning matter of fact and existence'. In *Philosophy* Carnap quotes this paragraph and adds:

> We agree with this view of Hume, which says – translated into our own terminology – that only the propositions of mathematics and empirical science have sense, and that all other propositions are without sense. (p. 36)

There, in a nutshell, is Carnap's appropriation of Hume's radical empiricism. It requires no further gloss at this juncture – save to note that what appeared to be a curiously unmotivated restriction in Hume, namely the restriction of the non-empirical to the mathematical (Ch. 4, §5), surfaces again here, only this time it appears to be, not merely unmotivated, but in direct opposition to its author's intent. For the very purpose of the lectures from which Carnap's quotation is taken is to demonstrate how the propositions that philosophers typically produce, though they are neither empirical nor mathematical, nevertheless have sense (see e.g. Lecture II, §8; and see further §5 below). Or so it seems. In fact the appearances are misleading. There is not really any opposition. As Carnap makes clear elsewhere, he has a broad conception of the mathematical. On that conception, analytic truths belong to 'the mathematics ... of language' (*Logical Syntax*, p. 284).

---

[10] This is an apt point at which to return to the contrast between the history of philosophy and the history of ideas which I mentioned in the Preface, and to emphasize that I am engaged in the former. I am not much concerned with conscious assimilations or repudiations on Carnap's part.

There is one respect in which, by pouring Hume's empiricism into an analytic mould, Carnap appears to consolidate it. He appears to make good Hume's claim that '[all] our thoughts or ideas, however compounded or sublime, ... resolve themselves into such simple ideas as were copied from a precedent [impression]' (Hume (1975a), p. 19). We saw little effort on Hume's part to justify or even to illustrate this claim, one notable exception being his attempt to locate the impression from which the crucial but troublesome idea of a causally necessary connection is copied (Ch. 4, §3). In his *Aufbau* Carnap appears to make up this deficiency. He appears to show, with painstaking ingenuity, using all the analytic tools at his disposal, how the various more or less sophisticated ways that we have of making sense of things can be reduced to the simple data of sense experience.[11] I say he *appears* to do these things. Not only is there the question of how far he succeeds in his project,[12] there is also the question of how far his project can in any case properly be said to be a Humean one. Hume was attempting an experimental science of human nature. He was interested in where our ideas actually come from. Carnap is attempting something that is really quite different, 'a rational reconstruction of the concepts of all fields of knowledge on the basis of concepts that refer to the immediately given' (*Aufbau*, p. v).[13] And, in keeping with his views about linguistic frameworks, he conceives this as just one of many possible reconstructions.[14] Still, on both accounts there is a sense (flexible enough to allow for *a priori* knowledge) in which all our sense-making derives from sense experience. And such is the basic empiricism that we find in both Hume and Carnap.

(b) Kant

The crucial break with Kant occurs in Carnap's rejection of the synthetic *a priori*. (See e.g. *Aufbau*, §106.) Kant's most compelling examples of the synthetic *a priori* were probably those that he culled from geometry. Yet ironically, it is from geometry that Carnap is able to draw some of the clearest illustrations of his own anti-Kantian stance.

There are mathematically coherent alternatives to the Euclidean geometry that Kant believed constituted a true synthetic *a priori* description of

---

[11] For a beautiful summary, see Quine (1995a), pp. 10–14.

[12] Quine famously expresses reservations in Quine (1961b), §5. For more detailed reservations, see Goodman (1977). For a fascinating criticism of a related project in A.J. Ayer, a criticism that identifies some fundamental problems for logical positivism more generally, see Williams (1981).

[13] Cf. n. 2 above. And see Stroud (1977), Ch. 10, §I, for a discussion that emphasizes how different these projects are.

[14] For discussion, see Goodman (1963), which is more sympathetic than Goodman (1977), cited in n. 12 above, and to which Carnap replies in 'Goodman'.

physical space. These 'non-Euclidean geometries' are *non-Euclidean* in that they include principles which, taken at face value, are straightforwardly incompatible with those of Euclidean geometry (e.g. that between two points there can be more than one straight line). They are *geometries* in that they nevertheless share sufficiently many principles with Euclidean geometry, and with one another, to constitute a mathematical family.[15]

The Carnapian view is that there are two equally legitimate ways of construing these different geometries. On one construal, they are themselves linguistic frameworks. This means that the choice between them is not a matter of truth or falsity. Once the choice has been made, however, *then* we can use whichever geometry has been selected to make claims that are true or false. And there are two ways in turn in which we can do this. First, we can articulate the principles that constitute the geometry. These are analytic truths, determined by the rules of the framework. They can be known *a priori*. (This is why I included the qualification 'taken at face value' in the previous paragraph. On this construal, no principle of any non-Euclidean geometry is strictly speaking incompatible with any principle of Euclidean geometry. For, strictly speaking, 'point', 'line', and the rest mean different things in the different contexts. Between any two *Euclidean* points there cannot be more than one straight *Euclidean* line.) Second, we can apply the concepts furnished by the geometry we have selected to make claims about physical reality. If our claims are true, then they are synthetically true, dependent for their truth on what physical reality is actually like. Their truth has to be determined empirically. Now although the original choice of geometry is not itself a matter of truth or falsity, even so one geometry is overwhelmingly the best, from a practical point of view, for making true claims of this second kind. It alone allows for a full and accurate description of physical reality that is not hopelessly unwieldy. And, as it happens, for reasons of which Kant could not have had the least idea, the geometry in question is non-Euclidean.

The second way of construing these different geometries is as rival descriptions of physical space that can be proffered within some other linguistic framework. On this construal the choice between them *is* a matter of truth or falsity. The true one is synthetically true. It is also empirically true. And, as it happens, again for reasons of which Kant could not have had the least idea, it is non-Euclidean. But that last fact is less significant, in this context, than the fact that nothing, on either way of construing these different geometries, is at once true, synthetic, and *a priori*.[16]

---

[15] Such geometries were developed in the late eighteenth and early nineteenth centuries. It is natural to wonder whether Kant knew of their existence. Unfortunately, we cannot be sure. But probably not: see Potter (2000), pp. 36–37.

[16] For a beautifully clear and concise account of this conception, see 'Introduction'. This supersedes Carnap's doctoral thesis, published as *Der Raum*, in which he still accedes to the synthetic *a priori*.

Adopting a linguistic framework, whether in connection with geometry or in any other connection, is *somewhat* akin to donning a pair of Kantian spectacles.[17] It provides a set of concepts for making empirical sense of things. But the very 'donning' indicates why this is to be sharply contrasted with anything advocated by Kant himself, whose concern was with native spectacles that could be neither donned nor removed. Furthermore, Kantian spectacles involved intuitions as well as concepts, which is why they were supposed to be themselves sources of synthetic knowledge. Carnap accepts nothing like that. Thus his neo-Humeanism.

(c) Frege[18]

Like any other analytic philosopher, Carnap inherits a huge amount from Frege – including, of course, the distinction between analytic truths and synthetic truths.[19] But Carnap differs from Frege in one fundamental respect. He is utterly hostile to Frege's conception of logic as the study of transcendent objects whose existence and character are independent of us. Frege held that the laws of logic are the laws that govern such objects, specifically thoughts and their truth or falsity. Carnap, by contrast, believes about the laws of logic just what he believes about analytic truths more generally, namely that they are truths fixed by the rules of a linguistic framework that we have adopted. Suppose we accept, what Frege would have said we have no alternative *but* to accept, that, bracketing any senses that lack corresponding *Bedeutungen*, every proposition – or thought, in Frege's terminology – is either true or false (see e.g. Frege (1997i), p. 300/p. 214 in the original German). For Carnap this is just a decision about how to speak. It indicates, or goes part way to indicating, our choice of framework. We could have adopted a framework whereby, not every proposition, but every proposition of this or that kind, is either true or false. Such an alternative would have had some advantages, perhaps, and some disadvantages. A possible advantage is that it would have allowed us to prove fewer things and would therefore have run less risk of allowing us to prove the contraries of claims

---

[17] Cf. Stroud (1984), pp. 195–196, though for reasons that I am about to sketch I think that Barry Stroud overstates the similarities. The whole of Chapter 5 of Stroud's book is concerned with Carnap's idea of a linguistic framework. He points to some deep problems that he thinks afflict the idea. We shall consider related problems in §§5 and 6.

[18] For a thorough comparison of Carnap with Frege, see Gabriel (2007). For a clear statement from Carnap himself of how he sees his own insights as amalgamating those of the classical empiricists and Frege, see *Aufbau*, p. vi.

[19] Mention should also be made of the influence on Carnap's semantics of Frege's distinction between sense and *Bedeutung*: see esp. *Meaning and Necessity*, where in §§28 and 29 Carnap compares and contrasts Frege's distinction with his own distinction between 'intension' and 'extension'.

we want to make, for instance claims about all truths. A possible disadvantage is that it would have been less user-friendly. But it would not have been either correct or incorrect. It would not have been answerable to anything independent of us – still less to anything transcendent.[20]

That even the laws of logic should fall within the ambit of Carnap's views about linguistic frameworks is a direct consequence of his attempt to combine Humean empiricism with some basic tenets of mainstream analytic philosophy. As we have seen, he is sufficiently Humean to insist that the only sense that we can make of things, except for whatever sense we make of things when we adopt a linguistic framework, is empirical sense (the kind of sense that we cannot make of transcendent things). On the other hand, he is sufficiently immersed in the analytic tradition to resist going all the way with Hume and counting our acceptance of the laws of logic as itself an example of our making empirical sense of anything.[21] So he takes the only course that remains for him to take. He counts our acceptance of the laws of logic as an example of our making sense of things by adopting a linguistic framework.[22]

(d) The Early Wittgenstein

Carnap's rejection of the synthetic *a priori* in favour of a simple binary classification of all truths is fully in keeping with Wittgenstein's *Tractatus*. But the specific account that he gives of what it is for a truth to fall on one side or the other of his divide is much less so. Indeed, there is tension between Carnap's understanding of what it is for a truth to be analytic and Wittgenstein's. This tension is clearest in the logical pluralism that we have just witnessed in Carnap. Wittgenstein is as keen as Carnap to insist that there is an arbitrary element in our use of language. But he also insists that

---

[20] See e.g. *Logical Syntax*, §17; 'Ontology', §5; and 'Autobiography', p. 49. Note the 'Principle of Tolerance' which Carnap formulates in the first of these passages: 'It is not our business to set up prohibitions but to arrive at conventions' (p. 51, emphasis removed). In the second and third passages he positively encourages the adoption of non-standard linguistic frameworks, in case unexpected benefits accrue. If they do not, no harm will be done: 'the work in the field will sooner or later lead to the elimination of those forms [of expression] which have no useful function' ('Ontology', p. 221).

[21] See Ch. 4, n. 36.

[22] Note that Carnap has an easy way with Frege's question whether Julius Caesar is a number or not (Ch. 8, §3). Accepting the existence of people and accepting the existence of numbers each involves adopting a linguistic framework that makes no reference to the other. So we are free to insist that people and numbers are *sui generis* and that Julius Caesar is therefore not a number: cf. 'Ontology', pp. 210–211. (But we are also free, if we so choose, to create and adopt a linguistic framework in which people *are* numbers: cf. *Philosophy*, Lecture III, §3. To that extent Frege was right to view this as a matter of stipulation. Unlike Frege, however, we now have some rationale for so viewing it.)

there is a non-arbitrary element in it, and that logic, which 'must look after itself' (Wittgenstein (1961), 5.473), pertains to the latter (ibid., 6.124; cf. 3.342).[23] Again, Carnap's insistence that it must always be possible to confirm a synthetic truth by appeal to sense experience has no precursor in the *Tractatus*. All we find there is the insistence that it must never be possible to confirm an analytic truth in that way (ibid., 6.1222).[24] Finally, Carnap's dichotomy is intended as an altogether cruder instrument of destruction than Wittgenstein's. Its destructive power should not be exaggerated, as I urged in §1. Nevertheless, as we shall see in §5, Carnap's use of it to expose illusions of sense shows much less respect than we find in Wittgenstein for the various impulses that make such illusions possible, impulses which, after all, Wittgenstein spent the *Tractatus* engaging, exploiting, and arguably even fostering (see Ch. 9, §§5–8).[25] All these differences bear witness to the Humean empiricism at work in Carnap – but not in Wittgenstein.[26]

Another difference, to which we shall return in §5, is that Carnap, unlike Wittgenstein, acknowledges a kind of nonsense in which perfectly meaningful words are combined in a way that violates their logical syntax, for example 'Caesar is and' ('Elimination', §4). What Wittgenstein would have said about this example is no different from what he would have said about 'Caesar is quirxaceous', namely that its nonsensicality is due simply to the fact that the third word in it, which is functioning here as an adjective, has no adjectival meaning; it is not that there is something somehow illegitimate about the very combination of words (Wittgenstein (1961), 5.473ff.; see Ch. 9, §3).

Finally, one very important similarity between the two is that Carnap shares Wittgenstein's conception of good philosophy as an activity rather than a body of doctrine ('Elimination', p. 77; cf. *Philosophy*, Lecture I, §1, and p. 31). Admittedly, they have somewhat different views about the scope of the activity. In particular, Carnap has higher hopes than Wittgenstein

---

[23] That Carnap overestimates what can be achieved by the arbitrary element in language, and specifically in the language of logic, is a theme of Quine's well-known attack on his views in Quine (1966b). 'The difficulty,' Quine writes, 'is that if logic is to proceed mediately from conventions [i.e. if it is to proceed in accord with Carnap's understanding of what is arbitrary about it], logic is needed for inferring logic from the conventions' (p. 98). See also Quine (1966c).

[24] See Ch. 9, n. 20.

[25] For a stark drawing of the contrast between logical positivists and Wittgenstein in this respect, see Engelmann (1967), pp. 97–98. See also n. 39.

[26] They also explain Wittgenstein's feeling of alienation with respect to the Vienna Circle, despite the popular view, originating with members of the Circle themselves, that he had been one of their primary inspirations. For two full and very instructive accounts of the philosophical relations between Wittgenstein and the Vienna Circle, see Baker (1988), Ch. 6, §1, and Hacker (1996), Ch. 3. For insight into their personal relations, see Monk (1991), pp. 242–242 and 283ff.

has for how much it can achieve and for how systematic it can be. For Wittgenstein, the proper function of philosophy is purely negative, to combat bad philosophy. For Carnap, it can also make a positive contribution to scientific enquiry. Indeed he goes as far as to say that it can 'lay logical foundations for factual science and for mathematics' ('Elimination', p. 77). He thinks it can do this by clarifying the workings of particular linguistic frameworks, so that scientists and mathematicians can then choose between them. Still, he agrees that what Wittgenstein identifies as the sole legitimate aim of philosophy is one of its principal aims: the elimination of what I called above 'bad philosophy' and what they both call 'metaphysics'.

(e) The Later Wittgenstein

The continuity in Wittgenstein's conception of philosophy means that this last cluster of comparisons applies equally to the later work. But the contrasts are now if anything more pronounced. Although Carnap distinguishes sharply between philosophy and other sciences, 'other' is the operative word. Philosophy is itself a scientific enterprise for him: systematic, governed by general principles, detached. This view is an anathema to the later Wittgenstein, for whom philosophy has to be piecemeal, contextual, engaged. Relatedly, we find in Carnap support for the objection that I brought against the later Wittgenstein in the previous chapter. Carnap sees no reason why philosophy should be restricted to clarifying extant linguistic frameworks that have been misunderstood in one way or another, why it should not present us with brand new linguistic frameworks. In fact such innovation is in Carnap's view the very business of philosophy. Precisely what philosophers should be doing is striving to provide (other) scientists with options for couching whatever sense they make of things, there being no obvious reason why the linguistic frameworks they already use are best suited to this purpose.[27]

But as for the very idea of a linguistic framework, that has much about it that would be congenial to the later Wittgenstein.[28] He too holds that there are rules determining how we are to represent things without themselves representing anything, and that whether or not we are right to adopt these rules is a matter of utility rather than a matter of truth or falsity.[29] And he too holds that for us to adopt such rules is, in part, for us to be prepared to affirm certain propositions, such as – to revert once more to our stock example – that aunts are female. Conversely, the Wittgensteinian idea that these very propositions may come to play a representative role instead

---

[27] Cf. n. 20.

[28] See also Wittgenstein (1961), 6.34ff., for something interestingly akin to it in the early Wittgenstein.

[29] Cf. Wittgenstein (1978), Pt I, §4.

(Ch. 10, §3) has its counterpart in Carnap, who acknowledges that linguistic and non-linguistic pressures can transform analytic truths determined by the rules of one framework into synthetic truths assertable within another (*Logical Syntax*, pp. 318–319).

4. Glances Ahead

(a) Quine

In the next chapter we shall see Quine taking possession of the empiricism handed down by the logical positivists, just as they take possession of that handed down by Hume.[30] We shall also however see him discarding some of its embellishments, which it has acquired from the analytic mould in which it has been cast. Quine will attempt to revert to something rawer. This is not because of any opposition to analytic philosophy. On the contrary. He wants to refashion analytic philosophy, not to reject it. It is as though he wants to reverse the functions: to let the basic empiricism that he inherits be the mould and to let the fundamental precepts of analytic philosophy (the respect for clarity, the methodical attention to language, etc.) be what gets poured into that mould. In particular, we shall see him invoking empiricist principles to challenge the very distinction between analytic truths and synthetic truths, as well as the idea, implicit in much of the logical positivist literature, that each meaningful statement stands in relations of confirmation and confutation to different possible courses of sense experience, independently of other statements.[31]

Full discussion of these matters will have to wait until the next chapter (see in particular §4). But it is relevant to note here that, whatever may be true of other logical positivists, *Carnap* is far from being a straightforward target for Quine. (I do not mean to suggest that Quine is under any illusions on this point.) Carnap's own analytic credentials are nuanced enough for him to be at least out of Quine's direct firing line, if indeed he is not himself already firing in the same direction. Thus concerning the analytic/synthetic distinction there is the subtlety mentioned at the very end of the previous section, whereby in Carnap's view a truth's status as one or other of these can change.[32] And concerning the point about the confirmation

---

[30] See §1 of that chapter for testimony to the high regard in which Quine held Carnap himself.

[31] See e.g. Hempel (1959) and Schlick (1959b). Carl Hempel himself subsequently has second thoughts about this idea: see Hempel (1951).

[32] For a suggestion that any differences between Carnap and Quine on this issue are due to Quine's having transposed the Humean empiricism into an epistemological key, if not back into a psychological key (see n. 2), see Friedman (2006), p. 48.

and confutation of meaningful statements, Quine's famous 'countersuggestion[, namely] … that our statements … face the tribunal of sense experience not individually but only as a corporate body,' can, as Quine himself notes, already be found in Carnap (Quine (1961b), p. 41).[33] Thus in *Logical Syntax* we find:

> [A] test applies, at bottom, not to a single hypothesis but to the whole system of physics as a system of hypotheses. (p. 318, emphasis in original)[34]

(b) Heidegger

Carnap thinks that, as often as not, the nonsense that metaphysicians produce involves violations of logical syntax. (For further discussion, including comparisons with Wittgenstein, see the next section.) In §5 of 'Elimination' he selects a passage from Heidegger as an especially graphic illustration of what he has in mind. The relevant passage occurs just after Heidegger has proclaimed that science is concerned with the investigation of what he calls 'beings'. Heidegger writes:

> What should be examined [i.e. in science] are beings only, and besides that – nothing; beings alone, and further – nothing; solely beings, and beyond that – nothing. (Heidegger (1993a), p. 95)[35]

He then asks, 'What about this nothing?' (ibid.) And he ventures various suggestions about it, including the notorious suggestion that 'the nothing … noths.'[36] In Carnap's view this is a paradigm of the kind of confusion against which a proper training in logic, in particular Fregean logic, can serve as a bulwark: Heidegger is treating the quantifier 'nothing' as a name and is getting into an unholy muddle about that whose name it is.[37] (Not that familiarity with logic is any guarantee against such confusion. As Carnap laments, Heidegger knows full well that he is flouting certain fundamental principles of received logical wisdom and thinks that the fault lies with

---

[33] It can also be found in Pierre Duhem, again as Quine notes: see Quine (1961b), n. 17. For two of Duhem's own statements of the doctrine, see Duhem (1991), pp. 183 and 258.

[34] Carnap too attributes the view to Duhem, and to Poincaré. For further discussion of the relations between Carnap and Quine, see Hookway(1988), Ch. 2, §§3–5; Isaacson (2004); Friedman (2006); and Creath (2007).

[35] This translation differs from that given in 'Elimination'. It is far preferable: it is both more accurate and a clearer indication of Heidegger's thinking.

[36] '*Das Nicht … nichtet*.' Here I am adopting the popular rendering of Heidegger's neologism '*nichtet*', which is translated in Heidegger (1993a) as 'nihilates' (p. 103) and in 'Elimination' as 'nothings' (p. 69). For discussion, see the entry on 'Nothing and Negation' in Inwood (1999a) and (1999b).

[37] Cf. again the well-known passage from Carroll (1982) cited in Ch. 7, n. 64.

received logical wisdom ('Elimination', pp. 71–72; see Heidegger (1993a), pp. 96ff.).)[38,39]

5. The Implications for Metaphysics

What are the implications of Carnap's views for metaphysics? As with some of our earlier protagonists, this question divides into two. What are the implications of his views for metaphysics on his own conception? What are their implications for metaphysics on mine?

(a) The Implications for Metaphysics on Carnap's Own Conception of Metaphysics

Carnap defines metaphysics as 'the field of alleged knowledge of the essence of things which transcends the realm of empirically founded, inductive science' ('Elimination', Supplementary Remarks, p. 80; cf. *Aufbau*, §182, and *Philosophy*, Lecture I, §2).[40] And his views immediately preclude such knowledge. There are only two kinds of knowledge for Carnap: *a priori* knowledge of analytic truths determined by the rules of some linguistic framework, and empirical knowledge of synthetic truths expressible within such a framework. Beyond these there is neither knowledge nor indeed sense-making. Metaphysics is a sham. It has to be exposed. And it has to be eliminated. (See 'Elimination', esp. §§5 and 6, and *Pseudoproblems*, esp. Pt II.)

[38] For a full and historically fascinating discussion of Carnap *vis à vis* Heidegger, see Friedman (2000). See also, for something much more compendious, Friedman (2002). For a sympathetic treatment of what Heidegger is doing that draws comparisons between Frege and Heidegger, see Witherspoon (2002). (There will be an indirect recurrence of these comparisons in Ch. 20, §§5 and 6, in connection with Derrida.)

[39] This material in Heidegger, to which incidentally we shall return in Ch. 18, §§6 and 7, may appear to be of just the sort that would likewise arouse opposition in Wittgenstein – in both his early and his later phases. In fact we find a curious but revealing open-mindedness on Wittgenstein's part. In notes dictated to Friedrich Waismann he says, 'If we want to deal with a proposition such as "The nothing nòths"..., then to do it justice we must ask ourselves: what did the author have in mind with this proposition? Where did he get this proposition from?' – and he then goes on to consider possible motivations for saying such a thing (Wittgenstein and Waismann (2003), pp. 69–75). Elsewhere in connection with Heidegger he comments, in a way that reminds us of his own ambivalent attitude towards nonsense, 'Man feels the urge to run up against the limits of language.... This ... is *ethics*.... [The] inclination, the running up against something, *indicates something*' (Wittgenstein (1979b), pp. 68–69, emphasis in original). For discussion, see Baker (2004d), esp. pp. 207ff. And see again Witherspoon (2002), mentioned in the previous note.

[40] Of the five philosophers whom Carnap singles out as adopting systems of metaphysics on this conception, two are from Part One of this book – Fichte and Hegel – and two are from Part Three – Bergson and Heidegger. (The fifth is Schelling.)

I said in the previous section that Carnap takes metaphysicians' non-sense often to involve violations of logical syntax. This can easily put us in mind of Wittgenstein. But there are two important reasons for resisting any simple assimilation of the two. The first and more basic reason is that, while the idea that metaphysicians misunderstand logical syntax is certainly Wittgensteinian, the idea that they violate it is not. Or at least, it is not early-Wittgensteinian. (It is arguably not later-Wittgensteinian, either.[41]) As I commented in §3(d), where Carnap sees logical syntax being violated, Wittgenstein sees only words being used without meaning. But second, and more significant in this context, Wittgenstein counts such deviant linguistic behaviour – the use of words without meaning due to a misunderstanding of logical syntax – as more or less a defining characteristic of metaphysics, whereas for Carnap it is but a symptom of metaphysics, as already defined. The essence of metaphysics, for Carnap, remains the underlying urge 'to discover and formulate a kind of knowledge which is not accessible to empirical science' ('Elimination', p. 76). He writes:

> Since metaphysics does not want to assert analytic propositions, nor to fall within the domain of empirical science, it is compelled to employ words for which no criteria of application are specified and which are therefore devoid of sense, or else to combine meaningful words in such a way that neither an analytic ... statement nor an empirical statement is produced.[42] In either case pseudo-statements are the inevitable product. ('Elimination', p. 76)

Sometimes, Carnap thinks, when we appear to be engaged in perfectly legitimate metaphysics, what is illusory is not that what we are engaged in is perfectly legitimate, but that what we are engaged in is metaphysics. Moreover, the source of the illusion in such cases is the same as in cases where the illusion is the other way round. It is a failure on our part properly to grasp the logical syntax of our own language. More specifically, it is a failure on our part to register that certain words are being used to draw attention, not to what they are standardly used to draw attention to, but to themselves. For instance, suppose I want to convey that the word 'rose' is a noun, or a 'thing'-word. Then one quite acceptable way for me to do this is to say, 'A rose is a thing.' Here it looks as though I am making a metaphysical claim about the essence of roses. Really, I am making an analytic claim

---

[41] See e.g. Wittgenstein (1967a), Pt I, §500. And see further Diamond (1991c), esp. pp. 106–107, which contain further pertinent quotations from the later work.

[42] The early Wittgenstein would demur at this point (even if he were prepared to equate the non-analytically true with the empirically true). He would invoke his sign/symbol distinction and, in line with the point that I made earlier in the main text, count the second of these kinds of nonsense as a species of the first. (See Ch. 9, §2.)

about how the word 'rose' functions.[43] (See *Philosophy*, p. 62.) In Carnap's own terminology, I am adopting *the material mode of speech*. Had I said, 'The word "rose" is a "thing"-word,' I would have been adopting the less misleading *formal mode of speech* (*Logical Syntax*, Pt V.A, and *Philosophy*, Lecture II, §8).[44]

The material mode of speech is in Carnap's view widespread. To take another of his own examples, if I say, 'This books treats of Africa,' I have adopted the material mode. Had I said, 'This book contains the word "Africa",' I would have adopted the formal mode.[45] The latter would have been less misleading because 'it is not a quality of Africa to be treated of in that book.... It is only a quality of the word "Africa" to be contained in the book' (*Philosophy*, p. 65). However, there is no suggestion in this case that I am engaged in metaphysics. That suggestion arises only when I am practising the kind of logical analysis that is characteristic of philosophy, that is when I am clarifying the workings of some linguistic framework. If I *then* use the material mode, I give the impression, not only that I am making claims about the entities that form the subject matter of the framework, but that I am concerned with what it is for them to *be* those entities. An especially striking variation on this theme is the case in which I present reasons for or against adopting a particular linguistic framework, that is for answering a particular external question in a certain way, and, by using the material mode, give the impression that I am addressing an internal question. Thus I might say, 'The indispensability of mathematics to physics is a good reason for believing that real numbers exist.'[46] The less misleading formal mode counterpart of this is: 'The indispensability of mathematics to physics is a good reason for adopting a linguistic framework that allows us to use the expression "real number" as we do.'[47] In a nutshell, then, while Carnap is at once the staunchest advocate of philosophy and the fiercest critic of metaphysics, he recognizes that, because of the material mode of speech, the one can all too easily appear as the other.[48]

---

[43] The claim is analytic because 'words', in this context, are being identified, not purely orthographically or phonemically, but in part by how they function. In Wittgensteinian terms they are being construed, not as signs, but as symbols (Ch. 9, §2).

[44] Wittgenstein notes a similar phenomenon in Wittgenstein (1969) where he writes, 'The characteristic of a metaphysical question [is] that we express an unclarity about the grammar of words in the *form* of a scientific question' (p. 35, emphasis in original). The difference is that Wittgenstein thinks that this already betokens confusion on our part and that what we are engaged in does (therefore) count as metaphysics.

[45] Here Carnap is presupposing a manifestly inadequate account of what it is for a book to treat of Africa, but we can prescind from that.

[46] See n. 64 of the previous chapter for the definition of a 'real' number.

[47] Cf. Wittgenstein (1967a), Pt I, §402.

[48] The distinction between the material mode and the formal mode looks as though it might serve as a 'bail-out' for some of our earlier protagonists. In particular, it looks as though

(b)　The Implications for Metaphysics on My Conception of Metaphysics

What are the implications of Carnap's views for metaphysics when metaphysics is conceived as the most general attempt to make sense of things? As in Wittgenstein's case (Ch. 9, §§2 and 8, and Ch. 10, §3) this question sub-divides according to what is meant by making sense of things. Its answers, too, are in line with those that it receives in Wittgenstein's case. If making sense of things is understood as arriving at truths about the world, then we can say that, by Carnap's lights, metaphysics is the most general of the natural sciences, and quite distinct from philosophy. If making sense of things is understood as providing for clarity in our thinking, which in Carnap's terms means clarifying linguistic frameworks that we use, or might use, then we can say that by Carnap's lights metaphysics is philosophy of the most general kind – where the generality in question is the generality of the concepts involved in the frameworks being clarified. On this second account the only truths that it is the prerogative of metaphysicians to assert are analytic truths determined by the rules of some framework. Metaphysicians are not in the business of discovering truths about the world. They are in the

---

it might serve to show that Frege had no need to admit the nonsensicality of his apparent talk about the *Bedeutungen* of predicates (Ch. 8, §7) nor the early Wittgenstein the nonsensicality of his apparent talk about internal properties (Ch. 9, §5). In each case cannot the talk in question be exposed as misleading talk in the material mode and its true sense thereby be revealed, in Frege's case by showing that it is really talk about predicates themselves and in Wittgenstein's case by showing that it is really talk about the properties of associated symbols? In Wittgenstein's case, Carnap thinks, it can (*Logical Syntax*, esp. pp. 282–283 and 295–296). But, as he makes clear, this is scarcely a bail-out for Wittgenstein, who, given the role played in his thinking by the nonsensicality of the remarks in question, could not readily have accommodated the suggestion that they in fact made sense. There is in any case the point that I made in Ch. 9, n. 27, that some of Frege's and Wittgenstein's problems are replicated in talk about linguistic items.

Elsewhere Carnap invokes his distinction in further departures from his two predecessors. Thus in *Philosophy* he considers the identity statement that Frege made famous: 'The evening star and the morning star are the same thing.' And he defends the view which Frege himself originally held and subsequently retracted, that this is really a statement about the two names involved, misleadingly expressed in the material mode (p. 66; and see above, Ch. 8, §4, esp. n. 39). Again, in *Logical Syntax* he lists some sentences from Wittgenstein's *Tractatus* which he takes to be in the material mode and gives their formal mode translations – notably, 'The world is the totality of facts, not of things' (Wittgenstein (1961), 1.1), which he translates as, 'Science is a system of sentences, not of names' (p. 303). But he does so as a prelude to urging that Wittgenstein himself is not always in command of his own language and that other sentences in his book, including many of those in the late 6s that purport to deal with 'what is higher', are likewise in the material mode – to whatever extent they are in any proper mode at all – though they lack any satisfactory translation. (Not, of course, that Wittgenstein need disagree.)

business of supplying suitably lucid frameworks from which to select the best for couching truths about the world that have already been discovered, or that may yet be discovered.

One interesting feature of this second account is that it allows for clear Carnapian answers to the three questions that I posed in §6 of the Introduction:

- (the Transcendence Question) there is no scope for metaphysicians to make sense of what is transcendent, if what is transcendent means what transcends sense experience, for there is no such sense to be made
- (the Creativity Question) metaphysics is an inherently creative enterprise

and, most significantly perhaps, redressing what I take to be the principal failing of the later Wittgenstein (see Ch. 10, §6, and §3(e)),

- (the Novelty Question) metaphysicians can, and sometimes should, make sense of things in ways that are radically new.[49]

There is also an important account that is intermediate between the two just considered. On this intermediate account, just as on the second, metaphysicians are in the business of supplying suitably lucid frameworks from which to select the best for couching truths about the world. *But they are also in the business of making the selection.* This is something they must do in the light of our various purposes and in the light of whatever truths about the world have already been discovered. In this respect the intermediate account is like the first: it gives metaphysicians some responsibility for telling the eventual story about what the world is like, albeit responsibility that they can discharge without dirtying their hands. The full significance of this intermediate account will become apparent at the very end of the chapter.

(c)   Carnap on Alternative Conceptions of Metaphysics

I have distinguished between where Carnap's views leave metaphysics on his own conception and where they leave it on mine. But I do not mean to suggest that Carnap is oblivious to the possibility of alternative conceptions to his own; nor indeed that he is oblivious to the possibility of alternative conceptions to his own that may lead to a sympathetic reassessment of the very material that, on his own conception, he is forced to decry. Here we do well to recall the point that I emphasized in §1: for a statement to lack what logical positivists call 'literal' meaning, in other words for it to fail to express a

---

[49] This is significant for me in that it is the first point in this narrative at which we find the triad of answers that I myself would give. For a somewhat more conservative approach to the Novelty Question, from a broadly similar point of view, see Ayer (1969).

truth or a falsehood, is by no means for it to lack all kinds of meaning. Some extremely significant possibilities are left open: witness the fact that logical positivists deny literal meaning to any statement of commendation or condemnation, whether ethical, aesthetic, or of any other kind; to any statement that serves as an optative, or a supplication, or a curse; to any statement of joy, wonder, or horror at the beauty and ravages of creation; and to countless other statements besides.[50] What if one of the thinkers under attack from Carnap insists that his metaphysics is not an attempt to discover and state transcendent truths about the essence of things; that it is not an attempt to discover and state *truths* at all; that it is an attempt, rather, to convey some of these other kinds of meaning, using statements that belong to some of these other classes; and that it is therefore best viewed, not as a scientific exercise, but as an artistic exercise?[51]

Carnap has plenty to say in response to such a suggestion. (See e.g. *Philosophy*, Lecture I, §5, and 'Elimination', §7.) But the gist of his response is gratifyingly straightforward and uncompromising. The metaphysical material that he has in his sights may well, he concedes, be an attempt to convey some of these other kinds of meaning; but if it is, then it is still subject to two serious criticisms. First, it is a *dissembling* attempt: it presents itself as what it is not, a system of logically interrelated truth-evaluable statements. Second, and much more damning, it is a *very poor* attempt: it is put to shame by other, more overtly artistic achievements. 'Metaphysicians,' Carnap writes with withering sarcasm, 'are musicians without musical ability' ('Elimination', p. 80).

6. Tu Quoque?

A common objection to logical positivism is that it cannot survive its own critique. Like Hume, Kant, and the early Wittgenstein, logical positivists seem to be under threat when they apply their own principles to their own espousal of them. Consider, in particular, the cardinal principle that a

---

[50] In Ch. 1, §3, I referred to what Simon Blackburn calls 'quasi-realism'. A quasi-realist recognizes the same variety of functions that statements can serve but differs from a logical positivist in holding that a statement can serve one of these functions and still express a truth or a falsehood: see Blackburn (1984), Ch. 5, §6, and Ch. 6, and Blackburn (1993a). (Cf. also n. 21 of the previous chapter.) I mention this because it is important to appreciate that the logical positivist account of truth and falsity is by no means uncontentious: see further the next section.

[51] Ironically, if my interpretation of Wittgenstein's *Tractatus* is correct (Ch. 9, §§6–8), then this question is especially pertinent to that work. I say 'ironically', because the *Tractatus* is far from being one of Carnap's principal targets. On the contrary, it is a work he greatly admires, though not on the grounds that this question suggests make it admirable: see e.g. *Logical Syntax*, p. 282. (And see again n. 26.)

statement has literal meaning if and only if either it or its negation expresses either an empirical truth or an analytic truth. Let us follow A.J. Ayer in calling this 'the verification principle' (Ayer (1992), p. 149).[52] What is the status of the verification principle itself? Does it express an empirical truth? Or does it express an analytic truth? Or does it not express a truth at all? All three options appear unattractive: the first because it seems plainly inadequate to the force of the principle, in particular by casting it as a mere contingency; the second because it suggests that there is nothing more to the principle than how certain words are used; and the third because it means that, unless the principle expresses a falsehood, it lacks any literal meaning, which, despite the many other kinds of meaning that logical positivists acknowledge, seems intolerable.

I shall argue in this section that there is indeed an embarrassment for logical positivists here – or rather, hereabouts. For it is not quite where the common objection locates it. And it is of an altogether subtler kind than the common objection would lead us to suppose.

The first thing to appreciate is that all three options can actually be made to look attractive. All three have at some time been espoused by philosophers of a broadly positivist persuasion. If logical positivists do experience any embarrassment here, then, initially at least, it is liable to be felt as an embarrassment of riches.

Let us call the three options, respectively, the 'empirical' option, the 'analytic' option, and the 'no-truth' option. And let us first consider the empirical option. That is perhaps, at first blush, the least appealing of the three. But it is noteworthy that, if we allow ourselves the anachronism of saying where Hume stood on this issue, then this is the option he espoused. In Hume's view, it was a matter of fact, confirmed by experience, that all our ideas are composed of simple ideas copied from previous impressions. Had that not been the case, then we could (for instance) have had, just as Descartes thought we did have, an innate idea of God, surpassing all our impressions in such a way as to furnish us with the knowledge that God exists, a truth that would have qualified neither as a relation of ideas nor as a matter of fact in Hume's terms.

In the next chapter we shall see Quine trying to distil from logical positivism the basic empiricism in which he takes its true worth to lie. And although this will involve his challenging the very terms of the current dispute, it is noteworthy, again, that he will count the empiricism with which he is left as itself an empirical truth. (See §3 of the next chapter.)

---

[52] Ayer also sometimes calls it 'the principle of verification' (see e.g. ibid.). In Ayer (1971), p. 7, he gives a different formulation of the principle, and, as I observed in n. 5, goes on to discuss some complications that these formulations glide over; but the differences between the formulations, and for that matter the complications, are for current purposes immaterial.

It is the other two options, however, that have found greatest favour with logical positivists. On the analytic option, the verification principle expresses a truth in virtue of how those who are party to this dispute use the relevant words. The worry about this is that it makes the principle trivial. But does it? In any troublesome sense? After all, logical positivists cast the whole of pure mathematics as analytic. There is room, given our psychological limitations, for a kind of substantiveness in such matters – as even Hume knew. The analytic option is certainly defensible. It is in fact Carnap's view (see *Philosophy*, Lecture I, §7, and Lectures II and III passim).

But Carnap also expressly considers the no-truth option. Or rather, he considers one version of the no-truth option, which is what he (wrongly) thinks we find in Wittgenstein's *Tractatus*.[53] This is to regard the verification principle as being of a piece with the metaphysical nonsense that it is supposed to help us banish, serving its purpose in some curiously indirect, self-abnegating way. Carnap sees no hope for such a view (*Logical Syntax*, pp. 283–284, and *Philosophy*, pp. 37–38).

He has not however considered the most compelling form of the no-truth option. The most compelling form of the no-truth option is something much less exotic: to regard the principle as a prescriptive definition of the expression 'literal meaning'. (This is not so different from Carnap's own view, of course, because such a definition can be regarded as part of a linguistic framework that straightway allows for the expression of analytic truths in accord with it.) Those who espouse this option will point to the importance of prescriptive definitions in other sciences, as a way of allaying any concern that such a thing cannot be of any scientific interest. This is the option that Carl Hempel espouses (Hempel (1959), p. 125). It is also the option that A.J. Ayer espouses. Admittedly, in *Language, Truth and Logic* Ayer is not clear about this. Though he calls the principle a 'definition', he also insists that 'it is not supposed to be arbitrary' (Ayer (1971), pp. 20–21). Later, however, in response to a direct challenge to say what status he takes the principle to have, he says that he was never inclined to regard the principle either as empirical *or* as analytic, then continues:

> Happily not everything that the verification principle failed to license was cast by me on the pyre of metaphysics. In my treatment of ethics, I made provision for prescriptive statements.... Accordingly, in ... *Language, Truth and Logic*, I treated the verification principle as a prescriptive definition. (Ayer (1992), p. 149)

We shall return shortly to some discomfort that Ayer nevertheless feels with this. But notice first that the choice between the no-truth option and the analytic option can be cast in terms of the Limit Argument which appeared

---

[53] He is wrong about this because the *Tractatus* is not concerned with the verification principle at all: see §3(d), and see again Ch. 9, n. 20.

in Chapter 5, §8. That argument purported to reveal an incoherence in the project of drawing a limit (in the sense of a limitation) to what we can make sense of – which is, in effect, the logical positivists' project.[54] We have already seen that, on a suitably thick conception of sense-making, the Limit Argument can be resisted. Such a conception brings both its premises, the Limit-Drawing Principle and the Division Principle, into question. Now the logical positivists have, in effect, a thick conception of sense-making, whereby making sense of something involves producing statements about it which have literal meaning and which either express empirically know-able truths about that thing or express analytic truths that make provision for such knowledge. In these terms, those who espouse the no-truth option could say that they have drawn a limit to what we can make sense of with-out making sense of that limit, *contra* the Limit-Drawing Principle; while those who espouse the analytic option could say that they have made sense of a limit to what we can make sense of without making sense of anything on its 'far' side, *contra* the Division Principle.

Logical positivists appear to have considerable room for manoeuvre then. So why Ayer's discomfort? Well, if the verification principle is a prescrip-tive definition, there is still the question of why the prescription should be obeyed. 'I avoided this awkward question,' Ayer says, 'by defying my critics to come up with anything better' (Ayer (1992), p. 149). Very well; but why is the question awkward? After all, insofar as it is an invitation to expound on the significance of the *definiens*, or on the work that might be done by the *definiendum*, there is plenty that Ayer can say in response to it. For instance, he can advert to some of the important differences that there are between matters that can be settled by appeal to some combination of sense experi-ence and conceptual analysis and matters that cannot be settled in that way.

Nonetheless, the question is awkward. And what makes it awkward is something that Michael Dummett forcefully argues in the essay to which Ayer is replying when he makes these remarks: namely, that no answer he gives will be fully satisfactory unless and until it is placed in the context of some general philosophical account of the different ways in which different matters can be settled and of what turns on these differences, an account that is of just the same character as what he (Ayer) wants to cast on the pyre of metaphysics (Dummett (1992), pp. 133–134).[55] Consider: as a logical pos-itivist, Ayer not only distinguishes between matters that can be settled by appeal to some combination of sense experience and conceptual analysis and matters that cannot be settled in that way; he also insists that matters of the latter kind, which is to say matters that are neither matters of empirical truth nor matters of analytic truth, *are not matters of truth at all*. In particular, he

---

[54] That Carnap is concerned with a *limitation* to what we can make sense of, not (just) with its essence, is interestingly highlighted in 'Elimination', pp. 72–73.

[55] Ayer partially concedes this point in Ayer (1992), p. 150.

insists that no evaluative matter is a matter of truth. But this requires some defence.[56] And the defence must be a contribution to what, on any remotely orthodox conception of metaphysics, counts as the metaphysics of value. The logical positivist must enter into debate with Spinoza (Ch. 2, §3), with Leibniz (Ch. 3, §1), with Hume (Ch. 4, §5), with Kant (Ch. 5, §§7 and 9), with Fichte (Ch. 6, §4), with Hegel (Ch. 8, passim), and with the early Wittgenstein (Ch. 9, §8)[57] – debate of just the kind that he is trying to dismiss as spurious. He must try to give an account of value and its place in the world.

To be sure, this enterprise is to some extent an attempt to arrive at what, in the logical positivist's own terms, counts as analytic truth of the most general kind, or at what, specifically in Carnap's terms, counts as clarity of linguistic frameworks of the most general kind. But it is not just that. Recall that in §5(b) I mentioned one of the activities which, even by Carnap's lights, might reasonably attract the label 'metaphysics': clarifying linguistic frameworks of the most general kind *and deciding which to adopt.* The enterprise identified above must include some such decision-making. It cannot be confined to (theoretical) reflection on the relations between different conceptions of evaluation and different conceptions of truth and falsity. It must include (practical) reflection on which of these conceptions are best suited to our various purposes.

Whatever label attaches to the activity of clarifying linguistic frameworks of the most general kind and deciding which to adopt, decisions of that sort must sooner or later be taken. We must sooner or later reflect, not only on how we make maximally general sense of things, but on how *to* make maximally general sense of things.[58] We must consider whether our current sense-making is all that we might have expected it to be; whether such and such alternatives might work better for us; how well we could cope with them; at what cost; with what gain. And in making our decisions – in putting our reflections into practice – we are neither trading in analytic truths nor trading in empirical truths. We are not trading in truths at all. We are, however, practising something at least akin to traditional metaphysics, something that certainly counts as metaphysics on my conception. It seems to me, then, that Carnap and the other logical positivists, like Hume before them, do not so much eliminate metaphysics as put us in mind of its importance.

---

[56] Quasi-realists, among others, disagree: see above, n. 50. For a sample of the debate, see Hooker (1996).

[57] This is not to mention all those from Part Three of my book with whom he must enter into debate.

[58] This is interestingly reminiscent of the Fichtean idea that metaphysics is grounded in a practical choice that we are forced to make between different systems of thought (Ch. 6, §2).

CHAPTER 12

Quine

The *Ne Plus Ultra* of Naturalism

1. Introduction

From Carnap we proceed naturally to Quine. We can get a good sense of the extraordinarily high esteem in which Quine held Carnap from the homage to Carnap that Quine delivered at a memorial meeting shortly after Carnap's death. In that homage Quine said:

> Carnap is a towering figure. I see him as the dominant figure in philosophy from the 1930s onwards.... Some philosophers would assign this role rather to Wittgenstein; but many see the scene as I do. ('Carnap', p. 40[1])

Much of Quine's own work can be seen as a direct response to Carnap's. There were parts that he thoroughly espoused and parts that he just as thoroughly opposed, but all of it had a deep and lasting influence on his philosophical thinking.

W.V. Quine (1908–2000) had, to an extent that I think is unrivalled in the analytic tradition, a profound synoptic vision. And an integral part of

---

[1] Throughout this chapter I use the following abbreviations for Quine's works: 'A Constructive Nominalism' for Goodman and Quine (1947); 'Austin' for Quine (1981d); 'Carnap' for Quine (1966a); 'Empirical Content' for Quine (1981b); 'Epistemology Naturalized' for Quine (1969b); 'Equivalent Systems' for Quine (2008b); 'Existence' for Quine (1969c); 'Facts' for Quine (2008c); 'Five Milestones' for Quine (1981c); *From Stimulus to Science* for Quine (1995a); 'Gibson' for Quine (1986a); 'Goodman' for Quine (1981e); 'Mathematization' for Quine (1981f); 'Meaning' for Quine (1961c); 'Naturalism' for Quine (2008f); 'Natural Kinds' for Quine (1969d); 'Ontological Relativity' for Quine (1969a); 'On What There Is' for Quine (1961a); *Philosophy of Logic* for Quine (1970); *Pursuit of Truth* for Quine (1992); 'Putnam' for Quine (1986b); 'Reactions' for Quine (1995b); 'Responses' for Quine (1981g); *Roots of Reference* for Quine (1974); 'Skolimowski' for Quine (1986c); 'Stroud' for Quine (1990); 'Structure' for Quine (2008e); 'Translation' for Quine (2008a); 'Translation Again' for Quine (2008d); 'Things' for Quine (1981a); 'Two Dogmas' for Quine (1961b); 'Universals', for Quine (1961e); 'Vuillemin' for Quine (1986d); *Web of Belief* for Quine and Ullian (1978); and *Word and Object* for Quine (1960).

302

that vision was the empiricism that had likewise been an integral part of Carnap's logical positivism. It is here in fact that we find the greatest continuity between the two thinkers. But while Quine accepted the empiricism itself, he rejected the various crucial modifications that it had undergone in Carnap's hands. To understand the role that it played in his own thinking we must first place it in the context of two other 'isms' that he famously embraced: naturalism and physicalism.

2.   Quine: Empiricist, Naturalist, Physicalist

In this section I shall comment on each of the three 'isms' in turn. In the next section I shall relate them to one another.[2]

(a)   Quine's Empiricism

Quine's empiricism, like Carnap's, and indeed like Hume's, has both an epistemic element and, more radically, a semantic element. Quine himself characterizes these two elements as follows:

> One is that whatever evidence there is for science is sensory evidence. The other ... is that all inculcations of meanings of words must rest ultimately on sensory evidence. ('Epistemology Naturalized', p. 75, emphasis removed)

In describing the semantic element as the more radical, I am simply rehearsing a point that I made in Chapter 4, §1: if there are empiricist reasons for denying the very meaningfulness of a statement, that is if there are empiricist reasons for denying that the statement expresses any belief at all,[3] then the question whether the belief that it expresses merits the title of knowledge, or whether it is fit to be included in science,[4] does not so much as arise. It does not follow, however, that the epistemic element is a simple corollary of the semantic element. Suppose we agree that a statement has to stand in some specified relation to sense experience in order to count as meaningful. It remains an open question in what further relation it has to stand to sense experience, if indeed it has to stand in any, in order to express an item of knowledge, or in order to be worthy of being added to a scientific theory.

---

[2] Much of the material in these two sections, and through to §7, derives from Moore (2009). I am grateful to the editors and publisher of the volume in which that essay appears for permission to make use of this material.

[3] Here I am construing meaning narrowly, to include only what the logical positivists called 'literal' meaning (see §1 of the previous chapter). But there are in any case Quinean reasons for doubting that there is meaning of any other kind: see esp. n. 37.

[4] See *Web of Belief*, p. 3, for Quine's broad conception of science.

I think this goes some way towards explaining a tendency on Quine's part to treat the semantic element in his empiricism as the more evident of the two, or better perhaps as the less negotiable of the two. In fact it is Quine's view that the semantic element in his empiricism is dictated by the very nature of language. He writes:

> Language is socially inculcated and controlled; the inculcation and control turn strictly on the keying of sentences to shared stimulation.... Surely one has no choice but to be an empiricist so far as one's theory of linguistic meaning is concerned. ('Epistemology Naturalized', p. 81; cf. *Pursuit of Truth*, pp. 37–38)

Later in this section we shall see the somewhat more guarded claim that he makes on behalf of the epistemic element in his empiricism. Be that as it may, both elements can usefully be captured in the deliberately loose formula that I used in Chapter 4 to capture Hume's empiricism:

all sense-making derives from sense experience.

(b)   Quine's Naturalism

Quine's naturalism likewise aligns him with Hume, and to a lesser extent with Spinoza. It sets him apart from Fichte,[5] and above all from Descartes. It is a variation on Hume's view that philosophy is nothing unless it is of a piece with the established empirical sciences, taking its place alongside physics, astronomy, botany, and the rest. (More specifically, Hume took philosophy to be an experimental science of human nature.) Descartes assigned to philosophy – in its guise as metaphysics – a very different role: to provide empirical science, including what would nowadays be called natural science, with *foundations*, in the form of a once-for-all *a priori* vindication. That is precisely what Quine abjures. Quine's naturalism consists in the conviction that natural science neither needs nor admits of any such vindication; that there is no higher authority, concerning the general character of reality, than what in fact serves as our authority concerning its general character, which is to say: natural science. This means, in particular, that questions about the authority of science are themselves scientific questions.[6] They are questions about 'how we, physical denizens of the physical world, can have projected our scientific theory of that whole world from our meagre contacts

---

[5] It is a direct descendant of the position that Fichte rejected in the primordial choice whereby he inaugurated his philosophy (Ch. 6, §2). This is one of the reasons why I dubbed that position too 'naturalism'. But they are not the same position: my usage here is not meant to be a mere resumption of my earlier usage.

[6] To the extent that they are legitimate questions at all.

with it: from the mere impacts of rays and particles on our surfaces and a few odds and ends such as the strain of walking uphill' (*From Stimulus to Science*, p. 16). Such questions are to be answered by appeal to the various relevant branches of science, as it may be optics or neurophysiology. In sum, 'it is within science itself, and not in some prior philosophy, that reality is to be identified and described' ('Things', p. 21).[7] In terms conducive to my project:

> the way to make sense of things is the way of (natural) science.[8]

(c) Quine's Physicalism

Quine's physicalism is the view that there are no facts, not even facts about our thoughts and experiences, that are not ultimately physical facts, that is facts about how things are physically. Among the natural sciences, which are privileged by Quine's naturalism, this view further privileges physics. But it is important to be clear about how exactly. Here is Quine's own, characteristically elegant way of putting the matter:

> Why ... this special deference to [physics]? This is a good question, and part of its merit is that it admits of a good answer. The answer is not that everything worth saying can be translated into the technical vocabulary of physics; not even that all good science can be translated into that vocabulary. The answer is rather this: nothing happens in the world, not the flutter of an eyelid, not the flicker of a thought, without some redistribution of microphysical states. ('Goodman', p. 18)[9]

Notice that there are really two versions of Quine's physicalism, depending on whether it is defined in terms of current physics or in terms of some ideal physics. If it is defined in terms of *current* physics, then it is a hypothesis that is liable to rejection in the face of evidence that challenges current physics itself. Quine does sometimes talk in this way. It is in this vein that he says, 'The science game is not committed to the physical' (*Pursuit of Truth*, p. 20). If, on the other hand, his physicalism is defined in terms of an *ideal* physics, then it is more of an evidence-insensitive methodological principle.

---

[7] For amplification, see 'Naturalism'.

[8] It is worth noting that the term 'naturalism' has many uses in contemporary analytic philosophy. On one other use that should be mentioned, it stands for the view that, while the scientific way to make sense of things may not be the only way to do so, there is nevertheless nothing that *cannot* be made sense of in that way. This is what David Papineau calls 'ontological naturalism'; Quine's view is more or less what Papineau calls 'methodological naturalism': see Papineau (2009), p. 1.

[9] For amplification, see 'Facts'.

And Quine sometimes talks in *this* way. It is in this vein that he says, 'If the physicalist suspected there was any event that did not consist in a redistribution of the elementary states of his physical theory, he would seek a way of supplementing his theory. Full coverage in this sense is the very business of physics, and only of physics' ('Goodman', p. 98).[10] When I need to distinguish I shall call the two versions 'provisional physicalism' and 'regulative physicalism', respectively. Often, however, this distinction does not matter. For there is no real rationale for provisional physicalism save regulative physicalism; and regulative physicalism, for its part, must for the time being issue in provisional physicalism, since current physics is, for the time being, our best guide as to what an ideal physics would look like. So I shall often talk indiscriminately just of physicalism.

Similarly, be it noted, in the case of naturalism. We can distinguish between a provisional and a regulative version of that too – though in the account above, where nothing hung on this, I played fast and loose with any such distinction, conflating considerations about where natural scientists are with considerations about where they aspire to be.

With this caveat we can define physicalism as follows, invoking a third formula that subserves my project. Where naturalism is the view that the way to make sense of things is the way of (natural) science, physicalism is the view that

> *the way to make the most fundamental sense of things is the way of physics.*[11]

3.   Relations Between Quine's Empiricism, Naturalism, and Physicalism

The relation between Quine's naturalism and his physicalism is comparatively straightforward. The latter is an application-cum-embellishment

---

[10] Cf. Hookway (1988), Ch. 4, §5, and Hylton (2007), pp. 314ff. (though I think that Peter Hylton underestimates how vulnerable to new evidence the first of these versions of physicalism is). In 'Stroud', p. 334, Quine insists that how we use the word 'physical' is not itself of any importance.

[11] Note that Carnap too eventually embraced a version of physicalism. But it was a more radical version than Quine's, inasmuch as it involved the claim from which Quine explicitly distances himself in the first quotation from 'Goodman' in the main text above: that 'every sentence of any branch of scientific language … can … be translated into the physical language without changing its content' (Carnap (1935), p. 89). For Carnap, this meant that one particular linguistic framework in science was powerful enough to do the work of any other, and he therefore appropriated that framework. Even so, in line with his general conception of frameworks, he claimed no *truth* on behalf of his appropriation. In the next section we shall see Quine recoiling from this conception. (Quine thinks that, when Carnap eventually adopted the physicalist stance that he did, he showed

of the former, having to do with the special role played by one particular branch of science. Neither strictly entails the other, though they do go naturally together.

It is more interesting, and more difficult, to consider how the two of them relate to his empiricism. This issue ramifies. For concerning his empiricism, there is the epistemic/semantic distinction to be taken into account. And concerning both his naturalism and his physicalism, there is the provisional/regulative distinction to be taken into account. The most interesting questions for our purposes, however, all have to do with the relation between the *epistemic* element in his empiricism, which concerns the scientific credentials of any given belief, and the *provisional* versions of his naturalism and his physicalism, which concern those beliefs whose scientific credentials we currently take to be the best, what I shall henceforth call 'our current beliefs'. It is on these questions that I shall therefore focus.

The first point to note is that the epistemic element in his empiricism does not itself privilege our current beliefs. It entails that, provided our current beliefs stand in a suitable relation to sense experience, they are warranted. But it does not entail that they do stand in that relation to sense experience. And, just as significantly, it does not entail that other, incompatible beliefs do not.[12]

Now unless things have gone badly, our current beliefs are in fact warranted. They represent the best that we have been able to do so far in trying, on the strength of our sense experience, to determine the general character of reality. But even if things have gone well, indeed as well as they could have, there will be incompatible beliefs that are no less warranted. Our account of the general character of reality has not been *dictated* to us. Sense experience does not rule out accounts that are in outright conflict with that account. For instance, it does not rule out accounts whereby physical space has a geometry that is different from that which we take it to have, with corresponding implications concerning the shrinking and stretching of bodies as they move about. Indeed it does not rule out accounts whereby reality is not fundamentally physical at all, but fundamentally mental.[13] The natural sciences in general, and physics in particular, are, as Quine says, *underdetermined* by the evidence. (See e.g. 'Equivalent Systems' and *Pursuit of Truth*, §§41–43.)

Nor is this just a question of the current evidence. Quine is prepared to entertain the extreme possibility of two accounts of the general character of

---

himself to be unwittingly sensitive to the *error* of his earlier stance: see *From Stimulus to Science*, p. 15.)

[12] I understand warrant in such a way that it falls short of an absolute guarantee of truth.

[13] See the next section for why Quine cannot avail himself of an appeal to Carnapian linguistic frameworks to show that there is not in fact any incompatibility here.

reality that are 'empirically equivalent', that is to say compatible with all the same *possible* evidence, yet still incompatible with each other ('Translation', pp. 209–210, and *Pursuit of Truth*, p. 96).[14]

So neither sense experience itself nor the claim that our current beliefs need to be suitably related to sense experience to merit the store that we set by them ensures that our route to those beliefs constitutes 'the' way to make sense of things, or 'the' way to make the most fundamental sense of things. We can summarize this part of the discussion by saying that the epistemic element in Quine's empiricism does not secure the status for our current beliefs that either the provisional version of his naturalism or the provisional version of his physicalism accords them. In particular, his (epistemic) empiricism does not yield his (provisional) naturalism.

It is rather the reverse. His (provisional) naturalism, given what our current beliefs actually are, yields his (epistemic) empiricism. Quine writes:

> It is a finding of natural science itself, however fallible, that our information about the world comes only through impacts on our sensory receptors.... Even telepathy and clairvoyance are scientific options, however moribund. It would take some extraordinary evidence to enliven them, but, if that were to happen, then empiricism itself ... would go by the board. (*Pursuit of Truth*, pp. 19–21)

Empiricism is itself an empirically testable hypothesis, then, a hypothesis which our current beliefs happen to support.[15] It is not part of some preliminary armchair methodology serving to justify the way in which we have arrived at those beliefs. (How could it be? That is just what naturalism precludes.)

This gives us our first insight into what is arguably the single most important feature of Quine's entire philosophy: *that its real driving force is his naturalism.* Everything else flows from that; everything else must be understood in terms of that; everything else needs to accommodate that. Quine's naturalism, we could say, is the consummation of all naturalisms.

There is a striking illustration of this in an issue that he addresses in connection with his views about underdetermination.[16] Quine imagines two accounts of the general character of reality that are empirically

---

[14] This means that, although the claim of underdetermination in the main text above was intended as a claim about the natural sciences in their current state, it would apply equally to the natural sciences in an ideal state.

[15] As I commented in §6 of the previous chapter, this is in line with Hume.

[16] The next two paragraphs draw on Moore (2007a), pp. 29ff. I am grateful to the editor and publisher of the volume in which that essay appears for permission to make use of the material cited.

equivalent but not, as in the extreme case alluded to above, incompatible; rather, compatible but expressed in irreducibly different terms.[17] The issue is what to say, if one of these accounts is ours, about the other – assuming the other 'is as neat and natural as our own' (*Pursuit of Truth*, p. 99).[18] Quine distinguishes two attitudes that we can take. The *sectarian* attitude, as he calls it, is to repudiate the alien terms and, despite the fact that the rival account could have served just as well as our own in helping us to make sense of things, to regard it as nonsense. The *ecumenical* attitude is to acknowledge the alien terms and to regard the rival account as true ('Gibson', pp. 156–157, and *Pursuit of Truth*, §42[19]). Quine has vacillated over the years between these alternatives. And the reason he has vacillated is that his naturalism, which privileges our own account, inclines him to sectarianism, while his empiricism, which cannot see past the empirical equivalence of the two accounts, inclines him towards ecumenism.[20] In the end his naturalism has won out: he has eventually settled for sectarianism ('Gibson', p. 157, and *Pursuit of Truth*, p. 100).[21] And that is just as it should be. His naturalism does see beyond the empirical equivalence of the two accounts: it privileges our own *as* our own. Those are the only terms, for Quine, in which the issue *can* be settled. (His sectarianism also accords better with what he is forced to say about the extreme possibility to which we have seen him accede, the possibility in which an account that is empirically equivalent to ours is also incompatible with it. In such a case, Quine is forced to say, not only must we *not* regard the rival account as true,

---

[17] Part of his interest in this less extreme case is that he thinks that the extreme case can be reduced to it, by reconstruing certain key terms that appear in the two incompatible accounts as pairs of distinct homonyms. Thus it may be that in one account 'shrinking' and 'stretching' mean one thing, while in the other account they mean something quite different: see *Pursuit of Truth*, pp. 97–98.

[18] What do neatness and naturalness have to do with anything? Quine sees these as criteria of truth. This is a further expression of his naturalism: it is part of the scientific way of making sense of things so to see them.

[19] Note that on p. 156 of the former he characterizes sectarianism as the view that the rival account is false rather than nonsense. But that is an aberration. It is subverted on the very next page.

[20] For an example of a swing to sectarianism, see 'Things', pp. 21–22. For an example of a swing to ecumenism, see the first edition of 'Empirical Content', p. 29. (This is altered in later editions. The earlier version is quoted in Gibson (1986), p. 153, n. 2. This is the essay that prompted the alteration: see 'Gibson'.)

Note: when I say that Quine's empiricism inclines him to ecumenism, it is important to remember that I am talking here about the epistemic element in his empiricism. The semantic element exerts pressure in the other direction; see 'Gibson', p. 157.

[21] Hence the alteration referred to in parentheses in the previous note. Cf. Rorty (1991), §2.

we must, on pain of surrendering our own account, regard it as false (cf. 'Equivalent Systems', p. 242).[22])

It is instructive, however, that this issue exercises him at all. A hard-core naturalist, one might think, should never have felt the tug of ecumenism in the first place. Yet Quine certainly does. He feels it from the outset; and he continues to feel it even once he has settled against ecumenism. There is, he senses, an invidiousness in regarding one account as true and another as nonsense even though there is no cosmically telling between them and even though it is nothing but a kind of historical accident that one of them has our allegiance rather than the other. So he salves his conscience by reminding us that we can change our allegiance. The sectarian, he tells us,

> is as free as the ecumenist to oscillate between the two [accounts].... In his sectarian way he does deem the one [account] true and the alien terms of the other meaningless, but only so long as he is entertaining the one [account] rather than the other. He can readily shift the shoe to the other foot. (*Pursuit of Truth*, p. 100)

This is not to concede, along with the ecumenist, that both accounts should be regarded as true. It is not even to concede that both accounts *can* be regarded as true. But it *is* to concede that *each* account can be regarded as true. And, as Quine himself admits, to concede this is but one terminological step away from conceding ecumenism. After all, sectarians and ecumenists alike are agreed that, whichever account has our allegiance, we are free to pay the other account every compliment we can short of giving it too our allegiance. The question whether this includes dignifying the other account with the label 'true' seems to 'simmer down, bathetically, to a question of words' (*Pursuit of Truth*, pp. 100–101).[23]

Here, I suggest, we see a dim recognition on Quine's part of something for which I shall argue in §8: that, contrary to the letter of the loose formulation of his naturalism that I ventured in the previous section, and contrary to the spirit of any decent formulation of it, the way of science is not 'the' way to make sense of things, because, in particular, it is not the way to make sense of making sense of things. His naturalism does not serve him well in making sense of his naturalism – despite all that he claims on behalf of it. More of this later.

---

[22] This seems to be controverted in 'Things', p. 22, where he seems to suggest that an account that is compatible with all the evidence cannot be false. But he is there talking about an account that we have accepted, an account that counts as *our* account. (I am indebted here to Gary Kemp.)

[23] There are connections between this question and the question how far truth is 'immanent' or 'transcendent' in various senses of those words that Quine identifies; see Davidson (2005b) and (2005c), and 'Reactions', §IV. For discussion of Quine's treatment of the main issue, see Bergström (2004) and Hylton (2007), pp. 320–323.

Meanwhile, we should consider what motivates his naturalism, this driving force in his philosophy. Can it be derived from other, yet more basic 'isms' that he embraces? Not really.[24] To an extent Quine is impressed by the sheer success that the natural sciences have enjoyed, indeed the quite *spectacular* success that they have enjoyed, when it comes to predicting the future and thereby controlling and modifying the environment. Here he shows his affinity to the American pragmatist tradition that extends back to Peirce, James, and Dewey and whose very defining feature might be said to be the view that success is the yardstick for assessing different ways of making sense of things.[25] But whatever the success of the natural sciences, Quine does not think that there is any serious alternative to naturalism.[26] Given that the natural sciences, in their current form, embody our best efforts hitherto to determine the general character of reality, they *must* be our point of departure for any further enquiry into its general character, including any further enquiry that has our own methods and principles of enquiry as part of its focus. They must be our point of *departure*: they may not be our destination. In a hundred years' time we may look back on our current beliefs and see them as fundamentally mistaken. But if so, then this will be because we have got there from here, and this in turn will be because we have done the only thing we can do starting from here, namely use the methods and principles of the natural sciences in their current form. If we were to step outside our current beliefs altogether, in an effort to raise questions about how they stand in relation to reality, then we should have no basis for any further progress. This is the purport of the famous 'ship' image that Quine so frequently invokes, an image due to the logical positivist Otto Neurath and captured by him in a quotation that Quine uses as an epigraph for his book *Word and Object*:

> We are like sailors who have to rebuild their ship on the open sea, without ever being able to dismantle it in dry dock and reconstruct it from its best components. (Neurath (1983), p. 92)[27]

[24] In 'Five Milestones', p. 72, he appears to suggest that it can. And this is how Roger Gibson likewise appears to present the matter in Gibson (1995) – an essay that Quine describes as 'Gibson's clear and penetrating exposition and defense of my position' ('Reactions', p. 347). But I remain unconvinced that there is any other 'ism' that is quite so fundamental to what Quine is doing. It is noteworthy that in the passage from 'Five Milestones' he talks of 'sources' of his naturalism rather than premises from which it can be derived, and he identifies these, in one case explicitly, as 'states of mind' (ibid.).

[25] Cf. 'Two Dogmas', p. 46.

[26] Quine's stance is therefore a kind of mirror image of that of Fichte, who, concerning the primordial choice to which I referred in n. 5, did not think that there was any serious alternative to what I dubbed 'transcendentalism' – the position that he opposed to his version of naturalism (Ch. 6, §2).

[27] Quine invokes this image throughout his writings: in *Word and Object* see, in addition to the epigraph, pp. 3–4 and 124. The idea behind the image, if not the image itself, is anticipated in Hegel's critique of Kant: see Ch. 8, §8.

4.   Some Distinctions Rejected ...

I indicated in §1 that there are elements in Carnap's logical positivism that Quine rejects. So far there has been no real evidence of this. We have seen him developing Carnap's ideas, but not yet seriously opposing them. How does he do so?

One useful way of broaching this question is to pick some basic kind of entity postulated by current physics and then to consider a statement to the effect that such entities exist. Take the statement that there are quarks, for instance. Now, what is Quine's attitude to this statement? He regards it as a fundamental truth about reality; at the same time he concedes that physics may later make him reconsider and regard it as a falsehood instead. That is the only attitude he believes he *can* take, given his (provisional) naturalism. Very well, what is Carnap's attitude to the statement? He regards it, at least on its most natural interpretation, as a decision, or, better, as the announcement of a decision, to adopt a particular linguistic framework, neither true nor false. The question whether there are quarks is for Carnap most naturally interpreted as an external question, not an internal question (see §2 of the previous chapter). Here, certainly, is a point of disagreement.

The fact is that Quine sees no rationale for Carnap's external/internal distinction. When the forces of the world impinge on people's surfaces, they sometimes hit back by making noises and marks on paper. They produce statements that record their conception of what is going on. And there are various dimensions of assessment for these statements. Two in particular are pertinent to this issue. One is with respect to truth. The other is with respect to desiderata in the systems of classification involved: power, elegance, economy, clarity, user-friendliness, and suchlike.[28] But there is neither need nor justification, in Quine's view, for keeping these separate, for seeing the latter as bearing on a choice of framework and the former as bearing on assertions made within the framework. If people respond to their sense experience by claiming that there are quarks, or that there are positive integers, or that the number of quarks in the solar system is less than some specified positive integer, then, in each case, they are simply asserting how they take things to be. Their classifications may or may not have the aesthetic-cum-utilitarian virtues advertised above, and other classifications may have these virtues to a greater or lesser extent. But what these people have claimed is in each case straightforwardly true or false. (See e.g. 'Two Dogmas', §6, and *Word and Object*, §56.)

For similar reasons Quine rejects the distinction between analytic truths and synthetic truths. In his celebrated essay 'Two Dogmas' he identifies the conviction that there is such a distinction as one of two dogmas that

---

[28] Cf. n. 18.

characterize what he calls 'modern empiricism', by which he means, pretty much, logical positivism.[29] And he urges that there is no satisfactory way of effecting the distinction. If we say that a statement is analytically true when its truth depends on the rules of some linguistic framework, or when its truth is not sensitive to what reality is like, or when it is true by virtue of meaning alone, or when it can be known to be true independently of sense experience, or when it cannot be denied without violating the principle of contradiction, or when it cannot be denied without betraying a misunderstanding of the language, then in every case we are, in Quine's view, playing out a variation on the same incoherent theme. We are presupposing that each individual statement has its own meaning, determining, by itself, what is required of reality to make the statement true.

Quine's view is that, when the forces of the world impinge on people's surfaces and they hit back by producing statements that record their conception of what is going on, they do so by producing statements that *collectively* record their conception of what is going on. None of their statements makes its own isolable contribution to the story they have to tell.[30] Suppose that, when the forces of the world impinge some more, these people find themselves reconsidering their earlier conception of what is going on. Perhaps they used to claim that all swans are white, and now they find themselves having what seems for all the world like an encounter with a black swan. There are all sorts of ways in which they might accommodate this sense experience. They might simply reject their earlier claim that all swans are white. They might continue to claim that all swans are white and dismiss this apparent counterexample as an illusion of some kind. They might continue to claim that all swans are white, *accept* that here is a black swan, and reject whatever principle they previously took to preclude doing both of these things at once. There is much to be said for or against each of these options, for instance in terms of how easy it would be to implement given its various repercussions. But there is nothing in the meaning of any of the claims these people used to make, considered in isolation, to force them to take one option rather than any other.

So the real object of Quine's censure, when he rejects the analytic/synthetic distinction, is the idea that each individual statement stands in its own relations of confirmation and confutation with different possible courses of sense experience. And in fact this is the second dogma that he identifies in his essay – though his very talk of 'two' dogmas is somewhat belied by his claim that 'the two dogmas are … at root identical' (p. 41).[31] An analytically

---

[29] We shall consider the second dogma shortly.

[30] But see §4 of the previous chapter: in this at least he is following Carnap.

[31] It is significant, however, that he only ever gives reasons why the second entails the first (reasons that I am about to sketch in the main text). It is significant because Carnap too rejects the second dogma: see the previous note. So Carnap may say that Quine's assault

true statement is a statement that is not only confirmed by the actual course of sense experience, but that would have been confirmed by any possible course of sense experience. For Quine that makes no sense. Any statement we accept, even the statement that aunts are female, is just part of our overall account of how things are, and, had our sense experience taken a different course, it would have been a candidate for rejection. Imagine, for instance, that we had discovered some tribe in which we had observed, among the siblings of parents, a very high correlation, but not an exceptionless one, between being female and playing some crucial social role. And imagine that we had found it more convenient, when talking about members of this tribe, to align aunthood with playing this role than with being female. Then, in acceding to this, we would have acknowledged a few male aunts. (It is natural to protest that we would at most have found it convenient to *call* a few people 'male aunts', but that this would have involved a change in the meaning of the word 'aunt'. Indeed, in later writings, Quine himself talks in such terms.[32] In 'Two Dogmas', however, his position is less compromising, and the idea that each expression has its own monadic meaning which it might retain or lose through any change of doctrine is itself part of what is under attack.) Likewise, a synthetically true statement is a statement that, although it is confirmed by the actual course of sense experience, would have been confuted by some other possible course of sense experience. But that too makes no sense for Quine. Any statement we accept we could still have accepted, no matter what course our sense experience had taken, if we had made suitable compensatory adjustments to the rest of what we accepted, most obviously if we had dismissed any apparent counterevidence as illusory.[33,34]

on the second dogma, an assault with which he concurs, leaves him free to accept the first. (Still, *unless* Carnap sees the first dogma as equivalent to the second, the onus is still on him it to explicate it.) For an insightful discussion of this matter, see Isaacson (2004), pp. 239ff. For an illuminating discussion that bears on other themes in this chapter, see George (2000). And for a penetrating discussion of how the first dogma might survive rejection of the second, see McDowell (1996), Afterword, Pt I, §9.

[32] See e.g. *Philosophy of Logic*, p. 81.

[33] Quine occasionally acknowledges some rare and artificial exceptions that do satisfy this criterion of synthetic truth (e.g. 'Vuillemin', p. 620, and 'Five Milestones', p. 71). But 'rare and artificial' is the operative phrase – these statements are able to satisfy the criterion only because they differ in certain fundamental respects from most statements – so I think we can afford to ignore them. He also sometimes says that 'observation' statements satisfy the criterion (e.g. 'Epistemology Naturalized', p. 89). But I see this as another relaxing of his position in 'Two Dogmas'.

[34] Note that my exegesis here brings me into conflict with Michael Dummett, who in Dummett (1978l), p. 375, argues that Quine is not denying the very coherence of the analytic/synthetic distinction, merely denying that, on one clear characterization of analytic and synthetic truths, there are any truths of either kind. For a counterargument see Moore

Consider Carnap's bifurcated treatment of how Euclidean geometry was superseded as a description of physical space. Carnap's view is that there are two equally legitimate ways of construing the geometries involved in this process – either as linguistic frameworks or as descriptions of physical space proffered within some other linguistic framework – each with its own implications concerning where the division between the analytically true and the synthetically true falls, each with its own implications concerning where the division between the truth-evaluable and the non-truth-evaluable falls, each with its own implications concerning what has been rejected and what has been retained (see §3 of the previous chapter). Quine is able to cut through all of this. On Quine's view, we used to think that physical space is Euclidean and we now think it is non-Euclidean: it is as simple as that.

Nor is it just the logical positivists' distinction that is under attack. There is a long, venerable history of similar distinctions with which Quine would have just as little sympathy:

- Leibniz' distinction between truths of reasoning and truths of fact
- Hume's distinction between relations of ideas and matters of fact
- Kant's original distinction, later appropriated and given sharper formulation by Frege, between analytic truths and synthetic truths[35]
- Kant's distinct distinction, likewise appropriated by Frege, between *a priori* truths and empirical truths

and

- various versions of the distinction between necessary truths and contingent truths, including those to be found in the early and the later Wittgenstein.[36,37]

(2002a), §I. For further attacks on the analytic/synthetic distinction, see White (1952) and Waismann (1968). For a defence of it, see Grice and Strawson (1956). And for discussion see Putnam (1975).

[35] Quine himself cites all three of these distinctions in 'Two Dogmas', p. 20.

[36] It is perhaps the distinction that we find in the later Wittgenstein that is least vulnerable to Quine's attack, given Wittgenstein's own sensitivity to the way in which various pragmatic forces can bring it about that the very statements we use at one time to say how things must be we may later find ourselves using to say how they are not: see Ch. 10, §3 (and see again the material cited in n. 37 of that discussion). But ironically, given that there is something strikingly similar to Wittgenstein's vision in Carnap (see §3(e) of the previous chapter), Carnap's distinction may also be a good deal less vulnerable than most: this relates to the points made in nn. 30 and 31.

[37] Note that Quine is similarly unsympathetic to the various other distinctions of meaning that we saw the logical positivists draw among statements, whereby some have 'non-literal' meaning and are therefore neither true nor false. For Quine, if a statement has meaning at all, its very form makes it true or false. This is because he accepts what he calls 'Tarski's paradigm', by which he means, roughly, the view that calling a statement

Quine is not averse to acknowledging associated distinctions of degree. He readily concedes that, among the statements we currently accept, some would be more resistant to rejection than others. In the eponymous metaphor of his co-authored book *The Web of Belief*, these statements are closer to the centre of the web of what we currently accept than the others are, and hence more directly connected to more of the rest of the web. So their rejection would necessitate more rejections elsewhere. And the more of the web we reject, the harder it is for us to maintain our grip on what we come to accept. Hence Quine's 'maxim of minimum mutilation' (*Pursuit of Truth*, p. 14). The fact remains that the sharp distinctions of kind that he finds in his predecessors are abhorrent to him.

There is one feature of these distinctions, which is accepted even by his empiricist predecessors, that may in any case always have seemed an offence to empiricism – it certainly seems that way to Quine – namely the idea that not all knowledge is grounded in sense experience.[38] On Quine's view, *all* knowledge is indeed grounded in sense experience (albeit no individual item of knowledge is grounded in any individual episode of sense experience). Quine's empiricism, he would insist, is empiricism of the purest strain, empiricism without any unempirical accessories.[39]

5. ... and a New One Introduced

In repudiating the various distinctions that we have just seen him repudiating, Quine at the same time repudiates all that subserves them, notably the Fregean notion of sense (see e.g. 'Meaning').[40] This in turn leads him to draw

---

true is equivalent to issuing it (e.g. *Philosophy of Logic*, p. 12; cf. 'Equivalent Systems', p. 242). '[This] paradigm,' he writes, 'works for evaluations ... as well as for statements of fact. And it works equally well for performatives. "Slander is evil" is true if and only if slander is evil, and "I bid you good morning" is true of us on a given occasion if and only if, on that occasion, I bid you good morning' ('Austin', p. 90). We might wonder whether this involves a thinning of the logical positivists' conception of sense-making which leaves Quine vulnerable to the Limit Argument (see §6 of the previous chapter). In fact, however, it involves an assimilation of all sense-making to scientific sense-making which allows him, harmlessly, to view the project of drawing a limit to our sense-making as the broadly scientific project of accounting for how interactions between us and our environment cause some of what we do to make sense and some of it not to.

[38] Cf. 'Epistemology Naturalized', p. 80, where he urges that logical positivists 'espoused a verification theory of meaning but did not take it seriously enough'.

[39] 'Unempirical' is a word that he uses to stigmatize the analytic/synthetic distinction ('Two Dogmas', p. 37). We can readily imagine him using it to stigmatize any of the rest of these distinctions.

[40] We saw how the Fregean notion of sense subserves Frege's own analytic/synthetic distinction in Ch. 8, §§4 and 5.

a distinction of his own. This distinction is best illustrated by appeal to what he calls 'radical translation', that is 'translation of the language of a hitherto untouched people' (*Word and Object*, p. 28).

Imagine that you are engaged in a project of such translation: you are trying to compile a bilingual dictionary for English and the language of some people with whom neither you nor any other English speaker has had any prior contact. And suppose you have got as far as speculating, perhaps on excellent grounds, that one of the statements they accept can be translated as 'All swans are white.' Now suppose that you see, for the first time, a group of them encountering a black swan, though this does not stop them from accepting the statement in question. There are all sorts of hypotheses you might form. Perhaps they allowed for this possibility all along and your translation was imperfect. Perhaps they take themselves to be subject to an illusion. Perhaps they have started using one of their terms in a new way, say the term that they previously used to denote swans. Perhaps they operate with some bizarre logic. To be sure, some of these hypotheses will come to mind much more naturally than others, depending on what exactly these people go on to say and do. But if Quine is right about the araneous nature of what they accept, and of what you accept, then *in principle* all of these hypotheses, and more besides, can, with suitable compensatory adjustments elsewhere, be kept alive. And this in turn will allow for incompatible ways of translating from their language into English, none of which is precluded by what you observe, or could observe, as you go about your interpretative project. If there were Fregean senses attaching to the expressions of their language, and to the expressions of English, then the correct way to translate their statement would be by means of an English statement that had the same sense, and your inability to choose between these various options would just betoken (irremediable) ignorance on your part. As it is, Quine does not believe that there *is* anything to make one option correct rather than any other. There is, as he famously puts it, 'no fact of the matter' concerning which is correct ('Things', p. 23).

He means this quite literally. As we saw in §2 he has a physicalist understanding of what a fact is. And he is denying that any *physical* features of how these people are disposed to use their language or to interact with their environment rule out any of the aforementioned options for translation. The whole point, in a way, is that we have the conceptual resources to discriminate more finely than the facts themselves can.

This is very reminiscent of the underdetermination of truth by evidence to which we saw Quine accede in §3. There is, however, a crucial difference. In that case Quine was prepared to say the very thing that he is not prepared to say in this case, namely that there *are* facts beyond what is settled by the evidence. Indeed, that is precisely what underdetermination consists in.

The picture is as follows then. The evidence leaves open different options for what to say about certain matters. In some cases this is because the facts discriminate more finely than the evidence can. Such is underdetermination. In some cases, however, including the translation case, it is because not even the facts can discriminate finely enough. Such is what Quine calls *indeterminacy*. (See *Pursuit of Truth*, §43.) And it is this distinction, the distinction between underdetermination and indeterminacy, to which I was referring.

But what motivates Quine to draw it? Why does he insist that the facts slice just so thinly and no thinner? (This question is especially pertinent in view of the regulative version of his physicalism, which warns against forming an overly narrow preconception of what the facts are.) It is not enough to advert to his repudiation of Fregean senses. Either his repudiation of Fregean senses deprives translation of just one source of determinacy, in which case the question remains as to why he is so sure that it has no other, or Fregean senses are construed as *whatever* would make translation determinate,[41] in which case the question remains as to why he is so sure that they are to be repudiated.

The key, once again, is his naturalism. To determine the general character of reality, or to determine what the general facts are, is the very business of the natural scientist. It is not the business of the radical translator. The radical translator is trying to find a way of interpreting certain people, and perhaps also of communicating with them. This is a practical exercise. It does not, in the present context, count as an exercise in making sense of things.[42]

6. Quinean Metaphysics I: An Overview

It is comparatively easy to see where Quine's views must leave metaphysics. Insofar as he regards metaphysics as a legitimate exercise at all,[43] he must

---

[41] This would be a stretching of Frege's own notion. But Quine does sometimes talk in such terms: see e.g. *Pursuit of Truth*, p. 102, where for 'propositions' we can read '(Fregean) thoughts'; and cf. 'Ontological Relativity', pp. 27–29.

[42] See *Word and Object*, Ch. 2. See also 'Translation', 'Facts', and 'Translation Again'. For a further indication of how much (or how little) counts as making sense of things in this context, see *Roots of Reference*, pp. 51–52. For discussion of Quine's views on indeterminacy, see Dummett (1978l); Kirk (1986); Gibson (1986); Hookway (1988), Pt III; Zabludowski (1989); Morris (2006), Ch. 11; and Hylton (2007), Ch. 8. In the Appendix to this chapter I shall suggest that there is tension between Quine's commitment to this new distinction and his rejection of the various others that we saw him reject in the previous section.

[43] Towards some metaphysics – and in particular, towards the sort of metaphysics which, in Wittgenstein's phrase, takes language 'on holiday' (Wittgenstein (1967a), Pt I, §38) – he has straightforward logical positivist antipathy. (Cf. *Word and Object*, p. 133, and 'Structure', p. 406.) There is a delicious example of this which I cannot resist quoting,

regard it as the sort of thing that I have defined it to be, that is to say the most general attempt to make sense of things. In his own terms, he must regard it as the most general of the sciences – and therefore as continuous with all the other sciences. As Quine himself says towards the beginning of 'Two Dogmas', referring to the eponymous doctrines that he is about to abandon, 'one effect of abandoning them is … a blurring of the supposed boundary between speculative metaphysics and natural science' (p. 20).

The idea that philosophy, or more particularly metaphysics when it is reckoned a proper branch of philosophy, should be both a contribution to sense-making and yet something of a fundamentally different kind from empirical science – the idea which we have seen so many of the rest of our protagonists embrace – is a direct breach of Quine's naturalism. And some of the specific tasks that have been assigned to philosophy in the name of this idea, such as providing a once-for-all *a priori* vindication of empirical science (Descartes), or promoting clarity of thought as opposed to discovering truths about reality (early and later Wittgenstein), or clarifying certain linguistic frameworks by articulating analytic truths that depend on the rules of those frameworks (Carnap), or addressing external questions about the costs and benefits of adopting such frameworks (Carnap again), are but further indications, for Quine, of just how wrong-headed the idea is. If metaphysics is anything, then it is maximally general science, different only in degree from the rest of science.[44]

Very well; what examples are there of tasks that can be properly assigned to metaphysics on this conception? Significantly, much of what we have already seen Quine undertaking serves as a paradigm. For Quine, as for so many of the rest of our protagonists, an integral part of the most general

---

since the quotation is a personal favourite of mine. Henryk Skolimowski, in his contribution to a book of essays on Quine (Skolimowski (1986)), makes a series of needling proposals about Quine's ideas, in a spirit of broad hostility, about which he himself comments, 'I can anticipate Professor Quine's response to my proposals. He is likely to say that he doesn't know what I mean by my assertions about the spiral of understanding as corresponding to the walls of our cosmos' (p. 489). Quine's response, in 'Skolimowski', is mischievously caustic: 'Skolimowski predicts that I will pretend not to understand what he means by his "assertions about the spiral of understanding as corresponding to the walls of our cosmos." I am tempted, perversely, to pretend that I do understand. But let us be fair: if he claimed not to understand me, I would not for a moment suspect him of pretending' (p. 493).

[44] Cf. 'Natural Kinds', pp. 126–127. Note: it follows that Quine's answers to the three questions that I posed in §6 of the Introduction are nowhere near as clear as the Carnapian answers proffered in §5(b) of the previous chapter. (This is especially true of the Creativity Question. The possibility alluded to in n. 26 of the Introduction is pertinent here: see *Word and Object*, p. 161. But Quine's sectarian commitment to certain evidence-transcendence facts means that even his attitude to the Transcendence Question is unstraightforward.) I shall not pursue this matter.

attempt to make sense of things is the self-conscious attempt to make sense of making sense of things.

But there are other tasks. Many of these have to do with the upkeep of our most general conceptual apparatus, that which is common to all the sciences. They involve the pursuit of various desiderata in this endeavour, the very desiderata that Carnap would have said we needed to pursue when choosing a linguistic framework: power, clarity, elegance, familiarity, user-friendliness, and the rest. Each science involves its own pursuit of these desiderata in the upkeep of the conceptual apparatus that is peculiar to it. The metaphysical pursuit differs only in being more general. And, *contra* both Carnap and Wittgenstein, it 'is not to be distinguished from a quest of ultimate categories, a limning of the most general traits of reality' (*Word and Object*, p. 161). Considerations that Carnap would have said were relevant only to one aspect of the project of making sense of things (choosing a linguistic framework) are on Quine's conception part of a package of considerations that are jointly relevant to the entire project: the single unified project of determining how things are.[45]

One very typical example of such a task, which is concerned with a concept that is as integral as any to our most general conceptual apparatus, namely the concept of a physical object, is to determine whether physical objects are three-dimensional objects that endure through time or four-dimensional objects with temporal parts. The former view is pretty much the view of common sense. The latter view assimilates objects to what we ordinarily think of as their 'histories', where these extend into the future as well as into the past. Quine himself favours the latter view, which for various reasons he thinks makes for greater simplicity and clarity (*Word and Object*, §36).

A closely related and equally representative example is to determine whether statements concerning the future are (already) true or false. Quine's view, consonant with his four-dimensionalism, is that they are (*Pursuit of Truth*, §38). This too, he thinks, makes for greater simplicity and clarity.[46] It is striking, however, that Quine is also prepared to advert unashamedly to the view's *ethical* payoff – as we saw in §7 of the Introduction. He evidently means what he says, in the very last sentence of 'Two Dogmas':

> The considerations which guide [a man] in warping his scientific heritage to fit his continuing sensory promptings are, where rational, pragmatic.

---

[45] See Hylton (2007), Ch. 9.

[46] Does it also receive support from Tarski's paradigm (see above, n. 37)? Quine explicitly argues not (*Pursuit of Truth*, pp. 90–91). For a contrary argument, see Williamson (1994a), §7.2.

7. Quinean Metaphysics II: Ontology

Perhaps the most characteristic metaphysical questions, however – on Quine's conception – are questions in ontology: questions about what exists. Quine's view is that there are things of a given sort if some true theory is 'ontologically committed' to things of that sort, that is, roughly, if some true theory *says* there are things of that sort (e.g. 'Universals', p. 103). In a way this is trivial, as Quine himself would be the first to concede.[47] It sounds less trivial, however, when the notion of ontological commitment is made less rough. To say that a given theory is ontologically committed to things of a given sort is to say that the theory cannot be true unless things of that sort are among the things about which the theory makes explicit generalizations once it has been suitably formalized, where an explicit generalization is a statement of the form 'Everything is thus and so,' or 'Something is thus and so' (*Word and Object*, §49, and 'Existence', p. 106). Anyone versed in contemporary formal logic will recognize this account as the purport of Quine's famous slogan 'To be is to be the value of a variable' ('On What There Is', p. 15).

Very well, what sorts of things are there? What does exist? That, we now see, is an issue to be broached by ascertaining which theories are actually true. So it is an issue largely for various specialists in the natural sciences – but not exclusively for them. For there is also the question of how any given theory is best formalized.[48] And that is in part (the part that has to do with the theory's most general conceptual apparatus) a metaphysical question. Typically, it will involve what Quine calls 'semantic ascent' (*Word and Object*, §56): the shift from talking in certain terms to reflecting on those terms instead. Thus if the issue is whether positive integers exist, it is settled by deciding whether we do well to include any arithmetical apparatus as part of the formalization of any of our scientific theories.[49] This is *precisely* the kind of shift that Carnap took to be constitutive of asking an external question about a linguistic framework. For Carnap, it was a characteristically philosophical move. There is a sense in which, for Quine too, it is a characteristically philosophical move. But Quine does not think that moves of this kind are only ever made by philosophers – any more than he thinks that moves made by philosophers are only ever of this kind. Nor, crucially,

---

[47] See e.g. 'Responses', pp. 174–175.

[48] There is room for concern about whether this compromises Quine's naturalism. For this issue, at least as Quine conceives it, is arguably not of the kind that exercises natural scientists themselves.

[49] 'Do well' may be too weak. There are those who think that we do well to include such apparatus for heuristic reasons, without its embodying any truth: see e.g. Field (1980) and Melia (1995). (For some comments relevant to the question of what 'do well' might come to in this context, see Soames (2009), p. 442.)

does he think that moves of this kind only ever issue in decisions about how to speak. Provided all goes well, they issue in insights into how things are (see the previous section).

Quine's own preference, both on aesthetic and on pragmatic grounds, is for theories that are ontologically committed to as few sorts of things, indeed to as few things, as possible. He describes this preference as 'a taste for desert landscapes' ('On What There Is', p. 4). It aligns him to William of Ockham, who is famously credited with the slogan known as Ockham's razor, that '*entia non sunt multiplicanda praeter necessitatem*' ('entities are not to be multiplied beyond necessity').[50] And it means that, if he could, Quine would gladly endorse formalizations of scientific theories that did *not* include any arithmetical apparatus. As it is, he reluctantly acknowledges that a good deal of heavy-duty mathematics – not just arithmetic – is indispensable to natural science. He concludes, against his own instincts, but in strict accord with his ontological principles, and in strict accord with his naturalism, that positive integers exist (see e.g. 'Mathematization').[51]

In some cases parsimony can be achieved by what might be called creative doubling. This occurs whenever we acknowledge entities of one kind by identifying them with entities of some other kind that we already acknowledge. For an example of this we can turn to a section of *Word and Object* with the remarkable title 'The Ordered Pair as Philosophical Paradigm' (§53). No great philosophical significance attaches to the *content* of this example; quite the opposite. But in its structure it serves as a particularly clear illustration of the phenomenon in question. The relevant background to the example is Quine's belief that, over and above whatever other things exist, there are also sets of these things. This in turn rests on his conviction that set theory is part of the heavy-duty mathematics that occurs in the best formalizations of the various natural sciences. Thus, given any two things a and b, there is also their *pair set* $\{a, b\}$, the set whose only two members they are. This is not the same as their *ordered pair* $\langle a, b \rangle$. The latter differs from the former in one crucial respect: the order matters. Thus, whereas $\{a, b\}$ is the same entity as $\{b, a\}$, $\langle a, b \rangle$ is not the same entity as $\langle b, a \rangle$. Suppose, then, that we acknowledge ordered pairs as well as sets. (Quine gives reasons for doing so.) Does this mean that we are acknowledging entities of an entirely new kind? Not necessarily. Given any two things a and b, the set $\{\{a\}, \{a, b\}\}$, which is the pair set of the single-membered set $\{a\}$ and the pair

---

[50] But 'credited with' is the operative phrase; see Thorburn (1918).

[51] For a sense of how deep his reluctance is, see his early essay 'A Constructive Nominalism', which is co-authored with Nelson Goodman and which the authors open by declaring, 'We do not believe in abstract entities' (p. 105). For a later retraction of that declaration, see *Word and Object*, p. 243, n. 5.

set {a, b}, can double as the ordered pair ⟨a, b⟩. For while a and b are peculiarly involved in this set, they are also asymmetrically involved in it: {{a},
{a, b}} is a different set from {{b}, {b, a}}. This allows us to identify ordered
pairs with sets that we already acknowledge. And Quine's proposal is that
we do precisely that. (Not that the specified method of identification is the
only one available. There are many others that would do just as well. Quine
thinks it is a matter of indifference which we adopt – so long as we are clear
about it, and faithful to it.)

This proposal, as Quine himself points out in the next section of his
book, is reminiscent of Frege's proposal that we identify numbers with sets
(Ch. 8, §3), except, of course, that Quine need not have any scruples about
whether the arbitrariness of the identification flouts the supposed analyticity of truths concerning the entities in question (Ch. 8, §5). Certainly, Quine
does not purport to be saying what ordered pairs 'really are' in some deep
philosophical sense. His proposal is intended in a spirit of legislation. It is
designed to help us systematize and formalize, in as elegant and economical
a way as possible, our various theories about what is going on. This helps to
explain why the example serves as a 'philosophical paradigm'. It is a paradigm, as we now see, of good metaphysics. And it contributes, as does all
good metaphysics on Quine's conception, to the overall project of determining the general character of reality.

But to repeat: no great philosophical significance attaches to the content
of this example. There are other examples that are of far greater philosophical interest. Consider mental states and processes. Many people follow
Descartes in taking these to be logically independent, if not causally independent, of all physical states and processes (Ch. 1, §6). This is in direct
violation of Quine's (provisional) physicalism. But suppose, what many of
these same people also believe, that physical states and processes always
at least *accompany* mental states and processes, and that they exhibit a
complexity that correlates perfectly with the complexity of the mental
states and processes themselves. In that case, Quine argues, whatever metaphysical rationale there was for insisting on a logical independence here
simply lapses. We can identify the mental states and processes with the
physical states and processes, in just the same spirit in which we identified
ordered pairs with sets. (See *Word and Object*, pp. 264–265.) This too can
be regarded as a piece of legislation. But, for reasons that should by now
be clear, it can also, in Quine's view, be said to lead to insights into how
things are. It can be said to be part of the most general attempt to make
sense of things.[52]

---

[52] For further views of Quine's in ontology, see *Word and Object*, Ch. 7, passim. For an illu-
minating discussion, see Hylton (2004).

8. Objections to Quine's Naturalism[53]

What, now, are we to make of what I earlier described as the driving force behind all of this, Quine's extreme naturalism? I voiced disquiet about it towards the end of §2. And I suggested that Quine's lax sectarianism, which is laxer than his naturalism warrants, exhibits a dim recognition that only something less extreme is ultimately sustainable. For in his lax sectarianism Quine allows himself to step back from the scientific way of making sense of things, which is the only way of making sense of things that the extreme view sanctions, and tries to make sense of that way of making sense of things *without* simply redeploying it. I think we see the same dim recognition when Quine concedes, of his unregenerate sectarian-naturalistic view – whereby 'there is … no higher truth than the truth we are claiming or aspiring to as we … tinker with our system of the world from within' – that it 'has the ring of cultural relativism,' and then further concedes, in unregenerate sectarian-naturalistic vein:

> That way … lies paradox. Truth, says the cultural relativist, is culture-bound. But if it were, then he, within his own culture, ought to see his own culture-bound truth as absolute. He cannot proclaim cultural relativism without rising above it, and he cannot rise above it without giving it up. ('Equivalent Systems', pp. 242–243)

There Quine leaves the matter.

Something, clearly, is amiss. And what is amiss, it seems to me, is that Quine's extreme naturalism has fallen foul of the following fundamental fact: the (natural-)scientific way to make sense of things is not the way to make sense of making sense of things. But what then of Neurath's image (§2), which suggests that all sense-making is of a piece? The image works well for scientific sense-making. If the ship in its current state represents what I called in §2 'our current beliefs', in other words those beliefs that we have arrived at so far by using the scientific way of making sense of things, then the image helpfully indicates what is required of us if we are to continue to use that way of making sense of things to arrive at new beliefs. But this does not preclude our using some quite different way of making sense of things to arrive at a conception of the beliefs themselves. We can jump overboard: we can look at the ship from outside. It is just that, if we do, we must remember to modify our procedures in an appropriate way – by treading water, say. I shall not develop this analogy; I do not want to stretch it to breaking point. But I shall advert to it again in Chapter 17,

---

[53] Much of the material in this section derives from Moore (2006b), §V. I am grateful to the editor and publisher of the issue of *Philosophical Topics* in which that essay appears for permission to make use of this material.

because I think it is very relevant to the fundamental cleavage between Quine and Husserl.

Meanwhile I want to return, by a somewhat different route, to the anti-naturalistic idea that there is a non-scientific way of making sense of making sense of things. I shall begin by considering two objections that have been levelled against Quine's naturalism.

The first of these is an objection to which John McDowell has given celebrated expression (see esp. McDowell (1996), Afterword, Pt I, §3). It pertains to Quine's naturalistic construal of our evidence for our current beliefs. On Quine's account, this evidence is a matter of impacts on our sensory receptors, patterns of ocular irradiation, and suchlike. The objection is that these entities do not intrinsically represent things as being a certain way; they are not *answerable to how things are*. This means that they cannot enter into logical or rational relations with our current beliefs. They can at most enter into causal relations with them. And this in turn means that they cannot act as *evidence* for our current beliefs.[54]

The second objection, which John Campbell has expressed very forcibly (Campbell (2002), Ch. 11, §5), and which likewise pertains to Quine's naturalistic construal of our evidence for our current beliefs, seems, initially, to run contrary to the first. For whereas the gist of the first objection was that Quine recognizes too much of a gap between our evidence for our current beliefs and the beliefs themselves, the gist of this objection is that he does not recognize enough of a gap between them. More precisely, the second objection is that, by construing our evidence for our current beliefs in terms that depend so heavily on those very beliefs, Quine has violated his own crucial insight that the beliefs are underdetermined by the evidence (see §3 above). '[Given that] patterns of ocular irradiation have to be described in terms of the physics of the day,' writes Campbell, 'how ... could they be consistent with some rival to the physics of the day?' (ibid., p. 233).

Now one might think that Quine has a perfectly satisfactory riposte to Campbell's rhetorical question. What matters, one might think, is not how the patterns of ocular irradiation are to be described, but what their *content* is. Here is an analogy. Imagine a human brain that is being kept alive in a vat of nutrients and that is being manipulated by computers in such a way that the subject thinks he is living the life of a Premier League footballer.[55] And suppose we have to draw on various principles of computerized neurotechnology to describe what is happening to the brain. It simply does not

---

[54] It is interesting to note in connection with this objection how evasive much of Quine's language is. In *Pursuit of Truth* he speaks of 'the flow of evidence from the triggering of the senses to the pronouncements of science' (p. 41). The word 'flow' here nicely epitomizes the very fudge of which McDowell takes him to be guilty.

[55] Cf. Putnam (1981), pp. 5–6.

follow that what is happening to the brain, whose content may have nothing to do with computerized neurotechnology, is enough to refute the subject's impression of what kind of life he is leading. Again, suppose we have to accept some basic assumptions about the mind-independence of physical objects in order adequately to describe the impact of Samuel Johnson's foot on a stone. It simply does not follow that this impact is enough to refute Berkeleian idealism (see Berkeley (1962a)).[56] Similarly, if we have to use the physics of the day to describe certain patterns of ocular irradiation, it simply does not follow that these patterns are enough to refute each and every rival to that physics. If there were people who, on broadly the same evidence as ours, accepted such a rival, then they could not acknowledge any such phenomenon as ocular irradiation (which would be a deficiency by our reckoning). They would have to tell their own rival story about what evidence they had for their theory. Yet, for all that, their evidence would in fact (by our reckoning) involve ocular irradiation. There is nothing incoherent in this. Nor, incidentally, does it mean that we cannot eventually come to accept a rival to the physics of the day. Campbell suggests that, without an Archimedean point, Quine's views lead to an unacceptable conservatism (ibid., p. 234). But Neurath's image shows that this is not so.

Is this a legitimate reply on Quine's behalf to Campbell's rhetorical question? Only granted one absolutely crucial proviso: that Quine is entitled to talk about the 'content' of the patterns of ocular irradiation. But that, of course, brings us back to the first objection. The first objection was precisely that Quine is *not* entitled to talk in such terms. That was why patterns of ocular irradiation were deemed unsuitable to play the role of evidence. McDowell thinks that Quine needs a fundamentally new and more commonsensical conception of evidence, whereby it is a matter of how we experience things as being. But really that is Campbell's point too. 'Scientific theorizing,' Campbell writes, 'can never let go of the idea that it is ultimately our experiences [as of macroscopic physical objects] that have to be explained' (ibid., p. 234).[57] The two objections, despite an initial appearance of disparity, are of a piece.

And they cut deep.[58] They suggest that there is after all room for some non-scientific way of making sense of the scientific way of making sense of things. Quine is able to see the scientific way of making sense of things as the only way of making sense of things because he presupposes a narrow conception of what it is to make sense of things. (There is a clear illustration of this in the point that I made at the end of §5: the attempt to interpret

---

[56] Johnson famously thought it was enough: see Boswell (1887), Vol. I, p. 471.

[57] Cf. also Stroud (1984), Ch. 6, esp. pp. 250–254.

[58] Roger Gibson, in Gibson (1995), §IV, cites further instances of this sort of objection, including that of Barry Stroud mentioned in the previous note, and tries to defend Quine against them. His defence seems to me question-begging.

people who speak some radically unfamiliar tongue does not, on this narrow conception, count as an attempt to make sense of things. This is why Quine thinks he has license to say that there is no fact of the matter where certain issues about the interpretation of such people are concerned, and, concomitantly, why he thinks he has license to repudiate Fregean senses.) But we need not share this narrow conception. And if we do not, then I think we can see all sorts of possibilities for sense-making that are invisible to Quine. Moreover, some of these possibilities, including some of the possibilities for self-conscious reflection on our own sense-making that we have just glimpsed in the two objections to Quine's naturalism, are crucial possibilities for the project of making maximally general sense of things, crucial possibilities, in other words, for metaphysics.[59]

Appendix: Can Quine Consistently Reject the Distinctions He Rejects and Espouse the Indeterminacy/ Underdetermination Distinction?

In §4 we saw Quine reject several distinctions. In §5 we saw him introduce a new one of his own. This was a distinction between two ways in which the evidence may fail to settle what to say about a given matter. First, there may be no fact of the matter: the matter may be *indeterminate*. Second, there may be a fact of the matter which nevertheless transcends the evidence: the matter may be, relative to the evidence, *underdetermined*. I tried to give Quine's reasons for espousing this distinction. But, be these reasons as they may, and be their appeal as it may (rather meagre, I submit, in the light of our subsequent discussion), there is also the question of whether Quine can consistently espouse this distinction granted his rejection of the various others.

I have argued elsewhere (Moore (1997b)) that he cannot. The purpose of this appendix is not much more than to allude to this argument, so as to convey one more misgiving about the extreme naturalism at work in all of this. But I also proffer the following very brief summary of my argument.

When Quine says that there is no fact of a given matter, either he means that there is no *truth* of the matter or he allows for the possibility that truth outstrips factuality, just as factuality, granted underdetermination, outstrips evidence. If the former, then he must think that the decision concerning what to say about the matter is a non-truth-evaluable decision whose implementation allows for the making of truth-evaluable claims about how things

---

[59] Cf. Hookway (1988), Ch. 12, esp. §6. Cf. also Williams (2006m). And for a strenuous defence of the idea that there is a non-scientific way of making sense of making sense of things, see Gadamer (2004). This idea will dominate Part Three: see esp. Chs 17 and 18.

are (as, for instance, the decision about how to translate a sentence from a foreign language allows for the making of true or false claims about what a speaker of the language has just said); and that sits ill with his rejection of the external/internal distinction. If the latter, then he must think that there are some truths whose truth is determined, not by the facts, but simply by what we decide to say about the matter; and *that* sits ill with his rejection of the analytic/synthetic distinction.[60],[61]

---

[60] Cf. Rorty (1972), p. 459.

[61] I have presented the argument in the form of a dilemma. But there is also the exegetical issue of which horn, if either, Quine is actually impaled on. In my essay I suggested the second. This fits the material in n. 37 which shows Quine prepared to assign truth to statements other than 'statements of fact'. One might protest that he is prepared to do this only when the statements in question have meaning. But in any relevant non-question-begging sense, statements about matters that Quine takes to be indeterminate do have meaning; witness his own freewheeling use of them (see e.g. the material straddling pp. 334–335 of 'Stroud'). It is noteworthy also that there are passages in which Quine treats sympathetically of the idea that mathematical truth outstrips factuality: see e.g. 'Putnam', p. 430; *Pursuit of Truth*, §40; and *From Stimulus to Science*, pp. 56–57. All of that said, there are reasons, also, for seeing Quine as impaled on the first horn – though I am not much moved by them. I know of only two, and I find neither decisive. (One reason why I find neither decisive is that we can always attribute to Quine a further, incidental inconsistency, of the sort that was noted in n. 19.) The first is Quine's enthusiastic reception in 'Gibson' of Roger Gibson (1986), where Gibson glosses 'indeterminate' as 'neither true nor false' (p. 152). The second is a passage in Burton Dreben (2004), in the opening paragraph of which Dreben claims that 'all except perhaps two of the sentences that follow are Quine's' (though he gives no references). The passage in question occurs on p. 291 and runs as follows: 'This [i.e. a case in which there are two rival ways of translating from one language into another, each of which is compatible with all the evidence] is where, by my lights, open-mindedness [gives] way to truth-valuelessness: there is no fact of the matter. Such is indeterminacy as distinct from underdetermination.'

CHAPTER 13

✦

Lewis

Metaphysics in the Service of Philosophy

1. Analytic Philosophy in the Immediate Aftermath of Quine

Quine changed the map of analytic philosophy. Or perhaps the perfect tense better captures the dynamic: Quine has changed the map of analytic philosophy. To be sure, his influence, like that of any great philosopher, has been marked no less by rebellion among his successors than by discipleship. Thus many of his specific proposals about meaning, to take one central example, have been subjected to sustained counterargument, but only because they have first been subjected to sustained scrutiny. And even when philosophers who have disagreed with him have not been particularly concerned to justify their disagreement, they have felt obliged to register it. It would be out of the question, now, for an analytic philosopher to make pivotal but uncritical use of the analytic/synthetic distinction, something that was commonplace before Quine's onslaught.[1]

David Lewis (1941–2001) was a student of Quine's. As well as being an extraordinarily engaging thinker in his own right, he is also an especially interesting representative of post-Quinean analytic philosophy. On the one hand, he epitomizes the naturalistic spirit that has dominated analytic philosophy since the middle of the twentieth century and that Quine did so much to propagate. On the other hand, he epitomizes one of the most signal features of analytic philosophy's more immediate past: a resurgence of

---

[1] David Lewis, the subject of the present chapter, accepts an (unsharp) analytic/synthetic distinction. But he also works hard at rebutting Quinean objections to what he accepts: see *Convention*, pp. 200–202 and Conclusion.

Note: throughout this chapter I use the following abbreviations for Lewis' works: 'Abstract' for Lewis (1986b); 'Anselm' for Lewis (1983c); 'Attitudes' for Lewis (1983f); 'Ayer on Meaning' for Lewis (1998b); *Convention* for Lewis (2002); *Counterfactuals* for Lewis (1986d); 'Counterpart Theory' for Lewis (1983d); 1st Introduction for Lewis (1983b); 2nd Introduction for Lewis (1986a); 'Knowledge' for Lewis (1999d); *Metaphysics and Epistemology* for Lewis (1999a); 'Observation' for Lewis (1998a); *Papers I* for Lewis (1983a); *Parts of Classes* for Lewis (1991); *Plurality* for Lewis (1986c); and 'Reduction' for Lewis (1999c).

the kind of mainstream metaphysics that was practised in the early modern period; a resurgence, that is, of armchair reflection on such topics as substance, identity, necessity, causation, time, space, freedom, and the relation between mind and body.[2]

Why 'on the other hand'? Because the armchair reflection in question was an attempt, by the early moderns, to make sense of these things. Yet naturalism, even in its less extreme forms, is a revolt against any attempt to make sense of such things in other than a broadly scientific way.[3] Armchair reflection on the corresponding *concepts* (the concept of time, the concept of space, and so forth) is another matter. That may be naturalistically quite acceptable. But then it cannot, on a simple naturalistic conception, result in sense's being made of the things themselves. True, Quine's assault on the very idea of a dichotomy between reflection on a topic and reflection on the concepts associated with that topic has muddied the naturalistic waters. But not everyone in the analytic tradition has been persuaded by that assault. And certainly among those who have not, the thought that one can turn one's philosophical gaze directly on, say, space, as opposed to the intellectual tools that people use to make sense of space, and then achieve insights into its character, rubs right against the naturalistic grain.

In some ways, if not in countless other ways, this situation is analogous to that which we witnessed in post-Kantian German philosophy. To develop the analogy in tandem with the cartoon sketch that I made at the beginning of Chapter 11: just as Kant modified Hume's reaction to earlier metaphysical excesses, and created a system which allowed others, whether by purporting to follow him or by reacting against him, to indulge in metaphysics of the very sort that Hume might have thought he had exorcized, so too Quine modified the logical positivists' reaction to earlier metaphysical excesses and created a system which has somehow allowed others to indulge in metaphysics of the very sort that the logical positivists might have thought they had exorcized, certainly of a sort that seems contrary to the naturalistic spirit that the logical positivists fostered and that has

---

[2] See esp. the essays in *Papers I* and *Metaphysics and Epistemology* for Lewis' own treatment of these topics. For samples of other classic treatments of them within the analytic tradition, from the second half of the twentieth century, see Strawson (1959); Armstrong (1968); Kripke (1981); van Inwagen (1981); Nagel (1986); McDowell (1996); Mellor (1998); and Wiggins (2002). Note: I talk about the resurgence of metaphysics as practised in the early modern period, though what Lewis epitomizes is also highly reminiscent of scholasticism, not least in its close attention to language. Were this comparison to be pushed, then we might further say that science plays the role that was played in scholasticism by theology, and Frege's varied legacy the role that was played in scholasticism by Aristotle's.

[3] Here and throughout this chapter I use the term 'naturalism' in more or less the Quinean way defined in §2 of the previous chapter. (Contemporary analytic philosophy exhibits other, less demanding uses of the term; see n. 8 of that chapter.)

itself survived this new-found interest in old-style metaphysics. One of my principal aims in the present chapter is to explain how this has happened, using Lewis as a paradigm case. And while it would be stretching things to say that Lewis plays Fichte or Hegel to Carnap's and Quine's Hume and Kant, I do believe that there are deep and important similarities between the story that I tried to tell at the end of Part One and the story that I have to tell here.

But first, I must mention one feature of the situation that makes my task especially difficult. I have in mind the curious (and in my view suspect[4]) lack of self-consciousness that accompanies this reversion to earlier metaphysical practices.[5] Recent work in analytic metaphysics has involved surprisingly little reflection on the nature of the enterprise.[6] This means that my story about what has been going on cannot be informed in any significant way by the practitioners' own sense of what has been going on. Lewis is a case in point. His metaphysical work has countless laudable features. It is fertile, deep, beautifully crafted, and endlessly fascinating. But it is not particularly self-reflective. It is, in the terms of my Preface, very much work in metaphysics rather than meta-metaphysics. Since my own primary concern is with meta-metaphysics, what follows will therefore be highly selective in what it draws from that work.

2. Lewis' Quinean Credentials; or, Lewis: Empiricist, Naturalist, Physicalist

Lewis is an empiricist. Or at least, he is an epistemic empiricist.[7] In his account of knowledge he equates basic evidence with 'perceptual experience and memory' ('Knowledge', p. 424) – although, just like Quine (see §3 of the previous chapter), he equates them non-dogmatically, the equation being, if correct, correct only because of contingent features of reality.

Lewis is also a naturalist. He is not perhaps an extreme Quinean naturalist, prepared to say that the scientific way to make sense of things is 'the' way to make sense of things. But he is enough of a naturalist to say that the

---

[4] Cf. Introduction, §5. See further §4.

[5] There are some notable exceptions. See in particular Davidson (1984b) and (2005a), Williamson (2007), and Papineau (2009) – the last of which is especially robust in its commitment to naturalism. I should also mention the many excellent essays in Chalmers et al. (2009). Note, however, that these essays are concerned specifically with questions in ontology. They do not exhibit the broader self-consciousness about metaphysics that I have in mind.

[6] Here the analogy with post-Kantian German philosophy certainly breaks down!

[7] In 'Observation' and 'Ayer on Meaning' he considers in detail certain problems that afflict the formulation of semantic empiricism and provides a solution to these problems. Even so, he remains non-committal as far as the *truth* of semantic empiricism is concerned.

scientific way to make sense of things is the paradigmatic way to make sense of things; and that it stands in no need of any kind of Cartesian vindication from philosophy. He never does say this, in so many words. It is nevertheless clear that he would be totally unsympathetic to the Cartesian project. One thing that helps to make this clear is his attitude to a related project concerning mathematics, the project of ridding mathematics of that which is philosophically problematical. He writes:

> That will not do. Mathematics is an established, going concern. Philosophy is as shaky as can be. To reject mathematics for philosophical reasons would be absurd. If we philosophers are sorely puzzled by the [entities] that constitute mathematical reality, that's our problem. We shouldn't expect mathematics to go away to make our life easier. (*Parts of Classes*, p. 58)[8]

Another thing that helps to make clear the hostility with which Lewis would greet the Cartesian project is a Quinean account that he gives, if not of our scientific beliefs, then at least of our (scientifically informed) common-sense beliefs. He writes:

> It is far beyond our power to weave a brand new fabric of adequate theory *ex nihilo*, so we must perforce preserve the one we've got. A worthwhile theory must be credible, and a credible theory must be conservative. It cannot gain, and it cannot deserve, credence if it disagrees with too much of what we thought before. And much of what we thought before was just common sense....
>
> Common sense has no absolute authority in philosophy.... [But] theoretical conservatism is the only sensible policy for theorists of limited powers, who are duly modest about what they could accomplish after a fresh start. (*Plurality*, p.134)[9]

I ascribe naturalism to Lewis, then, not because he anywhere explicitly commits himself to it, but because of how the naturalistic spirit that I mentioned in the previous section pervades his work and is manifest in what he does explicitly say about other, related matters.

---

[8] Later he writes, 'I'm moved to laughter at the thought at how *presumptuous* it would be to reject mathematics for philosophical reasons' (ibid., p. 59, emphasis in original), and goes on, very wittily, to present a catalogue of philosophy's more outrageous pronouncements as evidence of its credentials. (Here as elsewhere there is a curious convergence between Lewis' attitude and that of the later Wittgenstein: see Ch. 10, §5, where I cited Wittgenstein (1967a), Pt I, §124.) That Lewis' attitude to the presumptions of philosophy with respect to mathematics provides a clue to his attitude to naturalism is also proposed by Daniel Nolan in Nolan (2005), pp. 11–12. But Nolan is more circumspect in his proposal than I am inclined to be; see in particular p. 12.

[9] This passage evokes Neurath's image; see §3 of the previous chapter.

Finally, Lewis is a physicalist. He states his physicalism as follows:

> It is the task of physics to provide an inventory of all the fundamental properties and relations that occur in the world[10].... We have no *a priori* guarantee of it, but we may reasonably think that present-day physics already goes a long way toward a complete and correct inventory.... And we may reasonably hope that future physics can finish the job in the same distinctive style.... [That is,] if we optimistically extrapolate the triumph of physics hitherto, we may provisionally accept that all fundamental properties and relations that actually occur are physical. This is the thesis of [physicalism]. ('Reduction', p. 292)[11]

Lewis is an empiricist, a naturalist, and a physicalist, then. His Quinean credentials are impeccable. Later we shall see some significant differences between Quine and him. But these differences, I shall suggest, are altogether less significant and altogether less profound than the similarities. There is a continuity between the two thinkers that speaks volumes concerning the *Zeitgeist* within analytic philosophy to which I have already referred.

One very interesting and telling *difference* between them is as much temperamental as it is philosophical; it serves, in fact, to reinforce the impression of philosophical kinship. I have in mind the way in which Quine revels in the systematicity of his thinking, searching for ever more elegant and ever more economical ways of connecting the various elements of what I called in §1 of the previous chapter 'his profound synoptic vision'.[12] Lewis, by contrast, tells us in the Introduction to his first volume of essays, 'I should have liked to be a piecemeal, unsystematic philosopher, offering independent proposals on a variety of topics. It was not to be. I succumbed too often to the temptation to presuppose my views on one topic when writing on another' (1st Introduction, p. ix).[13] A couple of pages later he lists what he calls 'some recurring themes that unify the papers in this volume, thus

[10] 'The world' here – to anticipate the next section – stands elliptically for the actual world.

[11] Notice how, in the terms of the previous chapter, Lewis, like Quine, subscribes to both provisional physicalism and regulative physicalism. (But note that Lewis himself calls his thesis 'materialism' rather than 'physicalism', in combined acknowledgement of its ancestry and deference to earlier usage. (Fichte, for one, used the label 'materialism': see Ch. 6, §2.) 'Physicalism' is the better label, however. This is for a reason that Lewis himself gives: 'our best physics acknowledges other bearers of fundamental properties [than matter]: parts of pervasive fields, parts of causally active spacetime' (ibid., p. 293).)

[12] Two fine examples of this are provided by his two late works (Quine (1992) and (1995a)), each of which is only about a hundred pages long and in each of which we find a meticulously wrought compendium of all his main ideas.

[13] This is the passage to which I referred parenthetically in the Introduction, n. 17. See also *Parts of Classes*, p. 57, where he says, 'I am no enemy of systematic metaphysics,' – and the ensuing 'However' is already audible.

frustrating my hopes of philosophizing piecemeal' (ibid., p. xi). Lewis is a systematist *malgré lui*. It is almost as if the naturalistic spirit to which I have been referring, and which is one of the main sources of his systematicity, has taken possession of him.

That said, his aversion to system finds some sort of expression in the *content* of his overall vision, whereby 'all there is to the world is a vast mosaic of local matters of particular fact, just one little thing and then another' (2nd Introduction, p. ix). Lewis calls this thesis 'Humean', 'in honor of the great denier of necessary connections' (ibid.).[14] It leads him, for example, to endorse the Quinean view of physical objects mentioned in §6 of the previous chapter: the view that physical objects have temporal parts that are strictly distinct from one another, albeit united by various kinds of continuity, including, most notably, causal continuity (e.g. *Plurality*, pp. 204–206). It also has a curious echo – I put it no more strongly than that – in his work on what might fairly be described as the metaphysics of mathematics. Many philosophers of mathematics, and indeed many mathematicians, taking their lead largely from Frege, hold mathematics to be fundamentally about sets. But what exactly is a set? According to Cantor's two famous definitions, a set is 'any gathering into a whole … of distinct perceptual or mental objects' (Cantor (1955), p. 85) or 'a many that allows itself to be thought of as a one' (Cantor (1932), p. 204).[15] Lewis complains that this account fails in the basic case of a singleton, that is to say a set with only one member, such as the set of English popes or the set of terrestrial moons. (Where is 'the many' in either of these cases?) In *Parts of Classes* he develops a rival account, whereby the case of a singleton really is the basic case and bigger sets are quite literally made up of singletons. Thus your singleton and my singleton together constitute our pair set, the set whose only two members we are. Each of them is literally a part of it. Sethood, on this conception, is not fundamentally a matter of manies begetting ones; it is fundamentally a matter of ones begetting different ones, which in turn beget yet different ones, and so on. Thereafter the different little begotten ones make up bigger ones. It is all markedly atomistic.

Before we turn our attention to what is undoubtedly the most notorious of Lewis' metaphysical views, I want to mention one further respect in which he reveals his Quinean credentials. Although he shares Quine's sense of the arbitrariness of some of our decisions concerning what to assert in metaphysics, or more generally concerning what to assert in philosophy,[16] he

---

[14] Whether it is Humean or not, it is certainly profoundly anti-Hegelian: see Ch. 7, §§3 and 4.

[15] Do these definitions bypass the contradiction that afflicted Frege's conception of a set (Ch. 8, §7(a))? Arguably they do: see Hallett (1984) or, for something more sketchy, Moore (2001a), Ch. 8, §§5 and 6.

[16] Compare Quine's discussion of ordered pairs (Ch. 12, §7) with Lewis' discussion of the null set in *Parts of Classes*, §1.4.

is also resolutely Quinean in his insistence that they are decisions concerning *what to assert*, each objectively true or false as the case may be. Thus:

> Once the menu of well-worked-out theories is before us, philosophy is a matter of opinion. Is that to say that there is no truth to be had? Or that the truth is of our own making, and different ones of us can make it differently? Not at all! If you say flatly that there is no god, and I say that there are countless gods ..., then it may be that neither of us is making any mistake of method.... But one of us, at least, is making a mistake of fact. Which one is wrong depends on what there is. (1st Introduction, p. xi)[17]

3. Modal Realism

Aptly, the notorious view to which I referred towards the end of the previous section is a view about what there is. Lewis dubs it *modal realism* (*Plurality*, p. 2). It is the view – a throwback to Leibniz – that, as well as the actual world and all that constitutes it, there are countless other possible worlds and all that constitutes them.[18]

Lewis' conception of possible worlds and his philosophical interest in them are quite different from Leibniz'. For both of them, however, there is a basic link between possible worlds and modal notions such as necessity, possibility, and contingency. What is necessarily the case is what is the case in all possible worlds; what is possibly the case is what is the case in at least one possible world; and what is contingently the case is what is the case in this world, the actual world, but not in all of them.

For Lewis, each of these possible worlds is a spatio-temporally unified cosmos causally independent of each of the others. And the things that constitute it really do exist. Thus given that there *could have been* flying pigs, in other words given that there is at least one possible world in which there *are* flying pigs, then there really are flying pigs. True, there are no flying pigs in the actual world, a fact that we might naturally express by saying, 'There are no flying pigs.' But that is no embarrassment for Lewis. He points out that our talk of what there is or is not is often tacitly and quite legitimately restricted, in a way that the context makes clear. Someone who says, 'There are no flying pigs,' is naturally interpreted as making a claim about what there is in the actual world – just as someone who opens the fridge and

---

[17] Cf. the parenthetical remark in n. 44 of the previous chapter for how this bears on Lewis' answers to the Transcendence Question and the Creativity Question which I posed in §6 of the Introduction.

[18] Real worlds, not what Lewis would call '*ersatz* worlds'; not, that is, mere abstract representations of how the actual world might have been. See further below and see *Plurality*, Ch. 3.

says, 'There are no eggs,' is naturally interpreted as making a claim about what there is in the fridge. The former claim is no more vitiated by all the flying pigs in other possible worlds than the latter claim is by all the eggs in other people's fridges. (See *Plurality*, esp. §§1.1, 1.2, and 2.1; cf. also 'Counterpart Theory'.)[19]

Whatever we make of such modal realism, there are two respects in which it appears radically un-Quinean. First, it appears not even to make sense unless there is a distinction to be drawn between what is necessarily the case and what is contingently the case; but this is one of the distinctions that we saw Quine repudiate in §4 of the previous chapter. Second, such modal realism appears to be ontologically extravagant; but, as we saw in §7 of the previous chapter, Quine is keen to acknowledge the existence of as little as possible.

In fact, the offence against Quine is not as great in either case as it appears. As far as the first point is concerned, the mere claim that all these possible worlds and their constituents exist is not, by itself, under any direct threat from Quine's attack on the necessary/contingent distinction. It needs to be supplemented with the claim that there is a determinate yes/no answer to the question whether any given statement is true with respect to any given world. The real offender, in other words, is the idea of *what is the case in a possible world*. There is scope for an unregenerate Quinean to accept the first claim – to accede to the existence of countless possible worlds beyond the actual world – but to deny the second – to deny that we have any effective way of delineating, for anything that is the case, the range of possible worlds beyond the actual world in which it remains the case. (Quine himself toys with just such a view in Quine (1969e), pp. 147ff.[20]) Still, for reasons that we shall glimpse in due course, such a view would not be acceptable to Lewis. It might conform to his strict definition of modal realism, which only requires the first claim, but it would not satisfy most of the philosophical assertions that he makes on behalf of his own view, which require the second claim as well. So as far as the first point is concerned, the offence against Quine, though not as great as it appears, is still pretty great.

As far as the second point is concerned, the offence against Quine is really not great at all. Yes, Quine champions parsimony. He wants to acknowledge the existence of as little as possible.[21] But that means: as little as is

---

[19] This too bears on Lewis' answer to the Transcendence Question (n. 17), but more straightforwardly so. This is because other possible worlds, of which Lewis thinks that we metaphysicians can make perfectly good sense, are in several senses of the term transcendent.

[20] But note that Lewis would not count what Quine calls possible worlds as the real thing. He would count them as *ersatz* worlds: see n. 18 above and see *Plurality*, §3.2.

[21] In the previous chapter I put this in terms of his wanting to acknowledge, not only as few things as possible, but as few *sorts* of things as possible. Lewis adverts to this distinction and urges that modal realism, insofar as it is ontologically extravagant, is ontologically

compatible with the satisfaction of various other desiderata. Quine himself, as we saw in §7 of the previous chapter, reluctantly acknowledges the existence of mathematical entities, because of what he sees as the indispensable work that mathematics does in natural science. Lewis likewise acknowledges the existence of possible worlds and their constituents because of what he sees as crucial work that appeal to them does in our attempt to make overall sense of things. (More on this later.) He would hold no brief for modal realism were it not for that. *Methodologically*, his procedure is utterly Quinean. There may of course be disagreement between him and Quine concerning whether appeal to all these possible entities does do the work that he (Lewis) thinks it does. But that is another matter, more pertinent to the first point. As far as the second point is concerned, Lewis is no less keen to avoid extravagance than Quine is.[22]

This is symptomatic of the fact, as I see it, that the similarities between Lewis and Quine are far more profound than the differences. Each is concerned with providing an account of the most general character of reality. Each sees the need for a continual trade-off between various conflicting desiderata in the process of settling on such an account: conformity to common sense may have to be sacrificed for simplicity; simplicity may have to be sacrificed for accuracy, or, come to that, for conformity to common sense; parsimony may have to be sacrificed for explanatory power; and so forth. Each recognizes that what benefits outweigh what costs is a matter of non-codifiable judgment. Each refuses to draw the conclusion that the correct account is anything other than that: *the correct account*, unique, true, objectively affirmable. Each sees his project as broadly scientific. More fully, each sees his project as the project of making general sense of things in the only way in which sense can ever really be made of anything, which is to say in accord with broadly scientific methods and principles (this last point being an expression of their shared naturalism).

I mentioned conformity to common sense. We have already seen Lewis' attitude to this in the previous section. He regards conformity to common sense in precisely the way I have just been outlining: as a good, but not a supreme good, and therefore a good to be weighed against others. He is well aware that modal realism, according to which flying pigs really exist, is an infringement of common sense. He refers amusingly to the 'incredulous stares' with which his view tends to be greeted (*Counterfactuals*, p. 86; see further *Plurality*, §2.8). But sometimes an infringement of common sense is a reasonable price to pay for certain theoretical gains. It is common for natural scientists to pay this price. They tell us, for instance, that the earth

extravagant only in the first and less problematical of these respects: see *Counterfactuals*, p. 87. For current purposes this distinction does not matter; but for a rejoinder, see Melia (2003), pp. 113–114.

[22] Cf. *Plurality*, pp. 3–5, and 'Abstract'. See also Nolan (2005), pp. 203–204.

is continuously rotating, and that simultaneity is relative to a frame of reference. Some of them see fit to tell us that glass is a liquid. Lewis tells us that there are flying pigs. The reason, in each case, is the same: it makes for a better overall account of the general character of reality. 'We ought to believe in other possible worlds and individuals,' writes Lewis, 'because systematic philosophy goes more smoothly in many ways if we do' ('Abstract', p. 354).

It is unfortunately beyond the scope of this chapter to discuss the impressive list of ways in which Lewis is able to show that systematic philosophy does indeed go more smoothly if we accept his modal realism.[23] One representative example that I shall mention, though still not discuss, is the use of modal apparatus in analyzing counterfactual conditionals, that is statements of the form, 'If it had been the case that p, then it would have been the case that q.' On Lewis' account, a statement of this form is true if and only if, roughly, in the possible worlds most like the actual world in which the antecedent holds, the consequent holds too (*Counterfactuals*, passim, and *Plurality*, §1.3). As it happens, I do not myself believe that modal realism pays its way. But I am more concerned with what it shows us about Lewis' attitude and approach to metaphysics than with whether or not we should accept it. This is what I shall pursue in the next section.

A final point for this section. Since Lewis holds possible worlds to be spatio-temporally unified cosmoses that are causally independent of one another, there are grounds for the complaint that he is not properly attuned to all that might have been the case. Some of what might have been the case seems not to be the case in any of his possible worlds. For example, there might have been no space and no time. Again, there might have been (indeed, some physicists claim that there actually are) spatio-temporally unified cosmoses that are causally independent of one another, which means that there are possible worlds that Lewis can see only as pluralities of possible worlds.[24]

Lewis responds to this objection by simply denying the possibilities in question. In the case of the possibility of causally independent cosmoses he confesses that he 'would rather not' (*Plurality*, p. 71). But doing so, he thinks, is another infringement of common sense worth incurring for an overall gain in simplicity (ibid., pp. 71–72). This may seem cavalier on Lewis' part. But it makes sense in terms of his broad programme. After all, the alleged possibilities are not particularly relevant to the work that he takes his modal apparatus to perform. (The analysis of counterfactual conditionals is a pertinent case in point. This analysis is meant to apply, first

[23] See esp. *Plurality*, §§1.2–1.5. John Perry has remarked that Lewis' modal apparatus 'goes through philosophical problems the way a McCormick reaper goes through wheat' (quoted in van Inwagen (1998), p. 592).

[24] See Melia (2003), pp. 111–113.

and foremost, to counterfactual conditionals that are of real concern to us, never mind what would have been the case had there been neither space nor time.) If, as I suspect, this is the dominant factor in Lewis' preparedness to reject these possibilities, and if, as I have also been urging, the work that he takes his modal apparatus to perform is of a piece with the work performed by the theoretical apparatus in any branch of natural science, then we see once more how far Lewis epitomizes the naturalistic spirit of his philosophical time and place.

4. Concerns About Modal Realism. The Concerns Removed, but the Shortcomings of Lewis' Metaphysics Thereby Revealed

Lewis trumpets the various ways in which modal realism aids the smooth running of systematic philosophy. But he also considers various ways in which it seems positively to hinder it. For it seems to exacerbate certain philosophical problems (problems, it should be said, that are bad enough anyway). Thus consider the problem of induction: the problem of accounting for the reasonableness of certain inferences from the observed to the unobserved, such as the inference that someone instinctively makes when she assumes that the dog heard barking in the distance has only one head. If Lewis is right, then there are countless possible worlds, no different in kind from the actual world, in which everything is exactly as it is in the actual world until a time when dogs routinely start sprouting extra heads. How come we are so confident that our world is not one of those? (People in those worlds, let us not forget, are every bit as confident that neither is theirs.) Or consider the problem of accounting for the unreasonableness of certain courses of action, such as the infliction of gratuitous suffering. If Lewis is right, then any decision not to inflict gratuitous suffering in this world only means that gratuitous suffering is inflicted in countless other possible worlds instead. Why should it be preferable for the suffering to occur there rather than here?

Lewis shows admirably, it seems to me, that these worries are grounded in confusion. In fact his modal realism has no bearing whatsoever on these philosophical problems. Here is what he says about the first:

> As a modal realist, I have no more and no less reason than anyone else to give over groundless faith in inductive luck. I have the reason everyone has: it is possible, and possible in ever so many ways, that induction will deceive me. That reason is metaphysically neutral. It becomes no better and no worse if reformulated in accordance with one or another ontology of modality. ('Anselm', pp. 22–23)

Concerning the second problem, he fastens on variants of the commonsensical notion that the reasonableness or unreasonableness of what a person does is sensitive to what gratuitous suffering that person actually inflicts or refrains from inflicting, in a way in which it could never be sensitive to what gratuitous suffering that person might have inflicted or refrained from inflicting (*Plurality*, §2.6).[25]

The tactic that Lewis uses in both cases is akin to the tactic that I tried to use in Chapter 3, §4, to defuse the idea that each of Leibniz' possible worlds is the best by its own lights. The tactic is simply to stop thinking of possible worlds 'geographically', and to revert to a more homespun understanding of what it means to say that something might have been the case, must be the case, or is actually the case. True, the inhabitants of other possible worlds lead their own colourful lives, which bring them their own pleasures and pains, their own joys and sorrows; they even have their own (sometimes very alien) natural environments. But these can have no influence on us, nor ours on them. They are just ways things might have been.

I said that Lewis' modal realism has no bearing on the philosophical problems under consideration. In this context, that has to be taken as a compliment, since the bearing it would have, if it had any, could only be adverse. Nonetheless, in a broader context the comment should give pause. Here I am harking back to an observation that I made in §7 of the Introduction: that unless metaphysics makes a difference, it has no point. If modal realism were a way of thinking about necessity, possibility, contingency, and the rest that did not subserve any of the uses to which we put these notions, let alone if it were a way of thinking about them that positively thwarted the uses to which we put them, that would be objection enough to it. Leibniz' modal realism, granted the success of his system, subserves the use to which we put such notions in thinking about how an omniscient, omnipotent, perfectly good being could fail to prevent what seems to be (aptly enough, in the light of the example that we have just been considering) gratuitous suffering. What uses does Lewis' modal realism subserve?

Well, that, of course, takes us back to the previous section. But this discussion acts as a forceful reminder of how much turns on the philosophical work that Lewis takes his modal apparatus to perform. Deny that and, as Lewis would be the first to concede, you take away all reason to accept his modal realism. You do not refute it. You merely make it redundant.

What is striking – and this is the crucial point in the current context – is that both the work that Lewis takes his modal apparatus to perform and the damage that it briefly looked as though it might wreak are fundamentally *philosophical*. Descartes had a metaphysical system that was intended to subserve science; Spinoza, a metaphysical system that was intended to

---

[25] 'In a way in which' does crucial work here: obviously there *are* ways in which the reasonableness of what I do can be sensitive to what gratuitous suffering I might have inflicted, for example insofar as that in turn is relevant to alternatives between which I had to choose. For more on these matters, see also *Plurality*, §§2.5 and 2.7.

subserve ethics; Hegel, a metaphysical system that was intended to subserve everything. And the damage that their systems were in danger of
wreaking was similarly far-reaching. Even Leibniz, whose metaphysical
system came closest to being intended as an end in itself (Ch. 3, §1), was
in danger, partly indeed for that very reason, of fostering passive resig-
nation in the face of the world's evils. The positive or negative assessment of what Lewis offers, by contrast, seems very much a matter for the
philosophical study.

For Lewis, metaphysics is intended to subserve the rest of philosophy.
Thus even the example that I gave in §7 of the Introduction, of how Lewis
combines metaphysics with science in addressing questions about the existence and nature of properties and universals, showed him putting metaphysics to work in the service, not of science, but of the philosophy of
science, trying to make the best sense *of* science. Likewise, the example that
we considered in §2 above, of how Lewis combines metaphysics with mathematics, was an example of his putting metaphysics to work, in the service,
not of mathematics, but of the philosophy of mathematics, trying to make
the best sense *of* mathematics.[26] (This of course relates to the mathematical conservatism that we also saw him proclaim in that section.) Not that
the metaphysics in which Lewis engages need be viewed as anything other
than a maximally general attempt to make sense *of things*, of universals, for
instance, as opposed to the concept of a universal, or of sets, as opposed to
the concept of a set. It is just that its focus, as befits its place in the analytic
tradition, is as much on the sense that is being made of these things as it is
on the things themselves. In the offing are always philosophical questions
about the more particular sense that is available to be made of these things,
in the specific areas of human thought and experience in which they especially figure.

Let us return to the puzzle that I posed in §1. How is that, in the wake
of Quine, and against a fundamentally naturalistic backcloth, philosophers
have felt encouraged to revert to the kind of metaphysics that was practised
in the early modern period, to reflect, in their armchairs, on substance, universals, and the rest? The story, I suggest, goes something like this. Quine,
arch-naturalist that he was, believed that a crucial task for naturalism was
'[to blur] the supposed boundary between speculative metaphysics and natural science' (Quine (1961b), p. 20). He gave renewed respectability to the
idea that metaphysicians had a legitimate contribution to make to the overall project of making sense of things, of a piece with the various contributions made by natural scientists, but at a much higher level of generality than
most. Later, the boundary that he and many other analytic philosophers

---

[26] This is not to deny that he produces some deep and fascinating mathematics in the process: see esp. *Parts of Classes*, Ch. 4 and the Appendix, written jointly with John P. Burgess
and A.P. Hazen.

took his naturalism to have blurred seemed, in the eyes of a large proportion of the analytic community, perhaps even the majority, to be as sharp as ever. (It had rarely seemed *razor* sharp, certainly not when 'speculative metaphysics' had been recognized as a legitimate activity at all.) Analytic philosophers became altogether less suspicious than they had been under the sway of Quine of the various associated distinctions, most notably the distinction between what is necessarily the case and what is contingently the case. At the same time the idea that philosophers in general, and metaphysicians in particular, could muscle in with natural scientists in discovering truths about reality (and not just promoting clarity of thought, *a là* Wittgenstein, or articulating linguistic frameworks for the expression of other people's discoveries, *a là* Carnap) retained its allure. So philosophers, if they were to hold on to this idea, needed to conceive of the contribution that they had to make to the overall project of making sense of things as genuinely distinctive, not merely different in degree from the contribution that natural scientists had to make. The most obvious way for them to do this, if not the only way,[27] was to see it as their business to reflect on how reality must be, as opposed to finding out empirically how it happens to be. And in this way, or in some related way, they were able to reattain to a broad conception of philosophy, and in particular of metaphysics, that had been dominant in the early modern period, but that had been consigned to oblivion throughout most of the analytic tradition.

Why then did metaphysics in the early modern period have so many more repercussions beyond philosophy than its analytic descendant, metaphysics of the kind that Lewis practises, or 'naturalistic' metaphysics, as we might call it?

Part of the answer to this question is illustrated in what I said above about Lewis himself. The focus, when naturalistic metaphysicians attempt to make maximally general sense of things, is characteristically as much on the sense as it is on the things – which indeed connects with the idea that the project is one of saying how the things must be, not simply how they are. But that is only part of the answer. Even if it explains the special connection between naturalistic metaphysics and the rest of philosophy, it does not explain the broader connections enjoyed by metaphysics in the early modern period. What did the early moderns bring to their endeavour that naturalistic metaphysicians do not?

The answer to *this* question – to continue in the same dangerously glib vein – is that they brought a due regard, not only for the things, and not only for the things together with the sense made of them, but for the making of that sense. Metaphysics in the early modern period had a distinctive kind of self-consciousness that naturalistic metaphysics lacks. (Recall my

---

[27] For a striking alternative, see Papineau (2009).

complaint at the end of §1.) Every single one of my protagonists in Part
One of this book tried to make maximally general sense of things by making
sense, in particular, of making sense of things – as I tried to indicate in each
of their respective chapters. This enabled metaphysics to serve, for each of
them, as 'a humanistic discipline', to use Bernard Williams' phrase (Williams
(2006m)).[28] And this in turn enabled it to enjoy the broader connections it
did. It became inextricably bound up with the attempt to understand the
place of humanity in the larger scheme of things: to understand, for example, how human beings can arrive at *scientia* (Descartes); or how they can
achieve their highest virtue, by acquiring adequate knowledge of the essence
of things (Spinoza); or how they can acknowledge this world as the best of
all possible worlds, despite its appearing not to be (Leibniz); or so forth.
This is not *yet* to say that metaphysics was in the service of anything other
than philosophy. To substantiate that claim, some story needs to be told
about how understanding the place of humanity in the larger scheme of
things could in turn help humanity to live in that place. But each of my
protagonists did have such a story to tell. And because of the distinctive
self-consciousness that we find in early modern metaphysics, each such story
became a story about the use to which metaphysics could be put beyond the
philosophical study – provided, of course, that it was metaphysics of the sort
practised then.

No such story is relevant to metaphysics of the sort practised now, by
those of Lewis' ilk, that is to say naturalistic metaphysics.[29] For reasons that
I tried to make clear in the previous chapter, it is precisely this distinctive
self-consciousness that the naturalism at work in such metaphysics prevents
it from replicating – at least when that naturalism assumes anything like
the extreme form that it assumes in Quine's case.[30] Such naturalism badly

---

[28] Williams applies the phrase to philosophy as a whole, but I think he would be happy to
apply it specifically to metaphysics too: see Williams (2006l).

[29] It is worth emphasizing in this connection that naturalistic metaphysics by no means
exhausts contemporary analytic metaphysics. For examples of the latter that are not
examples of the former, see Nagel (1986); McDowell (1996); Cockburn (1997); and
Cooper (2002).

[30] This did not prevent Quine himself from trying to make sense of making sense of things.
In subsequent naturalistic metaphysics there has been little even by way of an *attempt*
to do so. At the limit is the view that we find in Churchland (1979), Stich (1983), and
Churchland (1986), that notions such as that of belief are as scientifically discredited as
that of phlogiston, and that there *is* no satisfactory sense ultimately to be made of them.
In company such as this Lewis counts as moderate. He, like Quine, tries to make sense of
making sense of things – and in fact produces some of his best work in the process. An
outstanding essay, which is also as it happens another example of his application of the
machinery of possible worlds, is 'Attitudes'. Still, the essay seems to me fundamentally
flawed, for the reasons to which I refer in the main text.

misconstrues, or at the very least fails to make adequate provision for, making sense of making sense of things. In Lewis, and in other metaphysicians of his stripe, we find insight, invention, and illumination. But we also find evidence, it seems to me, of the debilitating power of their naturalism, which, by forcing their metaphysics into an inappropriately scientific mould, seriously restricts its impact.

CHAPTER 14

✦

Dummett

The Logical Basis of Metaphysics

1. In Retrospect and in Prospect

This final chapter of Part Two brings it full circle, inasmuch as it directs our attention back to Frege. I do not mean to suggest that the subject of this chapter, Michael Dummett, is of importance to my narrative only to the extent that he is Fregean. The point is rather that Dummett himself wishes to direct our attention back to Frege. We have already seen (Ch. 8, §1) something of Dummett's enormous admiration for Frege, to the exposition and dissemination of whose work he has made an unrivalled contribution,[1] and whom he regards as having effected the revolution that made analytic philosophy possible.[2] Dummett is convinced that we need to reassimilate the

---

[1] See esp. *Frege* I, *Frege* II, and *Frege* III. There are also numerous articles, of which 'Frege', 'Frege and Analysis', and 'Frege as a Realist' stand out.

   Note: throughout this chapter I use the following abbreviations for Dummett's works: 'Allard' for Dummett (2007d); 'Analytical Philosophy' for Dummett (1978m); 'Autobiography' for Dummett (2007a); 'Beards' for Dummett (2007h); 'Campbell' for Dummett (2007e); 'Deduction' for Dummett (1978j); 'Fitch's Paradox' for Dummett (2009); 'Frege' for Dummett (1978c); *Frege* I for Dummett (1981a); *Frege* II for Dummett (1981b); *Frege* III for Dummett (1991a); 'Frege and Analysis' for Dummett (1991c); 'Frege and Kant' for Dummett (1991f); 'Frege and Wittgenstein', for Dummett (1991g); 'Frege as a Realist' for Dummett (1991d); 'Gödel's Theorem' for Dummett (1978f); 'Indeterminacy' for Dummett (1978l); *Intuitionism* for Dummett (2000); 'Intuitionistic Logic' for Dummett (1978g); 'Knowledge of a Language' for Dummett (1993c); *Logical Basis* for Dummet (1991b); 'Mathematics' for Dummett (1993e); 'McDowell' for Dummett (2007f); 'McGuiness' for Dummett (2007b); *Origins* for Dummett (1993a); 'Pears' for Dummett (1994); 'Preface' for Dummett (1978a); 'Realism and Anti-Realism' for Dummett (1993f); 'Rumfitt' for Dummett (2007g); 'Sense and Reference' for Dummett (1978d); 'Theory of Meaning (II)' for Dummett (1993b); 'The Past' for Dummett (1978k); *Thought and Reality* for Dummett (2006); 'Truth' for Dummett (1978b); *Truth and the Past* for Dummett (2004); 'Verificationism' for Dummett (1992); 'Victor's Error' for Dummett (2001a); 'Wang's Paradox' for Dummett (1978h); and 'Wittgenstein's Philosophy of Mathematics' for Dummett (1978e).

[2] See again the material cited in Ch. 8, §1.

insights that were integral to this revolution before there can be any serious prospect of progress in metaphysics.

Michael Dummett (born 1925[3]) holds philosophy in general, and metaphysics in particular, to be at root the analysis of thought; and he holds the analysis of thought to be at root the analysis of the means by which thought is expressed, which is to say language. This makes 'the philosophy of language ... the foundation of all other philosophy' ('Analytical Philosophy', p. 442; cf. p. 458).[4] Dummett takes that to be one of the principal lessons to be learned from Frege. And he takes it to be the fundamental tenet of analytic philosophy.[5]

Let us reflect on how this tenet relates specifically to metaphysics. In Dummett's view, metaphysical questions are questions about the most general character of reality. They are questions about what, in general, it *takes* for things to be the way they are.[6] That is, they are questions about what, in general, it takes for things to be the way we *think* they are, when what we think is true. For Dummett, then, the most general attempt to make sense of things is an attempt to make sense of the sense, in general, that we make of things, insofar as we make correct sense of them. But there is no access to that sense save through the means by which we express it, namely language; such is the lesson of Frege. So the most general attempt to make sense of things is an attempt to make sense of *linguistic* sense, where this embraces all our thought and all that constitutes our thought.[7]

Very well; but how well has analytic philosophy born witness to Dummett's conception of these matters? Certainly, Frege's own attention to linguistic sense has had an indelible impact on subsequent analytic philosophy. Nevertheless, little of what we have observed since has exhibited the smooth application of Frege's ideas to the addressing of traditional metaphysical questions which Dummett's conception suggests it could and should have done. On the contrary, attempts to make sense of linguistic sense, on the one hand, and attempts to make linguistic sense in response to traditional metaphysical questions, on the other, have tended to militate against each other, with now the former prevailing, now the latter.[8]

---

[3] Within a month of Frege's death.

[4] Cf. *Origins*, Chs 13 and 14 passim.

[5] This way of putting Dummett's thought is due to John McDowell: see McDowell (1996), p. 124.

[6] In the opening sentences of Ch. 1 of *Thought and Reality*, Dummett characterizes them as questions about what there is. This characterization looks somewhat different, but they are really equivalent. Within a couple of pages he explains that by 'what there is' he means not just 'what kinds of *object* there are' but 'what kinds of *fact* obtain' (pp. 2–3, emphasis in original).

[7] Linguistic sense includes what I called in Ch. 9, §7, 'propositional sense'. But it includes more besides; e.g. it includes sense of whatever kind attaches to linguistic items other than full declarative sentences.

[8] This is but one illustration, among the many that we have witnessed in this enquiry, of the inhibiting and disconcerting effect that heightened self-consciousness can have.

This was certainly true in the case of Wittgenstein, both early and late. Here it was the former that prevailed. The making of linguistic sense was perceived as an activity to be *protected*, and to be protected, moreover, against attempts to address traditional metaphysical questions. Traditional metaphysical questions were perceived as nothing but morasses of confusion, wrecking the making of linguistic sense and nourishing the production of nonsense. The same was true in the case of the logical positivists. There too the former prevailed. In Quine, his positivist pedigree notwithstanding, there was a shift in favour of the latter. Quine showed a readiness to reengage with traditional metaphysical questions, but only as facilitated by an *un*readiness to reflect on linguistic sense, which, at least in its Fregean guise, he went as far as repudiating. Similarly in the case of subsequent naturalistic philosophers. Here the unreadiness, which has often been as much a lack of due equipment as a lack of due willing, has been an unreadiness to reflect on sense-making more generally, so that it has become virtually impossible for these philosophers to see how the metaphysical questions that they are addressing connect with broader humanistic concerns; how they manage to be the big questions that they have always affected to be (see Ch. 13, §4).

Dummett finds all of this intolerable. 'The layman,' he writes,

> ... expects philosophers to answer deep questions of great import for an understanding of the world. Do we have free will? Can the soul ... exist apart from the body? ... Is there a God?[9] And the layman is quite right: if philosophy does not aim at answering such questions, it is worth nothing. (*Logical Basis*, p. 1)

The time has therefore come, in Dummett's view, to overcome the opposition between these two enterprises: to master the unsettling effects of reflection on linguistic sense and to put it to work in tackling those big questions, just as Frege put it to work in tackling fundamental questions in the philosophy of mathematics.

This will entail significant departures from all of the protagonists who have appeared so far in Part Two. Thus:

- unlike both Wittgenstein and Quine we shall need to take seriously the possibility of a systematic theory of linguistic sense[10,11]

---

[9] This is the triad of questions to which Kant assigned such central importance: see Ch. 5, n. 44.

[10] On Wittgenstein, see 'Analytical Philosophy', 'Frege and Wittgenstein', *Origins*, pp. 164–166, 'Pears', and 'McGuiness'. On Quine, see 'Sense and Reference', pp. 134–140, and 'Indeterminacy'.

[11] Unlike *Quine* we shall need to take seriously linguistic sense itself, suitably construed. Among other things this will entail a recoil from the idea that what are confirmed or confuted by different possible courses of sense experience are only ever entire bodies of theory (though not a recoil from the idea that the confirmation or confutation of individual statements by different possible courses of sense experience is sometimes

- unlike Carnap and other logical positivists we shall need to take seriously the possibility of contributions to the exercise of making sense of things that consist neither in conceptual analysis nor in empirical investigation[12]
- unlike Lewis and other naturalistic philosophers of his ilk we shall need to pay proper attention not just to sense, still less just to linguistic sense, but to the making of sense[13]

and indeed

- unlike naturalistic philosophers more generally we shall need to eschew naturalism.[14]

I said 'significant departures from all of the protagonists who have appeared so far in Part Two.' *All* of them? Even Frege? Even Frege. We shall consider Dummett's most significant departure from Frege in the next section. But as a foretaste I note that Dummett is among those who take Frege to accord an unreasonable degree of objectivity to linguistic sense (see Ch. 8, §6).[15] Dummett thinks that Frege spoils his own insights about the relations between linguistic sense and language itself. He thinks that, by casting linguistic sense as something that is completely independent of language, and indeed of us, Frege thwarts a satisfactory account of how such sense is grasped and conveyed in acts of linguistic communication, and of how our grasp of it furnishes us with knowledge of the *Bedeutungen* of linguistic expressions. We shall see in the next section how this relates to his fundamental departure from Frege.

The programme, then, is first to clear the way for a systematic theory of linguistic sense by reflecting on what such a theory must look like,[16] and then, in the light of this reflection, to address the metaphysical questions that analytic philosophers hitherto have tended either to shun or to tackle

---

intelligible only in relation to other statements): see e.g. 'Deduction', pp. 304–305; 'Indeterminacy', p. 382; *Logical Basis*, Ch. 10; and *Origins*, pp. 190–191. It will also entail a rehabilitation of the distinction between analytic truths and synthetic truths: see e.g. 'Indeterminacy', pp. 414–415. Both these points bear on what we saw Quine argue in Ch. 12, §4.

[12] See 'Verificationism'.

[13] This connects with something on which Dummett has time and again insisted, namely that a satisfactory theory of linguistic sense must deliver a satisfactory theory of the grasp of it; a satisfactory theory, in other words, of linguistic understanding. Among countless references, see e.g. *Origins*, p. 11.

[14] For Dummett's opposition to Quine's naturalism, see 'McGuiness', p. 51.

[15] See the references in the discussion in Ch. 8, §6, esp. those in n. 56. See also *Thought and Reality*, pp. 9ff.

[16] For a succinct account of what such a theory must *deliver*, see *Thought and Reality*, pp. 14–15.

with inadequate tools. A crucial part of the programme will be to reflect on the character of *truth*. This is not just because the concept of linguistic sense and the concept of truth are correlative and need to be explained together (see e.g. *Truth and the Past*, p. 107, and 'McDowell', pp. 372–373). It is also because, as indicated earlier, the connection between making maximally general sense of things and making sense of making linguistic sense is forged by reflecting on the contents of *true* thoughts. Here is how Dummett himself puts the matter, quoting the famous second sentence of Wittgenstein's *Tractatus* (Wittgenstein (1961), 1.1):

> The world is the totality of facts, not things, and facts are true [thoughts];[17] so the concept of truth is the hinge upon which the door from the philosophy of thought opens into metaphysics, that is, the range of philosophical problems that concern the general character of reality. ('Beards', p. 890)

To reflect on the character of truth will in turn be, in Frege's famous phrase, 'to discern the laws of truth' (Frege (1997l), p. 325/p. 58 in the original German). And that, as Frege just as famously observed, is the task of logic (ibid.). And so it is that metaphysics will come to have, as Dummett puts it in the title of his most pertinent book, a *logical basis*.[18,19]

---

[17] Dummett has 'propositions' where I have inserted 'thoughts'. But he shows elsewhere (e.g. *Thought and Reality*, p. 9) that he is equally comfortable with the identification of facts with true thoughts; and the reference to thoughts here makes the connections I wish to emphasize more graphic. For discussion of the relation between 'thoughts' and 'propositions', see *Thought and Reality*, pp. 4ff. and 29–30.

[18] Dummett (1991b) – which I am abbreviating as *Logical Basis*.

[19] Cf. *Frege* I, pp. 671–672; *Frege* II, pp. 66–67; and *Logical Basis*, pp. 10ff. Cf. also 'Preface', p. xl, where he writes, 'The whole point of my approach to these problems [i.e. fundamental problems about the relations between realty and our capacity to know it] has been to show that the theory of meaning underlies metaphysics.' But note that Dummett is thereby forced to conceive his own work, which is primarily concerned with what a systematic theory of linguistic sense must look like, less as a contribution to metaphysics than as a prolegomenon to metaphysics (cf. *Logical Basis*, pp. x–xi). At the end of his Introduction to *Logical Basis* he writes, 'The layman wants the philosopher to give him a reason for believing, or for disbelieving, in God, in free will, or in immortality.... I am not proposing to answer [such questions]. I propose only to try to provide a base from which we might set out to seek for the answers' (p. 19). Not that he is inclined to be apologetic about this. He goes on to remark, 'Philosophical writing of the past, and of the present day as well, supplies answers to the great questions of metaphysics; and the answers usually satisfy no one but their authors.... I believe that we shall make faster progress only if we go at our task more slowly and methodically' (ibid.). In this there is something at once curiously reminiscent of, and strikingly different from, the boldness that we saw in the prefaces to Kant's first *Critique* and Wittgenstein's *Tractatus*: see Ch. 5, §2, and Ch. 9, §2, respectively;

2. Realism and Anti-Realism

We were reminded in the previous section of the unsettling effects that reflection on linguistic sense can have. Dummett is well aware of these and of what it takes to come to terms with them. Coming to terms with them is a condition of pursuing metaphysical questions on his conception. But it is not a condition in the sense of a prerequisite, something that has to be satisfied *first*. It is itself part of the metaphysical enterprise. Dummett holds that reflection on linguistic sense forces us to reassess some of our most deeply entrenched convictions concerning the general character of reality. Determining what to do about these convictions, perhaps determining how to live without them, *is* engaging in metaphysics.

The best known and most elemental example is the conviction that every thought is either true or not true.[20] I say 'not true' rather than 'false'. This is because there are various innocuous ways of challenging the idea that every thought is either true or false. For instance, it is natural to say that a thought about something non-existent, say the thought that Atlantis was ruled by a confederation of kings, is neither true nor false. But, whether or not that is the correct thing to say – perhaps it is not even correct to say that there is a thought involved in such a case[21] – the conviction that every thought is either true *or not* remains unassailed. Is it not unassailable? An incontrovertible law of logic?[22] On what possible grounds could *this* conviction be abandoned? It certainly never crossed Frege's mind to abandon it (cf. Frege (1997i), p. 300/p. 214 in the original German).

Dummett nevertheless urges caution. Reconsider the idea that every thought is either true *or false*. The innocuous ways of challenging this idea concern recognizable relations, in particular recognizable misfits, between our thinking and reality, such as we arguably find in the Atlantis case. Dummett, by contrast, is exercised by the prospect of *un*recognizable relations between our thinking and reality ('Truth', p. 23). Thus suppose there is a thought whose truth or non-truth we have no way of settling.[23] (An example might be a thought concerning some distant and undocumented event in history,

---

and cf. Ch. 9, n. 21. – For opposition to Dummett's view that (all of) metaphysics has a logical base, see Blackburn (1996), pp. 76–79.

[20] Dummett himself would insert the word 'determinately' before 'either': see *Frege* II, pp. 435–436. I remain unconvinced that this makes the difference he says it makes. But if you agree with Dummett, then take as read the insertion of 'determinately' in all the relevant contexts hereafter.

[21] For discussion of some of the issues involved, see Russell (1993) and Strawson (1993). And see again Ch. 8, n. 41, for the controversy concerning what Frege would say.

[22] It is part of Leibniz' principle of contradiction, one of the two fundamental *a priori* principles that he recognized; see Ch. 3, §1.

[23] By what standards? Conclusively? Beyond reasonable doubt? For any relevant practical purposes? It is an extremely important feature of Dummett's line of thought that this

such as the thought that Aristotle sneezed on his first birthday. Another might be a thought concerning a counterfactual that we have no way of negotiating, such as the thought that Descartes would have loved Marmite.) And suppose we take for granted that such a thought is either true or not true. Then, Dummett argues, it is not clear that we can give a satisfactory account of our grasp of the thought.

The argument proceeds very roughly as follows. Our grasp of a thought involves our knowing both how reality must be in order for the thought to be true and, derivatively, how reality must be in order for the thought not to be true. But such a grasp has to admit of public ratification. This is because, if it did not, nobody could ever know whether anybody else grasped the thought. So the thought would be incommunicable. But it is of the very essence of a thought to be communicable. For a thought is what can be expressed by a declarative sentence. And a declarative sentence can express only what it can be perceived to express, only what it can be used to communicate. (Both language learning and language use more generally would be unintelligible otherwise.)[24] However, it is not clear how our grasp of a thought can admit of public ratification if the thought is either true or not true without our being able to tell which. We must not simply take for granted, then, that, even in default of our having some way of telling whether a thought is true or not, it is one or the other.[25]

The caution that Dummett is urging here is a caution against a basic realism. It is a caution against the idea that reality outstrips our capacity to know about it. This is what makes his circumspection, on any reasonable conception of metaphysics, a contribution to metaphysics.[26] Where Frege held that the thought expressed by a declarative sentence is a matter of how things must be in order for the sentence to be true, irrespective of us, Dummett urges us to take seriously the 'anti-realist' alternative that the

matter should remain unresolved. As will become clear, his concern is not with any one clearly delineated scruple. It is with a family of scruples.

[24] Cf. Wittgenstein (1967a), Pt I, §§133–143 and 242; and cf. Quine's semantic empiricism (Ch. 12, §2).

[25] See esp. 'Truth'; 'Intuitionistic Logic'; 'The Past'; *Frege* II, Ch. 20; 'Theory of Meaning (II)'; and 'Realism and Anti-Realism'. The literature on this argument is vast. See e.g. McDowell (1976) and (2007a); McGinn (1979); Craig (1982); Wright (1992); Williamson (1994b), (2007), pp. 281–284; and Campbell (2007). For suspicion of the whole project, see P.F. Strawson (1976–1977), p. 21, where Strawson writes, 'Few things are more implausible that [sic] the idea that we can be rapidly forced into a wholesale revision ... of our metaphysics ... by a dogmatic interpretation of the observation, in itself irreproachable, that our understanding of a language is manifested only in our use of it.' (Cf. Diamond (1993), Lecture Two, §XI.)

[26] Or if not a contribution to metaphysics, then at least part of a prolegomenon to metaphysics (see n. 19). For further discussion of the connection with metaphysics, see *Logical Basis*, pp. 325–327, and *Intuitionism*, p. 267.

thought expressed by a declarative sentence is a matter of how things must be in order for us to *recognize* that the sentence is true.[27,28]

Two things should be emphasized, however, lest his position appear more radical than it really is. First, 'circumspection' is the operative word. In developing the line of argument sketched above, Dummett is presenting realists with a challenge; he is not opposing them. Insofar as he is making an anti-realist proposal, it is a proposal *for consideration*. He does not want to preclude an eventual decision in favour of some version of the realism that he is querying. It is just that any such decision must, he thinks, be earned, in full awareness of the problems that afflict it and of the alternatives to it. That is, it is not something to which we can uncritically help ourselves. Thus in his valedictory lecture 'Realism and Anti-Realism' Dummett writes:

> I viewed [my proposal], and still continue to view it, as a research programme, not the platform of a new philosophical party.... I did not conceive myself as proposing for consideration, let alone sustaining, any precise thesis, to be accepted or rejected. I saw the matter, rather, as the posing of a question how far, and in what contexts, a certain generic line of argument could be pushed. (p. 464; cf. 'Preface', p. xxxix)[29]

[27] He also, less frequently, considers the idea that the thought expressed by a declarative sentence is a matter of how things must be in order for us to recognize that the sentence is false. This idea is well explored in Rumfitt (2007), to which Dummett responds (enthusiastically) in 'Rumfitt'.

[28] In *Frege* I, pp. 683–684, Dummett suggests that it was 'historically necessary', if not 'logically necessary', for Frege to be immune to this alternative. This is because the revolution that Dummett takes Frege to have effected involved a retreat from various mind-centred approaches to philosophy that were dominant at the time, and his realism helped him to keep these at bay. For further discussion, in relation to Kant, Fichte, and Hegel, see *Frege* II, pp. 496–500.

[29] But note that it is not difficult to find what appear to be forthright affirmations of a blanket anti-realism in Dummett's writings. For instance in *Truth and the Past* we find, 'What is true is what can be known to be true' (p. 92); in 'Campbell', 'Only what is knowable can be true' (p. 313); and in 'Beards', 'It makes no sense to speak of a world, or the world, independently of how it is apprehended' (p. 892; cf. *Thought and Reality*, p. 64). Part of the explanation for this is that Dummett is genuinely wrestling with these problems and has at different times in his career been more or less convinced by the anti-realist proposal. There is further evidence for his lack of a settled view in the Postscript to 'Truth', written for its reprinting, where he says, 'The text of the article espouses a frankly anti-realist position.... I am no longer so unsympathetic to realism' (p. 24). Similarly, in the Preface to *Thought and Reality*, where he writes, 'Chapters 5–7 express views I no longer hold. It will naturally be asked why I am publishing them ..., if I no longer agree with them.... In [*Truth and the Past*] I ... set out a modification of the views I had expressed [here]. All the same, if I was sure that I had improved on my earlier thoughts, why put

This quotation also highlights the second thing that needs to be emphasized. We must not think of realism and anti-realism as two absolute opposed positions. Each admits of degrees. And each needs to be relativized to an area of discourse. The issue is *how far* one should think realistically or anti-realistically *about* this or that subject matter. It would be entirely reasonable for an extreme anti-realist about mathematics, say, to be a relatively robust realist about history, say. Such a person may think that Dummett's challenge can be met in the case of history in a way in which it cannot be met in the case of mathematics, or perhaps that there is a variation on the line of argument sketched above that is compelling in the case of mathematics but that has no analogue in the case of history.[30] It is instructive to see how the quotation from Dummett continues:

> I saw the matter ... as the posing of a question how far, and in what contexts, a certain generic line of argument could be pushed, where the answers 'No distance at all' and 'In no context whatever' could not be credibly entertained, and the answers 'To the bitter end' and 'In all conceivable contexts' were almost as unlikely to be right. (Ibid.)[31]

those earlier thoughts into print? The answer is that I am *not* sure.... [The two books] offer a choice between two possible conceptions of truth, conceptions that I hope I have succeeded in delineating with reasonable clarity' (p. vii, emphasis in original). (For the record, *Thought and Reality* 'firmly repudiates' an anti-realism about the past, 'but the conception of truth that [it proposes] does not make so conciliatory an advance in a realist direction as does that proposed in [*Truth and the Past*]' (ibid.).)

A final point: in the quotations from both *Truth and the Past* and 'Campbell' above Dummett claims that only what is knowable is true. A familiar argument due to F.B. Fitch derives from this the seemingly absurd conclusion that only what is *known* is true: see Fitch (1963). Dummett discusses this argument in 'Victor's Error' and 'Fitch's Paradox'. An approach to the paradox that I myself find attractive is that of Joseph Melia in Melia (1991). What Melia urges, in effect, is that the anti-realist thought is not that only what is knowable is true, but that only what is *settleable* is *true or false*. Fitch's argument has no bearing on the latter. (Cf. in this connection Schlick (1959a), p. 56. As noted in Ch. 4, n. 10, logical positivism involves a similar anti-realism, but here at least Schlick formulates it in the latter way. I think this goes some way towards rebutting the objection that Melia is simply changing the subject.)

[30] Cf. Dummett's own (implicit) comparison of these two cases in *Thought and Reality*, p. 79.

[31] For an attempt to resist any slide from anti-realism about mathematics to anti-realism in other areas, see McDowell (1998); and cf. Green (2001), pp. 130–131. For an excellent discussion of the way in which *Frege* III presents a case for anti-realism about mathematics that cannot be generalized, see Sullivan (2007). Note, however, that Dummett's own interest in the anti-realist proposal stems largely from the belief that *some* forceful arguments for anti-realism about mathematics *can* be generalized: see e.g. 'Intuitionistic Logic', pp. 226–227, and 'Autobiography', p. 18. (This explains why John McDowell, in the essay cited above, represents himself as opposing Dummett.) The irony is that

Furthermore, the term 'realism' has many varied uses within philosophy other than to designate a commitment to the thesis that every thought is either true or not, and Dummett has over the years increasingly come to embrace some of these other uses – even to the extent of suggesting that innocuous challenges to the thesis that every thought is either true *or false* may count as retreats, however pedestrian, from some kind of realism (see *Logical Basis*, p. 325, and 'Realism and Anti-Realism, p. 468).[32] The main further ingredient that he now thinks a position needs to have, in order to attract the label 'realism' on its most compelling-cum-robust interpretation, is a commitment to the thesis that statements are to be taken at face value (*Logical Basis*, p. 325, and 'Realism and Anti-Realism', p. 468). Thus consider the following three arithmetical statements:

7 + 5 = 12.
7 + 5 = 13.
Every even number greater than 2 is the sum of two primes.

A realist about arithmetic, on *this* construal of realism, will still insist that each of these statements is either true or not true.[33] Such a realist will also, however, insist that '7', which appears to function as a singular term in the first two statements, does function as a singular term there and picks out a particular object; that 'prime', which appears to function as a sortal noun in the third statement, does function as a sortal noun there and applies to a particular kind of object; and that 'every even number greater than 2', which appears to function as a quantifier in the third statement, does function as a quantifier there and ranges over a particular domain of objects.[34] What does this add? Well, consider the expression 'Arthur's sake', as it occurs in the statement 'She did it for Arthur's sake.' We surely have to say the opposite

the anti-realist position in the philosophy of mathematics that first attracted Dummett's attention, that of Brouwer, is based on considerations that are directly opposed to those on which Dummett bases his own anti-realist proposal (as indeed Dummett acknowledges: see 'Intuitionistic Logic', p. 226). Brouwer holds that mathematical thoughts are grounded in mathematical experience, conceived as something essentially private, and are therefore not fully communicable: see Brouwer (1983).

Finally, for related views in the philosophy of mathematics in Wittgenstein, views with which Dummett's have some affinity though about which Dummett also has considerable reservations, see e.g. Wittgenstein (1974a), Pt II, §§35 and 39, and Wittgenstein (1978), Pt V; and for Dummett's discussion of these views, see 'Wittgenstein's Philosophy of Mathematics'.

[32] Cf. *Frege* II, pp. 437–438.

[33] The first we know to be true. The second we know not to be true. The truth value of the third, at the time of my writing this, we do not know. I shall have more to say about the third statement in the next section.

[34] Cf. *Logical Basis*, p. 326, and 'Allard', p. 148. (Frege emerges as a realist about arithmetic on this construal.)

in this case. Although that expression appears to function as a singular term in that statement, we surely have to deny that it really does function as a singular term there, or at any rate, as a singular term that picks out a particular object. (She did it so as to benefit Arthur. Only the two of them were involved.) This is a kind of anti-realism with respect to sakes.[35]

Be that as it may, the kernel of any realism, in Dummett's view, remains a commitment to the thesis that every thought is either true or not true, independently of any capacity on our part to tell which. That is the thesis, of all realist theses, that 'has the greatest metaphysical resonance' (*Logical Basis*, p. 326).

3.   Three Replies to Dummett's Anti-Realist Challenge

Dummett's anti-realist challenge to this thesis has met with all sorts of reactions, including all sorts of opposition. I shall consider three replies that are particularly relevant to our enquiry.[36]

(a)   First Reply

The first reply is as follows. Dummett's attempt to make metaphysical capital out of considerations about language depends on a broadly Wittgensteinian view of language, whereby both the meaning of an expression and our understanding of the expression should be open to public view in the use that we make of it in communicating with one another.[37] But what if our use of language is not itself metaphysically neutral – as it surely is not?[38] After

[35] One interesting version of anti-realism with respect to arithmetic, on this construal, is Hartry Field's view, to which I adverted in Ch. 12, n. 49. On that view, a mathematical statement such as '7 + 5 = 12' is indeed either true or not true, and the apparent singular terms that occur in it are indeed singular terms; but they pick nothing out, because there is nothing for them *to* pick out, numbers being a fiction (Field (1980)). This makes '7 + 5 = 12' *not* true. Dummett discusses this view in 'Mathematics', pp. 433ff.

[36] Others are to be found in the literature cited in n. 25.

[37] 'Broadly Wittgensteinian' here is an allusion to such passages as those cited in n. 24. Some care is called for, however. This view of language is often put in the form of a rough slogan, 'Meaning is use', which Dummett and others explicitly attribute to Wittgenstein (see e.g. 'Theory of Meaning (II)', p. 38). In fact, Wittgenstein himself would not endorse this slogan without serious qualification: cf. Wittgenstein (1967a), Pt I, §§43 and 139, and (1974a), §29; and see Hacker (1996), pp. 244–249. (Mind you, Dummett would not endorse it either, as anything other than the crudest of guidelines. In 'Gödel's Theorem' he writes, 'The general thesis that the meaning of an expression is to be identified with its use is not ... particularly helpful; until it is specified in what terms the use of the expression is to be described, the thesis is merely programmatic' (p. 188).)

[38] Cf. Bernard Williams (2006o), Ch. 7, where Williams argues that our use of ethical language harbours illusions about the metaphysics of value.

all, no one, not even a mathematician, who is unschooled in the philosophy of mathematics is liable to think twice about using the words 'or' and 'not' in accord with a basic mathematical realism (either every even number greater than 2 is the sum of two primes or it is not). Dummett must think that he is entitled to criticize certain aspects of our use of language. But on what grounds? Surely, it is part of his Wittgensteinian view that our use of language is a datum.

There is a counter-reply to this first reply which runs as follows. It is indeed part of Dummett's view that our use of language is a datum, but not an unquestionable, indissoluble datum.[39] Where our use of language betrays metaphysical commitments, or where it betrays beliefs of any other kind for that matter, it is vulnerable to criticism: the beliefs betrayed may be illusory. And there is nothing in Dummett's conception to prevent him from playing the role of critic. Similarly, where our use of language betrays the rules that we take to govern it. There too it is vulnerable to criticism: the rules may conflict with one another. And again there is nothing in Dummett's conception to prevent him from playing the role of critic. (Whether any given criticism can be sustained or not is another matter. That is to be determined on the merits of the case. This relates back to the point that the anti-realist challenge may be far more powerful in some contexts than in others.)[40]

This counter-reply seems to me to be perfectly adequate. But does it perhaps leave Dummett in the same difficult position as the one in which we found Wittgenstein in Chapter 10, §5? Wittgenstein was able to meet one problem about sense-making only at the price of confronting another: he had no independent leverage for distinguishing between those aspects of our use of language that contribute to successful sense-making and those that do not. Is the same not true of Dummett?

Arguably not. Arguably, Dummett does have an independent leverage, in the requirement to construct a systematic theory of sense for our language. This leaves him free to repudiate those aspects of our use of language that obstruct any such construction.[41,42]

---

[39] Cf. his opposition to Quine mentioned in n. 11. Cf. also 'Sense and Reference', pp. 136 ff.

[40] Cf. *Logical Basis*, pp. 246ff.; *Origins*, pp. 174–175; and 'Realism and Anti-Realism', pp. 477–478.

[41] See again n. 16 for material on what such a theory must deliver.

[42] This explains why Dummett has no patience for Wittgenstein's dictum that philosophy 'leaves mathematics as it is' (Wittgenstein (1967a), Pt I, §124): see *Origins*, pp. 174–175. There is a profound irony, however, which is itself symptomatic of the difficult position in which Wittgenstein found himself, in the fact that Wittgenstein was prepared to question a great deal in our mathematical practices that Dummett finds quite unexceptionable. Thus Dummett shares none of Wittgenstein's qualms (Ch. 10, §5) about our comparing infinite sets in size: see e.g. *Frege* III, pp. 315–316. Cf. also Dummett's

I use the word 'arguably' not just in deference to the controversial nature of the requirement that a systematic theory of sense be constructible for our language, but also to register the fact that, even granted this requirement, there will be cases where judgment is needed to decide where exactly the fault lies when our use of language blocks the construction of such a theory. For example, if two or more of our linguistic practices are in tension with one another, then there may well be an irremediable indeterminacy about which is to be rejected. Still, Dummett might concede this point while insisting that the problem is hardly peculiar to him. It is just the familiar problem, he might say, with which anyone trying to make sense of things has to reckon, the problem of choosing between various competing desiderata of sense-making. (We saw both Quine and Lewis reckoning with this problem in the previous two chapters, §§7 and 3, respectively.) There is no reason to think that Dummett's vulnerability to the lack of an Archimidean point in the implementation of his programme is special, still less that it is specially problematical – is there?

Well, perhaps there is. This is a cue for the second reply to Dummett's anti-realist challenge.

(b)   Second Reply

Let us once again consider arithmetic. And let us once again consider the thought that every even number greater than 2 is the sum of two primes. This is Goldbach's conjecture. No counterexample to the conjecture has ever been discovered. But neither has the conjecture ever been proved. Moreover, we have no algorithmic procedure for settling the matter. An anti-realist about arithmetic therefore refuses to take for granted that the conjecture is either true or not true. According to such an anti-realist, only what we can know to be arithmetically the case – or, equivalently, only what we can prove to be arithmetically the case – is arithmetically the case. (So Goldbach's conjecture cannot as it were just *happen* to be true, as a kind of infinite coincidence.) But now: 'only what we *can* know', not 'only what we *do* know'.[43] Thus consider a thought about some complex arithmetical calculation that no one has ever performed, say the thought that the result of the calculation contains fewer 6s than 7s. Such an anti-realist need have no qualms about taking for granted that *this* thought is either true or not true. The fact that no one has actually gone through the slog of ascertaining which does not

disparaging reference to Wittgenstein's remarks on Gödel's theorem in 'Wittgenstein's Philosophy of Mathematics', p. 166. (Wittgenstein's remarks occur in Wittgenstein (1978), Pt I, App. III.)

[43] Cf. Fitch's argument, mentioned in n. 29.

matter. What matters is that we do have, in this case, the very thing that we do not have in the case of Goldbach's conjecture: an algorithmic procedure for deciding the issue. That is enough to safeguard the public ratifiability of anyone's grasp of the thought.

But this now raises a further issue. With so much hanging on this use of the word 'can', the anti-realist needs to say some more about the sense in which it is intended.[44] 'Can in principle'? Or 'can in practice'? Each of these stands in need of further elucidation, of course, but the broad distinction between them is what is critical in this context. And it is clear that if the anti-realist means 'can in practice', then the resultant circumspection is going to be very radical indeed. In fact, we had better reconsider that complex calculation. What if it is not just complex? What if it is *horrendously* complex – so complex that performing it would take a trillion steps? Plainly, there is then no *practical* sense in which we can know its result. If the anti-realist means 'can in practice', then even the thought that the result of this calculation contains fewer 6s than 7s is liable to anti-realist circumspection.

This is where the second reply impinges. This reply has particular force in the case of anti-realism about arithmetic – and that is the form of anti-realism on which I shall focus throughout my discussion of it – but it applies in other cases too. The reply has two parts. The first part is that such extreme anti-realism, based on what is possible in practice, is totally unacceptable. The second part is that there is no rationale for a moderate anti-realism, based on what is possible in principle, that is not also, *mutatis mutandis*, a rationale for this extreme version.

Why is the extreme version unacceptable? Obviously, that needs to be argued. Not everyone would agree.[45] But in *this* context no argument is required. For Dummett himself is among those who find the extreme version unacceptable. He regards it not just as overly extreme, but as positively incoherent. There is, he believes, an irremediable and unintelligible vagueness afflicting the notion of practicability on which it rests ('Wang's Paradox'). So the second part of the reply is enough for it to carry *ad hominem* force.

Dummett is aware of the reply ('Wang's Paradox', pp. 248–249). To an extent he can meet it by reiterating the sheer nature of his programme, which, as I have been following him in emphasizing, is not to defend any single anti-realist thesis, but to investigate how well, and where, the basic anti-realist challenge can be met. But there are also some pertinent differences between what is possible in principle and what is possible in practice

---

[44] Recall the concentric circles of possibility introduced in Ch. 9, §4; and the issue addressed in that same section of who 'we' are. (For the connection between these, see Moore (1997a), p. 138.)

[45] Crispin Wright mounts a defence of the extreme version in Wright (1982).

on which he can fasten (see e.g. *Thought and Reality*, pp. 70–71). The problem, however, is that there is a significant further twist. The second reply is reinforced by a subsidiary reply which threatens the collapse of the entire anti-realist challenge.

That subsidiary reply is as follows. If practical possibility is *not* relevant here, then, given any arithmetical thought, we *can* determine whether it is true or not, and we are hence justified in taking for granted that it is one or the other. Thus reconsider the thought that every even number greater than 2 is the sum of two primes. We can determine whether this is true or not by checking successive even numbers greater than 2, ascertaining in each case whether or not it is the sum of two primes, and continuing until we either find a counterexample or have checked every such number. It is of no avail to protest, as the anti-realist no doubt will, that this procedure might never end. Something needs to be said to forestall the objection that if we spend half a minute checking 4, a quarter of a minute checking 6, an eighth of a minute checking 8, and so on, then the procedure will end in a minute – at most. Obviously, we cannot do this in any *practical* sense. But that is precisely beside the point.[46]

Dummett is equally aware of this subsidiary reply (*Logical Basis*, pp. 345–348, and *Thought and Reality*, p. 71, n. 1). My own view is that his counter-replies to it are question-begging, in that they deploy an anti-realist conception both of the infinite and of what is possible in principle. But I shall not now try to substantiate this view, since I am more interested in the fact that, even if it is correct, the counter-replies may, in their own way, be good ones, and the best available. This at last brings us back to the prospect to which I referred earlier, that Dummett is specially vulnerable to the lack of an Archimidean point in implementing his programme. 'Specially' vulnerable, I say. Problematically vulnerable? Well, yes, to whatever extent there was a problem for Wittgenstein in his analogous predicament (Ch. 10, §5). Who is to say what makes sense? Who knows but that arithmetical realists and arithmetical anti-realists make their own quite different, incommensurable, individually coherent sense of things; that this is why the former accede to assumptions for which the latter can see no justification; and that when they try to settle their differences, they are simply talking past each other? Here, as so often in our enquiry, self-consciousness plays havoc with self-confidence.[47]

---

[46] Bertrand Russell, who mooted something similar, famously declared that the impossibility of performing infinitely many tasks in a finite time was 'merely medical' (Russell (1935–1936), pp. 143–144).

[47] For an attempt to trace some of the connections between Dummett's problem and Wittgenstein's, albeit not quite in those terms, see Moore (2002c). For discussions of relations more generally between Dummett and Wittgenstein, distancing the latter from the former, see Hacker (1986), Ch. 11, §4.

(c)   Third Reply

The third reply likewise connects with the lack of an Archimedean point. It is as follows. Dummett's anti-realist challenge to the assumption that every thought is either true or not true poses a real threat to that assumption only if there are thoughts whose truth or non-truth we cannot settle (in some appropriate sense of 'cannot'). But *are* there any such thoughts? Some putative examples have been given (the thought involving Aristotle's first birthday, the thought involving Descartes' penchant for Marmite, Goldbach's conjecture). But what would it take for any of these to be a genuine example? Well, on an anti-realist conception, we should have to be able to *tell* that it was a genuine example. That is, we should have to be able to tell that we could not settle its truth or non-truth. But how could we do that? We should need, in particular, to tell that we could not tell that it was true. The only way of telling *that*, however, again on an anti-realist conception, would be by telling that it was not true. (On an anti-realist conception, if we could not tell that it was true, then it could not *be* true. So if we could tell that we could not tell that it was true, then we could tell that it was not true.) We therefore arrive at a contradiction. It follows that there cannot, on an anti-realist conception, be any genuine examples of thoughts whose truth or non-truth we cannot settle. Nor, therefore, can there be any harm in assuming that every thought is either true or not true.

Dummett has a number of ways of dealing with this third reply. Most straightforward, and most heroic, would be to admit that there cannot be any harm in assuming that every thought is either true or not true, but still not to assume it. This would itself be an instance of anti-realist circumspection. It would be to admit that the assumption cannot *fail* to be true, but still not to accept that it *is* true.[48]

This raises an intriguing prospect. If anti-realists have no satisfactory answer to the question, 'When exactly does assuming that every thought is either true or not true lead us astray?', then it may be that they have no option, in the face of realist intransigence, but to maintain a kind of stoic silence. Whenever realists make assumptions that they are not themselves prepared to make, they must withhold assent, but they may have no satisfactory way of saying what is holding them back. This in turn would mean that, as far as anything they can say is concerned, their restraint might just as well be attributable, not to nonconformity, but to sheer reticence. Their knowledge of correct linguistic practice, if that is what it is, would be an example of a category that we have encountered more than once in this enquiry: knowledge that is, at least partially, ineffable.[49]

---

[48] Cf. 'Preface', p. xxx. In general, proof by *reductio ad absurdum* has no anti-realist warrant.

[49] See Ch. 2, §6; Ch. 9, §6, esp. n. 55; and Ch. 10, n. 55. For Dummett's own views about knowledge of correct linguistic practice, see e.g. 'Knowledge of a Language', pp. 94–96.

There is a loud echo of something else that we have encountered more than once in this enquiry, namely the Limit Argument. Suppose we construe sense-making in such a way that making sense of something involves having thoughts about it that are uniformly either true or not true. Then Dummett's project, which is to see how far it is possible to sustain a realist understanding of things, looks as though it can be characterized as the project of drawing a limit (limitation) to what we can make sense of. If it can, then it is vulnerable to the Limit Argument, whose conclusion precisely precludes the proper drawing of any such limit. And that, in effect, is the third reply. The third reply, in effect, is that we cannot properly draw any such limit, since we cannot have thoughts about it that are true (or not true), since we cannot have thoughts about what lies on its far side that are true (or not true).

The counter-reply to the third reply proposed above is essentially to deny that the project *is* one of drawing any such limit. The project is rather to make sense of making linguistic sense. And the proposed embellishment of the counter-reply is to say that this is achieved by fostering a kind of knowledge which is practical and, at least in part, ineffable. As soon as an attempt is made to put this knowledge, or rather its ineffable part, into words, the result, here as in the early Wittgenstein (Ch. 9, §7), is nonsense about the drawing of a limit, and about our access to what lies beyond that limit. In the present case such nonsense has us entertaining thoughts that are neither true nor not true – an idea that anti-realists find as absurd as realists do.[50]

If these proposals are even roughly correct, then the similarity between what we find in Dummett and what we found in the early Wittgenstein is profound. In each case:

- knowledge of what it is to make linguistic sense[51] is practical and, in part, ineffable
- such knowledge includes a capacity to recognize failed attempts to make linguistic sense
- if someone has exercised such knowledge, by recognizing a particular failed attempt to make linguistic sense, and if that person then tries to express what he knows, by saying what the failure in the failed attempt

---

Dummett himself does not talk of ineffable knowledge. But I see no incompatibility between my proposal and what he says.

[50] Cf. again the problem to which I drew attention in the Introduction, §6, in connection with the Transcendence Question, and which I mentioned in Ch. 9, n. 60, in connection with Wittgenstein.

For a much fuller discussion of the ideas canvassed in the last two paragraphs, see Moore (1997a), Ch. 10, §4.

[51] In Ch. 9, §7, I spoke of understanding rather than knowledge, and of propositional sense rather than linguistic sense, but neither difference is important in this context: see e.g. Ch. 9, n. 55, and cf. n. 7 in this chapter.

consists in, then his very effort to engage with the attempt will in all likeli-
hood lead to his simply repeating it ('It does not make sense to say that ...,'
'There is no settling the truth or non-truth of the thought that ...')
- the correct way to implement such knowledge would, to paraphrase
  6.53 of the *Tractatus*, really be the following: to say nothing except
  what can be said, and then, whenever someone else attempted unsuccessfully to make linguistic sense (say by insisting that some statement
  was either true or not true), to demonstrate to him that he had failed
  to give a meaning to some of the words he was using (say by pointing
  out that he was not using the words 'or' and 'not' in accord with their
  standard meaning, as revealed in the agreed procedures for recognizing
  the truth of any statement involving them).

If this constellation of ideas really is to be found in Dummett, then that
helps to explain the problems to which I alluded, in connection with the
second reply, concerning the lack of an Archimidean point. When anti-
realists are confronted with what they take to be realist failures to make
linguistic sense, their choice, in exposing these failures, is either 'to say
nothing except what can be said', which in this case means begging all the
relevant questions, or to try to express their inexpressible understanding
of what is wrong with realism, which, at best, means repeating the realists'
mistakes.

But note that here, as in the early Wittgenstein, *the latter may be a rhetorically effective alternative*. Very revealing, from this point of view, is the
following passage from one of Dummett's discussions of anti-realism about
the past:

> There is a strong temptation to try and [*sic*] contrast [realism and anti-
> realism about the past] by saying that, for the anti-realist, the past exists
> only in the traces it has left on the present, whereas for the realist, the
> past still exists as past.... Such a way of drawing the contrast ought to be
> rejected by both disputants – certainly by the anti-realist: for it describes
> each opinion in the light of the opposed opinion; but it does succeed
> in conveying something of the psychological effect of the two opinions.
> ('The Past', p. 370)

4. Is Anti-Realism a Form of Transcendental Idealism?

It is now irresistible, given the various connections that I have been trying
to forge – with the Limit Argument, with the early Wittgenstein, and with
seeing limits-*qua*-essential-features as limits-*qua*-limitations – to wonder
whether anti-realism is a form of transcendental idealism. It can certainly
seem so. If sense-making is understood in the way proposed in the previous
section, whereby making sense of something involves having thoughts about

it that are uniformly either true or not true, then anti-realists seem committed to the view that the limits-*qua*-essential-features of what we can make sense of depend on the limits-*qua*-limitations of the sense we can make of it, in a way that does not itself lie within the ambit of what we can make sense of (for reasons that emerged in our discussion of the third reply).

This dependence is captured by Bernard Williams as follows:

> Our sentences have the meaning we give them, ... [so] their logic ... [cannot] determine reality beyond, so to speak, what was put into it in the first place. (Williams (2006k), p. 377)[52]

This is reminiscent of Kant's claim:

> We can cognize of things *a priori* only what we ourselves put into them. (Kant (1998), Bxviii)

True, there is a difference, as it were, of direction. Kant is interested in exploiting his claim in a *modus ponens*: we have a non-empirical guarantee that things are thus and so, therefore we must, in making sense of things, have put such and such into them. Anti-realists, on the other hand, are interested in exploiting their counterpart of Kant's claim in a *modus tollens*: we cannot, in making sense of things, have put such and such into them, therefore we have no non-empirical guarantee that things are thus and so. But both Kant and they seem to agree about the basic dependence. And this in turn *seems* to be a shared commitment to transcendental idealism.

It is certainly not difficult to find idealist-sounding pronouncements in Dummett's writings, whether in exposition of anti-realism or *in propria persona*. Consider each of these:

> We could have ... the picture of a mathematical reality not already in existence but as it were coming into being as we probe....
>
> Whether this picture is right or wrong for mathematics, it is available for other regions of reality as an alternative to the realist conception of the world. ('Truth', p. 18)

> Although facts ... impose themselves upon us, ... we cannot infer from this that they were there waiting to be discovered before we discovered them, still less that they would have been there even if we had not discovered them. The correct image, on [an anti-realist] view, is that of blind explorers encountering objects that spring into existence only as they feel around for them. (*Thought and Reality*, p. 92)

---

[52] Williams is in fact characterizing a view that he finds in the later Wittgenstein rather than Dummettian anti-realism, but his very next sentence, which is annotated with a reference to Dummett's essay 'Wittgenstein's Philosophy of Mathematics', suggests that he would view the latter in the same terms.

> Could the physical universe have existed quite devoid of sentient crea-
> tures? ... What would be the difference between God's creating such a
> universe and his merely conceiving of such a universe without bringing it
> into existence? It seems to me that the existence of a universe from which
> sentience was perpetually absent is an unintelligible fantasy. What exists is
> what can be known to exist. What is true is what can be known to be true.
> Reality is the totality of what can be experienced by sentient creatures and
> what can be known by intelligent ones. (*Truth and the Past*, p. 92)

> Cannot it be said that the limits of our language signify the limits of our
> world? (*Thought and Reality*, p. 26)

It is hard, surely, to deny that there is an idealism here.

Yes; but a transcendental idealism? That is not so clear. (Even the last
quotation is a gloss on the non-transcendental-sounding denial that 'there
are features of [reality] that we could never in principle comprehend' (ibid.).)
Why should we not say rather that Dummett is casting anti-realism as a
form of empirical idealism and, to the extent that he is himself subscribing
to anything idealistic, subscribing to that?[53]

I am not sure that there is anything sufficiently determinate in Dummett
to attract an unqualified application of either label. But I do believe that
there are forces at work in the idealism that he is canvassing which make
it much more natural to develop that idealism in a transcendental direction than in an empirical direction. This is perhaps easiest to see in relation to the third quotation. However sympathetic we might be to the idea
that the physical universe depends for its very existence on the existence of
sentient creatures, we will want to reconcile that with the following basic
common-sense beliefs: that it was the merest contingency that conditions
in the physical universe were such as to generate sentient life; and that it is
straightforwardly false to say that, had those conditions not been met, the
physical universe as a whole would never have existed. The natural way to
reconcile these is to distinguish between the sense we make of things from
our position of engagement with them and the sense we make of things
when we take a critical step back and indulge in philosophical reflection.
The common-sense beliefs can then be seen as part of the former. And the
idealism can be seen as part of the latter. It is a view *about* the former,
though not assimilable to the former. And that precisely makes it a kind of
transcendental idealism. In fact it makes it a kind of transcendental idealism
not radically different from Kant's own (Ch. 5, §10).[54]

---

[53] For the distinction between transcendental idealism and empirical idealism, see Ch. 5,
Appendix.

[54] This, I believe, is connected to a comment that Dummett makes shortly after the first of
the quotations above: 'We can abandon realism without falling into *subjective* idealism'
(ibid., emphasis added).

The problem that it confronts – in mimicry of Kant's view – is that there are deep reasons, which it itself fosters, for thinking that the only real sense we can make of things is sense of the former kind: the sense we make of things from our position of engagement with them.[55] And this of course is entirely of a piece with the problem we saw anti-realism confront in the previous section. Anti-realism is a view about the only real sense we can make of things that precludes its own assimilation to that sense. In the light of all of this, there may seem to be no option but to conclude that anti-realism is indeed a form of transcendental idealism; moreover, a form of transcendental idealism that is as self-stultifyingly incoherent as any that we have encountered in this enquiry.

In fact, however, the matter is more subtle than that. This conclusion is warranted only with respect to anti-realism *conceived as a theory*. What the material at the end of the previous section gave us was an alternative conception of anti-realism, akin to the early Wittgenstein's conception of philosophy. On that alternative conception, anti-realism is not a theory; it is a practice. Or in the words of the *Tractatus*, it 'is not a body of doctrine but an activity' (Wittgenstein (1961), 4.112). It is a kind of circumspection, based on ineffable insights, insights of such a kind that, if an attempt were made to put them into words, the result would be just such transcendentally idealistic nonsense. Making that attempt, and producing such nonsense, may be efficacious for certain anti-realist purposes. But that is no indictment of anti-realism, nor of its practitioners, who after all may be well aware that the attempt is doomed. And if they want only to utter truths, then they are at liberty not to make it.

As regards the question of how they resist the *temptation* to make it, here we can implement a lesson that I think we learned in our study of the later Wittgenstein. They can resist the temptation by having nothing to do with whatever constitutive questions of philosophy demand to be answered in those terms (Ch. 10, §4). These include any question about what it is for things to be a certain way, when asked with a certain philosophical intent. An example would be: 'What is it for the physical universe to exist?' It is in trying to answer this question that anti-realists about the physical universe confront the problems we witnessed above. Another example would be: 'What is it, in general, for things to *have been* thus and so?', understood as a question about the reality and character of the past. It is in trying to answer this question that anti-realists about the past are liable to produce nonsense about the past's being constituted by traces it has left on the present. This may be fine as a heuristic device for winning over realists about the past. It is not a legitimate contribution to a theory of what the past is.[56]

---

[55] This is loosely related to the anti-relativist point that Dummett makes in 'Frege and Kant', p. 135.

[56] I leave it to others to judge how far Dummett is guilty of trying to answer such questions: see e.g. – as well as the relevant material already cited – *Thought and Reality*, Ch. 1.

It is appropriate, I think, to conclude this section with two quotations
from Wittgenstein's earlier work:

> I can only speak *about* [objects]: I cannot *put them into words*. Propositions
> can only say *how* things are, not *what* they are. (Wittgenstein (1961),
> 3.221, emphasis in original)

> The limit of language is shown by its being impossible to describe the
> fact which corresponds to ... a sentence, without simply repeating the
> sentence.
>   (This has to do with the Kantian solution of the problem of philosophy.)
> (Wittgenstein (1980a), p. 10)

5.   In Further Retrospect and in Further Prospect

At the end of Part One I anticipated the intense concern that there would be,
in the second period in our history, with sense. We have now seen some of
the principal forms that this concern took, and some of the principal ways in
which it developed, in the analytic tradition. In Quine and other naturalistic
metaphysicians it eventually became separated from a due concern with the
making of sense, to the detriment, I argued, not only of the understanding
of metaphysics, but of the practice of metaphysics (Ch. 12, §8, and Ch. 13,
§4). Dummett tries to reconnect these two concerns, or rather to reintegrate
them,[57] and thereby to readdress some of the big questions that occupied
metaphysicians in the early modern period.

But he propagates the linguacentrism that has been such a striking feature of what we have observed so far of the late modern period. Here as
in all the other philosophers on whom we have focused in Part Two, the
concern with sense is a concern, first and foremost, with linguistic sense.
And here as in Wittgenstein, the concern with linguistic sense is a concern with its protection against certain natural impulses on our part to
disrupt and pervert it. In particular, Dummett urges us to look critically
at those of our linguistic practices that betray a basic, uncritical belief in
the mind-transcendence of reality. I have argued that – here again as in
Wittgenstein – this makes metaphysics a practical exercise. It is also a thoroughly self-conscious exercise. And like many a self-conscious exercise, it
is designed both to destabilize us and, thereby, in a quasi-Hegelian way, to
help us to a greater stability.

Be all that as it may, anyone who thinks that we should be trying to tackle
the big questions head-on is liable to see in this near obsession with linguistic sense, and in the subordination of the big questions to it, a fundamental

----

[57] See again n. 13.

failing of analytic philosophy. It is in this vein that Stephen Hawking issues the following memorable reproach:

> Philosophers reduced the scope of their inquiries so much that Wittgenstein, the most famous philosopher of [the twentieth] century, said, 'The sole remaining task for philosophy is the analysis of language.'[58] What a comedown from the great tradition of philosophy from Aristotle to Kant! (Hawking (1988), pp. 174–175)

This reproach is unwarranted. Dummett's own work shows how analytic philosophy has been able to continue that tradition.[59] Even so, there may be grounds for the complaint that, in its insistence that metaphysical questions be addressed via considerations about the protection of linguistic sense, his work is unduly conservative. Does it perhaps share the defect that I claimed to find in the later work of Wittgenstein (Ch. 10, §6): that it makes no provision for radical conceptual innovation in metaphysics,[60] or in other words that it returns a negative answer to the Novelty Question which I posed in §6 of the Introduction?[61]

One might think that it is quite immune to this complaint. After all, what greater conceptual revision could there be than to challenge our fundamental conviction that every thought is either true or not true? Furthermore, Dummett himself expressly says that, despite his great admiration for Wittgenstein, he sees no reason to share Wittgenstein's 'belief that philosophy, as such, must never criticise but only describe' (*Logical Basis*, p. xi).

But let us not forget that Wittgenstein too was prepared to criticize, when he thought that he was dealing with failed attempts to make linguistic sense. Indeed, in his reflections on mathematics, his criticisms were not unlike Dummett's.[62] The significant issue – here yet again as in Wittgenstein – is not what metaphysical rationale there is for correcting the use to which

---

[58] Hawking writes as though he is quoting Wittgenstein, but he gives no reference. To the best of my knowledge Wittgenstein never said this.

[59] So does the work of everyone else we have studied in Part Two. To pick just one example: there is, in Wittgenstein (1967a), Pt I, §§243–317 and 398–421, some of the most profound material ever produced on the relation between mind and body.

[60] The expression 'in metaphysics' is important here. Dummett is keen to acknowledge both the existence and the importance of radical conceptual innovation in the large: see e.g. *Thought and Reality*, p. 24.

[61] There is also incidentally the issue of where Dummett stands with respect to the other two questions. His stance with respect to the Transcendence Question, on one natural interpretation of the question, is clear. One of the main points of his work is to deny that metaphysicians can make sense of what is transcendent (see the previous section). His stance with respect to the Creativity Question is less straightforward. It raises many further fascinating issues which I shall not pursue here.

[62] In fact they were more radical. See nn. 31 and 42.

we put the concepts that we already have, but what metaphysical rationale there may be for having new concepts. What scope is there, to paraphrase the Novelty Question, for making sense of things in a way that is not only maximally general but also radically new? There is not quite the animus against such radical innovation in Dummett that there was in Wittgenstein; that is true. But for an enthusiastic reception of such innovation we must wait until Part Three.

PART THREE

✦

THE LATE MODERN PERIOD II
NON-ANALYTIC TRADITIONS

CHAPTER 15

✦

Nietzsche

Sense Under Scrutiny Again

1. Introduction

Frege made linguistic sense an object of philosophical scrutiny and thereby both generated and shaped the whole of what followed in Part Two of this book. In the first sentence of Deleuze's commentary on Nietzsche – the philosopher who initiates Part Three – he writes, 'Nietzsche's most general project is the introduction of the concepts of sense and value into philosophy' (Deleuze (2006a), p. 1).

Frege and Nietzsche, in their interests and style, could hardly be less alike as philosophers. Even so, Deleuze highlights what is more than just a quirky point of comparison between them. Both, in their incommensurably different ways, made crucial contributions to establishing a due concern with sense as a linchpin of any attempt to make maximally general sense of things – and of any attempt to make sense of making maximally general sense of things. This is one respect of many in which Part Three of this book will run in parallel with Part Two.

Nietzsche's concern with sense was nevertheless much broader than Frege's. He shared an interest in linguistic sense,[1] but, as the quotation from Deleuze intimates, his interest extended to sense more generally. It extended to all the ways in which things are accorded significance and value – or rather, to all the ways in which things are *or may yet be* accorded significance and value. For Nietzsche was no slave to extant forms of sense-making, still less a blinkered slave to them. Quite the contrary. He was one of philosophy's great iconoclasts, probably the greatest. Insofar as he was concerned to account for the sense that is actually made of things, this was primarily with a view to debunking it, dismantling it, and passing beyond it, so as to make radically new sense of them. This was in turn because one of the most pervasive features of the sense that is actually made of things, in much of the modern world, is a combined moralism and religiosity which Nietzsche thoroughly

---

[1] He was trained as a philologist and appointed to a professorship in classical philology in his early twenties.

371

deplored. He found it constricting, pusillanimous, importunate, petty, and noxious. His assault both on this and on other aspects of modern sense-making was vicious and uncompromising. And it was all the more effective for the sheer brilliance and rhetorical power of his prose. It is impossible to read him – properly and honestly to read him – without feeling profoundly ill at ease with oneself. Often that effect is accentuated by the knowledge that the unease was shared in the writing. Freud is reputed to have said, '[Nietzsche] had a more penetrating knowledge of himself than any other man who ever lived or was ever likely to live' (Jones (1953), p. 344).

That Nietzsche's work should have been, on the one hand, so life-affirming and so opposed to the debilitations of self-censure and guilt while, on the other hand, so capable of instilling those very affects in his readers is neither the paradox nor the indictment of Nietzsche that it may appear to be. Nietzsche himself knew only too well how that which is constitutionally creative and enhancing can become destructive and degrading when pitted against that which is itself bent on destruction and degradation. This is connected to the point that Deleuze makes when, drawing on the distinction between active forces and reactive forces that is so crucial to his reading of Nietzsche,[2] he writes:

> How do reactive forces triumph? … Nietzsche's answer is that even by getting together reactive forces do not form a greater force, one that

---

[2] See esp. Deleuze (2006a), Ch. 2. (I shall have more to say about this in Ch. 21, §§2(a) and 3.) I have deliberately expressed this in such a way as to maintain a certain distance. While I have learned much from Deleuze's book and am far from endorsing Michael Tanner's verdict that it is, though 'interesting about Deleuze,' 'quite wild about Nietzsche' (Tanner (1994), p. 83), I nonetheless see Deleuze more as a creative appropriator of Nietzsche's ideas (for which I applaud him) than as a faithful rehearser of them. One thing that seems to me significant, as far as this distinction between active and reactive forces is concerned, is that there is, to the best of my knowledge, only one explicit drawing of any such contrast in Nietzsche's entire corpus, and even then only in unpublished notes that did not make it into any of the early editions of his notes: see The Will to Power, p. 471, n. 7.

Note: throughout this chapter I use the following abbreviations for Nietzsche's works: Anti-Christ for Nietzsche (1990b); Beyond Good and Evil for Nietzsche (1973); Daybreak for Nietzsche (1982a); Ecce Homo for Nietzsche (1967b); Fragmente for Nietzsche (1978); Gay Science for Nietzsche (1974); Genealogy for Nietzsche (1967a); Human for Nietzsche (1986); 'Postcard to Overbeck' for Nietzsche (1982b); Tragedy for Nietzsche (1967d); 'Truth and Lies' for Nietzsche (1979); Twilight for Nietzsche (1990a); Untimely Meditations for Nietzsche (1983); Werke for Nietzsche (1967–); Will [to Power] for Nietzsche (1967c); and Zarathustra for Nietzsche (1969). In giving references to Ecce Homo I adopt the convention whereby 'II.vii.1' names the second part ('Why I Write Such Good Books'), the seventh section ('Thus Spoke Zarathustra'), §1, and so forth. In giving references to the Fragmente I adopt the convention whereby 'III.19.35' names Vol. III, Section 19, §35, and so forth. In giving references to the Genealogy I adopt the convention whereby 'III.28' names The Third Essay, §28 and so forth. In giving references to

would be active. They proceed in an entirely different way – they decompose; *they separate active force from what it can do*; they take away a part or almost all of its power. In this way reactive forces do not become active but, on the contrary, they make active forces join them and become reactive in a new sense. (Deleuze (2006a), p. 57, emphasis in original; cf. pp. 64–68)

2. Truth, the Pursuit of Truth, and the Will to Truth

Descartes acted out the first scene in this historical drama by taking a critical step back and calling all his beliefs into question. He even called into question those of his beliefs which, when he was focusing on the matters in hand, he found irresistible. This led him to pose what I dubbed in Chapter 1, §3, his Reflective Question, which can be reformulated as follows:

> Why should the fact that I cannot help believing something, when I give the matter my full attention, mean that it is true?

Friedrich Nietzsche (1844–1900) wants to take an even larger critical step back.[3] It may seem obscure what space there is behind Descartes for any further retreat. But Descartes only really stepped back as far as he needed in his pursuit of the truth. He did not have much to say about whether that was a reasonable pursuit in the first place, nor indeed about what it consisted in.[4] There is therefore space for Nietzsche to ask:

> Why should the fact that something is true mean that I do well to believe it?

Human I adopt the convention whereby 'II.ii.67' names Vol. II, Pt Two, §67, and so forth. In giving references to *Twilight* I adopt the convention whereby 'II.12' names the second part ('Maxims and Arrows'), §12, and so forth. In giving non-page references to *Untimely Meditations* I adopt the convention whereby 'III.3' names Pt 3, §3, and so forth. In giving references to the *Werke* I adopt the convention whereby 'VII.3.30.10' names Section VII, Vol. 3, Notebook 30, §10, and so forth. In giving non-page references to *Zarathustra* I adopt the convention whereby 'III.ii.1' names Pt III, the second part ('Of the Vision and the Riddle'), §1, and so forth. For discussion of the shortcomings of the (now standard) translation of '*Fröhliche Wissenschaft*' as '*Gay Science*', see Williams (2006g), pp. 313–314. And finally, a caveat concerning *Will*, on which I shall be drawing extensively in this chapter. To quote Bernard Williams, this is 'not a book by Nietzsche at all, but a selection from [his unpublished] notes tendentiously put together by his sister' (Williams (2006g), p. 319). On the tendentiousness, and for an account of the various editions of Nietzsche's notes, see Kaufmann (1967a) and (1967b). See also Schacht (1995b).

[3] Cf. *Beyond Good and Evil*, §280. For opposition to Descartes' own answer to the Reflective Question, see *Will*, §§436, 471, and 533.

[4] See Williams (1978), Ch. 2, passim; and see esp. the wonderful comments on the fungus analogy at pp. 54–55. Cf. *Gay Science*, §344; *Beyond Good and Evil*, §§1 and 16; *Genealogy*,

and, concomitantly,

What is it to do well to believe something?[5]

and indeed, à la Pilate,

What is truth?[6]

There is space, in other words, for Nietzsche to reflect at the most fundamental level about the very character of sense-making, its aims and its
rationale. This is part of his project of rendering sense itself, in its many
guises, an object of philosophical scrutiny. In a way his critical step back
involves asking how sense, in one of its guises, relates to sense in another
of its guises. On one way of construing sense, to make sense of things is to
arrive at a true conception of them. On another, it is to view them in a way
that makes them easier to live with, perhaps even makes them bearable.
Part of Nietzsche's concern is with what the first of these has to do with
the second.

Not that Descartes is Nietzsche's only target. He is not even his principal
target. We saw in Chapter 5 how Kant extended the enlightenment project
that Descartes had started, using his own reason as the supreme arbiter in
his attempts to make sense of things. In particular, like Descartes, he used his
own reason to vindicate his privileging his own reason in this way; but not,
as in Descartes' case, with a view to establishing *that* his reason carried the
authority that he accorded it; rather, taking this for granted, with a view to
establishing *how* it carried the authority that he accorded it. Thus it was for
Kant a datum that, by dint of our reason, we can know that 7 + 5 = 12 (Kant
(1998), B20–21). So too it was a datum that, by dint of our reason, we can
ascertain the fundamental demands of morality (Kant (1996c), 5: 36 and
161–162).[7] It was a datum that reason enables us to make sense of things in
each of these ways – and in sundry other ways besides. For Nietzsche these
can scarcely be data when, quite apart from any reservations that he might
have about the specific ways in which Kant thinks reason enables us to

---

III.24, concluding paragraphs; *Will*, §§587 and 588; and *Werke*, VII.3.30.10 (cited in
Poellner (1995), p. 113).

[5] Let us not forget, as far as this question is concerned, that not believing something need
not mean believing the opposite. It may involve having no belief about the matter at all. It
may even involve refusing to think in such terms. Recall in this connection the discussion
of thick ethical concepts in the Introduction, §7. There is room for the view that it can be
both true that a work of art is blasphemous, say, and better for me not to think that it is;
better for me not so much as to think in terms of blasphemy. (I shall return to these issues
in the Conclusion, §3(b).)

[6] See *Will*, §§532 (esp. the final paragraph) ff. Cf. *Beyond Good and Evil*, §177. Cf. also
Wittgenstein (1974b), §222. For the reference to Pilate, see John, 18:38.

[7] This is in effect what he called the sole fact of pure reason: see Ch. 5, §9.

make sense of things, he (Nietzsche) wants to question what making sense of things even *is*.[8]

Kant himself, of course, thought that, in some of these cases, making sense of things involves arriving at synthetic *a priori* knowledge about them, and that the project was to explain how this is possible. Here is a characteristically withering quotation by Nietzsche, in which he takes Kant to task for his attempted execution of this project:

> Kant asked himself: how are synthetic judgements *a priori possible*? – and what, really, did he answer? *By means of a faculty*: but unfortunately not in a few words, but so circumspectly, venerably, and with such an expenditure of German profundity and flourishes that the comical *niaiserie allemande* involved in such an answer was overlooked.[9] People even lost their heads altogether on account of this new faculty, and the rejoicing reached its climax when Kant went on further to discover a moral faculty in man....
>
> But ... it is high time to replace the Kantian question 'how are synthetic judgements *a priori* possible?' with another question: 'why is belief in such judgements *necessary*?' ... Or, more clearly, crudely and basically: synthetic judgements *a priori* should not 'be possible' at all: we have no right to them, in our mouths they are nothing but false judgements. (*Beyond Good and Evil*, §11, emphasis in original)[10]

If anyone is Nietzsche's principal target, Kant is.[11]

It is not just that Kant assumes too much for Nietzsche's liking. *What* Kant assumes is not to Nietzsche's liking. Nietzsche's scepticism, unlike Descartes', is not merely tactical. When he questions our pursuit of truth, for example, it is because he thinks there is a genuine case to be answered for our being better off acceding to falsehoods (see e.g. *Human*, I.517). Similarly, when he questions the various presuppositions that Kant makes it is because he thinks there is a genuine case to be answered against them. Nietzsche sees Kant's philosophy as an epitome of the moralism-cum-religiosity to which I referred in the previous section. He sees Kant as a philosopher of the heights, to invoke Deleuze's image (Deleuze (1990b), pp. 127ff.). That

---

[8] Cf. Deleuze (2006a), p. 1, and Ch. 2, §§7 and 8.

[9] This is an allusion, as Nietzsche subsequently makes clear, to the famous exchange between the first doctor and Argan in the Finale to Molière (1959): the doctor asks how opium induces sleep and Argan replies by invoking its power to do so.

[10] See also the rest of the section; *Genealogy*, III.25; and *Will*, §530.

[11] 'If anyone ...'. The qualification is important. There is a profound sense, which I hope will become clear in the course of the chapter, in which Nietzsche's principal target is not an individual at all, but a kind of sickness of which Kant happens to be an especially significant symptom. In fact Nietzsche would see this as testimony to Kant's greatness. Through all the seemingly irreverent rhetoric a clear respect for Kant is discernible.

is, he sees Kant as attempting to climb up beyond the mire of appearances to a place where there is unique access to what is ultimately real, to what is ultimately good, and to what is ultimately true; a place where he can embrace all that is higher in lieu of all that is base; a place where he can live out what Nietzsche calls 'the ascetic ideal' (*Genealogy*, III passim; see further §6 below). But it remains to be shown, in Nietzsche's view, that there *is* anywhere up there; *a fortiori* that there is anywhere up there affording unique access to any such ultimata. And, just as important, it remains to be shown why, even if there is, that should impel us to make the climb (*Beyond Good and Evil*, §2).[12]

But look, you might say, surely Nietzsche's own persistence with these questions indicates his own desire for the truth. Surely, when he asks whether we should pursue the truth, he is pursuing the *truth* about whether we should pursue the truth. Is there not something self-stultifying about his taking this critical step back?

There is much to be said in response to this. In the first place we cannot assume without question-begging that Nietzsche's own persistence with these questions does indicate a desire for the truth. Who knows, pending further study of what he says, but that it indicates a desire for peace of mind?[13] Second, even if Nietzsche does have a desire for the truth, there is nothing in the least self-stultifying about his wanting to know whether he would be better off not having it. But, you may reply, suppose he eventually decides that he *would* be better off not having it. And suppose he would never have reached this decision had he *not* had it.[14] Is *that* not self-stultification? Perhaps it is. But if it is, then it is self-stultification of a kind that can be seen in retrospect as benign. Third, we must in any case not forget that part of Nietzsche's attempt to take this critical step back is to question what truth *is*, to question what the desire for truth is. Let us not rule out the possibility that both truth and the desire for truth assume different forms, and that what is motivating him to take this critical step back is not the same as what he is most concerned to take it back from.

One thing that is significant as far as this third point is concerned – I shall expand on its significance below – is that Nietzsche himself does not talk about the desire for truth. He talks about 'the will to truth' (e.g. *Gay Science*, §344, and *Beyond Good and Evil*, §§1ff.). And he means by this considerably

---

[12] Nietzsche contrasts the moderns with 'those Greeks', who 'knew how to live' by '[stopping] courageously at the surface ... [and believing] in the whole Olympus of appearance'; 'those Greeks' who were, as he famously puts it, 'superficial – *out of profundity*' (*Gay Science*, Preface, §4, emphasis in original). Not that the modern attempt to escape appearances in this way can be said to be peculiarly modern: see Plato's *Republic*, Pt VII, §§5–7. For more on the need to stop at the surface, see §6 in this chapter.

[13] Cf. Ch. 1, n. 7.

[14] Cf. *Beyond Good and Evil*, §1, and *Genealogy*, III.27.

more than the desire for truth. The will to truth is a valuing of truth *above all else*. Moreover, it is a valuing of truth as something pure, something whose pursuit can be otherwise disinterested, something that provides refuge from what I earlier described as the mire of appearances.[15] It is an abhorrence of all deception, even where deception seems best attuned to the demands of life.[16] It is a commitment to what we might call the scientific ideal. And it is a prime manifestation of the commitment to the ascetic ideal.

Here is Nietzsche's own analysis of his conception:

> This unconditional will to truth – what is it? Is it the will *not to allow oneself to be deceived*? Or is it the will *not to deceive*? For the will to truth could be interpreted in the second way, too – if only the special case 'I do not want to deceive myself' is subsumed under the generalization 'I do not want to deceive.' But why not deceive? But why not allow oneself to be deceived?
>
> ... The faith in science ... must have originated *in spite of* the fact that the disutility and dangerousness of 'the will to truth,' of 'truth at any price' is proved to it constantly....
>
> Consequently, 'will to truth' does *not* mean 'I will not allow myself to be deceived' but – there is no alternative – 'I will not deceive, not even myself'; *and with that we stand on moral ground....*
>
> Thus the question 'Why science?' leads back to the moral problem: *Why have morality at all* when life, nature, and history are 'not moral'? No doubt, those who are truthful in that audacious and ultimate sense that is presupposed by the faith in science *thus affirm another world* than the world of life, nature, and history.... But you will have gathered what I am driving at, namely, that it is still a *metaphysical faith* upon which our faith in science rests – that even we seekers after knowledge today, we godless anti-metaphysicians still take our fire, too, from the flame lit by a faith that is thousands of years old, that Christian faith which is also the faith of Plato, that God is the truth, that truth is divine. (*Gay Science*, §344, emphasis in original)

Three features of this quotation are especially important for our purposes. First, notice that 'metaphysical' is once again being used more or less pejoratively. It is being used to signal what Kant would have counted as bad metaphysics, the attempt to make 'thick' sense of the transcendent (Ch. 5, §§2 and 6). But not only that. It is being used to signal a commitment of

---

[15] The word 'moreover' in this sentence is important. Nietzsche's conception has a number of separable components. The valuing of truth above all else does not *have* to be a valuing of truth conceived in this way.

[16] Nietzsche talks of a 'liberation from all illusion, as "knowledge," as "truth," as "being," as release from all purpose, all desire, all action, as a state beyond even good and evil' (*Genealogy*, III.17).

any kind to the transcendent. We 'anti-metaphysicians', who are supposed to have advanced (even) beyond Kant in our repudiation of the transcendent (much like the logical positivists; see further §5 below), are being invited to admit that there is still a lingering commitment to the transcendent in our own veneration of scientific sense-making and scientific truth.

Second, Nietzsche's questioning of scientific sense-making and his reflection on what kind of sense it involves have turned into a questioning of sense-making more generally and a reflection on what kind of sense *it* involves. The issue has become what manner of conviction and what manner of principle make us pursue the truth rather than accede to falsehoods that may very well be 'less harmful, less dangerous, less calamitous' (ibid.). In fact it has become an issue about *morality*. This reflects the point with which we began, that Nietzsche's project casts sense, in all its guises, as a focal point of philosophical enquiry.

The third important feature of the quotation brings us back to the third response mooted above to the suggestion that Nietzsche's efforts to take a critical step back from our sense-making are self-stultifying. What Nietzsche is really concerned to take a step back from, as the quotation helps to illustrate, is *the will to truth*: the valuing, for its own sake, above all else, of a truth that is rigorously scientific, utterly detached, and accessible only from on high. But it takes far less than *that* to sustain Nietzsche's critical reflection. Moreover, the less that it takes can still be classified, for all that has been said so far, as 'a desire for truth'. (This adumbrates ideas that we shall explore in the next section and again in §6.)

A fortiori the less that it takes can still be classified as 'an attempt to make sense of things'. Whatever self-stultification may or may not be involved in this critical reflection, there is absolutely nothing in it to impugn any claim that Nietzsche himself might make to be trying to make sense of things; nor, it seems to me, any claim that he might make to be trying to make maximally general sense of things. For only on some conceptions of sense-making need sense-making involve arriving at beliefs at all,[17] let alone beliefs that enjoy truth of such a demanding kind. I think Nietzsche is indeed trying to make maximally general sense of things. That is, I think Nietzsche is engaged in metaphysics, on my definition of metaphysics. And I think he would, could, and should feel quite comfortable about acknowledging this.[18] But what views would, could, or should he adopt concerning the *prospects* for any such endeavour, the prospects for metaphysics, on my definition of metaphysics?

---

[17] Cf. Clark (1990), p. 223, where Maudemarie Clark urges that Nietzsche is engaged in sense-making of a sort that does not.

[18] This is not the same as (though neither is it incompatible with) Heidegger's view. Heidegger argues that Nietzsche is engaged in metaphysics on yet another conception of metaphysics, but in such a way as to bring it (metaphysics) to an end: see Ch. 18, §4.

3. Prospects for Metaphysics I: Perspectivism

First, Nietzsche would deny that metaphysics can lead us to absolute truth, understood as that at which the will to truth is ultimately targeted. Nietzsche is a perspectivist. He denies the possibility of any disengaged, disinterested sense-making either in metaphysics or, come to that, anywhere else (including physics: see *Will*, §636). For Nietzsche, all sense-making is sense-making *from some point of view*, that is to say in relation to some constellation of needs, interests, sensibilities, concerns, values, and the like. This is because all sense-making involves some system of classification and organization, whereby it draws attention to some things and away from others, structuring the world into foreground and background; and it is only in relation to some constellation of needs *et cetera* that any such structuring has a point or is even possible.[19]

Moreover, all sense-making, in Nietzsche's view, really is sense-*making*. Sense is created, not discovered. (Nietzsche has a very clear answer to the Creativity Question which I posed in §6 of the Introduction.) Sense-making is not a recognition of something that is there anyway. The world is a dramatic text, and making sense of it is part of acting out a particular life, adopting a particular style, telling a particular story: the story that will become the narrator's autobiography.[20] Nor, therefore, is the creation limited to the sense that is made of things. It extends to the things of which the sense is made, which have their place in the story,[21] and to the agent making the sense, whose story it is. All sense-making is from a point of view that is itself, partly, a creature of that very sense-making. Sense-making creates the conditions for its own possibility. Its province is deep, very deep, in the mire of appearances – though if Nietzsche is right, the mire of appearances should no longer be thought of either as a mire or indeed as consisting of

---

[19] See Ch. 3, n. 22, for one crucial difference between this view and the perspectivism that we found in Leibniz. For an exploration of the whole idea of a point of view in this broad sense, see Moore (1997a), esp. Ch. 1. In that book I argue, *contra* Nietzsche, that there can be sense-making that is not from any point of view: see esp. Ch. 4. (I draw on the work of Bernard Williams: see esp. Williams (1978), pp. 64–68.) How does this consist with my claim in §4 of the previous chapter that it is not possible for us to make sense of things except from our position of engagement with them? The matter is complex. But summarily: I do not count our position of engagement with things as a point of view. This is precisely because it admits of no alternative. In my book I also discuss Nietzsche's views: see Ch. 5, §8, from which some of the present section is derived. For further discussion of Nietzsche's views, see Houlgate (1986), esp. pp. 56–67; Clark (1990), Ch. 5; Poellner (1995), Ch. 6, §2; and Gemes (2009), to which Christopher Janaway replies in Janaway (2009), §2.

[20] See Nehamas (1985), passim.

[21] See *Gay Science*, §58.

appearances, in any sense that suggests a contrast with some independently accessible reality.[22]

Here are two pertinent quotations:[23]

> Henceforth, my dear philosophers, let us be on our guard against the dangerous old conceptual fiction that posited a 'pure, will-less, painless, timeless, knowing subject'; let us guard against the snares of such contradictory concepts as 'pure reason,' ... 'knowledge in itself': these always demand that we should think of an eye that is completely unthinkable, an eye turned in no particular direction, in which the active and interpreting forces, through which alone seeing becomes seeing *something*, are supposed to be lacking.... There is *only* a perspectival seeing, *only* a perspectival 'knowing'. (*Genealogy*, III.12, emphasis in original)[24]

> Against positivism ... – 'There are only *facts*' – I would say: No, facts are precisely what there are not, only interpretations....
> 'Everything is subjective,' you say; but even this is interpretation. The 'subject' is not something given, it is something added and invented and projected behind what there is. – Finally, is it necessary to posit an interpreter behind the interpretation? Even this is invention....
> It is our needs that interpret the world; our drives and their For and Against. (*Will*, §481, emphasis in original; cf. ibid., §556)[25]

Nietzsche denies the possibility of absolute truth then. But does he deny the possibility of truth altogether? Or is he prepared to countenance 'perspectival' truth? (This relates back to the question of whether a 'desire for truth' can survive his onslaught against the will to truth.)[26]

There are several passages which suggest the former. This, for example:

> The world with which we are concerned is false ...; it is 'in flux' ... as a falsehood always changing but never getting near the truth: for – there is no 'truth'. (*Will*, §616; cf. ibid., §§480, 540, 567, and 625)

But we need to see past the rhetoric. The 'truth' that he abjures in such passages, as his own use of scare quotes helps to signal, is absolute truth, not truth as such. In the revealing preface to *Beyond Good and Evil* he casts those who are committed to absolute truth, in their pursuit of the ascetic

---

[22] See *Twilight*, V.6, and *Will*, §567.

[23] See also *Daybreak*, §243; *Gay Science*, §§54, 373, and 374; *Beyond Good and Evil*, §§14 and 16; and *Will*, §§477, 503–507, 555–568, 590, and 616.

[24] I have taken the liberty of replacing 'perspective' in Walter Kaufmann's and R.J. Hollingdale's translation by 'perspectival'.

[25] I have taken the liberty of replacing each occurrence of 'is' in the first sentence of Walter Kaufmann's translation by 'are'.

[26] There is a large literature on this question. For one very interesting discussion that bears on it, see Han-Pile (2009).

ideal, as *violators*, 'standing truth on her head' (p. 14).[27] Nietzsche denies the possibility of making disengaged, disinterested sense of things. But he does not deny the possibility of making true sense of things. Nor does he deny the desirability of making true sense of things. Nor indeed does he deny the desirability of expending the very great effort required to do so. We should not find it surprising that Nietzsche is capable of writing this:

> Greatness of soul is needed for [truth], the service of truth is the hardest service. – For what does it mean to be *honest* in intellectual things? That one is stern towards one's heart, that one despises 'fine feelings', that one makes every Yes and No a question of conscience! (*Anti-Christ*, §50, emphasis in original; cf. *Zarathustra*, p. 213, *Ecce Homo*, Pref., §3, and *Will*, §1041)

Nietzsche's perspectivism is emphatically not a license to count all attempts at sense-making as equally worthy, then. Attempts at sense-making may not be answerable to an independently accessible reality. But they are answerable to something. In a way, like all artistic endeavours, they are answerable to themselves. Furthermore, they are always vulnerable to what might be called, in Quine's famous phrase, 'recalcitrant experience' (Quine (1961b), p. 44). Sense-making is an exercise in negotiating the world's contingencies, in an effort to live with them. That is not the same as unbridled wishful thinking. There is something to be negotiated. This is why, despite Nietzsche's denial that there are any facts, he still celebrates what he calls the Greeks' 'sense for facts', as well as their 'integrity for knowledge', something which he thinks we have to '[win] back for ourselves today with an unspeakable amount of self-constraint' (*Anti-Christ*, §59, emphasis removed).[28] It is also why he has no reservations about championing the 'sacrifice [of] all desirability to truth, *every* truth, even plain, harsh, ugly, repellent, unchristian, immoral truth' (*Genealogy*, I.1, emphasis in original; cf. *Will*, §172). For, as he immediately goes on to insist, 'such truths do exist' (ibid.).[29] I shall have more to say about Nietzsche's repudiation of absolute truth and his championing of perspectival truth in §6.

Let us now consider a very common and natural objection to perspectivism, which runs as follows. Perspectivism is itself the result of sense-making. Either this sense-making is perspectival or it is not. If it is not, then

---

[27] He famously opens the preface by 'supposing truth to be a woman.'

[28] It seems to me that, in Williams (2002), Bernard Williams exaggerates the tension between these, and thereby infelicitously downplays the denial that there are facts: see p. 10 and nn. 10 and 23.

[29] For further discussion, see Deleuze (2006a), Ch. 3, §15; Craig (1987), pp. 273ff.; Clark (1990), Ch. 1 (which contains references to a further wealth of material); Schacht (1995a); and Tanesini (1995) – each of which differs in various striking ways from the others but all of which are very helpful.

perspectivism stands refuted. For perspectivism is the view that *all* sense-making is perspectival. If, on the other hand, the sense-making in question *is* perspectival, then it is possible to deny perspectivism by making sense of things from some opposed point of view. So we have no good reason to accept it.[30]

The objection can be rebutted.[31] The second horn of the dilemma contains several confusions. If the sense-making is perspectival, then it is certainly possible to make sense of things from some opposed point of view. But that is not to say that it is possible to deny perspectivism. It may be that what makes a given point of view an 'opposed' point of view is that the concepts needed even to address the question are not available from there, or that they are available from there but are not applicable with the same effect (as the concepts of left and right are not applicable with the same effect from opposite ends of a tennis court). Making sense of things from an opposed point of view is not the same as making opposed sense of things. And failing to accept perspectivism is not the same as denying it.[32] But still, the objector may say, if it is possible to make sense of things from an opposed point of view, and thereby even to fail to accept perspectivism, does it not still follow that we have no good reason to accept it? It does not. (It would not even follow if what were at stake were the denial of perspectivism.) We may have good reason to accept perspectivism insofar as we have good reason to acknowledge the relevant point of view – the point of view from which it holds – as our own, something over which we may have no more control, at least while we are thinking about these issues, than we have over our position in time, our temporal point of view. (To say that it is possible to make sense of things from an opposed point of view is not to say that *we* can make sense of things from an opposed point of view.)

I argued earlier that Nietzsche's own perspectivism, though it is a repudiation of the notion of absolute truth, is not a repudiation of the notion of truth *tout court*. It is worth noting that neither this objection to perspectivism nor my rebuttal of it stands in any simple relation to that issue. In a way, a perspectivist who countenances perspectival truth, and who

---

[30] See e.g. Copleston (1960), p. 410; Clark (1990), p. 151; and Poellner (1995), Ch. 6, §3. (I should add that, although I am at variance with all three writers concerning the force of this objection, there is much in their respective discussions that I admire. What gives me greatest pause in Maudemarie Clark's case is the emphasis that she places, throughout her book, on different stages in Nietzsche's thinking. I think that many of the tensions that she thinks can be resolved by appeal to these different stages can be resolved in any case.) Cf. the quotation from Quine (2008b), pp. 242–243, given in Ch. 12, §8. Cf. also Plato's *Theaetetus*, 171a–c; and Nagel (1997), pp. 14–15. Nietzsche, incidentally, is aware of the objection: see *Beyond Good and Evil*, §22, final sentence.

[31] Cf. Yovel (1989), p. 121.

[32] Cf. n. 5.

reckons perspectivism itself to be a perspectival truth, is especially vulnerable to the objection, if only because the first horn of the dilemma is then especially sharp. That said, a perspectivist who countenances perspectival truth can also consolidate my rebuttal of the objection by emphasizing the gap between making *different* sense of things, from different points of view, and making *opposed* sense of things, from different points of view. In the former case, such a perspectivist may say, all the sense-making concerned can be true; in the latter case, at most some of it can.[33] However that may be, we have seen nothing in this section to prevent Nietzsche from regarding perspectivism itself as a truth; and a deeply important truth at that, a truth which signals one of the most significant limitations of metaphysics.[34]

4. Prospects for Metaphysics II: Grammar

The second aspect of Nietzsche's attitude to metaphysics on which I wish to focus is his continual quarrel with attempts by metaphysicians, if only sometimes subliminal attempts, to infer the nature of what we make sense of from the grammar of how we make sense of it. (Here I am using 'grammar' in a very broad sense.) Nietzsche thinks that the grammar of our sense-making often tempts us into making false sense of things. But even when that is not so – even when the grammar of our sense-making is conducive to our making true sense of things – Nietzsche's work serves as a warning against our supposing that it reveals anything beyond itself. (The comparisons with Wittgenstein, to whom we shall return, are striking.[35]) This is not to say that the grammar of our sense-making *cannot* reveal anything beyond itself. It can. It may well reveal something about the points of view that our sense-making is from for instance. But there can be no general presumption that it will do even that.

We have witnessed many examples in this enquiry of the sort of thing that Nietzsche is opposing. One of the first and most glaring was Descartes' attempt to deduce characteristics of God, indeed God's very existence, from his own idea of God (Ch. 1, §§3 and 5). But even more telling, perhaps, was what Nietzsche would see as an equally unwarranted attempt on Descartes'

---

[33] I leave open whether this is what Nietzsche would say. What he would say, and what he continually does say, is that it is of vital importance to make sense of things from different points of view – the better (as I see it) to grasp the truth. See e.g. *Genealogy*, III.12, and *Ecce Homo*, I.1. Cf. Deleuze (1990b), pp. 174–175.

[34] The argument against regarding perspectivism as a truth lies, I believe, elsewhere: see n. 19.

[35] Cf. *Gay Science*, §354, where Nietzsche refers to 'the epistemologists who have become entangled in the snares of grammar (the metaphysics of the people).' Cf. also *Beyond Good and Evil*, Preface and §20.

part to deduce characteristics of himself, specifically his status as an immaterial thinking substance, from the workings of the first-person singular.[36] Here are two relevant quotations:[37]

> We ... ought to get free from the seduction of words! ... [The] philosopher must say to himself: when I analyse the event expressed in the sentence 'I think', I acquire a series of rash assertions which are difficult, perhaps impossible, to prove – for example, ... that it has to be something at all which thinks, ... that an 'I' exists. (*Beyond Good and Evil*, §16, emphasis in original)

> 'There is thinking: therefore there is something that thinks': this is the upshot of all Descartes' argumentation. But that means positing as 'true *a priori*' our belief in the concept of substance – that when there is thought there has to be something 'that thinks' is simply a formulation of our grammatical custom that adds a doer to every deed....
>
> The concept of substance is a consequence of the concept of the subject: not the reverse! (*Will*, §§484 and 485)

As before, however, it is Kant who is the main villain of the piece. Nietzsche thinks that Kant too was guilty of postulating structures in reality corresponding to grammatical structures in our sense-making.[38] Admittedly, Kant was self-conscious enough to acknowledge the latter structures as structures determined by our transcendental point of view – our spectacles – and, thereby, to acknowledge the former structures as structures in empirical reality only, not the reality of things in themselves. But for Nietzsche, that merely compounded the offence. For it introduced the unacceptable notion of a reality beyond all that we can ever experience. (See the next section.) Relatedly, Kant took our transcendental point of view to impose a non-negotiable framework on all our empirical investigations, and to be not itself open to empirical investigation. That made it very different from the kind of thing that Nietzsche wants to recognize as a point of view, which relates to the empirically investigable needs, interests, *et cetera* that accrue from flesh and blood.[39] It is in these terms that Nietzsche castigates the whole concept

---

[36] I referred parenthetically just now to the comparisons with Wittgenstein. Significantly, G.E.M. Anscombe, drawing heavily on the work of Wittgenstein, devotes a justly famous article to arguing that the word 'I' cannot function as a referring expression, in the way in which it appears to, precisely because, if it did, what it was used to refer to would have to be an immaterial thinking substance of the very kind that Descartes took himself to be (Anscombe (1983)).

[37] See also *Beyond Good and Evil*, §§12, 17, 34, and 54; *Genealogy*, I.13; *Twilight*, IV.5; and *Will*, §§371, 519, 531, 561, and 631.

[38] Kant (1998), A66/B91ff., is very pertinent here.

[39] See *Will*, §§314, 507, and 567. Cf. Yovel (1989), pp. 178–181, and Williams (2006h), pp. 325–326.

of the *a priori* on which Kant erected his philosophical edifice, including his belief in the synthetic *a priori*:[40]

> The most strongly believed *a priori* 'truths' are for me – *provisional assumptions*; e.g., the law of causality,[41] a very well acquired habit of belief, so much a part of us that not to believe in it would destroy the race. But are they for that reason truths? What a conclusion! As if the preservation of man were a proof of truth! (*Will*, §497)

In passages that adumbrate the later Wittgenstein's repudiation of a 'realist' model of necessary truth (Ch. 10, §§3 and 5), Nietzsche extends this critique to the logical laws that we accept, and warns against viewing these as symptomatic of anything other than our own rules and conventions designed for our own convenience and to meet our own needs. (Here Frege could have served as a prime target.) Thus:[42]

> In the formation of reason, logic, the categories, it was *need* that was authoritative: the need, not to 'know,' but to subsume, to schematize, for the purpose of intelligibility and calculation....
>
> ... If ... the law of contradiction is the most certain of all principles, ... then one should consider all the more rigorously what *presuppositions* already lie at the bottom of it. Either it asserts something about actuality, about being, as if one already knew this from another source; that is, as if opposite attributes *could* not be ascribed to it. Or the proposition means: opposite attributes *should* not be ascribed to it. In that case, logic would be an imperative....
>
> ... [But the former] is certainly not the case. (*Will*, §§515 and 516, emphasis in original)

> The world seems logical to us because we have made it logical. (*Will*, §521)

> Logicians ... posit *their* limitations as the limitations of things. (*Will*, §535, emphasis in original)[43]

---

[40] See again the quotation from *Beyond Good and Evil*, §11, given in §2. See also ibid., §§4, 21, and 22; and *Will*, Bk Three, Pt I.5, passim, and §520 – in the last of which Nietzsche writes that 'all human knowledge is either experience or mathematics', thereby anticipating the logical positivists' Humean repudiation of synthetic *a priori* knowledge. Note: in many of these passages we need to beware something that we have already witnessed, namely that sometimes (and not only when he is using scare quotes) Nietzsche means by 'truth' absolute truth.

[41] This is what I called in Ch. 5, §2, the Causal Principle. In *Beyond Good and Evil*, §4, Nietzsche suggests that this critique extends to synthetic *a priori* 'truths' in general.

[42] See also *Gay Science*, §§110 and 111; *Beyond Good and Evil*, §4; *Will*, Bk Three, Pt I.5, passim, and §§507 and 584.

[43] The Wittgensteinian element in these quotations is evident not least in the element of idealism (see Ch. 10, §§3 and 4). But Nietzsche is altogether less concerned than Wittgenstein

The dangers that we have seen Nietzsche highlight in this section can be partially overcome by our simply cultivating and adopting as many different points of view as possible, which is something that Nietzsche continually urges us to do.[44] For this can expose us to different grammars and thereby lessen the risk of our taking any one to be an image of reality. But the strategy has its limitations. Some of our points of view are ineluctably ours. 'The human intellect,' Nietzsche writes, 'cannot avoid seeing itself in its perspectives, and *only* in these. We cannot look round our own corner: it is a hopeless curiosity that wants to know what other kinds of intellects and perspectives there *might* be' (*Gay Science*, §374, emphasis in original).

5. Prospects for Metaphysics III: Transcendence

The third and final aspect of Nietzsche's attitude to metaphysics that I shall discuss, though independent of the other two, is a very natural accompaniment to them. Nietzsche repudiates the idea of that which is in any remotely ambitious sense transcendent: that which transcends experience; that which transcends knowledge; that which transcends *life*. In particular, though he is not a naturalist in Quine's sense, he is a naturalist in the more modest sense that he repudiates the idea of that which transcends the world of which the natural sciences treat.[45] So he denies that we have any prospect, in practising metaphysics, of making sense of any such thing. (His answer to the Transcendence Question which I posed in §6 of the Introduction is every bit as clear as his answer to the Creativity Question.)

Part of Nietzsche's reason for taking this anti-transcendent stance is an empiricism of sorts (see e.g. *Beyond Good and Evil*, §134, and *Twilight*, IV.3 and V.4–5) albeit an empiricism which, insofar as it is epistemic rather than semantic, precludes only our access to the transcendent, not the very idea of it (see e.g. *Human*, I.9; *Daybreak*, §117; and *Will*, §555). But the views discussed in the previous section are at work here too. Nietzsche thinks that

to disown the latter: in a passage omitted from the first quotation he talks of 'the axioms of logic' as 'a means and measure for us to *create* reality, the concept "reality," for ourselves' (emphasis in original). This helps to explain why, in Nietzsche's case, the idealism is as much an empirical idealism as a transcendental idealism (Ch. 5, Appendix). Cf. also *Will*, §522, where Nietzsche writes, 'We cease to think when we refuse to do so under the constraint of language' (emphasis removed). Frege, the early Wittgenstein, and the later Wittgenstein would all agree. But then Nietzsche immediately adds, in idealist vein, 'We barely reach the doubt that sees this limitation as a limitation.' Frege and the two Wittgensteins would try to resist the idea that there is any limitation here. What Nietzsche sees as a limitation of thought they would see rather as a *limit* of thought, in the sense of one of thought's essential features: see e.g. Ch. 9, §4.

[44] See n. 33.

[45] Cf. Ch. 12, n. 8.

one significant impetus for the belief in a transcendent world is that, when we try to read off features of reality from features of our sense-making, we often find, as both Kant and Frege notably found, that we cannot do so without breaking reality apart into a transcendent world and an empirical world, each equipped in its own way to bear some of these features.[46] This explains Nietzsche's memorable claim that 'we are not getting rid of God because we still believe in grammar' (*Twilight*, IV.5; cf. ibid., VII.3).

Another significant impetus for the belief in a transcendent world is of course the ascetic ideal. The urge to pursue what is higher fosters the belief that there is something higher to pursue. The transcendent is what has played this role. It is what has been elevated when life has been abased.[47]

The transcendent is what 'has' played this role; again, the transcendent is what has 'played this role'. The phraseology here is doubly significant. It indicates an extremely important feature of Nietzsche's rejection of the transcendent. I have in mind its historicism. To explain what I mean by this I need to return to Nietzsche's view that all sense-making is perspectival. I claimed above that this is independent of his rejection of the transcendent. And there is a sense, I believe, in which the former trumps the latter. In particular, I think there is provision in Nietzsche for saying the following: that when people in the past made sense of things in terms of the transcendent, and specifically in terms of God (understood as transcendent), the sense that they made of things embodied a truth, albeit a truth that was surrounded by trappings of falsehood and that is now irretrievably lost.[48]

It is a delicate matter how exactly to put this in terms of God's existence. It would be crass, for example, to say that God used to exist but no longer does, or that God existed from their point of view but does not exist from ours. Nietzsche would see any such prevarication as itself a betrayal of our point of view. It is nevertheless significant, and significant for more than rhetorical reasons, that he does not just deny God's existence. He says that *God is dead*, and, at least through the mouth of a 'madman' whom he depicts, that *we have killed Him* (*Gay Science*, §§108, 125, and 343; cf. *Will*, §331). Really, what Nietzsche is doing is rejecting not a hypothesis but a concept: a *way* of making sense of things.[49] He is calling time on something with a history, something which he thinks has run its course. This may seem to be belied by the fact that he himself makes use of the concept to achieve his

---

[46] In Kant's case the empirical world bore them all, at least insofar as the sense-making in question was 'thick': see Ch. 5, §§4 and 8. In Frege's case the transcendent world bore features corresponding to various logical features of our sense-making: see Ch. 8, §6. (Note: my talk of two worlds in Kant's case is to be interpreted with due caution. In particular it is not meant to beg any of the questions raised in Ch. 5, n. 36.)

[47] Cf. *Will*, §§576ff.

[48] Cf. *Anti-Christ*, §16.

[49] Cf. again n. 5.

end. But – rhetorical considerations once again aside – we can compare this with what Carnap would have seen as the use of the material mode of speech to reject a linguistic framework (Ch. 11, §5). (Not that this comparison captures *all* that Nietzsche is up to, of course. In particular it fails to do justice to an idea which Bernard Williams marvellously puts as follows: 'Nietzsche's saying, God is dead, can be taken to mean that we should now treat God as a dead person: we should allocate his legacies and try to write an honest biography of him' (Williams (2006o), p. 33).) Be all that as it may, the crucial point is that Nietzsche's brand of atheism is not just a piece of abstract metaphysics. It is a break, in its time but not of its time,[50] with a major cultural force in Western civilization that is itself more than just a piece of abstract metaphysics.[51]

6. Nietzsche's Vision. Truth Again

We have now witnessed some of the fundamental restrictions to which Nietzsche thinks the most general attempt to make sense of things is subject. But these still leave the attempt with considerable scope. And, as I claimed in §2, it is an attempt in which Nietzsche himself is engaged. My aim in this section is to sketch some of the main features of his own metaphysical vision.[52]

As we shall see, and as with so many of our protagonists, Nietzsche's meta-metaphysical views are deeply informed by his metaphysical views. In sketching his metaphysical vision I shall at the same time try to cast retrospective light on the material in the last three sections, and in particular on

---

[50] Cf. Deleuze (2006a), p. 100.

[51] The awkwardness explored in this paragraph concerning how to express Nietzsche's atheism is arguably an instance of a more general awkwardness concerning how to express any post-reflection state of enlightenment in which the reflection has, in accord with the controversial and provocative view that Bernard Williams defends in Williams (2006o), destroyed knowledge: see ibid., p. 148. (I discuss this further in Moore (2003c).) Two very pertinent passages in Nietzsche himself are *Beyond Good and Evil*, §211, and *Genealogy*, III.27. Also relevant, in particular to the question of what truth must be like if it is to vary in this way from one epoch to another, is the famous passage from 'Truth and Lies' in which Nietzsche characterizes truth as 'a movable host of metaphors, metonymies, and anthropomorphisms: in short, a sum of human relations which have been poetically and rhetorically intensified, transferred, and embellished, and which, after long usage, seem to a people to be fixed, canonical, and binding,' adding that 'truths are illusions which we have forgotten are illusions' (p. 84). Finally, for two fascinating discussions of Nietzsche's claim that God is dead, each of which emphasizes different aspects of the force of the claim, see Heidegger (1977) and Deleuze (2006a), Ch. 5, §3. (Heidegger connects Nietzsche's claim to the idea, which I mentioned in n. 18, that Nietzsche brings metaphysics of a sort to an end.)

[52] There is a helpful account in Poellner (1995), Ch. 6. See also Han-Pile (2006) for an interesting discussion of Nietzsche's metaphysics in his earliest work.

why Nietzsche thinks that the restrictions to which metaphysics is subject are felt as restrictions; that is, why he thinks there is an urge to transgress them. I also hope to say some more about the notion of (perspectival) truth to which I have claimed he is hospitable, and about how he is able to view his own attempts to make sense of things as attempts to do so truthfully.[53]

There is a famous section at the end of *The Will to Power* which serves as a wonderfully evocative summary of the core of his metaphysical vision. We can do no better than start there.

> And do you know what 'the world' is to me? ... This world: a monster of energy, without beginning, without end; a firm, iron magnitude of force that does not grow bigger or smaller, that does not expend itself but only transforms itself; ... enclosed by 'nothingness' as by a boundary; ... something ... set in a definite space as a definite force, and ... as force throughout, as a play of forces and waves of forces, at the same time one and many, increasing here and at the same time decreasing there; a sea of forces flowing and rushing together, eternally changing, eternally flooding back ..., still affirming itself in this uniformity of its courses and its years ..., as a becoming that knows no satiety, no disgust, no weariness: this my *Dionysian*[54] world of the eternally self-creating, the eternally self-destroying, ... my 'beyond good and evil,' without goal, unless the joy of the circle is itself a goal; ... – do you want a *name* for this world? A *solution* for all its riddles? ... – *This world is the will to power – and nothing besides!* And you yourselves are also this will to power – and nothing besides! (*Will*, §1067, emphasis in original; cf. ibid., §639)

Thus Nietzsche's vision. The world consists of a mass of interacting forces subject to continual change. There is no unity within the world, no identity, no stasis, save what is imposed on it by interpretation.[55] The will to power is not itself a force. It is a cosmological principle that produces and is manifest

---

[53] Two caveats before I proceed. First, Nietzsche's work resists being presented systematically. There are many reasons for this, among which his own suspicion of systematic theorizing in philosophy is paramount: see e.g. *Twilight*, II.26. (Is this akin to what we found in the later Wittgenstein? Not really. Nietzsche's suspicion of systematic theorizing in philosophy is grounded in his (utterly non-Wittgensteinian) conviction, of which more anon, that philosophy is an essentially creative enterprise that should be constantly on its guard against stagnation. For more on the relation between Nietzsche and Wittgenstein, see Williams (2006f), pp. 299–300.) That said, Nietzsche does have a story to tell, and it is that story that I shall try to summarize in this section. The second caveat is simply the caveat about *The Will to Power* that I have already issued in n. 2: I shall be making especially extensive use of Nietzsche's unpublished notes in this section.

[54] Dionysos was the Greek god of wine, who inspired ritual madness and ecstasy.

[55] But note that the very use of language involves such imposition. We cannot say what the world is like *apart from* interpretation: see *Will*, §§517 and 715. This of course relates to the seductions of grammar discussed in §4.

On Nietzsche's rejection of identity, see further n. 85.

in the ever-changing relations between forces. The will to power is what ultimately interprets or makes sense of things. It does this by literally making
the differences between forces and evaluating them in relation to one another.[56] Thus suppose there is a struggle between two forces which eventually
results in the triumph of one over the other together with the celebration of
this by some individual subject. Then both the struggle and its celebration
are manifestations of the will to power. Not that the will to power *is* the
will of any individual subject (cf. *Will*, §692).[57] It is manifest in the wills
of individual subjects, in what they feel as triumphs and disasters as they
make their own sense of things. Individual subjects are themselves nothing
more than creatures of the will-to-power's own ultimate sense-making (cf.
§3 above). And they make sense of things only insofar as that is how sense
is made of *them*. They interpret only insofar as they are interpreted as interpreting. (See *Will*, §§490, 556, 635, 643, 676, and 688.)

Now asceticism, the commitment to the ascetic ideal, is an act of sense-
making. It is a denigration of all that is bodily and unclean, all that is
fragmented, fractured, transitory, and unstable, in favour of that which is
abstract, fixed, and abiding. But all that we experience is of the former kind.
Therefore, by the lights of asceticism, it counts as inferior. But inferior to
what? To an atemporal reality that is posited beyond it, a reality relative to
which it is itself mere appearance. It is in this transcendent reality that true
value, true meaning, and true goodness are to be found (*Twilight*, IV.1–4).

But *why* this denigration of all that we experience in favour of something
beyond?

Because all that we experience is replete with horror, affliction, and misery.
It is replete with suffering. The thought that there is something beyond, and
that this is what really matters, provides solace. To believe in a transcendent, atemporal reality is one way of coping with life (*Will*, §§576, 579, and
585(A)).[58]

The *rejection* of any such reality, the killing of (a transcendent) God,
is a further act of sense-making. It is Nietzsche's act of sense-making.
And by usurping asceticism in the way in which it does, it leads to what
Nietzsche himself describes as 'the radical repudiation of value, meaning,

---

[56] Cf. Deleuze (2006a), Ch. 2, §7, and Deleuze (1989), pp. 139ff.

[57] Cf. Maudemarie Clark (1990), Ch. 7, §4, where Clark distinguishes between Nietzsche's
metaphysical doctrine, which she describes as a kind of 'construction', and his views
about the wills of individual subjects, which she accounts a contribution to the empirical
understanding of human psychology. (In *Will*, §692, Nietzsche rejects 'the will of psychology hitherto'. This is directed principally at Schopenhauer, whose view I mentioned
in Ch. 6, §1.)

[58] For a particularly graphic illustration of this, written as if to play straight into Nietzsche's
hands (especially in the light of what is still to come in this chapter), see Fichte (1956),
p. 101.

and desirability' (*Will*, §1.1). It is not just that it removes the one place where, according to asceticism, (true) value, (true) meaning, and (true) desirability are to be found. It also shares with asceticism its conviction that these are *not* to be found in what we experience. Thus Nietzsche is hostile both to Leibniz' cost-benefit analysis[59] and to Hegel's belief in a *telos* towards which what we experience has been striving,[60] each of which as it were concretizes the transcendent reality by whose means asceticism enables us to endure the suffering and purports to show that the suffering is, even in its own terms, ultimately worth it. Nietzsche's act of sense-making abnegates *all* of that. It leads to the conviction that there is nothing, nothing at all, but grievous pointless ceaseless change. In a word – in Nietzsche's word – it leads to *nihilism* (*Will*, §1.1; cf. ibid., Bk One, §I, passim, and §617).

Nihilism, however, is unbearable. Or at least, it is unbearable provided that we do not simply shut our eyes to the suffering, but rather confront it, with due honesty and with due courage, as Nietzsche exhorts us to do. If the suffering had a purpose, we might be able to bear it. But nihilism entails that it has no purpose. It is meaningless suffering. *That* is what is unbearable. (See *Genealogy*, II.7 and III.28.)[61]

The crucial question for Nietzsche is therefore how nihilism is to be overcome. How are we to face God's death and not be broken by it? How are we to confront the suffering in the world and not be crushed by it? This is at once a fundamental question about how we are to live and a fundamental metaphysical question. Perhaps it is the most fundamental question of either kind.

We must somehow overturn the sense-making that constituted asceticism without succumbing to the awful power of nihilism. Rather than condemn the world, we must affirm the world. But what is it to affirm the world? It cannot be to give the world some sort of favourable assessment. Nihilism itself already precludes our doing that. (To overcome nihilism is not to refute it.) Nihilism entails that there is no assessing the world, as a whole, without condemning it. This is precisely because of the suffering, which, given that it is not atoned in a superior transcendent reality, is not atoned at all. But there is in fact an even more basic reason why there is no assessing the

---

[59] See e.g. *Will*, §§411 and 419.

[60] That there is no such *telos* is in Nietzsche's view indicated by the very passage of time. For if there were such a *telos*, he argues, then the universe ought already to have reached it: there would be, as it were, no point to time (*Will*, §§55, 708, and 1062). Hegel of course thought that the universe *had* already reached it (just): see Ch. 7, §5. For further discussion of the relations between Hegel and Nietzsche, see the next section below.

[61] For a fascinating discussion of meaningless suffering in relation to Nietzsche, see Williams (2006i). Cf. also Williams (2006a), pp. 52–54, and (2006g), pp. 317–319. Other interesting discussions of Nietzsche's views on suffering, with a bearing on what is to come, include Neiman (2002), pp. 206–227, and Dews (2008), pp. 136–152.

world, as a whole, without condemning it. There is no assessing the world, as a whole, in the first place. There is no suitable point of view from which any such assessment can be made: there is no point of view outside the world (*Twilight*, III.2). It is in this vein that Nietzsche talks of 'the innocence of becoming' (*Twilight*, VII.8, and *Will*, §552) where 'becoming' is his word for the ever-changing relations between forces that constitute the world.[62]

Affirming the world does not involve assessing it then. But it cannot simply consist in resignedly accepting everything either. Nietzsche is adamant that such passive and indiscriminate acquiescence would itself be a concession to the meaninglessness of everything and would leave nihilism entirely undefeated (*Zarathustra*, IV.xvii).

So what *is* it to affirm the world?

It is, in spite of all the suffering, to remain committed to life. It is to *create* the meaning and value that are otherwise lacking, by suitably making sense of things. It is to make sense of things in such a way as to accentuate all three components of that phrase, that is:

- proactively to *make* sense of things – not to interpret and evaluate things simply by reacting to events as they occur, but to do so by acting out a particular life in its own terms
- to make discriminating *sense* of things – not to say 'yes' to everything, as though the world were some inert homogeneous plenum, but to say 'yes' to some things and 'no' to others, in accord with differences between them

and

- to make sense of *things*, in their singularity – not to interpret, evaluate, and say 'yes' or 'no' to the world as a whole, but to do so to specific episodes, occurrences, and relations between forces within the world.

(See *Gay Science*, §301; *Beyond Good and Evil*, §211; *Twilight*, II.12 and XI.5; and *Will*, §§12, 13, 567, 616, and 708.)

Nietzsche's most general attempt to make sense of things therefore assigns importance to more particular, local attempts to make sense of things; local attempts to make things bearable. A paradigm would be a subject's attempt to redeem his or her own past. The kind of redemption that is characteristic of asceticism is that which is born of guilt-ridden penitence. It involves a *renunciation* of the past, in favour of the subject's new-found commitment to what is higher. The kind of redemption that Nietzsche advocates is completely different. It occurs when 'It was,' which Nietzsche describes as 'the will's teeth-gnashing and most lonely affliction,' is transformed into 'Thus I willed it' (*Zarathustra*, II.xx). And this in turn occurs when the

---

[62] In *Will*, §765, he also talks of 'the innocence of all existence'.

subject, drawing on the power of his or her own past, appropriates it in the continuing saga of his or her life, acting out a life of which that past can come to be (interpreted as) an integral (if abhorrent) part; tracing out a line of which that line can come to be (seen as) an earlier (if crooked) segment.[63] This is a creation of value and meaning.

It follows that we must distinguish between two kinds of value and meaning: that which Nietzsche repudiates and that which he champions. This is entirely of a piece with the fact that we must distinguish between two kinds of truth: absolute truth, which he repudiates, and perspectival truth, which he champions (§§2 and 3). Absolute truth is for Nietzsche a perversion of perspectival truth.[64] It is an idealized version of the real thing, seen through the distorting lens of asceticism. Likewise in this case. The value and meaning that Nietzsche repudiates are such as to be:

- discovered
- located in the world as a whole
- viewed from somewhere outside the world.

The value and meaning that he champions are such as to be:

- created
- located in parts of the world
- viewed from somewhere within the world. (See *Will*, §556.)

Nor is this parallel between the case of truth and the case of value and meaning merely a parallel. Truth is itself a value. And it depends on meaning. The case of truth is in effect an instance of the case of value and meaning, as indeed sense-making of the kind that involves arriving at a conception of something is an instance of sense-making more generally. To make *true* sense of things, I suggest, is to arrive at a conception of things that will enable one, from one's point of immersion in them, with due honesty and with due courage, to say, 'Thus I will it' (*Will*, §§495, 534, and 568).[65]

This is not a definition, though. Or at any rate, it is not a non-circular definition. 'Due', 'honesty', and even 'courage' can all be said to presuppose the notion of truth. Indeed, I might just as well have written, in place of 'with due honesty and with due courage', 'truthfully'. (Nietzsche at one point defines truthfulness as 'the opposite of the cowardice of the "idealist" who flees from reality' (*Ecce Homo*, IV.3).[66]) But although it is not a

---

[63] The parenthetical references here to abhorrence and crookedness indicate that 'Thus I willed it' means nothing like 'I was glad that it was so,' nor even 'I am glad that it was so.'

[64] See again the material from *Beyond Good and Evil*, Preface, to which I referred in §3.

[65] Cf. Houlgate (1986), p. 74. Note: this requires a caveat similar to that in n. 63.

[66] But note that there is just the same equivocation, with respect to truthfulness, as there is with respect to truth itself. For a discussion of the opposed conception of truthfulness,

(non-circular) definition, it does, I believe, help to signal some important features of the notion of truth that Nietzsche embraces. There are three features in particular to which I wish to draw attention.

First, the attainment of truth is *not easy*.[67] If it were, other ways of contending with suffering, including asceticism, would not have held sway in the way in which they have done. Nor would metaphysicians have felt the urge that they have done to transgress the restrictions that I described in §§3–5.

Second, the pursuit of truth is more of an art than a science. Not only does it involve inventiveness and imagination (which science involves as well). Lacking science's truth fetish, it allows for *the inventive and imaginative appropriation of falsehood* (*Human*, I.146 and *Genealogy*, III.25).[68] Thus it is possible for someone who has arrived at a false conception of something, from a given point of view, to remedy that – or better, to move on from there – by adopting, not a new conception of this thing, but a new point of view, a point of view from which the conception is true.[69] And insofar as the new point of view is itself engendered in the process, this will constitute a kind of creative transformation of the false into the true.

Third, the pursuit of truth is subsidiary to the creation of value. This applies even, or especially, at the level of generality at which the sense-making characteristic of philosophy occurs. For philosophers are in Nietzsche's view nothing unless they are creators of value. The creation of value – the provision of value for more particular sense-making – is their contribution to the process of overcoming nihilism (*Beyond Good and Evil*, §§9, 204, and 211; and *Fragmente*, III.19.35 (cited in Han-Pile (2006), p. 394)). And philosophy here embraces metaphysics.[70]

A final point in this section. Asceticism, as we have seen, is a non-affirmative reaction to the meaninglessness of life's suffering. But it is not the only one. It is not even one of the commonest. There are countless others: countless ways of recoiling, hitting back, brooding, scapegoating, or trying

---

as a correlate of *absolute* truth, see *Untimely Meditations*, pp. 152–155; cf. *Gay Science*, §344, and *Will*, §§277 and 278.

[67] Cf. the quotation from §50 of the *Anti-Christ* which I gave in §3: see also *Ecce Homo*, Preface, §3, and *Will*, §538. Cf. Craig (1987), p. 281. But for the suggestion that its not being easy is an indication of something rotten, see *Twilight*, VII.2.

[68] Cf. *Beyond Good and Evil*, Pt One, passim, and *Will*, §§539–544 and 599–606. See also Deleuze (2006a), pp. 97ff.

[69] Here is a very crude model. (It is too crude to provide anything other than an initial steer, but it does provide that.) A man incorrectly thinks he is facing north; and he continues to think he is facing north after reorienting himself so that he is.

[70] I am still working with my own conception of metaphysics. Nietzsche himself talks only in terms of philosophy, though it is worth noting that, in his earliest work, he is also prepared to say, 'I am convinced that art represents … the truly metaphysical activity of this life' (*Tragedy*, 'Preface to Richard Wagner').

to contain the suffering other than by doing as asceticists[71] do, which is to say relegating the suffering to a world of mere appearance where nothing really matters. They include:

- vengefulness ('Somebody should pay for my suffering')
- self-pity ('I shall dwell on my suffering – may it never be forgotten')
- blame ('My suffering is all your fault')
- guilt ('Your suffering is all my fault, so I must suffer too')
- hope ('Suffering will eventually be a thing of the past')
- despair ('Suffering will never be a thing of the past – it is part of the very fabric of the world')
- acquiescence – which we briefly considered earlier ('I shall say "yes" to everything, including suffering')

and even (*Twilight*, III.6–7, and *Will*, §§429–433 and 441–443)

- Socratic dialectic, which combines various elements of the above ('I shall make you pay for my suffering, by wielding my intellect over yours, but at the same time I shall display my grasp of what really matters; my grasp of those values and resources beyond suffering which enable me to master it').[72]

None of these are ways of overcoming nihilism. They are just what a successful metaphysics must leave behind.

I close this section, much as I began it, with a quotation from *The Will to Power* that serves as a compendium of Nietzsche's vision:

Man seeks 'the truth': a world that is not self-contradictory, not deceptive, does not change, a *true* world – a world in which one does not suffer ...!

... [He believes:] the world as it ought to be exists; this world, in which we live, is an error – this world of ours ought not to exist....

The belief that the world as it ought to be *is*, really exists, is a belief of the unproductive who do *not desire to create a world* as it ought to be. They posit it as already available, they seek ways and means of reaching it. 'Will to truth' – *as the impotence of the will to create....*

This same species of man, grown one stage poorer, no longer possessing the strength to interpret, ... produces *nihilists*. A nihilist is a man who

---

[71] This unlovely coinage is meant simply as a term for those who embrace asceticism. 'Ascetics' would have had inappropriate connotations of monasticism.

[72] The last of these examples is also an example, as the references testify, of what Nietzsche calls '*ressentiment*'. *Ressentiment* in fact includes a number of these examples. It includes all those in which suffering is externalized and met with a resounding 'no': see *Genealogy*, I.10–11 and III.14; *Ecce Homo*, I.6; and *Will*, §579. (See Deleuze (1990b), p. 149, for a suggestion that even acquiescence, with its meaningless 'yes', is a form of *ressentiment*.)

judges of the world as it is that it ought *not* to be, and of the world as it ought to be that it does not exist. According to this view, our existence (action, suffering, willing, feeling) has no meaning....

It is a measure of the degree of strength of will to what extent one can do without meanings in things, to what extent one can endure to live in a meaningless world *because one organizes a small portion of it oneself.* (*Will*, §585(A), emphasis in original)

7. Nietzsche *Pro* Spinoza and *Contra* Hegel

In Chapter 7, §6, I tried to highlight some profound differences between Spinoza and Hegel. It is instructive, notwithstanding Nietzsche's many quarrels with Spinoza and notwithstanding his many convergences with Hegel, to look upon what we have just witnessed as an anti-Hegelian development of certain core Spinozist ideas.

(a) Nietzsche Pro Spinoza[73]

Both Spinoza and Nietzsche have on overriding concern with the affirmation of life, or with what I called in the previous section the affirmation of the world. In Chapter 2, §6, we saw Spinoza refer to 'an intellectual love of God', or, in the original Latin, '*amor dei intellectualis*'. Nietzsche repeatedly refers to '*amor fati*', literally 'a love of fate' (e.g. *Gay Science*, §276, and *Ecce Homo*, II.10). These, despite various important differences between them, are Spinoza's and Nietzsche's respective ways of referring to just such

---

[73] Cf. in what follows Schacht (1995c) – which also, incidentally, draws attention to some of the quarrels. What are these? There is an extensive list – so extensive that it can even seem to foreclose any *rapprochement*. Nietzsche is opposed to Spinoza's idea of a single substance with attributes of both thought and extension (*Will*, §523). He is suspicious of Spinoza's notion of conatus, whereby nature comprises unified individuals bent on their own self-preservation: on his own conception of the will to power, nature comprises, not unified individuals, but centres of force, bent not on their own self-preservation, but on the exertion and the increase of power, sometimes at their own expense (*Gay Science*, §349; *Beyond Good and Evil*, §13; and *Will*, §688; cf. also *Will*, §627). He thinks that there is something of the will to truth in Spinoza's pursuit of knowledge (*Gay Science*, §§37 and 333) and indeed, more generally, that Spinoza is in the grip of the ascetic ideal (*Will*, §578). He thinks that Spinoza is too concerned with the minimization of passion, too naïve about the ease with which this can be achieved (*Beyond Good and Evil*, §198). And he even sees an element of *ressentiment* in Spinoza (*Beyond Good and Evil*, §25; see previous note). There is obviously much to be said about each of these. In particular, there is an issue in each case about how fair and accurate Nietzsche's view of Spinoza is. But I shall not pursue these quarrels

affirmation.[74] Both thinkers take the affirmation of life to be our greatest ethical achievement. Both see it as a way of welcoming the future with joy, a way of being active rather than passive in the midst of life's afflictions.[75]

There is a famous postcard from Nietzsche to Franz Overbeck in which he records his own sudden realization of this kinship with Spinoza. He writes:

> I am utterly amazed, utterly enchanted. I have a *precursor*, and what a precursor! ... Not only is [Spinoza's] over-all tendency like mine – making knowledge the *most powerful* affect – but in five main points of his doctrine I recognize myself; this most unusual and loneliest thinker is closest to me precisely in these matters: he denies the freedom of the will, teleology, the moral world order, the unegoistic, and evil. Even though the divergences are admittedly tremendous,[76] they are due more to the differences in time, culture, and science. *In summa*: my lonesomeness, which, as on very high mountains, often makes it hard for me to breathe and made my blood rush out, is at least a twosomeness. ('Postcard to Overbeck', emphasis in original)

But does Nietzsche not fasten on quite different points of contact here from that which I emphasized above? Not at all. When he says that Spinoza makes knowledge 'the most powerful affect', he is referring to the way in

---

any further. – Not that they are the only reason why Spinoza and Nietzsche may appear unlikely bedfellows. Even the most casual reading of the *Ethics* and of Nietzsche's works supplies another. The austere, methodical disquisitions of the former, where theorems are derived from axioms and definitions *a là* Euclid (2002), stand in stark contrast to the florid and desultory tirades that we find throughout the latter. True, these are matters of style rather than matters of content, and misleading matters of style at that. (The *Ethics* lacks the mathematical rigour that its format suggests it has. Nietzsche's works follow a much more carefully wrought plan than they appear to do.) But the misleadingness does not prevent – in fact it provokes – a further recoil from Spinoza on Nietzsche's part. Nietzsche attacks what he calls 'that hocus-pocus of mathematical form in which, as if in iron, Spinoza encased and masked his philosophy' (*Beyond Good and Evil*, §5). He sees this as a terror-inducing sham designed to hide the fact that Spinoza is merely defending his prejudices, and he bemoans the 'personal timidity and vulnerability [which] this masquerade of a sick recluse betrays' (ibid.).

[74] See Yovel (1989), Ch. 5, for discussion of the differences between the two conceptions, as well as discussion of the similarities between them.

[75] In a remarkable passage in his notebooks Nietzsche gives an indication of his own distinctive conception of joy (a conception that is related to, if not identical with, Spinoza's). He describes joy as a feeling of 'the presence of eternal harmony', and as a 'sensation of contact with the whole of nature'. He also says that it is a 'clear and indisputable feeling', that it is 'not an emotion', and that it is 'superior to love.' And he suggests that the soul cannot bear it for more than 'five [or] six seconds' (*Werke*, II.3.11.337, trans. Béatrice Han-Pile, to whom I am indebted for drawing the passage to my attention).

[76] See n. 73.

which, on Spinoza's conception, the acquisition of knowledge, or more specifically knowledge of the third kind, gives us power over all our other affects (including what Spinoza would call our affects of sadness and what Nietzsche would call our affects of suffering). And it does this by enabling us to make sense of those affects, which in turn brings us both to our highest level of activity and to *amor dei intellectualis* (Ch. 2, §5). So Nietzsche is talking about precisely the same shared concern as I identified above.

As regards the other five points of contact that he mentions, these signal the two thinkers' common rejection of attempts to achieve power over all these affects by other means. Both reject the idea that nature has some purpose or *telos* towards which it is striving and in whose terms life's afflictions can be justified. Both reject the idea that there is refuge from life's afflictions in the transcendent. (Indeed, both reject the transcendent.) Both, in the contrast between ethics and morality that I drew in Chapter 2, §3, likewise reject the idea that there is refuge from life's afflictions in morality: the good that we pursue is as opposed to the bad, not as opposed to the evil.[77] The only one of Nietzsche's five points of comparison for which we have not already seen clear evidence is the first. This is because we have not hitherto considered Nietzsche's own denial of freedom of the will. But actually this denial is very much in keeping with what we have considered. For the belief in freedom of the will is an integral part of the belief in morality; and it is fostered, like the belief in an immaterial thinking substance, by the grammar of how we make sense of ourselves (see e.g. *Human*, I.39 and I.106; *Beyond Good and Evil*, §§19–21; and *Will*, §786).[78]

(b)   *Nietzsche* Contra *Hegel*[79]

Some of what Spinoza and Nietzsche share Hegel shares too. All three reject the transcendent, albeit in Hegel's case by rejecting the very distinction between the immanent and the transcendent. And this commits all three, as I see it, to atheism, albeit in each case atheism of a notably unstraightforward sort (Ch. 2, §2; Ch. 7, §6; and §5 above). All three also in some sense

---

[77] This is reflected in the very titles of *Beyond Good and Evil* and *Genealogy*, I ("Good and Evil," "Good and Bad"), each of which is a sustained discussion of this idea. Cf. also *Daybreak*, passim.

[78] It is fascinating in this connection to consider P.F. Strawson's celebrated avowal of freedom of the will, on pretty much the same grounds: see Strawson (2008). (Especially noteworthy, in view of Nietzsche's promotion of proactive sense-making over reactive sense-making, is Strawson's continual appeal, throughout this essay, to what he calls 'our reactive attitudes'.)

[79] Cf. in what follows Deleuze (2006a), 'Conclusion', and Turetzky (1998), Ch. 8, §2, to both of which I am indebted. (I have borrowed the title of the latter.) For a book-length study somewhat opposed to these, see Houlgate (1986). See also n. 60 above.

champion ethics over morality (cf. Ch. 7, §6[80]).[81] Nietzsche's philosophy nevertheless marks a fundamental break with that of Hegel.[82]

For Hegel there is ultimately no truth save the absolute truth of the whole. All that we experience – all that is 'fragmented, fractured, transitory, and unstable,' to reclaim my own phrase from the previous section – bespeaks falsehood. And it bespeaks falsehood of a kind that needs to be both sublated and reintegrated into that absolute truth by various processes of negation. This means that, although Hegel eschews any immanent/transcendent distinction, his philosophy contains something of the asceticist's depreciation of all that we experience in favour of what is ultimately true and ultimately real. Hegel takes the friction, opposition, and suffering that beset us to represent stages in a master process, stages which on the one hand we have to endure for the sake of its *telos*, but which on the other hand we can eventually put completely behind us. Nietzsche would see this as a failure of nerve, a failure to confront the suffering squarely and, through creation and affirmation rather than through prescission and negation, to defy it. There is in fact a sense in which Hegel serves as a paradigm of all that most deeply appals Nietzsche.

Another facet of the break between them is interestingly reflected in one of the contrasts between analytic philosophy and philosophy that we shall be exploring later in Part Three. Both Hegel and Nietzsche have a particular concern with *difference* and specifically with change. (For Hegel these are the means whereby the finite surpasses its own finitude. For Nietzsche they are the very character of reality.) In this respect they both anticipate what is to come. For in the work that we shall be exploring later there is likewise a particular concern with difference.[83] In analytic philosophy, by contrast, there is typically a greater emphasis on identity.[84] But not only that; there is also typically a *prioritization* of identity. It is extremely difficult for analytic philosophers to think of difference in anything other than negative terms; that is, to avoid thinking of what is different as what is *not* the same, or as what does *not* have some feature that some given thing does

---

[80] But see n. 50 of that section for an important qualification.

[81] A further interesting point of comparison between Hegel and Nietzsche, reflected in Nietzsche's doctrine of the death of God, is that they both believe that concepts have histories: see *Gay Science*, §357.

[82] One symptom of this is that Nietzsche would never dream of declaring the rational actual or the actual rational: see e.g. *Gay Science*, §109, and *Will*, §§12(B), 436, 480, and 488.

[83] See esp. Ch. 21, §§3 and 4.

[84] For examples of the interest in identity shown by our protagonists from Part Two, see Frege (1980), §§62ff.; Frege (1997c), pp. 151–152/pp. 25–26 in the original German; Wittgenstein (1961), 5.53ff.; Wittgenstein (1967a), Pt I, §§215 and 216; Carnap (1935), p. 66; Quine (1960), §24; Quine (1961d); Lewis (1983d); Lewis (1983e); and Dummett (1981a), Ch. 16. (In the case of Wittgenstein, both early and late, the interest is characteristically idiosyncratic.)

have.[85] The philosophers whose work we shall be exploring later reverse this prioritization. And in *this* respect Hegel is closer to the former. He too construes difference negatively. Not so Nietzsche.[86] Nietzsche fully anticipates what is to come. The *positive* construal of difference, as something that betokens affirmation and something that is itself to be affirmed, is profoundly Nietzschean.[87]

8. Eternal Return

So far I have said nothing about what is probably the best-known feature of Nietzsche's metaphysics, namely his idea of eternal return.[88] Nietzsche assigns very great significance to this idea. He describes it as the 'highest formula of affirmation that is at all attainable' (*Ecce Homo*, III.vi.1; cf. *Twilight*, XI.5).

There is nevertheless considerable exegetical controversy surrounding the idea. This controversy has two dimensions. First, there is a dispute about what the idea even consists in. Second, there is a dispute about whether Nietzsche intends it as part of an actual cosmology or whether he intends it merely as a thought experiment with a role to play in our attempts to overcome nihilism.[89]

As far as the first of these disputes is concerned, the vast majority of commentators take Nietzsche to be reviving the ancient idea of an endlessly recurring cosmic cycle in which everything is repeated in exact detail again and again.[90] And in fact to settle the first dispute in *that* way is surely, in

---

[85] Among the reasons for this are the fact that it would be impossible to recast the standard logic of numerical identity in terms of difference without the use of negation. (I shall have more to say about this in §4 of the next chapter.) Nietzsche, incidentally, would not so much take issue with such logic as take issue with the concept of numerical identity itself: see e.g. *Gay Science*, §111, and *Will*, §520. This is another example, along with his atheism, of his taking issue with a whole *way* of making sense of things. And even then he would take issue with it only in the sense of querying its fundamentality. He would not deny the usefulness of that way of making sense of things, nay its indispensability, for practical purposes: see ibid., and cf. *Beyond Good and Evil*, §4.

[86] Cf. *Human*, II.ii.67, and *Will*, §§581 and 853.

[87] Which incidentally brings this section full circle. For it is also profoundly Spinozist (Spinoza (2002c), Pt I, Def. 6 and Expl.).

[88] Sometimes it is called the idea of eternal recurrence. Nietzsche himself uses two words – '*Wiederkehr*' and '*Wiederkunft*' – though not, it seems, very systematically. (Occasionally, he uses '*Wiederholung*' as well. This is normally translated as 'repetition'.) Here I am indebted to Stambaugh (1972), pp. 29–31.

[89] Bernard Reginster registers this second dispute by distinguishing between a 'theoretical' interpretation and a 'practical' interpretation: see Reginster (2006), Ch. 5, §1.

[90] According to Simplicius, the Pythagoreans accepted this idea: see Barnes (1987), p. 88. Empedocles also accepted a version of it: see ibid., pp. 166–167.

effect, to settle the second dispute as well. For Nietzsche surely does not believe that the universe *actually* undergoes any such recurring cycle. There are passages, to be sure, in which he toys with arguments concerning the play of finite resources in infinite time, arguments whose intended upshot seems to be that all of the finitely many states that the universe can be in it will be in, and will be in again, infinitely many times (e.g. *Will*, §§1062 and 1066). But there are issues about what exactly Nietzsche is doing with these arguments, unconvincing and readily refutable as they are.[91] And elsewhere he all but explicitly denies that the universe undergoes any such recurring cycle (e.g. *Untimely Meditations*, III.1, opening paragraph, and *Gay Science*, §109).

On this account of eternal return, then, Nietzsche cannot reasonably be said to intend the idea as part of an actual cosmology. But he can reasonably be said to intend it as a thought experiment. There is a compelling interpretation whereby he is exhorting us to act out our lives *as if* there were such a cycle, the idea being that one test of whether we properly affirm the world is whether we make such sense of things as to be able, with due acknowledgement of the world's suffering, to bear the infinite repetition of all things; indeed to *will* their infinite repetition.[92]

This interpretation certainly chimes well with Nietzsche's frequent insistence that what is important about eternal return is whether we can will it (*Gay Science*, §§285 and 341; *Zarathustra*, III.ii.2, III.xvi, and IV.xix; *Ecce Homo*, II.10, final paragraph; and *Will*, §§1053–1060). The interpretation is not without its problems, however. There are passages in *Zarathustra* in which it is hard to see what Nietzsche is doing if not precisely distancing his idea from the idea of a recurring cycle: I have in mind Zarathustra's admonishments, first of the dwarf (III.ii.2) and later of the animals (III.xiii.2), when they severally proclaim the idea of just such a cycle.[93] Also, it is not clear, on this interpretation, why the idea of eternal return should be the idea of *eternal* return. A thought experiment involving just one repetition of the cycle would do the job as effectively as a thought experiment involving infinitely many. As Bernard Williams puts it, 'If you could overcome the "nausea" ... of the prospect that [the past] ... will come round again *even once*, and say "yes" to it, you would have taken the essential step: could willing all those further recurrences cost you very much more?' (Williams (2006g), p. 319, emphasis in original).[94]

---

[91] It is in any case worth recalling the caveat in n. 2. The passages in question occur in Nietzsche's unpublished notes. As for the refutation of these arguments, see e.g. Schacht (1983), pp. 263ff.

[92] For one of countless instances of this interpretation, see Williams (2006g), pp. 318ff.

[93] Hard to see, not impossible to see. An advocate of this interpretation might say that Zarathustra's reason for admonishing the dwarf and the animals is that they treat the idea, as he himself puts it to the dwarf, 'too lightly'.

[94] We might wonder about the force of Williams' rhetorical question. If willing one recurrence could cost you anything, then *could not* willing all those further recurrences cost

A diametrically opposed account of eternal return has been given by Deleuze. According to this account eternal return is not the eternal return *of* anything that is the same: it is itself the same, but it applies only to what is different (e.g. Deleuze (2006a), p. 45, and Deleuze (1994), p. 126). It is the inexhaustible renewal of the ever-differing moment of becoming, ensuring that the world is a world, not only of ceaseless change, but of ceaseless novelty. Furthermore, Deleuze takes Nietzsche to be claiming that this is a feature of the world as it is, not merely as we might suppose it to be in some heuristically useful thought experiment.

Unfortunately, it is far beyond the scope of this chapter to engage with Deleuze's exegesis – though the ideas themselves will come to the fore again in Chapter 21 (see esp. §2(a) of that chapter). I simply hereby record that, although the account I favour is very close to Deleuze's, and although I am indebted to Deleuze for it, there are certain core elements of his account with which I am uncomfortable. In particular, I am uncomfortable with the idea that eternal return is not the return of anything that is the same.[95]

What then is the account that I favour?[96] Like Deleuze, I believe that Nietzsche holds eternal return to be a feature of the world as it is and not merely as we might suppose it to be when trying to frame some sort of guide to living. I take as my starting point two ideas to which Nietzsche seems to me to be clearly committed: first, that everything is knotted together in such a way that each thing implicates every other thing and the affirmation of each is the affirmation of all (*Human*, I.208;[97] *Zarathustra*, III.ii.2 and IV.xix.10; and *Will*, §§293, 331, 584, and 1032); second, that change is ceaseless (*Will*, §688).[98] The idea of eternal return, I suggest, amalgamates these two ideas.

---

you very much more? But we must not forget that what is at issue here is the cost of willing the recurrences, not the cost of enduring them. In order to will even one recurrence you would already have to think in as much vivid detail as possible of all the horror, all the affliction, and all the misery: it would already cost you as much as that. As far as enduring the recurrences is concerned, its costs are beside the point. Affirming the world, as we saw in §6, is not a matter of balancing costs against benefits at all.

[95] This is not so much because I fail to see this idea in Nietzsche as because I fail to see *him* in *it*. If it can be seen there, this is not, I think, because he has put it there. See again my comments about Deleuze in n. 2. (You may be suspicious of the distinction between what can be seen in an author and what he or she has put there. We shall return to this kind of suspicion, which is associated especially with Derrida, in Ch. 20, §3.)

[96] It is an account that I have tried to defend elsewhere: see Moore (2006a). Some of the present section is derived from this essay. I am grateful to the editor of *Mind* for permission to make use of the relevant material. For something very similar, see the superb discussion in Lloyd (1993), pp. 107–122.

[97] This section is also incidentally relevant to the issue of whether it is possible to see something in a writer that he or she has not put there: see n. 95 above.

[98] I do not mean to suggest that Deleuze does not likewise see Nietzsche as committed to these two ideas: see e.g. Deleuze (2006a), Ch. 2, §15.

What the knotting together of things means is that the ceaseless change is a ceaseless change in *everything*, including everything that has been and everything that will be. The whole of the past and the whole of the future come together in each moment of change. And this is what I understand by eternal return. It is the eternal return of all things, but ever different.

Here is Nietzsche, in the words of Zarathustra:

> Behold this gateway ... : ... it has two aspects. Two paths come together here: no one has ever reached their end.
>
> This long lane behind us: it goes on for an eternity. And that long lane ahead of us – that is another eternity.
>
> They are in opposition to one another, these paths; they abut on one another: and it is here at this gateway that they come together. The name of the gateway is written above it: 'Moment'.
>
> ... From this gateway Moment a long, eternal lane runs *back*: an eternity lies behind us.
>
> Must not all things that *can* run have already run along this lane? Must not all things that *can* happen have already happened, been done, run past?
>
> And if all things have been here before: what do you think of this moment ...? Must not this gateway, too, have been here before?
>
> And are not all things bound fast together in such a way that this moment draws after it all future things? *Therefore* – draws itself too?
>
> For all things that *can* run *must* also run once again forward along this long lane.
>
> ... [Must] we not return and run down that other lane out before us, down that long, terrible lane – must we not return eternally? (*Zarathustra*, III.ii.2, emphasis in original; cf. *Gay Science*, §109)

What I am suggesting is that for all things that can happen to have already happened, and to happen again, *is* for everything to be, as Nietzsche later puts it, 'chained and entwined together' (*Zarathustra*, IV.xix.10). What happens at any moment, on this account, happens at every moment – albeit at some moments as future, at some moments as present, and at some moments as past. Each moment affords its own different perspective on the whole, its own different point of view from which to interpret the whole. Each moment enables the will to power to make associated sense of things. The world has, in Nietzsche's words, 'a differing aspect from every point; its being is essentially different from every point' (*Will*, §568).[99]

[99] There are two interesting precursors of this conception in earlier chapters. In Ch. 3, §3, we saw Leibniz defend the view that the world is a world of monads, each affording its own different perspective on the whole. And in Ch. 9, §8, we saw Wittgenstein defend the idea that viewing the world first one way and then another can, without altering the facts, make it become a different world. The latter is especially pertinent to how I am

On this interpretation, as on the interpretation considered above whereby the idea of eternal return is merely a thought experiment, eternal return is crucial to the overcoming of nihilism.[100] How so? Does it not in fact exacerbate nihilism? For, as Nietzsche himself insists, it presents the nihilistic spectre of meaninglessness in its most extreme and terrifying form, a form in which the meaninglessness recurs and recurs and recurs, *ad infinitum* (*Will*, §55; cf. *Zarathustra*, III.xiii.2).[101] – True; but eternal return is also the very condition of that sense-making, that ultimate act of the will to power which is manifest in our various individual efforts to create value and meaning, whereby each of us is able to affirm the world and thus contribute to the overcoming of nihilism. In its continual generation of new perspectives eternal return allows for the continual generation of new evaluations and new interpretations. Through these, things in the world, including things that are past, can be continually transformed, so that, although they keep returning, they keep returning differently. They can be continually developed, continually cultivated, continually lived afresh. That is to say, new sense can be continually made of them. And the horror of their objective meaninglessness[102] can be prevented from destroying us. But the eternity of the eternal return is vital. Nihilism can never be overcome once and for all. If ever the process were to cease, it would meet with an unanswerable 'So what?', and nihilism would have a standing invitation, which it would accept, to reassert itself. (See *Gay Science*, App., 'Towards New Seas'; *Beyond Good and Evil*, §56; *Twilight*, XI.5; *Ecce Homo*, III.i.3; and *Will*, §§575, 616, and 1067).[103]

Eternal return is a crucial feature of Nietzsche's metaphysics. But its importance to us lies as much in its relation to his meta-metaphysics. I remarked in §6 how the contribution of metaphysicians to overcoming nihilism is in Nietzsche's view the creation of value.[104] The comments above apply as much to this contribution as to any other. It too needs to be, as eternal return allows it to be, a continual contribution. Without an ever-renewed supply of value, adapted to an ever-changing world, sense-making at a lower level of generality would eventually give out (*Untimely Meditations*, III.3–4, and *Will*, §409).

---

about to develop the conception. (Wittgenstein, it should be added, was writing after Nietzsche. Was Nietzsche an influence on Wittgenstein? There is no reason to think so, though it is worth noting that Schopenhauer was a great influence on both: see Ch. 9, n. 65, and see e.g. *Untimely Meditations*, III.)

[100] As it is on Deleuze's interpretation: see Deleuze (2006a), Ch. 15 passim. (In fact no reasonable interpretation could gainsay this point.)

[101] This is marvellously captured in Kundera (1984), Pt One, §§1 and 2.

[102] The word 'objective' here is intended to signal the first of the two kinds of meaning distinguished in §6.

[103] Cf. Nehamas (1985), pp. 163–164. (But note that Nehamas adopts the popular first interpretation of Nietzsche's doctrine which I have rejected.)

[104] See n. 70: here again I intend my own conception of metaphysics.

Does this mean that Nietzsche's vision anticipates its own supersession? I think perhaps it does.[105] It certainly means – to echo my earlier parenthetical references to the questions that I raised in §6 of the Introduction – that Nietzsche has an answer to the Novelty Question which is every bit as clear as his answers to the Creativity Question and the Transcendence Question. There is plainly scope, on Nietzsche's view, for metaphysicians to make radically new sense of things.[106] In fact, there is not only scope for them to do so. There is call for them to do so.

---

[105] Its own supersession; not its own denial; still less its own refutation. See §§5 and 6: Nietzsche's vision can legitimately be superseded even if it is true.

[106] This makes Nietzsche the second of my protagonists after Carnap – historically, the first – to give the triad of answers that I myself would give. (See Ch. 11, n. 49.)

CHAPTER 16

Bergson

Metaphysics as Pure Creativity

1. Introduction

Many of our protagonists have distinguished, if only implicitly, between two
or more kinds of sense-making, in a way that has critically shaped their contribution to the saga.[1] Thus we have witnessed:

- Spinoza's distinction between his three kinds of knowledge
- Kant's broad distinction between what I called 'thick' sense-making
  and 'thin' sense-making
- Hegel's distinction between operations of understanding and operations of reason
- the early Wittgenstein's distinction between propositional sense-making
  and non-propositional sense-making
- the two variations on that theme in the later Wittgenstein and
  Dummett

and

- Carnap's distinction between the making of judgments within a linguistic framework and the adoption of the framework.

In each case there were important questions about where metaphysics
stood in relation to the distinction, either on the protagonist's own conception of metaphysics or on mine, or on both. (See respectively Ch. 2, §6; Ch. 5,
§§9 and 10; Ch. 7, §§7 and 9; Ch. 10, §3; Ch. 14, §4; and Ch. 11, §5.)

Nowhere in the history of metaphysics, however, has the drawing of
a distinction between different kinds of sense-making been more pronounced, or more relentlessly pursued, or more directly relevant to our
narrative, than in Bergson. Henri Bergson (1859–1941) distinguished
sharply between 'analysis' and 'intuition'. And he insisted that metaphysics

---

[1] And some have declined to draw such a distinction, in a way that has critically shaped
their contribution to it. I have in mind the naturalism of Quine and Lewis (see Ch. 12, §8,
and Ch. 13, §4, respectively).

consists of the latter. It remains to be seen how far his conception of meta-physics coincided with mine. But even if it did not coincide at all, the importance of his distinction to his overall vision and its ready application to the very idea of sense-making at the highest level of generality ensure that the distinction cannot fail to have a significant bearing on our own enquiry.

2.   Analysis (or Intelligence) versus Intuition

Here is how Bergson introduces the distinction:

> If we compare the various ways of defining metaphysics and of conceiving the absolute, we shall find, despite apparent discrepancies, that philoso-phers agree in making a deep distinction between two ways of knowing a thing. The first [sc. analysis] implies going all around it, the second [sc. intuition] entering into it. The first depends on the viewpoint chosen and the symbols employed, while the second is taken from no viewpoint and rests on no symbol. Of the first kind of knowledge we shall say that it stops at the *relative*; of the second that, wherever possible, it attains the *absolute*. ('Metaphysics', p. 159, emphasis in original[2])

Note that Bergson claims no novelty for his distinction. On the contrary, he claims it to have been generally recognized. This, it must be said, is wild. There are interesting analogues of this distinction elsewhere in the history of philosophy,[3] but there is nothing else quite like it. In our own enquiry we have seen much that would actually distance other philosophers from it, most notably and most recently in §3 of the previous chapter, where we saw Nietzsche argue strenuously for the impossibility of non-perspectival sense-making. (It is also worth noting that the most compelling subsequent attempts to defend the possibility of non-perspectival sense-making are quite unlike Bergson's, to the extent that they disentangle the two components in Bergson's way of drawing his distinction and envisage knowledge which, though not from any viewpoint, does make use of symbols.[4]) But let us put

---

[2] Throughout this chapter I use the following abbreviations for Bergson's works: 'Change' for Bergson (1965e); *Creative Evolution* for Bergson (1975); *Duration and Simultaneity* for Bergson (1965g); 'Introduction I' for Bergson (1965a); 'Introduction II' for Bergson (1965b); 'Intuition' for Bergson (1965d); *Matter and Memory* for Bergson (1991); 'Metaphysics' for Bergson (1965f); *Mind-Energy* for Bergson (1920); 'The Possible and the Real' for Bergson (1965c); and *Time and Free Will* for Bergson (1910).

[3] In §§5 and 6 we shall note similarities between this distinction and the distinction between Spinoza's second and third kinds of knowledge.

[4] See Williams (1978), pp. 64–65, to which I referred parenthetically in Ch. 15, n. 19. As I indicated in that same note, I try to develop and defend Williams' argument in Moore (1997a), Ch. 4.

to one side the question of how far Bergson has been anticipated or followed by others. Let us focus on what he himself proffers.

First, a point of taxonomy. Bergson not only contrasts 'analysis' with intuition. He also contrasts 'intelligence', or 'intellect', with intuition (e.g. *Creative Evolution*, Ch. 3, passim). Intelligence is not the same as analysis. Nevertheless, this is in effect the same distinction. For intelligence is the faculty corresponding to analysis, or the faculty whose operation is analysis, while the word 'intuition' stands ambiguously both for the faculty and for its operation (cf. 'Introduction II', pp. 30ff.).

Very well, what are the lineaments of these two kinds of sense-making?

Analysis is characteristic of the natural sciences. It is normally pursued for some practical purpose, and it is often pursued only as far as is necessary for the purpose in question (see e.g. *Creative Evolution*, p. 358). It involves *representations* of the things of which sense is being made. It also therefore involves comparisons of those things with other things that can be represented in relevantly similar ways. And it typically proceeds by drawing on what is already known about these other things. Its representations in turn involve symbols, and these symbols always admit of alternatives, alternatives that express different concepts or highlight different features of the things being represented. This is why Bergson maintains that analysis only ever results in knowledge that is perspectival and relative. It further means that both analysis itself and the knowledge in which it results are subject to never-ending refinement and supplement. For it is always possible to analyze things more subtly, or in more detail, or indeed in completely different terms, that is to say from some completely different point of view. (See 'Intuition', esp. pp. 126ff., and 'Metaphysics', esp. pp. 159–162.)[5]

Intuition is different in every respect. It is not normally pursued for some practical purpose. It is most characteristically pursued for its own sake. It dispenses with representations and symbols.[6] It seeks knowledge of things in their own terms. It also seeks knowledge of things in their full particularity. And its way of achieving such knowledge is by overcoming all separation between the knower and the known. The knowledge in which it results is complete, thorough, and absolute.

It is knowledge of this second kind that properly deserves to be called knowledge of the facts. The knowledge in which analysis results, involving as it does the abstractions of an intermediary veil of representation, is only ever knowledge of generalities and laws that can be extracted from the facts (cf. *Time and Free Will*, pp. 140–141). Similarly, whereas the properties of

---

[5] There is much here with which Nietzsche could and would have agreed. His principal quarrel would have been with what is to come.

[6] I have already remarked that Bergson takes intuition to be the method of metaphysics. At one point he accordingly defines metaphysics as 'the science which claims to dispense with symbols' ('Metaphysics', p. 162, emphasis removed).

things with which analysis is concerned are universals, the properties of things with which intuition is concerned are as particular and as concrete as the things themselves.[7] And whereas the concepts that analysis uses are context-independent meanings attaching to symbols, the concepts that intuition uses '[follow] reality in all its windings' ('Metaphysics', p. 190).

One consequence of all of this is that not only are analysis and intuition two very different kinds of sense-making, they are ways of making two very different kinds of sense. (They may also be – we shall come back to this issue – ways of making sense of two very different kinds of things.) Indeed, to make one of these kinds of sense is to do so at the expense of the other. Analysis, with its fixed forms, draws attention away from what is changing and fluid, away from the teeming particularity of what can be intuited. It 'substitutes the symbol for the reality' (*Time and Free Will*, p. 128; cf. *Creative Evolution*, p. 357).[8] Nevertheless, it also uses the symbol to *represent* the reality. Although the sense that is made of things in analysis is different from, even inimical to, the sense that is made of things in intuition, the latter is so to speak what the former aspires to be and is always available to be retrieved from the former by a suitable act of immersion in the thing itself.[9]

Put like that, Bergson's view seems to be a damning indictment of analysis. It portrays analysis as a forlorn pursuit of something that can be attained only by intuition and, worse, whose attainment it positively thwarts. Indeed, there is much else in Bergson to suggest hostility towards analysis. He says that analysis takes the life out of things (*Creative Evolution*, pp. 204ff.). And he argues that analysis involves elements of falsification that can engender deep confusion: an example to which we shall return in §6(a) is the confusion attending the ancient paradoxes of motion.

In fact, however, Bergson has nothing against analysis. The practical benefits that can accrue from knowledge attained through the simplification, categorization, and organization of data are obvious enough. And Bergson never tires of reminding us of them. His opposition is not to *analysis*. It is to the misappropriation of analysis. It is opposition to the belief that analysis is equal to all cognitive tasks. I remarked earlier that analysis is characteristic of the natural sciences. This makes Bergson's opposition, in effect, opposition to Quinean naturalism. He wants to free us from the idea that analysis is *the* way to make sense of things. (Cf. *Creative Evolution*, pp. 209–210, and 'The Possible and the Real', p. 95.)

---

[7] So indeed is its concern with them.

[8] Cf. the pitfall to which I referred at the end of Introduction, §4: even on a looser, non-Bergsonian conception of analysis and intuition, it is a familiar fact that making sense of something by analyzing it can militate against other, more intuitive ways of making sense of that same thing.

[9] Cf. Deleuze (1988b), p. 88, and Turetzky (1998), pp. 202–203.

But it is certainly *a* way to make sense of things. And it is a way to make sense of things which is in Bergson's view indispensable to our social life, nay to our very way of being. Language itself would be impossible without the abstractions of analysis. Come to that, *intuition* would be impossible without the abstractions of analysis. For despite the opposition between intuition and analysis, intuition requires a degree of sophistication that is unattainable to any non-language-using animal. True, intuition, as a faculty, is a modification of the instinct that we share with other animals. But it is 'instinct that has become disinterested, self-conscious, capable of reflecting upon its object and of enlarging it indefinitely,' and it has achieved this by '[utilizing] the mechanism of intelligence,' – albeit utilizing that mechanism 'to show how intellectual molds cease to be strictly applicable' (*Creative Evolution*, pp. 194–195).[10] Bergson writes:

> Though [intuition] … transcends intelligence, it is from intelligence that has come the push that has made it rise to the point it has reached. Without intelligence, it would have remained in the form of instinct, riveted to the special object of its practical interest, and turned outward by it into movements of locomotion. (*Creative Evolution*, p. 195)[11]

It is clear, then, that Bergson celebrates intelligence. What he deplores is the intelligence fetish. (Cf. 'Introduction II', pp. 66ff. and 79.)

But is there perhaps more to Bergson's celebration of intelligence than even these remarks suggest? Should there not be more? Recall that, on Bergson's account, intuition yields no knowledge in which there is any separation between knower and known. It seems to follow that the only object of intuitive knowledge is the self. And this is surely to the further advantage of intelligence. For surely there are objects of intellectual knowledge other than the self.

This train of thought is too quick. For one thing, the role of symbols in analysis – specifically, the way in which they take the place of what they symbolize, to the extent that they themselves become the focal point of analysis – means that nothing has claim to the title of being an 'object' of intellectual knowledge except in a rather oblique sense,[12] a sense in which, for all that has been said so far, it may have equal claim to the title of being an object of intuitive knowledge. But also, more important, even if that oblique sense is waived, Bergson is keen to resist the inference from there

---

[10] This goes some way towards accounting for an apparent anomaly in *Time and Free Will*, p. 129, where Bergson says that what is required, to recover the intuitable from the analyzed, is 'a vigorous effort of [further] analysis.' Cf. Mullarkey (2004).

[11] Cf. Deleuze (1988b), pp. 107ff., and Lacey (1989), Ch. 6, §4. (Not that analysis on its own can generate intuition. 'It cannot be too often repeated,' Bergson avers: 'from intuition one can pass on to analysis, but not from analysis to intuition' ('Metaphysics', p. 180).)

[12] Cf. 'Change', pp. 137–138.

being no separation, in intuitive knowledge, between knower and known to there being no object of intuitive knowledge except the self. On his developed vision, there is sometimes no separation between the self and other selves. 'Unreflecting sympathy and antipathy,' he writes, '... give evidence of a possible interpenetration of human consciousness' ('Introduction II', p. 32). He envisions intuitive knowledge of other people's consciousness, perhaps even of 'consciousness in general' (ibid.). More than that, he envisions intuitive knowledge of 'the vital' (ibid., p. 33). Indeed, in the full splendour of his developed vision there is intuitive knowledge that extends further still, to 'the material universe in its entirety' (ibid). It is to this complex of ideas and their rationale that we must now turn.[13]

3. Space versus Duration. The Actual versus the Virtual. The Real versus the Possible

It may not be obvious, but underlying everything that we have witnessed so far is a very distinctive conception of space and time. Indeed, to a first gross approximation, we can say that intellectual knowledge is knowledge of the spatial and intuitive knowledge knowledge of the temporal.

Let us begin with intellectual knowledge. Given any process of analysis, and given the system of classification it uses, there has to be some other way of distinguishing between the items being classified. For precisely what a system of classification does is to register certain differences between things by abstracting from all other differences between them. It leaves open the possibility, even if that possibility is not in fact realized, that two items are to be classified in exactly the same way; in other words, that, among the features with which the analysis is concerned, two items have exactly the same features.[14] Two such items may of course be distinguished in accord with some other system of classification. But then the same considerations apply to that. There has to be some way, Bergson thinks, in which the items are *ultimately* distinguished. But what way? The distinction between them cannot be 'brute'. The only way in which the items can be ultimately distinguished, Bergson argues, is by their respective positions and extensions in some space. This may be a space in the metaphorical sense that is familiar to mathematicians, an abstract structure in whose terms we can define relations of 'distance', 'congruence', and the like. Or it may be literal, physical space. The essential differences between things, within such a space, are all differences of degree: any item is more or less 'extended', any two items are more

---

[13] On the material towards the end of this section, and for an anticipation of what is to come, see Ansell Pearson (1999), pp. 35ff., and Sacks (2000), pp. 131ff.

[14] Can it foreclose this possibility by including among the features with which the analysis is concerned haecceities? No. That is simply not how analysis, as Bergson conceives it, works. Analysis, as Bergson conceives it, is concerned with *general* features of things.

or less 'far apart', and so forth. The space itself is completely homogeneous. The items occupying it constitute what Bergson describes as a discrete quantitative multiplicity. (See *Time and Free Will*, pp. 75–85 and 120–123.)

Now time itself can be construed as such a space. Indeed, for nearly all practical purposes, that is precisely how it is construed. Intelligence recognizes no difference, as far as these considerations go, between time and (physical) space.[15] But whatever practical advantages there may be in construing time in this way, it is false to the reality of time *as consciously experienced*. This is what Bergson calls *duration*. Things in duration constitute multiplicities of a completely different sort. Such multiplicities are heterogeneous: they are characterized by differences of kind rather than differences of degree. And they have parts that are not discrete but permeate one another. The past of duration does not terminate with the present, but continues into the present. In fact that continuation of the past into the present is what duration *is*. Duration is therefore in a never-ending state of growth.[16] In Bergson's own formulation, duration 'is the continuous progress of the past which gnaws into the future and which swells as it advances' (*Creative Evolution*, p. 7). It has the 'indivisible and indestructible continuity of a *melody* where the past enters into the present and forms with it an undivided whole which remains undivided and even indivisible in spite of what is added at every instant, or rather, thanks to what is added' ('Introduction II', p. 71, emphasis added). The reality of duration is inaccessible to intelligence, but not to intuition (*Creative Evolution*, pp. 371ff., and 'Introduction II', pp. 34–35). For intuition, which is itself an enduring faculty, yields knowledge by assimilation. What allows such knowledge to be more than merely self-knowledge is the fact that intuition's own duration is the duration of the entire universe. The universe is in fact essentially spiritual in character. Its 'inner life' encompasses the inner lives of individuals.[17] Here is a fuller extract from the paragraph from which I quoted at the end of the previous section:

> [Intuition] ... bears above all upon duration.... It is the direct vision of the mind by the mind.... [But] is it merely the intuition of ourselves? ... Unreflecting sympathy and antipathy ... give evidence of a possible interpenetration of human consciousness.... It may be that intuition opens the way for us into consciousness in general. – But is it only with consciousness that we are in sympathy? If every living being is born, develops, and dies, if life is an evolution and if duration is in this case a reality, is there not also an intuition of the vital ...? – Let us go still further.... The

---

[15] Cf. *Time and Free Will*, pp. 115ff.

[16] Cf. *Duration and Simultaneity*, p. 49.

[17] Cf. *Creative Evolution*, pp. 7–8, and *Duration and Simultaneity*, pp. 46–47. In the former he writes, 'What are we ..., if not the condensation of the history that we have lived from our birth – nay, even before our birth, since we bring with us prenatal dispositions?'

material universe in its entirety *keeps* our consciousness *waiting*; it waits
itself. Either it endures, or it is bound up in our own duration. Whether it
is connected to the mind by its origins or by its function, in either case it
has to do with intuition through all the real change and movement that it
contains.... Pure change, real duration, is a thing spiritual or impregnated
with spirituality. Intuition is what attains the spirit, duration, pure change.
Its real domain being the spirit, it would seek to grasp in things, even material things, their participation in spirituality. ('Introduction II', pp. 32–33,
emphasis in original; cf. 'Metaphysics', pp. 187–188)

It would be easy to read into Bergson a kind of Cartesian dualism: there
is matter, which is ultimately no different from space, and which therefore,
at the most fundamental level, is to be understood in mathematical terms;
and there are minds, or spirits, or consciousnesses, which, at the most fundamental level, are to be understood in terms of their duration, where this
in turn can be grasped only by participation in it.[18] But the passage above
belies any such reading. *Everything* participates in duration. Everything –
including, as Bergson indicates at the end of the passage, every material
thing – participates in spirituality.

That said, Bergson does see in Cartesian dualism an inchoate attempt
to reckon with the main components of his vision (*Creative Evolution*, pp.
375–377).[19] It may be incorrect to read a Cartesian dualism into that vision.
But is there perhaps a dualism of some related kind there?[20]

In fact, we do well not to think of the vision as dualistic at all, any more than
we would think of a vision as dualistic just because it involved an appeal to,
say, form and content. There is only nature. But, to quote Deleuze, 'duration

[18] Not that Bergson's use of the word 'intuition', to register such grasping, is anything like
Descartes': see Ch. 1, §4.

[19] This is a convenient excuse to mention an important objection to Bergson's account of the
difference between differences of degree and differences of kind. The objection concerns
non-spatial differences between material things: differences of colour, taste, heat, and
suchlike. On Bergson's account these must all be classified as differences of kind – a classification which this concession to Cartesian dualism, however minimal, serves to reinforce,
since Descartes would have said that such differences were not differences in the material
things themselves but differences in how the mind perceives them (Descartes (1985c), Pt
One, §§68–70). Yet some of them, surely, are differences of degree. Can a material thing
not be more or less hot, for example?

Later we shall see Deleuze develop this objection and turn it into the very cornerstone
of his own rival account (Ch. 21, esp. §3). Not that Bergson is unaware of the objection.
He addresses it in, e.g., *Time and Free Will*, pp. 57ff. Roughly, his response is that there
is nothing in these non-spatial differences between material things to warrant the measurement that genuine differences of degree require. (Cf. Moore (1996), Ch. 2, §F.) This
response, it must be said, has an air of special pleading.

[20] Deleuze raises this question and has characteristically fascinating things to say in response
to it, to which I am indebted: see Deleuze (1988b), Ch. 4.

is like naturing nature, and matter a natured nature' (Deleuze (1988b), p. 93). The past of duration exists *virtually*. It consists of tendencies. Duration is the never-ending *actualization* of these tendencies – in matter. Or rather, it is their never-ending actualization of themselves in matter. This never-ending process is nature's continuous creation of itself, 'the uninterrupted upsurge of novelty' ('Introduction I', p. 18). One way to think of this is topologically. Processes of bending, blending, stretching, breaking, twisting, piercing, and suchlike actualize various topologically characterizable tendencies in things. A spherical Plasticine ball, say, may become ovoid as a result of squashing or even toroid as a result of puncturing. And the actualization of these tendencies in turn generates new tendencies. A previously spherical, now ovoid Plasticine ball may bump down an inclined plane where previously it would have rolled smoothly down it. The past of duration is thus continually growing, which means that the virtual is never completely actualized. Intuition is a way of knowing nature as it is in itself, that is as it is in its enduring self. Analysis is a way of knowing nature as if it had eventually come to an end; as if there *had* been a complete actualization of its previously ever-expanding past of virtual tendencies. (See e.g. 'Metaphysics', pp. 162ff., and *Creative Evolution*, pp. 12–14 and 384–385.)[21]

It is important to appreciate that the virtual/actual distinction is not at all the same as another distinction that Bergson acknowledges, the possible/real distinction. (Here a caveat is required. Bergson's usage of these terms – or rather, his usage of their French equivalents – is awkwardly out of sync with a tendency in contemporary English usage, namely to contrast the virtual with the real and to contrast the possible, or the merely possible, with the actual. A graphic illustration of this was supplied in Ch. 13, where we saw Lewis arguing that all possible worlds are equally real though all but one of them is merely possible, the exception being the one that is actual. This is a frustrating terminological discrepancy that we must simply live with and beware of. Throughout this chapter, I adhere to Bergson's usage.) Bergson's distinctions cut right across each other. The virtual is as much a part of reality as the actual. The actual, conversely, is as much a part of various unrealized possibilities as the virtual.

One way to register the difference between the two distinctions is by reflecting on Lewis' modal realism, which furnishes a particularly extreme account of the second of them. On this account there are infinitely many possible worlds which, despite differences of detail between them, are no different in basic kind from one another. One of them, the real world (or the 'actual' world, in Lewis' own terminology), is the one that *we* inhabit. When we say that a possibility is realized, we mean that the real world belongs to some given range of possible worlds, which is of course equivalent to saying that it does not belong to the complement of that range. It follows that,

---

[21] See Turetzky (1998), Ch. 13, esp. pp. 207ff.

except in the limit case in which a possibility is also a necessity, the realization of one possibility is always *eo ipso* the non-realization of others.

Bergson would have deep misgivings about this account, as we shall see. But there are two core ideas here which are no less a feature of his own conception of the possible/real distinction:

(1) The possible, even the merely possible, is of the same basic kind as the real.

(2) The realization of a contingent possibility is always the non-realization of others.[22]

Neither has any analogue where the virtual/actual distinction is concerned. The virtual is of a completely different kind from the actual. And the actualization of a virtual tendency is never in any sense the non-actualization of others. Deleuze puts it as follows:

> The rules of actualization are not those of resemblance and limitation, but those of difference or divergence and of creation.... [In] order to be actualized, the virtual ... must *create* its own lines of actualization in positive acts.... [It] is forced ... to create its lines of differentiation in order to be actualized. (Deleuze (1988b), p. 97, emphasis in original)

Even the spherical Plasticine ball that sits still and retains its shape does so only in the context of change round about it. The identity of things, both through their own changes and through surrounding changes, is a product of those changes, not they of it. (See the next section.[23]) Actualization proceeds through the ceaseless creation of novelty.[24]

Might there be a marriage between Bergson and Lewis? Consider the following view, which I shall call the Hybrid View.

---

[22] I do not mean to suggest that these two ideas are a non-negotiable feature of *any* acceptable conception of the possible/real distinction: Wittgenstein (1967a), Pt I, §194, contains an apparent repudiation of (1). (I say 'apparent' because, as always with Wittgenstein, there is an issue about whether his target is the idea itself, or our mishandling of the idea. There is also an issue, especially in the light of ensuing sections, about whether his ultimate concern is in fact with something more like the virtual/actual distinction. Note in addition that Wittgenstein talks of the possible as being 'like a shadow' of the real. But that is not strictly part of (1). Indeed, Bergson himself insists that 'there is more and not less in the possibility of each of the successive states [of the world of life] than in their reality' ('The Possible and the Real', p. 100).)

[23] See also 'Change', p. 147.

[24] These differences between the possible/real distinction and the virtual/actual distinction allow for an interesting variation on a Kantian theme. I noted in the lengthy parenthesis in Ch. 5, §5, how Kant was concerned with conditions of experience, of a kind involving relations between the possible and the real. Bergson too is concerned with conditions of experience, but of an importantly different kind, a kind involving relations between the virtual and the actual. See Deleuze (1988b), pp. 27–28, and Turetzky (1998), p. 201.

The Hybrid View: The virtual/actual distinction is, just as Bergson insists it is, quite different from the possible/real distinction. But the former can be explained in terms of the latter, understood in a Lewisian way. The virtual tendencies in any given possible world w at any given time t can be considered as the set of possible worlds w^* such that (i) w^* is just like w up to t and (ii) w^* shares with w certain patterns of change, laws of nature, or the like.[25] The subsequent actualization of these tendencies in w consists in what happens in w beyond t.

The Hybrid View seems to give Bergson everything he wants. In particular, the virtual/actual distinction admits of no analogue of either (1) or (2). The virtual is of a completely different kind from the actual: the actual is a matter of what happens within a world; the virtual is a matter of how what has happened within a world, up to any given time, along with various principles of development that characterize that world, constrain the possibilities for what will happen thereafter, or, more strictly, delimit the set of worlds to which that world belongs. Again, the actualization of the virtual does not in any sense necessitate the non-actualization of some other virtual. The Hybrid View also makes clear why Bergson's two distinctions cut across each other. The virtual is as much a feature of the real world as what actually happens there. And conversely, actual happenings are as much a feature of other possible worlds as the worlds' ever-changing virtual tendencies.

Nevertheless, the Hybrid View would be an anathema to Bergson. The principal reason for this does not lie where it may appear to lie. It may appear to lie in how little the view retains of Bergson's distinctive conception of the virtual and its actualization. For instance, on Bergson's conception, the virtual, which is the past of duration, and which continues into the present, grows with its continual actualization. On the Hybrid View, the virtual, which is a particular set of worlds, and which is indexed to a time, *shrinks* with its continual actualization – in the sense that the set corresponding to any given time is a proper superset of the set corresponding to any later time.[26] (We could call this the 'zip fastening' view of actualization.) But this is not the discrepancy that it appears to be. It is in fact nothing more than a reflection of (2) above: there is no growth in reality except at the expense of other possibilities.

The principal reason why the Hybrid View would be an anathema to Bergson lies not in how little it retains of his conception of the virtual and its actualization. It lies in how little it retains of his conception of the possible and its realization. Bergson's conception of the possible is fundamentally different from Lewis'. On Lewis' conception, the possible is transcendent

---

[25] Much of *Matter and Memory* might be viewed as an attempt to make (ii) precise.

[26] A is a proper superset of B if and only if all members of B are members of A but not *vice versa*.

and abiding. On Bergson's conception, the possible is immanent and ever-changing. Bergson holds that the possible, no less than the virtual, grows over time. In particular, possibilities beyond a certain level of specificity do not antedate their realization. Thus consider some event that has occurred, say a football match. In Bergson's view, nothing so specific was even possible beforehand. True, something of this or that broad kind, say a victory for the away side, was possible; and something of that very particular kind can be said, in retrospect, to have been possible, in the quite different and quite innocuous sense that 'there was no insurmountable obstacle to its realization' ('The Possible and the Real', p. 102; cf. 'Introduction I', pp. 21–22). But in the sense that is of primary concern to Bergson, the sense that has been in play so far in this chapter and will remain in play hereafter, the match itself, in all its unforeseeable detail, actually brought in its train its own possibility, just as it brought in its train untold further possibilities, such as the possibility of that particular game's being discussed by television pundits a dozen years from now. (See 'The Possible and the Real', passim.)

It is plain how Lewis would respond to these suggestions. He would accuse Bergson of conflating epistemological issues with ontological issues, of illegitimately inferring from the fact that there was no knowing about some given possibility at some given time that there *was* no such possibility at that time. Once we have extricated the ontological from the epistemological, Lewis would say, we have licence to view possible worlds as spatio-temporally unified cosmoses, any one of which, including this world, exists in complete detail throughout all eternity.

And it is equally plain how Bergson would respond to this accusation. He in turn would accuse Lewis of committing the basic error of trying to understand through analysis what can be understood only through intuition, of trying to see *sub specie æternitatis* what can be seen only '*sub specie durationis*' ('Change', p. 158). But *can* that which is abstract, such as a possibility, come into existence at a particular time, as Bergson's view requires? To think not, Bergson would say, is severely to compromise the very idea of creation ('The Possible and the Real', pp. 92ff.).[27] It is to think, by implication, that there can be no pure creation except the creation *ex nihilo* of something concrete, that any other act of so-called creation is really an act of discovery, if only the discovery of some possibility of reconfiguration, perhaps accompanied by the relevant reconfiguring. How plausible, Bergson would ask, is that? Does a sculptor, by chipping away at a block of stone, discover a statue inside? Does painting involve discovering some arrangement of pigment on one's canvas? Are dramatic works discovered?[28]

---

[27] Cf. Deleuze (1988b), p. 98.

[28] Cf. Quine (1987a). (Actually, Michelangelo is reputed to have said that every block of stone does have a statue inside 'and it is the task of the sculptor to discover it'. The view is not absurd.)

It is certainly true that reflection on the idea of creation lends some intuitive support (in the colloquial, non-Bergsonian sense of 'intuitive') to Bergson's view. But I see nothing in these rhetorical questions to dislodge an inveterate opponent, who can simply hold fast to the idea that, insofar as pure creation consists in bringing something into existence without rearranging already available material,[29] then none of the examples in question *is* an example of pure creation. (Thus consider the passage in which Bergson describes a conversation in which he was asked, 'How do you conceive … the great dramatic work of tomorrow?' and replied, 'If I knew what was to be the great dramatic work of the future, I should be writing it' ('The Possible and the Real', p. 100). The fact is, his opponent can get just as much purchase out of that anecdote.) Note, however, something that will be especially pertinent to the discussion in §6(c), that there is one sort of innovation which, whether it is to be described as pure creation or as a kind of discovery, is marked by an unpredictability of the most extreme form. I am thinking of the introduction of radically new concepts or, more generally, of radically new ways of making sense of things.[30] Obviously, the writing of a dramatic work is unforeseeable in the sense that fully to foresee it would already be to have written the work. But the introduction of a radically new way of making sense of things is unforeseeable in the more profound sense that, until that way of making sense of things has been introduced, there is no way even of making sense of its introduction. It is at least natural to say, even if Bergson's opponent remains resolved not to say, that the introduction of a radically new way of making sense of things brings its own possibility with it and is an act of pure creation.[31]

For Bergson, it is not only an act of pure creation. It is a paradigm of freedom. He writes:

> Even those [philosophers] who have believed in free will, have reduced it to a simple 'choice' between two or more alternatives, as if these alternatives were 'possibles' outlined beforehand, and as if the will was limited to 'bringing about' … one of them.… They seem to have no idea whatever of an act which might be entirely new … and which in no way would exist, not even in the form of the purely possible, prior to its realization. But this is the very nature of a free act. ('Introduction I', p. 19)

He also goes on to insist that 'to perceive [freedom] thus, as indeed we must do with any creation, novelty or unpredictable occurrence whatever, we have to get back into pure duration' (ibid.). This illustrates a general feature of Bergson's conception of philosophy. The problem of how to make sense of freedom is one of many traditional philosophical problems which

---

[29] This excludes what van Gogh does when he brings a picture into existence.
[30] See Ch. 8, n. 11.
[31] See further Moore (2003a), pp. 122–124.

he believes can be solved only by an exercise of intuition.[32] Duration, the continuation of the virtual past into the actual present through nature's endlessly innovative self-creation, is in Bergson's view the very essence not only of freedom but also of consciousness and of life itself. A proper philosophical grasp of any of these phenomena requires an exercise of intuition.[33]

4. Identity versus Difference

In §7(b) of the previous chapter I drew attention to one important contrast between the analytic tradition in philosophy and some of the traditions represented in Part Three of this book. In the former there is a tendency to prioritize identity over difference. In the latter there is the opposite tendency. Bergson provides a striking illustration of this. Precisely what intelligence does, on Bergson's view, is to abstract from differences in things to arrive at stable concepts applicable to discrete entities. It imposes the concept of identity onto things. Their own unwrought reality is a reality of mutually permeating differences, graspable only by intuition.

Analytic philosophers, to hark back to that earlier section, find it difficult to think of difference save in negative terms. The reasons for this are many and complex, and they may not be entirely philosophical. But they centrally include the fact that it would be impossible to recast the standard logic of numerical identity in terms of difference without the use of negation. That logic comprises two principles: (i) if $a = b$ and a has feature F, then b has feature F; and (ii) $a = a$.[34] True, (i) can arguably be recast in terms of difference as follows: if a is qualitatively different from b, then a

---

[32] See *Time and Free Will*, Ch. 3, passim. He summarizes his discussion in that chapter as follows: 'Every demand for explanation in regard to freedom comes back ... to the following question: "Can time be adequately represented by space?" To which we answer: Yes, if you are dealing with time flown; No, if you speak of time flowing.... All the difficulties of the problem ... arise from the desire to endow duration with the same attributes as extensity, ... and to express the idea of freedom in a language into which it is obviously untranslatable' (p. 221).

[33] Helpful secondary literature on the material in this section, beyond that already cited, includes Kolakowski (1985), Chs 1–3; Lloyd (1993), pp. 96–107; and Ansell Pearson (1999), pp. 20–40.

[34] See Frege (1967), §§20 and 21.
    How does (i) accommodate, say, the fact that Wilfrid was once clean-shaven and is now bearded? Analytic philosophers disagree about how to answer such questions. Some would construe 'features' in such a way as to exclude being clean-shaven and being bearded in favour of being clean-shaven-at-t_1 and being bearded-at-t_2. Others, notably Lewis (see Lewis (1986c), pp. 204–206), would deny that the entity which was once clean-shaven is numerically identical to the entity which is now bearded. There are many other views besides. For a very helpful survey, see Gibson (unpublished), Ch. 4, §4. For an excellent contribution to the discussion, see Sattig (2006).

is numerically different from *b*. But then to give an adequate explication of this notion of qualitative difference would in turn be impossible without the use of negation.

So what attitude would Bergson adopt towards (i) and (ii)? Like Nietzsche,[35] he would not so much take issue with these principles, which effectively *define* the concept of numerical identity, as take issue with the concept of numerical identity itself. (And even then, again like Nietzsche, he would acknowledge the usefulness of the concept for practical purposes: cf. §2 above.) To take issue with the concept of numerical identity is to take issue with something at the very core of our linguistic sense-making. It is to take issue with the whole Fregean notion of an object, and therefore with those deep structural features of language which enable us to parse declarative sentences into Fregean names and their associated predicates. (See Ch. 8, §7.) Bergson writes:

> All our ways of speaking, thinking, perceiving imply in effect that ... immutability [is] there by right, that ... change [is] superadded, like [an accident], to things which, by themselves, do not ... change.... Such is the logic immanent in our language ...: the intelligence has as its essence to judge, and judgment operates by the attribution of a predicate to a subject. The subject, by the sole fact of being named, is defined as invariable; the variation will reside in the diversity of the states that one will affirm concerning it, one after another. In proceeding thus, by apposition of a predicate to a subject, ... we follow the bent of our intelligence, we conform to the demands of language. ('Introduction II', pp. 68–69)[36]

5.   Bergson Compared with Some of His Predecessors

In this section I shall briefly compare Bergson with some of his predecessors.

(a)   Bergson Compared with Fichte

There are striking parallels between Bergson and Fichte. Fichte presented us with, if not two kinds of sense-making, then two philosophical paradigms, one of which involved taking seriously the free subject's self-consciousness

---

[35] See n. 85 of the previous chapter and the passages from Nietzsche cited therein.

[36] For thought-provoking comments on Bergson's positive conception of difference, see Deleuze (1988b), pp. 46–47. Later, at pp. 75–76, Deleuze describes 'the Bergsonian project' as that of 'showing that Difference, as difference in kind, could and should be understood independently of the *negative*' (emphasis in original), while at p. 103 he writes that 'difference is never negative but essentially positive and creative.' In Chapter 21 we shall see how Deleuze develops these ideas on his own account.

and the other of which was a form of naturalism. And he argued that it was only the former that enabled us to do justice to what he called 'absolute, independent self-activity' (Fichte (1956), p. 84); only the former, indeed, that we could properly 'live'. (See Ch. 6, §2.)[37] Fichte further anticipated Bergson by describing exercise of self-consciousness as a kind of intuition of how things are in themselves. However, whereas Fichte, who knew that this was in defiance of Kant, argued that it was in defiance only of the letter of Kant, not the spirit (Ch. 6, §3), Bergson is involved in a much more straight-forward act of defiance (see e.g. 'Change', pp. 139ff., and 'Metaphysics', pp. 195ff.). This relates to the most fundamental difference between them. Fichte wanted to retain a Kantian idealism. Bergson, for whom intuition is not just a way of making sense of the self and its various aspects, but a way of making sense of what is beyond the self (see above, §2), does not.[38]

(b)   Bergson Compared with Spinoza and Nietzsche

There are echoes in Bergson of the joyful affirmation of life that we saw in both Spinoza and Nietzsche. These are due to the way in which, for Bergson, intuition brings us into an awareness of the very heartbeat of reality: it is an expression of our symbiotic relationship with reality. Bergsonian intuition can usefully be compared with Spinoza's third kind of knowledge, which he (Spinoza) characterized as adequate knowledge of the essence of things (cf. 'Intuition', p. 113).[39,40] There is no better way of capturing this evocation of Spinoza and Nietzsche than by quoting Bergson himself:

> To the eyes of a philosophy that attempts to reabsorb intellect in intui-
> tion, many difficulties vanish or become light. But such a doctrine does
> not only facilitate speculation; it gives us also more power to act and to
> live. (*Creative Evolution*, p. 295)
>
> If this [new kind of] knowledge is generalized, speculation will not be the
> only thing to profit by it.... Let us ... grasp ourselves afresh as we are ...;

---

[37] One passage in Bergson that is especially reminiscent of this is *Creative Evolution*, pp. 375–377.

[38] This is connected to the point that I made in n. 24.

[39] Note also, in the light of Spinoza's fundamental concern with the question of what a body is and can do (Ch. 2, §3), the subtitle of Ch. 1 of *Matter and Memory*: 'What Our Body Means and Does'.

[40] How does this comparison of Bergsonian intuition with Spinoza's third kind of knowl-edge consist with the fact that the former requires seeing things *sub specie durationis*, the latter *sub specie æternitatis*? The first of the many points that need to be made in response to this large question is that Spinoza's conception of seeing things *sub specie æternitatis* is not at all the same as Bergson's: see Spinoza (2002c), Pt V, Prop. 29, and accompanying material.

let us grasp afresh the external world as it really is.... [Let] us in a word
become accustomed to see all things *sub specie durationis*: immediately
in our galvanized perception what is taut becomes relaxed, what is dor-
mant awakens, what is dead comes to life again.... [Science,] with its
applications which aim only at the convenience of existence, ... gives us
the promise of well-being, or at most, of pleasure. But philosophy could
already give us joy. ('Intuition', pp. 128–129)[41]

6. The Implications for Metaphysics

As with previous protagonists who distinguished between two kinds of
sense-making, the implications of Bergson's various doctrines for metaphysics can be discussed under three headings.[42] There are the implications that
his doctrines have on his own conception of metaphysics. There are the
implications that they have on my conception of metaphysics, as the most
general attempt to make sense of things, applied to the first of his two kinds
of sense-making, analysis: call this the *analytic* conception of metaphysics.
And there are the implications that they have on my conception, applied to
the second of his two kinds of sense-making, intuition: call this the *intuitive*
conception of metaphysics. (I leave open, at this stage, the possibility of partial or total overlap between Bergson's own conception and either of these
other two conceptions.)[43]

(a) The Implications for Metaphysics on Bergson's
Own Conception of Metaphysics

I have already remarked in §5(a) that Bergson is in revolt against Kant.
His own conception of metaphysics is part of that revolt. Bergson holds, in
opposition to Kant, that we can have insight into how things are in themselves. And he holds that it is the business of metaphysics to pursue such
insight. It immediately follows, given the rest of what he thinks, that metaphysics must proceed by intuition. (See 'Introduction II', pp. 30ff. and 37.)

This in turn has a number of important consequences. The insights
achieved by intuition resist linguistic expression, linguistic expression presupposing as it does the abstractions of analysis. So metaphysical insights
must likewise resist linguistic expression on this conception.

---

[41] For a discussion of what Bergson means by joy, further indicating his kinship with Spinoza
and Nietzsche, see *Mind-Energy*, pp. 29–30. He there says that joy, which he distinguishes
from pleasure, 'always announces that life has succeeded, gained ground, conquered,' and
that 'wherever there is joy, there is creation; the richer the creation, the deeper the joy.' Cf.
n. 75 of the previous chapter.

[42] Cf. e.g. Ch. 9, §2, and Ch. 10, §3.

[43] For a discussion that bears on the material in this section, see Mullarkey (2007).

Does this mean that Bergson is committed to casting the metaphysician in the role of mystic – a casting that is liable to give pause even to those to whom the very role of mystic does not already give pause? In fact, as the material at the end of the previous section may already have intimated, Bergson does see such a role for the metaphysician.[44] Even so, the thought that metaphysical insights resist linguistic expression does not have to be taken in quite such a heady way, and is not always taken in quite such a heady way by Bergson. Nor is it without precedent in this enquiry. In our discussion of the early and the later Wittgenstein we considered a conception of metaphysics whereby metaphysics is an activity rather than a body of doctrine. On that conception too, metaphysical insights resist linguistic expression. What prevents metaphysics from being unduly mystical on that conception is that, although the insights themselves resist linguistic expression, they are insights into how to recognize and combat confusions of various kinds, and their implementation involves saying a very great deal. Furthermore, it involves saying a very great deal in connection with traditional metaphysical debates, which is where the original confusions lie. We find something similar in Bergson.

Bergson believes that a typical contribution to a traditional metaphysical debate consists of some confused response to some ill-conceived question based on some misapplication of analysis. And he believes that one of the benefits of (properly conducted) metaphysics, if not perhaps the principal benefit,[45] is that it enables us to see that this is so and to clear away the confusion by showing that we need intuition to understand what we could not understand by means of analysis.[46] Such understanding cannot itself be put into words. But much can be said about the role that it plays in equipping us to overcome the confusion.

A clear case in point is the traditional metaphysical debate about the nature of freedom and its relation to physical determinism: we glimpsed Bergson's views about these at the end of §3.[47] Another well-known case in point turns on the ancient paradoxes of motion which I mentioned in §6 of the Introduction. Bergson believes that these paradoxes arise directly from the attempt to understand duration through analysis. Inevitably, when we make such an attempt, we come to regard change and movement as constituted

---

[44] See also (e.g.) *Creative Evolution*, pp. 212–218.

[45] See the two quotations at the end of the previous section for an indication of what the principal benefit might be.

[46] Note that this gives metaphysics, and thereby intuition, a disciplinary role that somewhat mitigates the comparison that I drew in §5(b) between Bergson and the pair Spinoza and Nietzsche. Neither Spinoza nor Nietzsche would have been comfortable with Bergson's discussion of 'the power of negation', or with his likening of intuition – which gives its 'most clear-cut manifestations' when 'it forbids' – to 'the demon of Socrates' ('Intuition', pp. 109–110).

[47] See n. 32.

by infinitely many instantaneous states and as divisible into infinitely many discrete parts, and we are straightway ensnared in the paradoxes. Once we adopt an intuitive understanding of change and movement, Bergson insists, we shall be free of any such paradoxes. (See *Creative Evolution*, pp. 335ff., and 'Change', passim.)[48] It is in the light of cases such as these that Bergson is emboldened to say, much as Wittgenstein was emboldened to say:

> I believe that the great metaphysical problems are in general badly stated, that they frequently resolve themselves of their own accord when correctly stated, or else are problems formulated in terms of illusion which disappear as soon as the terms of the formula are more closely examined. ('The Possible and the Real', p. 95; cf. 'Introduction I', p. 17)[49]

But Bergson's conception of metaphysics also allows for a substantial positive linguistic component as well as this negative linguistic component. For although it precludes the use of language to express metaphysical insights, it does not preclude the use of language to talk around them (as we have been doing). Nor indeed does it preclude the use of language to *evoke* them. 'Comparisons and metaphors,' Bergson says, '[can] suggest what cannot be expressed' ('Introduction II', p. 42). A large part of metaphysical practice consists of attempts, by means of language, to evoke metaphysical insights.[50]

Metaphysicians who make such attempts naturally use the idioms of the epoch in which they find themselves ('Intuition', p. 111). But their use of these idioms can never be entirely straightforward. There is therefore no guarantee that they will use them in the same way as one another. So it can easily appear that metaphysicians are embroiled in dispute when really they are talking past one another, or that they are in accord when really they are trying to say quite different things. This is another consequence of Bergson's conception of metaphysics that he is at pains to emphasize (see e.g. 'Intuition', pp. 112ff.). And I do not doubt that such would have been

---

[48] For a brief discussion, see Moore (2001a), pp. 103–104.

[49] Cf. Wittgenstein (1961), p. 3 and 4.003; and Wittgenstein (1967a), Pt I, §122. Note that the comparisons with Wittgenstein are by no means confined to the methodological point that I have just been highlighting. One further extremely important comparison relates to what I said in Ch. 10, n. 15, about Wittgenstein's recognition of a deep distinction between that which is simple and that which is easy. Bergson recognizes just the same distinction. He frequently insists on the simplicity of metaphysical practice: see e.g. 'Intuition', pp. 109 and 126. He even more frequently insists on its difficulty: see e.g. 'Introduction II', pp. 41, 67–68, and 87–88. (As regards learning how to do this difficult thing, at one point he likens it to learning how to swim, where we must begin by fearlessly throwing ourselves into the water: see *Creative Evolution*, p. 211. This brooks comparison with the passage from Hegel (1975a), §10, which I quoted in Ch. 7, §8.)

[50] Cf. 'Introduction II', pp. 42–43, and 'Metaphysics', pp. 191–192. Cf. also of course Wittgenstein (1961), 6.54.

his verdict on the constellation of views concerning substance which we witnessed in the first three chapters of this book, and which I summarized at the beginning of Chapter 4.

(b) The Implications for Metaphysics on the Analytic Conception of Metaphysics

The analytic conception of metaphysics is clearly quite different from Bergson's. But what exactly does it come to? Is metaphysics, on this conception, merely the most general of the natural sciences, say physics? Or is it perhaps mathematics?

Here we need to remember how generous Bergson's notion of analysis is. The very use of language in attempting to make sense of things ensures that the sense-making in question consists of analysis. So on the analytic conception, metaphysics might in fact just be the sort of thing that Bergson himself engages in in works such as *Time and Free Will*. For that matter it might be the sort of thing that he engages in in works such as 'Metaphysics', where he discusses and promotes what he himself counts as metaphysics. The second of these possibilities would constitute something structurally analogous to what we saw in Chapter 2. In that chapter I represented Spinozist metaphysics as the sort of thing that Spinoza engages in in the main part of the *Ethics*: pursuit, at the highest level of generality, of knowledge of the second kind. But this in turn centrally includes discussion and promotion of knowledge of the third kind, which, like Bergsonian intuition, resists (finite) linguistic expression. (See Ch. 2, §6.)[51]

(c) The Implications for Metaphysics on the Intuitive Conception of Metaphysics

To turn finally to the intuitive conception of metaphysics: what does *this* come to? Does it simply equate with Bergson's own conception?

One reason not to accede to this conclusion without further ado is that, whereas my definition of metaphysics explicitly includes the idea of generality, intuition is by its very nature a way of making sense of what is particular. This does not of course mean that there is no such thing as its most general form. Nor does it mean that there is no such thing as pursuit of it in its most general form. There is such a thing and it may yet prove to be the

---

[51] The analogy extends even further. For just as Spinoza holds that knowledge of the third kind would be impossible without knowledge of the second kind, so too (§2 above) Bergson holds that intuition would be impossible without analysis. And I have already independently remarked (§5(b)) that Spinoza's third kind of knowledge can usefully be compared with Bergsonian intuition.

same as what Bergson counts as metaphysics. But even if it does, *just* to say this would run the risk of being seriously misleading. For it may be that the very attempt to apply my definition to intuition in this way is offensive to the spirit of my definition. Metaphysics, on the intuitive conception, may be completely unlike anything that my definition is intended to capture. Is this a genuine concern?

In fact, no – though there is a point here that is certainly worth registering. My definition is meant to be broadly in accord with standard uses of the word 'metaphysics'. That is precisely why it includes the idea of generality, which I take to be a common implication of such uses. But my definition is also meant to allow for just the kind of latitude that is exhibited here. It is meant to allow for the possibility that, because of the very nature of the sense-making involved, metaphysics lacks this or that generality.

Very well; what sort of generality does metaphysics lack on the intuitive conception? A very important sort, certainly; a sort which it has often been thought to possess. Metaphysics has often been thought to be concerned, not just with reality as it is, but with reality as it must be. On the intuitive conception it has no such pretension. On the intuitive conception, although metaphysics is concerned with the full sweep of the real, it is not concerned with the full sweep of the possible. So be it. As it happens, this is another hallmark of Bergson's own conception of metaphysics that he is at pains to emphasize ('Introduction II', pp. 31–32 and 44).[52]

I am inclined to think that Bergson's own conception does in fact equate with the intuitive conception, more or less; and that acknowledging this provides us with an instructive way of revisiting the former.

What then is the most general form, or the most general exercise, of Bergsonian intuition? Is it the turning of one's mind's eye, not just to one's own consciousness, or to consciousness in general, or to life in general, but to the duration of all that is real?[53] Yes, provided that this is done with suitable discipline, a proviso that has to be met if *sense* is to be made of anything and indeed if the exercise is properly to count as an exercise of *intuition*. What, then, counts as suitable discipline? The direction of concepts, provided – this is an equally important proviso – that concepts and their direction are both construed in an appropriate way. In what way? Not, obviously enough, so as to abnegate the fact that the sense-making involved is intuition rather than analysis. Concepts here, to echo the contrast that I drew in §2, need to be understood as features of the mind's immersion in the ever-changing reality that it intuits; they must not be understood as context-independent meanings whereby the mind judges this reality. And their direction needs to be so understood that it is as much a matter of their being directed as it is of

---

[52] This is connected to the point raised in n. 24.
[53] Cf. the passage from 'Introduction II', pp. 32–33, quoted in §3 in this chapter. Cf. also *Creative Evolution*, pp. 194–195.

their directing. The exercise of intuition needs to be entirely of a piece with what is being intuited. It must involve the evolution of new concepts, new ways of making sense of things, new forms of metaphysics itself. (It is here if anywhere in my book that its title is most apt.[54]) Here is Bergson:

> [Our mind] can be installed in the mobile reality, adopt its ceaselessly changing direction, in short, grasp it intuitively. But to do that, it must ... reverse the direction of the operation by which it ordinarily thinks, continually upsetting its categories, or rather, recasting them. In so doing it will arrive at fluid concepts, capable of following reality in all its windings and of adopting the very movement of the inner life of things. ('Metaphysics', p. 190; cf. 'Introduction I', p. 29, and 'Introduction II', p. 68)

Metaphysics involves bringing about radically new ways of making sense of things, then. That, indeed, is its core activity. And, as we saw in §3, it is an activity which on Bergson's view counts as an exercise of pure creativity.[55]

It seems to follow that Bergson has the clearest possible answer both to the Novelty Question and to the Creativity Question which I posed in §6 of the Introduction. To an extent he does. There is however a complication worth noting in connection with the Creativity Question. In my discussion of that question in the Introduction I suggested that it can be turned into a question about whether there is scope for our getting things right in metaphysics, whether our metaphysical sense-making can be an accurate reflection of reality itself. The thought was that, insofar as our metaphysical sense-making is creative, it is *not* an accurate reflection of reality itself. But such is the element of creativity involved in metaphysics on Bergson's conception that he would, or at least could, see it as both. The development of new ways of making sense of things in metaphysics is the development of new ways for things to be: in intuitive knowledge there is no separation between the knower and the known. So although Bergson does have a clear answer to the Creativity Question, narrowly interpreted, there is a broader interpretation of the question, whereby it has additional connotations concerning the accuracy of metaphysical sense-making, on which we do better to see him as rejecting the question altogether, à la Hegel.

Be that as it may, metaphysics is for Bergson a matter of free, creative self-development. It issues in radically new ways of making sense of things, including radically new ways of making sense of things that can be implemented in metaphysics itself. But 'including' is the operative word here. The transformative power of Bergsonian metaphysics is not just a power

---

[54] Cf. 'Intuition', pp. 111–112.

[55] Note that it involves novel questioning no less than novel understanding. Novel questioning is itself, Bergson urges, a matter of invention: see 'Introduction II', p. 51; and cf. ibid., pp. 47ff., and 'Intuition', p. 121. (Cf. Ch. 21, §6.)

to transform itself. As we saw earlier when drawing the analogy with Wittgensteinian therapy, Bergsonian metaphysics can have an influence on the operations of intelligence too. There is no reason whatsoever why it should not also issue in radically new ways of making sense of things that can be implemented in science.

This, in a curious way, harks back to Descartes, for whom metaphysics was in the service of science. And indeed Bergson does see metaphysics as capable of benefitting science (if not by providing it with Cartesian foundations) – just as he sees science as capable of benefitting metaphysics. Here is one representative passage:

> A truly intuitive philosophy would realize the union so greatly desired, of metaphysics and science.... It would put more of science into metaphysics and more of metaphysics into science. Its result would re-establish the continuity between the intuitions which the various positive sciences have obtained at intervals in the course of their history, and which they have obtained only by strokes of genius. ('Metaphysics', p. 192; cf. *Creative Evolution*, p. 218, and 'Introduction II', p. 44)

Nonetheless, Bergson's real predecessor, as far as these views on the creative power of metaphysics are concerned, is not Descartes. It is Nietzsche. I can draw this chapter to a close in much the same way as I drew the previous chapter to a close. Here we have a conception of metaphysics whereby not only is there scope for us, as practising metaphysicians, to make radically new sense of things; we have no proper claim to the title of metaphysicians unless we do.

✦

CHAPTER 17

Husserl

Making Sense of Making Sense; or, The *Ne Plus Ultra* of Transcendentalism

1. Husserl *Vis-à-Vis* the Analytic Tradition

Towards the end of Chapter 12 I argued that Quine's extreme naturalism, whereby the only way to make sense of things is the (natural-)scientific way, failed because that is not the way to make sense of making sense of things. Invoking Neurath's image of the ship, which Quine himself was so fond of invoking, and taking the ship to represent those of our beliefs that we arrive at by (natural-)scientific means, I suggested that understanding *how* we arrive at these beliefs, in contrast to actually arriving at them, requires something of an altogether different kind from staying on board and ensuring that the ship's parts are in proper working order; it requires jumping overboard and looking at the ship from the outside.

I shall not dwell on this analogy. It has several defects. (Not least of these is its implication that what is wrong with a naturalistic attempt to make sense of how we make sense of things is that it is not sufficiently detached from its subject matter. In due course we shall see reason to regard this implication as the very reverse of the truth.) The crucial point is that a standard scientific investigation of how sense is made of things, even an investigation that belongs to the psychological or social sciences, cannot account for the rudimentary way in which the things of which sense is made do not just affect the sense that is made of them, but manifest themselves in it; do not just cause the making of that sense, but are given in it; do not just stand in certain relations to the sense-maker, but are made sense of *as so standing*.

Analytic philosophers have recently made deep and important contributions to the quest for a suitable alternative,[1] thereby testifying to the fact that not all of them, by any means, are Quinean naturalists. But the earliest examples of the sort of thing that these analytic philosophers have been doing were provided some fifty years before Quine even began to proclaim his naturalism. They were provided by Husserl, founder of the

---

[1] E.g. Evans (1982) and McDowell (1996).

phenomenological tradition, a tradition that is often set in contradistinction to the analytic tradition.

Edmund Husserl (1859–1938) was only a decade or so from being an exact contemporary of Frege. He and Frege had many of the same interests. The title of Husserl's first book, *Philosophy of Arithmetic*,[2] bears witness to this. This book contained some criticisms of Frege's *Foundations of Arithmetic*. Frege wrote a trenchant review of it (Frege (1984b)) and the two of them corresponded about the issues. Husserl later retracted many of his earlier views, in favour of views much closer to Frege's. How far this was due to Frege's influence and indeed quite what the essence of his *volte-face* was are both matters of dispute. Concerning the question of influence, there is reason to think that Husserl had independently come to have reservations about his earlier position.[3] Concerning the question of what exactly his *volte-face* consisted in, the popular account is that he had earlier championed a psychologism of the sort that we saw Frege oppose in Chapter 8, §6: a grounding of arithmetical laws in psychological laws. Such indeed appears to be the lesson of Frege's review. Such, for that matter, appears to be the lesson of Husserl's own subsequent glosses on his first book (e.g. *Investigations* 1, 'Foreword to the 1st Edn' and Vol. I, §45). However, while it is certainly true that this would have represented a change of position, inasmuch as Husserl was later a vehement opponent of any such psychologism, there is reason to doubt whether he had ever really subscribed to it.[4]

Be that as it may, there was enough eventual convergence of philosophical doctrine, attitude, and interest between Frege and Husserl to make the later opposition between the analytic tradition and the phenomenological tradition, or rather the later sense of opposition between these two traditions, a matter of some mystery. There is much that might be said to quell the mystery.[5] My own first instinct is simply to emphasize that what there

---

[2] Throughout this chapter I use the following abbreviations for Husserl's works: *Basic Problems* for Husserl (2006); *Crisis* for Husserl (1970); *Husserliana* III for Husserl (1950); *Husserliana* VIII for Husserl (1959); *Husserliana* XIII for Husserl (1973a); *Husserliana* XIV for Husserl (1973b); *Ideas* I for Husserl (1962); *Ideas* II for Husserl (1952); *Investigations* 1 for Husserl (2001a); *Investigations* 2 for Husserl (2001b); *Logic* for Husserl (1969); *Meditations* for Husserl (1995), and *First Meditation, Second Meditation*, etc. for its separate parts; 'Phenomenology' for Husserl (1981b); *Philosophy* for Husserl (1965); *Philosophy of Arithmetic* for Husserl (2003); 'Pure Phenomenology' for Husserl (2002); *The Idea of Phenomenology* for Husserl (1964b); and *Time Consciousness* for Husserl (1964a). Page references for the *Meditations* are in duplicate, first to the translation itself and then to the standard German edition as indicated in its margins.

[3] See Mohanty (1982), Chs 1 and 2. Dagfinn Føllesdal, in Føllesdal (1958), p. 48, sees more of an influence.

[4] See Bell (1990), pp. 79ff. For discussion of Frege's and Husserl's shared opposition to psychologism, see Hanna (2006), Ch. 1.

[5] For an insightful discussion, see Glendinning (2006), esp. Ch. 4.

was later was merely a sense of opposition, and to bemoan it as a false sense. But even that leaves a puzzle about what begat the sense, and of course, relatedly, about what makes the two traditions *two* traditions at all.

In Chapter 8, §1, we considered Dummett's characterization of analytic philosophy as philosophy based on the tenet that the philosophy of language is a foundation for the rest of the discipline. To whatever extent this admittedly controversial characterization is correct, it goes some way towards addressing these puzzles, since Husserl, despite his philosophical interest in language, would not have privileged that interest in any such way. Analytic philosophy, on Dummett's characterization, has an elemental concern with sense, specifically with linguistic sense. Phenomenology has an elemental concern, not so much with sense – certainly not so much with linguistic sense – as with sense-*making*.[6] This suggests that the branch of philosophy that phenomenologists are most likely to regard as a foundation for the rest is the philosophy of mind. But sense-making in this context is not to be construed as an activity of the mind, at least not on any ordinary understanding of what an activity of the mind is. (This should be clearer by the end of the chapter.) If there is any branch of philosophy that phenomenologists are most likely to regard as a foundation for the rest, it is in fact metaphysics.[7,8]

More important than these differences between analytic philosophy and phenomenology, however, at least for current purposes, are their relations to naturalism. Although analytic philosophy does not carry any commitment to naturalism, neither, of course, does it preclude it. Phenomenology does. Phenomenology is an attempt to make sense of sense-making in a non-(natural-)scientific way, in direct violation of naturalism. An analytic philosopher may believe that a non-(natural-)scientific way is the only way to make sense of sense-making. A phenomenologist must believe this. Husserl's project was twofold. In the first place he wanted to justify this belief. In the second place he wanted, *pari passu*, to put the belief into practice. In other words he wanted to make sense of sense-making.[9]

---

[6] I am anticipating ideas that will come to the fore in §4 about how subjects relate to the things of which they make sense.

[7] This too should be clearer by the end of the chapter. What it comes to, as we shall see, is that what phenomenologists really regard as the foundation for the rest of philosophy, if indeed they do not regard it as identical with philosophy, is phenomenology.

[8] Note that Dummett himself has written extensively on relations between Husserl and analytic philosophy. See e.g. Dummett (1991c); (1991i); (1993a), passim; and (1993d). (He also contributes a brief Preface to Husserl's *Investigations* 1 – Dummett (2001b) – which he closes by asking whether work of the kind to which I referred in n. 1 gives us 'a means of reconciling the two traditions' (p. xix).)

[9] This is an apt point at which to flag the alternative title that I have given this chapter. It is intended to echo the titles that I gave the chapters on Fichte and Quine. The point is simply to register, by evocation of the choice with which Fichte presented us, that just as Quine

2. The Phenomenological Reduction

We make sense of things. How? What are the relations between us and the things of which we make sense that allow for and/or contribute to our making sense of them? How are things *given to us*? Such are the questions that concern Husserl. Here are two pertinent quotations:

> We have, on the one hand, the fact that all thought and knowledge have as their aim *objects* or *states of affairs*, which they putatively 'hit' in the sense that the 'being-in-itself' of these objects and states is supposedly shown forth … in a multitude of actual or possible meanings, or acts of thought. We have, further, the fact that all thought is ensouled by a thought-form which is subject to ideal laws, laws circumscribing the objectivity or ideality of knowledge in general. These facts … provoke questions like: How are we to understand the fact that the intrinsic being of objectivity becomes 'presented', 'apprehended' in knowledge, and so ends up by becoming subjective? What does it mean to say that the object has 'being-in-itself', and is 'given' in knowledge? How can the ideality of the universal *qua* concept or law enter the flux of real mental states and become an epistemic possession of the thinking person? What does the *adæquatio rei et intellectus* mean in various cases of knowledge …? (*Investigations* 1, Vol. II, Introduction, §2, emphasis in original)

> How can experience as consciousness give or contact an object? How can experiences be mutually legitimated or corrected by means of each other, and not merely replace each other or confirm each other subjectively? … Why are the playing rules, so to speak, of consciousness not irrelevant for things? How is natural science to be comprehensible …, to the extent that it pretends at every step to posit and to know a nature that is in itself – in itself in opposition to the subjective flow of consciousness? (*Philosophy*, pp. 87–88)[10]

Husserl's fundamental idea is that, in the case of our scientific sense-making, indeed in the case of all our normal sense-making concerning things in space and time – all our 'natural' sense-making, as I shall call it[11] – there is no prospect of our answering such questions, no prospect of our understanding

---

espouses an extreme naturalism, so too Husserl espouses an extreme anti-naturalism. The point is *not* to cast Husserl as Fichtean. To be sure, there is an important affinity between Husserl's position and Fichte's, as we shall see in §6. But the former is as much of a variation on the latter, that is to say the former is as much of a variation on what I called 'transcendentalism' in Ch. 6, as Quine's position is on what I called 'naturalism' there: see Ch. 12, n. 5. The word 'transcendentalism' will not appear again in this chapter.

[10]　At the root of these questions is the question concerning representation on which Kant placed such emphasis in his letter to Marcus Herz: see Ch. 5, n. 30.

[11]　In §5 I shall make this a little more precise.

what it is that we manage to do when we make such sense, by doing more of the same. Partly, he has in mind the threat of vicious circularity (*Philosophy*, pp. 88–89). But he also believes that our focus would be wrong if we tried to make sense of our natural sense-making by carrying on in the same vein.[12]

It is thus that Husserl urges on us what he calls 'the phenomenological reduction'.[13] This is a methodological tactic whereby we cease temporarily to engage in any natural sense-making. This leaves us free to reflect self-consciously on the sense-making itself. For us to cease to engage in any natural sense-making is not for us to call into question any of the beliefs that we have arrived at as a result of having engaged in it in the past, any of our 'natural' beliefs. Still less is it for us to replace any of these beliefs with others, something that in any case we could not wilfully do.[14] It is for us to stop being concerned with 'natural' matters at all. We are to refuse to allow such a concern, and the miscellaneous beliefs with which it has so far furnished us, to inform this upper-level sense-making project.

For example, many of us believe that the sun is an enormous ball of gas whose light takes approximately eight minutes to reach our eyeballs. And we have untold further beliefs that stand in various relations of entailment, justification, and the like to this belief. But to make sense of our conception of the sun we are to 'bracket' all of these beliefs. We are to reflect

---

[12] Cf. his assault on naturalism in *Philosophy*, pp. 80–81. Cf. also the fact that Frege, when he attempted to make sense of our arithmetical sense-making, and in particular when he attempted to determine how numbers are given to us, did not just do more arithmetic. His questions were not arithmetical questions.

[13] There is a second reduction, which he calls the 'eidetic' reduction and which I shall discuss in §5. But note that the language of reduction, both in Husserl himself and in his commentators, is by no means confined to these two. Thus, for example, Husserl frequently refers to the 'transcendental' reduction (e.g. *Crisis*, §41). Sometimes indeed he refers to the 'transcendental-phenomenological' reduction (e.g. *Meditations*, §8). David Bell and others refer to the 'abstractive' reduction (e.g. Bell (1990), pp. 216–218). There are many others besides. Moreover, it is far from clear which of these, if any, are intended to be equivalent to which. Some commentators talk as though there are only two reductions altogether, variously labelled. Others distinguish as many as eight. (Philip J. Bossert, in Bossert (1973) – cited in Moran (2000), p. 494, n. 20 – identifies eight reductions in the *Crisis* alone.) The situation is aggravated by two further facts: first, that Husserl sometimes talks of 'phenomenological reductions' in the plural (e.g. *Ideas* I, §61); and second, that he also frequently uses the ancient Greek term '*epoché*', which he himself glosses as 'bracketing' (*Ideas* I, §31), and which many commentators take him to use more or less interchangeably with 'reduction' (e.g. David Smith (2007), p. 443), while others see him as distinguishing them (e.g. Smith (2003), p. 27). I shall bypass these controversies. For our purposes all that matters is that the phenomenological reduction and the eidetic reduction are indeed two, and that each has a crucial role to play in Husserl's attempt to make sense of our sense-making. (That said, in §5 we shall also advert to issues connected to the suggestion that there is more than one phenomenological reduction: see n. 49.)

[14] See Williams (1973c).

instead on the beliefs themselves, and on what their significance for us is; on what they *come to* for us. How do our various beliefs about sunshine, say, never mind for the time being sunshine itself, relate to that familiar glare that each of us experiences when standing outdoors (as we suppose) on a bright summer's day? And what is the exact intrinsic nature of the experience itself, never mind for the time being the facts about light and sight that occasion it?

Here is how Husserl himself characterizes such bracketing:

> [It is] an *epoché*[15] of all participation in the cognitions of the objective sciences, an *epoché* of any critical position-taking which is interested in their truth or falsity, even any position on their guiding idea of an objective knowledge of the world....
>
> Within this *epoché*, however, neither the sciences nor the scientists have disappeared for us who practice the *epoché*.... [It is just that] we do not function as sharing [their] interests, as coworkers, etc. (*Crisis*, §35)
>
> When we pursue natural science, we *carry out* reflexions ordered in accord with the logic of experience.... At the phenomenological standpoint, ... we 'place in brackets' what has been carried out, 'we do not associate these theses' with our new inquiries; instead of ... carrying *them* out, we carry out acts of *reflexion* directed towards them.... We now live entirely in such acts of the second level. (*Ideas* I, §50, emphasis in original)

And here is how he justifies its implementation:

> How can the pregivenness of the life-world become a universal subject of investigation in its own right? Clearly, only through a *total change* of the natural attitude, such that we no longer live, as heretofore, as human beings within natural existence, constantly effecting the validity of the pregiven world; rather, we must constantly deny ourselves this. Only in this way can we arrive at the transformed and novel subject of investigation, 'pregivenness of the world as such': the world purely and exclusively *as* – and in respect to *how* – it has meaning and ontic validity, and continually attains these in new forms, in our conscious life.... What is required, then, is ... a *completely unique, universal* epoché. (*Crisis*, §39, emphasis in original)[16]

The temporary transformation of the 'natural attitude' to which Husserl refers here *is* the temporary suspension of all natural sense-making in favour

---

[15] See n. 13.
[16] See also *Basic Problems*, §15; *Ideas* I, esp. 'Author's Preface', pp. 13–14, Ch. 3, and §56; 'Phenomenology', §3; 'Pure Phenomenology'; and *First Meditation*.

of reflection on that very sense-making. It brings into focus how things are given to us: the appearance of things,[17] the significance of things.[18]

3. Why Husserl Is Unlike Descartes (But Not Unlike Wittgenstein)

There is much in what we have just witnessed, and elsewhere in Husserl, to put us in mind of Descartes. Husserl himself has plenty to say about the various ways in which Descartes anticipated his project (see e.g. *Meditations*, Introduction).[19] However, as in Bergson's case (see §3 of the previous chapter), it is easy to read elements of Descartes' philosophy into Husserl that are quite certainly not there. And although Husserl does see an anticipation of his project in Descartes, he is like Bergson in seeing an abortive anticipation of it. He is as concerned to distinguish himself from Descartes as he is to liken himself to him.

Prominent among the elements of Descartes' philosophy that we are especially liable to read into Husserl are:

(1) a preparedness not to take anything for granted, and in particular not to acquiesce in natural sense-making

(2) an attempt, nonetheless, having critically reflected on natural sense-making, to vindicate it, and more specifically to vindicate it by founding it on the data of consciousness

and

(3) a fundamental cleavage between mind, the locus of such data, and matter, the spatio-temporal reality beyond mind, at which (most of) our natural sense-making is targeted.

---

[17] For warnings against some of the misleading connotations of talk of 'appearance' here, see Heidegger (1962a), §7A. (I shall discuss this passage briefly in §2 of the next chapter, in the context of a more general discussion of Heidegger's conception of these matters: see esp., in the current connection, n. 2 of that discussion.)

[18] For helpful discussions of the phenomenological reduction, see Merleau-Ponty (1962), Preface; Heidegger (1962a), §7; Heidegger (1985), esp. Chs 1 and 2; Bell (1990), esp. pp. 153–172; Moran (2000), Ch. 4; Sokolowski (2000), pp. 47–51; Smith (2003), Ch. 1; and David Smith (2007), Ch. 6, passim. (The passage mentioned from Bell (1990) is particularly helpful – notwithstanding some occasional obtuseness and ill-motivated venom that seem to me totally out of keeping with the rest. I include the following extraordinary sentence: 'Well, I have tried to follow Husserl's instructions for the performance of the phenomenological reduction, and I have to report that nothing of any philosophical interest occurred' (p. 162).)

[19] The very title of the *Meditations* – *Cartesian Meditations: An Introduction to Phenomenology*, in its unabbreviated form – speaks volumes of course.

In fact, none of this is in Husserl, at least not in quite the same way as it is in Descartes. Some of it is not there at all.[20] To begin with (1). Descartes' preparedness not to acquiesce in natural sense-making was born of simple circumspection. It indicated a concern with the reliability of such sense-making. He was interested in the truth of his natural beliefs. (See Ch. 1, §3.) Husserl's preparedness not to acquiesce in natural sense-making, as we saw in the previous section and as Husserl himself is at pains to emphasize (*Ideas* I, §31), is born of something quite different. It indicates a (tactical) *lack* of concern with the reliability of such sense-making. *Qua* phenomenologist he is precisely *not* interested in the truth of his natural beliefs.[21]

It immediately follows that (2) is not in Husserl. Husserl does see his work as an attempt to found a kind of sense-making, but not natural sense-making, nor any instance of it. He is trying to found 'a new science' (*Ideas* I, 'Author's Preface', p. 5), not any of the extant sciences. (Husserl could agree with Quine that there is nothing more secure than the extant sciences on which to found them.[22]) Furthermore, it is quite misleading to talk of 'data' in connection with Husserl's project. True, Husserl is concerned with 'things that are given', inasmuch as he is concerned with how things are given. But this concern is quite general. It is not, as talk of 'data' suggests it is, a concern with some privileged things that are given or with things that are given in some privileged way. Moreover – this is a related point to which we shall return in §§4 and 6 – in the sense in which he takes anything to be capable of being given in consciousness, he takes everything to be capable of being given in consciousness (*Ideas* I, §50; cf. *Crisis*, §§48ff.). It is not as if what can be given in consciousness can serve as evidence for what can be given only in some other way, or for what cannot be given at all (*Ideas* I, §32).

This in turn relates to the most profound difference between Husserl and Descartes, which concerns (3). Descartes, reflecting on his natural beliefs,

---

[20] One person who I think sees too much of it there is Thomas Baldwin: see Baldwin (1988), §I.

[21] This is not of course to deny, what Husserl is equally keen to emphasize (ibid.), that neither he nor Descartes could suspend belief in the way he does were it not possible to suspend belief in the way the other does. Nor is it to deny that there is something of Descartes' attempt to return to basics in Husserl, and to do so, moreover, in a way that is – how to put it? – intellectually autonomous (e.g. *Meditations*, §2). It remains the case that Descartes and Husserl have fundamentally different projects. (One illustration of this is the fact, as I argued in Ch. 1, §4, that *structurally* Descartes' strategy is the same as the naturalist's.)

[22] As indeed he seems to in *Ideas* I, §30, and *Crisis*, §28. (It is true that elsewhere, notably in *Meditations*, §64 (see esp. p. 155/p. 181), he speaks about the founding of all 'genuine sciences of matters of fact'. But he does not mean this in a Cartesian sense. There is no question of providing these sciences with any kind of vindication. It is a matter rather of describing what is presupposed in their methods of investigation.)

recognized a distinction between those that enjoyed a certain indubitability, his beliefs about the contents of his own mind, and those that did not, his beliefs about material objects. This was what led him to regard his own mind and matter as two separate substances (Ch. 1, §6). But Husserl is simply not interested in any such distinctions among his natural beliefs. The *epoché* described above is a bracketing of all of them, be their subject matter as it may, be their indubitability as it may (*Ideas* I, §33, opening paragraph). Insofar as this leads him to a new domain of investigation (*Ideas* I, §32), this is not a question of his prescinding from one part of the natural world, that which lies beyond his own private mental life, and attending to another, the mental life itself. It is a question of his ceasing to attend to anything in that world in a 'natural' way, and attending instead to everything in that world in a new, self-conscious way.[23] The bracketed beliefs are no longer *operative*, but both they and their content are still in view: that is the very point of the exercise. So there is a sense in which, after the *epoché*, nothing has changed for Husserl, even though there is also a sense in which everything has changed. '[The world] goes on appearing,' he says, 'as it appeared before; the only difference is that I, as reflecting philosophically, no longer keep in effect ... the natural believing in existence involved in experiencing the world – though that believing too is still there and grasped by my noticing regard' (*Meditations*, §8). He also says that he has 'lost nothing', but has 'won the whole Absolute Being' (*Ideas* I, §50; cf. ibid., 31).[24]

It follows that Husserl, unlike Descartes, is not even tempted to see grounds for a mind/body dualism in his project. He thinks that Descartes was on the brink of the crucial insight that whatever exists in nature can be given in consciousness, but that he mistook this insight, which is an insight about natural sense-making, for an insight *of* natural sense-making, an insight about one more thing that exists in nature. Here is how Husserl himself famously summarizes his opposition to Descartes:

> It must by no means be accepted ... that, with our apodictic pure ego, we have rescued a little *tag-end of the world*, as the sole unquestionable part of it for the philosophizing Ego, and that now the problem is to infer the rest of the world by rightly conducted arguments, according to principles innate in the ego.

[23] Husserl is aware that his own formulations sometimes obscure this contrast. Cf. the material in his marginalia to *Ideas* I that appears in *Husserliana* III, p. 70, and that David Bell quotes in Bell (1990), p. 185.

[24] Cf. his use of inverted commas to indicate this simultaneous continuity and change (*Ideas* I, §§89 and 130). Thus he distinguishes between 'the tree' and 'the "tree"', or, as he also puts it, between 'the *tree plain and simple*' and '[the] *perceived tree as such*', claiming that the former, 'though it figures as "the same exactly"' in the latter, is nevertheless 'as different as it can be from [it]' (*Ideas* I, §89, emphasis in original). For a helpful discussion, see Moran (2000), pp. 148–152.

... Descartes erred in this respect.... [He] stands on the threshold of the greatest of all discoveries – in a certain manner, has already made it – yet he does not grasp its proper sense, the sense namely of transcendental subjectivity,[25] and so he does not pass through the gateway that leads into genuine transcendental philosophy. (*Meditations*, §10, emphasis in original, punctuation slightly altered; cf. ibid., §41, and *Crisis*, §§17 and 18)[26]

(As a parenthetical addendum to this section, notice how, by distancing himself from Descartes, Husserl draws attention to some similarities between himself and the later Wittgenstein. Husserl emphasizes that the point of his project, unlike Descartes' project, is 'not to secure objectivity but to understand it' (*Crisis*, §55). Wittgenstein too is concerned, not to settle objectively how anything is, but to understand what it is for anything to be thus or so.[27] This makes philosophy, for the later Wittgenstein, just as for the early Wittgenstein, an activity rather than a body of doctrine; something 'above or below the natural sciences, not beside them' (Wittgenstein (1961), 4.111–4.112). For Husserl too, philosophy is as much a practice as a straightforwardly theoretical undertaking. When talking about 'the phenomenological attitude', he goes as far as to say that it is capable of effecting 'a complete personal transformation, comparable ... to a religious conversion' (*Crisis*, §35). He too is led to deny that philosophy, or in his case phenomenology, is anything '*by the side of* the [natural sciences]' (*Ideas* I, §62-Note, emphasis in original).[28] Both seek a kind of clarity, then. And for both this means describing in a suitably careful way what is already open to view: nothing, in philosophy, is hidden, except as a result of our own inattentiveness (Wittgenstein (1967a), Pt I, §§129 and 435). Both therefore seek to clarify a sense that is there 'prior to any philosophizing, ... a sense which philosophy can uncover but never alter' (*Meditations*, §62, emphasis removed; cf. *Ideas* I, 'Author's Preface', p. 14).[29] It follows that, for both, philosophy 'leaves everything as it is' (Wittgenstein (1967a), Pt I, §124; cf.

---

[25] In *Logic*, p. 167, Husserl defines a 'transcendental subjectivity' as a 'subjectivity antecedent to all objective realities'. And in *Crisis*, §26, he indicates that he means by 'transcendental' pretty much what Kant meant by it (see Ch. 5, §4; cf. *Ideas* I, §97, final paragraph).

[26] See Glendinning (2007), pp. 49–54, for a very helpful discussion of these matters.

[27] Cf. Ch. 9, n. 7.

[28] The phrase that Husserl himself uses, where I have inserted 'natural sciences', is 'extra-phenomenological sciences of fact'. This is strictly wider, in that it also includes the social sciences. But that certainly does not register any difference between him and Wittgenstein, whose use of the term 'natural sciences', in this context, is extraordinarily broad: see Wittgenstein (1961), 4.11.

[29] Cf. Heidegger's definition of phenomenology as 'letting the manifest in itself be seen from itself' (Heidegger (1985), p. 85, emphasis removed). See further §2 of the next chapter.

ibid., §§128 and 129). Husserl summarizes these ideas in what he calls 'the principle of all principles': 'that whatever presents itself in "intuition" ... is simply to be accepted as it gives itself out to be, though only within the limits in which it then presents itself' (*Ideas* I, §24, emphasis removed).[30,31])

4. The Execution of the Project

Husserl's greatest achievements probably lie in his actual execution of the project, in the brilliant way in which he draws to our attention aspects of our natural sense-making that we have not noticed because of their sheer familiarity.[32] It is well beyond the scope of this chapter to do more than point up a few of the most salient features of the exercise. But I shall try in this section at least to do that.

Following Brentano, who in turn follows the scholastics, Husserl fastens on the notion of 'intentionality'.[33] By 'intentionality' is meant the distinctive way in which the mind is directed towards objects, so that what we call 'making sense of things' is indeed always, at root, making sense *of things*. For any perception, there is an object of perception; for any flash of understanding, an object of understanding; for any pang of remorse, an object of remorse; for any hallucination, an object of hallucination. But Husserl assigns this notion a primordiality that neither the scholastics nor Brentano did. He also understands it differently. (These two facts are related.) The crucial difference is that, for Husserl, no relation of intentionality, insofar as it is to be thought of as a relation at all, is to be thought of as a relation between two independently existing entities. Not even the relation of intentionality involved in a case of veridical perception is to be thought of in that way. In particular, it is not to be thought of as a relation between an event in the psychology of the perceiver and a feature of the perceived environment – on pain of flouting the phenomenological reduction. Rather, any such relation is to be thought of as an articulated whole of which the act

---

[30] By 'intuition' here Husserl means that which 'is a source of authority of knowledge'. He also sometimes uses 'intuition' as a sortal term (e.g. *Ideas* I, §4) – a usage that picks out a correspondingly broad category. See Smith (2003), pp. 46–49.

[31] A final incidental similarity (which is not unrelated to those already mentioned). Husserl writes, '[A] tree plain and simple can burn away.... But ... the meaning of [a] perception [of it] ... cannot burn away' (*Ideas* I, §89). Wittgenstein writes, 'When Mr N.N. dies one says that the bearer of the name dies, not that the meaning dies' (Wittgenstein (1967a), Pt I, §40).

[32] This obviously relates to the material in parentheses at the end of the previous section: cf. again Wittgenstein (1967a), Pt I, §129.

Particularly noteworthy is Husserl's work on our temporal sense-making: see esp. *Time Consciousness*, and for a superb discussion, see Turetzky (1998), Ch. 11.

[33] Brentano (1973), p. 88.

and the object are two aspects.[34] The object is intrinsic to the act; the act is intrinsic to the object. A given hallucination is a hallucination of a *tree*, for example, just insofar as it has an arboreous object. And likewise in the case of a veridical perception of a tree. As far as the relations of intentionality themselves are concerned, these two cases are of a piece.

Nevertheless there *is* a difference. The difference is that, in the latter case, there is a tree. So what, from a phenomenological point of view, makes this difference? To begin to answer this question, let us consider how the arboreous object of perception stands in relation to the tree itself.

We can *all but* say: they are the same thing. We cannot quite say this, for reasons implicit in the preceding discussion. (The tree is independent of the perception.) What we can say, however, is that the arboreous object of perception is the tree *as so perceived*. The tree *is* what is perceived. *It* is what is given in perception.[35]

But it is given *in some way*. The tree can be perceived by being seen, or it can be perceived by being touched. It can be perceived by being seen from the north, or it can be perceived by being seen from the south. It can be perceived *as* a tree, or it can be perceived through dense fog as a building. Again, it can be first perceived, then subsequently remembered as having been perceived. Many mental acts, one physical object. Physical objects are 'constituted' as unities in experience. (I shall say a little more about this shortly.) They are given in acts of perception – differently in different acts. And the different ways in which objects are given are roughly what Husserl means by '*noemata*', which are in turn close cousins of what Frege means by senses.[36] (See *Ideas* I, esp. Chs 4, 9, and 11, passim.)

Let us return to this notion of 'constitution'. Each perception of the tree has a 'sense' and carries, as part of its sense, retained perceptions of the tree, anticipated perceptions of the tree, and/or imagined perceptions of the tree. Each of these may in turn implicate the original perception in some

---

[34] Cf. *Ideas* I, §36.
[35] Cf. *Investigations* 2, Vol. II, Investigation V, Ch. 2, Appendix to §§11 and 20, and *Ideas* I, §43.
[36] How close? I shall not dwell on that question here. There are many dimensions of controversy (concerning Frege as well as Husserl – e.g. consider the issue of whether Frege acknowledges senses without corresponding *Bedeutungen*, mentioned in Ch. 8, n. 41). I merely note that Husserl's category differs from Frege's in at least the following respect: not all *noemata* are constituents of what Frege calls 'thoughts'. For helpful discussions, see Føllesdal (1969); Dreyfus (1970); Solomon (1970); Bell (1990), pp. 179–184; Dummett (1993a), esp. Chs 7, 8, and 11; Dummett (1993d); Sokolowski (2000), pp. 59–61 and 191–194; Moran (2000), pp. 155–160; Moran (2005), pp. 133–139; and David Smith (2007), pp. 257–286. (Note that there are also interesting questions about how Husserlian *noemata* relate to Kantian intuitions (Ch. 5, §4) and to Tractarian objects (Ch. 9, §3). And certainly Husserl's notion of a mental act as essentially intentional brooks comparison with Kant's notion of a cognition (Ch. 5, n. 13).)

analogous way. There is an elaborate nexus of intentionality, in which relations of intentionality and relations between relations of intentionality are
themselves objects of intentionality. It is these relations which, collectively,
constitute the identity of the tree. And they constitute it as something over
and above any one of them. That is to say, they constitute a kind of *transcendence*, but a transcendence which is itself given in experience. (See *Ideas* I,
Ch. 4, passim, esp. §§41–46, and *Meditations*, §§19 and 20.)[37]

I mentioned anticipated perceptions. When perceptions are anticipated,
the reality may of course be different from the anticipation. And when the
reality is different from the anticipation, 'positional components of the earlier course of perception suffer *cancellation* together with their meaning ...
[and] the whole perception *explodes*, so to speak' (*Ideas* I, §138, emphasis
in original). It is when the reality is not only different from the anticipation,
but different from it in a sufficiently drastic way, that an apparent perception
is exposed as a hallucination. Suppose, for example, that an apparent visual
perception of a tree is followed by a tactile perception of nothing, where a
tactile perception of the tree was anticipated. And suppose that something
relevantly similar holds upon further investigation. Then the apparent visual
perception is revealed to be but a hallucination of a tree, notwithstanding
its arboreous object.[38]

How does Husserl's belief that the tree itself is both given and constituted in experience relate to his prior bracketing of his natural belief in the
very existence of the physical world? Does it mean that that belief is back
in play? Yes. So is he arguing by *reductio ad absurdum*? No. He would be
arguing by *reductio ad absurdum* if he had first supposed his natural belief
in the existence of the physical world to be false and then, on that basis,
argued for its truth. But, as I insisted in §2, to bracket a belief is not to
suppose it to be false. It is to cease to engage in the very sense-making that
yielded the belief. If engaging in sense-making of a different kind yields the
belief afresh, so be it. As Husserl himself puts it in the penultimate sentence
of the *Meditations*: 'I must lose the world by *epoché*, in order to regain it by
universal self-examination.'

So far we have been considering Husserl's conception of how particulars
are given. But he also believes that universals, or essences, are given (*Ideas*
I, §3). Thus not only can there be a perception of the tree; there can be an
intuition[39] of the greenness exemplified by the tree. This intuition helps to
furnish such *a priori* knowledge as that nothing can be both red and green
all over (*Ideas* I, Chs 1 and 2, passim, and *The Idea of Phenomenology*,

---

[37] For doubt about whether such transcendence can be constituted in this way, see Sartre
(2003), Introduction, esp. §V.

[38] It is the ineliminable possibility of this kind of frustrated anticipation which in Husserl's
view allows for Cartesian doubt about the existence of the physical world (*Ideas* I, §46).

[39] See n. 30.

pp. 44–45).[40] Quite how essences are given on Husserl's conception is a matter of delicate exegesis. But it is not unlike the way in which physical objects
are given, in that many different perceptions of green things can all furnish
an intuition of one and the same essence. The crucial difference lies in the
fact that imagined perceptions of green things can serve this function just as
well as actual perceptions of them. This means that intuitions of essences are
secured largely through 'the play of fancy' (*Ideas* I, §4).[41]

I shall not further pursue Husserl's conception of how essences are given
beyond making four brief observations about how, in acceding to it, Husserl
differs from four of our protagonists. First, his conception sets him apart
from Hume, who thought that the nearest that the mind comes to grasping
a universal is grasping a particular which, through its annexation to a linguistic item, is able to represent other particulars. Thus a particular 'idea' of
green, in Hume's terminology, is able to represent all other particular ideas
of green through its annexation to the word 'green' (Ch. 4, §2).[42] Second,
and related, although Husserl agrees with Kant that there is synthetic *a priori* knowledge (*Ideas* I, §16), he is able, on his conception, to account for
such knowledge in terms of the intuition of essences and the apprehension
of certain truths concerning their broad generic features. He does not, he
believes, need to follow Kant in concluding that reality is viewed through
native spectacles (*Crisis*, §§30 and 31). Third, in accepting that *a priori*
knowledge such as the knowledge that nothing can be both red and green
all over answers to what essences are like, Husserl is in profound and direct
opposition to Wittgenstein (Ch. 10, §3). And fourth, in sharply separating
such knowledge from 'knowledge of facts' (*Ideas* I, §4), he is in profound
and direct opposition to Quine, since this is just the kind of separation that
Quine's araneous conception of belief leads him to repudiate (Ch. 12, §4).
We began this chapter by considering the opposition between Husserl and
Quine with respect to naturalism. The opposition just noted is really an
aspect of that. It is because of Quine's extreme naturalism that he is unsympathetic to the attempt to draw a sharp distinction of this (as he would see
it, unscientific) kind between two sorts of sense-making.

Finally, in this section I note that Husserl recognizes the need to include,
among the various objects of natural sense-making that he discusses, subjects of natural sense-making. For they too are made sense of. They too are
given and constituted. It is true that the very attention to natural sense-
making that is consequent upon the phenomenological reduction brings
to light what Husserl calls 'consciousness': that in which he takes things

---

[40] Is the knowledge that nothing can be both red and green all over 'natural' knowledge? For
the time being I will assume that it is. We shall return to this issue in the next section.

[41] For discussion, see Bell (1990), pp. 194–197, and David Smith (2007), pp. 330–333.

[42] However, by the time Hume has explained what he means by this, the difference between
him and Husserl looks less marked: see Hume (1978a), Bk I, Pt I, §VII.

to be given. But that is not what is at issue here. Construed in *that* way, consciousness is not one more thing of which natural sense is made. It is rather a transcendental limit to natural sense-making, somewhat like the 'I' of Wittgenstein's *Tractatus*, whose appearance in that book we observed in Chapter 9, §7. Here is what Husserl says about such consciousness:

> [It] must be reckoned as a *self-contained system of Being*, as a system of *Absolute Being*, into which nothing can penetrate, and from which nothing can escape; which has no spatio-temporal exterior, and can be inside no spatio-temporal system; which cannot experience causality from anything nor exert causality upon anything. (*Ideas* I, §49, emphasis in original; cf. ibid., §57)[43]

Elsewhere Husserl distinguishes between 'the transcendental Ego' and 'the psychological Ego':

> [The transcendental Ego], who necessarily remains for me, by virtue of [my free *epoché* with respect to the being of the experienced world], is not a piece of the world; and if he says, 'I exist ...,' that no longer signifies, 'I, this man, exist.' No longer am I the man who, in natural self-experience, finds himself *as* a man ...; nor am I [his] separately considered psyche.... Apperceived in this 'natural' manner, I and all other men are themes of sciences that are objective ... in the usual sense: biology, anthropology, and also ... *psychology*.... Phenomenological *epoché* ... excludes [the objective] world completely from the field of judgment.... Consequently for me, the meditating Ego who, standing and remaining in the attitude of *epoché*, posits exclusively himself as the *acceptance-basis* of all objective acceptances and bases, there is no psychological Ego....
>
> ... The objective world ... derives its whole sense and its existential status, which it has for me, from me myself, *from me as the transcendental Ego*. (*Meditations*, §11, emphasis in original, punctuation slightly adapted; cf. *Ideas* I, §54, and *Crisis*, §§53–55 and 58)

It is the transcendental Ego that the phenomenological reduction brings to light. It is the psychological Ego for whose givenness and constitution Husserl still needs to provide an account.

Not, of course, that the two are completely unrelated. In the passage above Husserl talks about them as if they were two separate things. But really they are one thing viewed in two separate ways. Here as elsewhere, to effect the phenomenological reduction is not to attend to something new. It

---

[43] If this calls to mind Leibnizian monads, in particular in respect of their windowlessness (Ch. 3, §3), then that is as should be: see the material at the end of §6. (But see also n. 70.)

is to attend to something familiar in a new way. (See 'Phenomenology', §9; and cf. *Meditations*, §45.)[44]

That is one reason why the execution of this part of Husserl's project is such a bedevilling matter. He has to wrestle with the basic 'paradox of human subjectivity', namely that a human subject is both 'a subject for the world and at the same time ... an object in the world' (*Crisis*, §53). Another reason why the execution of this part of his project is such a bedevilling matter is that each human subject also makes natural sense of other human subjects. Husserl therefore also needs to address fundamental issues about mutual interpretation and the constitution of the community and its culture. He undertakes all of these tasks in (among other places) *Fourth Meditation*, *Fifth Meditation*, and *Ideas* II.[45]

5. The Eidetic Reduction

So far there is no real indication why phenomenology should be thought to be part of *philosophy*. (Still less is there any indication why it should be thought to *be* philosophy, as Husserl evidently thinks it is: see e.g. *Meditations*, §64.) What we glimpsed of the execution of Husserl's project in the previous section certainly looked philosophical. But we have been given no indication why we should regard it as typical. Merely shifting attention from things in space and time to the way in which sense is made of such things does not, by itself, involve adopting any characteristically philosophical stance.

For one thing, it is not yet clear why phenomenology should be an *a priori* endeavour, as any philosopher opposed to naturalism is liable to think philosophy is. The phenomenological reduction allows for *a priori* enquiry, obviously. But it does not necessitate it. Consider the Humean story about where our idea of a causally necessary connection comes from (Ch. 4, §3). Could not a counterpart of that story be told, after the phenomenological reduction, about the workings of the transcendental Ego? And would not such a counterpart of Hume's story be *a posteriori*, an account, so to speak, of how the transcendental Ego happens, as a matter of fact, to work? Indeed, though Hume himself believed that he was engaged in an experimental science of human nature, which sounds for all the world like a species of natural sense-making, such was his somewhat idiosyncratic, introspective conception of a science of human nature that we may wonder whether

---

[44] In *Ideas* I, §76, Husserl is led to conclude that any phenomenological thesis that concerns the transcendental Ego (as all phenomenological theses do: see the next section) can be 'reinterpreted' as a thesis concerning the psychological Ego.

[45] For excellent discussions, see Smith (2003), pp. 108–115 and Ch. 5, passim; and Moran (2005), Ch. 7, passim. David Bell (1990), Ch. 4, is also strongly to be recommended, though once again (see n. 18) Bell occasionally displays a curious and incongruous lack of sympathy.

'counterpart' is too weak a word here. Certainly, Husserl sees Hume as engaged in phenomenology of a sort (e.g. *Crisis*, §24). Even so, he does not see him as a fellow traveller. He does not see him as engaged in phenomenology of the sort that *he* is trying to establish, the sort that he often distinguishes by calling it 'transcendental' phenomenology (see *Ideas* I, 'Author's Preface', p. 16).[46] And that is not because he sees him as engaged in natural sense-making. It is because, or it is principally because, he sees him as concerned with what Hume himself would describe as 'matters of fact' rather than 'relations of ideas'.[47]

The simple truth is that Husserl needs to say some more about what makes (transcendental) phenomenology the distinctive undertaking that he believes it to be. He needs to say what makes it *a priori*. But he needs to do more than that. He needs to say why, as he also believes, its field of enquiry is the transcendental Ego *and the transcendental Ego alone*.

Let us begin with this second point. What exactly is bracketed in the phenomenological reduction? Natural sense-making. But what – exactly – is that? The loose characterization that I gave in §2 was simply that it is normal sense-making concerning things in space and time. But among the many indeterminacies afflicting this characterization there is one in particular that is critical. Must natural sense-making concern things in space and time directly? Or can it concern them at, so to speak, one remove, by extending to the investigation of the *essences* of things in space and time?[48] The characterization, as it stands, can be heard either way. But the matter needs to be resolved. And if it is resolved in the first way (the narrower way), then less is bracketed and the phenomenological reduction allows for enquiry beyond the transcendental Ego. Husserl, some of whose own formulations of the phenomenological reduction share the same indeterminacy, spends the bulk of Chapter 6 of *Ideas* I explaining why phenomenologists should in fact undertake what he calls 'the phenomenological reduction *in its extended form*' (§61, emphasis added),[49] bracketing enough to preclude enquiry beyond the transcendental Ego. In effect he wants them to bracket all sense-making save for that which must be retained in order for the very aim of the exercise not to be thwarted: the aim of making sense of making sense of things. In particular, he does indeed want them to bracket investigation of the essences of things in space and time. When

---

[46] See n. 25.

[47] Cf. *Ideas* I, 'Introduction', p. 38.

[48] See n. 40: in the previous section I assumed the latter. The reasons for this will I hope soon be clear. Even so, I had not said anything at that stage to block the opposite assumption.

[49] 'In its extended form' implies that his own earlier formulations are to be interpreted in the first way, whereby less is bracketed. It also helps to account for his preparedness to talk of 'phenomenological reductions' in the plural, as he does in the opening sentence of §61 and, for that matter, in the very title of Ch. 6: see n. 13.

phenomenology is understood as resting on this extended reduction, it will
be the utterly pure science of the transcendental Ego that he takes it to be.
Here is Husserl:

> The controlling practical thought which this extension [of the phenom-
> enological reduction] brings with it ... [is] that, as a matter of principle,
> not only the sphere of the natural world but all these eidetic[50] spheres
> as well [i.e. spheres of the *essences* which are taken from the sphere of
> the natural world (such as 'thing,' 'bodily shape,' 'man,' 'person,' and so
> forth)] should, in respect of their true Being, provide no data for the phe-
> nomenologist; that as a guarantee for the purity of its region of research
> they should be bracketed in respect of the judgments they contain; that
> not a single theorem, not even an axiom, should be taken from any
> of the related sciences, nor be allowed as premises for phenomenolog-
> ical purposes. (*Ideas* I, §61, emphasis added, punctuation very slightly
> adapted)

But there is still the question of what makes phenomenology *a priori*. And the answer is that there is a second, different sort of reduction
that phenomenologists need to undertake: what Husserl calls 'the eidetic
reduction'.[51] The eidetic reduction involves prescinding from all but what is
open to view through the 'play of fancy' to which I referred in the previous
section. In other words, it involves prescinding from particulars and focusing on essences. This ensures that phenomenology is 'an *a priori* science,
which confines itself to the realm of pure possibility' (*Meditations*, §12). It
leads beyond investigation of the actual workings of the transcendental Ego
to investigation of its essential structure, that is its 'universal apodictically
experienceable structure' (ibid., emphasis removed). It also leads to a critique of any sense-making that can be erected on that structure. (See *Ideas*
I, 'Introduction', pp. 40–41; 'Phenomenology', §§4 and 5; and *Meditations*,
§§12, 13, and 34–37.)

Any sense-making that can be erected on that structure? Not just natural sense-making? Any. And this has important consequences. First, it
means that there will be provision for placing the critique of natural sense-
making in a broader context. Phenomenologists can reflect on what it takes
for sense-making to *be* natural sense-making (see *Ideas* I, §47). This will
involve the sort of thing we observed in the previous section: reflection on
how physical objects are given and constituted in experience. The second

---

[50] Husserl uses the term 'eidetic' in place of the more familiar '*a priori*'. See *Ideas* I,
'Introduction', pp. 41–42, for why he prefers the former.
[51] The eidetic reduction is parasitic on the phenomenological reduction, and to that extent
secondary. But it is still crucial. Cf. *Husserliana* VIII, p. 80. And cf. what Husserl says
about the extended phenomenological reduction in *Ideas* I, §60, final paragraph.

important consequence turns on the fact that 'any sense-making that can be erected on that structure' means, in effect, 'any sense-making'. For any sense-making has a subject, and the transcendental Ego is nothing but the subject viewed in a non-natural self-conscious way. So the broader critique will apply to sense-making of all kinds. (In particular, it will apply to itself. Phenomenologists can make sense of making sense of making sense of things. They can make sense of phenomenology.) Moreover, such are the efficacy and the efficiency of this phenomenological critique, Husserl believes, that it can survive the bracketing of all sense-making that is not *peculiarly* phenomenological. It can even survive the bracketing of the sense-making that is constitutive of (pure) logic. For although there can be no sense-making at all that does not make use of logic, 'the logical propositions to which [phenomenology] might find occasion to refer would ... be logical axioms such as the principle of contradiction, whose universal and absolute validity ... it could make transparent by the help of examples *taken from the data of its own domain*' (*Ideas* I, §59, emphasis added). Thus just as natural sense-making of a certain basic kind, once bracketed, can be recovered by the phenomenologist (see the previous section), so too logical sense-making of a certain basic kind, once bracketed, can be recovered by the phenomenologist. Phenomenology is ultimately a completely self-sustaining autonomous discipline, 'the theory of the essential nature of the transcendentally purified consciousness' (*Ideas* I, §60; cf. ibid., p. 13, and *Investigations* 1, Vol. II, Introduction, §1).

6. Idealism in Husserl

Husserl famously encapsulates both the aim and the methodology of phenomenology in the slogan: 'We must go back to the "things themselves"' (*Investigations* 1, Vol. II, 'Intro', §2; cf. *Philosophy*, p. 96). This is not, or at least not in any straightforward way, an exhortation to attain that knowledge of things in themselves which Kant took us to be incapable of attaining. What Husserl means, first and foremost, is something that might be heard, not as a rebuke to Kant, but (however anachronistically) as a rebuke to analytic philosophers: that we must not regard linguistic analysis, the exchange of one form of words for another, as a substitute for thinking about what those forms of words mean. Even so, the slogan carries the suggestion that phenomenology is a way of penetrating through to the true nature of things.[52] And where the things in question are things in space and time,

---

[52] And, despite what I say in the main text, it may indeed have been intended as a corrective to the slogan 'Back to Kant!' adopted in the late nineteenth century by neo-Kantians: see Copleston (1963), p. 361, and Cumming (1991), p. 37.

this in turn may seem puzzling. Surely, the only way to penetrate through to *their* true nature is by processes of natural sense-making, precisely what phenomenologists abstain from. Phenomenology is a way of establishing how such things are given to us rather than how they are – is it not?

Well, yes and no. How such things are given to us is after all an aspect of how they are. Phenomenology is a way of establishing how things are to at least the following extent: it is a way of establishing how they are *qua* given. Or better, reflecting the *a priori* nature of the discipline, it is a way of establishing how they must be *qua* giveable. To that extent it penetrates through to their true nature.

Still, this does not do justice to Husserl's own sense of how far it penetrates, which is to say, not just to how things must be *qua* giveable, but to how things must be *simpliciter*. For he also believes that such things *must be giveable*. He believes that it is of the very essence of the things of which we make natural sense that they are susceptible to just such sense-making, and that other essential features of theirs depend on this. He is, by the definition that I proffered in the Appendix to Chapter 5, an idealist.

Here are some forthright statements of his idealism:[53]

> Reality [i.e. the reality of which we make natural sense], that of the thing taken singly as also that of the whole world, essentially lacks independence.... Reality is not in itself something absolute ..., it is, absolutely speaking, nothing at all, it has no 'absolute essence' whatsoever, it has the essentiality of something which in principle is *only* intentional, *only* for consciousness, objective or apparent for consciousness. (*Ideas* I, §50, emphasis in original)[54]

> The existence of what is natural cannot condition the existence of consciousness since it arises as the correlate of consciousness; it *is* only in so far as it constitutes itself within ordered organization of consciousness. (*Ideas* I, §51, emphasis in original)

> The attempt to conceive the universe of true being as something lying outside the universe of possible consciousness, possible knowledge, possible evidence, related to one another merely externally by a rigid law, is nonsensical. They belong together essentially; and, as belonging together essentially, they are also concretely one, one in the only absolute concretion: transcendental subjectivity. (*Meditations*, §41)

---

[53] For further expressions of this idealism, see *Ideas* I, Ch. 5, passim, and 'Phenomenology', §11.

[54] I have taken the liberty of adapting Boyce Gibson's translation of the final clause of this passage, which, in the original German, reads as follows: '*es hat die Wesenheit von etwas, das prinzipell* nur *Intentionales,* nur *Bewußtes, bewußtseinsmäßig Vorstelliges, Erscheinendes ist*' (emphasis in original). I am indebted here to Robert Welsh Jordan.

And finally this, sounding for all the world as if it had been written by Fichte:[55]

> All wrong interpretations of being come from naïve blindness to the horizons that join in determining the sense of being, and to the corresponding tasks of uncovering implicit intentionality. If these are seen and undertaken, there results a universal phenomenology, as a self-explication of the ego.... Stated more precisely: first, a self-explication in the pregnant sense, showing systematically how the ego constitutes himself, in respect of his own proper essence, as existent in himself and for himself; then, secondly, a self-explication in the broadened sense, which goes from there to show how, by virtue of this proper essence, the ego likewise constitutes in himself something 'other', something 'objective', and thus constitutes everything without exception that ever has for him, in the ego, existential status as non-ego. (*Meditations*, §41, punctuation very slightly altered)[56]

What then motivates this idealism? Does it follow from anything that we have observed so far? There is a suggestion in Husserl that it does. 'The proof of this idealism,' he claims, 'is ... phenomenology itself' (*Meditations*, §41, emphasis removed). This suggestion seems to me incorrect. Either Husserl's claim betokens a conception of phenomenology that itself extends beyond what we have observed so far or – I see no alternative – we should take issue with it.[57] For I see no reason why someone should not accede to everything hitherto (the place of the various reductions in making sense of how we make sense of things *et cetera*) without acceding to this (the dependence of the things of which we make natural sense for some of their essential features on their susceptibility to just such sense-making).[58]

Suppose I am right. What then would induce someone to take the extra step, the step, in other words, from what we have observed so far of Husserl's phenomenology to his idealism? One thing that would at least point them in the right direction would be a dose of something like logical positivism or Dummettian anti-realism whereby the very idea of a reality beyond the reach of experience is called into question. What would propel them from

---

[55] On the comparison between Husserl and Fichte, whom Husserl greatly admired, see Moran (2003), pp. 60–62.

[56] Cf. Kant (1998), A129, and Wittgenstein (1961), 5.62. But see also the translator's n. 3 on p. 85: in Husserl's own copy of the text there are exclamation marks in the margin against this passage, which, from 'Stated more precisely ...' to the end, is marked as unsatisfactory. Perhaps what gave him pause was the intimation that objects of natural sensemaking depend for their very existence on that sense-making, an idea which goes beyond anything in the other quotations and to which he does not subscribe.

[57] As I think we should take issue with Dummett's thesis, in Dummett (1993a), Ch. 8, that the very introduction of *noemata* is an inducement to idealism.

[58] Cf. Bell (1988), pp. 57–58. Cf. also Harrison (1974), pp. 26–28.

there would be an understanding of this whereby the limits of reality are set by the limits of experience – in such a way that the former count as *limitations* (cf. Ch. 9, §4).

Do we find anything of this sort in Husserl? Indeed we do. See this for example:

> The hypothetical assumption of a Real Something outside this world [sc. the one spatio-temporal world which is fixed through our actual experience] is indeed a 'logically' possible one, and there is clearly no formal contradiction in making it. But if we question the essential conditions of its validity, *the kind of evidence demanded by its very meaning*[,] ... we perceive that the transcendent must needs be *experienceable*, and not merely by an Ego conjured into being as an empty logical possibility but by any *actual* Ego. (*Ideas* I, §48, emphasis adapted)[59]

There is also, relatedly, a loud echo of Fichte's rendition of the Limit Argument, which Fichte used to repudiate subject-independent things in themselves (Ch. 6, §3):

> We have here [an] ... idealism that is nothing more than ... an explication of my ego as subject of every possible cognition, and indeed with respect to every sense of what exists, wherewith the latter might be able to *have* a sense for me, the ego. (*Meditations*, §41, some emphasis removed)

Note, however, that if the sense-making involved here is understood in the ultra-thin way in which Fichte understood it, then this train of thought is not idealistic. (Fichte's own idealism was independently motivated.) It is only when the sense-making involved is understood in a suitably thick way, such as the 'natural' way in which Husserl himself understands it, that its limits, to echo this time the early Wittgenstein, can be said to determine the limits of the world (Wittgenstein (1961), 5.6ff.); only then that idealism beckons.

These various evocations of Dummett, Fichte, and the early Wittgenstein bring us conveniently to the next obvious question concerning Husserl's idealism, which is whether it is an empirical idealism or a transcendental idealism. And they do so by suggesting forcefully that it is the latter.

Is it? Certainly, Husserl himself calls his position 'transcendental idealism' (e.g. *Meditations*, §41, p. 86/p. 118). But this is not decisive. It is a further question how exactly he is using the term. We cannot take for granted that he is using it in a way that conforms, even roughly, with the Kant-inspired definition which I gave in the Appendix to Chapter 5 and which I have been

---

[59] In the rest of this section Husserl addresses the question that we saw to be of such critical significance in Dummett (Ch. 14, §3(b)): whether the possibility at stake here is a possibility 'in practice' or a possibility 'in principle'. He insists on the latter.

presupposing ever since. For one thing, he says that he intends the term 'in a fundamentally and essentially new sense' (ibid.).[60] And he is at pains to emphasize that his idealism is not 'a Kantian idealism' (ibid.; see also *Crisis*, §§28ff.). (This is largely for the Fichtean reason that he too rules out the possibility of subject-independent things in themselves.[61] But it is not exclusively for that reason.[62] Recall that Husserl sees no rationale for the Kantian belief in native spectacles: see §4.)

These caveats notwithstanding, Husserl's idealism surely is an instance of transcendental idealism on my definition – in fact, a paradigm of it. The dependence of things in space and time for some of their essential features on their susceptibility to our natural sense-making is not itself susceptible to our natural sense-making. It manifests itself when, and only when, we indulge in phenomenological sense-making (see *Ideas* I, 'Author's Preface', p. 15).

But it does not follow that there is not also an empirical idealism in Husserl. The idealism that has been at issue so far is with respect to natural sense-making. (Any idealism, recall, is with respect to some kind of sense-making: see Ch. 5, Appendix.) Our discussion therefore leaves open the possibility that Husserl is also an idealist with respect to some other kind of sense-making, in particular phenomenological sense-making, and that this second idealism is empirical. Given the capacity of phenomenological sense-making to replicate natural sense-making (§3), and given its capacity to reckon with itself (§4), I think this is a possibility that we must take very seriously. The thought is that, for Husserl, things in space and time depend for some of their essential features on their susceptibility to phenomenological sense-making in a way that is itself susceptible to phenomenological sense-making.

One of the reasons why this possibility is such a significant one is the bearing it has on the relation between Husserl and Berkeley. Berkeley's idealism is the very prototype of a certain kind of empirical idealism (see Berkeley (1962a)). And it is certainly hard not to be reminded of Berkeley when reading Husserl. The views canvassed in §4 about the difference between perceiving a tree and merely seeming to perceive a tree, for example, are entirely of a piece with what Berkeley would say about the same issue.[63] Are we not justified in seeing a fundamental affinity between the two thinkers – an affinity which Husserl's classification as an empirical idealist would surely serve to capture?

---

[60] But see again n. 25. I leave open whether there is internal tension here.

[61] See Ch. 6, §3: this is anti-Kantian, not because Kant insists that there *are* subject-independent things in themselves, but because Kant insists that we are not in a position to rule one way or the other.

[62] See *Meditations*, §41, p. 86/p. 118, n. 1.

[63] See e.g. Berkeley (1962a), §30.

Husserl himself insists not. He denies that he is Berkeleian. He writes:

> If anyone objects, with reference to these discussions of ours, that they
> transform the whole world into subjective illusion and throw them-
> selves into the arms of an 'idealism such as Berkeley's,' we can only make
> answer that he has not understood the *meaning* of these discussions....
> It is not that the real sensory world is 'recast' or denied, but that an
> absurd interpretation of the same ... is set aside. It springs from making
> the world absolute in a *philosophical* sense, which is wholly foreign to
> the way in which we naturally look out upon the world. (*Ideas* I, §55,
> emphasis in original)

But Husserl had better not rest his case there. The latter part of this quotation is precisely what Berkeley, a self-styled champion of common sense,
would say in defence of his own view.[64] Were Husserl to rest his case there,
either he would be guilty of having misunderstood Berkeley or he would
have an objection to how Berkeley peddles his view which would be no less
an objection to how he (Husserl) peddles *his* view.

Husserl does however have more to say (e.g. *Crisis*, §§21–24). There is
a genuine and important difference between him and Berkeley on which he
is fastening. On Berkeley's view, there is a sense, however sophisticated, in
which things in space and time depend for their very existence on their perception by subjects. There is no analogue of this on Husserl's view.[65] If there
is an empirical idealism in Husserl, as I am still inclined to think there is, it
is a tempered version of Berkeley's idealism, relating to the 'giveability' of
things in space and time, not to their existence.[66]

Be that as it may, the fact remains that there is *an* idealism in Husserl.
How comfortable should we be with it?[67] How well, for example, does it
square with our natural sense-making? Is there not perhaps an unrelievable
tension between it and the most basic of our natural convictions, that which
Husserl himself dignifies with the label 'the general thesis of the natural

---

[64] See e.g. Berkeley (1962a), §§34 and 35, and Berkeley (1962b), pp. 149ff. and 256–258.
(Philonous is Berkeley's representative in the latter.)

[65] Cf. n. 56.

[66] Cf. what Bernard Williams salvages from the argument in Berkeley (1962b) to which I
referred in Ch. 5, n. 70: see Williams (1973a).

   Note that there are other crucial differences between Husserl and Berkeley. One is the
difference noted in §4 between Husserl and Hume: Berkeley, like Hume, makes no provision for the mind's grasp of universals.

[67] One concern, which I shall not address in the main text, is that, in spite of Husserl's
appreciation of the need to explain how the Ego can be an object of sense-making – the
need, in other words, not to take the empirical Ego for granted – his readiness to say that
everything else can be an object of sense-making *for* the Ego shows that he takes the transcendental Ego too much for granted. For expressions of this concern, or something like
it, see Deleuze (1990b), pp. 98 and 102.

standpoint' (*Ideas* I, §30), namely the conviction that the spatio-temporal world 'has its being,' as Husserl puts it, 'out there' (ibid.)?

When we considered an analogous question in connection with Kant's idealism, and in connection with the closely related idealism to be found in Dummett, I suggested that there is indeed such a tension (Ch. 5, §10, and Ch. 14, §4). In their case there is an obvious way of trying to relieve the tension. This is to argue that our natural conviction is part of the sense we ordinarily make of things, from our position of engagement with them, whereas the idealism is part of the sense we make of things in our capacity as philosophers, from a position of *dis*engagement with them, a disengagement that equips familiar concepts to be exercised in unfamiliar ways. But this attempt to relieve the tension fails, I suggested, because it is not possible for us to make sense of things except from our position of engagement with them.

In Husserl's case there is no analogous way of even trying to relieve the tension. On Husserl's view, our philosophical (or phenomenological) sense-making, while fundamentally different in kind from our ordinary (or natural) sense-making, is still from our position of engagement with things. '[The world] goes on appearing,' we heard him say in §3, 'as it appeared before' (*Meditations*, §8). So where familiar concepts are exercised in our philosophical sense-making, there is no reason, or at any rate no analogous reason, to expect them to be exercised in anything but familiar ways.

Husserl does however have another way of trying to relieve the tension, a way that, while similar, is importantly different. He portrays the independence of things in space and time in which we naturally believe as a constituted independence, an independence with respect to each and every constituted (or psychological) Ego. This form of independence, to reecho the early Wittgenstein, is a form of dependence (Wittgenstein (1961), 2.0122). It is a form of dependence on the very constituting. In other words, it is a form of dependence on the sense-giving of the unconstituted (or transcendental) Ego.[68] And it becomes apparent only after the phenomenological reduction. Here is Husserl:

> Our phenomenological idealism does not deny the positive existence of the real world and of Nature.... Its sole task and service is to clarify the meaning of this world, the precise sense in which everyone accepts it, and with undeniable right, as really existing. *That* it exists – given as it is as a universe out there ... – that is quite indubitable.... [But] the phenomenological clarification of the meaning of the manner of existence of the real world ... is that only transcendental subjectivity has ontologically the meaning of Absolute Being ...; whereas the real world exists, but in respect of essence is relative to transcendental subjectivity, and in such a

---

[68] See e.g. *Ideas* I, §55.

way that it can have its meaning as existing reality only as the intentional meaning-product of transcendental subjectivity....

... But how could we ever be aware [that the world has this meaning] prior to the phenomenological reduction which first brings the transcendental subjectivity as our absolute Being into the focus of experience? So long as it was only the psychological subjectivity that was recognized, and one sought to posit it as absolute, and to understand the world as its correlate, the result could only be an absurd Idealism. (*Ideas* I, 'Author's Preface', pp. 14–15)

A time before all consciousness can only mean a time in which no animal was alive. That has a sense. But a time and no absolute consciousness: that has no sense. *Absolute* consciousness is 'before' objective time, and is the non-temporal ground for the constitution of infinite time and a world infinitely stretching out in time. (*Husserliana* XIII, p. 16, trans. in Smith (2003), pp. 201–202)

(The distinctions that Husserl invokes here, between psychological subjectivity and transcendental subjectivity, and between consciousness and absolute consciousness, are variants of the distinction between the psychological Ego and the transcendental Ego.[69]).

Granted the rest of Husserl's phenomenology, this may be enough to relieve the tension. Even so, his idealism still seems to me problematical. In particular, it seems to me to risk the same fate as other forms of transcendental idealism: that of trying to represent as limits, in the sense of limitations, what are merely limits in the sense of essential features, and thereby lapsing into nonsense. For it tries to represent the limits of the spatio-temporal world, the limits, in other words, of that which is susceptible to natural sense-making, as limitations determined by that very susceptibility. That there is nonsense in the offing is apparent when we consider the following question. What kind of sense-making does it take to represent these limits in this way? In particular, what kind of sense-making does it take to advert to what, *qua* limitations, these limits exclude? We could say that it takes phenomenological sense-making. But that really just defers the problem. For how is phenomenological sense-making supposed to be equal to the task?

We have seen several attempts to address this problem, or at any rate versions of it, in previous chapters. They have all been struggles. (See e.g. Ch. 5, §§8 and 9, and Ch. 9, §§5 and 7.) Likewise in Husserl's case. Here is a striking illustration of his struggle. At one point he says, in a memorable

---

[69] In the case of the distinction between consciousness and absolute consciousness, cf. *Ideas* I, §§33, 53, and 76.

sentence that is highly reminiscent of both the visionariness and the vision of Wittgenstein's *Tractatus*:

> If transcendental subjectivity is the universe of possible sense, then an outside is precisely – nonsense. (*Meditations*, §41, p. 84/p.117)

But he straightway adds, in a very telling sentence that is likewise reminiscent of the *Tractatus*, though this time of some of its contortions:

> But even nonsense is always a mode of sense and has its nonsensicalness within the sphere of possible insight. (Ibid.)

There is another illustration of Husserl's struggle with this problem, I submit, in his comparison of his idealism to Leibniz' monadology (see Ch. 3, §3; and for the comparison, see e.g. *Meditations*, §§60–62).[70] This comparison reinforces the idea that 'the [spatio-temporal] world and all I know about it' are subject to limitations, inasmuch as it casts that world as 'a mere "phenomenon"' (*Meditations*, §62, p. 149/p. 176). The trouble is that it also, *eo ipso*, threatens to undo the work that Husserl has previously done to reconcile his idealism with our natural conviction that the spatio-temporal world 'has its being out there'. Husserl, like other transcendental idealists before him, finds that his attempt to make sense of our most basic sense-making threatens to lead him, despite his best efforts, to flout that very sense-making. The suspicion persists that his idealism is not ultimately tenable.[71]

7.   Husserl as Metaphysician

Suppose that the suspicion is justified. And suppose, as I urged in the previous section, that the idealism is separable from the rest of Husserl's phenomenology. How might someone sympathetic to the rest of his phenomenology uncouple them?

By accepting that phenomenology, though it puts us in a position to say how things are given to us, or how we make sense of things, does not put us in a position to say what the intrinsic nature of things is. Or, to revert to the Wittgensteinian slogan that I pitted against Dummett's idealism in Chapter 14, §4, by accepting that phenomenology, though it puts us in a position to say *how* things are – *qua* given – does not put us in a position to say

---

[70] For discussion, see Smith (2003), pp. 200–210. But note one important respect in which Husserl departs from Leibniz. He holds that, insofar as there can be empathy between monads, they are not windowless: see *Husserliana* XIV, p. 260.

[71] For discussions of Husserl's idealism, see Philipse (1995); Smith (2003), pp. 30–32 and Ch. 4, passim; Moran (2003); and Glendinning (2007), pp. 17–20.

what things are (Wittgenstein (1961), 3.221).[72] Roughly, Husserl's idealism
is what accrues when we attempt to do the latter. If we want to accede to
his phenomenology without acceding to his idealism, then we must learn to
curb our metaphysical impulses.

This raises the question of how far Husserl himself is engaged in metaphysics. The question is pertinent not only to what he is doing when he is
defending his idealism, but also to what he is doing when he is practising the
rest of his phenomenology.

When he is defending his idealism, he is engaged in metaphysics of the
most rampant sort. That is clear. But even when he is practising the rest of
his phenomenology, he is, at least some of the time, attempting to make
maximally general sense of things. True, what he is principally doing, all
of that time, is attempting to make sense of making sense of things. But
as I claimed in §5 of the Introduction, and as I think has been evidenced
many times since, such 'second-order' sense-making and the corresponding
'first-order' sense-making always have a bearing on each other, at least at
the highest level of generality, which is the level at which Husserl is largely
operating. Indeed, we could say that precisely what is wrong with the excur-
sion into idealism is that it is an attempt to make maximally general sense of
things that is not suitably informed by the attempt to make sense of making
sense of things.[73]

These remarks obviously presuppose my own conception of metaphysics. But Husserl himself freely acknowledges a conception of metaphysics
on which, both when he is defending his idealism and when he is practising
the rest of his phenomenology, he is engaged in metaphysics. As far as his
defence of his idealism is concerned, as I noted at the end of the previous section, that involves him in a reversion to Leibniz' monadology, about which
he writes, 'Our monadological results are *metaphysical*, if it be true that
ultimate cognitions of being should be called metaphysical' (*Meditations*,
§60, emphasis in original). As far as the practice of the rest of his phenomenology is concerned, at one point he refers to 'the "ultimate and highest"
problems as phenomenological' ('Phenomenology', §15) while elsewhere he

---

[72] Towards the beginning of the previous section we saw how the concern not to mistake
linguistic analysis for thinking about what words mean acted as a partial impetus for
Husserl's idealism. What completed the impetus, it now appears, was the urge, not just to
think about what words mean, but to *say* (directly) what words mean. For a very clear
statement of the view that this concern and this urge together lead to metaphysical excess,
see Schlick (1959a), p. 57.

[73] How does this relate to the diagnosis mooted in the previous note? Roughly, when the
attempt to make maximally general sense of things *is* suitably informed by the attempt to
make sense of making sense of things, it becomes clear that the closest we can get to saying (directly) what words mean is saying how things must be for us to make the linguistic
sense of them that we do: see Moore (2010a).

characterizes metaphysics as 'the science of the ultimate and highest questions' (*Crisis*, §3).[74]

What Husserl does *not* see himself as engaged in is metaphysics 'in the customary sense' (*Meditations*, §60), an activity which he utterly abjures. He means the attempt to make sense of what is transcendent, not in *his* sense of what is transcendent (§4), but in the more colloquial and stronger sense whereby nothing transcendent can be given in consciousness. This includes much of what Kant would have counted as bad metaphysics (Ch. 5, §§2 and 6). But it also includes Kant's own concession that there may be subject-independent things in themselves. 'Phenomenology,' Husserl insists, '*excludes every naïve metaphysics* that operates with absurd things in themselves' (*Meditations*, §64, emphasis in original) – though revealingly, he straightway adds that it '*does not exclude metaphysics as such*' (emphasis in original).

It is worth pausing to reflect on where he thereby stands with respect to the Transcendence Question, which I posed in §6 of the Introduction. If transcendence is understood in this second sense, his answer is clear: there is no scope for metaphysicians to make sense of what is transcendent. If transcendence is understood in his own sense, his answer is less clear; or better, more subtle; or better still, in one respect more subtle. In another respect his answer is utterly straightforward: there *is* scope for metaphysicians to make sense of what is transcendent, for the simple reason that essences are transcendent (*Ideas* I, §59). The respect in which his answer is more subtle is that there is another, more oblique reason why metaphysicians can engage in transcendent sense-making, which has nothing to do with essences. They can engage in transcendent sense-making insofar as, having bracketed it, they are in a position to recover it (see §4 above; and see *Ideas* I, §76).[75]

We should consider, finally, what the point of the metaphysical exercise is for Husserl. The parenthetical comparison with Wittgenstein in §3 goes some way towards answering this question; but not far, because, as we have noted several times, for Wittgenstein – and I mean specifically the later Wittgenstein – there would be no rationale for anything of this sort were there not pernicious and debilitating confusions to combat. Husserl is much closer to Spinoza, Fichte, and Bergson, closer also to the early Wittgenstein,

---

[74] In *Ideas* I, §22, he also acknowledges that, insofar as it is 'metaphysical' to accept that there can be intuition of essences, phenomenology is metaphysical.

[75] A word also about where he stands with respect to the Novelty Question. In §6 of the Introduction I quoted P.F. Strawson's characterization of descriptive metaphysics as 'content to describe the actual structure of our thought about the world' (Strawson (1959), p. 9). In a way phenomenology is content to do that. But of course, Husserl believes that, in order to do that, it has to involve a radically new way of making sense of things. So one thing that Husserl does is to upset any simple assimilation of answers to the Novelty Question with Strawson's descriptive/revisionary contrast.

in recognizing a significance in the exercise beyond whatever restorative significance it has: an *ethical* significance. For the metaphysical exercise, properly conducted, brings us back from the factual questions with which the natural sciences are concerned to 'the questions which man … finds the most burning: questions of the meaning or meaninglessness of the whole of this human existence' (*Crisis*, §2). It brings us to 'the problems … of death, of fate, of the possibility of a "genuine" human life demanded as "meaningful" in a particular sense …, and all the further and still higher problems[:] … the *ethico-religious* problems' (*Meditations*, §64, some emphasis removed).

Further, because the metaphysical exercise is fundamentally a matter of self-exploration,[76] the proper conduct of it both fosters and contributes to individual integrity – which in turn, on Husserl's developed view, both fosters and contributes to the integrity of the wider community, even ultimately the community of man. In the final paragraph of the *Meditations* Husserl writes that 'the Delphic motto, "Know thyself!" has gained a new significance.' Early in the *Crisis* he gives a striking account of what this new signification is:

> We have … become aware in the most general way … that human philosophizing and its results in the whole of man's existence mean anything but merely private or otherwise limited cultural goals. In *our* philosophizing, then – how can we avoid it? – we are *functionaries of mankind*. The quite personal responsibility of our own true being as philosophers, our inner personal vocation, bears within itself at the same time the responsibility for the true being of mankind. (p. 17, emphasis in original)[77]

It is scarcely surprising that such metaphysical aspirations as these should lead to such metaphysical excesses as the espousal of idealism. Scarcely surprising, but not inevitable. In the next chapter we shall see Heidegger sharing many of the aspirations while avoiding many of the excesses.

---

[76] See again the passage from *Meditations*, §41, quoted in the previous section, where he refers to 'a universal phenomenology, as a self-explication of the ego.'

[77] See further *Crisis*, Pt I, passim, and Appendix, §I, passim. For a helpful discussion of Husserl's conception of philosophy, see Smith (2003), pp. 2–9.

CHAPTER 18

✦

Heidegger

Letting Being Be

1. Introduction

It was Husserl's great *protégé* Martin Heidegger (1889–1976) who did most, after Husserl, to propagate the phenomenological tradition. But he propagated it in ways that were at some remove from, indeed in certain critical respects opposed to, Husserl's own conception of the enterprise. He avoided many of Husserl's excesses, not by showing less ambition in the questions he addressed or in the spirit in which he addressed them, but by addressing them with more varied and more sophisticated tools. In the final section of this chapter we shall consider whether he avoided as much as he should have done.

2. Heidegger as Phenomenologist, *Pro* Husserl and *Contra* Husserl; or, Three Characterizations of Phenomenology

(a) First Characterization

Heidegger is an enthusiastic etymologist. Both in his own writing and in the attention he pays to the writing of others, he is very sensitive to how words speak to us through their origins.[1] So it is in the case of 'phenomenology'.

---

[1] This is a convenient excuse, at an early stage in this chapter, for me to say something about Heidegger's notorious writing style. Anyone previously unacquainted with his philosophy and opening *Being and Time* at random would be liable to have a harsh sense of linguistic butchery. (See e.g. the italicized paragraph at p. 437/p. 385 (referencing system explained below).) There are many points to be made in this connection. First, *Being and Time* is actually not all that typical, a fact that is somewhat obscured by one of the great curiosities of Heideggerian scholarship: the disproportionate amount of attention that is paid to this early, unfinished work. (I mean this less censoriously than it may sound. *Being and Time* is undoubtedly a central text.) Contrast, say, *History of the Concept of Time*, the supplemented text of a lecture course that Heidegger gave at the University of Marburg in 1925. The first two chapters of that book, i.e. §§4–9, provide an account of phenomenology whose language is, by philosophical standards, almost a model of unadulterated plain

The two Greek words at the roots of this word are '*phenomenon*' and '*logos*'. The first of these denotes that which shows itself.² The second has many meanings. It can be translated as 'reason', 'judgment', 'concept', 'word', and 'definition', among other things. On the interpretation that Heidegger takes to be most relevant in this context, it means 'discourse'. And it signals, in particular, that feature of a discourse whereby it makes its subject matter manifest, or lets its subject matter be seen. Phenomenology accordingly *lets*

speech – and which is incidentally far clearer than anything of comparable length and scope in Husserl. Second, Heidegger is very self-conscious both about his neologizing and about its aesthetic defects: see e.g. *Being and Time*, §7, final paragraph. Third, and related, early passages in *Being and Time* are much less likely to offend against anyone's linguistic sensibilities than later passages. Unorthodox language is used only once it has been defined. (The book is no different in this respect from an introductory logic text.) Finally, it is important to appreciate that Heidegger is often trying to make capital precisely out of his own wrenching of the language: see further §§6 and 7 below. Having said all of that in mitigation, I see no justification for Heidegger's belief, itself I suspect a contributory factor to his way of writing, that the Greek language is unique in being able to put us 'directly in the presence of the thing itself, not first in the presence of a mere word sign' (*What Is Philosophy?*, p. 45).

   Note: throughout this chapter I use the following abbreviations for Heidegger's works: 'Anaximander' for Heidegger (1984b); *Basic Concepts* for Heidegger (1993f); *Basic Problems* for Heidegger (1982b); *Basic Questions* for Heidegger (1994); *Being and Time* for Heidegger (1962a); *Contributions* for Heidegger (1999); 'Conversation' for Heidegger (1966); 'History of Being' for Heidegger (2003a); *History of the Concept of Time* for Heidegger (1985); 'Humanism' for Heidegger (1993c); 'Identity' for Heidegger (1969a); *Introduction* for Heidegger (1959); *Kant* for Heidegger (1962b); 'Logos' for Heidegger (1984c); *Metaphysical Foundations* for Heidegger (1992); *Nietzsche 1* for Heidegger (1979); *Nietzsche 2* for Heidegger (1984a); *Nietzsche 3* for Heidegger (1987); *Nietzsche 4* for Heidegger (1982a); 'Overcoming Metaphysics' for Heidegger (2003b); 'Technology' for Heidegger (1993d); 'The Constitution of Metaphysics' for Heidegger (1969b); 'The End of Philosophy' for Heidegger (1993e); *The Principle of Reason* for Heidegger (1991); 'The Question of Being' for Heidegger (1998); *Thinking* for Heidegger (1968b); 'Time and Being' for Heidegger (1972); 'Truth' for Heidegger (1993b); 'What Is Metaphysics?' for Heidegger (1993a); and *What Is Philosophy?* for Heidegger (1968a). Page references for *Being and Time* are in duplicate, first to the translation and then to the original German as indicated in the margins. All unaccompanied references are to *Being and Time*.

² We could also say that it denotes that which appears. But, as Heidegger warns, we must then beware that 'appearing' is also what is said to be done by that which, precisely without showing itself, is indicated by something else, as a disease is indicated by, or 'appears' in, its symptoms. The word 'appearance' can even be used to denote that which does the indicating, as the symptoms are an indication of, or an 'appearance' of, the disease. The ultimate example of this usage is to be found in Kant, where the word denotes that which does the indicating in contrast to that which is indicated and which *cannot* show itself, at least not to us (Kant (1998), A490/B518ff.; see Ch. 5, §4). A further complication is that something can be said to 'appear' precisely because there is no such thing: 'There is an appearance of bravado in his manner, but really he is extremely nervous.'

that which shows itself be seen. But we must be clear about the character of the seeing. There are indirect ways of seeing something, as when a doctor sees a disease by noticing its symptoms.[3] They are to be excluded. Phenomenology lets that which shows itself be seen 'from itself in the very way in which it shows itself from itself' (p. 58/p. 34).[4] 'But here,' Heidegger says, 'we are expressing nothing else than the maxim ...: "To the things themselves!"' (ibid.; see further, for the material in this paragraph, *Being and Time*, §7, and *History of the Concept of Time*, §9).

So far, then, so Husserlian.[5] In our own terms, and in evocation of the previous chapter, we can say that *phenomena* are what are immediately given in sense-making and that *logos* is sense-making. Phenomenology, in these terms, is making sense of that which is immediately given in sense-making, which is tantamount to making sense of making sense.[6] So far, to repeat, so Husserlian.

(b)   Second Characterization

Heidegger identifies the three 'decisive discoveries' of phenomenology as 'intentionality, categorial intuition, and the *a priori*' (*History of the Concept of Time*, p. 75). Intentionality we considered in §4 of the previous chapter. Categorial intuition is a species of the intuition of essences which we also considered in that section. It is the intuition of 'logical' essences, that is to say structural essences of the most general and most abstract kind, corresponding to such concepts as universality, number, and subjecthood.[7] As for the *a priori*, Heidegger believes that phenomenology has helped us beyond a conception of the *a priori* as a characteristic of certain ways of knowing to a conception of the *a priori* as a characteristic of certain ways of being. This third discovery is best understood in relation to the other two: the *a priori*, conceived ontologically, pertains to the intentional objects of categorial intuition. In fact, given the first discovery, the second and third can be regarded as variants of each other. As Heidegger himself puts it, 'these three discoveries ... are connected among themselves and ultimately grounded in the first' (*History of the Concept of Time*, p. 75). And together, afforced by the further idea that phenomenology is a descriptive exercise

---

[3] These correspond to the indirect ways indicated in the previous note in which a thing can appear.

[4] Cf. Husserl's 'principle of all principles', cited in parentheses at the end of §3 of the previous chapter.

[5] See the previous note, and see also the opening paragraph of §6 of the previous chapter.

[6] Cf. Hubert L. Dreyfus' claim, on p. 10 of Dreyfus (1991), that 'Heidegger's primary concern is ... to make sense of our ability to make sense of things.'

[7] There is much in this idea that would have given the early Wittgenstein pause: see Ch. 9, §§4 and 5.

rather than an explanatory exercise (p. 59/p. 35),[8] they suggest a second way of characterizing phenomenology: '*phenomenology is the analytic description of intentionality in its a priori*' (*History of the Concept of Time*, p. 79, emphasis in original). This too, Heidegger believes, serves to clarify the maxim 'To the things themselves' and is broadly in keeping with Husserl's own conception.

(c) Third Characterization

How then does Heidegger depart from Husserl? As phenomenologists, they have the same aim: to make sense of how we make sense of things. And they have the same basic methodological conviction: that making sense of how we make sense of things cannot be an exercise in what I dubbed in the previous chapter 'natural' sense-making. Husserl reacted by setting aside entirely the methods and principles of natural sense-making, then trying to replace them with those of a peculiarly phenomenological sense-making. There is one reading of Heidegger on which he thinks this was already a mistake, a drastic overreaction. On this reading, Heidegger agrees with Husserl that the tools of natural sense-making are inadequate for the phenomenological task in hand, but he does not agree that they are irrelevant to it. He is prepared to allow us, when we set about making sense of how we make natural sense of things, to avail ourselves of whatever natural sense of things we make; which is as much as to say that he eschews any phenomenological reduction. Such is the way in which he is often interpreted.[9]

This seems to me a misinterpretation.[10] The two thinkers seem to me far less opposed than that. As I see it, Heidegger accepts a version of the phenomenological reduction. He agrees with Husserl that phenomenological sense-making needs to be independent of mainstream natural sense-making. He even agrees that it can be pushed to a point of complete autonomy where it is independent of *all* other sense-making. Where he disagrees is over its field of enquiry, that is to say the transcendental Ego, the subject of all possible sense-making whose discovery Husserl takes to be the first and most important consequence of the phenomenological reduction. Heidegger does not deny that there is a subject of all possible sense-making, nor that it is in some sense the field of enquiry. But he differs from Husserl in how he construes it. For Husserl, the subject of all possible sense-making acts as a kind of limit of that of which any sense can be made: it neither need nor can be made distinctive phenomenological sense of in its own right. For Heidegger,

---

[8] Cf. the later Wittgenstein (Ch. 10, §1).
[9] See e.g. Copleston (1963), p. 435. Cf. Dreyfus (1991), p. 32, and Moran (2000), p. 228.
[10] I have been greatly helped by Crowell (1990). See also Jordan (1979) and Frede (2006), pp. 52ff.

as we shall see, making due phenomenological sense of the subject is itself a vital part of the phenomenological enterprise. Moreover, Heidegger does not think that there is any making sense of the subject independently of what lies beyond it. For Husserl, the subject is 'a self-contained system of Being ... which has no spatio-temporal exterior, and ... which cannot experience causality from anything nor exert causality upon anything' (Husserl (1962), §49, emphasis removed). For Heidegger,

> the idea of a subject which has intentional experiences merely inside its own sphere and is not yet outside it but encapsulated within itself is an absurdity which misconstrues the basic ontological structure of the being that we ourselves are. (*Basic Problems*, p. 64)[11]

It is wrong, then, to say that Heidegger eschews any phenomenological reduction. What we can say is that he eschews *Husserl's* phenomenological reduction, understood as a reduction to the transcendental Ego, itself understood in the attenuated sense highlighted above. We who make sense of things are planted firmly in the midst of the things of which we make sense. For Heidegger, there is no escaping this fact when it comes to making sense of how we do this. It is not that he denies that we must pay special attention to ourselves and to our peculiarities *vis-à-vis* the other things of which we make sense. On the contrary. 'We are ourselves the beings to be analyzed,' he says (p. 67/p. 41).[12] What Heidegger denies is that we must, nay can, pay the special attention to ourselves that we should have to pay in a pure phenomenology of the sort envisaged by Husserl; that which involves our prescinding from anything beyond ourselves.[13] If we accept the first 'decisive discovery' of phenomenology, namely that the way in which we are given things is through relations of intentionality, then we can rely on our phenomenological sense-making to reveal both the variety of things that we are thus given and the variety of forms that their givenness takes, and thereby work towards a synoptic account of our various ways of being in the world, our various ways of engaging with the world, our various ways of making sense of things (*Being and Time*, passim, esp. Pt One, Div. One, Chs II, IV, and VI).

---

[11] In Ch. 17, §6, we saw Husserl liken his view to Leibniz' monadology. That likeness is in effect what is at stake here. Heidegger unsurprisingly distances himself from it (the monadology): see *Basic Problems*, pp. 300–301.

[12] I have taken the liberty of replacing John Macquarrie's and Edward Robinson's 'entities' by 'beings' in their translation: see n. 15.

[13] This still leaves a great distance between Heidegger and naturalists. His own phenomenology, if not as pure as Husserl's, is still quite different from any of the standard human sciences – from human biology, most blatantly, but also from psychology or anthropology (p. 71/p. 45; cf. *History of the Concept of Time*, §4(c)) – albeit not different enough for Husserl's liking (see Husserl (1997)).

But what of the Husserlian ambition to go further than this, to proceed
from such an account to an account of the intrinsic nature of the things of
which we make sense? Heidegger shares this ambition. The slogan 'Back to
the things themselves' indicates, for Heidegger no less than for Husserl, a
concern to say, not just what it is for us to make sense of things in the various ways in which we do, but what it is for things to be the various ways
we make sense of them as being. In fact, his ambition is to go further still.
He distinguishes between the things of which we make sense, or at least of
which we make natural sense, and their very reality,[14] that which at the most
fundamental level they share with us and that which at the most fundamental level allows us to make sense of them. He distinguishes, as he himself
puts it, between beings and Being (see e.g. §2).[15] And he aspires to give an
account of the latter. He wants to understand what Being is, the different
forms it takes, and what its significance is. That is, he wants to make sense
of Being.

From the very outset of *Being and Time* he parades this as his aim:

> Do we in our time have an answer to the question of what we really mean
> by the word 'being' ['*seiende*'][16]? Not at all. So it is fitting that we should
> raise anew *the question of the meaning of Being*. But are we nowadays
> even perplexed at our inability to understand the expression 'Being'? Not
> at all. So first of all we must reawaken an understanding for the mean-
> ing of this question. Our aim in the following treatise is to work out the
> question of the meaning of Being and to do so concretely. (p. 19/p. 1,
> emphasis in original; cf. *History of the Concept of Time*, p. 85)[17]

Can Heidegger pursue this aim without lapsing into an idealism such as
Husserl's? We shall return to this issue in the final section. But it would
certainly not be absurd to suppose that he can. For, in crucial contrast
to Husserl, he will not be addressing his question within the framework

---

[14] I use the term 'reality' here in as neutral a way as possible. Heidegger himself uses it in
various more restricted ways: see e.g. pp. 166, 228, and 254–255/pp. 128, 183, and 211.

[15] The original German words are '*Seiendes*' and '*Sein*'. Translators differ in how they register this distinction. In *Being and Time* John Macquarrie and Edward Robinson usually
translate '*Seiendes*' as 'entities' and '*Sein*' as 'Being' with a capital 'B': see their n. 1 on
p. 19. I have altered their translations throughout as far as the former and its cognates are
concerned, because I prefer 'beings'. But I have followed their practice as far as the latter
is concerned. This is principally to avoid some potential confusions, e.g. in the phrase 'sort
of being' which will feature prominently in the following section. I shall also take the liberty of adapting the renderings of other translators to conform with this practice.

[16] This is the present participle, different from either of the nouns mentioned in the
previous note.

[17] Cf. the end of his essay 'What Is Metaphysics?', where he adverts to what he calls 'the
basic question of metaphysics', *viz*. 'Why are there beings at all, and why not rather

provided by the transcendental Ego, at least not as understood by Husserl. He will be addressing it in terms of the very things, including himself and other people, of which he and other people make sense.

Heidegger's project is therefore at once more sweeping than Husserl's and more piecemeal. It is at once more ambitious in its philosophical aims and less liable to metaphysical excess. By concerning himself with the variety of things of which we make sense, he will attempt to provide an account of Being itself. Here is his own elegant summary of how he departs from Husserl:

> Being is to be laid hold of and made our theme. Being is always Being of beings and accordingly it becomes accessible at first only by start-ing with some being.... Apprehension of Being ... always turns, at first and necessarily, to some being; but then, *in a precise way, it is led away* from that being *and back to its Being.* We call this basic component of phenomenological method ... *phenomenological reduction.* We are thus adopting a central term of Husserl's phenomenology in its literal word-ing though not in its substantive intent. *For Husserl,* phenomenological reduction ... is the method of leading phenomenological vision from the natural attitude of the human being whose life is involved in the world of things and persons back to the transcendental life of consciousness and its *noetic-noematic*[18] experiences, in which objects are constituted as cor-relates of consciousness. *For us* phenomenological reduction means lead-ing phenomenological vision back from the apprehension of a being ... to the understanding of the Being of this being. (*Basic Problems,* p. 21, emphasis in original)[19]

nothing?' (p. 110). – Note that the metaphor of concreteness, which occurs at the end of this quotation, recurs at p. 29/p. 9, where Heidegger asks, concerning his question, 'Does it simply remain – or *is* it at all – a mere matter for soaring speculation about the most general of generalities, *or is it rather, of all questions, both the most basic and the most concrete?'* (emphasis in original). He clearly hopes to convince us that it is the latter. Here there is a curious link with Wittgenstein. Wittgenstein, in Wittgenstein (1961), 5.5563, writes, 'Our problems are not abstract, but perhaps the most concrete that there are.'

[18] '*Noematic*' is the adjective corresponding to the noun '*noema*' which was introduced in its plural form in §4 of the previous chapter. '*Noetic*' is the adjective corresponding to the noun '*noesis*'. Where a *noema* is roughly some way in which an object can be given, a *noesis* is roughly some act of an object's being given in some way. See Husserl (1962), Ch. 10, passim.

[19] Immediately after this quotation Heidegger emphasizes the difficulty of the enterprise. 'Being,' he says, 'does not become accessible like a being. We do not simply find it in front of us.... [It] must always be *brought to view*' (ibid., pp. 21–22, emphasis added; cf. *History of the Concept of Time*, pp. 87–88). Again there are comparisons to be drawn with Wittgenstein: cf. Ch. 10, n. 15, and Ch. 17, §3, the material in parentheses at the end.

Heidegger is now able to give a third characterization of phenomenology: '*phenomenology is the science of the Being of beings*' (p. 61/p. 37, emphasis added).[20]

3. The Execution of the Project. *Dasein*

Heidegger's point of departure in his quest for an understanding of Being is the recognition that not only are there different sorts of beings, there are different kinds of Being.[21]

The 'not only' in this sentence may give pause. Is there any need to acknowledge differences between kinds of Being beyond whatever differences there are between sorts of beings? If the kind of Being that I enjoy is different from the kind of Being that Neptune enjoys, can this not be accounted for by differences between me and Neptune, or more generally by differences between people and planets? Or is the point that beings of the same sort, if not the very same being, can enjoy Being of more than one kind – as perhaps a living person and a dead person enjoy Being of two fundamentally different kinds?

These questions raise all manner of issues, some of them purely terminological, about how kinds of Being are individuated, about how sorts of beings are individuated, and about how beings themselves are individuated, which for current purposes we do not need to probe too deeply. (As it happens, Heidegger individuates the most fundamental sorts of beings, and indeed beings themselves, very finely. Thus reconsider the dead. Heidegger taps something at the very core of human sensibility by accounting a dead person – by which is meant here a corpse – a fundamentally different sort of being both from a living person and from a 'mere' physical object. And he uses that familiar philosophical device, the use of the word '*qua*', to distinguish between the person *qua* living and the person *qua* dead, the former of which can be said to end when the latter begins (§47, esp. pp. 281–282/p. 238). Elsewhere he even goes as far as to distinguish between 'the "source" which the geographer establishes for a river' and 'the "springhead in the dale"' (p. 100/p. 70).[22]) All that matters for current purposes is that we have a basic and relatively clear conception of a sort of being, likewise of a kind of Being, whereby, first, there is a plurality of each and, second, even if they are

---

[20] For very helpful discussions of the material considered in the section (albeit not always taking the same line as I do), see Dreyfus (1991), Introduction and Chs 1 and 2; Mulhall (1996), Introduction; Moran (2000), pp. 226–230; and Carman (2006).

[21] If it were not for connotations from elsewhere in this book (see esp. Ch. 2, §2), we would do well to call them not 'kinds' of Being, but 'modes' of Being. For they are different ways to be.

[22] We shall return to this, and to its significance, in the final section.

aligned, they are nevertheless distinct. This second point is all that the 'not only' was intended to signal.[23]

Now any being, Heidegger says, 'is either a *"who"* ... or a *"what"*' (p. 71/p. 45, emphasis in original). And the most fundamental difference between kinds of Being is the difference between the kinds of Being that are peculiarly enjoyed by 'whos' and the kinds of Being that are peculiarly enjoyed by 'whats'.

Let us begin with 'whos' and the most general kind of Being that is peculiarly enjoyed by them. Heidegger's own word for this sort of being is the German word '*Dasein*'.[24] This is a departure both from typical philosophical usage and from more everyday usage. On each of these the word pertains to Being rather than to beings. Thus philosophers typically use it as, in effect, another word for Being (of any kind). And in its more everyday usage, it is restricted to Being of one specific kind. In fact it is restricted to Being of the very kind that now concerns us: the most general kind that is peculiarly enjoyed by 'whos'. This makes Heidegger's usage closer to the latter. Even so, they are not the same. On Heidegger's usage, to repeat, the word designates, not that kind of Being, but that sort of being.[25] The word does nevertheless evoke, in its own way, what that kind of Being comes to; that is, what it can be seen, after due phenomenological work, to come to. It does this through its etymology, to which Heidegger is as ever sensitive and which he occasionally registers by hyphenating the word ('*Da-sein*'). For '*Dasein*' is constructed from '*Sein*', the word for Being, and '*da*', meaning 'here' or 'there'. And *Dasein*'s peculiar kind of Being is, in a sense, a way of being here or being there.[26]

In what sense though? What is *Dasein*? What does it take to be a 'who'?

Intentionality is primordial here.[27] *Dasein* is characterized by its various intentional relations to other beings. In fact it is constituted by such relations (e.g. pp. 73–74/p. 48 and *Metaphysical Foundations*, p. 167). They are in a sense antecedent to it. It follows that there is no conceiving of *Dasein* save in a way that involves the objects of its intentional acts: the things, as I put it in the previous section, in whose midst it is firmly planted and of which it makes sense. So the kind of Being that *Dasein* enjoys is indeed a way of

---

[23] Cf., in connection with the issues raised in this paragraph, Wittgenstein (1969), p. 58, and Quine (1960), pp. 241–242 (to which ibid., §27, is further relevant).

[24] In common with most Anglophone commentators, and indeed with most of his translators, I will leave this word untranslated. In what follows I have taken the liberty of amending the few translations in which this practice is not followed.

[25] Indeed he even occasionally uses it as a sortal noun to denote the beings themselves. See e.g. p. 92/p. 64, where he asks a question about 'every *Dasein*,' and p. 284/p. 240, where he says that 'one *Dasein* can ..., within certain limits, "be" another *Dasein*' (emphasis removed).

[26] Cf. the translators' n. 1 on p. 27; and Hofstadter (1982).

[27] As of course it was for Husserl.

being *here* or being *there*, among other beings. It is, in one of Heidegger's most celebrated and most expressive coinages, 'Being-in-the-world' (Pt One, Div. One, Ch. II).

This is clearly a non-Cartesian conception of *Dasein*.[28] In this respect it is in line with much that we have witnessed in this enquiry since its opening chapter. Where Heidegger is perhaps at his most innovative, as far as these ideas go, is in his insistence that these relations of intentionality are, 'primarily and for the most part',[29] *practical* (see e.g. *Basic Problems*, §15(c)). *Dasein* has concerns and projects, and it is fundamentally *engaged* with the world as it pursues these concerns and projects. It is related to things as to equipment, equipment that it uses thus or so and for this or that purpose. The *contemplative* relations of intentionality on which philosophers have tended to focus are arrived at only as a kind of abstraction from these practical relations, when 'concern holds back from any kind of producing, manipulating and the like' (p. 88/p. 61). Heidegger expresses this both forcefully and amusingly in the following passage:

> The ontological distinction … between ego and non-ego … cannot in any way be conceived directly and simply, as for instance in the form that Fichte uses … when he says, 'Gentlemen, think the wall, and then think the one who thinks the wall.'[30] There is already a constructive violation of the facts, an unphenomenological onset, in the request 'Think the wall'…. The request 'Think the wall,' understood as the beginning of a return to the one who is thinking the wall, as the beginning of the philosophical interpretation of the subject, is saying: Make yourselves blind to what is already given to you in the very first place…. But what is thus antecedently given? How do the beings with which we dwell show themselves to us primarily and for the most part? Sitting here in the auditorium, we do not in fact apprehend walls – not unless we are getting bored…. What is primarily given … is a thing-*contexture*.
>
> In order to see this we must formulate more clearly what *thing* means in this context and what ontological character the things have that are the initial beings here. The *nearest things* that surround us we call *equipment*. There is always already a manifold of equipment: equipment for working, for travelling, for measuring, and in general things with which we have to do. (*Basic Problems*, pp. 162–163, emphasis in original)

This difference between *Dasein*'s practical engagement with things and its contemplative engagement with things maps onto another fundamental difference that Heidegger wishes to draw between kinds of Being, this time between kinds of Being enjoyed by 'whats'. 'Whats' with which *Dasein* is

---

[28] And it goes with a non-Cartesian conception of what is not *Dasein*: cf. §§19–24.
[29] This phrase is taken from the quotation indented immediately below.
[30] See Smith (1889), p. 85.

practically engaged are 'ready-to-hand'[31] (p. 98/p. 69; cf. *Basic Problems*, pp. 162ff.). 'Whats' with which *Dasein* is contemplatively engaged are 'present-at-hand'[32] (p. 67/p. 42; cf. *Basic Problems*, p. 109).[33]

But let us return to *Dasein* itself and its various kinds of Being. One of the reasons why *Dasein* is an appropriate starting point for any enquiry into Being, as Heidegger points out, is that it is itself there from the start (§2; cf. *Basic Problems*, p. 19). *Dasein* is precisely the sort of being that conducts such an enquiry. It is the sort of being that raises and addresses the questions that we have been raising and are now addressing. It is the sort of being for which Being is an issue (cf. pp. 32 and 67–68/pp. 12 and 42).[34]

But there is another, more particular sense in which *Dasein* is the sort of being for which Being is an issue. *Its own* Being is an issue for it. It not only engages with that which is ready-to-hand or present-at-hand. It confronts questions about *how* to engage with such things, about which possibilities to realize, about how to act out its own Being. *Dasein* understands itself in terms of what it expects, including what it expects of its own future self, and in terms of what it retains, including what it retains of its own former self. Heidegger expresses this in terms of what he calls the 'ecstases' of temporality (pp. 376ff./pp. 328ff.). He is alluding to the Greek word '*ekstatikon*', which denotes a stepping outside of oneself. For by the ecstases of temporality he means the temporal aspects of *Dasein*'s intentional relations to beings and possibilities beyond its own present self, for instance the futurity of its expectations, whereby it so to speak steps outside itself. In the same vein, and yet again showing sensitivity to etymology, Heidegger reserves the word 'existence' (which derives from the Latin '*ex*', meaning 'out of', and '*sistere*', meaning 'to stand') for 'that kind of Being towards which *Dasein* can comport itself in one way or another, and always does comport itself somehow' (p. 32/p. 12). It follows that existence, so understood, is another kind of Being that is peculiar to 'whos'.

It is clear, even from this lightning summary of what Heidegger says about the Being of *Dasein*, that time is of crucial significance to it. And indeed, because of the centrality of *Dasein* to Heidegger's account of Being

---

[31] The German word is '*zuhanden*'. Translators differ in how they render it. I shall take the liberty of amending all translations in which it is not rendered as 'ready-to-hand'.

[32] The German word is '*vorhanden*'. Translators differ in how they render this too. I shall take the liberty of amending all translations in which it is not rendered as 'present-at-hand'.

[33] See further §§14–18 and *Basic Problems*, §15.

[34] Paul Ricoeur, in Ricoeur (1968), says in this connection that *Dasein*'s thinking of Being is 'a thinking of Being, in which the genitive "of Being" is at once both "subjective" and "objective"' (p. 91). That seems to me to sit uneasily with the fact that such thinking is an activity of beings, not of Being. But what we can say with respect to *Dasein* is that the question of its Being, in the sense of the question *about* its Being, is a question of its Being, in the sense of a question *emanating from* its Being.

more generally, time is likewise of crucial significance to what he says about the Being of 'whats'. It is in temporal terms that *Dasein* makes sense of anything. It is in temporal terms that anything, including *Dasein* itself, makes sense. *Dasein* is guided in everything it does by its own future possibilities, constrained in everything it does by its own past encounters and commitments, always engaged with what is currently given to it as ready-to-hand or as present-at-hand.[35] Such is the nature of its existence. Similarly, the way in which it is engaged with what is currently given to it is as enabling it to realize or to shun some of those future possibilities, or as tokens of some of those past encounters or commitments. Such is the nature of its sense-making. Such indeed is its nature. For it is of the very essence of *Dasein* to make sense of things. (See esp. *Basic Problems*, pp. 275ff.) Its own Being, which is an issue for it, is Being-in-the-world among other beings; and it can only address the issue of its own Being in terms of their Being, by grasping the possibilities that they afford it, which is to say by making sense of them. It must, to use one of Heidegger's most important words, *care* about them. (See esp. Pt One, Div. One, Ch. VI, entitled 'Care as the Being of *Dasein*'.) But such also is the nature of the things of which it makes sense. Their Being is their Being as made sense of by it. (Recall that 'the "source" which the geographer establishes for a river is not the "springhead in the dale".'[36]) The temporality of *Dasein* is therefore their temporality. The meaning of Being, which is what Heidegger has been seeking, is in a sense time.[37]

The remarks in this section do not of course begin to do justice to Heidegger's execution of his project, which includes countless achievements towards which I have not even gestured. Among these are:

- his treatment of the way in which existence, that kind of Being which is peculiarly *Dasein*'s, can be authentic or inauthentic, depending on whether the choices that *Dasein* makes are truly its
- his discussion of language and its role in *Dasein*'s making sense of things[38]
- his insights into mortality and the way in which it allows *Dasein*'s Being to be characterized, in yet another of the evocative terms that he coins, as 'Being-towards-death'

and many more. I must pass over all of these. One reason for this is that my primary concern remains with meta-metaphysics, and I need now to

---

[35] In Heidegger's own words, *Dasein*, 'resolutely open to what is to come and preserving what has been, sustains and gives shape to what is present' (*Nietzsche 2*, p. 99, adapted from plural to singular).

[36] Cf. also p. 34/p. 13.

[37] Cf. p. 38/p. 17. And cf. Sheehan (2003), §2.

[38] Note in particular his Wittgensteinian emphasis on the variety of 'language-games' we play at p. 204/p. 161 (see Ch. 10, §2). – I shall have a little to say about the role of language in *Dasein*'s making sense of things in Ch. 20, §3.

turn from how Heidegger executes his metaphysical project – let there be no doubt, incidentally, that the project that he executes *is* a metaphysical one, an attempt to make maximally general sense of things; I shall say some more about this in §5 – to how he conceives it. How he conceives it is a matter, very largely, of how he situates it in the history of metaphysics as a whole.[39]

4. Overcoming the Tradition

Heidegger's view is that, where the aim of metaphysicians should be to make sense of Being, and was at the inception of their discipline in the West to make sense of Being, they have for some two thousand years allowed this aim to become submerged by others and have been preoccupied instead with beings (see e.g. 'History of Being'). We need to recapture that feeling of mystery, that feeling of astonishment, that feeling of disturbance, which Being itself once induced.[40] And 'we' here does not just mean 'we metaphysicians'. The suppression of these feelings is part of *Dasein*'s 'everyday' encounters with things.[41]

---

[39] Among the many excellent discussions of how he executes it, and in particular of how he executes the parts of it that I have highlighted, see Dreyfus (1991), Ch. 3; Cooper (1996), Ch. 3; Mulhall (1996), Introduction and Ch. 1; Inwood (1997), Chs 3 and 4; Moran (2000), Ch. 7, passim; King (2001), Ch. 1; and Glendinning (2007), pp. 59–82. For a superb account specifically of how time features in the project, see Turetzky (1998), pp. 182–193. For a fascinating account of how language features in the project, see Brandom (2002e). (But this essay contains some flaws. In particular, beware a tendency to construe *Dasein* as a kind of Being. Also helpful, though suffering from the same flaw, is Brandom (2002d).)

[40] 'Once' induced? Heidegger begins *Being and Time* with a quotation from Plato's *Sophist*, 244a, in which one of Plato's protagonists expresses perplexity at what is meant by 'being' ['*seiende*' – see above, n. 16]. And in *What Is Philosophy?*, pp. 79 and 81, he cites Plato's *Theaetetus*, 155d, and Aristotle's *Metaphysics*, Bk A, Ch. 2, 982b 12ff., to show that both Plato and Aristotle saw philosophy as grounded in wonder and astonishment. But really Heidegger wants us to recapture something older still. Already in Plato there was, he believes, a wrong turn: see pp. 47–48/p. 25 and *Basic Questions*, p. 120.

[41] This is reminiscent of the anti-Wittgensteinian suggestion that I canvassed in Ch. 10, §6, that we need to return from the everyday to the properly metaphysical. The matter is complicated however. The everyday for Wittgenstein was to be understood as the authentic. Not so for Heidegger; precisely not. 'We understand ourselves in an everyday way,' he says at one point, immediately adding, 'or ... *not authentically* in the strict sense of the word, ... [i.e.] not as we at bottom are *able* to be own to ourselves' (*Basic Problems*, p. 160, emphasis in original; cf. *Kant*, §§42ff.). An additional complication within this complication is that Heidegger is at pains to distinguish between the inauthentic in *Dasein*'s everyday self-understanding and that which would prevent it from counting as genuine self-understanding. Given all of this, and given also the effort that we saw Wittgenstein expend in Ch. 10, §5, in trying to extricate the everyday in his sense from the

Heidegger talks a great deal about *Dasein*'s 'falling' (e.g. §38). He insists that 'this term does not express any negative evaluation' (p. 220/p. 175). But we can hardly fail to hear its religious overtones. Nor are these irrelevant to this neglecting of Being, or this 'forgetting' of Being, on our part.[42] Our situation as Heidegger conceives it is not unlike man's situation in the traditional Judæo-Christian myth of the Fall – even to the extent that it has been brought on by our pursuit of a certain way of making sense of things (Genesis:3).[43] We are, in Heidegger's view, in the grip of a kind of naturalism. We have been proceeding as if the only way to make sense of things is the (natural-)scientific way. But the only things that can be made sense of in that way are beings. In fact, within the parameters set by certain paradigms of scientific investigation, the only things that can be made sense of in that way are 'whats': 'whats' that are present-at-hand, of no intrinsic value, subject to invariant laws, and susceptible to our most fundamental categories of thought – even while remaining completely independent of that thought. And so it is that Being has either been ignored completely or been treated on the model of such 'whats', as something which, 'over against becoming … is permanence[,] over against appearance … is the always identical[,] over against thought … is … the already-there[,] over against the ought … is the datum …'; as something which, in sum, is 'enduring presence' (*Introduction*, p. 202).[44] We need to rekindle an awareness of Being as something *strange*, something which differs fundamentally from beings and resists any attempt on our part to make the same kind of sense of it as we make of them.[45] We need, in fact, to relearn the elemental lesson of phenomenology, a lesson of which ancient thinkers, it now appears, already had a rudimentary grasp. For granted that Being is 'that on the basis of which beings are already understood' (pp. 25–26/p. 6), to make sense of it is to make sense of how sense is made of things. In effect, then, we are being invited to consider afresh the truly remarkable and singular fact that sense is made of anything, and to try to make sense of that (cf. *Basic Problems*, p. 227).

---

everyday in any more colloquial sense, it would be rash indeed to jump to the conclusion that there is a direct opposition between the two thinkers here. It is far more probable, in fact, that they are offering variations on a single theme. (For a very helpful discussion of Heidegger's conception of the everyday, see Mulhall (1996), pp. 106–109. And see again Mulhall (1994), cited in Ch. 10, n. 9.)

[42] For Heidegger's definition of 'forgetting', see pp. 262 and 388–389/pp. 219 and 339, and *Kant*, pp. 241–242.

[43] Cf. 'Truth', §6. For a fascinating discussion of Heidegger in this connection, see Mulhall (2005), Ch. 2.

[44] Cf. §44 (a). In Chapter 20 we shall see Derrida develop this emphasis on presence.

[45] Cf. Bergson's pitting of intuition against analysis (Ch. 16, §2).

In describing Being as strange I am skirting one of the basic paradoxes of Being: that it is at once that which is most alien to us and that which is most familiar. It is that which is most alien to us precisely because we allow beings to occupy all our attention. It is that which is most familiar to us because it is that on the basis of which we understand beings. Indeed, as we saw in the previous section, and indirectly in the previous chapter, the investigation of Being must be at root a self-investigation.[46] (I shall come back to this point at the end of the section.)

To overcome the alienation – to let Being itself, in all its familiarity, become an object of attention – is classic phenomenology. It is to let that which shows itself properly be seen. It is also to let Being, in its own distinctive way, properly be.[47]

I said at the end of the previous section that Heidegger's conception of his own project is very largely a matter of how he situates it in the history of metaphysics. We are now in a position to see why. He sees it as a *recalling* of something forgotten. Much of his work is accordingly devoted to an exploration of how ancient thinkers managed to do what we should now be trying to do (e.g. 'Anaximander' and 'Logos'). But not only that. Much of it is also devoted to an account of what has happened in the interim. And so it must be. For although the aim is to recall something, this recalling has to be accomplished in the position in which we now find ourselves. We cannot simply put our circumstances to one side, as though the past two thousand years had never been. We must work through what has happened. We must work *with* what has happened. The project is in one sense very straightforward: to let that which is already fully visible be seen. But given that we are still not looking properly, the project is in another sense very far from straightforward.[48] We are like the sailors in Neurath's image.[49] We must refashion our ways of making sense of things

---

[46] Cf. p. 36/p. 15 and p. 69/p. 43, where Heidegger makes the related point that *Dasein* is that which is in one respect 'closest and well known', in another 'the farthest and not known at all.' Cf. also *Basic Concepts*, §2; *What Is Philosophy?*, p. 27; and *Thinking*, p. 110.

[47] Cf. 'Truth', §7. Cf. also Clark (1990), p. 19. But note that 'in its own distinctive way' is a crucial qualification. There is certainly a sense in which only beings, not Being, can be said to be: see e.g. 'Time and Being', pp. 3ff. and 18. (The phrase 'let Being be' is not Heidegger's own. He talks of letting *beings* be. Both here and in the very title of this chapter I am taking a liberty. But the point is really just to indicate, however schematically, that Being can be made sense of and that making sense of Being 'is itself a definite characteristic of *Dasein*'s Being' (p. 32/p. 12, emphasis removed).)

[48] See again the material in n. 19.

[49] But not, obviously, on the interpretation of that image in terms of scientific beliefs to which I alluded at the beginning of the previous chapter.

while continuing *pro tempore* to make sense of things in those very ways. Here is Heidegger:

> The ontological investigation which we are now conducting is determined by its historical situation and, therewith, … by the preceding philosophical tradition. The store of basic philosophical concepts derived from the philosophical tradition is still so influential today that this effect of tradition can hardly be overestimated…. [All] philosophical discussion, even the most radical attempt to begin all over again, is pervaded by traditional concepts and thus by traditional horizons and traditional angles of approach…. It is for this reason that there necessarily belongs to the conceptual interpretation of Being and its structures … a *destruction* – a critical process in which the traditional concepts, which at first must necessarily be employed, are deconstructed down to the sources from which they were drawn….
>
> … This is not a negation of the tradition or a condemnation of it as worthless; quite the reverse, it signifies precisely a positive appropriation of the tradition…. 'History of philosophy', as it is called, … belongs to the concept of phenomenological investigation. (*Basic Problems*, pp. 21–23, emphasis in original)[50]

Much of Heidegger's historical work is concerned with thinkers with whom this book too has been concerned. Thus Descartes' model of representation, Leibniz' idealism, Kant's subject-based conception of objectivity, and Hegel's belief in the subjectivity of the infinite all come under his scrutiny. All are symptomatic for Heidegger of a failure to reckon with Being and a consequent attempt to find relations between beings and/or properties of beings that can do its work (see e.g. §§6 and 82 and 'Overcoming Metaphysics').[51]

There is one respect in which the case of Hegel is especially instructive. Heidegger holds that *Dasein* always enjoys a radical particularity. As he himself puts it, '*Dasein* has in each case mineness' (p. 68/p. 42, emphasis removed). That is why 'one must always use a personal pronoun when one addresses it: "I am", "you are"' (ibid., emphasis removed). Not so for Hegel. Hegel believed in a 'who' that was a universal, not a particular. This 'who' had (historically situated) *instances*, or moments, which brought it to a full

---

[50] Cf. *Introduction*, pp. 44–45, and *What Is Philosophy?*, pp. 67–69. Cf. also 'Overcoming Metaphysics', §IX, where he writes, 'At first the overcoming of metaphysics can only be represented in terms of metaphysics itself, so to speak, in the manner of a heightening of itself through itself.'

[51] At the same time, of course, they are symptomatic of a sense of what that work is. Heidegger is far from believing that these thinkers had *no* idea what form proper metaphysics should take. For a sympathetic account of how (e.g.) Kant began to give metaphysics suitable reorientation, see *Kant*, esp. §One.

knowledge of itself (Hegel (1979), ¶¶793 and 797). From a Heideggerian point of view it could be regarded as a being drafted in to do the work of Being.

In another respect too the case of Hegel is especially instructive. By not registering this fundamental difference between Being and beings, still less any of the differences between kinds of Being, and by placing so much emphasis on the subject's progression from self-identity to self-knowledge, Hegel clearly lined up on one side of what has come to be a crucial dichotomy in this narrative: he prioritized identity over difference (cf. Ch. 15, §7(b), and Ch. 16, §4). Heidegger questions this prioritization (see e.g. 'Identity' and 'The Constitution of Metaphysics').

But the philosopher whose position in the prior history of metaphysics has greatest apocalyptic significance for Heidegger is Nietzsche, with whom he engages at especially great length (*Nietzsche 1* to *Nietzsche 4*). He argues that it was here in the history of metaphysics that traditional metaphysics really came to an end, not because Nietzsche managed to leave it behind, nor yet because he ensured that it would thereafter be left behind, but rather because he practised it in what had by then become the one remaining form that it could still take: an utter repudiation of anything transcendent; an utter revolt against Plato (see e.g. *Nietzsche 1*, Ch. 1; *Nietzsche 2*, Pt One, passim; and *Nietzsche 4*, Ch. 22). Traditional metaphysics had now 'gone through the sphere of prefigured possibilities' ('Overcoming Metaphysics', §XII). Nietzsche did not himself properly confront Being, then. But his idea of eternal return, which Nietzsche described as 'the closest approximation of a world of becoming to a world of being' (Nietzsche (1967b), §617, emphasis removed) was in Heidegger's view 'Nietzsche's attempt to think the Being of beings' (*Thinking*, pp. 109–110). And it prepared the way, through its exhaustion of what had prevailed thus far, for something radically new.[52]

Heidegger's excursions into the history of metaphysics, together with the anti-naturalism of which they are an expression, may suggest that what he is trying to reverse is something fundamentally intellectual. Not so. In fact, one thing that epitomizes what he is trying to reverse, if indeed it does not exhaust it, is *technology*. To be sure, Heidegger has an extremely broad conception of technology, which he takes to be (the use of) any means to some end, or (the instrument of) any human activity ('Technology', pp. 311–318).[53] That embraces the intellectual, certainly. But it embraces much else besides.

Precisely what technology has done in the past, Heidegger argues, and precisely what it increasingly does nowadays, is to make beings manifest

---

[52] For further discussion, see Sluga (2004).

[53] Cf. 'Overcoming Metaphysics', §X, where he writes that technology includes 'objectified nature, the business of culture, manufactured politics, and the gloss of ideals overlying everything.'

in a way that allows Being to remain concealed. It presents beings – even 'whos' – as nothing but an ever-available *resource*, or what Heidegger calls 'standing-reserve' (e.g. 'Technology', p. 329) And, as a result, it blinds us to what it is about them, namely their Being, that marks them out as more than that and that makes any of them worth caring about. It rams beings themselves, sometimes quite literally, down our throats. Indeed it does this so relentlessly that not only do we fail to reckon with Being, and in particular with our own Being, we place that very Being in jeopardy. Technology has the power to obliterate us altogether.[54] But even if it does not do that, there is something else that it both has the power to do and does do. It subjugates us and assimilates us to itself, reducing us to 'whats' rather than 'whos' ('Overcoming Metaphysics', §XXVI). It militates against that questioning of Being which is of our essence. As Heidegger puts it, in a sentence that will resonate in all sorts of ways within contemporary academia:

> An age which regards as real only what goes fast and can be clutched with both hands looks on questioning as 'remote from reality' and as something that does not pay, whose benefits cannot be numbered. (*Introduction*, p. 206)

That is the sort of thing that Heidegger is trying to reverse. (See 'Truth', §5, and 'Technology', passim.) It is in this vein that Heidegger is prepared to identify technology, in the form that it has nowadays assumed, with 'completed metaphysics' – where by 'metaphysics' he means traditional metaphysics, and where by 'completed' metaphysics he means, as we saw earlier, metaphysics that has exhausted all its possibilities, not metaphysics that will no longer be practised ('Overcoming Metaphysics', §X; cf. ibid., §XII).[55]

What is needed, then, is a restoration of metaphysics as it should be.[56] We need to let Being be, which is as much as to say that we need to let Being be seen to be. We need to 'shepherd the mystery of Being' ('Overcoming Metaphysics', §XXVII). This in turn requires us to be open to what Heidegger calls '*Ereignis*'. This German word is standardly translated as 'event'. But for Heidegger it serves as a technical term to designate the very givenness of what is given. The temporal overtones of the word are not lost, because

---

[54] 'The labouring animal,' Heidegger graphically writes, 'is left to the giddy whirl of its products so that it may tear itself to pieces and annihilate itself in empty nothingness' ('Overcoming Metaphysics', §III).

[55] For helpful discussions of Heidegger on technology, see Cooper (1996), Ch. 5; Young (2002), Ch. 3, esp. pp. 44–55; and Pattison (2005), Ch. 3.

[56] Here as in Kant, metaphysics as it should be is the only thing that can effectively be pitted against metaphysics of the misguided guide. Cf. 'Overcoming Metaphysics', §IX, where Heidegger himself makes the comparison with Kant. Cf. also the way in which 'the essential unfolding of technology harbours *in itself* what we least suspect, the possible rise of the saving power' ('Technology', p. 337, emphasis added).

what is given is given in time. But *Ereignis* is not itself an event, as ordinarily understood. It is what makes such events possible. (Cf. 'Time and Being', pp. 17–19.) And it creates a metaphorical space in which all that can appear can appear. If we enter that space and look properly, then metaphysics 'can return transformed, and remain in dominance as the continuing difference of Being and beings' ('Overcoming Metaphysics', §II, transposed from the third-person singular to the infinitive).

The demand to restore metaphysics as it should be is an ethical demand. It is a demand for us to make sense of Being, including, centrally, our own Being, and thereby to be true to ourselves. This is reminiscent of Spinoza, Fichte, Bergson, and especially Husserl (see Ch. 17, §7). Heidegger would agree with all four of these thinkers that practising metaphysics well is of a piece with living well. And he would agree in particular with Husserl that it brings us to 'the problems ... of death, of fate, and of the possibility of a "genuine" human life,' in such a way that 'the Delphic motto "Know thyself!" gains a new signification' (Husserl (1995), §64, slightly adapted). The connections are however even more intimate for Heidegger than they are for Husserl. Heidegger believes that

> metaphysics belongs to the 'nature of man'.... [It] is the basic occurrence of *Dasein*. It is *Dasein* itself. ('What Is Metaphysics?', p. 109; cf. *Being and Time*, p. 96/p. 67 and *Kant*, p. 251)[57]

Metaphysics, properly conducted, is *Dasein*'s most authentic interrogation of its own Being. (This is why, just as *Dasein* has its own nature as one of its central problems, so too metaphysics has its own nature as one of its central problems. These very reflections bear witness to that.) Metaphysics is a profoundly self-conscious discipline. It is, to reclaim the word from Bernard Williams that I used in Chapter 13, §4, a profoundly 'humanistic' discipline.

5.   Heidegger as Metaphysician

At the end of §3 I implied that there should be no doubt that Heidegger's project is a metaphysical one, by my lights. If anything counts as trying to make maximally general sense of things, this does. Someone might object that Heidegger is trying to make sense of Being, not of things. This objection, were it to have any force at all, would have to rest on an equation of 'things' in my formula with 'beings'. But, quite apart from the fact that Heidegger's project has significant implications for beings as well as for Being, such an equation would afford far greater determinacy to 'things' than was ever intended. My formula is to be taken in an utterly schematic way, precluding

[57] Cf. Kant (1998), B21.

at most the kind of high-level work in semantics that is the prerogative of
the (philosophical) logician. (See Introduction, §4.) So I am happy to repeat
that Heidegger's project is a metaphysical one.

That is, it is metaphysical on *my* conception of metaphysics. But what
about on Heidegger's own conception? In the previous section I several
times quoted Heidegger's views about what he calls 'metaphysics', without pausing to consider whether he uses the term in the same way as I do.
This will alarm many people. Does not 'metaphysics' serve as a derogatory
term for Heidegger, standing for something from which he wants (us) to
advance, not something to which he could cheerfully see his own work as a
contribution?[58] (Consider for example the very title of his essay 'Overcoming
Metaphysics'.[59]) Ought we not to say that, whether or not what he is doing
counts as metaphysics on my conception, it does not on his own?

Yes and no. It is true that Heidegger often uses the word 'metaphysics'
for something that is to be superseded. But the situation here is akin to that
which we have witnessed with other philosophers. When he uses the word
in this way he is using it elliptically to stand for metaphysics of the kind that
has actually prevailed in the past two thousand years, what I called in the
previous section 'traditional' metaphysics and what might also be called,
more clumsily, 'bad' metaphysics.[60] There really should be no doubt, in view
of the material from which I quoted towards the end of that section, that
Heidegger acknowledges the possibility of 'good' metaphysics as well.[61]

There is however an additional complication for Heidegger, as I further
tried to explain in the last section. He does not believe that bad metaphysics can be straightforwardly discarded in favour of good metaphysics.[62]

---

[58] See e.g. Cooper (1996), p. 61. Cf. Young (2002), p. 30.

[59] The German word translated as 'overcoming' is '*Überwindung*'. A striking fact, obscured
by the translation that I have been using, is that this is the same word as that used by Carnap
in the original title of Carnap (1959) where it is likewise coupled with '*der Metaphysik*' –
the whole phrase in that case being rendered 'The Elimination of Metaphysics'. (This is
the essay in which Carnap takes Heidegger to task for his pronouncements on 'nothing':
see Ch. 11, §4(b). We shall return to this *casus belli* in the next section.) For helpful comments on Heidegger's use of this word here, very relevant to the current issue, see Joan
Stambaugh's n. 1 to her translation.

[60] Cf. Hodge (1995), pp. 176ff. See Ch. 5, n. 9, for something similar in Kant; Ch. 9, n. 15,
for something similar in the early Wittgenstein (in that case with respect to the word
'philosophy' rather than the word 'metaphysics'); and Ch. 10, §1, for something similar
in the later Wittgenstein (again with respect to the word 'philosophy').

[61] Cf. 'What Is Metaphysics?', pp. 106ff.; *Contributions*, §83; and *Introduction*, p. 44,
where he writes that 'our asking of the fundamental question of metaphysics ... opens up
the process of human *Dasein* ... to unasked possibilities, futures, at the same time binds it
back to its past beginning, so sharpening it and giving it weight in its present.'

[62] In fact he does not believe that it can be straightforwardly discarded. In 'Time and
Being', p. 24, he writes, 'A regard for metaphysics,' – by which, as his previous sentence

He believes the former must yield to the latter by evolving into it. Thus he writes:

> Metaphysics cannot be abolished like an opinion. One can by no means leave it behind as a doctrine no longer believed and represented.
>
> The fact that man as *animal rationale* ... must wander through the desert of the earth's desolation could be a sign that metaphysics occurs in virtue of Being, and the overcoming of metaphysics occurs as the incorporation of Being....
>
> ... Metaphysics overcome in this way does not disappear. It returns transformed, and remains in dominance as the continuing difference of Being and beings. ('Overcoming Metaphysics', §II; cf. *Nietzsche 4*, Pt One, Ch. 22, and 'The End of Philosophy', passim)

In view of all of this I stand by my tacit assimilation of Heidegger's conception of metaphysics to my own.[63]

6. Metaphysics as Poetry

Where does Heidegger stand on the Creativity Question which I posed in §6 of the Introduction?[64] He certainly sees room for creativity in metaphysics. In many ways he sees the enterprise as more of an art than a science (see e.g.

---

indicates, he means bad metaphysics – 'still prevails even in the intention to overcome metaphysics. Therefore, our task is to cease all overcoming, and leave metaphysics to itself.' This bears directly on what I am about to say in the main text. For discussion, see Alweiss (2007).

[63] Compare my definition of metaphysics as the most general attempt to make sense of things with Heidegger's definition of it as 'inquiry beyond or over beings, which aims to recover them as such and as a whole for our grasp' ('What Is Metaphysics?', p. 106).

[64] While we are at it, where does he stand on the other two questions? First, the Novelty Question. We have already noted Heidegger's self-consciousness about his own neologizing (n. 1). This is in turn self-consciousness about his need to make sense of things in radically new ways, even, as he suggests, using a radically new 'grammar'. For an especially clear statement of his friendliness towards radical conceptual innovation in metaphysics, see *History of the Concept of Time*, §4(d), where he writes, 'It is not decisive, in philosophy, to deal with ... things ... by means of traditional concepts on the basis of an assumed traditional philosophical standpoint, but instead to disclose new domains of the matters themselves and to bring them under the jurisdiction of science by means of a productive concept formation.' (Cf. also the final sentence of 'The End of Philosophy'.) As for the Transcendence Question, there is a sense in which Heidegger does believe that metaphysicians have scope to make sense of what is transcendent, namely the sense, admittedly idiosyncratic, in which he believes that Being is transcendent – as indeed he does *Dasein* (see pp. 22 and 62/pp. 3 and 38, and *Basic Problems*, pp. 299–300). As we shall see, both of these stances bear directly on his stance on the Creativity Question.

'Humanism').[65] Even so, it is not entirely straightforward where he stands on the question – not least because the question itself is not entirely straight-forward. Heidegger may say, indeed surely would say, that there is scope for metaphysicians to be creative in their sense-making, not as opposed to looking for the sense that things themselves already make, but as a way of looking for the sense that things themselves already make. The creativity that he sanctions in metaphysics, nay requires of it, is necessary to let that which shows itself be seen.[66]

What sort of creativity is this? Heidegger several times suggests that metaphysicians should act as *poets* (e.g. *What Is Philosophy?*, pp. 91–97; 'Overcoming Metaphysics', §XXVIII; and 'Technology', pp. 339–341).[67] Poetry, in its most extreme forms, involves the wrenching of language from the norms and structures that allow it to be used in the formula-tion of propositions. This is significant. The assimilation of metaphysics to (natural) science which Heidegger takes to have bedevilled the last two millennia extends *even to the metaphysical use of propositions*. The sense-making required to make sense of Being is in Heidegger's view non-propositional. For only beings can be the subject matter of propositions. Only beings can be objects of representation. Here are some pertinent quotations.

We have come to confront something ineffable. ('Conversation', p. 88)

Our task is unceasingly to overcome the obstacles that tend to render [a saying of *Ereignis*] inadequate.

The saying of *Ereignis* in the form of a lecture remains itself an obsta-cle of this kind. The lecture[68] has spoken merely in propositional state-ments. ('Time and Being', p. 24)[69]

It is no longer a case of talking 'about' something and representing something objective, but rather of being owned over into *Ereignis*. This amounts to an essential transformation of the human from 'rational animal' ... to *Da–sein*. (*Contributions*, p. 3)[70]

---

[65] Recall that even Carnap, to whose censure of Heidegger we shall shortly be turning, conceded that metaphysicians can be thought of as artists, albeit third-rate artists (Ch. 11, §5).

[66] Cf. how the Creativity Question crumbled in Bergson's hands: see Ch. 16, §6(c).

[67] Cf. *The Principle of Reason*, p. 48, where he writes, 'The metaphorical exists only within metaphysics.'

[68] Heidegger is referring to the lecture that he has just given, i.e. the lecture of which this is the very last sentence

[69] I have taken the liberty of retaining the original German '*Ereignis*' in place of Joan Stambaugh's rendering of it as 'Appropriation': see §4 above.

[70] Cf. the previous note: this time I have taken the liberty of retaining the original German '*Ereignis*' in place of Parvis Emad's and Kenneth Maly's rendering of it as 'enowning'.

What is grasped here – and what is only and always to be grasped – is Be-ing[71].... The masterful knowing of this thinking can never be said in a proposition. But what is to be known can just as little be entrusted to an indefinite and flickering representation. (*Contributions*, §27; cf. ibid., §265)[72]

Language, if it is to convey the sense-making involved here at all, has to work in some radically new way. Hence the need for poetry, the need, as Heidegger says at one point, for 'the liberation of language from grammar' ('Humanism', p. 218).

It is impossible not to be reminded of the early Wittgenstein.[73] The similarities are both deep and numerous. Wittgenstein too is in the business of non-propositional sense-making, which, if it can be conveyed through the use of language at all, can be conveyed only through the 'aberrant' use of language, through uses that are more artistic than scientific. Relatedly, neither Wittgenstein nor Heidegger sees his work as an attempt to convey truth, on what Heidegger calls the traditional conception of truth whereby 'the "locus" of truth ... is judgment[, and] ... the essence of truth lies in the "agreement" of the judgment with its object' (p. 257/p. 214). Heidegger does see his work as an attempt to convey truth on what he considers the more primordial conception of truth, whereby its essence is to allow that which shows itself, but which has been covered, to be uncovered, and thereby properly to be seen (§44 passim and 'Truth'): that is precisely why his work counts as phenomenology by his lights. But Wittgenstein too sees his work as an attempt to display that which in some sense shows itself, so that his reader can 'see the world aright' (Wittgenstein (1961), 6.54). Again, not only are they both in the business of non-propositional sense-making, the actual sense that they try to make contains significant areas of overlap. Thus Wittgenstein writes:

> The 'experience' that something *is* ... is *not* an experience. (Wittgenstein (1961), 5.552, emphasis in original)
>
> At death the world does not alter but comes to an end.
> Death is not an event in life. (Wittgenstein (1961), 6.431–6.4311)

---

[71] The hyphen here is to register that the original German word is not '*Sein*', but the older '*Seyn*'. See Emad and Maly (1999), §I.2, for discussion of what difference Heidegger intends by this, or might intend by it.

[72] See Cooper (2002), pp. 292ff. Cf. also Dahlstrom (1994).

[73] Apart from what I am about to say in the main text, cf. Wittgenstein (1980a), p. 24, where we find: 'I think I summed up my attitude to philosophy when I said: philosophy ought really to be written as a *poetic composition*' (emphasis in original). Wittgenstein later adds, 'I was thereby revealing myself as someone who cannot quite do what he would like to be able to do' (ibid.). This too connects with what I am about to say in the main text.

It is not *how* things are in the world that is mystical, but *that* it exists. (Wittgenstein (1961), 6.44, emphasis in original)

There are things that cannot be put into words. They *make themselves manifest.* They are what is mystical. (Wittgenstein (1961), 6.522, emphasis in original)

and much else that evokes Heidegger's concerns with Being, *Dasein*, the essential finitude of the latter, and the relations between the two.

How far these comparisons between the two thinkers, which are of patent interest in their own right, also succeed in assuaging worries about Heidegger's assimilation of metaphysics to poetry depends largely, of course, on how far there remain unassuaged worries about the early Wittgenstein's own self-professed trafficking in nonsense. It depends largely on that, but not exclusively. Even someone broadly sympathetic to the project of the *Tractatus*, and broadly sympathetic to Heidegger's project, may balk at the idea that Heidegger's own work, or the kind of work that it fosters, should be construed in this non-propositional way. To be sure, Heidegger's use of language is unorthodox. But unorthodoxy is one thing; non-propositionality another. Heidegger *appears* to write in propositions. (Nor has anything hitherto in this chapter served to challenge such an appearance.) Where, if anywhere, is the appearance unsustainable – not through any incompetence on Heidegger's part but by design? How, if at all, does his writing replicate the deliberate self-destruction of the *Tractatus*?

Well, reconsider the material from 'What Is Metaphysics?' that we saw Carnap ridicule in Chapter 11, §4(b). In insisting that science is concerned with nothing but beings, then as it were hypostasizing that 'nothing' to draw attention to the Being of these beings, is Heidegger perhaps doing something analogous to what Wittgenstein does when he urges that propositions are concerned with nothing but objects, then affects to discuss the logical form which (though not itself an object) is a feature of the facts in which these objects participate?[74]

You may think that this is a needlessly elaborate account of what Heidegger is about. An alternative would be that he is simply making play with restricted quantification, that is with tacitly restricted talk about what things there are: he is making the point that, while there are, in one good sense, nothing but beings, and while there are certainly nothing but beings in any sense that is relevant to the concerns of science, we must also reckon with Being.[75] (If this is reminiscent of anyone in the analytic tradition, it is reminiscent of Lewis, who invoked restricted quantification to defend the

---

[74] Thus compare Heidegger's claim, on p. 105 of his essay, that the 'nothing' is the origin of logical negation with Wittgenstein (1961), 5.552–5.5521, part of which appeared in the list of quotations above.

[75] Cf. 'Humanism', p. 238, and 'The Question of Being', pp. 317–318.

claim that while there is, in one good sense, nothing but what is actual, we must also reckon with what is merely possible (Ch. 13, §3).)

But this alternative account does insufficient justice to the force of the 'nothing'.[76] For one thing, Heidegger is also alluding to that basic feature of *Dasein*'s existence whereby, among the possibilities that it acknowledges in stepping outside itself, is the possibility of its own non-existence. As Heidegger says in *Being and Time*, '*Dasein* finds itself *face to face* with the "nothing" of the possible impossibility of its existence' (p. 310/p. 266, emphasis in original). But also, more significantly in this context, Heidegger really does believe that 'beyond all … beings *there is nothing*' (*Basic Problems*, p. 10, emphasis in original) even on an unrestricted interpretation of the quantification. That is one reason why, in affecting to distinguish between the Being of beings and any being, he recognizes the need to introduce scare quotes into his text. He writes, 'The Being of beings "is" not itself a being' (p. 26/p. 6). In fact at one point he goes further. He uses not only scare quotes, but erasure. That is, he crosses out the very word 'Being' while allowing it to remain visible. He writes:

> Is it due to 'Being' that our saying fails in a telling manner in its response [to the question of Being], remaining only what is all too readily suspected as so-called 'mysticism'? Or does it have to do with our saying that such saying does not yet speak, because it is not yet able to respond in a fitting manner to the essence of 'Being'? …
>
> … [We are pointed] toward a realm that demands a different saying…. [A] thoughtful look ahead into this realm can write 'Being' only in the following way: B̶e̶i̶n̶g̶. The crossing out of this word initially has only a preventive role, namely, that of preventing the almost ineradicable habit of representing 'Being' as something standing somewhere on its own that then on occasion first comes face-to-face with human beings….
>
> … [The] sign of this crossing through cannot, however, be the merely negative sign of a crossing out….
>
> … The human essence also belongs to that which, in the crossing out of Being, takes thinking into the claim of a more originary call….
>
> Like B̶e̶i̶n̶g̶, the nothing would also have to be written – and that means, thought – in the same way. ('The Question of Being', pp. 309–311)[77]

Even in 'What Is Metaphysics?' Heidegger accedes to the impropriety of using the word 'nothing' as a noun in the way in which he does. He writes:

> What is the nothing? … In our asking we posit the nothing in advance as something that 'is' such and such; we posit it as a being. But that is

---

[76] Cf. Inwood (1999b). See also Glendinning (2007), Ch. 3, Pt III, whose conclusions I take to be very similar to mine, though they are not always expressed in the same way.

[77] Cf. *Basic Problems*, where he urges that Being, though it *is* not, 'is given' (pp. 10–11 and 18).

exactly what it is distinguished from. Interrogating the nothing – asking what and how it, the nothing, is – turns what is interrogated into its opposite. The question deprives itself of its own object.

Accordingly, every answer to this question is also impossible from the start. For it necessarily assumes the form: the nothing 'is' this or that. With regard to the nothing, question and answer alike are inherently absurd.

... Thinking, which is always essentially thinking about something, must act in a way contrary to its own essence when it thinks of the nothing. ('What Is Metaphysics?', pp. 96–99)

Elsewhere he makes clear that he does not hold thinking that acts in a way contrary to its own essence to be thinking of a peculiar kind; rather, in line with Frege and Wittgenstein, he holds it not to be thinking at all (*Metaphysical Foundations*, p. 19).[78]

It thus becomes increasingly difficult *not* to hear a Tractarian injunction to throw away the ladder, increasingly difficult, that is, to take everything in his texts at propositional face value. We really do seem to be dealing with self-conscious examples of what Wittgenstein calls, in a passage of express sympathy towards Heidegger's linguistic shenanigans, '[running] up against the limits of language' (Wittgenstein (1979b), p. 68).[79] And of course, here as in Wittgenstein, such examples must include some of the admonishments against trying to cross those very limits. If there really is no properly saying anything about the nothing, or thinking of the nothing, then, in particular, there is no properly saying or thinking that there is no properly saying anything about the nothing or thinking of the nothing. Small wonder that Heidegger believes metaphysicians need to be poets.

But what are the implications for what has gone before in this chapter? How much of what we have seen Heidegger say, or of what has been said about what he says, resists being construed propositionally?[80] Some central material survives, surely. Consider for example Heidegger's distinction between 'whos' and 'whats', or his distinction between 'whats' that are ready-to-hand and 'whats' that are present-at-hand. These still look as though they can be taken at face value.[81] On the other hand what about

---

[78] This of course casts retrospective light on the reference to thinking at the end of the previous quotation, from 'The Question of Being'.

[79] This occurs in the passage quoted in Ch. 11, n. 39. See again the other material cited there.

[80] A similar question arises with respect to the *Tractatus*, of course. In that case it is clear that nearly all of the book, if not all of it, must count as nonsense: see Ch. 9, n. 45.

[81] Or is Heidegger committed to the view that only 'whats' that are present-at-hand can be the subject matter of propositions? No, not unless he is inconsistent: see §33 and p. 267/ p. 224. (What I have in mind from §33 is particularly early material. Later in the same section, at pp. 200–201/pp. 157–158, there is material which some commentators have

Heidegger's very use of the word 'Being'? Or ours in reporting and discussing him? Must these already indicate something awry with any purported propositions in which they occur – rather like a Fregean use of the word 'property' (Ch. 8, §7(b))?

The matter is not at all straightforward. This is partly because there are many ways of not taking a proposition at face value without impugning its propositionality. Thus consider a proposition's grammar. This sometimes cannot be taken at face value. 'She did it for the sake of Arthur' does not state that she did it for something belonging to Arthur (cf. Ch. 14, §2). But we can still regard it as a bona fide proposition. Similarly, perhaps, in the case of 'We have forgotten the Being of beings.' Perhaps this is a bona fide proposition which nevertheless does not state that we have forgotten something belonging to beings. Or consider the way in which a word or phrase is sometimes used so that it is itself part of the subject matter of the proposition in which it occurs, even though syntax suggests otherwise. Examples are the use of 'George Eliot' in 'By 1857 she had become George Eliot' and (arguably) the use of 'fifty-two' in 'He has misremembered his six-times table and thinks that six nines are fifty-two.'[82] Whatever the correct story may be about Heidegger's own use of the word 'Being',[83] this second possibility is enough to safeguard the propositionality of much of what I have written about him, using that word. Thus 'Heidegger wants to make sense of Being' can at the very least be interpreted as a bona fide proposition concerning sense-making which Heidegger wants to achieve and which is such that imparting it, whether propositionally or not, involves the word 'Being'.

There is clearly far more to be said about these matters and their bearing on Heidegger's work. But I want now to focus on something of particular relevance to this enquiry: their bearing, more specifically, on his apparent idealism.

7.   Idealism in Heidegger?

We found a kind of idealism in Husserl, which I suggested was to Husserl's discredit (Ch. 17, §6). I also gave a diagnosis (Ch. 17, §7). We seem to find a kind of idealism in Heidegger. And we seem able to give the same diagnosis.

---

taken to show that Heidegger does in fact believe that only 'whats' that are present-at-hand can be the subject matter of propositions. For references and a corrective, see Schear (2007).)

[82] When I talk about the use of expressions here I am prescinding from the technical distinction that is sometimes drawn between using expressions and mentioning them. I shall return to this distinction in Ch. 20, Appendix.

[83] How significant is it, incidentally, that I feel justified in putting it in these terms, as opposed to referring to the German word 'Sein'?

Where is there an appearance of idealism in Heidegger? We have already seen one place, if only in passing. I commented parenthetically in §3 that Heidegger individuates beings very finely. He distinguishes between 'the "source" which the geographer establishes for a river' and 'the "springhead in the dale"' – as he does between 'the botanist's plants' and 'the flowers in the hedgerow' (p. 100/p. 70). It looks as though he is prepared, in idealistic vein, to carve up that of which sense is made in accord with the sense that is made of it. Such, more generally, appears to be the lesson of his distinction between things that are ready-to-hand and things that are present-at-hand. For this is a distinction that he draws by appeal to the different ways in which *Dasein* engages with things, where these in turn are, on a suitably broad construal of sense-making, different ways in which *Dasein* makes sense of things. Here is a striking passage in which Heidegger makes this very point and, in the course of doing so, seems to give it blatantly idealistic expression:

> World exists – that is, it is – only if *Dasein* exists, only if there is *Dasein*. Only if ... *Dasein* exists as being-in-the-world, is there understanding of Being, and only if this understanding exists are intra-worldly beings unveiled as present-at-hand and ready-to-hand. (*Basic Problems*, p. 297)

As far as the diagnosis is concerned, I suggested that Husserl's error was to think that he could address questions, not only about *how* things are, but about *what* things are. Precisely the same diagnosis seems to be available in this case. For surely Heidegger would never have individuated beings as finely as this if he had not wanted to go beyond an account of how things are to an account of what they are; if he had not been concerned, indeed, with Being. This suspicion seems to be confirmed when he writes:

> Beings are. Their Being contains the truth that they are. The fact *that* beings are gives to beings the privilege of the unquestioned. From here the question arises as to *what* beings are. ('The End of Philosophy', p. 81, emphasis in original; cf. *What Is Philosophy?*, pp. 35ff.)

But we need to tread very cautiously. I keep saying what there 'seems' to be in Heidegger – and with good reason. The appearances are misleading. Or at least they are partly misleading. Heidegger's fine individuation of beings *seems* to betoken a simple idealism. But actually, the very fact that he individuates beings as finely as he does can just as well be taken to show, nay should be taken to show, that he understands beings to be, not just what sense is made of, but what sense is made of *as* thus made sense of. They are objects of intentionality.[84] (Let us not forget that the individuation of beings is subject to the phenomenological reduction.) This is why he

---

[84] See *History of the Concept of Time*, §5(c)(α). Cf. Ch. 17, §4.

says that 'we must understand actuality, reality, vitality, existentiality, constancy in order to comport ourselves positively towards specifically actual, real, living, existing, constant beings' (*Basic Problems*, pp. 10–11). On this conception of beings, the claim that beings depend for their individuation on the sense that is made of them, so far from having to be heard as a commitment to some kind of idealism, can be heard as a tautology. The same is true of the claim that 'world' depends for its existence on the existence of *Dasein*. For by 'world' Heidegger means 'a determination of Being-in-the-world' (*Basic Problems*, p. 166), a determination, in other words, of *Dasein*'s peculiar kind of Being.[85] As for Heidegger's insisting that there is a question about what beings are, that too can be heard in a quite innocuous way. What I proffered above in connection with Husserl was just a slogan. Husserl's error was to attempt, by inappropriate phenomenological means, to say what the intrinsic nature of things was. Heidegger can be heard as asking, quite differently, and quite reasonably, how the notion of a being, as it occurs in his own work, is to be construed, in particular how beings are to be individuated: the very question that we have just been addressing.

This discussion is as pertinent to how the notion of Being is to be construed as it is to how the notion of a being is to be construed. For after all, Being is 'that which determines beings as beings, that on the basis of which beings are already understood' (pp. 25–26/p. 6). Being amounts to intelligibility or giveability. Or, as Heidegger himself puts it:

> Being 'is' only in the understanding of those beings to whose Being something like an understanding of Being belongs.... [There] is a necessary connection between Being and understanding. (p. 228/p. 183)[86]

This in turn gives the lie to further appearances of idealism in Heidegger, among which the most pertinent are in §44(c) of *Being and Time*. He there writes:

> Being ... is something which 'there is' only in so far as truth is.[87] And truth *is* only in so far as and only as long as *Dasein* is. (p. 272/p. 230, emphasis in original)

This too, on a correct understanding, can be heard as more or less tautologous.

Note that Heidegger very clearly distances his claim that Being depends on *Dasein* from the more idealistic-sounding claim, to which he emphatically does not subscribe, that beings depend on *Dasein*. Indeed in the ellipsis

---

[85] That is why it is appropriate to talk about the world's 'existing' (*Basic Problems*, p. 166). Cf. *Being and Time*, pp. 33–34/p. 13. (Cf. also Wittgenstein (1961), 5.621.)

[86] Cf. Dreyfus (1991), Ch. 1.

[87] This is truth on the conception of truth to which I alluded earlier, as that which allows that which shows itself to be seen.

in the quotation just given he writes in parentheses 'not beings'. And earlier
in the section he explains that:

> beings are uncovered only when *Dasein is*; and only as long as *Dasein is*,
> are they disclosed....
>
> [But] *once* beings have been uncovered, they show themselves precisely
> as beings which beforehand already were. (p. 269/pp. 226–227, emphasis
> adapted)

That beings are individuated in accord with the sense that is made of them,
and that their Being (i.e. their intelligibility, their susceptibility to sense-
making) is dependent on the sort of being that makes sense of them: neither of these facts gainsays the fact that they themselves enjoy, and indeed
are made sense of as enjoying, an objectivity whereby they are quite independent of that sort of being. Only when I turn my head slightly or reach
forward can I see or feel the pen on my desk, whose visibility and tangibil-
ity consist in the possibility of just such encounters. Moreover, I can distinguish between the pen *qua* seen and the pen *qua* felt. The fact remains that
what I see or feel is something that was there anyway, already available to
be seen or felt, which is indeed precisely how it strikes me when I see or
feel it.[88]

At one stage Heidegger, making clear that he holds individual truths such
as Newton's laws and the principle of contradiction to be aspects of Being
rather than beings, expresses the independence of beings with respect to
Dasein as follows:

> Newton's laws, the principle of contradiction, any truth whatever – these
> are true only as long as *Dasein is*. Before there was any *Dasein*, there
> was no truth; nor will there be any after *Dasein* is no more.... Before
> Newton's laws were discovered, they were not 'true'....
>
> [But to] say that before Newton his laws were [not true] ... cannot
> signify that before him there were no such beings as have been uncov-
> ered and pointed out by those laws. Through Newton the laws became
> true; and with them, beings became accessible in themselves to *Dasein*.
> (p. 269/pp. 226–227, emphasis in original)

Relatedly:

> *All truth is relative to* Dasein's *Being*. Does this relativity signify that all
> truth is 'subjective'? If one interprets 'subjective' as 'left to the subject's
> discretion', then it certainly does not. For uncovering ... takes asserting
> out of the province of 'subjective' discretion ... and brings the uncovering

---

[88] Cf. *Basic Problems*, pp. 115–116. And cf. the material from Husserl (1973a) quoted in
Ch. 17, §6.

Dasein face to face with the beings themselves. (p. 270/p. 227, emphasis in original)[89]

On closer scrutiny, then, the initial appearance of idealism in Heidegger begins to fade. But it does not disappear altogether. Still less are we in a position to conclude that there is no idealism in Heidegger. I believe that there is in fact an idealism in Heidegger: a variation of the idealism that we found in Husserl, whereby the things of which we make natural sense depend for their essential features on their susceptibility to just such sense-making. Heidegger's idealism is subtler than Husserl's, partly because of the subtleties in this notion of a being, in its contrast with that of Being, and partly because of the more restrained phenomenological reduction that underpins it. But it may still ultimately be subject to similar objections.

Note first that the subtleties in the notion of a being may be subtleties too far. There are various familiar niceties (aporiae?) associated with the use of the word '*qua*'. Is the pen *qua* seen 'the same thing' as the pen *qua* felt? Is the pen *qua* used, and thus ready-to-hand, 'the same thing' as the pen *qua* contemplated, and thus present-at-hand? In a sense, in each case, yes; in a sense, in each case, no.[90] But how satisfactorily can we both separate and maintain these different senses? More to the point, how satisfactorily can Heidegger do so, consonantly with what else he wants to say? The sense in which the pen was already available to be seen is surely the sense in which it *is* the same thing *qua* seen as *qua* felt, and the same thing *qua* used as *qua* contemplated. But that is not the sense that is pertinent to Heidegger's finely individuated notion of a being. One wonders whether he would have done better to invoke something like Frege's distinction between sense and *Bedeutung*, and to accept *only* the sense in which the pen *qua* used is the same thing as the pen *qua* contemplated, as indeed the source of the river identified by the geographer is the same thing as the springhead in the dale, albeit each of these things can be given, and can be made sense of, in more than one way. If somebody were to suggest that this is in effect what Heidegger is doing, and that his finely individuated beings are really nothing more than Fregean *Bedeutungen* indexed by Fregean senses, then that would raise a further concern. Heidegger's insistence that such beings do not depend on *Dasein* would seem to commit him to a Fregean objectivity about

---

[89] I have taken the liberty of dropping John Macquarrie's and Edward Robinson's capitalization of 'Interprets' in their translation. For their policy on this matter, see their n. 3 on p. 19.

[90] We noted parenthetically in §3 that Heidegger distinguishes between a person *qua* living and the person *qua* dead. Yet he also recognizes, not merely that something is common to each, but that some *being* is common to each. He says, 'The end of the being *qua Dasein* is the beginning of *the same being qua* something present-at-hand' (p. 281/p. 238, emphasis adapted). Cf. the material from Husserl (1962), §89, cited in n. 24 of the previous chapter.

sense; and that would sit ill with his radically non-Fregean insistence that truths such as Newton's laws do not antedate their discovery.

That view about Newton's laws is in any case problematical. One does not have to be all that Fregean to balk at the idea that Newton's laws 'became true' only when Newton discovered them. If they did, what previously kept the planets in orbit round the sun?[91] To be sure, there are various more or less dextrous ways of replying to this question, for instance in terms of a presently available explicans for a formerly instantiated explicandum. The question is, what could drive us to such dexterity? What could drive Heidegger to it?

Heidegger's main concern is to safeguard the connection between Being and *Dasein*'s understanding of Being. But why should that connection be forged at the level of individual human beings such as Newton? Why, for that matter, should it require the existence of human beings at all? Why should it require the existence of *any* actual 'whos' – as opposed to possible 'whos'? When Heidegger says that Being depends on *Dasein*, this is surely one point at which we do well to remind ourselves that '*Dasein*' is not the name of a particular being, but of a sort of being. Heidegger's claims about Newton's laws – claims, it should be noted, that are in tension with our natural, pre-phenomenological sense-making – suggest that he may himself need reminding of this.[92]

But now, this progression from the kinds of claims that Heidegger does occasionally make concerning individual human beings to the kinds of claims that he should surely confine himself to making concerning *Dasein* calls to mind the expansion of who 'we' are, from a particular group of human beings to a kind of infinite locus of sense-making, which we witnessed in connection with the later Wittgenstein in Chapter 10, §4. And here, much as there, the claims at the end of the progression can have the kind of bite that they are intended to have only if their subject (*Dasein* in Heidegger's case, 'we' in Wittgenstein's) is being said to determine the limits of that of which a certain kind of sense can be made, and only if such limits are understood as limitations. Otherwise the subject is redundant and the claims either lack any substance at all or have to be heard as claims about a subject-independent domain of sense such as would be an anathema to both Heidegger and Wittgenstein. We thus arrive at idealism of precisely the problematical kind which I argued Wittgenstein was only just able to avoid – and which Heidegger's mentor Husserl did not ultimately avoid.

---

[91] There is admittedly something glib about this way of expressing the concern. But any difficulties that there may be in finding a more careful way of expressing it do not detract from what is problematical about Heidegger's view; in fact they add to it.

[92] Elsewhere he is himself at pains to emphasize it: see e.g. *Metaphysical Foundations*, p. 188.

Heidegger himself defines 'idealism' as the thesis that 'Being can never be explained by beings but is already that which is "transcendental" for every being' (p. 251/p. 208). He both endorses this thesis and concedes that it is 'empty' without an account of how Being is internally related to *Dasein*'s understanding of Being (p. 251/p. 207). Heidegger's definition is not the same as mine. But the two are related. If we reserve the word 'ontic' for the kind of sense that can be made of beings, then idealism, on his definition, amounts to the thesis that susceptibility to ontic sense-making is a limit to that of which ontic sense can be made. This is indeed empty without an account of how *Dasein* relates to such sense-making. But given such an account, or more specifically, given the account that Heidegger gives, it amounts to idealism by my definition too: idealism of the problematical sort just identified.

There are several symptoms of this idealism in Heidegger. One of these involves Heidegger's conception of independence. As we have seen, he holds that the things of which we can make ontic sense (beings) are independent of such sense-making. But he also holds, as indeed he must – somewhat like Husserl – that such independence is a feature of the ontic sense of things we make. Thus he writes:

> When *Dasein* does not exist, 'independence' 'is' not either, nor 'is' the 'in-itself'. In such a case this sort of thing can be neither understood nor not understood. In such a case even beings within-the-world can neither be discovered nor lie hidden. *In such a case* it cannot be said that beings are, nor can it be said that they are not. But *now*, as long as there is an understanding of Being and therefore an understanding of presence-at-hand, it can indeed be said that *in this case* beings will still continue to be. (p. 255/p. 212, emphasis in original)

There we have it: '*in this case*'. The independence of beings with respect to us and our ontic sense-making is one of their essential features, *determined by* Dasein. And it is an independence that they enjoy *to the exclusion of* (not their failing to enjoy it, but) their not even admitting of it – nor for that matter failing to admit of it.

This is of a piece with other symptoms of Heidegger's idealism. Among these is his talk of the 'nothing' beyond beings which we considered in the previous section, his talk, as he also puts it at one point, of 'the complete negation of the totality of beings' ('What Is Metaphysics?', p. 98). How are these of a piece? In two ways. First, by casting that of which we can make ontic sense, which is to say the domain of beings, as a limited whole, beyond which there is that with respect to which ontic sense gives out. Second, and concomitantly, by falling prey to a version of the Limit Argument (Ch. 5, §8); that is, by themselves straining beyond the limit of ontic sense-making.

Heidegger says, 'As surely as we can never comprehend absolutely the whole of beings in themselves we certainly do find ourselves stationed in the midst of beings that are revealed somehow as a whole' ('What Is Metaphysics?', p. 99). We are reminded of what Wittgenstein says in the *Tractatus*:

> Feeling the world as a limited whole – it is this that is mystical. (6.45)
>
> There are ... things that cannot be put into words. They *make themselves manifest*. They are what is mystical. (6.522, emphasis in original)

And this at last brings us back to the material at the end of the previous section that heralded this discussion of idealism. I have been urging that Heidegger is involved in a problematical idealism which does not make ontic sense. This means that neither does it make propositional sense. That is precisely why I call it problematical. But of course, 'problematical' here really only serves as a term of condemnation to the extent that it (the idealism) is *supposed* to make propositional sense. It is open to Heidegger to take a leaf out of the early Wittgenstein's book and to say that all these symptoms of his idealism, and indeed the idealism itself, are deliberate manglings of propositional sense-making designed to convey non-propositional insights; to instil a non-propositional understanding of Being. It seems to me that this is an exegetical possibility that we have to take very seriously.

By this I do not mean that Heidegger would elect to take this leaf out of Wittgenstein's book. I am not at all confident that he would. I mean that he would do well to take this leaf out of Wittgenstein's book, given what else he is committed to. I think this would be his only fully integrated way of justifying the inclusion in his texts of propositions, or rather apparent propositions, which, by his own lights, resist being interpreted as such. Shall we conclude, then, on Heidegger's behalf if not in direct exposition of anything he says, that these ideas of his that we have been considering in this section are the stuff of poetry? That the passages in which he relativizes truth to the Being of *Dasein*, and suchlike, do not consist in assertions about how things are, but are moments of artistry?[93]

---

[93] I shall pursue these issues in Chs 20 and 21, in connection with Derrida and Deleuze (see esp. §6 and §4, respectively). I shall also come back to them in the Conclusion.

A very helpful discussion of Heidegger's views on reality and truth is Mulhall (1996), pp. 94–104. A very helpful discussion of Heidegger's idealism is Béatrice Han-Pile (2005), where, among other things, Han-Pile advances an interpretation of Heidegger that opposes that of Hubert L. Dreyfus, as found in Dreyfus (1991), pp. 253–265. (Han-Pile sees Heidegger as more Kantian than Dreyfus does.)

CHAPTER 19

✦

Collingwood

Metaphysics as History

1. Introduction

At the beginning of the finale of Beethoven's Ninth Symphony there is a brief quotation from each of the three preceding movements. Each is summarily rejected by an impassioned instrumental recitative. The whole episode helps to prepare the way for the burst of joy that is about to follow.

I hope it will not sound condescending towards either Collingwood or Derrida – it is certainly not intended to – if I liken the next two chapters to that episode. First, in this chapter, we shall hear fragmented repeats of certain ideas from previous chapters, repeats that I shall try to accentuate in §3. Then, in Chapter 20, Derrida will reject much of what generates these ideas. The two chapters between them will prepare us for something very different and quite extraordinary in the final chapter, much of which will constitute what may fairly be described as a hymn to joy.

I should straightway emphasize two important limitations of this analogy. First, it downplays the extent to which Collingwood's own thinking breaks with what has gone before. Second, and conversely, it downplays the extent to which Derrida's thinking is continuous with what has gone before. (Derrida is deeply Heideggerian.)

These two facts merit comment anyway. They make the present chapter something of an interlude. As a result, they might even be thought to raise questions about its positioning. But actually the chapter would have been something of an interlude wherever it had been positioned. Collingwood does not really belong to any of the traditions identified in this book.

2. Absolute Presuppositions and Metaphysics
as the Study of Them

R.G. Collingwood (1889–1943)[1] has a view of metaphysics that is grounded in his view of propositions (*Essay*, Ch. IV[2]). Let us therefore begin with the latter.

---

[1] The third of our protagonists to be born in 1889 (counting Wittgenstein only once).

[2] Throughout this chapter I use the following abbreviations for Collingwood's works: *Autobiography* for Collingwood (1944); *Essay* for Collingwood (1998a); 'Function of

493

Collingwood holds that every proposition is a potential answer to some question. And he holds that every question involves some presupposition. In fact it involves many. But only one of them directly makes the question 'arise'. Thus, to take the classic example, the question, 'Have you stopped beating your wife?', put to Albert, presupposes that Albert is married, that he is (therefore) of an age to be married, that he has been in the habit of beating his wife, and much else besides.[3] The presupposition that makes the question arise is the fullest of these, which is perhaps – 'perhaps', because there is a certain latitude in how the question is to be interpreted – that Albert has been in the habit of beating his wife and has resolved not to do so in the future. This presupposition does not need to be made consciously for the question to arise. But it does need to be made. If the question is put in a context in which the presupposition is *not* made, the question is, relative to that context, a 'nonsense question'. The presupposition needs to be made for the question to arise: it does not need to be *true* for the question to arise. Sometimes it is helpful to put a question knowing full well that it involves a presupposition that is false. Thus suppose you know that there is no football on television this evening, whereas I am convinced that there is, and you are trying to put me right. You can quite reasonably ask, as you reach for the television guide, 'Very well, which channel is it on?' You are presupposing, for the sake of argument, that there *is* football on television this evening, in which case it must be on one of the channels. If I reply that it is on BBC1, say, then you can show me straight away from the guide that I am wrong. If I am less committal in my reply, it will take you a while longer.

The examples given so far illustrate how one question's presupposition can be another question's answer. Both the proposition that Albert is married and the proposition that there is football on television this evening are, like any other propositions, potential answers to questions. This suggests that any given proposition will launch an infinite regress. Thus proposition p_1 is a potential answer to question q_1, which involves presupposition π_1, which is in turn proposition p_2, which is a potential answer to question q_2, which involves presupposition π_2, which is in turn proposition p_3, and so on *ad infinitum*. In fact, however, Collingwood does not believe that all presuppositions are propositions. Any that *is* must of course be the potential answer to some further question. But any that is not can block such a regress.[4]

Metaphysics' for Collingwood (1998b); *Philosophical Method* for Collingwood (2005); 'Philosophy of History' for Collingwood (1967); *Speculum* for Collingwood (1924); *The Idea of History* for Collingwood (1994); and *The Idea of Nature* for Collingwood (1945). All unaccompanied page references are to the *Essay*.

[3] For Collingwood's discussion of this example, see *Essay*, Ch. V.
[4] To the best of my knowledge he nowhere argues that there *cannot* be such a regress – either one that contains infinitely many propositions or one that contains an infinitely recurring loop.

Collingwood calls presuppositions that are themselves propositions *relative* presuppositions. And he calls presuppositions that are not themselves propositions *absolute* presuppositions. Absolute presuppositions are fundamentally different in kind from propositions, most fundamentally in not admitting of truth or falsity – though we can still use ordinary declarative sentences to express them.

Collingwood gives as an example of an absolute presupposition what I called in Chapter 5 the Causal Principle, the principle that whatever happens in nature has a cause. He holds that, when scientists make this presupposition (which, he observes, not all of them always do), that ensures that certain questions arise. For instance, it ensures that, given some explosion, the question arises as to what caused the explosion. Making the presupposition therefore has significant repercussions for scientific practice. It spurs scientists on in their quest for causes. But the presupposition is not itself true or false. Making it has more of the regulative about it than the constitutive, to borrow Kant's terminology (Ch. 5, §7). The presupposition cannot be tested, demonstrated, argued for, or argued against.[5] If we ask whether it is true, or if we ask what reason there is to believe it, we betray a basic misunderstanding.

It is Collingwood's further conviction that what *metaphysics* consists in is the study of the absolute presuppositions that are in fact made. Different absolute presuppositions are made in different settings, however. In particular, they vary from one period to another. Collingwood is accordingly quite explicit that metaphysics, so understood, is a fundamentally historical exercise (e.g. pp. 61–62). It is one of the human sciences. It sits alongside psychology and ethnography. To practise metaphysics (metaphysics itself, not just the history of metaphysics) is to investigate how human beings have actually conducted their enquiries in the past.

Now it is of course open to Collingwood to use the word 'metaphysics' in whatever way he chooses. But can he possibly think that what he thereby calls 'metaphysics' is anything like what the rest of us call 'metaphysics'?

Well, yes: this is not such an outrageous thing to think. A number of points need to be emphasized here. First, Collingwood has a distinctive conception of history. All history, he famously believes, is the history of thought (*The Idea of History*, p. 317). It is an attempt to understand past human activity by understanding past human thinking. And this in turn can be achieved only through a process of assimilation: that is, not by grasping such thinking 'as mere object' (ibid., p. 288), but by actually reenacting it in one's own mind and having the very same thoughts oneself (see *Autobiography*, p. 76). And to do this effectively one must achieve that articulated awareness of what it would be for the thoughts to be true, and of how they relate conceptually to other thoughts, at which philosophers characteristically aim

---

[5] But did not Kant argue for it? Collingwood thinks not. See §3(b).

(cf. pp. 38–39). Furthermore, this is bound to impact on how well one understands one's own thinking, especially where the presuppositions involved
are not the same as one's own (cf. *Autobiography*, p. 78). In any case – this
is the second point that needs to be emphasized – one's own thinking is fair
game for investigation in this metaphysical exercise. For one's own thinking belongs to the past: it just happens to belong to the 'relatively recent
past' (p. 70).[6] And when it comes to teasing out one's own absolute presuppositions, Collingwoodian metaphysics is not readily distinguishable from
what, in §6(b) of the Introduction, we saw P.F. Strawson call 'descriptive
metaphysics'.[7] To be sure, simply drawing attention to this likeness does
not eliminate the concerns about the former. It merely transfers them to the
latter. Strawson's account of descriptive metaphysics is itself subject to the
worry that it makes metaphysics too much like a human science, something
that we noted when we first considered it. But as I tried to argue then – this
is the third point that needs to be emphasized – a description of a given way
of thinking can be a self-conscious exercise in that very way of thinking. I
have called this the third point, but it is really the first point again, since that
is exactly what Collingwood thinks a description of a given way of thinking must be if it is to be properly historical. Finally, replace the references to
thinking in this paragraph by references to sense-making and the paragraph
will call to mind the point that I have laboured throughout this enquiry:
that making sense of things, at the highest level of generality, involves making sense of making sense of things. This in turn signals a direct connection between metaphysics as Collingwood conceives it and metaphysics as
I conceive it. Metaphysics as Collingwood conceives it, when it is focused
on one's own sense-making, is at the very least a staple of metaphysics as I
conceive it – even if the former does not exhaust the latter.

But still: is there not a great deal within what has traditionally passed for
metaphysics that Collingwood cannot possibly hope to convince us counts
as metaphysics on his conception?

There is less than you might think. Consider for example the so-called
ontological argument, in the version due to Anselm. This argument would
standardly be presented in something like the following way.

The Ontological Argument: God is by definition the greatest con-
ceivable being. And God exists at least in our minds. But for such

---

[6] That one's own thinking belongs to the past, as of course does the thinking of those with
whom one has immediate commerce, helps to explain Collingwood's belief in the ineluctability of history. 'The question,' he writes, 'is not "Shall I be an historian or not?" but
"How good an historian shall I be?"' ('Philosophy of History', p. 3).

[7] Michael Krausz alleges that 'Collingwood holds that one cannot be aware of one's own
absolute presuppositions' (Krausz (1972), p. 227). This rests on what seems to me a bizarre
reading of one passage in the *Essay*, at p. 96, which Krausz takes out of context. For a
corrective, see p. 43 of the *Essay*.

a being to exist in our minds without also existing in reality would not be as great as for it to do both. Therefore God also exists in reality. (See Anselm (1996), Ch. 2.)[8]

On almost any conception of a metaphysical argument, this is a paradigm case. On Collingwood's conception it appears not to be a metaphysical argument at all. But Collingwood insists that it is. He urges that the standard ways of presenting the argument are misleading. This argument is not really, as the standard ways of presenting it suggest it is, an argument for the existence of God. That God exists is an absolute presupposition, and there is no arguing for or against it. No, Anselm has not argued that our idea of God ensures the truth of that presupposition; he has argued that our idea of God ensures our commitment to that presupposition (pp. 189–190). This is history.[9]

Collingwood would in any case be happy to admit that a great deal within what has traditionally passed for metaphysics does not count as metaphysics on his conception. Just as other protagonists in this enquiry have offered their own accounts of proper metaphysics and have dismissed much of what has hitherto passed for metaphysics as bad metaphysics (see e.g. Ch. 5, §2, and, most recently, Ch. 18, §5), so too Collingwood offers his own account of proper metaphysics and dismisses much of what has traditionally passed for metaphysics as what he calls 'pseudo-metaphysics'. And by 'pseudo-metaphysics' he means, precisely, the attempt to argue for or against absolute presuppositions (pp. 47–48, 52–54, and 162–163).[10]

Let us reflect further on the nature of absolute presuppositions. Clearly, since they do not admit of truth or falsity, they cannot stand in relations of compatibility, incompatibility, and suchlike to one another (cf. pp. 67–68). There are however analogues of such relations in which they can stand to one another. Even if it makes no sense to say that one absolute presupposition is incompatible with another, it may be that nobody can simultaneously make both of them. Thus for example there is no presupposing both that whatever happens in nature has a cause and that some of what happens in nature, some human agency say, has no cause. Collingwood accordingly introduces

---

[8] This is rather different from the version due to Descartes to which I referred in Ch. 1, n. 29.

[9] Anyone who thinks, *contra* Collingwood, that the standard ways of presenting the argument are *not* misleading might marvel at the precision with which Collingwood's construal of the argument misses the point!

[10] Sometimes, interestingly, pseudo-metaphysics has not just taken the place of the real thing in Collingwood's view. It has arisen in reaction to the real thing. That is, it has been a kind of anti-metaphysics. Thus pseudo-metaphysicians, uncomfortable at having their own absolute presuppositions unearthed by genuine metaphysicians, have reacted by trying to adopt new absolute presuppositions (or absolute presuppositions that are new for them – in fact they are taken from yore) for which they have tried, pseudo-metaphysically, to argue (pp. 90ff.).

the relation of *consupponibility*, which holds between two absolute presuppositions when it *is* possible to make both of them together (p. 66). Granted this relation, granted that absolute presuppositions are expressed by declarative sentences, granted that we may *affect* to assert an absolute presupposition as a shorthand for actually asserting that 'in our ordinary thinking' we make it ('Function of Metaphysics', pp. 404–405), and granted that we may even go as far as to call an absolute presupposition 'true' as a shorthand for doing this (ibid., p. 409): one wonders how much, or rather how little, it would take to impel Collingwood into a quasi-realism of the sort championed by Simon Blackburn[11] whereby absolute presuppositions, despite their differences from ordinary descriptive propositions, are eventually accounted true or false in their own right.[12]

Be that as it may, absolute presuppositions have a regulative role that distinguishes them from scientific beliefs. Even if Collingwood were to accede to some sort of quasi-realism, he would still want to insist on this. Absolute presuppositions do not need to be justified in the way in which scientific beliefs do. They cannot be tested in the way in which scientific beliefs can. They do not *answer* to anything.

A natural question now is whether Collingwood holds any of them to be in any sense universal. Are there absolute presuppositions that human beings have always made? Or the making of which is somehow integral to their very humanity? Or even the making of which is a necessary condition of any coherent thought? The more ambitiously such questions are answered, the greater the prospects of a significant convergence between Collingwoodian metaphysics and Strawsonian descriptive metaphysics of the kind practised by Strawson himself. Collingwood leans the other way however. He writes:

> When [the metaphysician] has some knowledge about several different constellations of absolute presuppositions, he can set to work comparing them. This ... will convince [him] ... that there are no 'eternal' or 'crucial' or 'central' problems in metaphysics.... [And] it will give him a hint of the way in which different sets of absolute presuppositions correspond not only with differences in the structure of what is generally called scientific thought but with differences in the entire fabric of civilization.
>
> ... The metaphysician's business ..., when he has identified several different constellations of absolute presuppositions, is not only to study their likenesses and unlikenesses but also to find out on what occasions and by what processes one of them has turned into another. (pp. 72–73)

---

[11] We have encountered such quasi-realism in a number of contexts: Ch. 1, §3; Ch. 4, §3, esp. n. 32; and Ch. 11, n. 50.

[12] Cf. Mink (1969), pp. 144–145.

True, nothing here strictly precludes there being absolute presuppositions that are common to all the constellations identified. But the fact is that Collingwood never acknowledges, and never shows any inclination to acknowledge, absolute presuppositions that are universal.[13] He views the study of what absolute presuppositions are made not as the study of any constant in human nature, but as the study of contingently changing patterns of thought in their variation from one historical context to another.[14]

Very well, what governs such changing patterns? What form can they take? In particular, is it possible for a relative presupposition to become an absolute presupposition, as it shifts from one context to another? Or for the same thing to happen in reverse?[15]

You might think that such a thing is not possible, on the grounds that whether something admits of truth or falsity is independent of context. It is however a familiar fact that some ways of individuating truth bearers allow for the very same thing to have a truth value in one context and to lack a truth value in another. In fact this is how Collingwood himself views propositions. He urges that the truth or falsity of a given proposition, as used in a given context, depends on what question it is intended to answer, and that the proposition is neither true nor false if the question concerned does not arise (*Autobiography*, pp. 29–31). Thus when Albert says, 'I have stopped beating my wife,' he may speak truly. When Barry says, 'I have stopped beating my wife,' he may speak falsely. And when Charles says, 'I have stopped beating my wife,' he may speak neither truly nor falsely. Admittedly, being neither true nor false falls short of not even admitting of truth or falsity.

---

[13] Not even when he writes as follows? 'In part, the problems of philosophy are unchanging; in part, they vary from age to age, according to the special characteristics of human life and thought at the time; and in the best philosophers of every age these two parts are so interwoven that the permanent problems appear *sub specie sæculi*, and the special problems of the age *sub specie æternitatis*' (*The Idea of History*, pp. 231–232). Well, Collingwood is here talking about philosophy and philosophers rather than about metaphysics and metaphysicians. This is significant, because in another work, *Philosophical Method*, he defends a view of philosophy that is quite different from the view of metaphysics with which we are concerned in this chapter. In fact he goes as far as explicitly to distinguish it from history (ibid., Ch. X, §3). It is unfortunately beyond the scope of this chapter to consider in any detail what Collingwood says about philosophy.

[14] In Ch. II of the *Essay* Collingwood registers his agreement with Aristotle, or at least what he takes to be his agreement with Aristotle, that 'metaphysics ... deals with the presuppositions underlying ... science' (p. 11). Why my qualification? Well, the quoted sentence can be heard in two ways. Heard in one way it implies that there are some presuppositions that all scientists make. Heard in the other way it implies only that all scientists make some presuppositions or other. Given what I have said in the main text, Collingwood must intend it in the latter, weaker sense. But this is not the sense that one would naturally associate with Aristotle.

[15] Cf. Krausz (1972), p. 223.

Even so, it is a small step from here to the conclusion that a proposition that is true in one context and false in a second can lose its very status as a proposition in a third.

So *can* it? Can a relative presupposition become absolute, or an absolute one relative? Well, the following at least is surely possible (on Collingwood's conception of these matters). A declarative sentence that is used to express a relative presupposition in one context comes, through natural processes of semantic evolution, to express an absolute presupposition in another. What are we to say? That one thing is expressed, and that it is a proposition in the first context but not in the second? Or that different things are expressed in the two contexts? That one presupposition is involved, and that it is relative in the first context but absolute in the second? Or that two different presuppositions are involved?[16] This seems to be one of those cases where we do well to invoke Wittgenstein's dictum: 'Say what you choose, so long as it does not prevent you from seeing the facts' (Wittgenstein (1967a), Pt I, §79).[17]

3. A Second (Themed) Retrospective

In this section I shall consider Collingwood in relation to some of our earlier protagonists. I shall try to show how his ideas echo theirs. I hope at the same time to cast further light on what he means by an absolute presupposition.

(a)   Hume

Collingwood is the only one of our protagonists other than Hume who counts (acceptable) metaphysics as an empirical human science (cf. Ch. 4, §4). Despite my efforts in the previous section to demonstrate that this is not the aberration that it appears to be, it will act as an important constraint on how readily his views can be compared to those of other protagonists. Kant is an immediate case in point.

(b)   Kant

Let us call a constellation of consupponible absolute presuppositions an *outlook*.[18] And let us say that, when someone makes all the presuppositions

---

[16] These questions are reminiscent of questions that we have confronted before. Cf. the discussion in Ch. 10, §3, of whether necessities can cease to have that status. Cf. also Ch. 17, §7: are we to say that the game of chess came into existence when the pawn was first allowed to move forward two squares, or are we to say that the game had already existed for a long time and merely underwent a change then?

[17] For helpful discussion of the material considered in this section, see Mink (1969), Ch. 5 and Ch. 8, §3; and Williams (2006j), esp. pp. 351–355.

[18] Cf. pp. 66–67.

in a given outlook, he or she *accepts* that outlook. Then accepting an outlook is *somewhat* akin to donning a pair of Kantian spectacles: it provides a structure within which to make empirical sense of things. I said the same about adopting a Carnapian linguistic framework (Ch. 11, §3(b)). But I also straightway noted two respects in which that analogy was limited. First, Kantian spectacles are non-negotiable conditions of all human thinking. They cannot be 'donned' any more than they can be removed. Second, Kantian spectacles involve intuitions. They are themselves sources of synthetic knowledge. In both these respects they likewise differ from an outlook.

It is the first of these differences that is especially pertinent to the comparison just drawn with Hume. It is precisely because Collingwood denies that any outlook is a condition of all human thinking that Collingwoodian metaphysics is like Humean metaphysics in being an empirical science. This gives the lie to Louis Mink's claim, itself a deliberate allusion to Kant, that absolute presuppositions are *a priori* concepts (Mink (1969), Ch. 5, §5). The claim is not without justification. Absolute presuppositions certainly have something of the conceptual about them, inasmuch as they do not themselves answer truly or falsely to anything but are used in fashioning that which does. They also have something of the *a priori* about them, inasmuch as they give rise to questions concerning our experience without themselves being the answers to any questions concerning our experience. Nevertheless, as Mink himself clearly appreciates, they are not *a priori* in any fully Kantian sense.

The same point gives the lie to Collingwood's own project in Part IIIB of the *Essay*: to do, for the arguments in Kant's 'Transcendental Analytic' (Ch. 5, §5), what we saw him try to do for the ontological argument; that is, to show that, contrary to appearances, they are metaphysical arguments even on his own conception of a metaphysical argument as a piece of history. Kant himself would certainly recoil from this. Collingwood all but concedes as much. So much the worse, he suggests, for Kant. Here is his own summary of the situation as he sees it:

> It may be objected [that] ... we have only to look at the 'Transcendental Analytic' to see that it is not an historical essay....
>
> A second look will, I think, convince the reader that it is one; though I do not suggest its author was aware of this.
>
> ...
>
> The truth is that the 'Transcendental Analytic' is an historical study of the absolute presuppositions generally recognized by natural scientists in Kant's own time and ... for some time afterwards. I cannot add, 'and for some time before', because there is one of them [sc. the Causal Principle (see Ch. XXXIII of the *Essay*)] which I do not know that anybody ever accepted, in the precise form in which he states it, before himself. Some of them go back to Galileo. Some of them are to-day fallen into desuetude....

In the following four chapters I shall try to show how the 'Transcendental Analytic' can be read as a history of the absolute presuppositions of natural science from Galileo to Kant himself.... For Kant it would be hardly an exaggeration to say that the history of natural science from Galileo to his own time was equivalent to the history of natural science as a whole; and in that case the interpretation of the 'Transcendental Analytic' which I am about to offer would make it in Kant's eyes ... a comprehensive history of the entire subject. (pp. 243–246)[19]

The problem for Collingwood is that what he suggests would be hardly an overstatement of what was at stake here for Kant would in fact be a radical understatement of what was at stake here for Kant. Kant simply could not see his own work in these historical terms. It is no good Collingwood saying that he has provided an interpretation of Kant to which Kant would find it hard to subscribe simply because of his parochialism. He has not provided an interpretation of Kant at all.

All of that said, the original limited analogy, between accepting an outlook and donning a pair of Kantian spectacles, survives.[20]

(c)   Hegel (and Bergson)

In the previous section I raised the question of what governs changing patterns of thought from one historical context to another. This is just the sort of question which, on Collingwood's view – as he explicitly says (p. 73) – it is the metaphysician's business to address. He suggests that the question admits of a broadly Hegelian answer.

> One phase changes into another because the first phase was in unstable equilibrium and had in itself the seeds of change, and indeed of that change. Its fabric was not at rest; it was always under strain. If the world of history is a world in which *tout passe, tout lasse, tout casse*, the analysis of the internal strains to which a given constellation of historical facts is subjected, and of the means by which it 'takes up' these strains, or prevents them from breaking it to pieces, is not the least part of an historian's work.
>
> ... If Hegel's influence on nineteenth-century historiography was on the whole an influence for good, it was because historical study for him was first and foremost a study of internal strains. (pp. 74–75)

---

[19] I have taken the liberty of replacing Collingwood's references to 'the Transcendental Analytics' by references to 'the "Transcendental Analytic"' in conformity with my own earlier usage.

[20] There is a related but much more powerful analogy, which I anticipated in Ch. 7, n. 20, between Collingwood and Foucault. See again Foucault's characterization of the 'historical *a priori*' which I quoted in that note.

How much further in a Hegelian direction Hegel's undoubtedly large influence on Collingwood takes him is a matter of substantive exegetical debate.[21] The characteristic way in which tensions among absolute presuppositions can lead to their supersession by new absolute presuppositions is certainly reminiscent of Hegelian *Aufhebung* and its dialectical processes. But more than that would be required for Collingwood's position to merit classification as a kind of Hegelianism. There is no suggestion, for instance, that such change constitutes any kind of advance in the self-understanding of a world-spirit.[22] In fact there is no suggestion that it constitutes any kind of advance. (See further §4.) Collingwood himself insists that the only such advance that we can expect is in the actual practice of metaphysics: 'not a process by which errors *in* our presuppositions are corrected[, but] ... a process by which errors *about* our presuppositions are corrected' ('Function of Metaphysics', p. 401, emphasis in original). (This of course connects with his insistence that absolute presuppositions are neither true nor false.)[23]

If anything, the essentially unpredictable processes in question, which Collingwood takes to be retrospectively but not antecedently intelligible, and which he takes to issue in a novelty whereby 'the past lives in the present' (*Speculum*, p. 301), are more reminiscent of Bergson than they are of Hegel. See for example the following passage:

> History ... is not a sheer flux of unique and disconnected events.... And, on the other hand, it is not a barren cyclical repetition of the same pattern over and over again, still less a shuffling of rearranged units like repeated throws of dice, every new event an arbitrary selection from a given number of possibilities. It is a process in which method or regularity does not exclude novelty; for every phase, while it grows out of the preceding phase, sums it up in the immediacy of its own being and thereby sums up implicitly the whole of previous history. Every such summation is a new act, and history consists of this perpetual summation of itself. (*Speculum*, p. 56)

(d)   The Later Wittgenstein

There are clear similarities between Collingwood and the later Wittgenstein. I am thinking in particular of the later Wittgenstein's work on how our

---

[21] Louis Mink is particularly keen to emphasize the Hegelianism in Collingwood's thinking. See Mink (1969), Pt I passim, and Ch. 5, §6; and Mink (1972), esp. §III. The works on which Mink especially draws in defence of his view are *Speculum* and *Philosophical Method*, both of which are earlier than the *Essay*.

[22] On the contrary: see *Speculum*, p. 298.

[23] The advance in question does count as part of 'a self-knowing process' (*Speculum*, p. 301). But again it is a matter of substantive exegetical debate in quite how Hegelian a way Collingwood intends this, or can reasonably intend it: see *Speculum*, Ch. VII, passim.

forms of life determine what makes sense to us and what questions can arise for us (Ch. 10, §3). The most signal point of comparison is between Collingwood's very notion of an absolute presupposition and Wittgenstein's notion of what has come to be called, by courtesy of the following passage from *On Certainty*,[24] a 'hinge proposition'.

> The *questions* that we raise and our *doubts* depend on the fact that some propositions are exempt from doubt, are as it were like hinges on which these turn.
>
> That is to say, it belongs to the logic of our scientific investigations that certain things are *in deed* not doubted.
>
> But it isn't that the situation is like this: We just *can't* investigate every-thing, and for that reason we are forced to rest content with assumption. If we want the door to turn, the hinges must stay put.
>
> My *life* consist in my being content to accept many things. (§§341–344, emphasis in original)[25]

But how far does this comparison extend? Hinge propositions are, after all, *propositions*. At least, Wittgenstein calls them 'propositions'. Is that not a crucial difference between what he has in mind and what Collingwood has in mind?

Well, is it? There is an issue about whether hinge propositions admit of truth or falsity. (Some sections of *On Certainty*, such as §§4 and 403, can be taken to suggest that they do; some, such as §§94, 204, and 205, can be taken to suggest that they do not.) But even if they do, we saw in the previous section how little it might take for Collingwood to resile and to concede that absolute presuppositions likewise admit of truth or falsity. One suspects that this is another of those cases in which Wittgenstein, at least, will be indifferent to what we say – provided that certain relevant features of the case have been made clear and remain clear. And central among these features is the fact that it is at any rate problematical to say that such propositions are *known* (e.g. §347). They are rather *acted on* (e.g. §§148, 196, 204, and 232). But that too is comparable to what we find in Collingwood (e.g. p. 43). In fact, in the context of everything else that Wittgenstein says about such propositions, it helps to strengthen our grip on what we find in

---

[24] Wittgenstein (1974b): all unaccompanied section references in this sub-section are to this book.

[25] There is much in Collingwood that is reminiscent of this (or rather, of which this is reminiscent – Collingwood's work predates *On Certainty*). Cf. esp. p. 173, where he writes, 'We do not acquire absolute presuppositions by arguing; on the contrary, unless we have them already arguing is impossible to us. Nor can we change them by arguing; unless they remained constant all our arguments would fall to pieces.'

Note: it was to hinge propositions that I was referring in Ch. 10, n. 27.

Collingwood. It gives us another handle on what he means by an absolute presupposition.[26]

There are also points of comparison between the two thinkers' methodologies. Collingwood is prepared to say about some of his own work in metaphysics that he is not 'trying to convince the reader of anything, but only to remind him of what he already knows perfectly well' (p. 23; cf. *The Idea of Nature*, pp. 59–60). He also dissociates metaphysics from the propounding of 'doctrines' (p. 68) and expresses approval of Samuel Alexander's conviction that 'a metaphysician's business is not to argue but to recognize facts[, facts which] … are not recondite or remote … but simple and familiar' (p. 172). In all of this there are echoes of §§124–129 of Part I of Wittgenstein's *Investigations*.[27]

There is one respect in which Collingwood is perhaps more secure in his metaphysical practice than Wittgenstein. Nothing in that practice constitutes any kind of inducement to embrace transcendental idealism. Any 'we' that appears in Collingwood's texts and whose absolute presuppositions are under investigation is a historically rooted 'we': that is precisely the point of the exercise. The reader is not tempted to construe any such 'we' as the source of all possible sense-making, still less to think that it provides some kind of boundary around the domain of all possible sense-making. (See Ch. 10, §4.)[28]

(e)   Carnap and the Logical Positivists

The obvious comparison between Collingwood and Carnap was alluded to in §3(b). Insofar as accepting what I have called an outlook and adopting a Carnapian linguistic framework are each akin to donning a pair of Kantian spectacles, each is akin to the other. Each, as I put it earlier, provides a structure within which to make empirical sense of things. There are countless differences between them however. The most important of these is that adopting a linguistic framework is something that one typically does by making a conscious choice from a range of options. Accepting an outlook, by contrast, is something that one typically does by assimilating one's 'cultural equipment': one's 'outfit of social and political habits,

---

[26] It is worth noting also, in view of our earlier discussion about whether a presupposition can change its status as absolute from one context to another, that Wittgenstein does allow for a proposition to change its status as a hinge proposition from one context to another: see e.g. §§94–98, 349, and 622.

[27] But Collingwood had better allow *some* room for the remote and unfamiliar in metaphysics. The absolute presuppositions under investigation may be those of a remote and unfamiliar people.

[28] Cf. Williams (2006j), pp. 355–358.

... religion, ... education, and so forth' (p. 60). In the former case one can elect to stop doing it, perhaps in favour of another of the options. In the latter case one might not be able to stop doing it while maintaining a sane grip on reality. And certainly one will not be able to stop doing it by simply selecting an alternative outlook of which one happens to be aware and accepting that instead. Even the most empathetic twentieth-century historian cannot just *take on* the outlook of a medieval monk, say.

There is another point of comparison between Collingwood and Carnap, in a type of illusion that they both recognize. Both think that a sentence can appear to be being used straightforwardly, to discuss its regular subject matter, when really it is being used obliquely, to discuss one of its own functions or a function of one of the expressions in it, with the result that a quite legitimate intellectual exercise assumes the guise of a piece of improper metaphysics, or of what Collingwood would call 'pseudo-metaphysics'. A Carnapian example would be this: Smith, using the sentence 'There are positive integers,' appears to be defending the view that there are positive integers, but is really defending the view that there are advantages in adopting a linguistic framework that allows us to use the expression 'positive integer' in certain ways (cf. Ch. 11, §5(a)). A Collingwoodian example would be the very example we saw him give in the previous section: Anselm, using the sentence 'God exists,' appears to be arguing for the existence of God, but is really arguing that this sentence expresses an absolute presupposition to which he and his audience are committed. Both Smith and Anselm, on Carnap's and Collingwood's respective views, appear to be attempting the impossible. Both appear to be trying to verify that which admits of neither verification nor falsification because it is neither true nor false. In fact each is involved in an unexceptionable exploration of some structure within which to make empirical sense of things.

Collingwood thinks that, had logical positivists more generally had a better sense of this type of illusion, they would not have had the antipathy towards proper metaphysics that they had. Precisely their error, he argues, was to mistake proper metaphysics, the attempt to identify absolute presuppositions, for pseudo-metaphysics, the attempt to verify absolute presuppositions. They did not realize that, when they argued that the latter was a forlorn endeavour and that the relevant sentences (those expressing the absolute presuppositions in question) were literally meaningless, in the sense that they did not express anything either true or false, this was, or at least it should have been, music to their opponents' ears. (See *Essay*, Ch. XVI.[29])

The final irony, to which I do not think Collingwood ever draws attention, is this. To the question which is often taken to present a damning objection

---

[29] And for further criticism of logical positivism, see ibid., Chs XIV and XVIII.

to logical positivism, namely, 'What is the status of the principle of verification itself?' (see Ch. 11, §6), logical positivists can turn to Collingwood for
an attractive answer: it is an absolute presupposition.

(f)   The Phenomenologists

A couple of points, lastly, in connection with the phenomenologists.[30]

First, Collingwood is interestingly poised with respect to the phenomenologists' anti-naturalism. Like them, he is concerned to make sense of
how we make sense of things. Moreover, he is no more inclined than they
are to believe that this can be done using the methods and principles of the
natural sciences. But, unlike them, he does believe that it can be done (and
must be done) using the methods and principles of the social sciences, of
which he takes metaphysics to be one. There is not a *hint* here of any phenomenological reduction.

This brings us to the second point. Collingwood may show no inclination
to pursue any such reduction. But, just as he has the resources to furnish
logical positivists with an attractive answer to the question of what the status of their principle of verification is, so too, I contend, he has the resources
to furnish phenomenologists with an attractive account of what their phenomenological reduction consists in: it is the suspension of a set of absolute
presuppositions, or of what I have been calling an outlook. When Husserl
discusses his pre-phenomenological commitment to 'the general thesis of
the natural standpoint', in other words the thesis that the spatio-temporal
world 'has its being out there' (Husserl (1962), §30) – which is of course the
most basic of his convictions to be suspended in his reduction – he makes
that thesis, *qua* object of that pre-phenomenological commitment, sound
very much like an absolute presupposition. Without it, there are various
questions that do not so much as arise. But it is not itself in any straightforward sense the answer to any question.[31]

---

[30] And an incidental third point. Collingwood opposes Heidegger by arguing that the very
idea of an enquiry into pure being is incoherent: see *Essay*, Chs II and III. But Heidegger
anticipates Collingwood's arguments: see Heidegger (1962a), pp. 22–23/p. 3 in the original German.

[31] See e.g. Husserl (1981b), §7. (As with the later Wittgenstein, there is an issue about
whether Collingwood's insistence that absolute presuppositions are neither true nor false,
and in particular not true, is enough to scupper this comparison. But, again as with the
later Wittgenstein, this issue may not be as significant as it appears.) Cf. Collingwood's
discussion of the absolute presupposition 'that there is such a thing as "nature"[, i.e.] ...
that there are things that happen quite irrespectively of anything [anyone does]' (p. 192).
Beware, however, that Collingwood has in mind a quite particular contrast between
'nature' and 'art' and is talking about an absolute presupposition that not everyone has
made. Husserl, though he thinks he can cease to adopt the natural standpoint, never

(g)   Coda

Finally, though it may still not be clear what exactly an absolute presupposition is, I think this section has at least left us with the following schematic
idea:

> *an absolute presupposition is a non-propositional way of making
> propositional sense of things.*

That idea is enough to carry us forward to the next section.

4.   Collingwood's Conservatism. The Possibilities Afforded by Non-Propositional Sense-Making

On Collingwood's conception of metaphysics, it is the metaphysician's
business to study absolute presuppositions that are made; no more, no less;
in particular, no more. That makes the conception a profoundly conservative one. To the Novelty Question which I posed in §6 of the Introduction
Collingwood has a clear answer: there is no scope for metaphysicians to
make sense of things in ways that are radically new. True, a metaphysician
studying the absolute presuppositions of a remote and unfamiliar people
will have to make sense of things in ways that are correspondingly remote
and unfamiliar.[32] For, as we saw in §2, the study of those presuppositions
will be successful only to the extent that it is empathetic. But the remote
and the unfamiliar here are the remote and the unfamiliar merely from the
standpoint of the metaphysician's own community. The metaphysician is
not entering sense-making territory that no one has ever previously entered;
precisely not.

Why this restricted conception of metaphysics? Why should a metaphysician not investigate absolute presuppositions that *may be* made, even
though they never have been, and, where appropriate, promote them, by
pointing out the advantages that may accrue from making them? Admittedly,
for reasons that I gave in §3(e), merely pointing out the advantages that may
accrue from making new absolute presuppositions cannot by itself achieve

---

doubts that to do so is, precisely, unnatural; that he is talking about convictions that are
common to everyone (see e.g. Husserl (1962), §27).

There is a further comparison attendant on this one. We saw in Ch. 17, §4, how Husserl
thought that beliefs bracketed in the phenomenological reduction could be regained by
other means. Collingwood likewise thinks that a proposition that is a potential answer
to one question may also be, nay will also be, a potential answer to some other question
(*Autobiography*, pp. 29–30).

[32] Cf. n. 27.

much: call this *low-grade* promotion. For a community to accept a new outlook, the outlook must actually be put to work within the community in such a way that those for whom it is initially alien can, by absorbing the effects of accepting it, gradually come to accept it themselves: call this *high-grade* promotion. But why should metaphysicians not be involved in high-grade promotion too? This is what scientists are involved in, however unwittingly, whenever scientific practice changes a community's outlook. Why should metaphysical practice not likewise change a community's outlook?

Collingwood, as we have seen, has his own quasi-Hegelian story to tell about how one outlook, or at least one set of absolute presuppositions,[33] yields to another (§3(c)). He may defend his conservatism by saying that the 'internal strains' that govern such a process cannot be in any way controlled, nor the process itself in any way directed. But remember, even Hegel had his 'world-historical individuals' who helped to instigate whatever advances in our fundamental sense-making reason's growth in self-understanding demanded (Ch. 7, §5).[34]

A second thing that Collingwood may say, in fact does say, this time putting himself at a greater distance from Hegel, is that no set of absolute presuppositions is superior to another. The metaphysician can observe how one set yields to another, but has no business *making* one set yield to another, having no basis on which to do so. This is a dominant theme of 'Function of Metaphysics', in which Collingwood states his position as starkly as anywhere.

> [It] will be asked ... whether it is in *no* sense the business of the metaphysician to criticize or suggest improvements in the ... presuppositions which he discovers by analysis to be implied in the thought of his community. 'What is his business,' it will be asked, 'if he finds out that among these presuppositions there are some that are altogether silly ...? Is he to refrain from saying what he thinks of them, and may he not suggest improvements, granted that he can think of improvements? Or again, what if he discovers some that are to the best of his belief untrue? Is he not to denounce them and propose their replacements by true ones? In a word has he no kind of *critical* rights or duties with regard to these presuppositions?'

---

[33] A set of absolute presuppositions falls short of being an outlook if the presuppositions in it are not consupponible. But lack of consupponibility is liable to be just what is at stake here.

[34] For some recognition on Collingwood's part that an individual can indeed direct the transition from one outlook to another, see 'Function of Metaphysics', p. 410, where he suggests that this is what Kant did with respect to the Causal Principle.

> The answer to these questions is in my opinion a simple *no*. ('Function
> of Metaphysics', pp. 394–395, emphasis in original)

As Collingwood goes on to defend this answer, much of his effort is devoted
to establishing what is for us by now a familiar point, namely that such
presuppositions are neither true nor false. But that is not the sum of his
argument. He makes clear that he sees no other rationale for preferring one
set to another either.

Collingwood has various ways of defending his conservatism then. It
seems to me, however, that a significant factor in his recoil from the possibility of metaphysicians promoting new absolute presuppositions is a tacit
(relative) presupposition of his own: that any sense which it is the prerogative of metaphysicians to make must be propositional sense. Call this the
Propositional Assumption. Note that, even if the Propositional Assumption
is true, it is not decisive in this matter. For it is not clear why either the
low-grade promotion of new absolute presuppositions, through talking
about them, or the high-grade promotion of new absolute presuppositions,
through actually making them, should involve doing anything other than
justifying and asserting propositions; should involve, in other words, making anything other than propositional sense. Even so, how much greater will
the scope of metaphysicians for promoting new absolute presuppositions be
if the Propositional Assumption is false?

I am not just making the simple point that metaphysicians can then avail
themselves of non-propositional means of expressing the presuppositions
in question – which, on Collingwood's own view, will include declarative
sentences. (Mind you, the simple point does deserve to be made, especially
when we find Collingwood seemingly taking for granted that a metaphysician's use of the sentence 'God exists' can *only* be of the oblique kind
considered in §3(e), to express the proposition that God's existence is an
absolute presupposition made by certain people. (See e.g. *Essay*, Ch. XVIII;
and cf. 'Function of Metaphysics', pp. 404–405.)) There is a broader point.
If metaphysicians are not subject to the shackles of propositional sense-
making – if they need not always be trying to utter truths – then who knows
what imagination they may show, or what means they may devise, perhaps
of an essentially artistic nature, to impart, instil, and generally promote new
absolute presuppositions?[35] This broader point is itself an instance of what

---

[35] Cf. *Philosophical Method*, Ch. X, §2.9, where Collingwood argues that philosophy is
unlike science, especially in its use of language; and Ch. X, §4, where he goes on to say
why it is more like poetry. This is certainly conducive to the point that I am making.
Recall, however, that his view of philosophy in that work is quite different from the view
of metaphysics with which we have been concerned: see n. 13. Furthermore, even in the
passages mentioned, he does not go as far as I am recommending. Thus on p. 214 he
writes, 'The philosopher's word-patterns are constructed only to reveal the thought which
they express.'

has come to be a recurring theme in this enquiry. Insofar as there are possibilities afforded by non-propositional sense-making which are not afforded by propositional sense-making, the prospects for the most general attempt to make sense of things, and the prospects, more specifically, for radical innovation in the most general attempt to make sense of things, will be that much greater if the attempt does not have to be an exercise in sense-making of the latter (propositional) kind.[36]

---

[36] Compare some of the ideas in this section with Martin (1998), pp. xlvii–li. But Rex Martin is more sympathetic to Collingwood than I am. He also sees greater scope in Collingwood than I do for acknowledging progress in the transition from one outlook to another.

CHAPTER 20

✦

Derrida

Metaphysics Deconstructed?

1. A Foretaste

At the end of each of the two previous chapters I adverted to the important difference that it can make, in the most general attempt to make sense of things, if the sense concerned need not be propositional, if the aim of the exercise need not be to produce true declarative sentences, as in the sciences, but to produce something closer to artwork. I urged that Collingwood would have done well to acknowledge this possibility and that Heidegger may have shown in his practice that he did acknowledge it, however unself-consciously. But it was Chapter 9 that provided the model.[1] The maximally general sense-making in which the early Wittgenstein was engaged was non-propositional, and the way in which he tried to convey it was through a creative use of nonsense.

Wittgenstein was still using language however. He may not have been intending to produce true declarative sentences, but he was still affecting to do so. The sense that he was trying to convey may not have been linguistic,[2] but his medium was. (Similarly in Heidegger's case.) This chapter will provide a further indication of how linguistic resources might be used to convey non-propositional sense.

2. Derrida *Vis-à-Vis* Phenomenology; or, Derrida *Pro* Heidegger and *Contra* Husserl

(a)   Derrida Pro *Heidegger*

On certain fundamental matters that are especially pertinent to our enquiry Jacques Derrida (1930–2004) is a card-carrying Heideggerian.[3] In particular,

---

[1] Though see also Ch. 16, §6(a), on the use of language to evoke inexpressible metaphysical insights.

[2] See Ch. 14, n. 7, for the relation between linguistic sense and propositional sense. (Note that, on a very attenuated conception of linguistic sense, the sheer fact that he was using language in the way in which he was would be enough to make any sense he conveyed linguistic.)

[3] I shall be focusing on Derrida's early work in this chapter – that being what is most directly relevant to our enquiry. (See Ch. 9, n. 5.)

he accepts Heidegger's distinction between Being and beings, and he shares Heidegger's repudiation of traditional metaphysics. 'What I have attempted to do,' he says in an interview with Henri Ronse, 'would not have been possible without the opening of Heidegger's questions[,] … would not have been possible without the attention to what Heidegger calls the difference between Being and beings' ('Implications', p. 8[4]). And he agrees with Heidegger that precisely what traditional metaphysics has done is to ignore this difference. Metaphysics is a legitimate activity only if it treats of Being. But traditional metaphysics has proceeded as though it were a natural science. And natural sciences can treat only of beings. (See Ch. 18, §4; and cf. 'Violence and Metaphysics', pp. 140ff.)

One concept that becomes pivotal to this critique in Derrida's hands is that of presence. In fact he refers to traditional metaphysics as 'the metaphysics of presence' (e.g. 'Structure', p. 281). There is a passage in *Being and Time* in which Heidegger says, in connection with the ancients:

> Beings [were] grasped in their Being as 'presence'; this means that they [were] understood with regard to a definite mode of time – the '*present*'. (Heidegger (1962a), p. 47/p. 25 in the original German, emphasis in original; cf. Heidegger (1972), passim)[5]

Derrida fastens on this passage (e.g. '*Ousia* and *Grammē*', p. 31). He takes Heidegger to be signalling how and where things began to go wrong (though, as we shall see, he is less sympathetic to the idea that there was an earlier golden age in which they had gone right). He thinks that the fundamental error of traditional metaphysics has been to identify Being with presence, usually understood very narrowly as applying only to that which is given, in the present, as present, to consciousness; and that this is what has made it so difficult for metaphysicians properly to come to terms with the

---

[4] Throughout this chapter I use the following abbreviations for Derrida's works: 'Baldwin' for Derrida (2001b); 'Cogito' for Derrida (1978a); '*Différance*' for Derrida (1982a); 'Following Theory' for Derrida (2004); 'Form and Meaning' for Derrida (1982c); *Grammatology* for Derrida (1976); 'Hospitality' for Derrida (1999); 'Implications' for Derrida (2002a); 'Interview' for Derrida (1984); 'Letter to a Friend' for Derrida (1988b); 'Limited Inc' for Derrida (1988a); *Memoires* for Derrida (1986); 'Moore' for Derrida (2001a); '*Ousia* and *Grammē*' for Derrida (1982b); 'Phenomenology' for Derrida (1978c); 'Positions' for Derrida (2002c); 'Reason' for Derrida (1983); 'Semiology' for Derrida (2002b); '*Sec*' for Derrida (1982e), an abbreviation incidentally proposed by Derrida himself in 'Limited Inc', p. 37, and further explained in the accompanying n. 1 (pp. 108–109); *Speech and Phenomena* for Derrida (1973); 'Structure' for Derrida (1978d); 'The Original Discussion' for Derrida et al. (1988); *The Post Card* for Derrida (1987); 'Violence and Metaphysics' for Derrida (1978b); and 'White Mythology' for Derrida (1982d).

[5] I have taken the liberty of dropping John Macquarrie's and Edward Robinson's capitalization of 'Present' in their translation. For their policy on this matter, see their n. 2 on p. 47 of ibid.

difference between Being and beings. It is this error that he thinks Heidegger
has helped us overcome. (See e.g. 'Structure', pp. 278ff., and 'Ousia and
Grammē', passim.)

One way in which he thinks Heidegger has helped us overcome this error
is by helping us to think properly about absence (e.g. 'Ousia and Grammē',
pp. 63–67; cf. Grammatology, pp. 166–167).[6] Another is by helping us to
think properly about something which, though it is intimately related to
both presence and absence, is different from each of them, namely the trace
of what is not present within what is (cf. Grammatology, p. 70). Metaphysics
has not taken due account of this trace. On the contrary, it has '[striven]
toward [its] reduction' (Grammatology, p. 71). And this trace has ironically
included the trace of the very difference between Being and beings to which
metaphysics has at the same time been oblivious, the trace which it has itself
created. Here is Derrida:

> What Heidegger wants to mark is this: the difference between Being and
> beings, the forgotten of metaphysics, has disappeared without leaving a
> trace. The very trace of difference has been submerged. If we maintain
> that [the difference between Being and beings is itself] other than absence
> and presence, ... then when it is a matter of the forgetting of the differ-
> ence (between Being and beings), we would have to speak of a disappear-
> ance of the trace of the trace....
>
> ... [But] the erasure of the early trace ... of difference is ... the 'same'
> as its tracing in the text of metaphysics. The latter must have maintained
> the mark of what it has lost, reserved, put aside. The paradox of such a
> structure, in the language of metaphysics, is an inversion of metaphysical
> concepts, which produces the following effect: the present becomes ...
> the trace of the trace. ('Différance', pp. 22–23)[7]

We can put it in terms of the Transcendence Question which I posed in
§6 of the Introduction. In some sense traditional metaphysicians have not
tried properly to make sense of what is transcendent. That is, they have not
tried properly to make sense of what, on their own narrow conception of

---

[6] Note: we must not confuse absence with the 'nothing' whose connections with Being we
saw Heidegger forge in Ch. 18, §6. The latter is something altogether more basic. The paradigmatic way in which Dasein confronts absence is by anticipating something and then
failing to perceive that thing. (Cf. Sartre's famous discussion of the absence of his friend
Pierre from the café in Sartre (2003), pp. 9–11.) The paradigmatic way in which Dasein
confronts the nothing is by acknowledging the possibility of its own non-existence.

[7] The material that I have inserted in the first set of square brackets is not strictly faithful
to Derrida's text, where he uses his coinage 'différance'. But introduction of that coinage
must wait until later: see §5. For now I hope that this deviation from the original does no
great harm. (There is some justification for it elsewhere in the same essay, e.g. p. 26. This
too will receive attention in §5.)

presence, is not present. What they have done, in their inchoate awareness that too little of metaphysical concern is present on that narrow conception, is to conjure up a transcendence of their own. They have followed Plato in conceiving a realm of beings that are indeed present, on that narrow conception, but by being eternal, that is by being always present, thus transcending the sensible and the transitory; and they have allowed what should have been an attempt to make sense of Being to become an attempt to make sense of just such beings, in particular those that supposedly equip them to arrive at a maximally general understanding of things. Here is Derrida again:

> [The matrix of the history of metaphysics] is the determination of Being as *presence* in all senses of this word. It could be shown that all the names related to fundamentals, to principles, or to the centre have always desig-nated an invariable presence – *eidos, archē, telos, energeia, ousia* (essence, existence, substance, subject), *alētheia*, transcendentality, consciousness, God, man, and so forth. ('Structure', pp. 279–280)[8]

Metaphysics, in Derrida's view, should be rid of its obsessive concern with such beings; rid, in fact, of the idea that such beings exist at all.

This is reminiscent of Nietzsche, whose revolt against that same Platonism[9] Heidegger, whilst fully acknowledging it, nevertheless saw as itself a contribution, albeit the last remaining possible contribution, to tra-ditional metaphysics. This gives Derrida pause. On the one hand he thinks that this is an injustice of sorts to Nietzsche, whom he takes to have broken with the tradition in ways for which Heidegger gives him insufficient credit (*Grammatology*, pp. 18ff.). On the other hand he thinks that two can play at Heidegger's game: there is as much rationale for us to say that Heidegger's struggles with the tradition constitute a contribution to it as there is for him to say that Nietzsche's do (e.g. 'Structure', pp. 281–282 and *Ousia and Grammē*, pp. 47–48; cf. 'Positions', pp. 48–49).[10]

Derrida's Heideggerianism is far from unqualified then. The quarrel over Nietzsche illustrates what is perhaps his principal departure from Heidegger. He is altogether more pessimistic than Heidegger about the prospects for what I called in Chapter 18 'good' metaphysics. By the same token he is suspicious of Heidegger's belief that a form of good metaphysics prevailed among the pre-Socratics. Where Heidegger believes that we can make sense

---

[8] The Greek words '*eidos*', '*archē*', '*telos*', '*energeia*', and '*alētheia*' would standardly be translated as 'form', 'origin', 'purpose', 'activity', and 'truth', respectively. '*Ousia*' has the meanings indicated in Derrida's own parentheses.

[9] For what is intended by the label 'Platonism' here, see Plato's *Republic*, esp. Bks V – VII. (Cf. Ch. 8, n. 55, and accompanying text.)

[10] Up to a point Heidegger can agree with this: see Ch. 18, §4, esp. the lengthy quotation from Heidegger (1982b), pp. 21–23. This is connected to issues that we shall address later concerning Derrida's own relation to the tradition: see §4.

of Being by determining its meaning – '[by naming] the essential nature of
Being, ... [by] finding in thought the word for Being' (Heidegger (1984b),
p. 52) – Derrida, in much more Nietzschean vein, believes that we can at
most make sense of Being by supplying ever new interpretations of it from
ever changing points of view. It is in the same vein that he writes:

> There will be no unique name, even if it were the name of Being. And we
> must think this without *nostalgia*, that is, outside of the myth of ... a lost
> native country of thought. On the contrary, we must *affirm* this, in the
> sense in which Nietzsche puts affirmation into play, in a certain laughter
> and a certain step of the dance.
>
> From the vantage of this laughter and this dance, ... the other side
> of nostalgia, what I will call Heideggerian *hope*, comes into question.
> ('*Différance*', p. 27, emphasis in original)[11]

(b)   *Derrida* Contra *Husserl*

Although Derrida's Heideggerianism means that there is a line of descent
from Husserl to Derrida, Husserl is actually one of Derrida's primary targets, if not the primary one. Recall Husserl's 'principle of all principles',
quoted at the end of the lengthy parenthetical addendum to Chapter 17,
§3. Derrida takes this to be a way of acceding to what he calls '[the] *presence* of sense to a full and primordial intuition' (*Speech and Phenomena*,
p. 5, emphasis in original).[12] In other words – in the words that I used
in the previous sub-section – he takes the principle to be a way of acceding to the idea that Being amounts to being given, in the present, as
present, to consciousness.[13] If anything belongs to the metaphysics of
presence, Derrida insists, this does. (At one point he refers to 'the embed-
ding of transcendental phenomenology in the metaphysics of presence'
('Cogito', p. 60).)

Now Heidegger too took issue with Husserl, as we saw in Chapter 18,
§2(c). Indeed he rejected Husserl's very phenomenological reduction, along
with its concomitant the transcendental Ego, at least as Husserl himself
understood these. And really Derrida is just playing out a variation on that
Heideggerian theme, albeit a variation in which many of the original contrasts

---

[11] Cf. Norris (1987), pp. 160–161. Generally helpful for this sub-section is Spivak
(1976), §II.

[12] See Ch. 17, n. 30, for an explanation of the broad sense of 'intuition' intended here.

[13] See also *Speech and Phenomena*, p. 40, and 'Form and Meaning', p. 172. As far as 'in
the present' is concerned, cf. Husserl (1962), §111, which Derrida cites in *Speech and
Phenomena*, p. 58. But see below for reservations about how fair Derrida's portrayal of
Husserl is.

are accentuated in important ways. Thus Derrida rails against the idea of a transcendental Ego, conceived as a self-contained world-independent consciousness which is brought to light by the reduction and which, though distinct from the psychological Ego, is nevertheless curiously in tandem with it (e.g. *Speech and Phenomena*, pp. 10ff.; 'Violence and Metaphysics', pp. 134–135; and 'Phenomenology', p. 165). 'Between consciousness and ... the "world",' Derrida writes, with somewhat uncharacteristic understatement, 'the rupture, even in the subtle form of the reduction, is perhaps not possible' (*Grammatology*, p. 67). And he thinks that one crucial symptom of consciousness' inextricability from the 'world' is its relation to that which lies beyond it in the past or future:

> Does not everything that is announced already in [the] reduction to 'solitary mental life' ... appear to be stricken in its very possibility by what we are calling time [i.e. by time conceived as transcending what is immediately present to consciousness]? ... Is not the concept of pure solitude – of the monad in the phenomenological sense – *undermined* by its own origin, by the very condition of its self-presence, that is, by 'time,' to be conceived ... on the basis ... of difference within auto-affection[14] ...?
> (*Speech and Phenomena*, p. 68, emphasis in original)

Finally, taking his lead once again from Heidegger, he thinks that the most pungent and most elemental instance of the subject's relation to what lies beyond it in the past or future is its relation to its own eventual nonexistence, something else for which he thinks Husserl is unable to give a satisfactory account (e.g. *Speech and Phenomena*, p. 54, and 'Phenomenology', pp. 167–168).

But, as I have already intimated, Derrida's recoil from Husserl is more extreme than Heidegger's. Though he claims at one point to be providing a critique of phenomenology 'in the name of phenomenology' ('Hospitality', p. 81), it is hard ultimately to see him as remaining in the camp. Elsewhere his critique takes the form of an assault on the very possibility of a phenomenological reduction:

> Auto-affection supposed that a pure difference comes to divide self-presence. In this pure difference is rooted the possibility of everything we think we can exclude from auto-affection: space, the outside, the world, the body, etc. As soon as it is admitted that auto-affection is the condition for self-presence, no pure transcendental reduction[15] is possible. (*Speech and Phenomena*, p. 82)

[14] For current purposes we can understand 'difference within auto-affection' as a reference to the way in which the subject is given what is not temporally present.

[15] For current purposes we can ignore any difference between this term and 'phenomenological reduction': cf. Ch. 17, n. 13.

Elsewhere again, in an allusion to the phenomenological slogan 'Back to the things themselves' he writes:

> Contrary to what phenomenology … has tried to make us believe, contrary to what our desire cannot fail to be tempted into believing, the thing itself always escapes. (*Speech and Phenomena*, p. 104)

Derrida may be Heideggerian on crucial points of doctrine. He may even be Heideggerian on crucial points of methodology. But for reasons that we glimpsed at the end of the previous sub-section, and that we shall explore further in the next section, he is unable to commit himself to the phenomenological project in the way in which Heidegger does.[16]

Derrida's criticisms of Husserl put him at a greater remove than Heidegger then. But how fair are they? On many issues, most notably on the issue of how the subject relates to the past and the future, there is good reason to think that they are not fair.[17] But that is because there is good reason to think that the exegesis underlying them is not fair.[18] If we consider Derrida's criticisms as criticisms of the views themselves, irrespective of whether these views are Husserl's, then they seem to me to constitute some of his most penetrating writing.[19]

3.   Speech and Writing

As we have seen, the fact that Derrida is, as I put it in the previous section, a card-carrying Heideggerian on certain fundamental matters does not make him a card-carrying Heideggerian on all matters, still less an unregenerate card-carrying phenomenologist. In this section we shall reconsider the way in which he distances himself from phenomenology, and especially from Husserl. 'Reconsider' is the operative word. The ideas that we shall see him parade in this section are not essentially different from the ideas that we saw him parade in the previous section. But we shall see him give importantly new expression to them. Heidegger will once again provide the initial inspiration.

---

[16] For a very helpful and nuanced discussion of Derrida's relation to phenomenology, see Glendinning (2007), Ch. 7.

[17] See esp. *Speech and Phenomena*, §5. For counters, see Wood (2001), pp. 122–126, and Turetzky (1998), pp. 172–173.

[18] Perhaps wilfully? One possibility, highlighted by what we shall be exploring later in this chapter, is that Derrida is doing deliberate violence to some of Husserl's texts as a way of reworking the concepts operative in them so as to create something new (cf. 'Semiology', p. 22, a passage to which we shall return in §4).

[19] See *Speech and Phenomena*, passim.

Heidegger held language to be of utmost significance in how we make sense of things, and therefore in the character of Being. He wrote:

> Language is the house of Being. In its home man dwells. Those who think and those who create with words are guardians of this home. (Heidegger (1993c), p. 193)

He was not making the Whorfian point that the fundamental categories people use to make sense of things are affected by the language they happen to use.[20] That is an anthropological point. Heidegger's point is a phenomenological point: the very structure of language reflects how things are given to us. (See Heidegger (1962a), §§33 and 34.)

Derrida too comes to regard language as a focal point both in the project of making sense of how we make sense of things and in his own more specific project of saying why he wants to keep phenomenology at bay. He uses linguistic notions to provide an alternative characterization of the metaphysics of presence. This enables him not only to explain further what he rejects in Husserl, but to explain further what he rejects in the whole tradition of which he takes Husserl to be a prime representative. (It also establishes important connections between his work and work that we studied in Part Two of this enquiry.)

Derrida's starting point is the distinction between speech and writing.[21] I say 'the' distinction between speech and writing. In fact this is already misleading. The first thing that needs to be emphasized is that Derrida is not using the two terms 'speech' and 'writing' with their customary meanings. We do best, really, to think of them as two terms of art for him.[22] Indeed from now on I shall adopt the convention of writing both terms, and their cognates, in small capitals – 'SPEECH', 'WRITING', 'WRITTEN', and so forth – whenever they are being used in Derrida's sense. It is not that the normal associations of the two terms are irrelevant to what he is doing with them. But their relevance is largely a matter of how he situates himself with respect to other thinkers. Derrida, as we shall see, wants to challenge the prioritization, within traditional metaphysics, of SPEECH over WRITING.

---

[20] See Whorf (1956). Cf. Collingwood's views, discussed in §2 of the previous chapter.

[21] Despite my comment in parentheses at the end of the previous paragraph, this is a distinction to which analytic philosophers have paid surprisingly little attention (though for one interesting if cursory reference to the distinction in the analytic tradition, see Davidson (2005d), p. 249). For reasons that should soon be clear, however, even if analytic philosophers had paid the distinction more attention, this might well have had less relevance to what Derrida does with it than their actual preoccupations have had.

[22] Cf. *Grammatology*, p. 9, and Wood (2001), p. 260. (Sometimes Derrida talks of 'arche-writing' instead of 'writing' to emphasize that he does not have in mind 'the vulgar concept of writing' (*Grammatology*, p. 56).) But note: some of what follows will itself cast doubt on the very idea of a term's 'customary meaning'.

And he is able to cite a range of thinkers whose prioritization of speech over writing importantly reflects this: Plato, Aristotle, Rousseau, Condillac, and Saussure, among others.[23]

Very well, how does Derrida use these two terms? By extrapolating from the most basic structural feature of the more familiar distinction, as it is understood by those who accept the prioritization just mentioned. Those who accept this prioritization will say that, whereas speech involves the use of signs to represent things, writing has an extra level of mediation: it involves the use of signs to represent those signs, and hence only indirectly to represent the corresponding things.

Derrida is interested in a variation of this which he calls 'logocentrism' or 'phonocentrism' (see e.g. *Grammatology*, pp. 11–12). This is the idea that some entities that represent things do so of their very essence – they have representational powers that are intrinsic to them – whereas other entities that represent things do so only because they have been associated by artifice and by convention with entities of the former kind – they have representational powers that are not intrinsic to them. Let us call entities of the former kind *direct marks*. And let us call entities of the latter kind *indirect marks*.[24] Direct marks cannot be misinterpreted. They 'speak for themselves', as we aptly say. Indirect marks can be misinterpreted. Their meanings need to be learned, and the learning process is fallible. Examples of direct marks are, arguably, Descartes' clear and distinct perceptions, Kant's intuitions, Frege's senses, and Husserl's noemata.[25] Examples of indirect marks are, arguably, the words and expressions of any natural language.[26] Thus, for instance,

---

[23] See e.g. respectively: '*Sec*', pp. 316–317; *Grammatology*, pp. 11 and 141ff.; '*Sec*', pp. 311ff.; and *Grammatology*, pp. 30ff. For samples of what Derrida has in mind, see respectively: Plato's *Phaedrus*, 274bff.; Aristotle's *De Interpretatione*, Ch. 1; Rousseau (1959), Vol. 2, pp. 1249–1252; Condillac (2001), Pt II, §1, Ch. 13; and Saussure (1983), Introduction, Ch. VI, §2.

    Note: there are grounds for saying that Heidegger too prioritizes speech over writing (see e.g. Heidegger (1962a), §34). It is here, if anywhere, that Derrida is at his most innovative.

[24] This terminology is mine, not Derrida's. (Likewise in the case of the term 'non-direct mark' which I shall introduce shortly.) We shall see at the end of the section how Derrida himself refers to direct marks.

[25] 'Arguably', because in each case there are some delicate exegetical issues. For instance, Derrida himself would count Husserl's noemata as clear examples, but only because of his radically subjectivist interpretation of Husserl on which I have already cast doubt. As far as the other three cases are concerned, cf., respectively: Descartes (1985c), Pt One, §§45 and 46; Kant (2000), 5:351–352; and Dummett (1978d), p. 131, and (1981b), pp. 50–51, in each of which Dummett adverts to what he calls the 'transparency' of Fregean senses (though he means something rather different by this in each of the two cases).

[26] 'Arguably', this time, because something qualifies as an indirect mark only if it has been associated with a direct mark, and, as we shall see, precisely what is at issue is whether the

Frege would say that to understand the English word 'salt' is to grasp the sense which, by convention, has been associated with that word; and that to grasp this sense *just is* to think of salt, or to be 'presented' with salt, in a certain way. Now by 'SPEECH' Derrida intends exercise of direct marks. By 'WRITING' he intends, among other things – the reason for this qualification will become apparent in due course – exercise of indirect marks.

And it is in these terms that he provides his alternative characterization of the metaphysics of presence. The metaphysics of presence is metaphysics that presupposes just such a distinction, along with its implicit prioritization. You may wonder how this connects with the characterization given in the previous section. The point is this. The sense that is made of things in SPEECH depends only on what is present to consciousness when the sense-making is itself present to consciousness. By contrast the sense that is made of things in WRITING depends on what is absent from consciousness when the sense-making is present to consciousness: it depends on relations between itself and other, distinct entities. In a way, therefore, when sense is made of things in SPEECH, those things are themselves *made present* to consciousness, whereas when sense is made of things in WRITING, those things are at most related to what is present in consciousness. And the metaphysics of presence rests on the presupposition that for sense to be made of things in any way at all is ultimately for it to be made of things in SPEECH; in other words, that when sense is made of things in WRITING, this is parasitic on its being made of them in SPEECH. (See e.g. '*Sec*', pp. 311ff.; and cf. 'Semiology', pp. 19ff.)

Derrida rejects this picture. The very idea of a direct mark is an anathema to him. (See esp. *Speech and Phenomena*, passim.)[27] There can be no such thing as SPEECH.

It may appear to follow that there can be no such thing as WRITING either. After all, do not indirect marks depend for their existence on direct marks? They do. But that is why the definition of WRITING needed to be qualified. Derrida's notion of WRITING survives his rejection of the picture above. It embraces the use of any signs whose meanings are not intrinsic to them, not just those which – *per impossibile*, as it now appears – are associated with direct marks, in other words not just those which qualify as indirect marks. (See e.g. *Grammatology*, pp. 8–10.) Let us call any sign whose use his notion of WRITING embraces a *non-direct* mark.

words and expressions of any natural language, or any other things for that matter, satisfy this condition. For the same reason we should resist the temptation to include Humean ideas as examples of indirect marks, despite the fact that the representational power of any given Humean idea depends on its association with something else (Ch. 4, §2).

[27] His assault on this idea is highly reminiscent of the later Wittgenstein: see e.g. Wittgenstein (1967a), Pt I, §§73 and 74, 139–141, 205, and 452–461. For discussion of the relations between Derrida and the later Wittgenstein, see Sonderreger (1997). See also Baldwin (2001), §2, to which Derrida responds briefly in 'Baldwin', pp. 105–106.

Very well, but how can anything *be* a non-direct mark if not by association with a direct mark, that is to say if not by qualifying as indirect? What
else can breathe semantic life into it?[28]
This metaphor of life and breath is one that Derrida himself uses in this
connection (*Speech and Phenomena*, pp. 76 and 81). Aptly enough, so does
the later Wittgenstein (Wittgenstein (1967a), Pt I, §432). I say 'aptly enough',
because the answer that Derrida gives to these questions is likewise reminiscent of the later Wittgenstein. He adverts to the repeated use of signs.[29] For
signs to be meaningful they need to be applied again and again, in different
contexts, so that relevant connections can be established.
One feature of signs that is critical here, as Derrida himself is at pains
to emphasize, is their *iterability* (e.g. '*Sec*', p. 315). But we must straightway note a curiosity in Derrida's handling of the notion of iterability.
Philosophers in the analytic tradition distinguish between 'sign-types' and
'sign-tokens'. This distinction is to be understood in such a way that the
following list – 'tiger', 'lion', 'tiger' – contains two sign-types and three
sign-tokens, one of the sign-types appearing twice. Talk of the iterability of
signs naturally puts us in mind of sign-types. Precisely what the list above
illustrates is the iterability of the sign-type 'tiger'. And that iterability does
indeed seem indispensable to the connection of that sign-type with tigers.
It is the fact that the sign-type 'tiger' can be repeatedly applied in suitable
contexts, for instance contexts where there are tigers, or contexts that stand
in relations of historical dependence on contexts in which it has previously
been applied and where there have been tigers, that its connection with
tigers is able to be established. But Derrida, whose notion of WRITING never
quite loses the connotations of the more familiar notion of writing on which
it is modelled,[30] reminds us that even sign-*tokens* are amenable to a sort of
iteration. If someone makes an inscription on paper and sends it to someone
else, then that very inscription can survive both the person who made it and
the recipient and can be reassessed in contexts that are quite distinct from
any that surrounded the original transaction. Part of what it is for a sign's
meaning not to be intrinsic to it, even in the case of a sign-token, is for there
never to be a definitive, once-for-all interpretation of the sign. WRITING, on
Derrida's conception, involves putting something meaningful in the public
domain, something whose interpretation is thereafter at the continual mercy
of what lies in the future. This is fundamentally different from entertaining

---

[28] Actually, we might just as well ask what could breathe semantic life into a sign even if
it *could* be associated with a direct mark. Any such association would still need to be
established. (Cf. my reference earlier to artifice and convention.) This is one of the many
reasons for being suspicious of the very idea of a direct mark: cf. again Wittgenstein
(1967a), Pt I, §§139–141.

[29] Cf. Ch. 14, n. 37.

[30] Cf. *Grammatology*, pp. 56–57. Cf. also '*Sec*', p. 329.

an aspect of transcendental subjectivity. We can now see more clearly, then, how Derrida's insistence that all meaning is meaning of this WRITTEN kind serves as an expression of his anti-Husserlianism.[31] (See e.g. *Speech and Phenomena*, §4, and '*Sec*', pp. 314ff.)[32]

Let us reflect further on the idea that all meaning is meaning of this WRITTEN kind. One thing that follows from this is that there is no saying what a given piece of WRITING represents, no indicating what a given piece of WRITING represents, no *thinking* what a given piece of WRITING represents, except by producing more WRITING. Whatever the relation between the sign 'tiger' and tigers, for example, nobody is going to be able to get any purchase on that relation except by producing, in WRITING, some definition of 'tiger', or some equivalent of 'tiger' in another language, or some way of locating 'tiger' in a lexical network, or something else along those lines. There is no Fregean sense attaching to the sign, no Platonic form of tigerhood, nothing which, by its very nature, directs attention to tigers.[33]

Meaning, on Derrida's view, is determined by the repeated use of signs in WRITING. It is also, we now see, *given* by the use of signs in WRITING – in the sense illustrated in the previous paragraph. This in turn means that it is given by a kind of perpetual deferral: the connection of any given sign with what it represents is given through its connection with other signs, whose connection with what they represent is given through their connection with other signs, whose connection with what they represent is given through their connection with other signs, and so on indefinitely (see e.g. *Grammatology*, Pt I, Ch. 1, passim).

It is easy sometimes, when reading Derrida, to get the impression that he denies that there is any such thing as meaning. And it is easy sometimes, when reading him, to get the impression that he denies that there is anything *but* meaning. Both impressions are faulty. But I think we can now account for both. The first is due to his rejection of SPEECH, together with our engrained tendency to think that, if meaningful activity is anything, then SPEECH, ultimately, is what it is. The second impression is due to his commitment to the line of thought sketched in the previous paragraph, *together with that same engrained tendency in us*. Thinking that meaningful activity is ultimately SPEECH, that is the exercise of signs whose representational powers are intrinsic to them, and reflecting on the fact that, for Derrida, meaningful activity is ultimately the exercise of signs whose representational

---

[31] 'Meaning' here, like 'WRITING', is to be understood very broadly: cf. 'Semiology', p. 26.

[32] For an extremely helpful discussion of Derrida on WRITING and iterability, see Glendinning (2007), pp. 197–202.

[33] I have been highlighting similarities between Derrida's views and those of the later Wittgenstein. Here we see similarities between his views and those of Quine, whose repudiation of Fregean senses we witnessed in Ch. 12, §§4 and 5. Cf. esp. Quine (1969a), pp. 48ff. And for discussion, see Putnam (1985).

powers are given through their relations to other such signs, we conclude that, for Derrida, all there is, ultimately, to be represented in meaningful activity is the meaning of other meaningful activity.

This conclusion may seem to be corroborated by such pronouncements on Derrida's part as '*Il n'y a pas de hors-texte*' (*Grammatology*, p. 158) translated by Gayatri Chakravorty Spivak as 'There is nothing outside the text' (ibid.). In fact this translation is misleading.[34] Derrida is not claiming that everything is text, still less that everything is text as that term is ordinarily understood, still *less* that everything is meaning. On the contrary. He is adverting to context, the extralinguistic reality within which, as he is at the same time reminding us, every meaningful activity occurs, the point being that there is no meaningful activity which, of its very essence, irrespective of its relations to things in the contexts in which it occurs, and irrespective in particular of its relations to other associated meaningful activity, homes in on that which is being represented in it. There are no direct marks.

Here are two crucial quotations, the weariness in which is audible:

> I never cease to be surprised by critics who see my work as a declaration that there is nothing beyond language, that we are imprisoned by language; it is, in fact, saying the exact opposite. ('Interview', p. 123)

> The phrase which for some has become a sort of slogan, in general so badly understood, of deconstruction[35] ('*il n'y a pas de hors-texte*'), means nothing else: there is nothing outside context....
>
> ... The concept of text or of context which guides me embraces and does not exclude the world, reality, history. Once again (and this probably makes a thousand times I have had to repeat this, but when will it finally be heard, and why this resistance?): as I understand it ..., the text is not the book, it is not confined in a volume itself confined to the library. It does not suspend reference – to history, to the world, to reality, to Being, and especially not to the other, since to say of history, of the world, of reality, that they always appear ... in a movement of interpretation which contextualizes them according to a network of differences and hence of referral to the other, is surely to recall that alterity (difference) is irreducible. ('Limited Inc', pp. 136–137)[36]

I need to say something about the references to difference in the second of these quotations. Derrida's insistence that there are no direct marks means that a sign's relations to things other than itself are crucial to its meaning.

---

[34] For one thing it misses a pun in the original: '*hors-texte*' is a technical term used by printers to denote plates. For discussion, see McDonald (2006), pp. 222ff.

[35] See the next section for discussion of what Derrida means by 'deconstruction'.

[36] I have taken the liberty of altering Samuel Weber's translation by leaving '*il n'y a pas de hors-texte*' in the original French, and by capitalizing 'Being' as a reminder of the background Heideggerianism.

In particular, as we have seen, its relations to other signs are crucial to its meaning. Meaning does not attach, atomistically, to individual signs. It is a feature of systems of signs, and of the structure of their interrelations.[37] But that structure in turn resides in the differences between the signs and in how these differences themselves relate to one another.

Here Derrida's ideas echo those of Saussure. (This despite the fact noted above, that Saussure is a prime representative of the prioritization of speech over writing, and, indirectly, of SPEECH over WRITING.) Saussure holds that there is nothing to the elements of language beyond the systems in which they occur, rather as there is nothing to the rook in chess beyond the moves it can make in any given chess position. He applies this idea in the first instance to the phonetic elements of a language. A phoneme can only be identified by where it stands in relation to other phonemes in a system of contrasts. Phonemes are not 'sounds', in any neutral language-independent sense of that term. (Think how in some Asian languages there are distinctions between tonemes to which nothing corresponds in English, and conversely, how in English there is a distinction between the liquid consonants *l* and *r* to which nothing corresponds in those Asian languages. And note, incidentally, how this, in its own modest way, further threatens the metaphysics of presence. As Derrida himself puts it, 'the difference which establishes phonemes and lets them be heard remains in and of itself inaudible, in every sense of the word' ('*Différance*', p. 5).) It follows that there is no identifying one phoneme in one system with another in another, just as there is no saying how the ace of spades moves in chess. Likewise, Saussure argues, in the case of the semantic elements of a language. The meaning of a sign can only be identified by where it stands in relation to the meanings of other signs in a system of contrasts. (See Saussure (1983), passim.) Derrida, as we have seen, repeats much of this at the level of meaningful signs, though of course without the suggestion, implicit in what has just gone and explicit in Saussure himself, that meaningful signs are indirect marks and their meanings the direct marks with which they are associated (see *Grammatology*, Pt I, Ch. 2, esp. pp. 44–65, and pp. 141–143).[38]

I shall close this section with some quotations from Derrida that helpfully summarize all these ideas. But first I must note a couple of points of terminology, themselves derived from Saussure. Derrida uses the term 'signifier' to stand for something that is meaningful in virtue of its relation to something else that is meaningful. (This is obviously a variation on what I have been calling a 'non-direct mark'.) Given any signifier, so defined, there are two possibilities. The first possibility is that it launches an infinite regress. There is the signifier itself; then there is some other signifier to which it is appropriately related; then there is a third signifier to which the second signifier is

---

[37] Again the comparison with Quine is irresistible: see Ch. 12, §4.

[38] For helpful discussions, see Priest (1995), pp. 236ff, and Moran (2000), pp. 461–463.

appropriately related; and so on indefinitely (perhaps in an infinitely recurring loop). The second possibility is that any such regress is eventually arrested with something whose meaning is intrinsic to it: what I have been calling a 'direct mark' and what Derrida himself calls 'the transcendental signified' (e.g. *Grammatology*, p. 20). Derrida's view, in these terms, is that it is always the first possibility that obtains. There is no transcendental signified. Or, as he also puts it at one point, there is no signifier 'signifying a signifier itself signifying an eternal verity, eternally thought and spoken in the proximity of a present logos' (*Grammatology*, p. 15). Now for the quotations:

> WRITING is not a sign of a sign, except if one says it of all signs.... If every sign refers to a sign, and if 'sign of a sign' signifies WRITING, certain conclusions ... will become inevitable.... [A] certain model of WRITING [will be] necessarily ... imposed ... as instrument and technique of representation of a system of language. (*Grammatology*, p. 43)

> The maintenance of the rigorous distinction ... between the *signans* and the *signatum* [i.e. the signifier and the signified], the equation of the *signatum* and the concept ..., inherently leaves open the possibility of thinking a *concept signified in and of itself*, a concept simply present for thought, independent of a relationship to language, that is of a relationship to a system of signifiers. By leaving open this possibility ... Saussure ... accedes to the classical exigency of what I have proposed to call a 'transcendental signified,' which in and of itself, in its essence, would refer to no signifier, would exceed the chain of signs, and would no longer itself function as a signifier.... Of course [questioning the possibility of such a transcendental signified] is an operation that must be undertaken with prudence for ... it must pass through the difficult deconstruction[39] of the entire history of metaphysics which imposed ... upon semiological science in its entirety this fundamental quest for a 'transcendental signified' and a concept independent of language; this quest not being imposed from without by something like 'philosophy,' but rather by everything that links our language, our culture, our 'system of thought' to the history and system of metaphysics. ('Semiology', p. 19, emphasis in original)

> From the moment that there is meaning there are nothing but signs. We *think only in signs*.... One could call *play* the absence of the transcendental signified as limitlessness of play, that is to say as the destruction of ... the metaphysics of presence. (*Grammatology*, p. 50, emphasis in original)[40]

---

[39] See n. 35.

[40] See further *Grammatology*, Pt I and Pt II, Ch. 2; '*Sec*', passim; and 'Positions', p. 68. (On p. 49 of *Grammatology* he defines the metaphysics of presence as 'the exigent, powerful, systematic, and irrepressible desire for [a transcendental signified].') Cf. (as a further reminder of how Wittgensteinian much of this is) Wittgenstein (1967a), Pt I, §§380ff. Cf.

4. Deconstruction

Derrida rejects the prioritization of SPEECH over WRITING then. We might be tempted to say that he reverses it, prioritizing WRITING over SPEECH instead. But that would be wrong.[41] It would be wrong even if denying the existence of SPEECH, and concluding that all there is is WRITING, could count as a limiting case of prioritizing WRITING over SPEECH. Derrida denies the very idea of a distinction between the exercise of direct marks and the exercise of indirect marks. That is why, when he eventually concludes that all there is is WRITING, the notion of WRITING involved is an extended notion of WRITING that does not need to be understood in terms of that distinction. In the terminology that I used in the previous section it comprises not indirect marks, but non-direct marks. (Cf. *Grammatology*, pp. 68–69, and 'Structure', p. 281.)

On the other hand, as I tried to make clear, Derrida does not completely dissociate his notion of WRITING from that distinction either. The notion of WRITING as it occurs in that distinction is a kind of prototype of his notion of WRITING. And while there is a clear sense in which he rejects the former, as he does its complementary notion of SPEECH, there is another clear sense in which he does not: the sense in which 'reject' means something like 'have nothing to do with' (cf. *Grammatology*, pp. 13–14). For those two notions are his starting point. He subjects them to scrutiny, reflects on their history, and considers what may become of them. In particular, he considers whether either of them can adapt and evolve in such a way as to survive the discredited distinction between them, with its own implicit prioritization. And he believes that one of them can. Hence his own extended notion of WRITING.[42]

We see here an instance of a practice that Derrida adopts more widely, the practice to which he gives the name 'deconstruction'.[43] I use the word 'practice' advisedly. Derrida expressly denies that deconstruction is a 'method', or that it '[can] be transformed into one[,] especially if the technical and procedural significations of the word are stressed,' or that it

---

also Putnam (1981), esp. Ch. 2. Finally, for helpful discussions of all of the material in this section, see Norris (1987), Chs 3–5, esp. Ch. 4, and Hobson (1988), pp. 9–41 (much of which is also relevant to the next section). See also Murdoch (1993), Ch. 7 – altogether less sympathetic, frequently uncomprehending, annoyingly glib, yet somehow riveting.

[41] Cf. 'Implications', p. 10.

[42] It may appear irresistible at this point to invoke the Hegelian notion of *Aufhebung*. But we can and should resist. Derrida explicitly distances the processes involved from processes of *Aufhebung*: see e.g. 'Positions', pp. 38–41.

[43] Both the name and to some extent the idea are appropriated from Heidegger, whose corresponding '*Destruktion*' – sometimes translated simply as 'destruction' – we encountered in the lengthy passage from Heidegger (1982b) quoted in Ch. 18, §4. See also Heidegger (1962a), §6.

'[can] be reduced to ... a set of rules and transposable procedures,' or even that it is 'an *act* or an *operation*' ('Letter to a Friend', p. 3, emphasis in original).

Roughly,[44] deconstruction involves focusing on some prioritization in how sense has been made of things, whether on a large scale or on a small scale, and then, with the help of forces at work in the very sense-making concerned, to ask questions of the prioritization: to challenge it, to unsettle it, to consider what goes unsaid as a result of it, if appropriate to reverse or reject it, at the very least to toy with its reversal or rejection, and to see what new or renewed ways of making sense of things may emerge from the process. (See e.g. *Grammatology*, p. 24; 'Structure', passim; and 'Implications', passim.) Such new or renewed ways of making sense of things may or may not be an improvement on what preceded them. This is an exploratory exercise, not some foolproof recipe for coming to a better understanding of things.

Nor is it as iconoclastic or as bloody as it is sometimes presented as being.[45] 'It is not,' Derrida insists, 'a question of junking [certain] concepts, nor do we have the means to do so' ('Semiology', p. 22). Rather, as he goes on to say,

> it is more necessary ... to transform concepts, to displace them, to turn them against their presuppositions, to reinscribe them in other chains, and little by little to modify the terrain of our work and thereby produce new configurations. (Ibid.; cf. '*Sec*', p. 329)

'I do not believe in decisive ruptures,' he adds (ibid.; cf. 'Positions', pp. 37ff.). In any case, deconstruction is largely a matter of allowing extant ways of making sense of things to run their own course, to succumb to their own inner logic. 'There is,' Derrida says, 'always already deconstruction, at work in works.... Texts deconstruct *themselves* by themselves' (*Memoires*, p. 123).

The repudiation of traditional metaphysics is for Derrida a paradigmatically deconstructive project – which means that, here again, he is following Heidegger. In Chapter 18, §4, we saw how for Heidegger the repudiation of traditional metaphysics involved appropriating traditional metaphysical concepts and traditional metaphysical methods. It was not, in other words, a simple matter of turning one's back on the tradition. It was a matter of using the tradition's own resources to subvert it from

---

[44] 'Roughly', because shortly after the material just quoted Derrida also talks of the difficulty of defining deconstruction, a fact which itself, ironically, illustrates the power of deconstruction (ibid., p. 4).

[45] See e.g. Scruton (2004), pp. 478–479. It is worth noting in this connection the following quotation: 'Everything that I deconstruct – presence, living, voice and so on – is exactly what I'm after in life. I love the voice, I love presence' ('Following Theory', p. 8).

within.[46] Likewise for Derrida, who never tires of reminding us of how the project is situated within its own target area. Here are some pertinent quotations:[47]

> In order to exceed metaphysics it is necessary that a trace be inscribed within the text of metaphysics. ('*Ousia* and *Grammē*', p. 65; cf. *Grammatology*, p. 162)

> The revolution against reason, in the historical form of classical reason …, … can be made only within it. ('Cogito', p. 36)

> I have insisted again and again that I am not 'rejecting' metaphysics. I do not 'reject' metaphysics. Not even Platonism. Indeed, I think there is an unavoidable necessity of reconstituting a certain Platonic gesture. ('Baldwin', p. 105)[48]

> There is no sense in doing without the concepts of metaphysics in order to shake metaphysics. We have no language – no syntax and no lexicon – which is foreign to [the history of metaphysics]; we can pronounce not a single destructive proposition which has not already had to slip into the form, the logic, and the implicit postulations of precisely what it seeks to contest. To take one example from many: … we cannot do without the concept of the sign, for we cannot give up [its] metaphysical complicity without also giving up the critique we are directing against this complicity.… [The] metaphysical reduction of the sign needed the opposition it was reducing. ('Structure', pp. 280–281)[49]

---

[46] See esp. the lengthy quotation from Heidegger (1982b) given in that section. Cf. *Grammatology*, p. 24.

[47] Cf. Sheppard (2001).

[48] Cf. my distinction earlier between the sense in which Derrida rejects the discredited notions of SPEECH and WRITING and the sense in which he does not.

[49] There are many similar quotations throughout Derrida's corpus. There are also many places where he illustrates his thesis by appeal to specific thinkers, both among his predecessors and among his contemporaries, who he thinks have been concerned to repudiate traditional metaphysics and who he also thinks have worked within the very structures that they set out to repudiate (whether intentionally or unintentionally). See e.g. *Grammatology*, pp. 19–20, on Nietzsche; *Speech and Phenomena*, p. 5, 'Phenomenology', p. 166, and 'Form and Meaning', pp. 157–158, on Husserl; 'Implications', p. 8, on Heidegger; and 'Violence and Metaphysics, pp. 82–83 and 111–112, on Levinas.

It is interesting, particularly in the light of my remarks in §1 and in the light of some of what will follow in this chapter, to compare Wittgenstein's project in the *Tractatus*, where he uses, or rather 'uses', some more or less mainstream analytic tools (such as the idea of logical form) to dispose of those very tools. More generally, it does not take much to see the *Tractatus* as an exercise in deconstruction, perhaps directed at the prioritization of propositional sense-making over non-propositional sense-making. (For another comparison with the *Tractatus*, see Norris (1987), p. 17.)

All of this notwithstanding, the Platonic ideals listed in §2(a) – those abiding presences in whose name much of traditional metaphysics has been practised, all of which presuppose some variation of the prioritization of presence over absence[50] – are ultimately to be rejected. Each of the following, in its capacity as a member of the Platonic pantheon, gets defied, dumbfounded, and eventually deposed at Derrida's deconstructive hands:

- rationality (e.g. 'Reason', p. 9, and 'Ousia and Grammē', p. 38)
- consciousness (e.g. 'Différance', pp. 16ff.)
- truth (e.g. Grammatology, pp. 10ff.; 'Différance', p. 18; and 'Ousia and Grammē', p. 84; cf. also 'Moore', p. 84)
- identity (e.g. Speech and Phenomena, pp. 81–82, and 'Semiology', pp. 21–22)[51]

and of course

- presence (e.g. Grammatology, pp. 46ff.).[52]

5. Différance

Derrida's most famous coinage is the word 'différance', which differs by one letter from the familiar French word 'différence'.[53] Why this addition to the lexicon?

The French verb 'différer' can be translated either as 'to differ' or as 'to defer'. The noun 'différence', with an 'e', corresponds to only one of these. It can be translated as 'difference' but not as 'deferral'. Derrida wants a noun that does double duty – not, however, simply by standing ambiguously for both difference and deferral, but in what we shall see to be a much more

---

[50] Cf. Grammatology, pp. 82–83.

[51] Here we see another instance of what I have already signalled as one of the great recurring themes of Part Three of this book (cf. Ch. 15, §7(b); Ch. 16, §4; and Ch. 18, §4). It will find its most resounding expression in §§3 and 4 of the next chapter.

[52] Interesting discussions of deconstruction are Rorty (1992) and Priest (1995), Ch. 14. But I take issue with both. Graham Priest seems to me to have an overly systematic conception of deconstruction. Richard Rorty seems to me to achieve the remarkable feat of erring in the other direction. Moreover, both (see pp. 240–241 of the Rorty and p. 238 of the Priest) infelicitously liken the processes involved to those of Hegelian Aufhebung (see n. 42 in this chapter).

A further discussion of deconstruction, with particular reference to traditional metaphysics, and ultimately critical of Derrida, is Frank (1992).

[53] In what follows I shall simply appropriate Derrida's word rather than devise an equivalent.

subtle way that involves having connotations of both. Hence his coinage. (See '*Différance*', esp. pp. 3–9.[54])[55]

How then does Derrida use his new word?

Multifariously. Here are some of the uses to which he puts it. First, he exploits the fact that it evokes both the temporal and the spatial (deferral being primarily understood in temporal terms, difference being naturally understood in spatial terms[56]) to characterize the most basic kind of representation: representation of that which is *pro tempore* absent; representation, in other words, of that which is presently elsewhere, evoking the possibility of its being present elsewhen ('*Différance*', pp. 8–9). Second, he applies the word to the forgotten difference between Being and beings, to convey that we are destined never fully to grasp that difference ('*Différance*', pp. 23–24 and 26).[57] Third, he uses it in connection with the very deconstruction of presence, whose temporality is part of what is deconstructed, which makes '*différance*', with its particular play of associations, a peculiarly apt term for referring back, after the deconstruction, to the difference between it (presence) and its erstwhile subordinate absence (*Grammatology*, p. 143, and '*Semiology*', pp. 22–26). Fourth, he uses it to indicate the joint significance of both difference and deferral to his account of the meanings of signs: difference, in the way in which a sign's meaning is determined in contradistinction to that of other signs; deferral, in the way in which a sign's meaning is given by its connection with other signs whose meanings are given by their connection with other signs whose meanings are given by their connection with other signs and so on indefinitely ('*Semiology*', pp. 22–26; and see §3).

This is all very well, you may say, but these are just examples of rhetorical effects that Derrida achieves with his new word and/or of contexts in which he applies it. What does the word actually *mean*?

A natural enough question, but a question that should ring almost every Derridean alarm bell. Even if the very form of the question does not betray a kind of logocentrism (cf. *Grammatology*, pp. 74–75), there are special reasons why we should be wary of asking such a thing of '*différance*'. For

---

[54] This essay is the *locus classicus* for Derrida's views about *différance*. But the word occurs in earlier works: see e.g. *Speech and Phenomena*, pp. 82 and 88, and *Grammatology*, p. 84. The first occurrence is in 'Phenomenology', p. 161.

[55] An incidental benefit of the coinage, given that '*différence*' and '*différance*' are spelt differently but pronounced the same way, is that it provides a nice reminder of the advantages that writing can have over speech, which is itself a reminder of what Derrida does with his own notion of WRITING ('*Différance*', pp. 3ff).

[56] On the second of these cf. Bergson's account of how objects of analysis are ultimately distinguished (Ch. 16, §3).

[57] It is interesting to note that in Heidegger (1993b) Heidegger himself uses a special word in connection with this difference. In fact he invokes the old German word '*Seyn*' which we encountered in Ch. 18, n. 71.

there is a sense in which the word is used *just* for its rhetorical effects, not to designate anything. There is no such 'thing' as *différance*. The point of the word is not to draw attention to some super-being of relevance to each and every context in which the word is applied; precisely not. The point of the word is rather, by signalling a range of concerns, problems, and aporiae, to assist the deconstructive project of challenging, disrupting, and questioning that which makes the postulation of such super-beings so enticing: the metaphysics of presence. (See '*Différance*', pp. 21–22.)[58]

So should we say that, rhetorical effects aside, the word does not strictly mean anything?

No. Let us not say that. The word does mean something. But it does not mean some thing. We might put it this way: what the word means can never be the subject of any proposition.[59]

So is the point that its superficial grammar is misleading? That it does not really function as a singular noun phrase? Is what the word means incapable of being the subject of a proposition in the same way in which what the word 'unless' means is incapable of being the subject of a proposition?

No; not that either. The word '*différance*' does function as a singular noun phrase.[60] The point is rather that *différance* itself is a non-thing. Like Being, it is not itself a being. It is never present; not because it is somehow transcendent and resists any of the finite categories in terms of which we might make it present, nor yet because it is always absent, but because it acts as a kind of precondition of any presence, and, for that matter, of any absence. It is what 'makes the opposition of presence and absence possible' (*Grammatology*, p. 143). 'It exceeds the order of truth at a certain precise point,' Derrida writes, 'but without dissimulating itself as something, as a mysterious being, in the occult of a nonknowledge or in a hole with indeterminate borders (for example, in a topology of castration)' ('*Différance*', p. 6). It is not so much that '*différance*' cannot be a name of anything, then, as that *différance* cannot have anything as a name. Here again is Derrida:

> Such a *différance* has no name in our language. But we 'already know' that if it is unnameable, it is not provisionally so, not because our language has not yet found or received this *name*, or because we would have to seek it in another language, outside the finite system of our own. It is rather because there is no *name* for it at all, ... not even [the name] of '*différance*', which is not a name. ('*Différance*', p. 26, emphasis in original; cf. '*Ousia* and *Grammē*', pp. 66–67)[61]

[58] Cf. Wood (2001), pp. 261–264.
[59] Equivalently, what the word means is not an 'object' in Frege's and Husserl's sense: see Ch. 8, §7(b), including n. 71. Cf. also Wittgenstein (1967a), Pt I, §304.
[60] Cf. 'Moore', p. 85.
[61] Earlier in the same essay he is more forthright. He writes, '*Différance* ... is neither a word nor a concept' (ibid., p. 7). Cf. Geoffrey Bennington (1993), pp. 73–74, where Bennington

But, you may protest, is this not all horribly self-stultifying? If we are to accede to all of this talk about what *différance* is or is not, can or cannot be, does or does not do, then had there better not be such a *thing* as *différance*? Had *différance* better not be *the thing* that we are talking about? Indeed, is there not already self-stultification in the very claim that what the word '*différance*' means cannot be the subject of any proposition? For is that not *itself* a proposition whose subject is what the word '*différance*' means?[62]

This protest is well taken. But of course, we have been here before. Can the Fregean *Bedeutung* of the predicate '... is a horse' be the subject of any proposition (Ch. 8, §7(b))? Can Wittgensteinian logical form (Ch. 9, §5)? Can Heideggerian Being (Ch. 18, §6)?

Derrida is every bit as self-conscious about the self-stultification as his predecessors were. In one respect it is less of a threat to him than it was to them. For part of the aim of the exercise is to upset the very models of meaning that underpin the protest – models that are arguably imbued with the metaphysics of presence – and to do so, moreover, as much by illustrating their shortcomings as by stating them. If he has created something which, on the one hand, exhibits a kind of meaning and which, on the other hand, resists being understood in accord with those models, all well and good. (Let us not forget that a lot of the time Derrida is *teasing* his readers. He is defying them to make the kind of sense of what he is saying that their preconceptions lead them to think is the only kind of sense there is, while at the same time achieving a sufficiently integrated effect through what he is saying to prevent them from dismissing it as so much empty verbiage.) Still, there is a certain amount of self-stultification here that is independent of the models, and, in another respect, Derrida is in just the same predicament as his predecessors. He too is under pressure to express his understanding of things in ways which that very understanding exposes as unfit for purpose.

Furthermore, there are, in Derrida, echoes of each of his predecessors' reactions to the predicament. Thus Frege admitted that 'by a kind of necessity of language' he had said something other than he intended, and asked his reader not to begrudge a pinch of salt. Likewise Derrida, considering the difference between Being and beings, writes:

> In reality, there is not even a *distinction* in the usual sense of the word, between Being and being. For reasons of essence, and ... because Being is nothing outside the being ..., it is impossible to avoid the ontic metaphor in order to articulate Being in language [i.e. it is impossible to articulate

writes, 'This "word" or "concept" can be neither a word nor a concept, naming the condition of the possibility ... of *all* words and concepts' (emphasis in original).

[62] This is not to mention the many paradoxes with which Derrida deliberately saddles *différance*. For instance, having told us that it makes the opposition of presence and absence possible, he goes on to highlight its place in the deconstructive project by telling us that what it makes possible is 'the very thing that it makes impossible' (*Grammatology*, p. 143).

Being in language except as a being]. ('Violence and Metaphysics', p. 138, emphasis in original; cf. '*Différance*', p. 25[63])[64]

Again, Heidegger used the technique of erasure, crossing out words that resisted being understood in accord with their normal function while nevertheless allowing them to remain visible. Derrida uses the same technique:

> *Différance* i̶s̶ ... what makes possible the presentation of the being-present. ('*Différance*', p. 6)

Wittgenstein confessed at the end of the *Tractatus* that what he had written was nonsense. He likened it to a ladder that had to be thrown away after it had been climbed. Here is Derrida:

> I try to WRITE (in) the space in which is posed the question of SPEECH and meaning.... [It] is necessary in such a space, and guided by such a question, that WRITING literally means nothing.[65] Not that it is absurd in the way that absurdity has always been in solidarity with metaphysical meaning. It simply tempts itself, tenders itself, attempts to keep itself at the point of the exhaustion of meaning.... [It means] nothing *that can simply be heard*. ('Implications', p. 11, first emphasis in original, second emphasis added; cf. *Grammatology*, p. 93)[66]

It seems to me that by far the most compelling story about what is going on here, a story whereby Derrida is able both to have his cake and to eat it, is the one that I adumbrated in §1: Derrida, like the early Wittgenstein, like Bergson,

---

[63] Cf. also 'Cogito', p. 37, where, in a different connection (that of writing about madness), Derrida talks of '[the] difficulty, or [the] impossibility, [that] must reverberate within the language used,' and goes on to comment, 'One could perhaps say that the resolution of this difficulty is *practised* rather than *formulated*' (emphasis in original).

[64] I have taken the liberty of replacing 'existent' in Alan Bass' translation by 'being'. The original French is '*étant*'. For justification for this departure from the original, see Bass (1978), pp. xvii–xviii.

[65] Does this cast doubt on my earlier insistence that '*différance*' does mean something? I think not. Derrida is not specifically talking about the word '*différance*' here. But in any case, more importantly, as the rest of the quotation testifies and as I hope will become clearer in the next section, there is meaning and there is meaning.

[66] I have taken some liberties with the material in square brackets, where Derrida's original has 'I risk meaning', but I think the context justifies my making the link I have. The quotation continues, incidentally, in a way that exhibits Derrida's fine sense of humour: 'To be entangled in hundreds of pages of a WRITING simultaneously insistent and elliptical, imprinting ... even its erasures, carrying off each concept into an interminable chain of differences, surrounding or confusing itself with so many precautions, references, notes, citations, collages, supplements – this 'meaning-to-say-nothing' is not, you will agree, the most assured of exercises' (ibid.).

and arguably like Heidegger, is making play with linguistic resources to convey non-propositional sense. I shall pursue this story in the next section.[67]

6. How to Do Things with Words

Part of what makes such a story especially compelling in Derrida's case is that it fits well with his own reflections on what can be achieved with linguistic resources. He himself draws attention to the possibilities opened up by what might be thought of as abnormal uses of language, in particular by uses with a significant ludic dimension.[68] (Rather as with his assault on certain models of meaning that we noted in the previous section, he does this as much by exemplifying these possibilities as by discussing them.) Just as significantly, he emphasizes the continuity between the supposedly abnormal and the supposedly normal. He forestalls any impression that, just because there are criteria by which the former lacks sense, it cannot possibly count as legitimate linguistic activity and it cannot possibly contribute to the broad project of making sense of things.

The key essay is 'Sec'.[69] One of Derrida's main concerns in this essay is to discuss the ideas of J.L. Austin, who was himself preoccupied with how to do things with words ('Sec', pp. 32ff.).[70] Austin famously wanted to account for various features of what Wittgenstein called 'language-games' (Ch. 10, §2). Derrida complains that Austin's conception of a language-game is over-sanitized and thus unduly restrictive. Austin writes as if we can cleanly separate contexts in which it is possible to play any given language-game from those in which it is not. (One example that Austin gives of a context in which it is not possible to play a given language-game is that of a race which has been completed, where it is no longer possible to use the formula 'I bet ...' to bet on the outcome of the race (Austin (1975), p. 14). But what if each of the parties concerned knows that each of the others is still ignorant of the outcome?) In any other than the 'right' contexts there can at most be, on Austin's view, secondary or parasitic uses of the vocabulary associated with the language-game. This suggests, by extension and analogy, that we can cleanly separate the contexts in which it is possible to

---

[67] For very helpful discussions of *différance*, see Wood (1988) and Moran (2000), pp. 463ff., the former of which is more critical. A further fascinating read is 'The Original Discussion': this is a transcript of the discussion with Derrida that took place after he first delivered '*Différance*'.

[68] Cf. 'Positions', pp. 37–38.

[69] Much of what follows in this section derives from Moore (2001b). I am grateful to the editor and publisher of the volume in which that essay appears, and to the editor of the special issue of *Ratio* on which the volume is based, for permission to make use of this material.

[70] See esp. Austin (1975), whose very title is *How to Do Things with Words*.

use any given word – with its (standard) meaning – from those in which it is not. Derrida, by contrast, urges a much more fluid understanding of the relationship between how words are used and how they mean what they do. For a word to have meaning, it must be capable of being used in *any* context in a way that depends on, and at the same time extends, that meaning. Its meaning is, more or less, its infinite potential for iterability in new contexts, to new effects, for new purposes, in playing new games – or in playing old games in new ways (see §3 above). It would be an abrogation of a word's meaning to try to circumscribe in advance the contexts that could or could not tolerate its application, the contributions that it could or could not make to the playing of different games. We might try to rule out a word's use in certain *linguistic* contexts, as being in violation of its meaning. For example, we might try to rule out the use of the word 'green' in the context 'green is or', on the grounds that this combination of words was gibberish. But even in doing this, we would be belying our purpose. For precisely in saying that the combination of words in question was gibberish, we would be using the word 'green' in the supposedly forbidden context. True, we would be quoting it. But it would be begging the question against Derrida to insist that our use of the word therefore did not count; that it was somehow secondary. As Derrida himself puts it,

> every sign … can be *cited*, put between quotation marks; thereby it can break with every given context, and engender infinitely new contexts in an absolutely nonsaturable fashion.… This citationality, … this iterabil- ity of the mark is not an accident or an anomaly, but is that (normal/ abnormal) without which a mark could no longer even have a so-called 'normal' functioning. ('*Sec*', pp. 320–321, emphasis in original)[71]

There are indefinitely many things that can be done with words in accord with their meanings then. So we should not be surprised if there are rela- tively undemanding criteria for what it is to have sense whereby some uses of words, though they count as lacking sense, are still straightforward exam- ples of what can be done with the words in accord with their meanings. Think, for instance, of an ungrammatical string of words such as 'hunger eat bread', whose use, in a poem say, might, in virtue of the words' meanings, conjure up all sorts of images and have all sorts of associations and thereby convey all sorts of ideas. (Cf. '*Sec*', p. 319.) Indeed *any* criteria for what it is to have sense will allow for this (i.e. for the possibility of uses of words that lack sense even though they are in straightforward accord with the words' meanings), provided only that the criteria are not so undemanding that each

---

[71] It is interesting to compare this with a passage from Quine, someone who might be expected to be utterly hostile to Derrida's views on these matters: Quine (1961c), pp. 55–56. – For an excellent discussion of the debate between Austin and Derrida, see

use of a word that works its meaning to some effect *ipso facto* counts as having sense.[72]

Why then, provided that there is such a thing as non-propositional sense, should there not also be a creative if unorthodox use of language which, given the meanings of the words in play, succeeds in conveying such sense? That is, why should there not be a use of language, perhaps involving language-games in what might antecedently have been thought of as unsuitable contexts, perhaps involving neologisms, perhaps involving contradictions, perhaps involving nonsense, whose effect, because of the meanings of the words in play, is, if only as a matter of brute psychological fact, that those who encounter it, or some of those who encounter it, come to achieve a corresponding non-propositional understanding of things? And if such a use of language is indeed possible, then who is to say that much of Derrida's work, including his work on *différance*, cannot be viewed as a case in point?[73]

(I close this section by raising an incidental point of comparison with the later Wittgenstein. If this suggestion about Derrida's work is correct, then it *looks* as though he is doing something radically un-Wittgensteinian, namely deliberately taking words 'on holiday' (Wittgenstein (1967a), Pt I, §38). There can be no doubt that there is much here to distance Derrida from Wittgenstein, including, at times, a kind of revelling in confusion (e.g. '*Différance*', pp. 19 and 22–23). Let us not forget, however, that Wittgenstein too would have been happy to sanction our taking words on holiday, even our generating confusion, if it served some suitable purpose; for example, if it took us from a piece of disguised nonsense to a piece of patent nonsense, and thereby enabled us to recognize the former for what it was (see Wittgenstein (1967a), Pt I, §464). In fact the most significant difference between the two thinkers, in this regard, may be as much temperamental as it is doctrinal. Derrida, in true deconstructive spirit, is proactive. He is prepared to make play with concepts in order to promote new forms of understanding, or just to see what comes of it. Wittgenstein, the conservative, is reactive. He

---

Glendinning (2001). For a famously belligerent defence of Austin, see Searle (1977). For Derrida's reply, see 'Limited Inc'. For an excellent discussion of the exchange between Derrida and Searle, see Sarah Richmond (1996) (in §§IV–VI of which Richmond draws some interesting comparisons between Derrida's ideas and those of Donald Davidson). Finally, for further discussion of the issues surrounding the quotation of words, see the Appendix.

[72] Nor, incidentally, should we equate the nonsensical with the non-scientific, still less with the non-serious. There is a perfectly respectable view of mathematics, for instance, according to which it consists of the manipulation of nonsensical symbols. In fact I take this to be the view of the early Wittgenstein: see Ch. 9, n. 37.

[73] Cf. the story that I told in Ch. 2, §6, about Spinoza's *Ethics*: that it mainly involves his imparting knowledge of the second kind, but in such a way as to instil in those who read it knowledge of the third kind. Cf. also Moore (1997a), Ch. 9, where I explore some of these ideas in greater depth. Finally, cf. 'White Mythology', pp. 258ff.

countenances a playful use of concepts (at least by philosophers) only as and when this serves as a corrective to a damaging misuse of them.)

7. Whither Metaphysics?

I argued in §§2 and 3 of the Introduction that there is no disputing the possibility of metaphysics, on my definition of metaphysics. Derrida's deconstruction of traditional metaphysics, whatever else it may achieve, therefore does nothing, and can do nothing, to suggest that such an enterprise is illusory. Nevertheless it is perhaps here, more than anywhere else in this enquiry, that we confront real questions about whether such an enterprise is worthwhile. For one thing, there are questions about what sort of generality is attainable in our sense-making and how well it is liable to satisfy our metaphysical aspirations. There is one sort of generality in our sense-making that is certainly not attainable, on Derrida's view. We cannot make the kind of sense of things that is so impervious to the vicissitudes of individual circumstances that it demands, or even just invites, expression in language that is intelligible independently of context; not if the demand or invitation is to be understood in such a way that it can be met. For on Derrida's view no language is intelligible independently of context.

Derrida himself at any rate shows little enthusiasm for trying to make maximally general sense of things (not even when he is discussing such heady matters as the difference between Being and beings) *except* insofar as this subserves his own meta-metaphysical aspirations. Like many of our protagonists, he earns his place in this drama because of the implications that his views have *about* metaphysics rather than *within* metaphysics. But unlike any of the others, this is because he maintains a kind of ironic detachment from the ground-level exercise, which he is concerned, if not to escape, or to deprecate, or even to criticize, then certainly to question. 'Although I am professionally a philosopher,' he remarks at one point, 'everything I do is *something else* than philosophy. No doubt it is *about* philosophy, but it is not simply "philosophical" through and through' ('Moore', p. 83, emphasis in original).[74] Again:

> I have attempted more and more systematically to find … a non-philosophical site, from which to question philosophy. But the search for a non-philosophical site does not bespeak an anti-philosophical attitude. My central question is: how can philosophy as such appear to itself as other than itself, so that it can interrogate and reflect upon itself in an original manner. ('Interview', p. 98; cf. 'Violence and Metaphysics', pp. 79ff.)

---

[74] For discussion of how being 'something else than philosophy' is consistent with being, in some sense, a prerogative of philosophers, see Sheppard (2001).

I think he would say something similar with respect to metaphysics (on my conception of metaphysics).[75] Now, suppose we accept the value and significance of Derridean questioning. Suppose, in particular, we accept its value and significance when targeted at the value and significance of metaphysics. Are we then bound to conclude that metaphysics is of no value and of no significance? Clearly not. (To think that we are would not be to take seriously the status of Derridean questioning as *questioning*.) Very well, suppose we do not. That is, suppose we hold fast to the view that metaphysics is both valuable and significant. The issue then is what specific lessons we can learn from Derrida about the prospects for metaphysics – be his own engagement in the enterprise as it may.

One of the most important lessons, I suggest, is the one that I heralded in the opening section of this chapter: that we do well to think of metaphysics, not just as an attempt to make sense of things, but as an attempt, more specifically, to make non-propositional sense of things; and that we *can* so think of it without surrendering the view that the best medium for conveying whatever sense is thereby made is language. This lesson is by no means unique to Derrida. It has been passed on in different ways by many of our protagonists, however unintentionally (sometimes, indeed, in spite of them[76]). Derrida does however reinforce the lesson. He does not reinforce it explicitly. In fact he reinforces it as much through example as through doctrine: that is precisely what I have been trying to show in the last few sections of this chapter. But given his own discussions of *différance*, and given his own reflections on meaning – the former of which help to show what is possible in this arena, the latter of which help to account for its possibility – he engenders a lively appreciation of how a suitably artful use of language can serve to convey non-propositional insights. In his own playful way he ushers metaphysics along in a non-naturalistic direction.[77]

Appendix: The Distinction Between Using an Expression and Mentioning It

I have suggested elsewhere (Moore (1997a), Chs 7 and 9[78]) that any metaphysician who is squeamish about indulging in such artful use of language, and who thinks that it is his or her business soberly to affirm truths, can always resort to talking *about* such use of language and whatever it serves to

---

[75] Cf. his reflections on what becomes of metaphysics after the deconstruction of the metaphysics of presence, e.g. in *Speech and Phenomena*, pp. 102–104.

[76] See esp. the final section of the previous chapter.

[77] I shall return to these issues in the Conclusion.

[78] See also Moore (2001b), §§8–11, of which this Appendix is a summary; and see again n. 69.

convey.[79] But in the context of what we saw Derrida argue in §6, this suggestion is immediately problematical. The distinction in question, between actually engaging in this kind of linguistic abnormality and talking, in a perfectly normal way, about it, is just the kind of distinction that Derrida challenges.

There is a more general distinction at stake here, a distinction that many analytic philosophers would regard as a basic tool of their trade. This is the distinction between 'using' an expression and 'mentioning' it.[80] A fairly standard way of characterizing this distinction would be in the following, broadly semantic terms:

The Distinction Between Using an Expression and Mentioning It: Using an expression involves putting it to service in a way that exploits whatever meaning it has, in order to draw attention to some aspect of reality. Mentioning an expression involves putting it to service in a way that waives whatever meaning it has, in order to draw attention to the expression itself. Among the various means of mentioning an expression, one of the commonest, and one of the clearest, is to put the expression between quotation marks. An expression that is mentioned may lack sense, without this impugning whatever is said in the course of mentioning it. Thus we can say, truly, that 'green is or' consists of three words. Indeed we can say, truly, that 'green is or' is gibberish. (Mentioning gibberish does not entail talking gibberish.)

Derrida, as we have seen, recoils from much of this. In particular, he recoils from the idea that putting an expression between quotation marks is fundamentally different from, or even secondary to, doing what an advocate of this distinction would count as using the expression.

But actually, I too recoil from much of this. That is to say, I recoil from much of the thinking behind this broadly semantic characterization of the distinction in question. It does not follow, however, that there is no such distinction to be drawn. (This is a point on which I think Derrida would agree.[81]) We can oppose this way of characterizing the distinction without opposing the distinction itself. We can characterize the distinction in *narrowly*

---

[79] Cf. exercising Spinozist knowledge of the second kind concerning Spinozist knowledge of the third kind (Ch. 2, §6, and n. 73 above) or engaging in Bergsonian analysis of Bergsonian intuition (Ch. 16, §6(b)).

[80] This is one of the distinction that J.R. Searle accuses Derrida of failing to heed, in Searle (1977), to which I referred in n. 71: see p. 203.

[81] In *The Post Card*, pp. 97ff., he alludes, very amusingly, to the obsession that some philosophers have with the distinction between using an expression and mentioning it, and he gently mocks their convoluted efforts to keep the distinction clearly in focus. But in 'Limited Inc' – his reply to Searle (1977), cited in the previous note – he concedes, only half-jokingly, that confusing these two things 'might very well be [a radical evil]' (p. 81).

syntactic terms instead. A little more precisely, we can characterize the distinction in such a way that putting an expression between quotation marks, to form a singular noun phrase, is sufficient for mentioning the expression,[82] whether or not the expression's meaning is being waived. (Thus in the sentence 'The only word for this is "preposterous",' the adjective 'preposterous' is mentioned.)[83] Moreover, *unless* we characterize the distinction in this way, it will be of no avail in buttressing my original suggestion. For if mentioning an expression really did involve putting it to service in a way that waived whatever meaning it had, so as to draw attention to the expression itself, then a good translation of a text in which a given expression was mentioned would, all else being equal, leave that expression intact. Yet clearly, if we describe, in English, the relationship between some given non-propositional insight and some given artful use of language, then any examples of that use of language that we give will themselves be in English; and any translation of what we say into French will involve their French equivalents. So, on the first (broadly semantic) characterization of the distinction, we shall not have mentioned the expressions concerned. But mentioning the expressions concerned was precisely what was supposed to enable us to engage with that use of language while keeping a suitable distance from it.

What then becomes of my original suggestion? Well, I think I can stand by it. Mentioning expressions, and in that quasi-technical sense talking about them, does enable us to engage with artful uses of language while keeping a suitable (syntactic) distance from them. But the very fact that it does not determine what we are drawing attention to, nor, more generally, what effect we are achieving, means that it also leaves us free, with due skill and artistry of our own, to accomplish much of what can be accomplished by the very uses of language with which we are dealing. In particular, it means that we can, without ceasing at any point 'soberly to affirm truths', both identify some non-propositional insight as what is conveyed by some artful use of language that we have described and, if all goes really well, convey the insight. All that matters from Derrida's point of view is that we should not at the same time claim to have done something fundamentally different from whatever someone does if he or she actually indulges in the use of language in question. But that is fine. We need claim no such thing.

---

[82] I do not say that it is necessary for doing so. It is possible to mention an expression by, for example, italicizing it rather than putting it between quotation marks.

[83] For amplification and discussion, see Moore (1986). And note that, on this characterization, just as it is possible to mention an expression without waiving its meaning, so too it is possible to use an expression *while* waiving its meaning, in order to draw attention to the expression itself. Thus consider what Carnap called the material mode of speech (Ch. 11, §5(a)). And by the way, I just used the word 'material'.

CHAPTER 21

Deleuze

Something Completely Different

1. Introduction

For the second time in this narrative something extraordinary happens.[1] Gilles Deleuze (1925–1995)[2] was a remarkable thinker, a polymath whose capacity for innovation was matched only by his capacity to assimilate ideas from others, each capacity reinforcing the other. He took philosophy in general and metaphysics in particular in all sorts of new directions. And he did so largely by releasing forces at work in his predecessors. The image of a figure 'X' which I used at the beginning of Chapter 5 has a certain aptness here too.

Foucault famously wrote, in a 1970 review of two of Deleuze's most influential books,[3] 'Perhaps one day, this century will be known as Deleuzian' (Foucault (1998), p. 343). Admittedly, Deleuze himself later suggested that this was 'a joke meant to make people who like us laugh, and make everyone else livid' ('Letter to a Critic', p. 4) – the joke being, as James Williams insightfully puts it, that Foucault, 'a friend and inspiration to Deleuze', was

---

[1] This is a reference back to the opening sentence of Ch. 5.

[2] Deleuze's death in 1995 was by suicide. Having become debilitated by various pulmonary ailments he threw himself from his apartment window. In a subsequent internet discussion thread Greg J. Seigworth commented, 'I'm betting his eyes were open the whole way.' This chapter may go some way towards explaining the significance of Seigworth's comment.

[3] The books were *Difference and Repetition* and *Logic of Sense*.

   Note: throughout this chapter I use the following abbreviations for Deleuze's works: *A Thousand Plateaus* for Deleuze and Guattari (1987); *Bergson* for Deleuze (1988b); 'Breaking Open' for Deleuze (1995b); *Dialogues* for Deleuze and Parnet (1987); *Difference and Repetition* for Deleuze (1994); *Foucault* for Deleuze (2006b); *Hume* for Deleuze (1991); 'Immanence' for Deleuze (2001); *Kant* for Deleuze (1984); *Leibniz* for Deleuze (1993); 'Letter to a Critic' for Deleuze (1995a); 'Letter to Bensmaïa' for Deleuze (1995e); *Logic of Sense* for Deleuze (1990b); 'Mediators' for Deleuze (1995c); *Nietzsche* for Deleuze (2006a); 'Philosophy' for Deleuze (1995d); *Practical Philosophy* for Deleuze (1988a); *Spinoza* for Deleuze (1990a); and *What Is Philosophy?* for Deleuze and Guattari (1994). All unaccompanied page references are to *Difference and Repetition*.

deliberately flouting 'Deleuze's opposition to the cult of the origin, to the dominance of the human self in the definition of values and to the limitation of thoughts to epochs' (Williams (2003), p. 3). Yet, as Williams also goes on to observe, 'Foucault's mock prediction is turning out to be accurate' (ibid.). There is a growing interest in Deleuze's work which makes it increasingly difficult for anyone aspiring to make general sense of things not to reckon with his ideas.

Increasingly difficult; also, I think, increasingly inappropriate. Bernard Williams once listed as 'the various qualities of great philosophers' the following: 'intellectual power and depth; a grasp of the sciences; a sense of the political, and of human destructiveness as well as creativity; a broad range and a fertile imagination; an unwillingness to settle for the superficially reassuring; and, in an unusually lucky case, the gifts of a great writer' (Williams (2006b), p. 180). By these criteria, Deleuze is certainly a great philosopher, indeed one of the greatest.

2.   A Third (Themed) Retrospective

One of the qualities just listed was a broad range. Deleuze has that, as they say, in spades, especially if we include his collaborative work with the psychoanalyst Félix Guattari. One of his dominant concerns, however, albeit a concern that is itself hardly narrow, is with the history of philosophy. In fact his early work, spanning between a third and a half of his career, consists almost exclusively of studies of great philosophers of the past. There are books by him on six of our own protagonists: Spinoza, Leibniz, Hume, Kant, Nietzsche, and Bergson.[4]

Deleuze's engagement with the history of philosophy has two especially noteworthy features. First, the philosophers whose work he admires most and to whom he is most indebted tend to be outsiders, thinkers who neither conform to any of the great traditions of their time nor instigate great traditions of their own but who have an impact of a more oblique kind. Certainly, this is true of the three figures who may fairly be described as his three great heroes: Spinoza, Nietzsche, and Bergson.[5,6] What is striking is the

---

[4] Respectively: *Spinoza* (but see also, more briefly, *Practical Philosophy*); *Leibniz*; *Hume*; *Kant*; *Nietzsche*; and *Bergson*.

[5] The way Deleuze himself puts it is by saying that he 'likes writers who seem to be part of the history of philosophy, but who escape from it in one respect, or altogether' (*Dialogues*, pp. 14–15, transposed from the first person to the third person and from the past tense to the present tense). He then lists the same three figures together with Lucretius and Hume. We shall return to the idea that philosophy, at its best, is always 'untimely', in §6.

[6] The fact that Spinoza, Nietzsche, and Bergson are three of the philosophers to whom Deleuze devotes books prompts the following question: is his affinity to any given philosopher proportional to the amount that he writes about that philosopher? The answer

way in which, despite the fact that these three thinkers are out on various limbs, Deleuze traces significant connections between them. He shows how each of them, in his own way, produces something profoundly life-affirming, a cultivation of joy and a celebration of power (cf. 'Letter to a Critic', p. 6; and cf. Ch. 15, §7(a), and Ch. 16, §5).[7]

The second noteworthy feature of Deleuze's engagement with the history of philosophy is something at which I hinted in the previous section: the very form it takes. Deleuze is an extraordinary exegete. Many of the philosophers on whom we have focused in this enquiry have reacted violently against what preceded them, especially what preceded them under the title 'metaphysics', convinced that it was more or less worthless. Deleuze, while not immune to the thought that certain fundamental errors have prevailed and that they still need to be redressed (see esp. §§3 and 5 below), is altogether more positive in his approach to his predecessors. He is both more generous to them and more creative in his use of them. His aim is always to make as much as he can, in every sense of that phrase, of what they have to offer. Often he combines generosity and creativity by playing out variations on their themes: variations which are of great interest in their own right, but which also allow the themes themselves to be heard in invigoratingly new ways. Here is Deleuze's own very different metaphor for what he is doing (or rather, for what he was doing – the following passage is from a piece written in 1972, after the publication of all but one of his major historical works[8]).

> [I saw] the history of philosophy as a sort of buggery or (it comes to the same thing) immaculate conception. I saw myself as taking an author from behind and giving him a child that would be his own offspring, yet monstrous. It was really important for it to be his own child, because the author had to actually say all I had him saying. But the child was bound to be monstrous too, because it resulted from all sorts of shifting, slipping, dislocations, and hidden emissions that I really enjoyed. ('Letter to a Critic', p. 6)

is: only very roughly. Take Kant. Kant is another of the philosophers to whom Deleuze devotes a book. But Deleuze himself contrasts that book with the rest, claiming, '[This one] is different; ... I did it as a book on an enemy that tries to show how his system works' ('Letter to a Critic', p. 6). Conversely, there is great affinity between Deleuze and the Stoics, even though he has no single study of them. (The book in which he engages most with the Stoics, and in which his debt to them is clearest, is *Logic of Sense*.)

[7] It is in this connection that Philip Turetzky uses his very apt metaphor of a 'distaff tradition': see Introduction, n. 44. Cf. also Rajchman (2000), pp. 39–40, and Duffy (2006), pp. 2–3 and 249–254.

[8] The exception is *Leibniz*, the original version of which was published in 1988. (For these purposes I am not counting *Foucault* as a historical work, though it should be noted that the original version of that was published in 1986, which was two years after its subject's death.)

Here we see as clearly as anywhere in this enquiry, in fact with a clarity matched only in Bergson, what it is for metaphysics to *evolve*.[9]

This reference to Bergson is a good cue for me to begin an overview, which will occupy the rest of this section, of how Deleuze situates himself with respect to some of his predecessors.

(a)   Deleuze's Three Great Heroes: Bergson, Nietzsche, Spinoza

What Deleuze principally takes from Bergson is the distinction between the virtual and the actual, as contrasted with the distinction between the possible and the real. Deleuze too acknowledges a virtual past consisting of tendencies that are endlessly actualized. He too counts the virtual as no less real than the actual, while the possible, or the merely possible, comprises alternatives to the real. And for Deleuze, just as for Bergson, every one of these categories – the virtual, the actual, the real, and the possible – is subject to never-ending change. Thus the endless actualization of virtual tendencies not only generates new virtual tendencies, which are of course themselves part of a continually changing reality, it opens up new possibilities (see pp. 208–214).[10]

The endless actualization of the virtual, and the endless passage of the actual into the past to enlarge the virtual, together comprise a kind of perpetual splitting of the actual from the virtual, the one forever being replaced, the other forever growing. It is in his account of this perpetual splitting that Deleuze turns to Nietzsche. In particular he turns to Nietzsche's idea of eternal return. I mentioned Deleuze's interpretation of this idea in Chapter 15, §8. I also made clear that the interpretation I favour is different from Deleuze's, albeit very closely related to his and very heavily indebted to his. For now the question of whether he is being exegetically faithful is less important than the question of what he does with the idea as he conceives it (a contrast whose importance is in any case compromised by his approach to the history of philosophy).

For Deleuze, eternal return is the guarantor of ceaseless novelty. We are not to think of 'return' here in its standard sense as the coming back of something that retains its identity from an earlier time. Eternal return is not the return *of* anything, that is of anything that is the same. It applies to

---

[9] Cf. Williams (2008), p. 203. And cf. 'Breaking Open', pp. 88–89, for Deleuze's own reflections on his non-revolutionary approach to the history of philosophy.

[10] For one of the many commentaries on Deleuze that especially emphasize his inheritance from Bergson, see Ansell Pearson (1999). See also Boundas (1996) – pp. 85–86 of which contain a good summary of how Deleuze wants to reorient philosophy. (An interesting essay that explores the 'biophilosophical' aspects of Deleuze's work *without* reference to Bergson is Caygill (1997).)

what is ever different. And it applies only to what is different. (Identities, that is to say identities other than its own identity,[11] are wrought from it, not presupposed by it. Thus suppose that I step twice into the same river. Even so, different waters flow over me on the two occasions.[12] For that matter, the river is disturbed by different human cells on the two occasions. What makes it true to say that I step twice into the same river is a constellation of ever-changing processes of articulation and organization, processes of a kind that we shall explore more fully in §4.) Here is Deleuze:

> [Eternal return] is not to be interpreted as the return of something that is, that is 'one' or the 'same'. We misinterpret the expression 'eternal return' if we understand it as 'return of the same'.... It is not some one thing which returns but rather returning itself is the one thing which is affirmed of diversity or multiplicity. In other words, identity in the eternal return does not describe the nature of that which returns but, on the contrary, the fact of returning for that which differs. (*Nietzsche*, p. 45)[13]

Deleuze further relates this to a distinction that he finds in Nietzsche between active forces and reactive forces. He describes active forces, forces of domination and subjugation, as forces that affirm their own difference from other forces and go to the limit of what they can do. And he describes reactive forces, forces of adaptation and limitation, as forces that deny themselves and separate active forces from what they can do. The distinction is a relative one. That is, it applies to forces in relation to one another. One force may be active in relation to a second, reactive in relation to a

---

[11] I refer rather breezily to 'its own identity'. But we need to tread very carefully here. Eternal return does have an identity of its own. There is sheer linguistic pressure on us to say that. (I have in mind the fact that the phrase 'eternal return' functions as a singular term: cf. §5(a).) Moreover, Deleuze identifies a sense of 'the same' in which the same is 'indistinguishable from the eternal return itself' (p. 126). He amplifies on this as follows: 'The same is said of that which differs and remains different. The eternal return is the same of the different' (ibid.). (There is something similar in the quotation about to follow in the main text and in *Logic of Sense*, pp. 300–301.) All of that granted, Deleuze wants to resist any intimation of Platonism (e.g. pp. 126–128). He also insists that eternal return 'denounces' every appeal to identity other than whatever identities it itself produces (pp. 301–302; and see the material immediately following this note in the main text). The only safe conclusion, it seems to me, is that, although it is true that eternal return has an identity of its own, there is something deeply paradoxical about this. In §4 we shall be exploring another paradox, at the very core of reality. These paradoxes, I submit, are of a piece.

[12] This is a reference to Heraclitus' famous saying, 'On those who enter the same rivers, ever different waters flow' (Barnes (1987), p. 116).

[13] Deleuze's conception of time is articulated most fully in *Difference and Repetition*, Ch. II. For an excellent account, see Turetzky (1998), Ch. XIV.

third. Now when reactive forces separate active forces from what they can do, those active forces themselves 'become reactive' (*Nietzsche*, p. 59). But we must be careful how we interpret this. Deleuze does not mean that the active forces change from being active to being reactive. Rather, this is his way of saying that they are prevented from going to the limit of what they can do (*Nietzsche*, p. 53). He is highlighting a particular kind of process in which both the active and the reactive are involved. (It is partly to avert the natural misunderstanding that he always hyphenates the gerund 'becoming-reactive'.) Such a process, such becoming, is becoming of the only kind that we can know (*Nietzsche*, pp. 38 and 59). This is symptomatic of the fact that the relevant forces of cognition at work in us are themselves, in this context, reactive.[14] Such becoming is not becoming of the only kind there is however. Reactive forces can also become active, where, as before, this does not mean that reactive forces can change from being reactive to being active, but rather that there can be a certain kind of process in which 'reactive forces deny and suppress themselves' and 'strong spirits ... destroy the reactive inside themselves' (*Nietzsche*, p. 65). Moreover, eternal return applies ultimately to this second kind of becoming. For, 'however far [reactive forces] go, however deep the becoming-reactive of forces' (ibid., p. 66), endless becoming, or endless novelty, is a matter, ultimately, of ever-changing forces affirming their difference from other forces and going to the limit of what they can do. Endless becoming is both the form of being and the form of this affirmation. It is also the object of the affirmation. (See *Nietzsche*, Ch. 2, passim, and Ch. 5, §§12 and 13; and for more on this, see the next section.)[15]

In Chapter 15, §7(a), I discussed the affinity between Nietzsche and Spinoza. Deleuze emphasizes this affinity and endorses all that these two thinkers most fundamentally share. This is reflected in the ideas that we have just been considering. For at the heart of what they most fundamentally share is a celebration of activity, an affirmation of life, in all its diversity. Deleuze, like both of them, rejects the idea that life needs somehow to be justified, whether by some *telos* towards which everything is striving or by some transcendent structure in terms of which everything makes sense. Nature has no grand design. Nor is there anything transcendent to it. The celebration of activity and the affirmation of life are the celebration and the affirmation of immanence. And they reside in an ethic of empowerment, a

---

[14] But see also *Nietzsche*, Ch. 5, §8.

[15] For an excellent discussion, see Turetzky (1998), pp. 109–116. Also very helpful on Deleuze on eternal return is May (2005), Ch. 2, §IX.

Note: to say that eternal return applies ultimately to the second kind of becoming must not be allowed to obscure the fact that 'everywhere [reactive forces] are triumphant' (*Nietzsche*, p. 59). Roughly: only active forces return, but by no means all active forces return.

concern with how things can be,[16] not in a morality of obligation, a concern with how things ought to be (Ch. 2, §3).[17]

Deleuze is able, using resources that he has culled from Nietzsche, to recast many of Spinoza's key ideas. Thus recall Spinoza's notion of an affect, a person's felt transition from one degree of power to another (Ch. 2, §4). Affects are becomings.[18] They involve active forces becoming reactive and reactive forces becoming active. The sad passive affect that a man feels if he loses a limb, for example, is a disempowerment in which previously active forces are separated from what they can do. (But the man has new capacities *qua* amputee. He can now operate a prosthetic limb for instance. He can also relate empathetically to other amputees. He can even forgive the perpetrators of his misfortune, if such there be. There is now a new man in whom new active forces can go to the limit of what they can do.[19])

Here is another example, this time harking back to Bergson as well. Consider Spinoza's and Nietzsche's shared concern with how things can be. And consider Spinoza's third kind of knowledge. These are intimately related. Such knowledge is knowledge, in some sense, of how things can be (or, as Deleuze is apt to put it, of what bodies can do[20]). But in *what* sense? After all, such knowledge is particular, not general. So it cannot be, in the first instance, knowledge of possibilities that extend beyond the real. There is, however, a compelling alternative. It is knowledge of virtual powers that are part of the real.[21]

There is one crucial respect, however, in which Deleuze uses Nietzschean resources not so much to recast what he finds in Spinoza as to extend it. In fact in many ways this is the very heart of his own philosophy, the very heart of his own most general attempt to make sense of things. I shall close this sub-section with an outline of what I have in mind. (The rest of the chapter should further clarify it.)

Spinoza, Nietzsche, and Deleuze all reject the radically transcendent.[22] Or in terms that Deleuze borrows from the scholastic philosopher Duns Scotus, they are all committed to 'the univocity of being' (Duns Scotus (1987), pp. 19–20). (To say that being is univocal is equivalent to saying that there is nothing radically transcendent because both are ways of saying that there is nothing whose being has to be understood differently from the

---

[16] Recall Deleuze's emphasis, in his commentary on Spinoza's *Ethics*, on the question of what a body can do (Ch. 2, §3; and see *Spinoza*, Ch. XIV).

[17] Cf. Daniel Smith (2007).

[18] See *A Thousand Plateaus*, p. 283.

[19] Cf. *Nietzsche*, Ch. 2, §13.

[20] See n. 16.

[21] Cf. Duffy (2006), pp. 109ff.

[22] For part of the reason why I include the word 'radically', see Ch. 2, n. 11.

being enjoyed by us and by the things with which we interact.) Yet Spinoza believes in an infinite substance of which we and the things with which we interact are but finite modes. And although finite modes express the essence of substance, they are of a radically different kind from it. So is this not, already, a repudiation of the univocity of being? No. Spinoza is able to accede to the univocity of being by counting substance itself as expressive. Here the attributes are crucial. Just as finite modes express the essence of substance through its attributes, in the sense, for example, that a body expresses the essence of substance *qua* extended, so too, Deleuze urges, substance expresses itself through its attributes (e.g. *Spinoza*, pp. 27 and 59). On Spinoza's view, not only is substance extended, it is extended *in just the same sense in which bodies are extended* (e.g. *Spinoza*, pp. 46ff.). Substance may be of a radically different kind from finite modes, but its being does not have to be understood any differently from theirs.[23]

So far, for Deleuze, so good. But this is where he thinks that Nietzsche enables us to take a vital step further. For Nietzsche shows that we can understand the univocity of being involved here in terms of difference, of becoming, of endless novelty. It is as if, for Nietzsche, the modes assume a priority which brings us to a reconception of substance. Substance, for Spinoza, retains its identity throughout all change. On Nietzsche's view, nothing retains its identity throughout all change except eternal return itself.[24] This is consonant with the univocity of being because it makes all being the being of difference, of becoming, of endless novelty. (Eternal return itself is ever different, ever new.) Moreover, for reasons sketched above, it is integral in making all being an object of affirmation. And so it is that Nietzsche is able to develop the ethics to which Spinoza gave prior expression. In a famous sentence on the final page of *Difference and Repetition* Deleuze summarizes his thinking as follows:

> All that Spinozism needed to do for the univocal to become an object of pure affirmation was to make substance turn around the modes – *in other words, to realise univocity in the form of repetition in the eternal return*. (p. 304, emphasis in original; cf. ibid., pp. 40–42, and the quotation from Deleuze in Joughin (1990), p. 11)

For all that, it is Spinoza who in Deleuze's view deserves credit for having first helped us to a proper understanding of the univocity of being. This is why Spinoza is, for Deleuze, 'the "prince" of philosophers' (quoted in Joughin (1990), p. 11; cf. *What Is Philosophy*, p. 48).[25]

---

[23] For a helpful discussion, see May (2005), Ch. 2, §§I–III.

[24] But see n. 11.

[25] For helpful discussions of Deleuze on the univocity of being, see Hardt (1993), Ch. 4, and Smith (2001).

(b)   Hegel

If Spinoza is the prince of philosophers, then Hegel is the villain among them. 'What I most detested,' writes Deleuze, reflecting on his historical work, 'was Hegelianism and dialectics' ('Letter to a Critic', p. 6). We saw part of the explanation for this in Chapter 7, §6, where I emphasized the profound differences that separate Hegel from Spinoza. Chief among these differences, and chief among the reasons for Deleuze's opposition to Hegel, is the fact that for Spinoza substance does not involve any negation, whereas for Hegel the life of substance is played out precisely through processes of negation, through what Hegel calls 'the labour of the negative' (Hegel (1979), Preface, ¶19). The same chasm separates Hegel from Nietzsche (cf. Ch. 15, §7(b)). Deleuze writes:

> Three ideas define the dialectic: the idea of a power of the negative as a theoretical principle manifested in opposition and contradiction; the idea that suffering and sadness have value … ; the idea of positivity as a theoretical and practical product of negation itself. It is no exaggeration to say that the whole of Nietzsche's philosophy, in its polemical sense, is the attack on these three ideas. (*Nietzsche*, pp. 184–185; see also ibid., pp. 185ff.)[26]

(c)   Leibniz

I mentioned earlier that Leibniz is one of the philosophers to whom Deleuze devotes a book. But Deleuze makes frequent reference to Leibniz elsewhere too. Mostly, Leibniz appears as another source of inspiration. Thus Deleuze draws instructive and fascinating parallels between the notion of expression involved in Leibniz' idea that each monad is an expression of the whole world and the notion of expression involved in Spinoza's idea that each attribute, and each mode of each attribute, is an expression of the essence of substance (*Spinoza*, Conclusion). And he puts Leibniz' notion of a possible world to creative work in an account of the relation between the self and the other. Here is his summary of the central idea:

> [The] terrified face [of the other] (under conditions such that I do not see and do not experience the causes of this terror) … expresses a possible world: the terrifying world. (p. 260; cf. *What Is Philosophy?*, pp. 17ff.)

Deleuze is here fastening on a very basic link between our encounters with others expressing how they take things to be and our very conception of a

---

[26] Deleuze's own opposition to Hegel is well brought out in Hardt (1993), passim, and Duffy (2006), passim.

way things might be.[27] Deleuze's greatest Leibnizian inspiration, however, may well lie, not in Leibniz' philosophy, but in his mathematics, in his pioneering work on the calculus.[28] I shall have more to say about this in the next section.

(d)   Hume

Hume is another philosopher whom Deleuze champions, not least because Deleuze sees himself as a radical empiricist (see e.g. *What Is Philosophy?*, pp. 47–48). But his reading of Hume leads him to a striking new definition of empiricism. In Chapter 4, §1, I gave a more or less standard definition of empiricism as the view that all sense-making derives from sense experience. Deleuze would take exception to this definition. Not that he would have any quarrel with its accuracy. His quarrel would be with how useful it is. This quarrel would in turn be due, in large part, to how much the definition presupposes. In particular, it presupposes whatever is required for there to be sense-making in the first place, including a sense-maker. But no position that deserves the title 'empiricism' can acknowledge a sense-maker that is not just as much within 'the given', or the immanent,[29] as the data of sense

---

[27] Purists will insist that Deleuze should be talking here, not about possible worlds, but about ranges of possible worlds. (To say that a world is terrifying is to leave open many questions about how else it is. There is no such thing as 'the' terrifying world.) But such purism arguably misses the point, which is that Deleuze is putting Leibniz' notion to work by *adapting* it, thereby showing just the kind of creative appropriation of ideas that I have been applauding in this section (see *What Is Philosophy?*, pp. 17ff.). Why 'arguably'? Well, it is a real question how far this kind of licence can extend. Consider the related Leibnizian notion of incompossibility. Incompossibility is a relation between possible monads (Ch. 3, §3). Deleuze, however, without signalling any departure from Leibniz, allows it a much wider application. For instance, he sometimes treats it as a relation between what he calls events (e.g. *Logic of Sense*, p. 172 – see below, §4, for an account of how he uses the word 'event'), and sometimes indeed as a relation between possible worlds (e.g. ibid., pp. 111ff.). Nor is that the worst of it. Elsewhere he treats its complement, compossibility, as a non-relational property of worlds (e.g. *Leibniz*, p. 63) – the sort of thing that a suitably donnish critic would call a 'howler'. Can *this* be regarded as a creative appropriation of Leibniz' ideas? (A genuine question, not a rhetorical question. Part of what is going on here is that Deleuze is treating as primary, in his conception of worlds, the idea that they are what monads express, rather than the more familiar idea that they are sets of monads. As we saw in Ch. 3, §3, there are delicate exegetical issues about how these relate to each other. For Deleuze's own contribution to the exegesis, see e.g. *Leibniz*, pp. 25–26.)

[28] See Smith (2005).

[29] This is not to be confused with the notion of the given famously attacked by Wilfrid Sellars in Sellars (1997). Sellars' notion is intended to capture whatever is experienced, independently of how it is conceptualized, and there are good reasons, as Sellars argues, to doubt the very applicability of such a notion. Deleuze's notion is much wider and quite

experience themselves. What really marks a position out as empiricist, therefore, in Deleuze's view, is that it has some account of how the sense-maker,
or the subject, is 'constituted inside the given' (*Hume*, p. 109). And what
consolidates it in its empiricism, he further urges, taking his inspiration from
Hume, is that it holds the subject to be constituted, not so to speak at the
origin of the given, but downstream, where it constitutes *itself* (ibid., p. 87).
Thus Hume insists that the subject is not itself a datum of sense experience.
Rather, there are associations between the data of sense experience which
issue in the idea of a subject which is in turn conceived as that which makes
the associations.[30]

When an empiricist says that all sense-making derives from sense experience, then, really this is secondary in Deleuze's view. It is just a way of registering that all sense-making must 'await' the constitution of a sense-maker
somewhere beyond what is originally given. And it serves its purpose – if it
does – by in effect acting as an implicit definition of 'derives from' and 'sense
experience'. (See *Hume*, Ch. 6, passim.)[31]

(e)   Kant

This brings us naturally to Kant, who in these terms is certainly not an
empiricist (*Hume*, p. 111). This in turn signals the chief respect in which
Deleuze departs from Kant. For Kant, the subject is antecedent to the given.
What is given is given, *ab initio*, to the subject.[32] And what is given to the
subject *in experience*, as Kant understands that notion, is always independent of the subject. This enables Kant to identify conditions of experience
that are not themselves given in experience. Relatedly, it enables him to identify conditions of experience that determine, not just how experience is, but
how it must be. (See *Kant*, Ch. 1, passim.)[33]

A radical empiricism of the kind that Deleuze favours recoils from the
idea that experience has conditions of either of these kinds. It can accede
only to conditions of experience that (i) *are* themselves given in experience

---

immune to Sellars' attack. See further §7(a). (One person who arguably does accept the
notion of the given attacked by Sellars is Carnap: see Carnap (1967a), p. v.)

[30] This doctrine did not feature in Ch. 4. For Hume's discussion, see Hume (1978a), Bk I,
Pt IV, §VI.

[31] For discussion, see Buchanan (2000), pp. 75–87. And concerning the idea that the core
thesis of empiricism, as standardly construed, is really an implicit definition of 'derives
from' and 'sense experience', cf. Williams (2006l), pp. 29–33.

[32] The key phrase here is '*ab initio*'. The empiricist too can say that what is given is given
to the subject. (That is precisely what makes the language of givenness appropriate.) For
the empiricist, however, the subject is not at the origin of the given. Cf. 'Immanence',
pp. 25ff.

[33] Cf. Ch. 16, n. 24.

and (ii) apply exclusively to what is real, not also to what is merely possible. Not that Deleuze denies that experience has conditions. On the contrary, he would be the first to insist that it does have them. So how can he sustain his empiricism? By appeal to the virtual. Virtual conditions satisfy both (i) and (ii). (Cf. p. 69, and *Logic of Sense*, Appendix 3.[34])[35]

(f) Heidegger

Daniel W. Smith notes that the title of Heidegger's great work *Being and Time* is echoed in the title of Deleuze's great work *Difference and Repetition* (Smith (2001), p. 170). This is significant. There is a profound sense in which Deleuze is addressing Heidegger's question of Being. And there is a profound sense in which his answer to that question involves identifying Being with difference and time with repetition (as we have already glimpsed, and as the rest of this chapter should help to clarify).

In his long and elaborate defence of this answer Deleuze remedies what he sees as a lack in Heidegger himself. He thinks that Heidegger has shown afresh how being (or Being) can be univocal,[36] but without showing how, in Foucault's words, this 'permits difference to escape the domination of identity' (Foucault (1998), p. 364). One way to think of this is in terms of a striking pair of images that Deleuze presents at the very beginning of the first chapter of *Difference and Repetition*. He distinguishes between what he calls 'the black nothing' and 'the white nothing' (p. 28). The black nothing is a nothing in which there are no differences.[37] The white nothing is a nothing in which, though there are differences, they are not connected in any way: they do not *make sense*. If difference is to escape the domination of identity, there must be a way of avoiding the black nothing without ceding to the white nothing. There must, so to speak, be a way of attaining colour. Repudiating the radically transcendent in favour of a world of differences is certainly a way of avoiding the black nothing. That is what Heidegger has helped to show. But he has not shown how this in turn can become a way of avoiding the white nothing. (See pp. 64–66.) That, in a nutshell, is Deleuze's

---

[34] Cf. also Turetzky (1998), p. 221.

[35] Note that the basic Kantian error of construing what is given as what is given *ab initio* to the subject is one which, in different forms, Deleuze finds in other philosophers too, notably Descartes and Husserl: see e.g. *What Is Philosophy?*, p. 46, and *Logic of Sense*, p. 98; and cf. Williams (2008), pp. 133–134.

[36] Has he? What about all those kinds of Being? (Cf. also Heidegger (1982b), p. 176. And see McDaniel (2009) for a discussion that takes for granted that Heidegger opposes the univocity of Being.) The matter is complex and merits far more extensive treatment than I can give it here. I simply note the following: for there to be different kinds of Being is one thing; for there to be different ways of understanding Being is another.

[37] Cf. Hegel (1979), Preface, ¶16.

project. He wants to make sense of how differences become connected, of how they generate resemblances, identities, and unities. He wants to make sense of how things make sense.

3. Difference

This series of snippets from Deleuze's work on the history of philosophy may have appeared as something of a farrago. I hope that the remainder of this chapter will indicate the extent to which they are not.

An excellent starting point is provided by the observation that I made at the very end of the previous section: Deleuze's project is to make sense of how differences come to make sense. (It follows that he is attempting to make sense of things at the highest level of generality. In my terms this is a paradigmatically metaphysical project.[38])

Why does the project take this form? Because, in common with Nietzsche (Ch. 15, §7(b)), Bergson (Ch. 16, §4), Heidegger (Ch. 18, §4), and Derrida (Ch. 20, §4), Deleuze wants to reject the prioritization of identity over difference that has been a characteristic of most of Western philosophy – and that is still indeed a characteristic of most of analytic philosophy. (Cf. p. xv.[39])

What form does this prioritization take? It has two components. First, various discrete entities and their features are presumed given. These in turn afford a relation of numerical identity and a relation of qualitative identity. Numerical identity is that relation which each entity bears to itself and to itself alone. Qualitative identity is that relation which each entity bears to any entity that shares all its features.

Before we proceed to the second component let us reflect on how numerical identity and qualitative identity are themselves related. Everyone agrees, as a matter of logic, that the former entails the latter. But what about the converse? Does qualitative identity entail numerical identity, so that they are in fact equivalent? This is more controversial. If features are understood as including haecceities, then certainly the converse entailment holds. But what if they are not? Then many philosophers would say that qualitative identity falls short of numerical identity, or at least that it may do so. Many, not all. Even with haecceities excluded, this converse entailment has had its adherents, notably Leibniz, who thought that it followed from his principle of sufficient reason (e.g. Leibniz (1973d), pp. 88–89). Be that as it may, it is clear that qualitative identity is an extremely demanding relation. This means that, in practice, it tends to be understood in a more relaxed way, with respect to some restricted range of features. Thus two photographic prints are said to be qualitatively identical just because they *look*

---

[38] In his own terms too: see the quotations given by Daniel W. Smith in Smith (2001), p. 175 and n. 22.

[39] See also McMahon (2005).

alike, never mind that one was made before the other. Understood in this restricted way, qualitative identity can clearly fall short of numerical identity, as the example illustrates.

Now to the second component in the prioritization of identity over difference. Difference is thought of derivatively and negatively, simply as *non-identity* in one or other of the two senses just distinguished. Thus qualitative difference is thought of as that relation which holds between two entities when there is some feature that they do not share. (Again, in practice, this tends to be understood with respect to some restricted range of features.) And numerical difference is thought of as that relation which holds between two entities just by virtue of their being two entities, that is just by virtue of their not being one.[40]

Deleuze, unlike some others who have queried this prioritization,[41] is happy to accede to the first component. He does not deny the propriety of talk about discrete entities and their features, nor therefore of talk about numerical identity and qualitative identity. Nor indeed does he deny that discrete entities and their features are in some sense given, in the sense, namely, that they are part of what is immanent; in other words, that they are part of that in which, as an empiricist, he takes reality to consist. His concern is rather with the second component; with the idea that these things are fundamental and that difference can only be thought of in terms of them. This, for Deleuze, is the wrong way round. He wants to think of them in terms of it.[42,43]

For Deleuze, then, difference is not to be thought of derivatively. It is to be thought of as the fundamental character of what is given, indeed as the Being of what is given. This is not to say that difference is *itself* given. It is not. But it is that *by which* what is given is given. (See p. 222.) What is given includes discrete entities and their various features, as well as assemblages in which discrete entities are interconnected in various

---

[40] Cf. Hume (1978a), Bk I, Pt I, §V, the final paragraph of which looks like a clear statement of just this prioritization (though it uses different terminology). In fact, however, the case of Hume is complicated by his idiosyncratic conception of how discrete entities and their features are constituted. Recall in this connection the idea that we considered in §2(d): that the subject of sense-making needs to be constituted inside the given. There is a more uncompromising commitment to the prioritization both in Hegel (1975a), §38Z, p. 63, and Lewis (1986a), p. x.

[41] But in common with Nietzsche and Bergson: see Ch. 15, n. 85, and Ch. 16, §4, respectively.

[42] He wants to effect a straightforward reversal of prioritization, in other words. This is not Derridean deconstruction. Derrida is someone who would be as interested in challenging the first component as he would the second.

[43] Here the material in §2(d) is again relevant: see n. 40. Cf. also Wood (2001), p. 31.

Note: Deleuze goes as far as to say that the givenness of discrete entities and their features involves a kind of *illusion* (though not a kind of error: p. 126).

ways.[44] But it also includes something more basic, a multiplicity of differences, in terms of which everything that is given must ultimately be explained. And any such explanation must therefore eschew appeal to the subject, to God, to Platonic forms (see Plato's *Republic*, esp. Bks V–VII), to a transcendent structure holding everything together, even to persisting physical objects. (Cf. *Difference and Repetition*, Introduction, passim, and 'Philosophy', pp. 145–146.)

But how is this possible? How can difference be thought of positively? That is the basic challenge.

Before we look at how Deleuze meets the challenge, it is worth reflecting that those who accept the standard prioritization face challenges of their own. Consider: do they take an entity's difference from other entities, whether numerical or qualitative, to be itself one of the features of that entity which is presumed given? If so, then in what sense do they take it to be derivative? If not, then why not? What is their criterion for what counts as a feature? (Plato struggled with this problem: see e.g. his *Sophist*, 254ff.[45]) This is of course connected to the question that we considered above, whether qualitative identity entails numerical identity. For if an entity's numerical difference from other entities is itself a feature of that entity, then the entailment trivially holds. But this brings us to a second challenge for those who accept the standard prioritization. Do they think that the entailment continues to hold even on a suitably restricted conception of what counts as a feature? If, along with Leibniz, they do, then why do they? Presumably not for Leibniz' own antiquated reasons? If, on the other hand, they think that there could be two qualitatively identical entities, say two events in separate occurrences of an endlessly recurring cycle, then on what grounds do they hold numerical identity to be more basic than numerical difference?[46] It seems altogether more natural, when thinking about this sort of example, to invoke temporal separation as a basic discriminator, something more fundamental than any articulation of reality into discrete entities and their various features, a kind of difference that is to be thought of positively. And this indeed is part of what Deleuze is getting at with his notion of *repetition*, introduced right at the very beginning of *Difference*

---

[44] Cf. *A Thousand Plateaus*, p. 4. Cf. also Spinoza's definition of an 'individual thing' in Spinoza (2002c), Bk II, Prop. 13, Def.

[45] Both Plato and Aristotle also struggled with a range of related problems. Thus Plato was exercised by the question how the relation between a Platonic form and its instances bore on the relation between each such instance and its simulacra (e.g. *Timaeus*, 28bff.) And Aristotle was exercised by the question how being, genera, and species were related (e.g. *Metaphysics*, Bk B, Ch. 3, 998b 20–27). Deleuze discusses each of these ancient concerns in connection with his own concerns about difference at, respectively, pp. 126–128 and pp. 30ff.

[46] A comment in Wittgenstein's *Tractatus* seems pertinent here, namely 2.0233. See also 5.5302, which is in effect a flat denial that qualitative identity entails numerical identity.

and Repetition and at work throughout the rest of the book (see p. 1; and thereafter see esp. the Introduction and Ch. II passim).[47]

But by far the greatest challenge confronting those who accept the standard prioritization – something that also supplies our first clue as to how Deleuze meets his own challenge – is a sort of difference that simply resists being thought of in that negative way. In fact it is a sort of difference that likewise, and just as significantly, resists being thought of in a Bergsonian way. I mention this link with Bergson because it provides us with the ideal terms in which to broach the sort of difference that I have in mind.

Recall how Bergson argued that the essential differences between objects of analysis, or between things in space, whether literal space or metaphorical space, were all differences of degree, whereas the essential differences between objects of intuition, or between things in duration, were all differences of kind (Ch. 16, §3). The sort of difference I have in mind slips through Bergson's net.[48] On the one hand it is a difference of degree. On the other hand entities that differ in this way cannot *thereby* be thought of as occupying a space of the type that Bergson was envisaging. (They *can* be thought of as occupying a space of a much more limited type, with a much more limited structure. For example, given any such difference, the sheer fact that it is a difference of degree means that one entity can be thought of as lying 'between' two others with respect to it.[49] But they cannot thereby be thought of as occupying a space with a metric. There is no saying 'how far' the first entity is from either of the others.) Furthermore, again *contra* Bergson, the sort of difference I have in mind, though it is a difference of degree, is as much a feature of the virtual as it is of the actual.

I am talking about *intensive* difference. Examples of intensive difference are difference in heat, difference in brightness, and difference in speed.[50] It is true that, granted certain empirical assumptions and mathematical idealizations, such differences can be *represented* by Bergsonian differences of degree, or by what are sometimes called extensive differences. Differences in heat, for example, can be represented by differences in the height of a

---

[47] At one point Deleuze talks of repetition appearing as 'difference without a concept' (p. 13). This serves as an expression of his own anti-Leibnizian stance. In the same context he cites Kant's example of exact mirror images, or what Kant calls 'incongruous counterparts', which both he and Kant think show a further way in which numerical difference can consist with qualitative identity (see Kant (2002a), §13: but note that Kant uses the example to support his view that space and time are *a priori* intuitions, a view to which Deleuze does not subscribe). Again some comments in Wittgenstein's *Tractatus* seem pertinent (though they are also highly cryptic): 6.3611–6.36111.

[48] See Ch. 16, n. 19.

[49] For extended discussion, see Russell (2009), Pts III and IV.

[50] The scholastics, notably Oresme, were much exercised by such differences: see Oresme (1968). Kant too paid special attention to them: see Kant (1998), A166–176/B207–218 (the section entitled 'Anticipations of Perception').

column of mercury. This enables us to assign a numerical value to a thing's heat, as indeed we can to its brightness, or to its speed. But this must not be allowed to obscure the fact that intensive differences are intrinsically different from extensive differences. The former cannot be measured in their own terms.[51] Different intensive differences, even with respect to the same quality, are incommensurable, unlike different extensive differences with respect to the same quality.

There are many further differences between intensive differences and extensive differences, some empirical, some conceptual, some poised somewhere between the two. Here are a few more. Combining entities between which there is an extensive difference yields something of an aggregate extensity. Combining entities between which there is an intensive difference typically yields something of an intermediate intensity. Again, conversely, dividing an entity with a given extensity yields two entities of lesser extensity. Dividing an entity with a given intensity can yield all sorts of things. It can yield two entities of the same intensity; it can yield two entities of straddling intensities; it can yield two entities of some completely different kind. (There is a productivity about the intensive that is not to be found in the extensive.[52]) Finally, and crucially for our purposes, intensive differences, unlike extensive differences, cannot be understood in terms of the prioritization of identity over difference. If one entity is brighter than another, this is a qualitative difference that nevertheless does not consist in the entities' failing to share some feature: the only relevant feature here, namely brightness, is one that they precisely do share. To be sure, if we have assigned some measure, we may say that one of the entities, but not the other, has the feature of being bright to degree x, for some numerical value x. But then we are once again representing an intensive difference by an extensive difference, not treating it as it is in itself. (See *Difference and Repetition*, Ch. V, passim.)[53]

It is largely in terms of intensive difference that Deleuze will meet his challenge, as we shall see in the next section. I shall close this section by registering some connections with material in the foregoing retrospective. There are many. Take Spinozist affects, felt transitions from one degree of power to another. We can now say that these are felt intensive differences: power itself is an intensity (*Spinoza*, Pt Three, passim).[54] Relatedly, Nietzschean force is an intensity (*Nietzsche*, Ch. 2, §§2ff.). The fact that Nietzschean force is an intensity, admitting of greater and lesser, is incidentally related to

---

[51] Not even speed? Not even speed. Let us not forget how much is presupposed in assigning a measure to time.

[52] Cf. DeLanda (2002), pp. 69ff.

[53] For very helpful discussions, see Williams (2003), Ch. 7, and Turetzky (2005). See also Duffy (2006), pp. 240–248, for how this further distances Deleuze from Hegel.

[54] See Duffy (2006), Chs 4 and 5.

the fact that there is a difference between active forces and reactive forces. For, given any two forces, considered in relation to each other, the active force is always the greater and the reactive force is always the lesser. Not that this means that an active force must always prevail over a reactive force. A lesser force can prevail over a greater one (*Nietzsche*, p. 54). It is just that, if it does so, then it does so in the way that is characteristic of reactivity. Thus, whereas an active force prevails over a reactive force by doing what it can, a reactive force prevails over an active force by *preventing the active force* from doing what *it* can.[55] This reflects the fact that active forces affirm their difference from other forces, whereas reactive forces are forces of denial which separate other forces from what they can do. And, as I pointed out in the previous section, the endless difference of eternal return is then the prerogative of activity, that is of reactive forces becoming active and of active forces differing as much as they can.

To return to the connection with material in the retrospective: of especial interest is the connection with Leibniz' calculus. I have been talking about intensive difference as though it were exclusively a matter of difference between degrees of intensity. But the calculus, especially as conceived in its early days under Leibniz' own influence, rather than as conceived later through its rigourization in the nineteenth century,[56] reminds us that each degree of intensity is *itself* a sort of intensive difference (cf. p. 237). To see why, consider an extensity with different degrees of some intensity distributed across it. For instance, consider a poker, on which each point has some degree of heat: those at one end, perhaps, are very hot; those at the other end much cooler. Now the sheer fact that any given point on the poker *has* a degree of heat depends on the distribution of heat around it. It would be impossible, for instance, for one particular (indivisible) point to be very hot if it lay within a section of the poker that was otherwise uniformly cold – just as it would be impossible for one particular (indivisible) point to be red if it lay within a section that was otherwise uniformly grey. What are fundamentally given as differing in heat are sections of the poker, not points on it, albeit sections that may themselves have sub-sections of variable heat, in which case their own heat is some kind of mean. A yet clearer case, perhaps, is that of speed. Thus consider an ant running continuously along the poker from left to right, accelerating all the while. What are fundamentally given as differing in speed are portions of its journey, not points on the journey. Thus we talk of its (mean) speed along a given section of the poker, by construing this as the ratio of the length of that section to the time that the ant takes to traverse it, under some suitable measure. (And the ant's acceleration

---

[55] Cf. the discussion, at p. 28, of how something can 'make a difference' by 'distinguishing itself', even though 'that from which it distinguishes itself does not distinguish itself from it'.

[56] See Moore (2001a), Ch. 4, §§1 and 2.

means that the different speeds along different sections increase from left to right.) To talk of its speed *at a particular point* on the poker, as it were the reading on its internal speedometer at that point, is derivative. Very well, but how is it derived? How does talk of the ant's speed along different sections of the poker subserve talk of its speed at different points on the poker? Here at last we see the relevance of the calculus. The calculus answers just this sort of question. That is its genius. It enables us to construe the ant's speed at a particular point on the poker as the limit of its speeds along ever smaller sections of the poker that include that point.[57] And the very fact that such questions are answered in this way, nay the very fact that they are answered at all, is the kind of thing that I have in mind when I say that a degree of intensity is itself a sort of intensive difference: there can be no 'punctual' instance of any given intensity save insofar as there are suitable intensive differences between 'regional' instances of it.[58]

4.   The Execution of the Project. Sense

Deleuze's attempt to account for how things make sense in terms of a positive conception of difference begins with intensive difference then: a sort of difference that not only *can* be conceived positively but *must* be conceived positively. Intensive differences ground what he calls 'the transcendental field' (*Logic of Sense*, p. 98, and 'Immanence', pp. 25–26[59]). The project is to show how, within this field, all discrete entities, including the subject, are constituted along with their various features.[60] I shall try in this section to give a sketch of how Deleuze executes his project. (But I must issue a warning. Even the word 'sketch' is presumptuous. The project is colossal.)

I said in the previous section that intensive difference is as much a feature of the virtual as it is of the actual. In fact it is on the cusp. It is a feature of that actualization of the virtual (or, as we should rather perhaps put it, that actualization-of-the-virtual) of which the virtual and the actual are themselves ultimately abstractions. Consider again some point on the poker with a particular degree of heat. The sheer fact that the point has this degree of heat, I argued, depends on the distribution of heat around it. I had in mind sections of the poker. But the considerations that I invoked apply as much to the temporal as they do to the spatial. Just as it would be impossible

---

[57] See again the material cited in the previous note.
[58] For Deleuze's own reflections on the calculus, see pp. 170–182. See also Smith (2005), esp. §5, and Duffy (2006), Ch. 2.
[59] See also *Logic of Sense*, p. 344, n. 5.
[60] There is a very similar project, to which Deleuze is much indebted, in Simondon (1964) (see *Logic of Sense*, 15th Series, n. 3). Note: the fact that the subject too needs to be constituted is what makes the project empiricist (§2(d)). It also means that the field cannot itself have the form of a subject (*Logic of Sense*, pp. 98–99).

for this point to be very hot if it lay within a section of the poker that was otherwise uniformly cold, so too it would be impossible for some (indivisible) instant in the point's history to be an instant at which it was very hot if that instant lay within a period during which the point was otherwise uniformly cold. This is part of the reason why the instantiation of heat has both a virtual aspect and an actual aspect. Not that any *particular* history is a precondition of the point's having the degree of heat it has. The point could have that degree of heat while heating up, or while cooling down, or while enjoying a period of uniform heat – which for current purposes we may as well regard as a limit case of its cooling down. In itself, the degree of heat, construed as an intensive temporal difference, is a change of heat that is neither a heating up nor a cooling down. It is what Deleuze calls a 'pure event', a becoming that '[pulls] in both directions at once' (*Logic of Sense*, p. 1). Deleuze deliberately uses this more paradoxical formulation, saying that the becoming pulls in both directions rather than in neither, because he thinks we do well to acknowledge a paradox in reality itself, a paradox that is 'resolved' – the reason for the scare quotes should become clear in due course – in the actualization of the virtual, that is to say in a distribution of further degrees of heat in favour of one direction over the other. (Cf. *Logic of Sense*, 12th Series.) But of course, any such actualization of the virtual merely involves further instantiations of heat to which the same considerations apply. The perpetual splitting of the actual from the virtual is the perpetual 'resolution' of paradox in the creation of fresh paradox. It is as if paradox itself, the paradox inherent in intensive difference, is the driving force of eternal return (see pp. 119–124 and *Logic of Sense*, pp. 66–67).

Now I have been talking about instantiations of intensities as though these always had to be part of some smooth transition from one degree of intensity to another. In fact, however, a point on some surface may be bright because it lies on the very edge between two smaller adjacent surfaces, each of which is itself uniformly bright though one is brighter than the other. It is in this connection that Deleuze invokes what he calls 'singularities', pure events of a special kind. He characterizes these as follows:

> Singularities are turning points and points of inflection; bottlenecks, knots, foyers, and centres; points of fusion, condensation, and boiling; points of tears and joy, sickness and health, hope and anxiety, 'sensitive' points. (*Logic of Sense*, p. 52)

The actualization of the virtual involves countless singularities. And these critically shape the development of the virtual and its further actualization.

To get a sense of how, consider the fact that intensities are instantiated correlatively and conjointly. For instance some cooling down may be correlated with a transition from red to grey, indeed from bright red to dull grey. Virtual tendencies, if we abstract from their dynamism, may then be thought of as journeys through spaces of possibilities – what are technically known as 'state spaces' – where these are metaphorical spaces of the limited kind which, as I observed parenthetically in the previous section, are apt even for the characterization of intensive difference. Each point in any such space represents some combination of degrees of intensity (heat, redness, brightness, …). The space therefore has a dimension corresponding to each intensity involved (cf. pp. 182ff.). What the singularities associated with the space serve to do, in their virtual aspect, is to determine the geometry of the space. For example, they can determine its limits. An increase in heat and a correlated increase in redness, in the context of a further complex of correlations, will be able to proceed only so far. At the limit it will issue in a singularity that so to speak prevents continuation of the journey. This in turn bears on how the virtual is actualized. If the poker is heated enough, it will start to melt and eventually disintegrate. Again, relatedly, singularities can ensure that the space has certain 'holes' that voyagers 'fall down'. An increase in heat and redness, in the context of other relevant changes in intensity, will eventually be accompanied by a sharp decline in rigidity.

Here we see the way in which singularities shape, fashion, and generally work the virtual. But now recall two cardinal features of Bergson's account of the virtual: first, that the virtual is continually changing; and second, that the actualization of the virtual can be thought of topologically, as involving processes of blending, stretching, breaking, twisting, piercing, and suchlike. In Deleuze's account of the virtual, which shares these two features, they can be seen as more or less equivalent to each other. For the continual change of the virtual can be seen as the blending, stretching, and so forth of state spaces of the sort that we have just been considering. A singularity, in the splitting of its virtual aspect from its actual aspect, may 'dent' such a space and create a hole into which the relevant virtual tendencies must now descend. Once the poker has disintegrated, for example, further increases in surrounding heat will have new targets and will result in crises of a different kind elsewhere, say the combustion of nearby furniture.

Recall also a cardinal feature of Bergson's account of the possible, that the possible, no less than the virtual, is continually changing; in particular, that new possibilities are continually coming into existence. This too is an idea that Deleuze embraces. This too is an idea that we can now see anew. We can see it as involving the inception of new connections between intensities, or the inception of new state spaces with extra dimensions. Part of the significance of this is that it signals an extremely important way in which the navigation of these spaces, in the actualization of virtual tendencies, can surmount obstacles. Thus consider a journey along one dimension that leads to some sort of limit. Continuation of the journey along that one dimension seems impossible. But perhaps it is not. Perhaps it is possible by climbing a second dimension and 'jumping over' the limit. Thus a substance's melting point can increase when there is an increase in atmospheric pressure. So too someone's ability to play the piano can extend beyond previous limits when accompanied by instances of a hitherto completely absent form of encouragement.

We now begin to get a sense of how discrete individuals are constituted. In the actualization of virtual tendencies various singularities play a more or less direct role. (Note here that any inception of a new connection between intensities of the sort discussed in the previous paragraph is itself a kind of singularity.) The actualization of these tendencies can accordingly be seen as a more or less clear expression of these singularities, which Deleuze likens to the more or less clear expression that obtains between a Leibnizian monad and any given part of the rest of reality (*Logic of Sense*, pp. 110–111). Individuals are constituted as having something like a Leibnizian point of view on reality. (See ibid., 16th Series.)[61]

The account extends to subjects and to features of things (*Logic of Sense*, 16th and 17th Series; see also *Difference and Repetition*, pp. 256ff.). In fact it extends to space and time themselves. Although the endless actualization of virtual tendencies involves the distribution of intensities across extensities, we are not to think of this as occurring within two pre-given containers. 'Time itself unfolds,' Deleuze writes, '… instead of things unfolding within it' (p. 88; cf. p. 236).

Let us now retell the story that has just been told, but in different terms, to see better the role that sense plays in it.

The pure events that we considered above are connected in what Deleuze calls 'the Event' (*Logic of Sense*, p. 11; see further ibid., 9th and 10th Series). This is the very form of change, on the cusp between the virtual and the actual. Now in the splitting of the virtual from the actual, or in the actualization of the virtual, each of the events involved, as we saw, requires some distribution of further events, each of which in turn requires some distribution of further events, and so on indefinitely. It is through such distributions that the paradoxical element that inheres in all of these events is continually 'resolved'. Its 'resolution' can be thought of as a movement along and between series of events, selecting distributions. The movement never ceases. It cannot. It always involves new pure events in which the paradoxical element inheres. Or rather, it always involves *anew* pure events in which the paradoxical element inheres. The events themselves are not new, inasmuch as, simply *qua* pure events, they must already be connected with all others in the Event. There are thus continual changes in the relations between the events in the Event. And these changes are themselves changes in degree of intensity. For example, a change in heat comes to stand now in a more critical relation to a change of rigidity, now in a much less critical relation to it (as the poker is pulled away from the fire, say).

---

[61] Cf. *What Is Philosophy?*, pp. 153–154. For helpful discussions of the material so far in this section, see Hardt (1993), Ch. 4; DeLanda (2002), passim, esp. Chs 1 and 3; Williams (2003), Chs 6 and 7; and Duffy (2006), pp. 227ff.

One model for these continual changes in the relations between events is that of a musical theme and its variations. (The model is especially apt if the variations are thought of as improvised. That avoids undue connotations of stasis.) The theme and its variations have a kind of topological equivalence. Certain elements are invariant from one variation to the next. But relations between them vary, in different kinds of intensity. In one variation, for example, a modulation is accentuated. In another a pause is prolonged. In yet another the original accompaniment becomes the principal melody and vice versa. In a fourth the original principal melody shifts to a new key, with corresponding differences of resonance with respect to the home key. And so on. The changing *sense* of the theme and its variations consists in the changing significance of this nexus of relations, whereby not only can the invariant elements be heard afresh but the theme itself can become an object of renewed (retrospective) attention. This in turn is a model for what Deleuze himself means by sense. As the relations between pure events vary in different degrees of intensity, through the actualization of the virtual, ever new sense is created. And part of what such sense does is to constitute individuals, including subjects, and their various features. Thus the fact that the relation between that change of heat and that change of rigidity becomes more critical in that context is partly constitutive of the identity of that poker. (See e.g. *Logic of Sense*, 14th and 15th Series.)[62]

This notion of sense is related to, but importantly different from, various other notions of sense that we have encountered in this enquiry. In particular, while it bears on the relation between propositions and reality (as we are about to see), it is not the same as Frege's notion of sense. Nor is it the same as the development of Frege's notion of sense in the early Wittgenstein. I single out these two because it is especially instructive to contrast Deleuze's notion with each of them.[63]

We have glimpsed how subjects and other entities are constituted along with their various features. In the 3rd Series of *Logic of Sense* Deleuze discusses how propositions stand in relation to what is constituted.[64] Suppose, for example, that I see next-door's cat in our garden. And suppose that I straightway tell you that next-door's cat is in our garden. Then I utter a proposition which Deleuze would say:

- *denotes* a state of affairs that involves next-door, their cat, and our garden (hence denotes a state of affairs that involves suitably constituted individuals)
- *manifests* my belief about where next-door's cat is (hence manifests the belief of a suitably constituted subject)

and

---

[62] See Williams (2008), Ch. 1, for a helpful discussion of these ideas.
[63] Deleuze himself considers Frege's notion of sense in *What Is Philosophy?*, pp. 135ff.
[64] See also 19th Series and *Difference and Repetition*, pp. 153ff.

- *signifies* what else must be the case or may be the case if the proposition is true (hence signifies where the proposition is located in logical space as a result of the interrelations of suitably constituted features).

In the notion of denotation we hear echoes of Frege's notion of *Bedeutung*. In the notion of signification we hear echoes of both Frege's and the early Wittgenstein's notions of sense. And in the notion of manifestation, or at least in notions that underpin the notion of manifestation, we hear echoes of both Frege's and the early Wittgenstein's notions of the grasp of sense. But Deleuze insists that, in addition to all of this, my proposition *expresses* what he calls sense. This is a matter of complex relations between pure events, in which much else is at stake beyond those three more familiar dimensions of my proposition. It has to do with what *difference* it makes whether my proposition is true. Thus part of the sense expressed is a heightened danger now connecting a change in feline aggression with a change in avine safety. Furthermore, my very uttering of the proposition, itself an occurrence like any other in which virtual tendencies are actualized, will have a bearing on the sense expressed. For instance, a heightened danger may now also connect a change in human aggression with a change in feline safety. In fact the sense is nothing apart from its expression (cf. *Logic of Sense*, pp. 21–22). In these and many other ways Deleuzian sense and Fregean or early-Wittgensteinian sense are very different from each other.

There are two striking differences that merit particular mention. First, a proposition and its negation can express the very same Deleuzian sense (e.g. p. 156 and *Logic of Sense*, p. 33).[65] If I see next-door's cat in our garden and I tell you that next-door's cat is *not* in our garden, then I say something false, where in the original example I said something true; I lie, where in the original example I told it as I saw it; I leave open the possibility that there are no animals at all in our garden, where in the original example I foreclosed that possibility; but the same complex relations between pure events as were at stake in the original example, with their manifold implications for what matters to what else, can still be at stake here, expressed just as they were there. That is, it can make the same difference whether what I say is true as it did in the original example.

Second, Deleuze has a positive conception of nonsense whereby sense, so far from excluding nonsense, depends on it (e.g. *Logic of Sense*, 11th Series). Nonsense, as Deleuze conceives it, is a characteristic of the paradoxical element that inheres in events, that from which all sense ultimately arises. As far as language is concerned, this means that combinations of words that the early Wittgenstein in particular would have counted as straightforwardly lacking sense can for Deleuze be said to express sense of a special kind, enabling them to highlight just such nonsense. Examples are

---

[65] It is instructive here to look at Wittgenstein (1961), 4.023 and 4.06ff.

'Becoming pulls in both directions at once' and 'Alice does not grow without shrinking' (see *Logic of Sense*, p. 1). Indeed Deleuze is prepared to say that even a word to which no conventional meaning has been assigned, such as Lewis Carroll's 'snark' (Carroll (1974)), can be said to express sense, in this case by denoting the very sense that it expresses – a feature that words do not normally have, of course, and one that itself creates a distinctive movement in associated series of events whenever the word in question is used (*Logic of Sense*, pp. 66–67). Deleuze therefore has an extremely generous notion of sense, and correlatively of what it is for words to express sense, more reminiscent of Derrida's generous notion of what it is for words to be put to effective use (Ch. 20, §6) than of either Frege's notion or the early Wittgenstein's notion of what it is for a proposition to have a sense.[66] Relatedly, Deleuze recognizes all sorts of distinctions between the ways in which words express sense, and indeed the ways in which they highlight nonsense, to which nothing corresponds in either Frege or the early Wittgenstein. To be sure, the early Wittgenstein drew a distinction between two ways in which a combination of words could lack what *he* called sense, distinguishing between what he called nonsensicality, which attaches to a combination of words to which no meanings have been assigned, and what he called senselessness, which attaches to a proposition that is either necessarily true or necessarily false (Ch. 9, §3). Deleuze certainly has a distinction akin to that (*Logic of Sense*, p. 35). But he has plenty more besides. Part of the significance of this, in the context of our enquiry, is its bearing on the recurring idea, which surfaced most recently in §6 of the previous chapter but which is itself associated principally with the early Wittgenstein, that there may be a good story to tell about how a creative use of language might succeed in conveying what I have been calling a non-propositional understanding of things. For there might be a use of language expressing a Deleuzian sense of such a kind that whoever is suitably attuned to that sense will share the non-propositional understanding in question. Indeed that seems to me precisely the story that Deleuze himself must tell about his own use of language to highlight nonsense – as for instance when he says, 'Becoming pulls in both directions at once.' (I shall say a little more about this in the next section.)[67]

Finally in this section I want to allude very briefly to the ethical implications of these ideas, which Deleuze discusses in, among other places, the 20th to the 22nd Series of *Logic of Sense*, and which hark back especially to Spinoza.

---

[66] Very pertinent in this context, especially given the broader context, is Wittgenstein (1975), §V.

[67] There are very helpful and insightful discussions of Deleuze's views about sense in relation to language in both May (2005), Ch. 3, esp. §§VIII–XI, and Williams (2008), Ch. 2, passim. Also helpful is Poxon and Stivale (2005).

We have encountered often enough in this enquiry the idea that representing how things are is not the only way of making sense of them. We first encountered the idea near the very beginning, in connection with Descartes, where I adverted to an alternative to representation, namely expression (Ch. 1, §6). I suggested that, on the assumption that things themselves make sense (the very assumption that it is Deleuze's project to substantiate), sense can be made of things by participating in their sense-making, that is by expressing the sense that they themselves make. This is the notion of expression that Deleuze finds in Spinoza and Leibniz. And it is the notion that we have now seen him develop on his own account, in connection with propositions. But the connection with propositions is only one of many. Any actualization of the virtual serves as an expression both of the pure events involved and of the complex interplay between them wherein sense consists. We are, in a way, continually expressing sense. We are continually making sense of things.

For Spinoza, making sense of things was the stuff of ethics (Ch. 2, §3). Likewise for Deleuze. For Deleuze, just as for Spinoza, we come into our own, or 'we become those that we are',[68] when we are the agents of our own sense-making, or in other words when we see the virtual tendencies that are being actualized in our lives, appropriate them, experiment with them, creatively extend them, trigger the intensities at work in them,[69] release the sense expressed through them, and learn to surrender whatever cherished categories they may serve to destabilize (God, the self, the world of abiding values, the world of abiding physical objects[70]). And it is in passing from the actual to the virtual, or in seeing the virtual in the actual – this is what Deleuze means by 'counteractualization' (*Logic of Sense*, pp. 150ff.) – that we achieve our most intense activity and display our greatest power. We attain to Spinoza's third kind of knowledge.

Here, in summary, is Deleuze:

> Either ethics makes no sense at all, or this is what it means and has nothing else to say: not to be unworthy of what happens to us. To grasp whatever happens as unjust and unwarranted ... is, on the contrary, what renders our sores repugnant – veritable *ressentiment*[71].... What does it mean then to will the event? Is it to accept war, wounds, and death when they occur? It is highly probable that resignation is only one more figure of *ressentiment*.... We are faced with ... a transmutation. 'To my inclination for death,' said Bousquet, 'which was a failure of the will, I

---

[68] This is a Nietzschean phrase: see e.g. Nietzsche (1974), §§270 and 335, and the motto to Nietzsche (1967b), p. 215. It derives from Pindar (1980), Pythan 2, l. 71.

[69] I borrow the terminology of 'triggering intensities' from Williams (2003), p. 20.

[70] Cf. *Logic of Sense*, p. 176.

[71] See Ch. 15, n. 72.

will substitute a longing for death which would be the apotheosis of the will.' From this inclination to this longing there is, in a certain respect, no change except a change of the will, a sort of leaping in place ... of the whole body which exchanges its organic will for a spiritual will. It wills now not exactly what occurs, but something *in* that which occurs, something yet to come which would be consistent with what occurs, in accordance with the laws of an obscure, humorous conformity: the Event.... The splendour and magnificence of the event is sense. The event is not what occurs (an accident), it is rather inside what occurs, the purely expressed.... Nothing can be said, and no more has ever been said: to become worthy of what happens to us, and thus to will and release the event, to become the offspring of one's own events, and thereby to be reborn, ... and to break with one's carnal birth. (*Logic of Sense*, pp. 149–150, emphasis in original)[72,73]

5.   The Dogmatic Image of Thought

The ideas in the last two sections undoubtedly put a strain on some of our normal ways of thinking, and hence on some of our deepest self-conscious preconceptions about the nature of thought. Deleuze concedes this. In fact he proclaims it. He identifies a cluster of paradigms and assumptions concerning the nature of thought that have dominated the history of philosophy, groups them together under the label 'the dogmatic image of thought', and challenges them. In this section I shall consider four of the paradigms, then identify four of the most central of the assumptions.

(a)   Representation

The first paradigm is that of representation. This is a paradigm in which thought is separate from its object, and is successful or unsuccessful to the extent that it does or does not suitably correspond to its object. As I intimated in the previous section, we first encountered this paradigm in Descartes, where we also first noted how expression serves as an alternative to it.

One of the principal ways in which Deleuze puts pressure on this paradigm is through his very prioritization of difference over identity. For representing how things are *eo ipso* involves operating at the level of constituted

---

[72] There are two interesting echoes here: of John 3:1–8; and of Wittgenstein (1961), the 6.4s, esp. 6.41–6.43. In each case there is room for fascinating debate about how clear or how muffled the echo can be said to be.

[73] Helpful reading on Deleuze's ethics include: Hardt (1993), Ch. 4; Buchanan (2000), Ch. 3; and Williams (2008), Ch. 4.

identities. This is because the very idea of a correspondence between thought and its object is an idea of shared features between discrete entities. Or at any rate such is how Deleuze construes representation. At one point he refers to what he calls representation's 'dearest task', which he characterizes as '[relating] difference to the identical' (p. 235). He further insists that 'difference is not and cannot be thought in itself, so long as it is subject to the requirements of representation' (p. 262).

It by no means follows that there can be no such thing as representing how things are. What follows is that there can be no such thing as representing how things most fundamentally are, in their raw difference.[74] The assault is not an assault on the very idea of representation. It is an assault on the idea that representation is a paradigm that reveals the ultimate character of reality.

These considerations about representation extend to linguistic sensemaking more generally. For, as Bergson noted (Ch. 16, §4), the very articulation of propositions into subjects and predicates already bespeaks discrete entities and their features. Moreover, there is reason to think that such an articulation is not just a peculiarity of linguistic sense-making as we know it, but that it is of the very essence of linguistic sense-making; that simply making linguistic sense of things already involves identifying discrete entities and their features.[75] To whatever extent this is true, it poses no more of a threat to the sheer idea of making linguistic sense of things than was posed above to the sheer idea of representation. The threat, as before, is only to the idea of making linguistic sense of things as they most fundamentally are. And even that does not preclude a more oblique use of language to achieve and to convey an understanding of things at the most fundamental level, the sort of thing to which I adverted in the previous section and the sort of thing which, I urged then and I urge again now, we need to acknowledge on Deleuze's own pages.

(b)   Common Sense and Good Sense

The second and third paradigms form a pair. They are the paradigm of what Deleuze calls 'common sense' and the paradigm of what he calls 'good sense'. By 'common sense' he means a faculty of thought which, by bringing other faculties, such as the various sensory faculties and the faculty of imagination, under a certain unity, allows for recognition both of the subject of thought and of the object of thought. By 'good sense' he means an

---

[74] See pp. 55–56 for a fuller account of this. At p. 262 he says that difference 'can become thinkable only when tamed – in other words, when subject to the ... iron collars of representation.'

[75] For a sketch of an argument to this effect, see A.W. Moore (1996), pp. 157–158. See also *Difference and Repetition*, p. 121.

exercise of thought designed to organize the diversity of the given. (Error, in these terms, is 'a kind of failure of good sense within the form of a common sense which remains integral and intact' (p. 149).) Good sense is characteristically concerned with *progression*. It seeks, in the unruly diversity of the given, diachronic patterns, whereby things proceed from the remarkable to the unremarkable, from the less orderly to the more orderly, from the more differentiated to the less differentiated. Good sense requires common sense, because 'it could not fix any beginning, end, or direction …, if it did not … [relate] the diverse to the form of a subject's identity, or to the form of an object's or a world's permanence, which one assumes to be present from beginning to end' (*Logic of Sense*, p. 78). But common sense likewise requires good sense, because there can be no recognizing either a subject of thought or an object of thought without the orderliness that good sense makes available.

As with the paradigm of representation, to say that these are casualties of Deleuze's critique is not to say that he denies them a place in the operations of thought. What he denies them is a place in thought's most fundamental operations. At the most fundamental level, the level of pure difference, there is something that eludes them both: the paradox inherent in pure events. Where the paradox inherent in pure events has events going in both directions at once, good sense acknowledges only what goes in one direction. Where the paradox inherent in pure events contests all identities, through its driving of eternal return, common sense searches for and fastens on the identity of thought's subject and the identity of thought's object. (See pp. 132–138 and 223–228; and *Logic of Sense*, 12th Series.)

(c)   Clarity and Distinctness

The fourth paradigm is the Cartesian paradigm of clear and distinct perception. This is a paradigm in which every aspect of some given object of attention is itself an object of attention (Ch. 1, §3). This paradigm is not in the same sort of conflict with the execution of Deleuze's project as the other three are. Rather it is, Deleuze avers, in conflict with itself. For the two elements in the Cartesian paradigm, so far from complementing or reinforcing each other, actually militate against each other. The more a thing's several aspects can be said to be objects of attention, the less it can itself be said to be. Thus a computer image is an object of attention precisely insofar as its myriad component pixels are not: the image is clearly perceived precisely insofar as it is not distinctly perceived.[76]

---

[76] Descartes himself understood distinctness in such a way that it entailed clarity (Ch. 1, n. 13). In Descartes' terms, then, Deleuze is challenging the very legitimacy of the notion of distinctness. – Question: even if what Deleuze says is by and large true of perception, is it true of the sort of perception for which Descartes reserved the label 'intuition'

It follows that this paradigm, unlike the other three, is one that Deleuze does not just exclude from the most fundamental level of thought: he rejects it altogether. In fact there is a paradigm of his own that he pits against it. In Deleuze's paradigm thought operates precisely by converting obscurity (unclarity) into confusion (indistinctness) for the sake of greater clarity. It does this by taking the myriad distinctly perceived elements of some obscure multiplicity in the virtual and so actualizing them as to achieve a kind of unity in the actual that can be perceived as such – though only at the price that the many aspects of that unity meld into confusion. (See pp. 213–214, 252–254, and 280.)

(d)   Four Assumptions

Central among the assumptions that constitute the dogmatic image of thought are the following four, in which the paradigm of representation is especially visible.

(1)   The goal of thought is true representation.

(2)   The anathema of thought is false representation.

(3)   Thought is of such a nature that, with suitable 'good will' on the part of its subject, it tends to achieve its goal.[77]

(4)   The problems addressed by thought are defined by their solutions, where these in turn are the truths that thought seeks. Equivalently, the problems addressed by thought take the form of questions and the solutions to those problems are the answers to those questions.[78]

Deleuze thinks that every one of these assumptions both can and must be challenged. It will be the main burden of the next section to show how and why.

The dogmatic image of thought has in Deleuze's view been as pernicious as it has been prevalent. At the end of the chapter in *Difference and Repetition* devoted to it,[79] he writes that its assumptions 'crush thought,'

(Ch. 1, §4)? – Well, perhaps it is: consider, for example, the great pains taken in Whitehead and Russell (1927) to make our perception that $1 + 1 = 2$ more distinct, nicely encapsulated in the comment at *54.43. Nevertheless, the application of Deleuze's critique to Cartesian intuition, or to anything like Cartesian intuition, requires the support of further argument.

[77] Cf. Descartes' account of error (Ch. 1, §4).

[78] Cf. p. xvi (where Deleuze refers to the 'traditional' image of thought, but it is the same thing). There is a fuller list, highlighting connections with the paradigms of common sense and good sense, on p. 167. See also pp. 262–272.

For discussion of these assumptions, and of the dogmatic image of thought more generally, see Williams (2003), pp. 120ff., and May (2005), Ch. 3, passim.

[79] Ch. III – which, on p. xvii of his preface to the English edition of the book, he describes as 'the most necessary and the most concrete' of all the chapters.

and that it 'profoundly betrays what it means to think and alienates the two powers of difference and repetition' (p. 167). Deleuze's assault on the prioritization of identity over difference and his consequent attempt to show, in terms of pure difference, how things make sense are part of a much broader reorientation in philosophy.

6. The Nature of Problems, the Nature of Concepts, and the Nature of Philosophy; or, Metaphysics as the Creation of Concepts

Let us begin with assumptions (1) and (2). Deleuze acknowledges something far more precious to thought than truth. 'The notions of relevance, necessity, the point of something, are a thousand times more significant than the notion of truth,' he says, 'Not as substitutes for truth, but as a *measure* of the truth of what I'm saying' ('Philosophy', p. 130, emphasis added). Relatedly, he thinks that a far worse fate can befall thought than to issue in falsehoods. It can issue in 'nonsensical sentences, remarks without interest or importance, banalities mistaken for profundities, ordinary "points" confused with singular points, badly posed or distorted problems' (p. 153). These, he says, are 'all heavy with dangers, yet the fate of us all' (ibid.).

Assumption (4) is vulnerable to the same considerations. On assumption (4) thought is primarily a matter of trying to answer questions, questions whose answers are antecedently identifiable propositions ('What is the least number of colours that suffices to paint any given map, so that no two adjacent regions are painted the same colour?' 'How much weight can this bridge take?'). But in Deleuze's view there is a much deeper and much more important level at which thought, insofar as it is concerned with questions at all, is as much a matter of trying to pose them as trying to answer them. At that level thought tries to orient itself in significant new ways, something it may do by providing the wherewithal to frame questions which have hitherto been unframeable and which, because of their array of associations and implications, raise all manner of further questions.[80] This is a reflection of the fact that the most important and the most engaging problems addressed by thought do not themselves take the form of questions. They take the form of imperatives ('Extend the line of investigation that led to the discovery of this mathematical function,' 'Connect the actions of human beings to climate change,' 'Make sense of this calamity').[81] Moreover, where the solution to a problem on the dogmatic conception effectively kills the problem, a solution to a problem on Deleuze's conception – we no longer have any licence to talk about 'the' solution to a problem – can serve rather to invigorate it.

---

[80] Cf. Deleuze's comments on the calculus on p. 177.
[81] Cf. pp. 161–162 and 197–198.

(To extend a line of investigation is to present opportunities for further such extension; to connect events is to set them in a context that allows for further such connections; to make sense of a situation is to make something of it of which further sense can be made.) A problem on Deleuze's conception can play a heuristic role, akin to the essentially inexhaustible heuristic role played by a Kantian regulative principle (Ch. 5, §7).[82]

There is a related difference between what Deleuze would say about problems and their solutions and what someone under the sway of the dogmatic image of thought would say. On Deleuze's conception we may not even be in a position properly to formulate a problem until we have a solution to it. Take the familiar cake cutting problem: how to divide a cake fairly between two people. The equally familiar solution to this problem is that one person cuts and the other person chooses. So far, so straightforward – even on the dogmatic conception. But now suppose someone gives us the following instruction: 'Generalize that to more than two people.' This requires something of a different order. It requires us to think through what is achieved in the two-person case. And as we do so we shall soon see that there is a deep unclarity in the word 'that'. What is to be generalized? Is it a question of one person's being able to cut in such a way as to be immune to other people's choices? Is it a question of no one's ending up with a smaller portion than anyone else except by virtue of either cutting badly or choosing badly? What are the rules? There is no prospect of clarifying what is at stake here, nor therefore of formulating this problem well, except in tandem with actually working out some solution to it. Assumption (4) makes no provision for this sort of thing.[83]

Deleuze is working with a much broader notion of a problem than that which occurs in assumption (4) then. Elsewhere his notion appears broader still. For Deleuze, problems are objective features of the virtual. They present themselves as challenges: how to actualize the virtual in suitably creative ways. (Thus the challenge in the cake cutting case is to extend the virtual tendencies involved in our coming to see that two people can share a cake fairly by one cutting and the other choosing.) And they are solved to whatever extent the virtual *is* so actualized. Most of them are quite independent of human beings, certainly of the epistemic state of any particular human being (p. 280 and *Logic of Sense*, p. 54). A problem and its solution are as liable to involve plant mutations or geological shifts as they are to involve,

---

[82] This is a comparison to which Deleuze himself is alive. He frequently relates problems to the Kantian ideas of reason in terms of which regulative principles are framed (e.g. pp. 168ff.).

See further, for the rest of the material in this paragraph, pp. 158ff. and 176–182; and *Logic of Sense*, pp. 121–123. See also Williams (2008), pp. 106–115.

[83] For a classic discussion of a similar but far more interesting example, see Lakatos (1976). See further *Difference and Repetition*, pp. 158–164.

say, mathematical calculations or articulated programmes of research or
the machinations of some wily politician. They may involve something's
'jumping' over some obstacle by moving into a new state space, in the way
described in §4 above. They may involve an obscure virtual multiplicity's
being actualized in a clear whole, in the way described in §5(c) above. The
general form of a problem is not, 'How do things stand here?' but, 'Proceed
from here,' where proceeding from here is understood in a such a way as to
involve expressing anew the sense that is expressed here, playing out variations on these themes, tapping the virtual. The problematical, we now see, is
deeply related to the ethical (see §4 above).[84]

It follows that problems and their solutions are not essentially propositional – though they may of course involve the production of propositions
(cf. pp. 267–268). It does not follow that they are not essentially conceptual,
at any rate not on the broad construal of a concept that Deleuze advocates.
By a concept Deleuze means '[a set] of singularities that each extend into
the neighbourhood of one of the other singularities,' or 'a set of singularities ... [that lead] on from one another' ('Philosophy', p. 146). A concept,
on this construal, is an articulated area on what Deleuze calls 'the plane of
immanence', that is the virtual plane on which all singularities and all other
events, in their virtual aspect, are located (*What Is Philosophy?*, Ch. 2, passim; cf. 'Philosophy', p. 147). This means that anyone who traces connections between singularities is making use of a concept; and anyone who
establishes such connections is creating a concept.[85] Deleuze's notion of a
concept is therefore both importantly different from the notion standardly
invoked by analytic philosophers and importantly similar to it. It is different inasmuch as, on the notion invoked by analytic philosophers, a concept is a universal corresponding to a region of the possible rather than a
region of the virtual. It is similar inasmuch as, on either notion, the creation of concepts and the sustaining of concepts themselves constitute a kind
of sense-making. More specifically, they constitute a sense-making which,
while not itself propositional, serves, among other things, to make propositional sense-making possible.[86] What is crucial in the present context is that,

---

[84] For a fuller account of problems, see *Difference and Repetition*, Ch. IV, passim. See also
DeLanda (2002), Ch. 4, passim; Williams (2003), pp. 124–137, and (2008), pp. 7–13.
  Note: Deleuze further and very interestingly relates his account of problems to a non-
propositional account of learning, which he sees as a kind of assimilation of the problem-
atical. See e.g. pp. 165 and 192, and for discussion, see Williams (2003), pp. 135–137, and
May (2005), Ch. 3, §XII.

[85] In 'Philosophy', p. 149, Deleuze is unafraid to put a physiological gloss on such an act of
creation. He talks about the 'twisting, folding, [and] fissuring' of the brain's matter and
refers to 'new connections, new pathways, new synapses.'

[86] Cf. Ch. 19, §3(g). On the non-propositionality in Deleuze's notion, see *What Is
Philosophy?*, pp. 137–138.

on Deleuze's notion,[87] the creation and the sustaining of concepts are also a way of instigating, developing, formulating, assimilating, addressing, and solving problems.[88]

The solution of problems is, as we have seen, a response to life itself. It is a response to that which 'forces' thought. There is something accidental about it. 'Do not count upon thought,' Deleuze warns, 'to ensure the relative necessity of an act of thought or a passion to think' (p. 139). He then refers to 'the destruction of an image of thought which presupposes itself and the genesis of the act of thinking in thought itself' (ibid.). Elsewhere, commenting specifically on the exercise of thought in philosophy, he[89] writes:

> The birth of philosophy required an *encounter* between the Greek milieu and the plane of immanence of thought.... [Philosophy] does have a principle, but it is a synthetic and contingent principle – an encounter, a conjunction.... Even in the concept, the principle depends upon a connection of components that could have been different, with different neighbourhoods. The principle of reason such as it appears in philosophy is a principle of contingent reason and is put like this: there is no good reason but contingent reason. (*What Is Philosophy?*, p. 93, emphasis in original; cf. ibid., pp. 41–42 and 82)

This is the kernel of Deleuze's assault on assumption (3). He rejects the idea that thought can be suitably *directed* to achieve whatever basic aims its subject may have. That is to ignore the thousand natural shocks that thought is heir to.

These references to philosophical thinking provide us with a good cue to turn to Deleuze's account of philosophy itself. Much of what we have heard him say about thinking in general can be straightforwardly applied to philosophical thinking in particular. Here is a pertinent quotation:

> Philosophy does not consist in knowing and is not inspired by truth. Rather, it is categories like Interesting, Remarkable, or Important that determine success or failure.... [And] this cannot be known before being constructed. We will not say of many books of philosophy that they are false, for that is to say nothing, but rather that they lack importance or interest, precisely because they do not create any concept. (*What Is Philosophy?*, pp. 82–83; cf. *Hume*, p. 106, emphasis in original)

This quotation provides the telling clue as to how Deleuze conceives philosophy. Philosophy, for Deleuze, '*is the art of forming, inventing, and*

---

[87] This is not to suggest that what follows is not likewise true on the analytic notion.

[88] See further *What Is Philosophy?*, Ch. 1 and Pt Two, passim. For discussion of how concepts can be symptomatic of something deeper, see *Nietzsche*, pp. 72–73.

[89] Here as hereafter I am prescinding from the fact that the passage that follows is co-authored by Guattari,

fabricating concepts' (*What Is Philosophy?*, p. 2, emphasis added; cf. 'Philosophy', p. 136). Not just any concepts, mind; certainly not if it is to be truly worthwhile. Its concepts must disturb, challenge, provoke. They must be anachronisms of a sort. 'Philosophy,' Deleuze writes, '… is always against its time, critique of the present world. The philosopher creates concepts that are neither eternal nor historical but untimely…. And in the untimely there are truths that are more durable than all historical or eternal truths put together: truths of times to come' (*Nietzsche*, p. 100; cf. *Difference and Repetition*, p. xxi). In a similar vein he continues the preceding quotation set as an extract as follows:

> Concepts must have irregular contours moulded on their living material. What is naturally uninteresting? Flimsy concepts, … or, on the other hand, concepts that are too regular, petrified, and reduced to a framework. In this respect, the most universal concepts, those presented as eternal forms or values, are the most skeletal and least interesting. Nothing positive is done, nothing at all, … when we are content to brandish ready-made old concepts like skeletons intended to intimidate any creation, without seeing that the ancient philosophers from whom we borrow them were already doing what we would like to prevent modern philosophers from doing: they were creating their concepts. (*What Is Philosophy?*, p. 83)

The philosopher, on Deleuze's conception, provides new ways of making sense of things then. Those new ways of making sense of things need not be ways of making sense of new things. The aim is not to see new sights. It is to see sights anew. P.M.S. Hacker proposes that the chief insight of Wittgenstein's later work is that 'philosophy contributes not to human knowledge, but to human understanding' (Hacker (1996), p. 110). There is a sense in which, for Deleuze, philosophy contributes neither to human knowledge *nor* to human understanding, but rather to human[90] *thinking*, which may very well promote both knowledge and understanding but which may equally well disrupt them and force them out of both their complacence and their complaisance.[91]

Philosophy, on this conception, is certainly an attempt to make sense of things, on a suitably non-propositional, virtual-centred construal of making sense of things. It follows that Deleuze's account of philosophy can be readily adapted to an account of metaphysics, on my definition of

---

[90] See below, §7(c), for a qualification even concerning 'human'.

[91] Cf. 'Letter to Bensmaïa', pp. 164–165, where there is also talk of new ways of feeling and new ways of perceiving. Cf. also *What Is Philosophy?*, p. 11, where, among other things, we find the following wonderful observation: 'The more philosophy comes up against shameless and inane rivals and encounters them at its very core, the more it feels driven to the task of creating concepts that are aerolites rather than commercial products. It gets the giggles, which wipe away its tears.'

metaphysics: metaphysics is simply that part of philosophy in which the concepts created are of the most general kind.

There may now appear to be an anomaly *vis-à-vis* Spinoza however. For it now appears that Deleuze is presenting us with a vision of metaphysics as pursuit of Spinoza's third kind of knowledge. Certainly, there seems to be a strong hint of Spinoza's third kind of knowledge, and of the inexpressibility that I have argued attaches to it, in passages such as the following:

> Thought as such produces something *interesting* when it accedes to the infinite movement that frees it from truth as supposed paradigm and reconquers an immanent power of creation. But to do this it would be necessary to return to the interior of scientific states of affairs ... in order to penetrate into ... the sphere of the virtual, a sphere that is only actualized in them.... But it is the sphere of the virtual ... that logic can only *show*, according to a famous phrase,[92] without ever being able to grasp it in propositions. (*What Is Philosophy?*, p. 140, emphasis in original; cf. ibid., p. 160)

Why do I speak of an anomaly? Because in Chapter 2, §6, I argued that metaphysics, for Spinoza himself, with whom we might expect Deleuze to be in broad agreement on this issue, is a pursuit, not of knowledge of the third kind, but of knowledge of the second kind.

In fact, however, Deleuze no more presents us with a vision of metaphysics as a pursuit of knowledge of the third kind than Spinoza did. Knowledge of the third kind is by definition particular. Metaphysics is by definition general. What Deleuze presents us with is something which, in one critical respect, is just the same as what Spinoza presented us with: a vision of metaphysics as *conducive* to knowledge of the third kind, a vision of metaphysics as in the service of ethics, and thus itself an integral part of the good life. Deleuze nevertheless goes beyond Spinoza in his account of *how* metaphysics conduces to knowledge of the third kind. What Deleuze adds to the Spinozist vision is the idea of metaphysics as the creation of concepts.[93]

General references for Deleuze's account of philosophy are 'Philosophy', passim, and *What Is Philosophy?*, passim. (Each of these, preeminently the latter, includes discussion of how philosophy both differs from and relates to both science and art. All three of philosophy, science, and art confront the infinitude of virtual chaos: philosophy wants to preserve it, but by establishing connections within it; science is prepared to relinquish it, in order to define various finite features of the actual; and art wants to restore it, through the creation of finite sensory aggregates (see esp. *What Is Philosophy?*, pp. 197–199, and cf. 'Mediators', p. 123).) For discussion, see Rajchman (2000), pp. 42–45; DeLanda (2002), pp. 215–223; and Duffy (2006), pp. 257ff.

[92] This is a clear allusion to Wittgenstein's *Tractatus*.

[93] This is not of course to deny that Spinoza himself was a creator of concepts.

7.   Three Answers

Deleuze supplies clear answers to the three questions that I posed in §6 of the Introduction. A synoptically useful way of bringing this chapter to a close will be to say briefly what they are.

(a)   The Transcendence Question

Deleuze denies that there is scope, in metaphysics, for making sense of what is transcendent: it is not for nothing that the plane on which concepts are constructed is called 'the plane of immanence' (see the previous section). Indeed Deleuze denies that there is scope *anywhere* for making sense of what is transcendent. He denies that there is anything transcendent.

This is a consequence of his empiricism. He describes his empiricism as both 'a superior empiricism' (p. 57) and 'a radical empiricism' (*What Is Philosophy?*, p. 47). It is an empiricism in which nothing is taken for granted save what is given, and according to which nothing is given, at the most fundamental level, save differences: not discrete entities, not their features, not even the subject (see §4(d)).[94]

Deleuze also frequently describes his empiricism as 'transcendental empiricism' (e.g. p. 144). Here there is a deliberate echo of Kant. At first blush this is surprising. Does not Deleuze exclude from his position the very elements that would invite such a Kantian label: a pre-given subject, for instance, or a radical separation between experience and its conditions? Well, he certainly excludes those two elements. But he retains a dependence of experience on its conditions (§4(e)). And he makes capital out of the interplay between our various mental faculties, just as Kant did (cf. Ch. 5, §4, and Ch. 7, §8).[95] This is arguably enough to make the label apposite. At any rate it seems to be as much as Deleuze wants to evoke with the label (see pp. 135ff.).

A version of the concern that arises with respect to this label arises anyway. If Deleuze denies that there is anything transcendent, then with what right does he continue to talk of the immanent? Surely, the immanent is to be understood precisely in contrast to the transcendent, as that which is in some sense immanent *to* something else, such as the subject. Ought not Deleuze to follow Hegel's lead and repudiate the very distinction between the immanent and the transcendent? Surely, he could achieve all he wants

---

[94] It is interesting to note that, when Deleuze first introduces sense in *Logic of Sense* as a fourth dimension of the proposition alongside denotation, manifestation, and signification, and asks why we have to acknowledge any such thing, his answer involves a direct appeal to empiricism (3rd Series, esp. p. 20).

[95] One of the most noteworthy features of his book on Kant is the emphasis it places on this aspect of Kant's philosophy: see *Kant*, passim.

to achieve with his talk of the immanent by resting with the idea that being is univocal.

Several points can be made here. First, it is not obvious that rejection of the transcendent need occasion rejection of the very distinction between the immanent and the transcendent. Must someone who denies that there is anything unknowable, for instance, reject the very distinction between the knowable and the unknowable? There are in any case obvious historical reasons for continuing to talk of immanence, not least its theological connotations. (Deleuze's rejection of the transcendent is very much of a piece with Nietzsche's rejection of the transcendent, which found celebrated expression in Nietzsche's claim that God is dead (Ch. 15, §5): when God was still alive, what is now reckoned to be all there is was immanent to Him.) Deleuze helpfully discusses these issues in 'Example 3' of *What Is Philosophy?* (pp. 44–49). He rebukes Plato and his followers for casting the immanent as that which is immanent to the One; he rebukes Descartes, Kant, and Husserl for casting the immanent as that which is immanent to the subject;[96] and he applauds Spinoza, whom he sees as being followed in this respect by Bergson, for casting the immanent as that which is immanent only to itself.[97]

A final question for this sub-section: in urging that we can make sense only of what is immanent, is Deleuze vulnerable to the Limit Argument (Ch. 5, §8)? No – precisely because he rejects the transcendent. His project is not to draw a *limit* to what we can make sense of, not in the sense of 'limit' in which a limit is a limitation separating one terrain from another (cf. Ch. 9, §4).

(b)   The Creativity Question

Deleuze believes that metaphysics is a creative exercise; he could scarcely make his position on that any plainer. Indeed he follows Bergson in seeing it as a creative exercise of the purest kind (Ch. 16, §§3 and 6). At one point he goes as far as to say that 'to think is to create – *there is no other creation*' (p. 147, emphasis added). True, he has an extremely broad conception of thought (cf. pp. 252–253). Even so, the implications for metaphysics, in which thought is taken to a kind of pinnacle of what it can do, are clear.

Whether or not we accede to Deleuze's views about metaphysics, we cannot deny the creativity of his own practice, nor the richness of what he creates. Consider, for instance, the list of notions that he himself invents

---

[96] There may be a sense, for Deleuze, in which the immanent *is* immanent to the subject, but only insofar as the subject itself is understood as immanent, and indeed as given in just the same way as everything else that is immanent (cf. n. 32). This is not how Descartes, Kant, or Husserl understood it.

[97] See May (2005), Ch. 2, §II.

(event, sense, ...) as well as his appropriation and extension of other philosophers' ideas (eternal return, the univocity of being, ...). Here as elsewhere, his practice, in this case his contributions to metaphysics, can be seen as a striking endorsement of his theory, in this case his stance in meta-metaphysics.

(c)   The Novelty Question

Deleuze likewise believes that there is scope for (radical) innovation in metaphysics: this too is a point on which he leaves no room for doubt. Not only that; he thinks the metaphysician had *better* innovate. And he thinks the metaphysician had better not stop innovating. Once the new is established, it needs to be replaced by a new new.[98]

Part of the rationale for such innovation, as we saw in the previous section, is to upset traditional ways of making sense of things, which are in danger, as they stagnate, of ceasing to be ways of making sense of things at all. A certain bemusement, if only transitional bemusement, is thus to be expected when metaphysicians get to work. In fact it is to be applauded. This is both profoundly non-conservative and profoundly un-Wittgensteinian.[99]

In §6(b) of the Introduction I quoted P.M.S. Hacker's appeal to 'concepts and categories that we could not abandon without ceasing to be human' (Hacker (2001b), p. 368). Part of Hacker's reason for making this appeal is to defend a Wittgensteinian conservatism. But Deleuze might well accede to the idea of concepts and categories that we could not abandon without ceasing to be human and draw an entirely different conclusion. There are real practical questions about what our humanity consists in, about how beholden to it we should be, and about who, come to any of that, 'we' are.[100] When Deleuze urges that we should aspire, in metaphysics, to make sense of things in ways that are radically new, let us not forget the variety of ways in which our making sense of things (i.e. the *making* of *sense* of *things* by *us* – all four components are pertinent) can be radically new.

---

[98] Cf. p. 136. This is very Nietzschean of course: see the very end of Ch. 15. It is also very Bergsonian: see the very end of Ch. 16.

[99] It is not just un-Wittgensteinian. On p. 116 of *Logic of Sense* there is a memorable reproach to Leibniz for his 'shameful declaration' that philosophy can create new concepts 'provided that they do not overthrow the "established sentiments"'. (Cf. my comments about Leibniz' eclecticism in Ch. 3, §1.)

[100] Cf. Rajchman (2000), p. 42. And cf. Deleuze's discussion of 'becoming-animal' and 'becoming-woman' in *A Thousand Plateaus*, Ch. 10. (For discussion of the latter, see Sotirin (2005).)

Conclusion

1. Varieties of Sense-Making

In §4 of the Introduction I emphasized how much falls under the umbrella term 'making sense of things'. I also said that I did not want to rule any of it out of consideration in what followed. It was important for me that there should be a great deal that might legitimately be classified as 'the most general attempt to make sense of things'; a great deal, in other words, that might legitimately qualify as metaphysics on my definition of metaphysics.

What has happened since then has borne ample witness to this. One by one our protagonists have focused on different forms of sense-making, often, as I pointed out at the beginning of Chapter 16, by themselves distinguishing between two or more forms. And this in turn has left us free in each case to consider what the most general attempt to make sense of things might thereby come to. Thus Descartes was concerned with systematic well-founded knowledge, which he called '*scientia*' (Ch. 1, §1). Spinoza distinguished between three kinds of knowledge, which he characterized as inadequate knowledge, adequate knowledge based on common notions, and adequate knowledge of the essence of things (Ch. 2, §3); the most general of these was the second. Hume made play, sometimes by *not* clearly distinguishing them, with sense-making of a broadly epistemic kind, that which was involved in arriving at a knowledgeable or reliable conception of things, and sense-making of a broadly semantic kind, that which was involved in simply expressing meaning (Ch. 4, §1). Kant made play with a distinction between what I called 'thick' sense-making and 'thin' sense-making, the former being sense-making that could qualify as knowledge, the latter being sense-making that could only ever qualify as 'empty' thinking (Ch. 5, §8); but he also made clear that the latter could fulfil a vital regulative function, notably when it took the form of active faith. Hegel distinguished between processes of reason, the very stuff of reality, and processes of understanding, whereby human beings, using fixed forms of thought and well-entrenched logical principles such as the principle of contradiction, analyzed reality (Ch. 7, §7). The early Wittgenstein made it his business to

581

determine the limits of propositional sense-making, but he also acknowledged non-propositional sense-making, such as evaluation of various kinds, understanding of various kinds, and indeed the very sense-making involved in determining the limits of propositional sense-making (Ch. 9, esp. §8); in addition he revealed in his own practice how he thought the latter could sometimes affect to be the former, finding pseudo-expression in pseudo-propositions. The later Wittgenstein had a related distinction between arriving at truths about the world and making provision for clarity in our thinking (Ch. 10, §3), though he had untold subsidiary distinctions too, and there was no analogue in his case of the non-propositional feigning the propositional. Carnap too had a distinction between arriving at truths about the world and making provision for clarity in our thinking, but in his case underpinned by a distinctive account of the latter which he saw as the clarifying of linguistic frameworks (Ch. 11, esp. §2). Nietzsche was interested in all kinds of sense-making (Ch. 15, §2); one of his principal concerns was how far those that made life bearable could be subsumed under those that involved arriving at the truth. Bergson distinguished sharply between analysis, which involved symbolic representations of things, and intuition, which involved non-symbolic assimilation of them (Ch. 16, §2). Husserl distinguished between natural sense-making, that is sense-making of a more or less normal and/or scientific kind concerning things in space and time, and phenomenological sense-making, that is sense-making of a distinctively philosophical kind which he conceived as completely drained of the former and which he thought was needed to make sense of the former (Ch. 17, §2). Likewise Heidegger (Ch. 18, §2); but Heidegger also came to regard the latter as being, at least in part, non-propositional, appearances to the contrary, here as in the early Wittgenstein, notwithstanding (Ch. 18, §6). Collingwood drew attention to sense-making of a non-propositional kind in his account of absolute presuppositions, though he did not make quite the capital out of it that he might have done (Ch. 19, §4). Derrida too drew attention to sense-making of a non-propositional kind, in his case largely through his own practice, though also through his ruminations on the use of language exemplified in that practice (Ch. 20, §§5 and 6). Deleuze too drew attention to sense-making of a non-propositional kind, or rather of two non-propositional kinds: that involved in understanding how things most fundamentally are, in their raw difference (Ch. 21, §4), and that involved in the creation of what he called concepts (Ch. 21, §5).

With so many different forms of sense-making in play, an obvious question is whether any one of them, or any family of them, is peculiarly well suited to act as input in my definition of metaphysics, say because the resultant conception of metaphysics is peculiarly fecund, or because the resultant conception of metaphysics is peculiarly natural, or because the resultant use of the word 'metaphysics' conforms better than any other to standard uses of the word – uses to which I have never taken myself to be beholden, but to which I have tried not to be insensitive either. I think the answer is no. I am inclined to be as non-prescriptive in connection with this issue as possible. I see no reason why there should not be a range of equally legitimate claimants to the title of metaphysics.

What about the opposite question? Is any of these forms of sense-making peculiarly ill-suited to act as input in my definition? This time I think the answer is yes: I shall return to this issue in §5. But even here I favour as much latitude as possible. There are very few forms of sense-making that I am prepared to dismiss as straightforwardly unfit to be fed into my definition.

One thing that I insist is that we allow for, and indeed take very seriously, conceptions of metaphysics in which the input is sense-making of a non-propositional kind: I shall call these non-propositional conceptions of metaphysics. Not to take such conceptions seriously, and to think that metaphysics must be a pursuit of truth,[1] is to be in the grip of a kind of scientistic prejudice. There is no good rationale for it. In particular, we should not balk at the idea that metaphysics consists in the protection, nurturing, adaptation, rejection, or replacement of some of our most general concepts, systems of classification, ways of thinking, and the like; hence that its success does not consist in, though it may of course involve and/or assist, the production of true propositions. (We considered versions of this idea in the chapters on Wittgenstein, Carnap, Dummett, Collingwood, Derrida, and Deleuze, with in some cases a resistance to innovation, most prominently in the case of the later Wittgenstein, and in other cases an enthusiasm for innovation, most prominently in the case of Deleuze.) I would go further. I would suggest that even someone wedded to a conception of metaphysics whereby it is a pursuit of truth should acknowledge that it has a substantial non-propositional component of this kind. This is because I take metaphysics of any stripe to involve a significant element of self-consciousness (Introduction, §5).[2]

If we accede to a non-propositional conception of metaphysics, it is then a further obvious question what role language has to play in its practice. Not that there need be any puzzle about this. On a later-Wittgensteinian conception, for example, whereby metaphysics is the attempt to achieve clarity of understanding at the highest level of generality, language has an utterly straightforward, utterly unmysterious role to play in its practice. Distinctions need to be drawn, confusions exposed, questions raised, examples constructed, grammars described, rules stated (cf. Ch. 10, §2). In some of these cases, including that of stating rules, the metaphysician's task

---

[1] 'And' to think that metaphysics must be a pursuit of truth? Is this something additional? Strictly speaking, yes. There are propositional ways of making sense of things which are successful in their own terms but in which the propositions concerned have some desideratum other than truth, such as solace. (Cf. the comment about Nietzsche above.)

[2] I take any remotely sophisticated science to involve a significant element of self-consciousness too. This kind of reflection is by no means peculiar to metaphysics.

is to produce truths. A case in point may be: 'Only you can know if you had that intention' (see Wittgenstein (1967a), Pt I, §247). In *some* of these cases, not this time including that of stating rules, the metaphysician may even see fit to produce truths that are in some fairly robust and intuitive sense 'about the world'. This will simply be to demonstrate how certain concepts work (Ch. 10, §1). Such truths will certainly not be theses to be debated or defended. On the contrary, the more commonplace they are, the better they will fulfil their function. They will not themselves be of any metaphysical significance. Language has a straightforward and unmysterious role to play in the practice of such metaphysics, then, but it is not the direct role of expressing whatever sense the metaphysician makes of things. It cannot be. If the sense the metaphysician makes of things could be expressed – if there were propositions whose production could count as putting that sense into words – then neither the sense-making itself nor the conception of metaphysics that is based on it would count as non-propositional.

Other non-propositional conceptions of metaphysics afford language a more oblique role, but a role nonetheless. Recall Bergson's idea that, through 'comparisons and metaphors', language can evoke what it cannot express, and that metaphysical practice consists largely of attempts to put language to just such use (Ch. 16, §6(a)). We have seen similarly oblique and often dissembling uses of language in relation to non-propositional conceptions of metaphysics in Heidegger (Ch. 18, §§6 and 7), Derrida (Ch. 20, §§5–7), and Deleuze (Ch. 21, §§4 and 5), but above all in the early Wittgenstein (Ch. 9, esp. §§7 and 8). What I think the early Wittgenstein in particular bequeaths is the following bipartite idea: first, that even where non-propositional sense-making is concerned, be it in metaphysics or, come to that, elsewhere, there may be such a thing as the (linguistic) result of a (necessarily unsuccessful) attempt to express it; and second, that even if this result is by the strictest semantic criteria a kind of word salad, producing it may help to impart the sense-making in question.

One final point for this section. To think that metaphysics must be a pursuit of truth is not the limit of scientism concerning metaphysics. Scientism concerning metaphysics finds its fullest expression in the idea that metaphysics must be, not just a pursuit of truth, but a pursuit of truth *of fundamentally the same kind as the natural sciences*. This is obviously a more demanding idea. It is equally obviously a variant of what I have been calling 'naturalism'. And, as we have seen, it is vehemently opposed by phenomenologists. But it is vehemently opposed by phenomenologists because of that extra clause: Husserl in particular would have no qualms about saying that metaphysics must be a pursuit of truth. What this serves to remind us is that, even among propositional forms of sense-making, there are crucial distinctions to be drawn.[3]

---

[3] For one very interesting contribution to the project of drawing such distinctions, see Skorupski (1999). See also, for an extremely wide-ranging discussion of the issues that

2. History

One way to think about how metaphysics differs from the natural sciences is to consider its relation to its own history. That is what I aim to do in this section.

There is in any case good reason for me, now, to reflect on the relation between metaphysics and its history, because this is the conclusion to what has been, in its own limited way, a history of metaphysics. In its own limited way? There are three reasons for this qualification (even leaving aside whatever limitations may have afflicted the actual execution of the project). First, and most obviously, my narrative has been concerned exclusively with the modern era. Second, it has been highly selective, even within that period. And third, it has been more of a history of meta-metaphysics than a history of metaphysics. Still, reflection on the relation between metaphysics and its own history is of patent relevance to all that has happened in my book up to here. For one thing, as far as the third of these points is concerned, there is, as I have repeatedly tried to make clear, no sharp distinction between metaphysics and meta-metaphysics.

That there is no sharp distinction between metaphysics and meta-metaphysics is related to the first principal point that I want to make in this section: neither is there any sharp distinction between either of them and either of their histories. This is because, in Bernard Williams' useful contrast to which I drew attention in the Preface, these two histories are part of the history of philosophy rather than the history of ideas. They are philosophy before they are history.

That philosophy in general and metaphysics or meta-metaphysics in particular should admit of any such history, that is to say a history that is in the first instance a contribution to the discipline rather than a contribution to history, is one of the most significant respects in which all three of them differ from the natural sciences. The natural sciences have no history that is not in the first instance history. Thus the history of physics, whatever interest it may hold for a physicist, has little claim on his or her attention *qua* *physicist*. And the little claim it does have is to indicate pitfalls into which physicists have fallen in the past and which they must now try to avoid. The history of physics is a history of discovery. It is a partial vindication of what physicists think and say and do today, as opposed to what they thought and said and did before.

arise here, the superb Wright (1992). For an account of philosophy in general and metaphysics in particular that is firmly opposed to the liberalism that I have advocated in this section – an account that strikes me as highly scientistic – see Williamson (2007). Someone else who would be unsympathetic to my stance, despite proclaiming a kind of liberalism, is Dean W. Zimmerman: see Zimmerman (2004). Finally, see n. 7 for an indication of how I also find myself in disagreement with Dummett.

The history of metaphysics is nothing like that. True, there has been progress. And certainly there has been evolution. Some ideas have developed in
ways that have made them better equipped to survive the ravages of hostile
cross-examination; others have died out because they were not equipped to
survive these ravages. (In the first case, think of Frege's sharpening of Kant's
idea of an analytic truth.[4] In the second case, think of Descartes' idea of
an uncreated substance having dominion over one created extended substance and a multitude of created thinking substances.) Indeed there is very
little in what we have observed whose historical positioning does nothing
to account for it; very little that might just as easily have preceded what it
in fact succeeded. Nevertheless, it would be preposterous to think either
that there has been progress of the same sort as there has been in physics or,
insofar as there has not, that this is to the detriment of metaphysics. *We still
have a great deal to learn from Spinoza* – to pick just one notable example.
And while we may also have a great deal to learn from Derrida – to pick
another – we certainly have no more to learn from him just because he wrote
some three hundred years later. The historian of metaphysics engages philosophically with past metaphysical ideas in a way in which only a crackpot
historian of physics could think it appropriate to engage scientifically with
past physical ideas. The historian of metaphysics is involved in an attempt to
derive positive lessons from past ideas and thereby to be assisted in making
his or her own maximally general sense of things.

So is metaphysics in this respect more like an art form than like a natural
science? Is the historian of metaphysics who engages with some great metaphysical idea of the past like an artist who engages with some great work
of art of the past, as it may be a contemporary pianist playing Beethoven's
'Hammerklavier'? Well, there are some important similarities here. But there
are important differences too. Let us not lurch from one infelicitous analogy
to another. In particular, let us not think that the relation between metaphysics and its own history is any more like the relation between an art form and
its own history than it is like the relation between a natural science and its
own history – something which we are in any case given no encouragement
to think by the similarities to which I have just adverted. For even if great
metaphysical ideas of the past have an enduring value that great works of
art of the past have and that great scientific theories of the past, for all their
greatness, lack, that is obviously not what makes a contemporary metaphysician's engagement with them a *historical* exercise. Playing Beethoven's
'Hammerklavier' is not a historical exercise, at least not in anything like the
way in which writing a commentary on Spinoza's *Ethics* is. (We must not
lose sight of the fact that the history of metaphysics, though it is metaphysics

---

[4] I take this to be an apposite example even for those who think that Quine was right subsequently to repudiate the idea; for at least Frege made clear what was to be repudiated.
(Quine would have had a softer target if he had had only Kant's idea to reckon with.)

before it is history, is still history.) What makes the contemporary metaphysician's engagement with past metaphysical ideas a historical exercise is that it is the very thing that Collingwood took all history to be: an attempt to reenact a former way of making sense of things by attending to its questions, assimilating its propositions, and suchlike. It has a crucial transchronological aspect.[5]

This in turn gives the lie to yet another enticing and prevalent misconception about the history of metaphysics: that its principal value lies in its indicating voices of yore that can be heard as participating in contemporary metaphysical discussions. On the contrary, its principal value lies in its indicating voices of yore that *cannot* be heard as participating in contemporary metaphysical discussions. It indicates voices that challenge whatever presuppositions make contemporary metaphysical discussions possible. The impetus that it provides for the project of making one's own maximally general sense of things is to signal alternatives to what, if one remains rooted in the present, one will unthinkingly take for granted (even if it ultimately reinforces one's confidence in what one takes for granted).

There are several paradigms, then, that are inappropriate for thinking about the history of metaphysics, and specifically for thinking about its relation to metaphysics itself. That relation is unlike the relation between the history of physics and physics. It is unlike the relation between the history of music and music. It is unlike the relation between reading the latest issues of the journals to see what sense other people make of something and trying to make sense of it oneself. Nor, unless we are committed Hegelians, shall we think of the history of metaphysics as the telling of some grand dialectically necessary story that is destined to end with the hero's arriving at a kind of self-knowledge. But there is another important paradigm that we still need to consider. There is the Deleuzian view that the history of metaphysics indicates virtual tendencies which we can actualize in various more or less creative ways, or themes on which we can play out more or less innovative variations, by establishing connections between singularities. How does *that* relate to what I have been arguing?

I think it can be readily grafted on to what I have been arguing, or rather that what I have been arguing can be readily grafted on to it. When the historian of metaphysics hears voices of yore that challenge the presuppositions of contemporary metaphysical discussions, and is thereby spurred into participating in alternative metaphysical discussions, those alternative discussions are not simply the discussions in which metaphysicians used to

---

[5] Note: I have focused on the example of Beethoven's 'Hammerklavier' in order to downplay the assimilation of metaphysics to an art form. But I do not mean to suggest that an artist's engagement with a great work of art of the past is always of that kind. Sometimes it is far more like the engagement of a historian of metaphysics with a great metaphysical idea of the past. Consider Lichtenstein *vis-à-vis* Monet.

participate. There is no reliving the past. And even if there were, there would be no clear motive for doing so. No; what those voices do is to disrupt our living of the present, and thereby to help us find better ways of living the future. The right response to them is not to try to join in with them, any more than it is to turn a deaf ear to them. The right response is to connect what they are saying with what is being said now, and to search for ways of saying something that makes creative use of both. This is just the kind of thing that Deleuze has in mind. It is part of what he means when he suggests, as we saw him suggest in Chapter 21, §6, that the metaphysician should be working in a way that is 'untimely', attempting to create concepts for a time to come.

A final brief observation for this section. In view of what I have just been arguing, it is surely no accident that Wittgenstein, whose conservatism I have several times emphasized and several times bemoaned (see esp. Ch. 10, §6), showed relatively little interest in the history of philosophy.[6] For Wittgenstein, the aim of philosophy was to protect extant forms of sense-making. This certainly did not preclude engaging with alternatives (if only imaginary alternatives: cf. Wittgenstein (1978), Pt I, §§143–153). But it did, trivially, preclude engaging with alternatives in a deliberate attempt to upset the *status quo*.[7]

3.   The Wittgenstein Question

(a)   Consent

The brief addendum to the previous section was an example of something that has characterized this book ever since Chapters 9 and 10. Wherever

---

[6] But it may be all the more surprising, conversely, that Collingwood was as conservative as he was. All I can do in response to any such surprise is to repeat the diagnosis that I gave in Ch. 19, §4: Collingwood overlooked the possibility of metaphysical sense-making that was non-propositional.

[7] This section owes a huge amount to Bernard Williams: see esp. Williams (2006d), (2006m), and (2006n). Also very helpful are Simons (2000), §3; Wood (2001), Pt 4, Ch. 6; Ameriks (2006), esp. the Introduction and Essays 1, 8, and 13; and Dummett (2010), Ch. 16. Dummett draws some conclusions very different from mine because he takes for granted precisely what I wish to query, namely that philosophy, and by implication metaphysics, 'is a sector in the quest for truth, or ... a search for a clearer understanding of the truths we already know' (p. 148). That, to echo my complaint against Wittgenstein, is what *some* metaphysics is; it is not what all of it is. (I also incidentally have a very different view from Dummett's even about the metaphysics that is of that kind. His view is far too progressivist for my liking. I find it astonishing that he can write the following: 'There seems to me every reason to think that [metaphysics can settle the question whether there are rational grounds for believing in the existence of God] ..., and will even do so in the lifetimes of our great-grandchildren' (ibid., p. 151).)

possible, I have tried to situate Wittgenstein with respect to developments in my narrative and to situate them with respect to him. None of the rest of my protagonists has served as a touchstone in the same way. Why is this? Why have I been so concerned to keep drawing the discussion back to him in particular?

In the case of the later Wittgenstein the reason is very simple. Despite this crucial reservation that I have concerning his conservatism, there is no one else with whom I find myself in such deep agreement. Certainly, I would be happy to label my approach to any of the familiar metaphysical conundrums by which students of analytic philosophy are typically introduced to the discipline as a Wittgensteinian approach. (I shall illustrate this point shortly.) But even with respect to meta-metaphysics I am largely in agreement with Wittgenstein. I have broadly Wittgensteinian reasons for answering two of the three questions from §6 of the Introduction in the way in which I do. Thus concerning the Transcendence Question I agree that, for the metaphysician, 'everything lies open to view' (Wittgenstein (1967a), Pt I, §126).[8,9] And concerning the Creativity Question I accept the Wittgensteinian reasons canvassed in Chapter 10, §3, for thinking that our making maximally general sense of things, insofar as it is a matter of our acknowledging necessities, is a matter of our reckoning with the grammar of our own language and not with anything that is in any remotely robust sense independent of us. The later Wittgenstein seems to me to have a more compelling account of our grasp of necessary truths than anyone else in this enquiry.

What then of the early Wittgenstein? My reason for constantly bringing the discussion back to him is somewhat different. It is that he provides the model for the bipartite idea, which I have been intermittently trying to motivate since Chapter 9, and which I trumpeted most recently in §1, that:

- included in the maximally general non-propositional sense that can be made of things there is some that finds pseudo-expression in pseudo-propositions

and

- providing such pseudo-expression may serve to convey the sense in question.

---

[8] I am however less inclined to agree with a sentiment implicit in the last sentence of that section, namely that metaphysics is possible '*before* all new discoveries and inventions' (ibid., emphasis in original). That sentence encroaches too much for my liking into the arena of the Novelty Question.

[9] I also incidentally see *some* rationale for simply defining the immanent/transcendent distinction as the distinction between what we can make sense of and what we cannot make sense of, which would settle the Transcendence Question by *fiat*: cf. Moore (1997a), pp. 110–114.

One of the most signal features of this idea, a feature for which again Wittgenstein provides the model, is its relation to one of the recurring themes of this book: transcendental idealism. For precisely what transcendental idealism is, I would contend, is the pseudo-expression of certain non-propositional sense that can be made of things at the highest level of generality. This too is a view that I have tried to motivate at various points in the enquiry, ever since I first introduced it in §§7 and 8 of Chapter 9 (see Ch. 14, §4; Ch. 17, §§6 and 7; and Ch. 18, §7).[10]

An Interlude on Vagueness

I want to use this interlude as it were to illustrate my Wittgensteinian credentials. I shall briefly address a very familiar metaphysical puzzle, and try to show how a broadly Wittgensteinian approach can help to solve it. I have deliberately chosen a puzzle about which Wittgenstein himself said next to nothing, to give an indication of how he left us with something that might fairly be described as, if not a method for solving such puzzles (cf. Wittgenstein (1967a), Pt I, §133, final sentence), then a way of approaching them.

The puzzle I am going to address concerns vagueness.[11] It is the sorites paradox. The sorites paradox takes its name from the Greek adjective 'sorites', which in turn corresponds to the Greek noun 'soros', meaning 'heap'. It is illustrated in the following argument.

(P1) One grain of sand is not enough to make a heap.

(P2) For any number n, if n grains of sand are not enough to make a heap, then $n + 1$ grains of sand are not enough to make a heap.

---

[10] It is a view that I have tried to defend elsewhere too: see esp. Moore (1997a), Chs 6–9.

Note: in Ch. 18 I talked merely about idealism, not about transcendental idealism; but the idealism at stake was a descendant of the transcendental idealism that I had earlier found in Husserl.

[11] I count it a *metaphysical* puzzle because it raises some highly general questions about the relations between our language, our thought, and reality. Note that although Wittgenstein himself did not discuss this puzzle, he did make a number of interesting observations (not irrelevant to the puzzle) about vagueness: see e.g. Wittgenstein (1967a), Pt I, §§84 and 88.

There has been much written recently both about the puzzle and about vagueness more generally. Preeminent is Williamson (1994a). An excellent collection is Keefe and Smith (1997). I myself have contributed to the discussion in Moore (2002a), §§V and VI. This interlude provides an abridged version of the argument in the second of those two sections. (Note that my argument places me in a very different position from Timothy Williamson. In Williamson (1994a) he argues that vagueness is an epistemic phenomenon, a matter of our ignorance concerning what are in fact sharp cut-off points. That is very un-Wittgensteinian. It violates the principle that, in metaphysics, 'everything lies open to view'.)

Therefore:

> (C) There is no number of grains of sand that are enough to make
> a heap.

This is a paradox because the argument appears valid, both its premises
appear true, yet its conclusion appears false. And an analogous argument
can be constructed for any other similarly vague concept. Thus consider the
number of seconds that someone needs to live to survive childhood. But I shall
focus on the argument above, which can serve as a representative case.

Now, why does (P2) appear true? What makes us think we should accept
a principle such as that? I suggest that the reason why we think we should
accept (P2) is that we do accept the following, which looks equivalent to it:

> (P2*) There is no number n such that $n + 1$ is the least number of
> grains of sand that are enough to make a heap.

And we accept (P2*) because we want to rule out any sharp cut-off points
here. This in turn is because part of the point of a vague concept such as that
of a heap is that there should be enough latitude in its application for that
application to rest on relatively casual observation.[12]

On a Wittgensteinian approach, however, we have a way of seeing how
(P2) and (P2*) can come apart, or more strictly how accepting (P2) and
accepting (P2*) can come apart. How so? Consider what we would be
doing if we accepted (P2). On a suitably Wittgensteinian view, *we would be
endorsing a rule of application for the concept of a heap*: not to count any
number of grains of sand as too few to make a heap unless we also count
the next largest number as too few to make a heap (cf. Ch. 10, §3). Very
well, what are we doing in accepting (P2*)? We are *refusing* to accept the
following:

> (Neg-P2*) There is a number n such that $n + 1$ is the least number
> of grains of sand that are enough to make a heap.[13]

---

[12] Cf. Dummett (1978h), p. 264. Note: this is the essay in which Dummett argues that the
notion of practicability is unintelligible (see Ch. 14, §3(b)). His argument is essentially
that the notion of practicability is a vague notion which we cannot regard as intelligible
without succumbing to a version of the sorites paradox, this paradox being in Dummett's
view insoluble.

[13] Someone might say that we are doing something less radical than that, namely refusing to
accept any of the following:
(Neg-P2*-1) Two is the least number of grains of sand that are enough to make a heap.
(Neg-P2*-2) Three is the least number of grains of sand that are enough to make a heap
...
(Neg-P2*-n) $n + 1$ is the least number of grains of sand that are enough to make a heap.
...

And what would we be doing if we accepted (Neg-P2*)? Again, on a suitably Wittgensteinian view, we would be endorsing a rule of application for
the concept of a heap: to recognize that there is such a thing as the least
number of grains of sand required to make a heap. Two rules are now in
play then. *And there is no reason whatsoever why, having refused to endorse
one of them, we should not refuse to endorse the other.* To think that we
must endorse one or other of these two rules is like thinking that either 'The
opening move shall be a pawn move' or 'The opening move shall not be a
pawn move' must be a rule of chess. We can refuse to accept (Neg-P2*), on
the grounds that we want the concept of a heap to admit of a certain latitude in its application; and we can refuse to accept (P2), on the grounds that,
combined with (P1), it yields (C). (Cf. Wittgenstein (1978), Pt V, §13.[14])

What it comes to, then, is this. In accepting (P2*) we register our refusal
to accept (Neg-P2*). We endorse a kind of second-order rule that precludes
our adopting that first-order rule. But this does not commit us to accepting (P2). We can refuse to accept (Neg-P2*) *and* refuse to accept (P2) and
thereby avoid paradox.

This is all very well, you may say, but even if we accede to the idea that,
on the most natural interpretation of these sentences, accepting them is tantamount to endorsing the rules specified, what about an interpretation of
the sentences on which the meaning of the word 'heap' is simply taken as
given and the sentences are used, in accord with that meaning and perfectly straightforwardly, to say how things are? Will the paradox not
then rearise?

Well, but *is* there any such interpretation? We cannot uncritically appeal
to 'the meaning' of the word 'heap', along with some principle of compo-
sitional semantics, say, and imagine that we thereby fix what claim somebody would be making in asserting one of these sentences. (Cf. Wittgenstein
(1967a), Pt I, §350.) True, there are various claims in the offing that someone *might* make; various claims, therefore, that someone asserting one of
these sentences might, with more or less violence, be interpreted as making.
But none of them, as far as I can see, threatens paradox. For instance, it is
unproblematically true that the removal of one grain of sand from a heap
makes no readily discernible difference to it. It is unproblematically false
that the removal of one grain of sand from a heap makes no difference at all

---

This is less radical because it merely involves our refusing to accept, of any particular
number, that it is the least number of grains of sand required to make a heap. That falls
short of refusing to accept that there *is* such a number. And on some views this distinction
is crucial. (In particular it is crucial on a 'supervaluational' view: see Fine (1975).) Even so
I shall continue to assume that we are doing the more radical thing. If in fact we are doing
this less radical thing, my argument needs to be modified, but not, I think, abandoned
altogether.

[14] Cf. also Williams (1995b), p. 217.

to it. It is unproblematically true that no number has ever in fact been specified as the minimum number of grains of sand required to make a heap. It may also be unproblematically true that, if grains of sand are laid down one by one, there will be a first point at which you (or I, or both of us, or everyone in a certain group, or a majority of people in that group) are inclined to say that there are enough to make a heap. (Or it may be unproblematically false.) What is not clear, and what would have to be the case for there to be a paradox, is that there is any claim in this vicinity that both looks as if it must be true and looks as if it can be used to derive, by an argument that looks as if it must be valid, a claim that looks as if it must be false.

(b) Dissent

Back to Wittgenstein himself.

My preoccupation with Wittgenstein is not confined to the ways in which he promotes a correct understanding of metaphysics. It extends to the principal way in which, as I see it, he thwarts a correct understanding of metaphysics. His influence concerning the third of the questions from §6 of the Introduction, the Novelty Question, seems to me essentially malign (Ch. 10, §6).

I agree that we need to think clearly and carefully about how we make sense of things. But we also need to think clearly and carefully about how *to* make sense of things. And there is no reason why the second of these activities should not be as much a part of sense-making at the highest level of generality as it is lower down. Perhaps there are, even at the highest level, forms of sense-making that are both radically different from any we now have and an improvement on any we now have. Perhaps, unless we deliberately disrupt those we now have, they will atrophy.

And note that the thought that we do well to renounce some of our current forms of sense-making does nothing to impugn the Wittgensteinian thought that, in some sense, the very fact that we have those forms of sense-making ensures their correctness; ensures that they cannot be gainsaid. There is a distinction that is helpful to invoke here, between, as I shall put it, *rejecting* a proposition and *denying* it.[15] To reject a proposition is to decline to think in such terms: it is to repudiate some or all of the very concepts involved in the proposition. To deny a proposition, by contrast, *is* to think in such terms, but to count the proposition false. On this way of speaking, it is certainly possible to reject a proposition that it is not possible to deny. Suppose, for instance, that it is one of our rules that difference should count as an irreflexive relation. Then *there is no denying* that difference is an

---

[15] Essentially the same distinction is drawn, using that same terminology, in Harman (1967), p. 134. See also Dummett (1978i), p. 283.

irreflexive relation. If someone appears to deny that difference is an irreflexive relation,[16] then this only goes to show that he is not really – not properly, not strictly – using *those* concepts. He may proclaim, with complete ingenuousness, and with a clear grasp of what he is doing, 'Difference is not an irreflexive relation.' But then either the word 'difference' or the word 'irreflexive' or some other feature of the sentence has a use in his mouth that is, relative to our rule, non-standard. That, however, may be the very point of his pronouncement. He may be rejecting what he cannot deny. He may be repudiating some of the relevant concepts in favour of others which, though strictly distinct from them, are sufficiently closely related to them for the use of this sentence, in this context, to be the most effective way of introducing them. This is just the kind of thing that I argued was going on when Hegel appeared to deny the law of contradiction (Ch. 7, §7).[17]

In any case, to make sense of things in a way that is radically new is not necessarily to renounce any extant way of making sense of things. The new way of making sense of things may be intended to supplement what we have already, not to replace it. Someone might cheerfully accede to the proposition that difference is an irreflexive relation, and even accede to the merits of thinking in such terms, while insisting that there is another sense of difference, of particular importance to philosophy, say, in which we need to acknowledge the existence of that which differs from itself.

However that may be, I firmly believe that Wittgenstein's conservatism can be divorced from the rest of his account of sense-making. The answers that I have gleaned from that account to the Transcendence Question and the Creativity Question mark out metaphysics as an autonomous exercise whose aim is neither to dig beneath any surface nor to probe beyond any horizon but to ensure that the conceptual instruments that we use to dig and to probe, and to gain an overview of all that we have dug and probed, are fit for purpose. It is not an attempt to achieve insight into anything beyond those instruments, and it answers to no authority but the authority of their serviceability. This can easily seem to entail that the metaphysician, as such, has no business contriving new instruments. In other words, it can easily seem to entail a conservative answer to the Novelty Question. But it does not. Or rather – there is an ambiguity here – it entails such an answer only on one disambiguation of it. The ambiguity resides in the phrase 'ensure that the instruments we use are fit for purpose'. This phrase can be heard in two ways. It can be heard in such a way that 'the instruments we use' has wide scope, in which case the claim is that, given the instruments we use, the aim of metaphysics is to ensure that they are fit for purpose. If it is heard in this

---

[16] The example is not an arbitrary one. In Deleuze (2004), p. 38, Deleuze writes that 'duration differs from itself.'

[17] Cf. also Ch. 15, §5: in these terms Nietzsche is rejecting the proposition that God exists, not denying it.

way, then conservatism does indeed beckon. But it can also be heard in such a way that 'the instruments we use' has narrow scope, in which case the claim is that the aim of metaphysics is to ensure the following: that we use instruments that are fit for purpose. If it is heard in *this* way, which is the way in which I intend it, then conservatism does not beckon; just the opposite in fact. What beckons is something much more Deleuzian.[18]

4. Creation and Innovation in Metaphysics

Deleuze presents us with a vision of metaphysicians as creators of new concepts (Ch. 21, §6). I applaud that. True, Deleuze has his own distinctive understanding of 'concepts'. When I, as an analytic philosopher, talk about the creation of new concepts, I do not mean quite the same by it as he does. As I tried to make clear in the last chapter, however, Deleuze's understanding of 'concepts' is not *entirely* different from an analytic philosopher's. In any case, my own view is that metaphysicians can be creative and innovative in a way that includes both what Deleuze understands by the creation of new concepts and what an analytic philosopher would understand by it. Here I revert to the versatility of the term 'sense-making': metaphysicians can be creative and innovative *in all forms of sense-making*. They can create new Deleuzian concepts; they can create new concepts of a sort that an analytic philosopher would recognize; they can create new ways of thinking; they can create new ways of evaluating; they can arrive at new truths. And 'new' in each of these cases embraces the radically new.

It is worth noting also that they can be innovative without being creative. They can be destructive, subverting extant forms of sense-making. We have witnessed many examples in this enquiry of the innovative power of destruction in metaphysics – from Hume's empiricist assault on sense-making that is not suitably grounded in sense experience to Derrida's Heideggerian repudiation of the metaphysics of presence.[19] There is good reason, and in

---

[18] Both in this section and elsewhere I have emphasized Wittgenstein's conservatism. But it is interesting to note two examples of philosophers who can be said to be more or less Wittgensteinian in their outlook, but who are prepared to accept an element of revisionism. The first is Friedrich Waismann: see Waismann (1959), §§VII and VIII, helpfully discussed by G.J. Warnock in Warnock (1969), Ch. 10. The second is P.M.S. Hacker, an ardent defender of Wittgenstein, who acknowledges (without, I think, seeing this as a departure from Wittgenstein) that 'in practical philosophy there is room for the introduction of novel ... concepts and for the remoulding of existing concepts' (Hacker (2009), p. 150, emphasis removed).

[19] Cf. also how Nietzsche, in Nietzsche (1982b), cited in Ch. 15, §7(a), likens himself to Spinoza by specifying 'five main points of his [Spinoza's] doctrine' in which he recognizes himself, each of which is the *rejection* of something. (Walter Kaufmann in his translation has 'denies' rather than 'rejects', but in terms of the distinction that I drew in the previous

particular good Deleuzian reason, for thinking that such destruction counts for nothing except in the context of, or as a prelude to, creation. (A metaphysician needs as it were to earn the right to destroy.) Even so, the fact is that a metaphysician may see grounds for concern about some extant form of sense-making, which he or she therefore wants to subvert, without – yet – having any idea how to plug the gaps that this will leave behind.

But let us now take stock by reconsidering a few of the many striking examples from what has preceded this of metaphysical innovation that has also been creative.

Three relatively simple examples were given in §7 of the Introduction. We saw Lewis connect the ancient problem of universals with the question of what the purpose of physics is, thereby providing a new way of thinking both about universals and about physics. We saw Quine connect tenseless quantification with practical questions concerning the impact of what we do on future generations, thereby providing a new way of articulating the intuitive significance of the distinction between affecting how things will be for those who come later and affecting who comes later. And we saw P.T. Geach introduce a new conception of numerical identity whereby numerical identity is a three-place relation, not a two-place relation: on this conception, x can be numerically identical to y with respect to kind K_1 yet numerically different from y with respect to kind K_2.[20]

Once the main narrative had begun, wider-ranging and more powerful examples abounded. Right from the outset Descartes provided us with a set of interlocking ideas about the project of making sense of things – the project of arriving at an integrated science of man and nature – that was unprecedented in the extent to which it met all its own explanatory needs. His vision of how we make best sense of things, which could be applied, in particular, to how we arrive at that very vision, served as an important model for subsequent thinkers, however differently they may have conceived the sense-making involved. In particular, it served as a model for the arch-naturalist Quine (Ch. 1, §4) and, less remarkably perhaps, because at less chronological or doctrinal distance, for Quine's forerunner Hume (Ch. 4, §4). Neither Quine nor Hume shared Descartes' foundationalism, however, whereby metaphysics was an independent part of the project on

section it is certainly rejection, not denial, that is involved here.) See also Ch. 15, n. 78, for a reminder of how one of these five points, the rejection of freedom of the will, goes against the non-revisionary grain of P.F. Strawson's work.

[20] I adverted to another relatively simple example in Ch. 21, §2(d): the way in which empiricists, in effect if not perhaps by design, introduce their own concepts of derivation and sense experience in order to formulate their empiricism. (See again the reference to Williams (2006l) in n. 31 of that discussion.) A fifth relatively simple example, I would contend, is Bernard Williams' novel use of realism: see Moore (2007a), esp. §4. (This is the example to which I referred in the Introduction, n. 39.)

which the rest of it was to be erected. Nor, relatedly, did either of them share his demand for certainty. It was in trying to meet that demand, and in trying to sustain that foundationalism, that Descartes arrived at one of his other great metaphysical innovations, the idea that man and nature, or more strictly mind and matter, are of two fundamentally different kinds, jointly comprehensible only insofar as the former is conceived as providing a window on to the latter, which is as much as to say only insofar as the former is conceived as successfully making sense of the latter, or as producing correct representations of the latter (Ch. 1, §6).

This second great innovation, despite being of enormous influence beyond the metaphysical study, had much less influence on metaphysicians themselves. Or rather, it had much less positive influence on metaphysicians themselves. It had a profound negative influence on them. For it was something that they struggled hard, for the most part, to avoid. And many of their own greatest innovations were born of their struggles. Thus Spinoza and Hegel, in their very different ways, were both concerned to reenchant the world that Descartes had left disenchanted (Ch. 1, §6); to show that man is part of nature, that nature itself makes sense, and that man makes sense of nature by suitably expressing the sense that nature makes. Spinoza's most profound innovation was to make provision for this by introducing a conception of nature on which everything finite[21] is not only a part of nature but a mode of a single substance, expressing, in its own particular way, the essence of that substance. Hegel made very different provision for it. Although he too acknowledged a single substance, he differed from Spinoza in conceiving this substance as a subject. He also identified it with reason. One of *his* many great innovations was thus to cast reason itself in the role of subject. And he sought to reenchant the world by construing nature as the forum in which, through various dialectical processes involving human beings, this subject progresses towards self-knowledge.

Leibniz reacted to Descartes' separation of mind and matter in a much more direct way: he denied matter any existence beyond how things appear to certain minds. In this he instigated one of the great traditions of modern metaphysics, a kind of idealism in which the non-mental depends for its very existence on the mental. Kant espoused a particularly sophisticated version of such idealism. On Kant's version the material world depends for its very existence on us, who experience and make sense of it, but the sense that we make of it has no application to the dependence itself, which is utterly different from anything *within* the material world. To grasp such idealism therefore requires a form of sense-making that lies beyond whatever equips us to arrive at knowledge of the workings of that world. In fact it requires a form of sense-making that lies beyond whatever equips us to arrive at

---

[21] Or more strictly, everything finite with which we are acquainted: see Ch. 2, §2, for discussion of what 'nature' means here.

knowledge, period. This is because knowledge of the workings of that world is the only kind of knowledge, in Kant's view, at which we can arrive. Here we see two of his own great innovations: the very idea of a 'transcendental' idealism, whose significance to this enquiry, by now, I need not labour; and a form of sense-making, or at least what he took to be a form of sense-making, that consisted in thinking what could never be known, this being what I have dubbed 'thin' sense-making.

Later philosophers found both of these innovations problematical. But they also acknowledged enough of an advance beyond Descartes' original dualism not to be prepared simply to jettison either of them in favour of a return to the previous order. They demonstrated their own creativity in the variety of ways in which they parted company with Kant without retreating. Fichte developed a 'thicker' version of the second (supposed) form of sense-making (Ch. 6, §3). Hegel, as we have just seen, called for a reconsideration of the very subject of knowledge, or at least of the ultimate subject of knowledge. At the same time he called for a reconsideration of the forms of sense-making available to it (Ch. 7, §§2 and 3). This enabled him to accede to forms of sense-making that were as suitable for grasping the idealism to which he subscribed as they were for grasping the workings of nature. Such were the forms of sense-making involved in the subject's progression towards knowledge of itself. And if my account of the early Wittgenstein is correct, then he too is an example of a later philosopher who demonstrated his creativity in the way in which he grappled with the Kantian aporia – if not under that description. He too developed his own version of the second (supposed) form of sense-making, which he displayed, in his own unique and artful way, as a non-propositional form of sense-making and which he separated even more sharply than Kant had done from its 'thick' counterpart, in his case propositional sense-making, of which it acted as a Kantian precondition. (If anything deserves to be seen as the kind of metaphysical innovation to which his later self would take such exception, this does.)

Frege and Nietzsche, like Hume before them, helped to advance the most general attempt to make sense of things by ensuring that a certain self-conscious attention to sense itself would have a role to play in the enterprise. In Frege's case the sense concerned was linguistic sense. And had he done nothing more than introduce his ground-breaking account of how names and predicates combine to form declarative sentences, he would have made a signal contribution to the drama, not least by helping metaphysicians to see how much is involved, by way of a commitment to the existence of discrete entities and their features, in the very use of such sentences, nay in the very business of representation (cf. Ch. 8, §7(b); Ch. 12, §7;[22] Ch. 16, §4; and Ch. 21, §5(a)). Nietzsche, whose interest in sense extended to all

---

[22] The formalization of theories that Quine envisages presupposes the Fregean account of how declarative sentences function.

its varieties, but who also refused to take anything about it for granted, demonstrated his own capacity for innovation in the extraordinary extent to which, and relentlessness with which, he pursued the general critique of sense. He called into question far more than Descartes had done. He did so, moreover, in a spirit of genuine scepticism, as opposed to Descartes' merely tactical scepticism. Among other things this meant that it would never again be possible, when attempting to make maximally general sense of things, to do so with uncritical confidence in the sense (the point, the purpose, the value) of that very project: the project of making maximally general sense of things. This is yet another example of something on which I have commented often: the enervating power of self-consciousness.

Bergson introduced the concept of the virtual. This was a concept which, in the form in which he introduced it, had no real precursor in the history of Western philosophy.[23] This in turn subserved his idea of intuition, a whole form of sense-making of which he took metaphysics in particular to be a paradigm and which he distinguished from the sense-making involved in the natural sciences. Bergson claimed that this idea of intuition had always been prominent on the philosophical radar. In this he did a disservice to his own originality (Ch. 16, §2). Meanwhile Husserl too had the idea of a form of sense-making, in his case phenomenological sense-making, of which metaphysics (suitably understood) was a paradigm and which was to be distinguished from the sense-making involved in the natural sciences. But unlike Bergson he did not divorce such sense-making from the use of language. So he was free, as Bergson was not, not only to promote it in his own written work, but straightforwardly to practise it there.

As I indicated in §7(b) of the last chapter, Deleuze, whose meta-metaphysical stance I take this flurry of examples to corroborate, was himself responsible for creating many new concepts, both in his own sense of 'concept' and in the analytic philosopher's sense, as well as reworking many more familiar concepts (event, sense, possible world,[24] …). He also displayed a great capacity for the creative redeployment of philosophical ideas, sometimes producing results quite unlike what the originators of the ideas could themselves ever have envisaged. In general, Deleuze was both a supreme innovator and a supreme eclectic. What was remarkable about his work was the way in which he managed to be each of these by being the other.

In the light of all of this, that is to say in the light of this array of self-conscious attempts by metaphysicians over the past four hundred years to make sense of things in ways that are radically new, one would need

---

[23] 'In the form in which he introduced it' is an important qualification. Bergson's concept was one of many variations on a theme that had been familiar since at least the time of Aristotle: see e.g. Aristotle's *Metaphysics*, Bk Θ, Ch. VI, and the concept of potentiality introduced therein.

[24] See Ch. 21, n. 27.

to take an astonishingly dim view both of what has been perpetrated in modern metaphysics and of the levels of self-understanding achieved by those who perpetrated it to return a negative answer to the Novelty Question.

5. Metaphysics as a Humanistic Discipline

Whether or not a given metaphysical undertaking results in a radically new way of making sense of things, indeed whether or not it results in a way of making sense of things at all, there are other grounds on which it can be assessed. Here again I take myself to be largely in agreement with Deleuze, who reminds us that the principal dimensions of assessment for a metaphysical undertaking have to do with such factors as its interest, its relevance to other undertakings, and its capacity to stimulate and to empower (Ch. 21, §6). This connects with what I argued in §7 of the Introduction, namely that metaphysics matters, and that it matters not principally because of whatever intrinsic value it has, but because of the various ways in which it can *make a difference*. That said, the most important and the most exciting way in which it can make a difference is by enabling us to make radically new sense of things, or more specifically – this is something that I urged in that same section – by providing us with radically new concepts by which to live. As for the idea of 'living by' a concept, I explained that what I had in mind was the action-guidingness of some concepts. The paradigmatic action-guiding concepts are what Bernard Williams calls 'thick' ethical concepts. I briefly discussed these. But they are not the only examples.[25] And even if they were, this would be enough, I argued, to account for the capacity of metaphysics to make this kind of difference. In sum: metaphysics can have, does have, and had better have, repercussions for what we think and do beyond metaphysics.[26]

It certainly has had. Here is a list of especially prominent examples:

- the way in which the image that many of us have of ourselves, as embodied souls, has been fostered both by the Cartesian view that each of us is part physical object and part mental substance and by the Kantian variation on that theme whereby each of us appears now in the guise of animal, now in the guise of free rational agent

---

[25] See Introduction, n. 41, and the accompanying text: there is a case for saying that *all* concepts are action-guiding.

[26] This gives the lie to the contrast that P.M.S. Hacker tries to draw, in the context of the quotation that I gave in n. 18, between 'theoretical philosophy', which he clearly takes to include metaphysics, and 'practical philosophy' (ibid., pp. 149–150). When Hacker makes provision for innovation in the latter, he also, willy-nilly, makes provision for innovation in metaphysics.

- Hume's empiricist assault, and its refinement in the hands of the logical positivists, on the more speculative aspects of religious thought
- the recovery of those aspects from that assault under the restorative influence, first of Kant's separation of faith from knowledge, and later of Wittgenstein's appeal to the many different kinds of sense that we can make
- the materialistic development, in Marx's theory of history, of Hegel's vision of a world spirit progressing through dialectical stages towards its ultimate fulfilment[27]

and

- the secularist legacy of Nietzsche's work, in particular his devastating critique of a God-fearing morality and his own attempt, in the wake of that, to overcome nihilism.[28]

But having repercussions is one thing. Having beneficial repercussions is another. We need to beware of ways in which metaphysics can inflict damage beyond itself. (It seems scarcely deniable that it *has* on occasion inflicted damage beyond itself. After all, some of the examples above act as correctives to others.[29]) Nothing that I have just said is intended to give metaphysicians *carte-blanche* to make whatever difference they will and to expect to escape all censure.

We need to beware, for that matter, of ways in which metaphysics can inflict damage, not only beyond itself, but also upon itself. I have tried at various points in this enquiry to signal ways in which, as it seems to me, metaphysics has indeed inflicted damage upon itself, and ways in which such damage has later been repaired. Here again is a list of especially prominent examples:

- Descartes' separation of the mind from a disenchanted world and his associated commitment to the paradigm of representation, subsequently challenged by Spinoza, among others (Ch. 1, §6)
- Leibniz' and Hegel's shared idea that metaphysics can bring good news, in that it can show that affliction, anguish, and adversity are a finite

---

[27] See Cohen (1978), Ch. I.

[28] Another interesting if more marginal example is provided by the theory and practice of Derridean deconstruction and their influence on literary criticism (see Culler (2008)). This is more marginal for two reasons. First, there is an issue about how far Derridean deconstruction counts as a contribution to metaphysics. Second, the repercussions in this case are less far-reaching than in any of those cited in the main text.

[29] Not that this is decisive. One might think, with Hegel, that metaphysics has to achieve what it does through the resolution and *Aufhebung* of opposition. Or one might think, with Dummett, that it has to achieve what it does by following 'a meandering [path] that twists and turns upon itself' (Dummett (2010), p. 149).

price to be paid for something of infinite value,[30] an idea subsequently challenged by Nietzsche (Ch. 3, §5, and Ch. 15, §6)

- Hume's and the logical positivists' shared idea that the only way to make sense of things is by analyzing concepts and/or depicting and predicting the contingent course of sense experience, an idea challenged by Kant and Dummett (Ch. 5, §3, and Ch. 11, §6)
- Quine's descendent idea that the only way to make sense of things is the (natural-)scientific way, an idea espoused in a less extreme form by Lewis but challenged by the phenomenologists (Ch. 13, §4, and Ch. 17, §2)

and of course

- the later Wittgenstein's conservatism, indirectly challenged by Deleuze (§§3 and 4).

The failure in some of these cases is a failure of due self-consciousness.[31] I suggested in §5 of the Introduction that the most general attempt to make sense of things is bound to involve an element of self-consciousness. But I also urged in §4 of Chapter 13 that this element of self-consciousness can have an overly narrow focus. Its focus can be on the sense that is being made to the exclusion of the making of it. Similarly, the tools that are brought to bear on the project, though they may be suitable for the investigation of the former (the sense that is being made), may be unsuitable for the investigation of the latter (the making of that sense). Such was the charge that I levelled against the naturalistic metaphysics practised by Quine and Lewis. Those who engage in such metaphysics either have no real concern with the making of sense or treat it in an inappropriately (natural-)scientific way. They fail to register the extent to which metaphysics is, in a phrase of Bernard Williams that I have invoked a couple of times before (Ch. 13, §4, and Ch. 18, §4), a humanistic discipline.

The idea that metaphysics is a humanistic discipline has been exemplified throughout this enquiry. Most of our protagonists have been explicitly concerned in one way or another with the place of humanity in the larger scheme of things. When I was discussing these matters in §4 of Chapter 13 I mentioned how this was true in particular of Descartes, Spinoza, and Leibniz. There are many other examples in what preceded that chapter which I could just as readily have invoked – as of course there are in what has come since in Part Three.

---

[30] Cf. Williams (2006a), p. 49.

[31] This is related to a wider failure to which metaphysics is prone: the failure, as Bernard Williams puts it in a wonderful passage on these and related matters, '[to] listen to what it is saying' (Williams (2006n), §5, in which the quoted phrase occurs on p. 213). This is a failure to which the later Wittgenstein is especially sensitive: cf. the injunction in Wittgenstein (1967a), Pt I, §66, not to think, but to look.

It is because I take metaphysics to be a humanistic discipline that I am prepared to dismiss certain forms of sense-making as unfit to act as input in my definition (see §1). The most obvious casualty is natural-scientific sense-making. If that is fed into my definition, then the result is just high-level physics or something of the sort. (Cf. Ch. 9, §2; Ch. 12, §6; and Ch. 16, §6(b).)

But natural-scientific sense-making is not the only casualty. I am also prepared to dismiss any sense-making that is peculiar to any of the empirical human sciences, such as history. This has to do with the *kind* of humanistic discipline that I take to metaphysics to be. Both Hume and Collingwood gave us a vision of metaphysics as an empirical human science, and in Collingwood's case specifically as a branch of history (Ch. 4, §4, and Ch. 19, §2). I tried to show that this is not quite the aberration that it appears to be. Nevertheless it is an aberration, born in each case of what seems to me a distorted conception of the sort of sense-making that is available to the metaphysician (Ch. 4, §5, and Ch. 19, §4).

The truth is, metaphysics is not a *science* at all. It is no more a kind of history, or sociology, or anthropology, than it is a kind of physics.[32] Its humanistic aspect is of a different sort. It does nonetheless have a humanistic aspect; and it needs to be true to that aspect. Metaphysics may not be anthropological, but it does need to be anthropocentric. That is, it needs to be from a human point of view. It needs to be an attempt to make the sort of general sense of things that we its practitioners can appropriate as distinctively ours. Only then can it involve the kind of self-consciousness that it should.[33] Only then can it enjoy the kind of *importance* that it should. Importance, where human beings are concerned, is importance to human beings.[34]

But am I not now begging the recurrent question, which I first advertised in §6(a) of the Introduction, of who 'we' are? Even granted that metaphysics, as 'we' practise it, needs to be from 'our' point of view, and even granted that metaphysics throughout this discussion can be understood as elliptical for metaphysics as 'we' practise it, is it not a further question whether 'we' in this context are best understood as we humans?

Well, but who else could 'we' be? If a narrower constituency is entertained, say humans in the modern Western world, then that poses an

---

[32] This is not to deny, what my argument in §2 prevents me from denying, that metaphysics can be hard to distinguish from history – as indeed it can be hard to distinguish from sociology or anthropology. But it can also be hard to distinguish from physics.

[33] This is part of the reason why I answer the Creativity Question in the way I do. See Introduction, §6(c).

[34] Here I take myself to be in agreement with Bernard Williams, despite an initial appearance to the contrary: see Williams (2006o), pp. 182–183. See also the splendid passage in Lovejoy (1964), pp. 22–23.

immediate threat to the generality of metaphysics.[35] If a wider constituency is entertained, say rational beings, then that falls foul of the brute fact that we humans are not in dialogue with any other rational beings, which means that there are no other rational beings with whom we can arrive at a suitably self-conscious conception of a shared activity of sense-making targeted at results of shared importance. Human metaphysics needs to be anthropocentric. And human metaphysicians need to be unashamed about that. In fact they can glory in it. There seems to me truth in what we saw Husserl say about metaphysics in Chapter 17, §7: that it brings us to 'questions of the meaning or meaninglessness of the whole of this human existence' (Husserl (1970), §2), and that 'the quite personal responsibility [of metaphysicians] ... bears within itself at the same time the responsibility for the true being of mankind' (ibid., p. 17).

But what about the point that we considered at the very end of the last chapter in connection with Deleuze, that 'we' should be open to non-human possibilities? Well, so we should. But what this means, or at least what I think it had better mean, is that we *humans* should be open to non-human possibilities. In particular, we should be open to the possibility that our metaphysics will one day no longer need to be anthropocentric. Even so, we cannot oversee its becoming non-anthropocentric except by overseeing its evolution from something anthropocentric. And 'evolution' is the right word here. Nothing can happen in a metamorphic flash. Quite apart from whatever gradual transformation may have to be involved in our coming to embrace non-human possibilities beyond metaphysics, there is a gradual transformation that will certainly have to be involved in our coming to embrace them within metaphysics. This is really just the point captured in Neurath's image: we cannot come to make sense of things in ways that are radically new save through a progressive piecemeal process. (This is a conceptual point, not an anthropological point. There is a limit to how drastic and how rapid an upheaval in our sense-making can be while still counting as an upheaval in our sense-making – as opposed to our being as it were magically transported to some new ship on the intellectual sea.) So *for now* our metaphysics needs to be anthropocentric.

One of the exciting features of Deleuze's metaphysics is how little it presupposes. He has an account of sense that appears utterly neutral, dependent neither on a prior conception of universals nor on a prior conception of particulars nor on a prior conception of the subject. Indeed, if his account is successful, then it can be used to explain how universals, particulars, and the subject are all constituted (Ch. 21, §4). But am I not now challenging all of that by in effect suggesting that there can be no satisfactory account of sense

---

[35] Here there is an important difference between metaphysics and other branches of philosophy: see Williams (2006m), esp. §7.

that is not at least dependent on a prior conception of whose sense it is – that is, given that it is 'our' sense, on a prior conception of who 'we' are? I am not sure. And I do not mean this rhetorically. I am genuinely not sure. The supposed neutrality of Deleuze's account of sense does concern me. It is here especially that I have Wittgensteinian misgivings about what he offers us. (See Ch. 10, §3.[36]) But quite what relations of priority obtain between us and whatever sense we make of things is an enormous question for another occasion. My concern in this final section has been with other relations that obtain between us and whatever sense we make of things. It has been with relations that need to obtain between us and whatever sense we make of things for our sense-making to constitute good proper metaphysics.

I have been trying to reinforce the claim of importance that I have made on behalf of metaphysics. That is a claim that I hope the enquiry as a whole has helped to illustrate. The unexamined life, Socrates said, is not worth living (Plato's *Apology*, 38a). He may have overstated his case. But even if he did, his remark is very pertinent here. For what is it to examine life if not to try to make sense of it? And how can we try to make sense of life without trying to make sense, more generally, of things? To whatever extent the unexamined life is not worth living, neither is the life without metaphysics.

---

[36] Wittgenstein (1967a), Pt II, §xi, is very relevant here.

Bibliography

Adams, Robert Merrihew (1994), *Leibniz: Determinist, Theist, Idealist* (Oxford: Oxford University Press)

Adorno, Theodor W. (1973), *Negative Dialectics*, trans. E.B. Ashton (New York: Seabury Press)

Al-Azm, Sadik J. (1972), *The Origins of Kant's Arguments in the Antinomies* (Oxford: Oxford University Press)

Allison, Henry E. (1983), *Kant's Transcendental Idealism: An Interpretation and Defense* (New Haven, Conn.: Yale University Press)

(1990), *Kant's Theory of Freedom* (Cambridge: Cambridge University Press)

Alweiss, Lilian (2007), 'Leaving Metaphysics to Itself', *International Journal of Philosophical Studies* 15

Ameriks, Karl (2000), 'The Practical Foundation of Philosophy in Kant, Fichte, and After', in Sally Sedgwick (ed.), *The Reception of Kant's Critical Philosophy: Fichte, Schelling, and Hegel* (Cambridge: Cambridge University Press)

(2006), *Kant and the Historical Turn: Philosophy as Critical Interpretation* (Oxford: Oxford University Press)

Anscombe, G.E.M. (1971), *An Introduction to Wittgenstein's* Tractatus*: Themes in the Philosophy of Wittgenstein*, 3rd edn (South Bend, Ind.: St Augustine's Press)

(1981), 'The Question of Linguistic Idealism', reprinted in her *From Parmenides to Wittgenstein: Collected Philosophical Papers*, Vol. 1 (Oxford: Blackwell)

(1983), 'The First Person', reprinted in her *Metaphysics and the Philosophy of Mind: Collected Philosophical Papers*, Vol. 2 (Oxford: Blackwell)

Anscombe, G.E.M., and P.T. Geach (1961), *Three Philosophers* (Oxford: Blackwell)

Ansell Pearson, Keith (1999), *Germinal Life: The Difference and Repetition of Deleuze* (London: Routledge)

Anselm (1996), *Proslogian*, in his *Monologian and Proslogian with the Replies of Gaunilo and Anselm*, trans. Thomas Williams (Indianapolis, Ind.: Hackett Publishing)

Ariew, Roger (1992), 'Descartes and Scholasticism: The Intellectual Background of Descartes' Thought', in John Cottingham (ed.), *The Cambridge Companion to Descartes* (Cambridge: Cambridge University Press)

Aristotle (1924), *Metaphysics*, trans. W.D. Ross (Oxford: Oxford University Press)

(1936), *Physics*, trans. W.D. Ross (Oxford: Oxford University Press)

(1975), *De Interpretatione* in his *Categories and De Interpretatione*, trans. J.L. Ackrill (Oxford: Oxford University Press)

Armstrong, D.M. (1968), *A Materialist Theory of Mind* (London: Routledge & Kegan Paul)

Armstrong, Robert L. (1965), 'John Locke's "Doctrine of Signs": A New Metaphysics', *Journal of the History of Ideas* 26

Arnauld, Antoine, and Pierre Nicol (1996), *Logic or the Art of Thinking, Containing, Besides Common Rules, Several New Observations Appropriate for Forming Judgment*, trans. and ed. Jill Vance Buroker (Cambridge: Cambridge University Press)

Austin, J.L. (1970), 'A Plea for Excuses', reprinted in his *Philosophical Papers*, ed. J.O. Urmson and G.J. Warnock (Oxford: Oxford University Press)

(1975), *How to do Things with Words*, ed. J.O. Urmson and Marina Sbisà, 2nd edn (Oxford: Oxford University Press)

Ayer, A.J. (1969), 'Metaphysics and Common Sense', reprinted in his *Metaphysics and Common Sense* (London: Macmillan)

(1971), *Language, Truth and Logic*, 2nd edn (Harmondsworth: Penguin)

(1992), 'Reply to Michael Dummett', in L.E. Hahn (ed.), *The Philosophy of A.J. Ayer* (La Salle, Ill.: Open Court)

Ayers, Michael (1998), 'Theories of Knowledge and Belief', in Daniel Garber and Michael Ayers (eds), *The Cambridge History of Seventeenth Century Philosophy*, Vol. 2 (Cambridge: Cambridge University Press)

Baker, Gordon (1988), *Wittgenstein, Frege and the Vienna Circle* (Oxford: Blackwell)

(2004a), *Wittgenstein's Method: Neglected Aspects*, ed. Katherine J. Morris (Oxford: Blackwell)

(2004b), 'Wittgenstein on Metaphysical/Everyday Use', reprinted in his *Wittgenstein's Method: Neglected Aspects*, ed. Katherine J. Morris (Oxford: Blackwell)

(2004c), 'A Vision of Philosophy', reprinted in his *Wittgenstein's Method: Neglected Aspects*, ed. Katherine J. Morris (Oxford: Blackwell)

(2004d), 'Wittgenstein's Method and Psychoanalysis', reprinted in his *Wittgenstein's Method: Neglected Aspects*, ed. Katherine J. Morris (Oxford: Blackwell)

(2004e), 'Italics in Wittgenstein', reprinted in his *Wittgenstein's Method: Neglected Aspects*, ed. Katherine J. Morris (Oxford: Blackwell)

Baker, G.P., and P.M.S. Hacker (1984), *Frege: Logical Excavations* (Oxford: Blackwell)

Baldwin, Thomas (1988), 'Phenomenology, Solipsism and Egocentric Thought', *Proceedings of the Aristotelian Society*, Suppl. Vol. 62

(2001), 'Death and Meaning – Some Questions for Derrida', in Simon Glendinning (ed.), *Arguing with Derrida* (Oxford: Blackwell)

Barbone, Steven (2002), 'What Counts as an Individual for Spinoza?', in Olli Koistinen and John Biro (eds), *Spinoza: Metaphysical Themes* (Oxford: Oxford University Press)

Barnes, Jonathan (1987), *Early Greek Philosophy* (Harmondsworth: Penguin)

Bass, Alan (1978), 'Translator's Introduction', in Jacques Derrida, *Writing and Difference*, trans. and ed. Alan Bass (London: Routledge & Kegan Paul)

Beaney, Michael (1996), *Frege: Making Sense* (London: Duckworth)

Beck, Lewis White (1960), *A Commentary on Kant's Critique of Practical Reason* (Chicago: University of Chicago Press)

Beiser, Frederick C. (1993), 'Introduction: Hegel and the Problem of Metaphysics', in Frederick C. Beiser (ed.), *The Cambridge Companion to Hegel* (Cambridge: Cambridge University Press)

Bell, David (1984), 'Reference and Sense: An Epitome', in Crispin Wright (ed.), *Frege: Tradition and Influence* (Oxford: Blackwell)

(1988), 'Phenomenology, Solipsism and Egocentric Thought', *Proceedings of the Aristotelian Society*, Suppl. Vol. 72

(1990), *Husserl* (London: Routledge)

(2001), 'Some Kantian Thoughts on Propositional Unity', *Proceedings of the Aristotelian Society*, Suppl. Vol. 75

Benacerraf, Paul (1983), 'What Numbers Could Not Be', reprinted in Paul Benacerraf and Hilary Putnam (eds), *Philosophy of Mathematics: Selected Readings*, 2nd edn (Cambridge: Cambridge University Press)

Bennett, Jonathan (1966), *Kant's Analytic* (Cambridge: Cambridge University Press)

(1971), *Locke, Berkeley, Hume: Central Themes* (Oxford: Oxford University Press)

(1974), *Kant's Dialectic* (Cambridge: Cambridge University Press)

(1982), 'The Age and Size of the World', reprinted in Ralph C.S. Walker (ed.), *Kant on Pure Reason* (Oxford: Oxford University Press)

(1984), *A Study of Spinoza's Ethics* (Cambridge: Cambridge University Press)

(1998), 'Descartes' Theory of Modality', reprinted in John Cottingham (ed.), *Descartes* (Oxford: Oxford University Press)

(2001), *Learning from Six Philosophers: Descartes, Spinoza, Leibniz, Locke, Berkeley, Hume*, Vol. 2 (Oxford: Oxford University Press)

(2003), *Learning from Six Philosophers: Descartes, Spinoza, Leibniz, Locke, Berkeley, Hume*, Vol. 1, revised edn (Oxford: Oxford University Press)

Bennington, Geoffrey (1993), 'Derridabase', in Geoffrey Bennington and Jacques Derrida, *Jacques Derrida* (Chicago: University of Chicago Press)

Bergmann, Gustav (1964), *Logic and Reality* (Madison: University of Wisconsin Press)

Bergson, Henri (1910), *Time and Free Will: An Essay on the Immediate Data of Consciousness*, trans. F.L. Pogson (London: George Allen & Unwin)

(1920), *Mind-Energy: Lectures and Essays*, trans. H. Wildon Carr (Westport, Conn.: Greenwood Press)

(1965a), 'Introduction (Part I): Retrograde Movement of the True Growth of Truth', in his *An Introduction to Metaphysics: The Creative Mind*, trans. Mabelle L. Andison (Totowa, N.J.: Littlefield, Adams)

(1965b), 'Introduction (Part II): Stating the Problems', in his *An Introduction to Metaphysics: The Creative Mind*, trans. Mabelle L. Andison (Totowa, N.J.: Littlefield, Adams)

(1965c), 'The Possible and the Real', reprinted in his *An Introduction to Metaphysics: The Creative Mind*, trans. Mabelle L. Andison (Totowa, N.J.: Littlefield, Adams)

(1965d), 'Philosophical Intuition', reprinted in his *An Introduction to Metaphysics: The Creative Mind*, trans. Mabelle L. Andison (Totowa, N.J.: Littlefield, Adams)

(1965e), 'The Perception of Change', reprinted in his *An Introduction to Metaphysics: The Creative Mind*, trans. Mabelle L. Andison (Totowa, N.J.: Littlefield, Adams)

(1965f), 'Introduction to Metaphysics', reprinted in his *An Introduction to Metaphysics: The Creative Mind*, trans. Mabelle L. Andison (Totowa, N.J.: Littlefield, Adams)

(1965g), *Duration and Simultaneity: With Reference to Einstein's Theory*, trans. Leon Jacobson (Indianapolis, Ind.: Bobbs-Merrill)

(1975), *Creative Evolution*, trans. Arthur Mitchell (Westport, Conn.: Greenwood Press)

(1991), *Matter and Memory*, trans. N.M. Paul and W.S. Palmer (New York: Zone Books)

Bergström, Lars (2004), 'Underdetermination of Physical Theory', in Roger F. Gibson (ed.), *The Cambridge Companion to Quine* (Cambridge: Cambridge University Press)

Berkeley, George (1962a), *The Principles of Human Knowledge*, in his *The Principles of Human Knowledge with Other Writings* (London: Fontana)

(1962b), *Three Dialogues Between Hylas and Philonous, in Opposition to Sceptics and Atheists*, in his *The Principles of Human Knowledge with Other Writings* (London: Fontana)

Berlin, Isaiah (1978), 'The Hedgehog and the Fox', reprinted in his *Russian Thinkers* (London: Hogarth Press)

Bird, Graham (2006), *The Revolutionary Kant: A Commentary on the* Critique of Pure Reason (La Salle, Ill.: Open Court)

Biro, John (1993), 'Hume's New Science of the Mind', in David Fate Norton (ed.), *The Cambridge Companion to Hume* (Cambridge: Cambridge University Press)

Black, Max (1964), *A Companion to Wittgenstein's 'Tractatus'* (Ithaca, N.Y.: Cornell University Press)

Blackburn, Simon (1984), *Spreading the Word: Groundings in the Philosophy of Language* (Oxford: Oxford University Press)

(1993a), *Essays in Quasi-Realism* (Oxford: Oxford University Press)

(1993b), 'Morals and Modals', reprinted in his *Essays in Quasi-Realism* (Oxford: Oxford University Press)

(1996), 'Metaphysics', in Nicholas Bunnin and E.P. Tsui-James (eds), *The Blackwell Companion to Philosophy* (Oxford: Blackwell)

(2000), 'Hume and Thick Connexions', in Rupert Read and Kenneth A. Richman (eds), *The New Hume Debate* (London: Routledge)

Blumberg, Albert E., and Herbert Feigl (1931), 'Logical Positivism: A New Movement in European Philosophy', *Journal of Philosophy* 23

Blumenfeld, David (1981), 'Leibniz's Theory of the Striving Possibles', reprinted in R.S. Woolhouse (ed.), *Leibniz: Metaphysics and Philosophy of Science* (Oxford: Oxford University Press)

(1995), 'Perfection and Happiness in the Best Possible World', in Nicholas Jolley (ed.), *The Cambridge Companion to Leibniz* (Cambridge: Cambridge University Press)

Bolton, Derek (1982), 'Life-Form and Idealism', in Godfrey Vesey (ed.), *Idealism Past and Present* (Cambridge: Cambridge University Press)

Bossert, Philip J. (1973), 'The Origins and Early Development of Edmund Husserl's Method of Phenomenological Reduction,' Ph.D. thesis, Washington University

Boswell, James (1887), *The Life of Samuel Johnson, LL.D.* (Oxford: Oxford University Press)

Boundas, Constantin V. (1996), 'Deleuze-Bergson: An Ontology of the Virtual', in Paul Patton (ed.), *Deleuze: A Critical Reader* (Oxford: Blackwell)

Bradley, F.H. (1930), *Appearance and Reality: A Metaphysical Essay*, 2nd edn (Oxford: Oxford University Press)

Brandom, Robert B. (2002a), *Tales of the Mighty Dead: Historical Essays in the Metaphysics of Intentionality* (Cambridge, Mass.: Harvard University Press)

(2002b), 'Adequacy and the Individuation of Ideas in Spinoza's *Ethics*', reprinted in his *Tales of the Mighty Dead: Historical Essays in the Metaphysics of Intentionality* (Cambridge, Mass.: Harvard University Press)

(2002c), 'Leibniz and Degrees of Perception', reprinted in his *Tales of the Mighty Dead: Historical Essays in the Metaphysics of Intentionality* (Cambridge, Mass.: Harvard University Press)

(2002d), 'Heidegger's Categories in *Sein und Zeit*', reprinted in his *Tales of the Mighty Dead: Historical Essays in the Metaphysics of Intentionality* (Cambridge, Mass.: Harvard University Press)

(2002e), 'Dasein, the Being that Thematizes', reprinted in his *Tales of the Mighty Dead: Historical Essays in the Metaphysics of Intentionality* (Cambridge, Mass.: Harvard University Press)

Breazeale, Daniel (1994), 'Circles and Grounds in the Jena *Wissenschaftslehre*', in Daniel Breazeale and Tom Rockmore (eds), *Fichte: Historical Contexts/ Contemporary Controversies* (Atlantic Highlands, N.J.: Humanities Press)

Brentano, Franz (1973), *Psychology from an Empirical Standpoint*, ed. L.L. McAlister and trans. A.C. Rancurello, D.B. Terrell, and L.L. McAlister (London: Routledge & Kegan Paul)

Brewer, Bill (2004), 'Stroud's Quest for Reality', in *Philosophy and Phenomenological Research* 68

Broackes, Justin (2002), 'Hume, Belief, and Personal Identity', in Peter Millican (ed.), *Reading Hume on Human Understanding: Essays on the First Enquiry* (Oxford: Oxford University Press)

Brouwer, L.E.J. (1983), 'Intuitionism and Formalism', trans. Arnold Dresden, reprinted in Paul Benacerraf and Hilary Putnam (eds), *Philosophy of Mathematics: Selected Readings*, 2nd edn (Cambridge: Cambridge University Press)

Buchanan, Ian (2000), *Deleuzism: A Metacommentary* (Edinburgh: Edinburgh University Press)

Burbidge, John (1993), 'Hegel's Conception of Logic', in Frederick C. Beiser (ed.), *The Cambridge Companion to Hegel* (Cambridge: Cambridge University Press)

Burnyeat, Myles (1981), 'Aristotle on Understanding Knowledge', in Enrico Berti (ed.), *Aristotle on Science: The Posterior Analytics* (Padua: Editrice Antenore)

(1982), 'Idealism and Greek Philosophy: What Descartes Saw and Berkeley Missed', in Godfrey Vesey (ed.), *Idealism Past and Present* (Cambridge: Cambridge University Press)

Campbell, John (2002), *Reference and Consciousness* (Oxford: Oxford University Press)

(2007), 'If Truth Is Dethroned, What Role Is Left for It?', in R.E. Auxier and L.E. Hahn (eds), *The Philosophy of Michael Dummett* (Chicago and La Salle, Ill.: Open Court)

Cantor, Georg (1932), *Gesammelte Abhandlungen Mathematischen und Philosophischen Inhalts*, ed. Ernst Zermelo (Berlin: Springer)

(1955), *Contributions to the Founding of the Theory of Transfinite Numbers*, trans. Philip E.B. Jourdain (New York: Dover)

Carman, Taylor (2006), 'The Principle of Phenomenology', in Charles B. Guignon (ed.), *The Cambridge Companion to Heidegger*, 2nd edn (Cambridge: Cambridge University Press)

Carnap, Rudolf (1922), *Der Raum: Ein Beitrag zur Wissenschaftslehre* (Berlin: Reuther & Reichard)

(1935), *Philosophy and Logical Syntax* (Bristol: Thoemmes Press)

(1937), *The Logical Syntax of Language*, trans. Amethe Smeaton (London: Kegan Paul, Trench, Trubner)

(1956a), *Meaning and Necessity: A Study in Semantics and Modal Logic*, 2nd edn (Chicago: University of Chicago Press)

(1956b), 'Empiricism, Semantics, and Ontology', reprinted as Appendix A to his *Meaning and Necessity: A Study in Semantics and Modal Logic*, 2nd edn (Chicago: University of Chicago Press)

(1958), 'Introductory Remarks to the English Edition', in Hans Reichenbach, *The Philosophy of Space and Time*, trans. Maria Reichenbach and John Freund (New York: Dover)

(1959), 'The Elimination of Metaphysics Through Logical Analysis of Language', trans. Arthur Pap, in A.J. Ayer (ed.), *Logical Positivism* (Glencoe: Free Press)

(1963a), 'Intellectual Autobiography', in P.A. Schilpp (ed.), *The Philosophy of Rudolf Carnap* (La Salle, Ill.: Open Court)

(1963b), 'Nelson Goodman on *Der Logische Aufbau der Welt*', in P.A. Schilpp (ed.), *The Philosophy of Rudolf Carnap* (La Salle, Ill.: Open Court)

(1967a), *The Logical Structure of the World*, trans. Rolf A. George, in his *The Logical Structure of the World and Pseudoproblems in Philosophy* (London: Routledge & Kegan Paul)

(1967b), *Pseudoproblems in Philosophy*, trans. Rolf A. George, in his *The Logical Structure of the World and Pseudoproblems in Philosophy* (London: Routledge & Kegan Paul)

Carr, David (1999), *The Paradox of Subjectivity: The Self in the Transcendental Tradition* (Oxford: Oxford University Press)

Carroll, Lewis (1974), *The Hunting of the Snark: An Agony in Eight Fits* (Harmondsworth: Penguin)

(1982), *Through the Looking-Glass, and What Alice Found There*, in his *Alice's Adventures in Wonderland and Through the Looking Glass* (Oxford: Oxford University Press)

Carruthers, Peter (1989), *Tractarian Semantics: Finding Sense in Wittgenstein's Tractatus* (Oxford: Blackwell)

Cavell, Stanley (2002), 'Must We Mean What We Say?', reprinted in his *Must We Mean What We Say?*, updated edn (Cambridge: Cambridge University Press)

Caygill, Howard (1997), 'The Topology of Selection: The Limits of Deleuze's Biophilosophy', in Keith Ansell Pearson (ed.), *Deleuze and Philosophy: The Difference Engineer* (London: Routledge)

Chalmers, David J., David Manley, and Ryan Wasserman (eds) (2009), *Metametaphysics: New Essays on the Foundations of Ontology* (Oxford: Oxford University Press)

Churchland, Patricia S. (1986), *Neurophilosophy: Toward a Unified Science of the Mind/Brain (Computational Models of Cognition and Perception)* (Cambridge, Mass.: MIT Press)

Churchland, Paul M. (1979), *Scientific Realism and the Plasticity of Mind* (Cambridge: Cambridge University Press)

Clark, Maudemarie (1990), *Nietzsche on Truth and Philosophy* (Cambridge: Cambridge University Press)

Cockburn, David (1997), *Other Times: Philosophical Perspectives on Past, Present and Future* (Cambridge: Cambridge University Press)

Cohen, G.A. (1978), *Karl Marx's Theory of History: A Defence* (Oxford: Oxford University Press)

Collingwood, R.G. (1924), *Speculum Mentis, or The Map of Knowledge* (Oxford: Oxford University Press)

(1944), *An Autobiography* (Harmondsworth: Penguin)

(1945), *The Idea of Nature*, ed. T.M. Knox (Oxford: Oxford University Press)

(1967), 'The Philosophy of History', in his *Essays in the Philosophy of History*, ed. William Debbins (New York: McGraw Hill)

(1994), *The Idea of History*, revised edn, ed. Jan van der Dussen (Oxford: Oxford University Press)

(1998a), *An Essay on Metaphysics, in his An Essay on Metaphysics with an Introduction and Additional Material*, ed. Rex Martin (Oxford: Oxford University Press)

(1998b), 'Function of Metaphysics in Civilization', in his *An Essay on Metaphysics with an Introduction and Additional Material*, ed. Rex Martin (Oxford: Oxford University Press)

(2005), *An Essay on Philosophical Method*, in his *An Essay on Philosophical Method with an Introduction and Additional Material*, ed. James Connelly and Giuseppina D'Oro (Oxford: Oxford University Press)

Comte, Auguste (1988), *Introduction to Positive Philosophy*, ed. and trans. Frederick Ferré (Indianapolis, Ind.: Hackett Publishing)

Conant, James (1989), 'Must We Show What We Cannot Say?', in Richard Fleming and Michael Payne (eds), *The Senses of Stanley Cavell* (Lewisburg, Pa.: Bucknell University Press)

(1991), 'The Search for Logically Alien Thought: Descartes, Kant, Frege, and the *Tractatus*', *Philosophical Topics* 20

(2000), 'Elucidation and Nonsense in Frege and Early Wittgenstein', in Alice Crary and Rupert Read (eds), *The New Wittgenstein* (London: Routledge)

(2004), 'Why Worry About the *Tractatus*?', in Barry Stocker (ed.), *Post-Analytic Tractatus* (Aldershot: Ashgate)

Conant, James, and Cora Diamond (2004), 'On Reading the *Tractatus* Resolutely: Reply to Meredith Williams and Peter Sullivan', in Max Kölbel and Bernhard Weiss (eds), *Wittgenstein's Lasting Significance* (London: Routledge)

Condillac, Etienne Bonnot de (2001), *Essay on the Origin of Human Knowledge*, trans. and ed. Hans Aarsleff (Cambridge: Cambridge University Press)

Cooper, David E. (1996), *Thinkers of Our Time: Heidegger* (London: Claridge Press)

(2002), *The Measure of Things: Humanism, Humility, and Mystery* (Oxford: Oxford University Press)

Copleston, Frederick (1960), *A History of Philosophy*, Vol. 6: *Wolff to Kant* (New York: Doubleday)

(1963), *A History of Philosophy*, Vol. 7: *Fichte to Nietzsche* (New York: Doubleday)

Costello, Diarmuid (2004), '"Making Sense" of Nonsense: Conant and Diamond Read Wittgenstein's *Tractatus*', in Barry Stocker (ed.), *Post-Analytic* Tractatus (Aldershot: Ashgate)

Cottingham, John (1986), *Descartes* (Oxford: Blackwell)

Couturat, Louis (1901), *La Logique de Leibniz: d'Après des Documents Inédits* (Paris: Félix Alcan)

Craig, Edward (1982), 'Meaning, Use and Privacy', in *Mind* 91

(1987), *The Mind of God and the Works of Man* (Oxford: Oxford University Press)

Cranefield, Paul F. (1970), 'On the Origin of the Phrase: Nihil Est in Intellectu Quod Non Prius Fuerit in Sensu', *Journal of the History of Medicine* 25

Crary, Alice, and Rupert Read (2000), *The New Wittgenstein* (London: Routledge)

Creath, Richard (2007), 'Quine's Challenge to Carnap', in Michael Friedman and Richard Creath (eds), *The Cambridge Companion to Carnap* (Cambridge: Cambridge University Press)

Crompton, Richmal (1922), *Just – William* (London: George Newnes)

Crowell, Steven Galt (1990), 'Husserl, Heidegger, and Transcendental Philosophy: Another Look at the Encyclopædia Britannica Article', *Philosophy and Phenomenological Research* 50

Culler, Jonathan (2008), *On Deconstruction: Theory and Criticism After Structuralism* (London: Routledge)

Cumming, R.D. (1991), *Phenomenology and Deconstruction*, Vol. 1: *The Dream Is Over* (Chicago: University of Chicago Press)

D'Agostino, Fred (1981), 'Leibniz on Compossibility and Relational Predicates', reprinted in R.S. Woolhouse (ed.), *Leibniz: Metaphysics and Philosophy of Science* (Oxford: Oxford University Press)

Dahlstrom, Daniel O. (1994), 'Heidegger's Method: Philosophical Concepts as Formal Indications', *Review of Metaphysics* 47

Davidson, Donald (1980), 'Mental Events', reprinted in his *Essays on Actions and Events* (Oxford: Oxford University Press)

(1984a), 'On the Very Idea of a Conceptual Scheme', reprinted in his *Truth and Interpretation* (Oxford: Oxford University Press)

(1984b), 'The Method of Truth in Metaphysics', reprinted in his *Truth and Interpretation* (Oxford: Oxford University Press)

(2005a), 'Method and Metaphysics', reprinted in his *Truth, Language, and History* (Oxford: Oxford University Press)

(2005b), 'Pursuit of the Concept of Truth', reprinted in his *Truth, Language, and History* (Oxford: Oxford University Press)

(2005c), 'What Is Quine's View of Truth?', reprinted in his *Truth, Language, and History* (Oxford: Oxford University Press)

(2005d), 'The Socratic Concept of Truth', reprinted in his *Truth, Language, and History* (Oxford: Oxford University Press)

(2005e), 'Spinoza's Causal Theory of the Affects', reprinted in his *Truth, Language, and History* (Oxford: Oxford University Press)

Dejnožka, Jan (2007), 'Dummett's Backward Road to Frege and Intuitionism', in R.E. Auxier and L.E. Hahn (eds), *The Philosophy of Michael Dummett* (Chicago and La Salle, Ill.: Open Court)

DeLanda, Manuel (2002), *Intensive Science and Virtual Philosophy* (London: Continuum)

Deleuze, Gilles (1980), 'Spinoza', lecture delivered on 25 November 1980, available at http://www.webdeleuze.com

—— (1984), *Kant's Critical Philosophy: The Doctrine of the Faculties*, trans. Hugh Tomlinson and Barbara Habberjam (London: Athlone Press)

—— (1988a), *Spinoza: Practical Philosophy*, trans. Robert Hurley (San Francisco, Calif.: City Light Books)

—— (1988b), *Bergsonism*, trans. Hugh Tomlinson and Barbara Habberjam (New York: Zone Books)

—— (1989), *Cinema 2: The Time-Image*, trans. Hugh Tomlinson and Robert Galeta (London: Athlone Press)

—— (1990a), *Expressionism in Philosophy: Spinoza*, trans. Martin Joughin (New York: Zone Books)

—— (1990b), *The Logic of Sense*, trans. Mark Lester and Charles Stivale and ed. Constantin V. Boundas (New York: Columbia University Press)

—— (1991), *Empiricism and Subjectivity: An Essay on Hume's Theory of Human Nature*, trans. Constantin V. Boundas (New York: Columbia University Press)

—— (1993), *The Fold: Leibniz and the Baroque*, trans. Tom Conley (London: Athlone Press)

—— (1994), *Difference and Repetition*, trans. Paul Patton (New York: Columbia University Press)

—— (1995a), 'Letter to a Harsh Critic', in his *Negotiations, 1972–1990*, trans. Martin Joughin (New York: Columbia University Press)

—— (1995b), 'Breaking Things Open, Breaking Words Open', in his *Negotiations, 1972–1990*, trans. Martin Joughin (New York: Columbia University Press)

—— (1995c), 'Mediators', in his *Negotiations, 1972–1990*, trans. Martin Joughin (New York: Columbia University Press)

—— (1995d), 'On Philosophy', in his *Negotiations, 1972–1990*, trans. Martin Joughin (New York: Columbia University Press)

—— (1995e), 'Letter to Réda Bensmaïa, on Spinoza', in his *Negotiations, 1972–1990*, trans. Martin Joughin (New York: Columbia University Press)

—— (2001), 'Immanence: A Life', in his *Pure Immanence: Essays on a Life*, trans. Anne Boyman (New York: Zone Books)

—— (2004), 'Bergson's Conception of Difference', in his *Desert Islands and Other Texts, 1953–1974*, ed. David Lapoujade and trans. Michael Taorima (Los Angeles, Calif.: Semiotext(e))

—— (2006a), *Nietzsche and Philosophy*, trans. Hugh Tomlinson (London: Continuum)

(2006b), *Foucault*, trans. Sean Hand (London: Continuum)
Deleuze, Gilles, and Félix Guattari (1987), *Capitalism and Schizophrenia*, Vol. 2: *A Thousand Plateaus*, trans. Brian Massumi (London: Continuum)
(1994), *What Is Philosophy?*, trans. Hugh Tomlinson and Graham Burchill (London: Verso)
Deleuze, Gilles, and Claire Parnet (1987), *Dialogues*, trans. Hugh Tomlinson and Barbara Habberjam (New York: Columbia University Press)
Derrida, Jacques (1973), *Speech and Phenomena: Introduction to the Problem of Signs in Husserl's Phenomenology*, in his *Speech and Phenomena and Other Essays on Husserl's Theory of Signs*, trans. David B. Allison (Evanston, Ill.: Northwestern University Press)
(1976), *Of Grammatology*, trans. Gayatri Chakravorty Spivak (Baltimore, Md.: Johns Hopkins University Press)
(1978a), 'Cogito and the History of Madness', in his *Writing and Difference*, trans. and ed. Alan Bass (London: Routledge & Kegan Paul)
(1978b), 'Violence and Metaphysics: An Essay on the Thought of Emmanuel Levinas', in his *Writing and Difference*, trans. and ed. Alan Bass (London: Routledge & Kegan Paul)
(1978c), '"Genesis and Structure" and Phenomenology', in his *Writing and Difference*, trans. and ed. Alan Bass (London: Routledge & Kegan Paul)
(1978d), 'Structure, Sign and Play in the Discourse of the Human Sciences', in his *Writing and Difference*, trans. and ed. Alan Bass (London: Routledge & Kegan Paul)
(1982a), *'Différance'*, in his *Margins*, trans. and ed. Alan Bass (Brighton: Harvester Press)
(1982b), '*Ousia* and *Grammē*: Note on a Note from *Being and Time*', in his *Margins*, trans. and ed. Alan Bass (Brighton: Harvester Press)
(1982c), 'Form and Meaning: A Note on the Phenomenology of Language', in his *Margins*, trans. and ed. Alan Bass (Brighton: Harvester Press)
(1982d), 'White Mythology: Metaphor in the Text of Philosophy', in his *Margins*, trans. and ed. Alan Bass (Brighton: Harvester Press)
(1982e), 'Signature Event Context', in his *Margins*, trans. and ed. Alan Bass (Brighton: Harvester Press)
(1983), 'The Principle of Reason: The University in the Eyes of Its Pupils', in *Diacritics* 19
(1984), 'Interview with Richard Kearney', in Richard Kearney (ed.), *Dialogues with Contemporary Continental Thinkers: The Phenomenological Heritage* (Manchester: Manchester University Press)
(1986), *Memoires for Paul de Man*, trans. Cecile Lindsay and Jonathan Culler (New York: Columbia University Press)
(1987), *The Post Card: From Socrates to Freud and Beyond*, trans. Alan Bass (Chicago: University of Chicago Press)
(1988a), 'Limited Inc a b c ...', trans. Samuel Weber and reprinted in his *Limited Inc*, ed. Gerald Graff (Evanston, Ill.: Northwestern University Press)
(1988b), 'Letter to a Japanese Friend', trans. David Wood and Andrew Benjamin, in David Wood and Robert Bernasconi (eds), *Derrida and* Différance (Evanston, Ill.: Northwestern University Press)

(1999), 'Hospitality, Justice and Responsibility: A Dialogue with Jacques Derrida', in Richard Kearney and Mark Dooley (eds), *Questioning Ethics: Contemporary Debates in Philosophy* (London: Routledge)

(2001a), 'Response to Moore', in Simon Glendinning (ed.), *Arguing with Derrida* (Oxford: Blackwell)

(2001b), 'Response to Baldwin', in Simon Glendinning (ed.), *Arguing with Derrida* (Oxford: Blackwell)

(2002a), 'Implications: Interview with Henri Ronse', in his *Positions*, trans. Alan Bass, 2nd edn (London: Continuum)

(2002b), 'Semiology and Grammatology: Interview with Julia Kristeva', in his *Positions*, trans. Alan Bass, 2nd edn (London: Continuum)

(2002c), 'Positions: Interview with Jean-Louis Houdebine and Guy Scarpetta', in his *Positions*, trans. Alan Bass, 2nd edn (London: Continuum)

(2004), 'Following Theory', in Michael Payne and John Schad (eds), *Life.After. Theory* (London: Continuum)

Derrida, Jacques, et al. (1988), 'The Original Discussion of "*Différance*"', trans. David Wood, Sarah Richmond, and Malcolm Bernard, in David Wood and Richard Bernasconi (eds), *Derrida and* Différance (Evanston, Ill.: Northwestern University Press)

Descartes, René (1984a), *Meditations on First Philosophy*, in *The Philosophical Writings of Descartes*, Vol. 2, trans. John Cottingham, Robert Stoothoff, and Dugald Murdoch (Cambridge: Cambridge University Press)

(1984b), *Replies*, in *Objections and Replies*, in *The Philosophical Writings of Descartes*, Vol. 2, trans. John Cottingham, Robert Stoothoff, and Dugald Murdoch (Cambridge: Cambridge University Press)

(1985a), *Rules for the Direction of the Mind*, in *The Philosophical Writings of Descartes*, Vol. 1, trans. John Cottingham, Robert Stoothoff, and Dugald Murdoch (Cambridge: Cambridge University Press)

(1985b), *Discourse on the Method of Rightly Conducting One's Reason and Seeking the Truth in the Sciences*, in *The Philosophical Writings of Descartes*, Vol. 1, trans. John Cottingham, Robert Stoothoff, and Dugald Murdoch (Cambridge: Cambridge University Press)

(1985c), *Principles of Philosophy*, in *The Philosophical Writings of Descartes*, Vol. 1, trans. John Cottingham, Robert Stoothoff, and Dugald Murdoch (Cambridge: Cambridge University Press)

(1985d), 'The Passions of the Soul', in *The Philosophical Writings of Descartes*, Vol. 1, trans. John Cottingham, Robert Stoothoff, and Dugald Murdoch (Cambridge: Cambridge University Press)

(1991), *The Philosophical Writings of Descartes*, Vol. 3: *The Correspondence*, trans. John Cottingham, Robert Stoothoff, Dugald Murdoch, and Anthony Kenny (Cambridge: Cambridge University Press)

Dews, Peter (2008), *The Idea of Evil* (Oxford: Blackwell)

Diamond, Cora (1988), 'Losing Your Concepts', *Ethics* 98

(1991a), 'Wittgenstein and Metaphysics', in her *The Realistic Spirit: Wittgenstein, Philosophy, and the Mind* (Cambridge, Mass.: MIT Press)

(1991b), 'Frege and Nonsense', reprinted in her *The Realistic Spirit: Wittgenstein, Philosophy, and the Mind* (Cambridge, Mass.: MIT Press)

(1991c), 'What Nonsense Might Be', reprinted in her *The Realistic Spirit: Wittgenstein, Philosophy, and the Mind* (Cambridge, Mass.: MIT Press)

(1991d), 'What Does a Concept-Script Do?', reprinted in her *The Realistic Spirit: Wittgenstein, Philosophy, and the Mind* (Cambridge, Mass.: MIT Press)

(1991e), 'Throwing Away the Ladder: How to Read the *Tractatus*', reprinted in her *The Realistic Spirit: Wittgenstein, Philosophy, and the Mind* (Cambridge, Mass.: MIT Press)

(1993), 'Seeking the Logical Basis of Metaphysics', the Alfred North Whitehead lectures

(2000), 'Ethics, Imagination and the Method of Wittgenstein's *Tractatus*', in Alice Crary and Rupert Read (eds), *The New Wittgenstein* (London: Routledge)

(2004), 'Saying and Showing: An Example from Anscombe', in Barry Stocker (ed.), *Post-Analytic* Tractatus (Aldershot: Ashgate)

(2011), '"We Can't Whistle It Either": Legend and Reality', *European Journal of Philosophy* 19

Dostoevsky, Fyodor (1982), *The Brothers Karamazov*, trans. David Magarshack (Harmondsworth: Penguin)

Dreben, Burton S. (2004), 'Quine on Quine', in *The Cambridge Companion to Quine* (Cambridge: Cambridge University Press)

Dreyfus, Hubert L. (1970), '*Sinn* and Intentional Object', in Robert C. Solomon (ed.), *Phenomenology and Existentialism* (New York: Harper & Row)

(1991), *Being-in-the-World: A Commentary on Heidegger's* Being and Time, *Division I* (Cambridge, Mass.: MIT Press)

Duffy, Simon (2006), *The Logic of Expression: Quality, Quantity and Intensity in Spinoza, Hegel and Deleuze* (Aldershot: Ashgate)

Duhem, Pierre (1991), *The Aim and Structure of Physical Theory*, trans. Philip P. Wiener (Princeton, N.J.: Princeton University Press)

Dummett, Michael (1978a), 'Preface', in his *Truth and Other Enigmas* (Cambridge, Mass.: Harvard University Press)

(1978b), 'Truth', reprinted in his *Truth and Other Enigmas* (Cambridge, Mass.: Harvard University Press)

(1978c), 'Frege's Philosophy', reprinted in his *Truth and Other Enigmas* (Cambridge, Mass.: Harvard University Press)

(1978d), 'Frege's Distinction Between Sense and Reference', reprinted in his *Truth and Other Enigmas* (Cambridge, Mass.: Harvard University Press)

(1978e), 'Wittgenstein's Philosophy of Mathematics', reprinted in his *Truth and Other Enigmas* (Cambridge, Mass.: Harvard University Press)

(1978f), 'The Philosophical Significance of Gödel's Theorem', reprinted in his *Truth and Other Enigmas* (Cambridge, Mass.: Harvard University Press)

(1978g), 'The Philosophical Basis of Intuitionistic Logic', reprinted in his *Truth and Other Enigmas* (Cambridge, Mass.: Harvard University Press)

(1978h), 'Wang's Paradox', reprinted in his *Truth and Other Enigmas* (Cambridge, Mass.: Harvard University Press)

(1978i), 'Is Logic Empirical?', reprinted in his *Truth and Other Enigmas* (Cambridge, Mass.: Harvard University Press)

(1978j), 'The Justification of Deduction', reprinted in his *Truth and Other Enigmas* (Cambridge, Mass.: Harvard University Press)

(1978k), 'The Reality of the Past', reprinted in his *Truth and Other Enigmas* (Cambridge, Mass.: Harvard University Press)

(1978l), 'The Significance of Quine's Indeterminacy Thesis', reprinted in his *Truth and Other Enigmas* (Cambridge, Mass.: Harvard University Press)

(1978m), 'Can Analytical Philosophy Be Systematic, and Ought It to Be?', reprinted in his *Truth and Other Enigmas* (Cambridge, Mass.: Harvard University Press)

(1981a), *Frege: Philosophy of Language*, 2nd edn (London: Duckworth)

(1981b), *The Interpretation of Frege's Philosophy* (London: Duckworth)

(1991a), *Frege: Philosophy of Mathematics* (London: Duckworth)

(1991b), *The Logical Basis of Metaphysics* (London: Duckworth)

(1991c), 'Frege and the Paradox of Analysis', in his *Frege and Other Philosophers* (Oxford: Oxford University Press)

(1991d), 'Frege as a Realist', reprinted in his *Frege and Other Philosophers* (Oxford: Oxford University Press)

(1991e), 'Objectivity and Reality in Lotze and Frege', reprinted in his *Frege and Other Philosophers* (Oxford: Oxford University Press)

(1991f), 'Frege and Kant on Geometry', reprinted in his *Frege and Other Philosophers* (Oxford: Oxford University Press)

(1991g), 'Frege and Wittgenstein', reprinted in his *Frege and Other Philosophers* (Oxford: Oxford University Press)

(1991h), 'Frege's Myth of the Third Realm', in his *Frege and Other Philosophers* (Oxford: Oxford University Press)

(1991i), 'Thought and Perception: The Views of Two Philosophical Innovators', reprinted in his *Frege and Other Philosophers* (Oxford: Oxford University Press)

(1991j), 'More About Thoughts', reprinted in his *Frege and Other Philosophers* (Oxford: Oxford University Press)

(1992), 'The Metaphysics of Verificationism', in L.E. Hahn (ed.), *The Philosophy of A.J. Ayer* (La Salle, Ill.: Open Court)

(1993a), *Origins of Analytical Philosophy* (London: Duckworth)

(1993b), 'What Is a Theory of Meaning? (II)', reprinted in his *The Seas of Language* (Oxford: Oxford University Press)

(1993c), 'What Do I Know When I Know a Language?', reprinted in his *The Seas of Language* (Oxford: Oxford University Press)

(1993d), 'Frege and Husserl on Reference', in his *The Seas of Language* (Oxford: Oxford University Press)

(1993e), 'What Is Mathematics About?', in his *The Seas of Language* (Oxford: Oxford University Press)

(1993f), 'Realism and Anti-Realism', in his *The Seas of Language* (Oxford: Oxford University Press)

(1994), 'Reply to Pears', in Brian McGuiness and Gianluigi Oliveri (eds), *The Philosophy of Michael Dummett* (Dordrecht: Kluwer Academic Publishers)

(2000), *Elements of Intuitionism*, 2nd edn (Oxford: Oxford University Press)

(2001a), 'Victor's Error', *Analysis* 61

(2001b), 'Preface', in Edmund Husserl, *Logical Investigations*, trans. J.N. Findlay and ed. Dermot Moran (London: Routledge)

(2004), *Truth and the Past* (New York: Columbia University Press)

(2006), *Thought and Reality* (Oxford: Oxford University Press)

(2007a), 'Intellectual Autobiography', in R.E. Auxier and L.E. Hahn (eds), *The Philosophy of Michael Dummett* (Chicago and La Salle, Ill.: Open Court)

(2007b), 'Reply to Brian McGuiness', in R.E. Auxier and L.E. Hahn (eds), *The Philosophy of Michael Dummett* (Chicago and La Salle, Ill.: Open Court)

(2007c), 'Reply to Jan Dejnožka', in R.E. Auxier and L.E. Hahn (eds), *The Philosophy of Michael Dummett* (Chicago and La Salle, Ill.: Open Court)

(2007d), 'Reply to James W. Allard', in R.E. Auxier and L.E. Hahn (eds), *The Philosophy of Michael Dummett* (Chicago and La Salle, Ill.: Open Court)

(2007e), 'Reply to John Campbell', in R.E. Auxier and L.E. Hahn (eds), *The Philosophy of Michael Dummett* (Chicago and La Salle, Ill.: Open Court)

(2007f), 'Reply to John McDowell', in R.E. Auxier and L.E. Hahn (eds), *The Philosophy of Michael Dummett* (Chicago and La Salle, Ill.: Open Court)

(2007g), 'Reply to Ian Rumfitt', in R.E. Auxier and L.E. Hahn (eds), *The Philosophy of Michael Dummett* (Chicago and La Salle, Ill.: Open Court)

(2007h), 'Reply to Andrew Beards', in R.E. Auxier and L.E. Hahn (eds), *The Philosophy of Michael Dummett* (Chicago and La Salle, Ill.: Open Court)

(2009), 'Fitch's Paradox of Knowability', in Joe Salerno (ed.), *New Essays on the Knowability Paradox* (Oxford: Oxford University Press)

(2010), *The Nature and Future of Philosophy* (New York: Columbia University Press)

Duns Scotus, John (1987), *Philosophical Writings*, trans. Allan Wolter (Indianapolis, Ind.: Hackett Publishing)

Edwards, Jeffrey (2000), 'Spinozism, Freedom, and Transcendental Dynamics in Kant's Final System of Transcendental Idealism', in Sally Sedgwick (ed.), *The Reception of Kant's Critical Philosophy: Fichte, Schelling, and Hegel* (Cambridge: Cambridge University Press)

Einstein, Albert (1920), *Relativity: The Special and the General Theory*, trans. Robert W. Lawson (London: Methuen)

Emad, Parvis, and Kenneth Maly (1999), 'Translators' Foreword', in Martin Heidegger, *Contributions to Philosophy (From Enowning)*, trans. Parvis Emad and Kenneth Maly (Bloomington: Indiana University Press)

Engelmann, Paul (1967), *Letters from Ludwig Wittgenstein, with a Memoir*, ed. B.F. McGuiness and trans. L. Furtmüller (Oxford: Blackwell)

Engstrom, Stephen (1996), 'Happiness and the Highest Good in Aristotle and Kant', in Stephen Engstrom and Jennifer Whiting (eds), *Aristotle, Kant and the Stoics* (Cambridge: Cambridge University Press)

Euclid (2002), *Elements*, ed. Dana Densmore and trans. Thomas L. Heath (Santa Fe: Green Lion Press)

Evans, Gareth (1982), *The Varieties of Reference*, ed. John McDowell (Oxford: Oxford University Press)

Everson, Stephen (1988), 'The Difference Between Thinking and Feeling', *Mind* 97

Fausto-Sterling, Anne (2000), *Sexing the Body: Gender, Politics and the Construction of Sexuality* (New York: Basic Books)

Fichte, J.G. (1956), *The Vocation of Man*, ed. and trans. Roderick M. Chisholm (Indianapolis, Ind.: Bobbs-Merrill)

(1964–), *Gesamtausgabe der Bayerischen Akademie der Wissenschaften*, ed. Reinhard Lauth, Hans Jacobs, and Hans Gliwitzky (Stuttgart-Bad Cannstatt: Friedrich Frommann)

(1982), *The Science of Knowledge*, ed. and trans. Peter Heath and John Lachs (Cambridge: Cambridge University Press)

(1992), *Foundations of Transcendental Philosophy: (Wissenschaftslehre) Nova Methodo (1796/99)*, trans. and ed. Daniel Breazeale (Ithaca, N.Y.: Cornell University Press)

Field, Hartry H. (1980), *Science Without Numbers: A Defence of Nominalism* (Princeton, N.J.: Princeton University Press)

Findlay, J.N. (1958), *Hegel: A Re-examination* (London: George Allen & Unwin)

Fine, Kit (1975), 'Vagueness, Truth and Logic', *Synthese* 30

Fitch, F.B. (1963), 'A Logical Analysis of Some Value Concepts', *Journal of Symbolic Logic* 28

Floyd, Juliet (2000), 'Wittgenstein, Mathematics and Philosophy', in Alice Crary and Rupert Read (eds), *The New Wittgenstein* (London: Routledge)

Fogelin, Robert J. (1987), *Wittgenstein*, 2nd edn (London: Routledge & Kegan Paul)

Føllesdal, Dagfinn (1958), *Husserl und Frege: Ein Beitrag zur Beleuchtung der Entstehung der Phänomenologischen Philosophie* (Oslo: Aschehoug)

(1969), 'Husserl's Notion of Noema', *Journal of Philosophy* 66

Forster, Michael N. (2004), *Wittgenstein on the Arbitrariness of Grammar* (Princeton, N.J.: Princeton University Press)

Foucault, Michel (1972), *The Archeology of Knowledge*, trans. Alan Sheridan (London: Tavistock Publications)

(1982), 'The Order of Discourse', trans. Ian McLeod, in Robert J.C. Young (ed.), *Untying the Text: A Poststructuralist Reader* (London: Routledge & Kegan Paul)

(1998), 'Theatrum Philosophicum', trans. D.F. Brouchard and Sherry Simon, in his *Aesthetics, Method, and Epistemology: Essential Works of Foucault, 1954–1984*, ed. J.D. Faubion (Harmondsworth: Penguin)

Frank, Manfred (1992), 'Is Self-Consciousness a Case of *Présence à Soi*? Towards a Meta-Critique of the Recent French Critique of Metaphysics', in David Wood (ed.), *Derrida: A Critical Reader* (Oxford: Blackwell)

Franklin, James (1993), 'Heads of Pins', *Australian Mathematical Society Gazette* 20

Frede, Dorothea (2006), 'The Question of Being: Heidegger's Project', in Charles B. Guignon (ed.), *The Cambridge Companion to Heidegger*, 2nd edn (Cambridge: Cambridge University Press)

Frege, Gottlob (1964), *The Basic Laws of Arithmetic: Exposition of the System*, trans. and ed. Montgomery Furth (Berkeley and Los Angeles: University of California Press)

(1967), Begriffsschrift: *A Formula Language, Modeled upon That of Arithmetic, for Pure Thought*, trans. Stefan Bauer-Mengelberg, in Jean van Heijenoort (ed.), *From Frege to Gödel: A Source Book in Mathematical Logic, 1879–1931* (Cambridge, Mass.: Harvard University Press)

(1979), '[Diary Entries on the Concept of Numbers: 23.3.1924–25.3.1924]', in his *Posthumous Writings*, ed. Hans Hermes, Friedrich Kambartel, and Friedrich Kaulbach and trans. Peter Long and Roger White (Oxford: Blackwell)

(1980), *The Foundations of Arithmetic: A Logico-Mathematical Enquiry into the Concept of Number*, trans. J.L. Austin, 2nd edn (Oxford: Blackwell)

(1984a), 'On Formal Theories of Arithmetic', trans. E.-H.W. Kluge, in his *Collected Papers on Mathematics, Logic, and Philosophy*, ed. Brian McGuiness (Oxford: Blackwell)

(1984b), 'Review of E.G. Husserl, *Philosophie der Arithmetik* I', trans. Hans Kaal, in his *Collected Papers on Mathematics, Logic, and Philosophy*, ed. Brian McGuiness (Oxford: Blackwell)

(1984c), 'On the Foundations of Geometry: Second Series', trans. E.-H.W. Kluge, in his *Collected Papers on Mathematics, Logic, and Philosophy*, ed. Brian McGuiness (Oxford: Blackwell)

(1997a), 'Function and Concept', trans. Peter Geach, reprinted in his *The Frege Reader*, ed. Michael Beaney (Oxford: Blackwell)

(1997b), 'Letter to Husserl, 24.5.1891', trans. Hans Kaal, an extract reprinted in his *The Frege Reader*, ed. Michael Beaney (Oxford: Blackwell)

(1997c), 'On *Sinn* and *Bedeutung*', trans. Max Black, reprinted with revisions in his *The Frege Reader*, ed. Michael Beaney (Oxford: Blackwell)

(1997d), '[Comments on *Sinn* and *Bedeutung*]', trans. Peter Long and Roger White, reprinted in his *The Frege Reader*, ed. Michael Beaney (Oxford: Blackwell)

(1997e), 'On Concept and Object', trans. Peter Geach, reprinted with revisions in his *The Frege Reader*, ed. Michael Beaney (Oxford: Blackwell)

(1997f), 'Review of E.G. Husserl, *Philosophie der Arithmetik* I', trans. Hans Kaal, an extract reprinted in his *The Frege Reader*, ed. Michael Beaney (Oxford: Blackwell)

(1997g), 'Logic', trans. Peter Long and Roger White, an extract reprinted with revisions in his *The Frege Reader*, ed. Michael Beaney (Oxford: Blackwell)

(1997h), 'Letter to Russell, 22.6.1902', trans. Hans Kaal, an extract reprinted in his *The Frege Reader*, ed. Michael Beaney (Oxford: Blackwell)

(1997i), 'A Brief Survey of My Logical Doctrines', trans. Peter Long and Roger White, an extract reprinted in his *The Frege Reader*, ed. Michael Beaney (Oxford: Blackwell)

(1997j), 'Letter to Jourdain, Jan. 1914', trans. Hans Kaal, an extract reprinted in his *The Frege Reader*, ed. Michael Beaney (Oxford: Blackwell)

(1997k), 'My Basic Logical Insights', trans. Peter Long and Roger White, reprinted in his *The Frege Reader*, ed. Michael Beaney (Oxford: Blackwell)

(1997l), 'Thought', trans. Peter Geach and R.H. Stoothoff, reprinted in his *The Frege Reader*, ed. Michael Beaney (Oxford: Blackwell)

(1997m), '[Notes for Ludwig Darmstaedter]', trans. Peter Long and Roger White, reprinted in his *The Frege Reader*, ed. Michael Beaney (Oxford: Blackwell)

(1997n), 'Sources of Knowledge of Mathematics and the Mathematical Natural Sciences', trans. Peter Long and Roger White, an extract reprinted in his *The Frege Reader*, ed. Michael Beaney (Oxford: Blackwell)

(1997o), 'Numbers and Arithmetic', trans. Peter Long and Roger White, reprinted in his *The Frege Reader*, ed. Michael Beaney (Oxford: Blackwell)

(2003), 'Frege's Letters to Wittgenstein About the *Tractatus*', trans. R.H. Schmitt, *The Bertrand Russell Society Quarterly* 120

Friedman, Michael (2000), *A Parting of the Ways: Carnap, Cassirer, and Heidegger* (Chicago: Open Court)

(2002), 'Carnap, Cassirer, and Heidegger: The Davos Disputation and Twentieth Century Philosophy', *European Journal of Philosophy* 10

(2006), 'Carnap and Quine: Twentieth-Century Echoes of Kant and Hume', *Philosophical Topics* 34

Gabriel, Gottfried (2007), 'Carnap and Frege', in Michael Friedman and Richard Creath (eds), *The Cambridge Companion to Carnap* (Cambridge: Cambridge University Press)

Gadamer, Hans-Georg (2004), *Truth and Method*, revised trans. Joel Weinsheimer and Donald G. Marshall (London: Continuum)

Galileo Galilei (1967), *Dialogue Concerning the Two Chief World Systems, Ptolemaic and Copernican*, trans. Stillman Drake (Berkeley: University of California Press)

Gardner, Sebastian (1999), *Kant and the Critique of Pure Reason* (London: Routledge)

Garrett, Don (2009), 'Spinoza on the Essence of the Human Body and the Part of the Mind That Is Eternal', in Olli Koistinen (ed.), *The Cambridge Companion to Spinoza's Ethics* (Cambridge: Cambridge University Press)

Garver, Newton (1994), *This Complicated Form of Life: Essays on Wittgenstein* (La Salle, Ill.: Open Court)

(1996), 'Philosophy as Grammar', in Hans D. Sluga and David G. Stern (eds), *The Cambridge Companion to Wittgenstein* (Cambridge: Cambridge University Press)

Gatens, Moira (1999), *Collective Imaginings: Spinoza, Past and Present* (London: Routledge)

Geach, P.T. (1972), 'Identity', reprinted in his *Logic Matters* (Oxford: Blackwell)

(1976), 'Saying and Showing in Frege and Wittgenstein', *Acta Philosophica Fennica* 28, a special issue entitled *Essays on Wittgenstein in Honour of G.H. von Wright*, ed. Jaakko Hintikka

Gemes, Ken (2009), 'Janaway on Perspectivism', *European Journal of Philosophy* 17

George, Alexander (2000), 'On Washing the Fur Without Wetting It: Quine, Carnap, and Analyticity', *Mind* 109

Gibson, Ian (2007), 'Time, Objects, and Identity', D.Phil. thesis, Oxford University

Gibson, Roger F. (1986), 'Translation, Physics, and Facts of the Matter', in L.E. Hahn and P.A. Schilpp (eds), *The Philosophy of W.V. Quine* (La Salle, Ill.: Open Court)

(1995), 'Quine on the Naturalizing of Epistemology', in Paolo Leonardi and Marco Santambrogio (eds), *On Quine: New Essays* (Cambridge: Cambridge University Press)

Gilbert, Neal W. (1960), *Renaissance Concepts of Method* (New York: Columbia University Press)

Glendinning, Simon (2001), 'Inheriting "Philosophy": The Case of Austin and Derrida Revisited', in Simon Glendinning (ed.), *Arguing with Derrida* (Oxford: Blackwell)

(2006), *The Idea of Continental Philosophy: A Philosophical Chronicle* (Edinburgh: Edinburgh University Press)

(2007), *In the Name of Phenomenology* (London: Routledge)

Gödel, Kurt (1983), 'What Is Cantor's Continuum Problem?', in Paul Benacerraf and Hilary Putnam (eds), *Philosophy of Mathematics: Selected Readings*, 2nd edn (Cambridge: Cambridge University Press)

Goethe, Johann Wolfgang von (1893), 'Polarität', in *Goethes Werke* (Böhlau: Weimar)

Goldfarb, Warren (1997), 'Metaphysics and Nonsense: On Cora Diamond's *The Realistic Spirit*', *Journal of Philosophical Research* 22

Goodman, Nelson (1963), 'The Significance of *Der Logische Aufbau der Welt*', in P.A. Schilpp (ed.), *The Philosophy of Rudolf Carnap* (La Salle, Ill.: Open Court) (1977), *The Structure of Appearance*, 3rd edn (Dordrecht: Kluwer Academic Publishers)

Goodman, Nelson, and W.V. Quine (1947), 'Steps Toward a Constructive Nominalism', *Journal of Symbolic Logic* 12

Green, Karen (2001), *Dummett: Philosophy of Language* (Cambridge: Polity Press)

Grice, H.P., and P.F. Strawson (1956), 'In Defence of a Dogma', *Philosophical Review* 65

Guyer, Paul (1987), *Kant and the Claims of Knowledge* (Cambridge: Cambridge University Press) (2000), 'The Unity of Nature and Freedom: Kant's Conception of the System of Philosophy', in Sally Sedgwick (ed.), *The Reception of Kant's Critical Philosophy: Fichte, Schelling, and Hegel* (Cambridge: Cambridge University Press)

Hacker, P.M.S. (1986), *Insight and Illusion Themes in the Philosophy of Wittgenstein* (Oxford: Oxford University Press) (1996), *Wittgenstein's Place in Twentieth-Century Analytic Philosophy* (Oxford: Blackwell) (2000), 'Was He Trying to Whistle It?', in Alice Crary and Rupert Read (eds), *The New Wittgenstein* (London: Routledge) (2001a), 'Frege and the Early Wittgenstein', in his *Wittgenstein: Connections and Controversies* (Oxford: Oxford University Press) (2001b), 'On Strawson's Rehabilitation of Metaphysics', reprinted in his *Wittgenstein: Connections and Controversies* (Oxford: Oxford University Press) (2007), 'Gordon Baker's Late Interpretation of Wittgenstein', in Guy Kahane, Edward Kanterian, and Oskari Kuusela (eds), *Wittgenstein and His Interpreters: Essays in Memory of Gordon Baker* (Oxford: Blackwell) (2009), 'Philosophy: A Contribution, Not to Human Knowledge, but to Human Understanding', in Anthony O'Hear (ed.), *Conceptions of Philosophy* (Cambridge: Cambridge University Press)

Hale, Bob (2001), 'A Response to Potter and Smiley: Abstraction by Recarving', *Proceedings of the Aristotelian Society* 101

Hallett, Michael (1984), *Cantorian Set Theory and Limitation of Size* (Oxford: Oxford University Press)

Hampshire, Stuart (1962), *Spinoza*, revised edn (Harmondsworth: Penguin)

Hanna, Robert (1996), 'From an Ontological Point of View: Hegel's Critique of the Common Logic', in Jon Stewart (ed.), *The Hegel Myths and Legends* (Evanston, Ill.: Northwestern University Press) (2006), *Rationality and Logic* (Cambridge, Mass.: MIT Press)

Han-Pile, Béatrice (2005), 'Early Heidegger's Appropriation of Kant', in Hubert L. Dreyfus and Mark A. Wrathall (eds), *A Companion to Heidegger* (Oxford: Blackwell)

(2006), 'Nietzsche's Metaphysics in the *Birth of Tragedy'*, *European Journal of Philosophy* 14

(2009), 'Transcendental Aspects, Ontological Commitments and Naturalistic Elements in Nietzsche's Thought', *Inquiry* 52

Hardt, Michael (1993), *Gilles Deleuze: An Apprenticeship in Philosophy* (Minneapolis: University of Minnesota Press)

Hardy, G.H. (1929), 'Mathematical Proof', *Mind* 38

Harman, Gilbert (1967), 'Quine on Meaning and Existence, I: The Death of Meaning', *The Review of Metaphysics* 21

Harrison, Ross (1974), *On What There Must Be* (Oxford: Oxford University Press)

Hartmann, Klaus (1972), 'Hegel: A Non-Metaphysical View', in Alasdair MacIntyre (ed.), *Hegel: A Collection of Critical Essays* (New York: Doubleday)

Hatfield, Gary (2002), *Descartes and the Meditations* (London: Routledge)

Hawking, Stephen W. (1988), *A Brief History of Time: From the Big Bang to Black Holes* (London: Bantam Press)

Hegel, G.W.F. (1942), *Philosophy of Right*, trans. T.M. Knox (Oxford: Oxford University Press)

(1969), *Science of Logic*, trans. A.V. Miller (London: George Allen & Unwin)

(1970), 'Philosophy of Nature', i.e. Part Two of *The Encyclopedia of the Philosophical Sciences*, trans. M.J. Petry, Vol. 1 (London: George Allen & Unwin)

(1971), 'Philosophy of Mind', i.e. Part Three of *The Encyclopedia of the Philosophical Sciences*, trans. William Wallace and A.V. Miller (Oxford: Oxford University Press)

(1975a), 'Logic', i.e. Part One of *The Encyclopedia of the Philosophical Sciences*, trans. William Wallace (Oxford: Oxford University Press)

(1975b), *Lectures on the Philosophy of World History; Introduction: Reason in History*, trans. H.B. Nisbet (Cambridge: Cambridge University Press)

(1977a), *The Difference Between Fichte's and Schelling's System of Philosophy*, trans. and ed. H.S. Harris and W. Cerf (Albany: State University of New York Press)

(1977b), *Faith and Knowledge or the Reflective Philosophy of Subjectivity*, trans. W. Cerf and H.S. Harris (Albany: State University of New York Press)

(1979), *Phenomenology of Spirit*, trans. A.V. Miller (Oxford: Oxford University Press)

(1984), *Lectures on the Philosophy of Religion*, Vol. 1: *Introduction and the Concept of Religion*, ed. and trans. Peter C. Hodgson (Berkeley and Los Angeles: University of California Press)

(1988), *Lectures on the Philosophy of Religion*, Vol. 3: *The Consummate Religion*, ed. and trans. Peter C. Hodgson (Berkeley and Los Angeles: University of California Press)

(1995), *Lectures on the History of Philosophy*, Vol. 3: *Medieval and Modern Philosophy*, trans. E.S. Haldane and Frances H. Simson (Lincoln: University of Nebraska Press)

Heidegger, Martin (1959), *An Introduction to Metaphysics*, trans. Ralph Manheim (New Haven, Conn.: Yale University Press)

(1962a), *Being and Time*, trans. John Macquarrie and Edward Robinson (Oxford: Blackwell)

(1962b), *Kant and the Problem of Metaphysics*, trans. James S. Churchill (Bloomington: Indiana University Press)

(1966), 'Conversation on a Country Path About Thinking', in his *Discourse on Thinking*, trans. John M. Anderson and E. Hans Freund (San Francisco, Calif.: Harper & Row)

(1968a), *What Is Philosophy?*, trans. Jean T. Wilde and William Kluback (London: Vision Press)

(1968b), *What Is Called Thinking?*, trans. J. Glenn Gray (San Francisco, Calif.: Harper & Row)

(1969a), 'The Principle of Identity', in his *Identity and Difference*, trans. Joan Stambaugh (Chicago: University of Chicago Press)

(1969b), 'The Onto-Theo-Logical Constitution of Metaphysics', in his *Identity and Difference*, trans. Joan Stambaugh (Chicago: University of Chicago Press)

(1972), 'Time and Being', in his *On Time and Being*, trans. Joan Stambaugh (San Francisco, Calif.: Harper & Row)

(1977), 'The Word of Nietzsche: "God Is Dead"', in his *The Question Concerning Technology and Other Essays*, trans. William Lovitt (San Francisco, Calif.: Harper & Row)

(1979), *Nietzsche*, Vol. 1: *The Will to Power as Art*, trans. David Farrell Krell (San Francisco, Calif.: Harper & Row)

(1982a), *Nietzsche*, Vol. 4: *Nihilism*, trans. David Farrell Krell (San Francisco, Calif.: Harper & Row)

(1982b), *The Basic Problems of Phenomenology*, trans. Albert Hofstadter (Bloomington: Indiana University Press)

(1984a), *Nietzsche*, Vol. 2: *The Eternal Recurrence of the Same*, trans. David Farrell Krell (San Francisco, Calif.: Harper & Row)

(1984b), 'The Anaximander Fragment', in his *Early Greek Thinking: The Dawn of Western Philosophy*, trans. David Farrell Krell and Frank A. Capuzzi (San Francisco, Calif.: Harper & Row)

(1984c), 'Logos (Heraclitus, Fragment B 50)', in his *Early Greek Thinking: The Dawn of Western Philosophy*, trans. David Farrell Krell and Frank A. Capuzzi (San Francisco, Calif.: Harper & Row)

(1985), *History of the Concept of Time: Prolegomena*, trans. Theodore Kisiel (Bloomington: Indiana University Press)

(1987), *Nietzsche*, Vol. 3: *The Will to Power as Knowledge and Metaphysics* (San Francisco, Calif.: Harper & Row)

(1991), *The Principle of Reason*, trans. Reginald Lilly (Bloomington: Indiana University Press)

(1992), *Metaphysical Foundations of Logic (Studies in Phenomenology and Existential Philosophy)*, trans. Martin Heim (Bloomington: Indiana University Press)

(1993a), 'What Is Metaphysics?', trans. David Farrell Krell, in his *Basic Writings from Being and Time (1927) to The Task of Thinking (1964)*, revised edn, ed. David Farrell Krell (London: Routledge)

(1993b), 'On the Essence of Truth', trans. John Sallis, in his *Basic Writings from Being and Time (1927) to The Task of Thinking (1964)*, revised edn, ed. David Farrell Krell (London: Routledge)

(1993c), 'Letter on Humanism', trans. Frank A. Capuzzi and J. Glenn Gray, in his *Basic Writings from* Being and Time *(1927) to* The Task of Thinking *(1964)*, revised edn, ed. David Farrell Krell (London: Routledge)

(1993d), 'The Question Concerning Technology', trans. William Lovitt and David Farrell Krell, in his *Basic Writings from* Being and Time *(1927) to* The Task of Thinking *(1964)*, revised edn, ed. David Farrell Krell (London: Routledge)

(1993e), 'The End of Philosophy and the Task of Thinking', trans. Joan Stambaugh, in his *Basic Writings from* Being and Time *(1927) to* The Task of Thinking *(1964)*, revised edn, ed. David Farrell Krell (London: Routledge)

(1993f), *Basic Concepts*, trans. Gary E. Aylesworth (Bloomington: Indiana University Press)

(1994), *Basic Questions of Philosophy: Selected 'Problems' of 'Logic'*, trans. Richard Rojcewicz and André Schuwer (Bloomington: Indiana University Press)

(1998), 'On the Question of Being', trans. William McNeill in his *Pathmarks*, ed. William McNeill (Cambridge: Cambridge University Press)

(1999), *Contributions to Philosophy (From Enowning)*, trans. Parvis Emad and Kenneth Maly (Bloomington: Indiana University Press)

(2003a), 'Metaphysics as History of Being', in his *The End of Philosophy*, trans. Joan Stambaugh (Chicago: University of Chicago Press)

(2003b), 'Overcoming Metaphysics', in his *The End of Philosophy*, trans. Joan Stambaugh (Chicago: University of Chicago Press)

Hempel, Carl G. (1951), 'The Concept of Cognitive Significance: A Reconsideration', *Proceedings of the American Academy of Arts and Sciences* 80

(1959), 'The Empiricist Criterion of Meaning', reprinted in A.J. Ayer (ed.), *Logical Positivism* (Glencoe, Ill.: Free Press)

Hintikka, Jaakko (1969), 'On Kant's Notion of Intuition (Anschauung)', in Terence Penelhum and J.J. MacIntosh (eds), *The First Critique: Reflections on Kant's Critique of Pure Reason* (Belmont, Calif.: Wadsworth Publishing)

Hobson, Marian (1988), *Jacques Derrida: Opening Lines* (London: Routledge)

Hodge, Joanna (1995), *Heidegger and Ethics* (London: Routledge)

Hofstadter, Albert (1982), 'Translator's Appendix: A Note on the Da and the Dasein', in Martin Heidegger, *The Basic Problems of Phenomenology*, trans. Albert Hofstadter (Bloomington: Indiana University Press)

Hooker, Brad (ed.) (1996), *Truth in Ethics* (Oxford: Blackwell)

Hookway, Christopher (1988), *Quine: Language, Experience and Reality* (Cambridge: Polity Press)

(1996), 'Perspicuous Representations', in Robert L. Arrington and Hans-Johann Glock (eds), *Wittgenstein and Quine* (London: Routledge)

Hopkins, James (1982), 'Visual Geometry', reprinted in Ralph C.S. Walker (ed.), *Kant on Pure Reason* (Oxford: Oxford University Press)

Houlgate, Stephen (1986), *Hegel, Nietzsche and the Criticism of Metaphysics* (Cambridge: Cambridge University Press)

(2006), *The Opening of Hegel's Logic: From Being to Infinity* (West Lafayette, Ind.: Purdue University Press)

Hume, David (1741–1742), 'Of the Rise and Progress of the Arts and Sciences', in his *Essays Moral and Political* (Edinburgh: Kincaid)

(1975a), *An Enquiry Concerning Human Understanding*, in his *Enquiries Concerning Human Understanding and Concerning the Principles of Morals*, ed. L.A. Selby-Bigge, revised P.H. Nidditch, 3rd edn (Oxford: Oxford University Press)

(1975b), *An Enquiry Concerning the Principles of Morals*, in his *Enquiries Concerning Human Understanding and Concerning the principles of Morals*, ed. L.A. Selby-Bigge, revised P.H. Nidditch, 3rd edn (Oxford: Oxford University Press)

(1976), *The Natural History of Religion*, ed. A. Wayne Colver, in his *The Natural History of Religion and Dialogues Concerning Natural Religion*, ed. A. Wayne Colver and John Vladimir Price (Oxford: Oxford University Press)

(1978a), *A Treatise of Human Nature*, ed. L.A. Selby-Bigge, revised P.H. Nidditch, 2nd edn (Oxford: Oxford University Press)

(1978b), 'An Abstract of a Book Lately Published, Entituled, *A Treatise of Human Nature*, &c', in his *A Treatise of Human Nature*, ed. L.A. Selby-Bigge, revised P.H. Nidditch, 2nd edn (Oxford: Oxford University Press)

Husserl, Edmund (1950), *Husserliana – Edmund Husserl, Gesammelte Werke*, Vol. 3: *Ideen zu Einer Reinen Phänomenologie und Phänomenologischen Philosophie. Erste Buch: Allgemeine Einführung in die Reine Phänomenologie*, ed. Walter Biemel (The Hague: Nijhoff)

(1952), *Husserliana – Edmund Husserl, Gesammelte Werke*, Vol. 4: *Ideen zu Einer Reinen Phänomenologie und Phänomenologischen Philosophie. Zweites Buch: Phänomenologische Untersuchungen zur Konstitution*, ed. Walter Biemel (The Hague: Nijhoff)

(1959), *Husserliana – Edmund Husserl, Gesammelte Werke*, Vol. 8: *Erste Philosophie (1923–1924). Zweiter Teil: Theorie der Phänomenologischen Reduktion*, ed. Rudolf Boehm (The Hague: Nijhoff)

(1962), *Ideas: General Introduction to Pure Phenomenology*, trans. W.R. Boyce Gibson (New York: Collier)

(1964a), *The Phenomenology of Internal Time Consciousness*, ed. Martin Heidegger and trans. James S. Churchill (The Hague: Nijhoff)

(1964b), *The Idea of Phenomenology*, trans. W.P. Alston and G. Nakhnikian (The Hague: Nijhoff)

(1965), *Philosophy as Rigorous Science*, in his *Phenomenology and the Crisis of Philosophy*, trans. Quentin Lauer (New York: Harper & Row)

(1969), *Formal and Transcendental Logic*, trans. Dorion Cairns (The Hague: Nijhoff)

(1970), *The Crisis of European Sciences and Transcendental Phenomenology: An Introduction to Phenomenological Philosophy*, trans. David Carr (Evanston, Ill.: Northwestern University Press)

(1973a), *Husserliana – Edmund Husserl, Gesammelte Werke*, Vol. 13: *Zur Phänomenologie der Intersubjectivität. Texte aus dem Nachlaß, Erster Teil*, ed. Iso Kern (The Hague: Nijhoff)

(1973b), *Husserliana – Edmund Husserl, Gesammelte Werke*, Vol. 14: *Zur Phänomenologie der Intersubjectivität. Texte aus dem Nachlaß, Zweiter Teil*, ed. Iso Kern (The Hague: Nijhoff)

(1981a), 'Husserl's Inaugural Lecture at Freiburg im Breisgau', trans. Robert Welsh Jordan, in his *Husserl: Shorter Works*, ed. Peter McCormick and Frederick A. Elliston (Notre Dame, Ind.: University of Notre Dame Press)

(1981b), 'Phenomenology', an article for *Encyclopædia Britannica* (1927), revised trans. Richard E. Palmer, reprinted in his *Husserl: Shorter Works*, ed. Peter McCormick and Frederick A. Elliston (Notre Dame, Ind.: University of Notre Dame Press)

(1995), *Cartesian Meditations: An Introduction to Phenomenology*, trans. Dorion Cairns (Dordrecht: Kluwer Academic Publishers)

(1997), 'Phenomenology and Anthropology', trans. Thomas Sheehan and Richard E. Palmer, Appendix Three to his *Psychological and Transcendental Phenomenology and the Confrontation with Heidegger (1927–1931)*, ed. Thomas Sheehan and Richard E. Palmer (Dordrecht: Kluwer Academic Publishers)

(2001a), *Logical Investigations*, Vol. 1, trans. J.N. Findlay and ed. Dermot Moran (London: Routledge)

(2001b), *Logical Investigations*, Vol. 2, trans. J.N. Findlay and ed. Dermot Moran (London: Routledge)

(2002), 'Pure Phenomenology, Its Method, and Its Field of Investigation', trans. Robert Welsh Jordan, reprinted in Dermot Moran and Timothy Mooney (eds), *The Phenomenology Reader* (London: Routledge)

(2003), *Philosophy of Arithmetic: Psychological and Logical Investigations* in his *Philosophy of Arithmetic: Psychological and Logical Investigations with Supplementary Texts from 1887–1901*, trans. Dallas Willard (Dordrecht: Kluwer Academic Publishers)

(2006), *The Basic Problems of Phenomenology: From the Lectures, Winter Semester, 1910–1911*, trans. Ingo Farin and James G. Hart (Dordrecht: Springer)

Hylton, Peter (2004), 'Quine on Reference and Ontology', in Roger F. Gibson (ed.), *The Cambridge Companion to Quine* (Cambridge: Cambridge University Press)

(2007), *Quine* (London: Routledge)

Inwood, Michael (1983), *Hegel* (London: Routledge & Kegan Paul)

(1992), *A Hegel Dictionary* (Oxford: Blackwell)

(1997), *Heidegger* (Oxford: Oxford University Press)

(1999a), *A Heidegger Dictionary* (Oxford: Blackwell)

(1999b), 'Does the Nothing Noth?' in Anthony O'Hear (ed.), *German Philosophy Since Kant* (Cambridge: Cambridge University Press)

Isaacson, Daniel (2004), 'Quine and Logical Positivism', in Roger F. Gibson (ed.), *The Cambridge Companion to Quine* (Cambridge: Cambridge University Press)

Ishiguro, Hidé (1972), *Leibniz's Philosophy of Logic and Language* (London: Duckworth)

Jacobi, F.H. (1995), 'Concerning the Doctrine of Spinoza in Letters to Herr Moses Mendelssohn', in his *The Main Philosophical Writings and the Novel 'Allwill'*, ed. and trans. George di Giovanni (Kingston and Montreal: McGill-Queen's University Press)

James, Susan (1998), 'Reason, the Passions, and the Good Life' in Daniel Garber and Michael Ayers (eds), *The Cambridge History of Seventeenth Century Philosophy*, Vol. 2 (Cambridge: Cambridge University Press)

(2012), *Spinoza on Philosophy, Religion and Politics* (Oxford: Oxford University Press)

James, William (1978), *The Meaning of Truth*, ed. I.K. Skruoskelis (Cambridge, Mass.: Harvard University Press)

Janaway, Christopher (2009), 'Responses to Commentators', *European Journal of Philosophy* 17

Janik, Allan, and Stephen Toulmin (1973), *Wittgenstein's Vienna* (New York: Touchstone)

Johnston, Colin (2007), 'Symbols in Wittgenstein's *Tractatus*', *European Journal of Philosophy* 15

Jones, Ernest (1953), *The Life and Work of Sigmund Freud*, Vol. 2: *Years of Maturity: 1901–1919* (New York: Basic Books)

Jordan, Robert Welsh (1979), 'Das Transzendentale Ich als Seiendes in der Welt', *Perspektiven in der Philosophie 5*, available in translation at http://lamar.colostate.edu/~rwjordan/

(2004), 'Multiple Heideggers? An Early, Still Prevalent Misinterpretation', *Current Studies in Phenomenology and Hermeneutics*, available at http://lamar.colostate.edu/~rwjordan/

Joughin, Martin (1990), 'Translator's Preface', in Gilles Deleuze, *Expressionism in Philosophy: Spinoza*, trans. Martin Joughin (New York: Zone Books)

Kant, Immanuel (1992a), 'The Blomberg Logic', trans. J. Michael Young, in his *Lectures on Logic*, trans. and ed. J. Michael Young (Cambridge: Cambridge University Press)

(1992b), 'The Dohna-Wundlacken Logic', trans. J. Michael Young, in his *Lectures on Logic*, trans. and ed. J. Michael Young (Cambridge: Cambridge University Press)

(1992c), 'The Jäsche Logic', trans. J. Michael Young, in his *Lectures on Logic*, trans. and ed. J. Michael Young (Cambridge: Cambridge University Press)

(1993), *Opus Postumum*, ed. Eckart Förster and trans. Eckart Förster and Michael Rosen (Cambridge: Cambridge University Press)

(1996a), 'An Answer to the Question: What Is Enlightenment?', trans. Mary J. Gregor, in his *Practical Philosophy*, trans. and ed. Mary J. Gregor (Cambridge: Cambridge University Press)

(1996b), *Groundwork of the Metaphysics of Morals*, trans. Mary J. Gregor, in his *Practical Philosophy*, trans. and ed. Mary J. Gregor (Cambridge: Cambridge University Press)

(1996c), *Critique of Practical Reason*, trans. Mary J. Gregor, in his *Practical Philosophy*, trans. and ed. Mary J. Gregor (Cambridge: Cambridge University Press)

(1996d), 'On the Miscarriage of all Philosophical Trials in Theodicy', trans. George di Giovanni, in his *Religion and Rational Theology*, trans. and ed. Allen W. Wood and George di Giovanni (Cambridge: Cambridge University Press)

(1996e), *Religion Within the Boundaries of Mere Reason*, trans. George di Giovanni, in his *Religion and Rational Theology*, trans. and ed. Allen W. Wood and George di Giovanni (Cambridge: Cambridge University Press)

(1997), *Lectures on Metaphysics*, trans. Karl Ameriks and Steve Naragon (Cambridge: Cambridge University Press)

(1998), *Critique of Pure Reason*, trans. and ed. Paul Guyer and Allen W. Wood (Cambridge: Cambridge University Press)

(1999), *Correspondence*, trans. and ed. Arnold Zweig (Cambridge: Cambridge University Press)

(2000), *Critique of the Power of Judgment*, trans. Paul Guyer and Eric Matthews and ed. Paul Guyer (Cambridge: Cambridge University Press)

(2002a), *Prolegomena to Any Future Metaphysics That Will Be Able to Come Forward as a Science*, trans. Gary Hatfield, in Immanuel Kant, *Theoretical Philosophy After 1781*, ed. Henry Allison and Peter Heath (Cambridge: Cambridge University Press)

(2002b), *On a Discovery Whereby Any New Critique of Pure Reason Is to Be Made Superfluous by an Older One*, trans. Henry Allison, in Immanuel Kant, *Theoretical Philosophy After 1781*, ed. Henry Allison and Peter Heath (Cambridge: Cambridge University Press)

Kaufmann, Walter (1960), *From Shakespeare to Existentialism*, 2nd edn (New York: Doubleday)

(1967a), 'Editor's Introduction', in Friedrich Nietzsche, *The Will to Power*, trans. Walter Kaufmann and R.J. Hollingdale and ed. Walter Kaufmann (New York: Random House)

(1967b), 'On the Editions of *The Will to Power*,' in Friedrich Nietzsche, *The Will to Power*, trans. Walter Kaufmann and R.J. Hollingdale and ed. Walter Kaufmann (New York: Random House)

Keefe, Rosanna, and Peter Smith (1997), *Vagueness: A Reader* (Cambridge, Mass.: MIT Press)

Kierkegaard, Søren (1941), *Concluding Unscientific Postscript to the Philosophical Fragments*, trans. David F. Swenson and Walter Lowrie and ed. Walter Lowrie (Princeton, N.J.: Princeton University Press)

King, Magda (2001), *A Guide to Heidegger's* Being and Time, ed. John Llewelyn (Albany: State University of New York Press)

Kirk, Robert (1986), *Translation Determined* (Oxford: Oxford University Press)

Kolakowski, Leszek (1985), *Bergson* (Oxford: Oxford University Press)

Krausz, Michael (1972), 'The Logic of Absolute Presuppositions', in Michael Krausz (ed.), *Critical Essays on the Philosophy of R.G. Collingwood* (Oxford: Oxford University Press)

Krell, David Farrell (1986), *Intimations of Mortality: Time, Truth, and Finitude in Heidegger's Thinking of Being* (London: Pennsylvania State University Press)

Kremer, Michael (2001), 'The Purpose of *Tractarian* Nonsense', *Noûs* 35

Kripke, Saul (1981), *Naming and Necessity*, 2nd edn (Oxford: Blackwell)

Kundera, Milan (1984), *The Unbearable Lightness of Being*, trans. Michael Henry Heim (New York: Harper & Row)

Kuusela, Oskari (2005), 'From Metaphysics and Philosophical Theses to Grammar: Wittgenstein's Turn', *Philosophical Investigations* 28

Lacey, A.R. (1989), *Bergson* (London: Routledge)

Lakatos, Imre (1976), *Proofs and Refutations: The Logic of Mathematical Discovery*, ed. John Worrall and Elie Zahar (Cambridge: Cambridge University Press)

Lear, Jonathan (1984), 'The Disappearing "We"', *Proceedings of the Aristotelian Society* Suppl. Vol. 58

(1986), 'Transcendental Anthropology', in Philip Pettit and John McDowell (eds), *Subject, Thought, and Context* (Oxford: Oxford University Press)

(1988), *Aristotle: The Desire to Understand* (Cambridge: Cambridge University Press)

Leibniz, G.W. (1875–1890), *Die Philosophischen Schriften von Gottfried Wilhelm Leibniz*, ed. C.I. Gerhardt (Berlin: Weidemann Buchhandlung)

(1923–), *Sämtliche Schriften und Briefe*, ed. German Academy of Sciences (Darmstadt and Berlin: Akademie Verlag)

(1948), *Textes Inédits*, ed. Gaston Grua (Paris: Presses Universitaires de France)

(1956), 'Reflections on the Common Concept of Justice', in his *Philosophical Papers and Letters*, trans. and ed. Leroy E. Loemker (Chicago: University of Chicago Press)

(1962), 'Correspondence Between Leibniz and Arnauld', in his *Basic Writings*, trans. and ed. George Montgomery (La Salle, Ill.: Open Court)

(1973a), 'An Introduction to a Secret Encyclopedia', in his *Philosophical Writings*, ed. G.H.R. Parkinson and trans. Mary Morris and G.H.R. Parkinson (London: J.M. Dent & Sons)

(1973b), 'Of Universal Synthesis and Analysis; or, of the Art of Discovery and of Judgement', in his *Philosophical Writings*, ed. G.H.R. Parkinson and trans. Mary Morris and G.H.R. Parkinson (London: J.M. Dent & Sons)

(1973c), 'A Specimen of Discoveries About Marvellous Secrets of a General Nature', in his *Philosophical Writings*, ed. G.H.R. Parkinson and trans. Mary Morris and G.H.R. Parkinson (London: J.M. Dent & Sons)

(1973d), 'Primary Truths', in his *Philosophical Writings*, ed. G.H.R. Parkinson and trans. Mary Morris and G.H.R. Parkinson (London: J.M. Dent & Sons)

(1973e), 'Necessary and Contingent Truths', in his *Philosophical Writings*, ed. G.H.R. Parkinson and trans. Mary Morris and G.H.R. Parkinson (London: J.M. Dent & Sons)

(1973f), 'On Freedom', in his *Philosophical Writings*, ed. G.H.R. Parkinson and trans. Mary Morris and G.H.R. Parkinson (London: J.M. Dent & Sons)

(1973g), 'New System, and Explanation of the New System', in his *Philosophical Writings*, ed. G.H.R. Parkinson and trans. Mary Morris and G.H.R. Parkinson (London: J.M. Dent & Sons)

(1973h), 'On the Ultimate Origination of Things', in his *Philosophical Writings*, ed. G.H.R. Parkinson and trans. Mary Morris and G.H.R. Parkinson (London: J.M. Dent & Sons)

(1973i), 'A Résumé of Metaphysics', in his *Philosophical Writings*, ed. G.H.R. Parkinson and trans. Mary Morris and G.H.R. Parkinson (London: J.M. Dent & Sons)

(1973j), 'Metaphysical Consequences of the Principle of Reason', in his *Philosophical Writings*, ed. G.H.R. Parkinson and trans. Mary Morris and G.H.R. Parkinson (London: J.M. Dent & Sons)

(1973k), 'Monadology', in his *Philosophical Writings*, ed. G.H.R. Parkinson and trans. Mary Morris and G.H.R. Parkinson (London: J.M. Dent & Sons)

(1973l), 'Principles of Nature and Grace', in his *Philosophical Writings*, ed. G.H.R. Parkinson and trans. Mary Morris and G.H.R. Parkinson (London: J.M. Dent & Sons)

(1985), *Theodicy*, ed. Austin Farrar and trans. E.M. Huggard (La Salle, Ill.: Open Court)

(1989), 'On Contingency', in his *Philosophical Essays*, trans. Roger Ariew and Daniel Garber (Indianapolis, Ind.: Hackett Publishing)

(1996), *New Essays on Human Understanding*, trans. and ed. Peter Remnant and Jonathan Bennett (Cambridge: Cambridge University Press)

(1998), 'Discourse on Metaphysics', in his *Philosophical Texts*, trans. Richard Francks and R.S. Woolhouse (Oxford: Oxford University Press)

Leibniz, G.W., and Samuel Clarke (1956), *The Leibniz-Clarke Correspondence*, ed. H.G. Alexander (Manchester: Manchester University Press)

Lewis, David (1983a), *Philosophical Papers*, Vol. 1 (Oxford: Oxford University Press)

(1983b), 'Introduction', in his *Philosophical Papers*, Vol. 1 (Oxford: Oxford University Press)

(1983c), 'Anselm and Actuality', reprinted with postscripts in his *Philosophical Papers*, Vol. 1 (Oxford: Oxford University Press)

(1983d), 'Counterpart Theory and Quantified Modal Logic', reprinted with postscripts in his *Philosophical Papers*, Vol. 1 (Oxford: Oxford University Press)

(1983e), 'Survival and Identity', reprinted with postscripts in his *Philosophical Papers*, Vol. 1 (Oxford: Oxford University Press)

(1983f), 'Attitudes *De Dicto* and *De Se*', reprinted with postscripts in his *Philosophical Papers*, Vol. 1 (Oxford: Oxford University Press)

(1986a), 'Introduction', in his *Philosophical Papers*, Vol. 2 (Oxford: Oxford University Press)

(1986b), 'Abstract of *On the Plurality of Possible Worlds*', in 'Bibliography of the Writings of David Lewis', in his *Philosophical Papers*, Vol. 2 (Oxford: Oxford University Press)

(1986c), *On the Plurality of Worlds* (Oxford: Blackwell)

(1986d), *Counterfactuals*, 2nd edn (Oxford: Blackwell)

(1991), *Parts of Classes*, with an appendix written jointly with John P. Burgess and A.P. Hazen (Oxford: Blackwell)

(1998a), 'Statements Partly About Observation', reprinted in his *Papers in Philosophical Logic* (Cambridge: Cambridge University Press)

(1998b), 'Ayer's First Empiricist Criterion of Meaning: Why Does It Fail?', reprinted in his *Papers in Philosophical Logic* (Cambridge: Cambridge University Press)

(1999a), *Papers in Metaphysics and Epistemology* (Cambridge: Cambridge University Press)

(1999b), 'New Work for a Theory of Universals', reprinted in his *Papers in Metaphysics and Epistemology* (Cambridge: Cambridge University Press)

(1999c), 'Reduction of Mind', reprinted in his *Papers in Metaphysics and Epistemology* (Cambridge: Cambridge University Press)

(1999d), 'Elusive Knowledge', reprinted in his *Papers in Metaphysics and Epistemology* (Cambridge: Cambridge University Press)

(2002), *Convention: A Philosophical Study* (Oxford: Blackwell)

Lloyd, Genevieve (1993), *Being in Time: Selves and Narrators in Philosophy and Literature* (London: Routledge)

(1994), *Part of Nature: Self-Knowledge in Spinoza's* Ethics (Ithaca, N.Y.: Cornell University Press)

(1996), *Spinoza and the* Ethics (London: Routledge)

Locke, John (1965), *Essay Concerning Human Understanding*, ed. John Yolton (London: Dent)

Loeb, Louis E. (1990), 'The Priority of Reason in Descartes', *Philosophical Review* 98

(1992), 'The Cartesian Circle', in John Cottingham (ed.), *The Cambridge Companion to Descartes* (Cambridge: Cambridge University Press)

Lovejoy, Arthur O. (1964), *The Great Chain of Being: A Study of the History of an Idea* (Cambridge, Mass.: Harvard University Press)

Lowe, E.J. (1998), *The Possibility of Metaphysics: Substance, Identity, and Time*, 2nd edn (Oxford: Oxford University Press)

(2008), 'Two Notions of Being: Entity and Essence', in Robin Le Poidevin (ed.), *Being: Developments in Contemporary Metaphysics* (Cambridge: Cambridge University Press)

McDaniel, Kris (2009), 'Ways of Being', in David J. Chalmers, David Manley, and Ryan Wasserman (eds), *Metametaphysics: New Essays on the Foundations of Ontology* (Oxford: Oxford University Press)

McDonald, Peter (2006), 'Ideas of the Book and Histories of Literature: After Theory?', *Publications of the Modern Languages Association of America* 121

McDonough, Jeffrey K. (2010), 'Leibniz and the Puzzle of Incompossibility: The Packing Strategy', *Philosophical Review* 119

McDowell, John (1976), 'Truth Conditions, Bivalence and Verificationism', in Gareth Evans and John McDowell (eds), *Truth and Meaning: Essays in Semantics* (Oxford: Oxford University Press)

(1986), 'Singular Thought and the Extent of Inner Space', in Philip Pettit and John McDowell (eds), *Subject, Thought, and Context* (Oxford: Oxford University Press)

(1993), 'Wittgenstein on Following a Rule', in A.W. Moore (ed.), *Meaning and Reference* (Oxford: Oxford University Press)

(1996), *Mind and World*, 2nd edn (Cambridge, Mass.: Harvard University Press)

(1998), 'Mathematical Platonism and Dummettian Anti-Realism', reprinted in his *Meaning, Knowledge, and Reality* (Cambridge, Mass.: Harvard University Press)

(2007a), 'Dummett on Truth Conditions and Meaning', in R.E. Auxier and L.E. Hahn (eds), *The Philosophy of Michael Dummett* (Chicago and La Salle, Ill.: Open Court)

(2007b), 'On Pippin's Postscript', *European Journal of Philosophy* 15

McGinn, Colin (1979), 'An A Priori Argument for Realism', *Journal of Philosophy* 76

McGinn, Marie (1997), *Wittgenstein and the* Philosophical Investigations (London: Routledge)

(1999), 'Between Metaphysics and Nonsense: Elucidation in Wittgenstein's *Tractatus*', *Philosophical Quarterly* 49

(2006), *Elucidating the* Tractatus: *Wittgenstein's Early Philosophy of Logic and Language* (Oxford: Oxford University Press)

McGuiness, Brian (1990), *Wittgenstein: A Life – Young Ludwig (1889–1921)* (Harmondsworth: Penguin)

McMahon, Melissa (2005), 'Difference, Repetition', in Charles J. Stivale (ed.), *Gilles Deleuze: Key Concepts* (Chesham: Acumen)

McManus, Denis (2006), *The Enchantment of Words: Wittgenstein's* Tractatus Logico-Philosophicus (Oxford: Oxford University Press)

Makin, Gideon (2000), *The Metaphysics of Meaning: Russell and Frege on Sense and Denotation* (London: Routledge)

Malcolm, Norman (1982), 'Wittgenstein and Idealism', in Godfrey Vesey (ed.), *Idealism Past and Present* (Cambridge: Cambridge University Press)

Marion, Mathieu (1998), *Wittgenstein, Finitism, and the Foundations of Mathematics* (Oxford: Oxford University Press)

Martin, Rex (1998), 'Editor's Introduction', in R.G. Collingwood, *An Essay on Metaphysics with an Introduction and Additional Material*, ed. Rex Martin (Oxford: Oxford University Press)

Martin, Wayne M. (1997), *Idealism and Objectivity: Fichte's Jena Project* (Stanford, Calif.: Stanford University Press)

Matthews, H.E. (1982), 'Strawson on Transcendental Idealism', reprinted in Ralph C.S. Walker (ed.), *Kant on Pure Reason* (Oxford: Oxford University Press)

May, Todd (2005), *Gilles Deleuze: An Introduction* (Cambridge: Cambridge University Press)

Melia, Joseph (1991), 'Anti-Realism Untouched', *Mind* 100

(1995), 'On What There's Not', *Analysis* 55

(2003), *Modality* (Chesham: Acumen)

Mellor, D.H. (1998), *Real Time II* (London: Routledge)

Mercer, Christia (2001), *Leibniz's Metaphysics: Its Origins and Development* (Cambridge: Cambridge University Press)

Merleau-Ponty, M. (1962), *Phenomenology of Perception*, trans. Colin Smith (London: Routledge & Kegan Paul)

Millican, Peter (2002), 'Hume's Sceptical Doubts Concerning Induction', in Peter Millican (ed.), *Reading Hume on Human Understanding* (Oxford: Oxford University Press)

(2007), 'Humes Old and New: Four Fashionable Falsehoods, and One Unfashionable Truth', *Proceedings of the Aristotelian Society*, Suppl. Vol. 81

(2009), 'Hume, Causal Realism, and Causal Science', *Mind* 118

Mink, Louis O. (1969), *Mind, History, and Dialectic: The Philosophy of R.G. Collingwood* (Middletown: Wesleyan University Press)

(1972), 'Collingwood's Historicism: A Dialectic of Process', in Michael Krausz (ed.), *Critical Essays on the Philosophy of R.G. Collingwood* (Oxford: Oxford University Press)

Mohanty, J.L. (1982), *Frege and Husserl* (Bloomington: Indiana University Press)

Molière (1959), 'The Imaginary Invalid', in his *The Misanthrope and Other Plays*, trans. John Wood (Harmondsworth: Penguin)

Monk, Ray (1991), *Ludwig Wittgenstein: The Duty of Genius* (London: Vintage)

Moore, A.W. (1986), 'How Significant Is the Use/Mention Distinction?', *Analysis* 46

(1992), 'A Note on Kant's First Antinomy', *Philosophical Quarterly* 42

(1996), 'Philosophy of Logic', in Nicholas Bunnin and E.P. Tsui-James (eds), *The Blackwell Companion to Philosophy*, 2nd edn (Oxford: Blackwell)

(1997a), *Points of View* (Oxford: Oxford University Press)

(1997b), 'The Underdetermination/Indeterminacy Distinction and the Analytic/Synthetic Distinction', *Erkenntnis* 46

(2001a), *The Infinite*, 2nd edn (London: Routledge)

(2001b), 'Arguing with Derrida', in Simon Glendinning (ed.), *Arguing with Derrida* (Oxford: Blackwell)

(2002a), 'What Are These Familiar Words Doing Here?', in Anthony O'Hear (ed.), *Logic, Thought and Language* (Cambridge: Cambridge University Press)

(2002b), 'Quasi-Realism and Relativism', *Philosophy and Phenomenological Research* 65

(2002c), 'A Problem for Intuitionism: The Apparent Possibility of Performing Infinitely Many Tasks in a Finite Time', reprinted in Dale Jacquette (ed.), *Philosophy of Mathematics: An Anthology* (Oxford: Blackwell)

(2003a), *Noble in Reason, Infinite in Faculty: Themes and Variations in Kant's Moral and Religious Philosophy* (London: Routledge)

(2003b), 'Ineffability and Nonsense', *Proceedings of the Aristotelian Society*, Suppl. Vol. 77

(2003c), 'Williams on Ethics, Knowledge, and Reflection', *Philosophy* 78

(2006a), 'Williams, Nietzsche, and the Meaninglessness of Immortality', *Mind* 115

(2006b), 'The Bounds of Sense', *Philosophical Topics* 34, issue ed. James Conant

(2007a), 'Realism and the Absolute Conception', in Alan Thomas (ed.), *Bernard Williams* (Cambridge: Cambridge University Press)

(2007b), 'Wittgenstein and Transcendental Idealism', in Guy Kahane, Edward Kanterian, and Oskari Kuusela (eds), *Wittgenstein and His Interpreters: Essays in Memory of Gordon Baker* (Oxford: Blackwell)

(2009), 'Quine', in Christopher Belshaw and Gary Kemp (eds), *Twelve Modern Philosophers* (Oxford: Blackwell)

(2010a), 'Transcendental Idealism in Wittgenstein, and Theories of Meaning', reprinted in Daniel Whiting (ed.), *The Later Wittgenstein on Language* (London: Macmillan)

(2010b) 'Transcendental Doctrine of Method', in Paul Guyer (ed.), *The Cambridge Companion to Kant's 'Critique of Pure Reason'* (Cambridge: Cambridge University Press)

(2011), 'Wittgenstein on Infinity', in Marie McGinn and Oskari Kuusela (ed.), *The Oxford Handbook on Wittgenstein* (Oxford: Oxford University Press)

(forthcoming), 'Was the Author of the *Tractatus* a Transcendental Idealist?', in Michael Potter and Peter M. Sullivan (eds), *The* Tractatus *and Its History* (Oxford: Oxford University Press)

Moore, A.W., and Andrew Rein (1986), '*Grundgesetze*, Section 10', in Leila Haaparanta and Jaako Hintikka (eds), *Frege Synthesized: Essays on the Philosophical and Foundational Work of Gottlob Frege* (Dordrecht: Reidel)

Moore, F.C.T. (1996), *Bergson: Thinking Backwards* (Cambridge: Cambridge University Press)

Moore, G.E. (1953), 'What Is Philosophy?', in his *Some Main Problems of Philosophy* (London: George Allen & Unwin)

(1959), 'Wittgenstein's Lectures in 1930–33', reprinted in his *Philosophical Papers* (London: George Allen & Unwin)

Moran, Dermot (2000), *Introduction to Phenomenology* (London: Routledge)

(2003), 'Making Sense: Husserl's Phenomenology as Transcendental Idealism', in Jeff Malpas (ed.), *From Kant to Davidson: Philosophy and the Idea of the Transcendental* (London: Routledge)

(2005), *Edmund Husserl: Founder of Phenomenology* (Cambridge: Polity Press)

Morris, Michael (2006), *An Introduction to the Philosophy of Language* (Cambridge: Cambridge University Press)

(2008), *Wittgenstein and the* Tractatus (London: Routledge)

Morris, Michael, and Julian Dodd (2009), 'Mysticism and Nonsense in the *Tractatus*', *European Journal of Philosophy* 17

Moyal-Sharrock, Danièle (ed.) (2004), *The Third Wittgenstein: The Post-Investigations Works* (Aldershot: Ashgate)

Moyal-Sharrock, Danièle (2007), 'The Good Sense of Nonsense: A Reading of Wittgenstein's *Tractatus* as Non-Self-Repudiating', *Philosophy* 82

Mulhall, Stephen (1994), *Stanley Cavell: Philosophy's Recounting of the Ordinary* (Oxford: Oxford University Press)

(1996), *Heidegger and* Being and Time (London: Routledge)

(2005), *Philosophical Myths of the Fall* (Princeton, N.J.: Princeton University Press)

(2007), 'Words, Waxing and Waning: Ethics in/and/of the *Tractatus*', in Guy Kahane, Edward Kanterian, and Oskari Kuusela (eds), *Wittgenstein and His Interpreters: Essays in Memory of Gordon Baker* (Oxford: Blackwell)

Mullarkey, John (2004), 'Creative Metaphysics and the Metaphysics of Creativity', *Journal of the British Society for Phenomenology* 35

(2007), '"The Very Life of Things": Thinking Objects and Reversing Thought in Bergsonian Metaphysics', in Henri Bergson, *An Introduction to Metaphysics*, trans. T.E. Hulme and ed. John Mullarkey and Michael Kolkman (Basingstoke: Palgrave)

Murdoch, Iris (1993), *Metaphysics as a Guide to Morals* (Harmondsworth: Penguin)

Nagel, Thomas (1986), *The View from Nowhere* (Oxford: Oxford University Press)

(1997), *The Last Word* (Oxford: Oxford University Press)

Nehamas, Alexander (1985), *Nietzsche: Life as Literature* (Cambridge, Mass.: Harvard University Press)

Neiman, Susan (2002), *Evil in Modern Thought: An Alternative History of Philosophy* (Princeton, N.J.: Princeton University Press)

Neurath, Otto (1983), 'Protocol Statements', in his *Philosophical Papers 1913–1946*, ed. and trans. Robert S. Cohen and Marie Neurath (Dordrecht: Reidel)

Nietzsche, Friedrich (1967a), *On the Genealogy of Morals: A Polemic*, trans. Walter Kaufmann and R.J. Hollingdale, in his *On the Genealogy of Morals and Ecce Homo* (New York: Random House)

(1967b), *Ecce Homo: How One Becomes What One Is*, trans. Walter Kaufmann, in his *On the Genealogy of Morals and Ecce Homo* (New York: Random House)

(1967c), *The Will to Power*, trans. Walter Kaufmann and R.J. Hollingdale and ed. Walter Kaufmann (New York: Random House)

(1967d), *The Birth of Tragedy, or Hellenism and Pessimism*, trans. Walter Kaufmann, in his *The Birth of Tragedy and the Case of Wagner* (New York: Random House)

(1967–), *Werke: Kritische Gesamtausgabe*, ed. Giorgio Colli and Mazzino Montinari (Berlin: de Gruyter)

(1969), *Thus Spoke Zarathustra: A Book for Everyone and No One*, trans. R.J. Hollingdale (Harmondsworth: Penguin)

(1973), *Beyond Good and Evil: Prelude to a Philosophy of the Future*, trans. R.J. Hollingdale (Harmondsworth: Penguin)

(1974), *The Gay Science, with a Prelude in Rhymes and an Appendix of Songs*, trans. Walter Kaufmann (New York: Random House)

(1978), *Nachgelassene Fragmente: Herbst 1869–Herbst 1872*, ed. Giorgio Colli and Mazzino Montinari (Berlin: de Gruyter)

(1979), 'On Truth and Lies in a Nonmoral Sense', in his *Philosophy and Truth: Selections from Nietzsche's Notebooks of the Early 1870s*, trans. and ed. Daniel Breazeale (Sussex: Harvester Press)

(1982a), *Daybreak: Thoughts on the Prejudices of Morality*, trans. R.J. Hollingdale (Cambridge: Cambridge University Press)

(1982b), 'Postcard to Franz Overbeck from Sils Maria, 30 July 1881', in his *The Portable Nietzsche*, ed. and trans. Walter Kaufmann (New York: Viking Penguin)

(1983), *Untimely Meditations*, trans. R.J. Hollingdale (Cambridge: Cambridge University Press)

(1986), *Human: All Too Human: A Book for Free Spirits*, trans. R.J. Hollingdale (Cambridge: Cambridge University Press)

(1990a), *Twilight of the Idols, or How to Philosophize with a Hammer*, in his *Twilight of the Idols and The Anti-Christ*, trans. R.J. Hollingdale (Harmondsworth: Penguin)

(1990b), *The Anti-Christ*, in his *Twilight of the Idols and the Anti-Christ*, trans. R.J. Hollingdale (Harmondsworth: Penguin)

Nolan, Daniel (2005), *David Lewis* (Chesham: Acumen)

Norris, Christopher (1987), *Derrida* (London: Fontana)

Novalis (1892), *Schriften*, ed. Paul Kluckhohn (Leipzig)

Olson, Eric T. (2009), 'The Rate of Time's Passage', *Analysis* 69

O'Neill, Onora (1989), 'Reason and Autonomy in *Grundlegung* III', reprinted in her *Constructions of Reason* (Cambridge: Cambridge University Press)

Oresme, Nicole (1968), *Nicole Oresme and the Medieval Geometry of Qualities and Motions: A Treatise on the Uniformity and Difformity of Intensities Known as Tractatus de Configurationibus Qualitatum et Motuum*, trans. and ed. Marshall Clagett (Madison: University of Wisconsin Press)

Papineau, David (2009), 'The Poverty of Analysis', *Proceedings of the Aristotelian Society*, Suppl. Vol. 83

Parfit, Derek (1984), *Reasons and Persons* (Oxford: Oxford University Press)

(2004), 'Why Anything? Why This?', reprinted in Tim Crane and Katalin Farkas (eds), *Metaphysics: A Guide and Anthology* (Oxford: Oxford University Press)

Pattison, George (2005), *Thinking About God in an Age of Technology* (Oxford: Oxford University Press)

Pears, David (1971), *Wittgenstein* (London: Fontana)

(1987), *The False Prison: A Study of the Development of Wittgenstein's Philosophy*, Vol. 1 (Oxford: Oxford University Press)

(1990), *Hume's System: An Examination of the First Book of His Treatise* (Oxford: Oxford University Press)

Peirce, C.S. (1931–1958), *Collected Papers*, ed. Charles Hartshorne, Paul Weiss, and A.W. Burks (Cambridge, Mass.: Harvard University Press)

Philipse, Herman (1995) 'Transcendental Idealism', in Barry Smith and D.W. Smith (eds), *The Cambridge Companion to Husserl* (Cambridge: Cambridge University Press)

Pindar (1980), *Pindar's Victory Songs*, trans. Frank J. Nisetich (Baltimore: Johns Hopkins University Press)

Pinkard, Terry (1985), 'The Logic of Hegel's *Logic*', reprinted in Michael Inwood (ed.), *Hegel* (Oxford: Oxford University Press)

Pippin, Robert (1989), *Hegel's Idealism: The Satisfactions of Self-Consciousness* (Cambridge: Cambridge University Press)

(1996), 'Hegel's Metaphysics and the Problem of Contradiction', in Jon Stewart (ed.), *The Hegel Myths and Legends* (Evanston, Ill.: Northwestern University Press)

(2000), 'Fichte's Alleged Subjective, Psychological, One-Sided Idealism', in Sally Sedgwick (ed.), *The Reception of Kant's Critical Philosophy: Fichte, Schelling, and Hegel* (Cambridge: Cambridge University Press)

Plato (1961a), *Socrates' Defense (Apology)*, trans. Hugh Tredennick, in his *The Collected Dialogues of Plato, Including the Letters*, ed. Edith Hamilton and Huntington Cairns (Princeton, N.J.: Princeton University Press)

(1961b), *Meno*, trans. W.K.C. Guthrie, in his *The Collected Dialogues of Plato, Including the Letters*, ed. Edith Hamilton and Huntington Cairns (Princeton, N.J.: Princeton University Press)

(1961c), *Phaedrus*, trans. R. Hackforth, in his *The Collected Dialogues of Plato, Including the Letters*, ed. Edith Hamilton and Huntington Cairns (Princeton, N.J.: Princeton University Press)

(1961d), *Republic*, trans. Paul Shorey, in his *The Collected Dialogues of Plato, Including the Letters*, ed. Edith Hamilton and Huntington Cairns (Princeton, N.J.: Princeton University Press)

(1961e), *Theaetetus*, trans. F.M. Cornford, in his *The Collected Dialogues of Plato, Including the Letters*, ed. Edith Hamilton and Huntington Cairns (Princeton, N.J.: Princeton University Press)

(1961f), *Sophist*, trans. F.M. Cornford, in his *The Collected Dialogues of Plato, Including the Letters*, ed. Edith Hamilton and Huntington Cairns (Princeton, N.J.: Princeton University Press)

(1961g), *Timaeus*, trans. Benjamin Jowett, in his *The Collected Dialogues of Plato, Including the Letters*, ed. Edith Hamilton and Huntington Cairns (Princeton, N.J.: Princeton University Press)

Plutarch (1976), *Platonic Questions*, in his *Moralia*, Vol. 13, Pt I, trans. Harold Cherniss (Cambridge, Mass.: Harvard University Press)

Poellner, Peter (1995), *Nietzsche and Metaphysics* (Oxford: Oxford University Press)

Popper, Karl (1972), 'Epistemology Without a Knowing Subject', reprinted in his *Objective Knowledge: An Evolutionary Approach* (Oxford: Oxford University Press)

Potter, Michael (2000), *Reason's Nearest Kin: Philosophies of Arithmetic from Kant to Carnap* (Oxford: Oxford University Press)

Potter, Michael, and Timothy Smiley (2001), 'Abstraction by Recarving', *Proceedings of the Aristotelian Society* 101

Poxon, Judith L., and Charles J. Stivale (2005), 'Sense, Series', in Charles J. Stivale (ed.), *Gilles Deleuze: Key Concepts* (Chesham: Acumen)

Priest, Graham (1995), *Beyond the Limits of Thought* (Cambridge: Cambridge University Press)

Prior, Arthur N. (1993), 'Changes in Events and Changes in Things', reprinted in Robin le Poidevin and Murray MacBeath (eds), *The Philosophy of Time* (Oxford: Oxford University Press)

Proops, Ian (2001), 'The New Wittgenstein: A Critique', *European Journal of Philosophy* 9

——— (2005), 'Kant's Conception of an Analytic Judgment', *Philosophy and Phenomenological Research* 70

Putnam, Hilary (1975), 'The Analytic and the Synthetic', reprinted in his *Mind, Language and Reality: Philosophical Papers*, Vol. 2 (Cambridge: Cambridge University Press)

——— (1981), *Reason, Truth and History* (Cambridge: Cambridge University Press)

——— (1983), 'Analyticity and Apriority: Beyond Wittgenstein and Quine', reprinted in his *Realism and Reason: Philosophical Papers*, Vol. 3 (Cambridge: Cambridge University Press)

——— (1985), 'A Comparison of Something with Something Else', *New Literary History* 17

Quine, W.V. (1960), *Word and Object* (Cambridge, Mass.: MIT Press)

——— (1961a), 'On What There Is', reprinted in his *From a Logical Point of View: Logico-Philosophical Essays* (New York: Harper & Row)

——— (1961b), 'Two Dogmas of Empiricism', reprinted with amendments in his *From a Logical Point of View: Logico-Philosophical Essays* (New York: Harper & Row)

——— (1961c), 'The Problem of Meaning in Linguistics', in his *From a Logical Point of View* (New York: Harper & Row)

——— (1961d), 'Identity, Ostension, and Hypostasis', in his *From a Logical Point of View* (New York: Harper & Row)

——— (1961e), 'Logic and the Reification of Universals', in his *From a Logical Point of View* (New York: Harper & Row)

——— (1966a), 'Homage to Rudolf Carnap', reprinted in his *The Ways of Paradox and Other Essays* (New York: Random House)

——— (1966b), 'Truth by Convention', reprinted in his *The Ways of Paradox and Other Essays* (New York: Random House)

——— (1966c), 'Carnap and Logical Truth', reprinted in his *The Ways of Paradox and Other Essays* (New York: Random House)

——— (1969a), 'Ontological Relativity', in his *Ontological Relativity and Other Essays* (New York: Columbia University Press)

——— (1969b), 'Epistemology Naturalized', in his *Ontological Relativity and Other Essays* (New York: Columbia University Press)

——— (1969c), 'Existence and Quantification', in his *Ontological Relativity and Other Essays* (New York: Columbia University Press)

——— (1969d), 'Natural Kinds', in his *Ontological Relativity and Other Essays* (New York: Columbia University Press)

——— (1969e), 'Propositional Objects', reprinted in his *Ontological Relativity and Other Essays* (New York: Columbia University Press)

——— (1970), *Philosophy of Logic* (Englewood Cliffs, N.J.: Prentice-Hall)

——— (1974), *The Roots of Reference* (La Salle, Ill.: Open Court)

——— (1981a), 'Things and Their Place in Theories', in his *Theories and Things* (Cambridge, Mass.: Harvard University Press)

(1981b), 'Empirical Content', in his *Theories and Things* (Cambridge, Mass.: Harvard University Press)

(1981c), 'Five Milestones of Empiricism', in his *Theories and Things* (Cambridge, Mass.: Harvard University Press)

(1981d), 'On Austin's Method', reprinted in his *Theories and Things* (Cambridge, Mass.: Harvard University Press)

(1981e), 'Goodman's *Ways of Worldmaking*', reprinted in his *Theories and Things* (Cambridge, Mass.: Harvard University Press)

(1981f), 'Success and Limits of Mathematization', in his *Theories and Things* (Cambridge, Mass.: Harvard University Press)

(1981g), 'Responses', reprinted in his *Theories and Things* (Cambridge, Mass.: Harvard University Press)

(1986a), 'Reply to Roger F. Gibson, Jr', in L.E. Hahn and P.A. Schilpp (eds), *The Philosophy of W.V. Quine* (La Salle, Ill.: Open Court)

(1986b), 'Reply to Hilary Putnam', in L.E. Hahn and P.A. Schilpp (eds), *The Philosophy of W.V. Quine* (La Salle, Ill.: Open Court)

(1986c), 'Reply to Henryk Skolimowski', in L.E. Hahn and P.A. Schilpp (eds), *The Philosophy of W.V. Quine* (La Salle, Ill.: Open Court)

(1986d), 'Reply to Jules Vuillemin', in L.E. Hahn and P.A. Schilpp (eds), *The Philosophy of W.V. Quine* (La Salle, Ill.: Open Court)

(1987a), 'Creation', in his *Quiddities: An Intermittently Philosophical Dictionary* (Cambridge, Mass.: Harvard University Press)

(1987b), 'Future', in his *Quiddities: An Intermittently Philosophical Dictionary* (Cambridge, Mass.: Harvard University Press)

(1990), 'Comment on Stroud', in Robert B. Barrett and Roger F. Gibson (eds), *Perspectives on Quine* (Oxford: Blackwell)

(1992), *Pursuit of Truth*, revised edn (Cambridge, Mass.: Harvard University Press)

(1995a), *From Stimulus to Science* (Cambridge, Mass.: Harvard University Press)

(1995b), 'Reactions', in Paolo Leonardi and Marco Santambrogio (eds), *On Quine: New Essays* (Cambridge: Cambridge University Press)

(2008a), 'On the Reasons for Indeterminacy of Translation', reprinted in his *Confessions of a Confirmed Extensionalist and Other Essays*, ed. Dagfinn Føllesdal and Douglas B. Quine (Cambridge, Mass.: Harvard University Press)

(2008b), 'On Empirically Equivalent Systems of the World', reprinted in his *Confessions of a Confirmed Extensionalist and Other Essays*, ed. Dagfinn Føllesdal and Douglas B. Quine (Cambridge, Mass.: Harvard University Press)

(2008c), 'Facts of the Matter', reprinted in his *Confessions of a Confirmed Extensionalist and Other Essays*, ed. Dagfinn Føllesdal and Douglas B. Quine (Cambridge, Mass.: Harvard University Press)

(2008d), 'Indeterminacy of Translation Again', reprinted in his *Confessions of a Confirmed Extensionalist and Other Essays*, ed. Dagfinn Føllesdal and Douglas B. Quine (Cambridge, Mass.: Harvard University Press)

(2008e), 'Structure and Nature', reprinted in his *Confessions of a Confirmed Extensionalist and Other Essays*, ed. Dagfinn Føllesdal and Douglas B. Quine (Cambridge, Mass.: Harvard University Press)

(2008f), 'Naturalism; or, Living Within One's Means', reprinted in his *Confessions of a Confirmed Extensionalist and Other Essays*, ed. Dagfinn Føllesdal and Douglas B. Quine (Cambridge, Mass.: Harvard University Press)

Quine, W.V., and J.S. Ullian (1978), *The Web of Belief*, 2nd edn (New York: Random House)

Rajchman, John (2000), *The Deleuze Connections* (Cambridge, Mass.: MIT Press)

Ramsey, F.P. (1931), 'General Propositions and Causality', in R.B. Braithwaite (ed.), *F.P. Ramsey: The Foundations of Mathematics* (London: Routledge & Kegan Paul)

Rawls, John (1971), *A Theory of Justice* (Oxford: Oxford University Press)

Read, Rupert, and Kenneth A. Richman (2000), *The New Hume Debate* (London: Routledge)

Reginster, Bernard (2006), *The Affirmation of Life: Nietzsche on Overcoming Nihilism* (Cambridge, Mass.: Harvard University Press)

Reid, Lynette (1998), 'Wittgenstein's Ladder: The *Tractatus* and Nonsense', *Philosophical Investigations* 21

Rein, Andrew (1982), 'A Note on Frege's Notion of *Wirklichkeit*', *Mind* 91

Rescher, Nicholas (2000), *Kant and the Reach of Reason: Studies in Kant's Theory of Rational Systemization* (Cambridge: Cambridge University Press)

Rhees, Rush (ed.) (1984), *Recollections of Wittgenstein* (Oxford: Oxford University Press)

Richmond, Sarah (1996), 'Derrida and Analytical Philosophy: Speech Acts and Their Force', *European Journal of Philosophy* 4

Ricoeur, Paul (1968), 'The Critique of Subjectivity and Cogito in the Philosophy of Heidegger', in Manfred A. Fings (ed.), *Heidegger and the Quest for Truth* (Chicago: Quadrangle Books)

Rockmore, Tom (1994), 'Antifoundationalism, Circularity, and the Spirit of Fichte', in Daniel Breazeale and Tom Rockmore (eds), *Fichte: Historical Contexts/Contemporary Controversies* (Atlantic Highlands, N.J.: Humanities Press)

Roget, P.M. (1987), *Thesaurus of English Words and Phrases*, prepared by Betty Kirkpatrick (Harlow: Longman Group UK)

Rorty, Richard (1972), 'Indeterminacy of Translation and of Truth', *Synthese* 23

(1991), 'Is Natural Science a Natural Kind?', reprinted in his *Objectivity, Relativism, and Truth: Philosophical Papers*, Vol. 1 (Cambridge: Cambridge University Press)

(1992), 'Is Derrida a Transcendental Philosopher?' in David Wood (ed.), *Derrida: A Critical Reader* (Oxford: Blackwell)

Rousseau, Jean-Jacques (1959), *Oeuvres Complètes* (Paris: Gallimard)

Rumfitt, Ian (2007), 'Asserting and Excluding', in R.E. Auxier and L.E. Hahn (eds), *The Philosophy of Michael Dummett* (Chicago and La Salle, Ill.: Open Court)

Russell, Bertrand (1935–1936), 'The Limits of Empiricism', *Proceedings of the Aristotelian Society* 36

(1961), *History of Western Philosophy and Its Connection with Political and Social Circumstances from the Earliest Times to the Present Day*, 2nd edn (London: George Allen & Unwin)

(1980a), 'Letter to Frege, 16.06.1902', in Gottlob Frege, *Philosophical and Mathematical Correspondence*, ed. Brian McGuiness and trans. Hans Kaal (Chicago: University of Chicago Press)

(1980b), 'Letter to Frege, 12.12.1902', in Gottlob Frege, *Philosophical and Mathematical Correspondence*, ed. Brian McGuiness and trans. Hans Kaal (Chicago: University of Chicago Press)

(1992a), *A Critical Exposition of the Philosophy of Leibniz*, 2nd edn (London: Routledge)

(1992b), 'The Philosophy of Logical Atomism', in his *Logic and Knowledge* (London: Routledge)

(1992c), *The Principles of Mathematics* (London: Routledge)

(1993), 'Descriptions', reprinted in A.W. Moore (ed.), *Meaning and Reference* (Oxford: Oxford University Press)

(1998), *The Autobiography of Bertrand Russell* (London: Routledge)

(2009), *The Principles of Mathematics* (London: Routledge)

Sacks, Mark (2000), *Objectivity and Insight* (Oxford: Oxford University Press)

Sartre, Jean-Paul (2003), *Being and Nothingness: An Essay on Phenomenological Ontology*, trans. Hazel E. Barnes (London: Routledge)

Sattig, Thomas (2006), *The Language and Reality of Time* (Oxford: Oxford University Press)

Saussure, Ferdinand de (1983), *Course in General Linguistics*, trans. Roy Harris (London: Duckworth)

Savile, Anthony (2000), *Leibniz and the* Monadology (London: Routledge)

Schacht, Richard (1983), *Nietzsche* (London: Routledge)

(1995a), 'Beyond Nihilism: Nietzsche on Philosophy, Interpretation, and Truth', reprinted in his *Making Sense of Nietzsche: Reflections Timely and Untimely* (Chicago: University of Illinois Press)

(1995b), 'Beyond Scholasticism: On Dealing with Nietzsche and His *Nachlaß*', in his *Making Sense of Nietzsche: Reflections Timely and Untimely* (Chicago: University of Illinois Press)

(1995c), 'The Nietzsche-Spinoza Problem: Spinoza as Precursor?', reprinted in his *Making Sense of Nietzsche: Reflections Timely and Untimely* (Chicago: University of Illinois Press)

Schear, Joseph K. (2007), 'Judgment and Ontology in Heidegger's Phenomenology', *New Yearbook for Phenomenology and Phenomenological Philosophy* 7

Schelling, F.W.J. (1993), *System of Transcendental Idealism (1800)*, trans. Peter Heath (Charlottesville: University of Virginia Press)

Schiller, F.C.S. (1912), 'The Ethical Basis of Metaphysics', in his *Humanism: Philosophical Essays*, 2nd edn (London: Macmillan)

Schlick, Moritz (1938), 'Meaning and Verification', *Philosophical Review* 45

(1959a), 'The Turning Point in Philosophy', trans. David Rynin, reprinted in A.J. Ayer (ed.), *Logical Positivism* (Glencoe, Ill.: Free Press)

(1959b), 'Positivism and Realism', trans. David Rynin, reprinted in A.J. Ayer (ed.), *Logical Positivism* (Glencoe, Ill.: Free Press)

Schopenhauer, Arthur (1969a), *The World as Will and Representation*, Vol. 1, trans. E.F.J. Payne (New York: Dover)

(1969b), *The World as Will and Representation*, Vol. 2, trans. E.F.J. Payne (New York: Dover)

Scruton, Roger (2004), *Modern Philosophy: An Introduction and Survey* (London: Pimlico)

Searle, J.R. (1977), 'Reiterating the Differences: A Reply to Derrida', *Glyph* 1

Sellars, Wilfrid (1963), 'Philosophy and the Scientific Image of Man', reprinted in his *Science, Perception and Reality* (London: Routledge & Kegan Paul)

(1997), *Empiricism and the Philosophy of Mind* (Cambridge, Mass.: Harvard University Press)

Sheehan, Thomas (2003), 'Heidegger, Martin (1889–1976)', in Edward Craig (ed.), *Routledge Encyclopedia of Philosophy* (London: Routledge)

Sheppard, Darren (2001), 'The Reading Affair: On Why Philosophy Is Not '"Philosophical" Through and Through', in Simon Glendinning (ed.), *Arguing with Derrida* (Oxford: Blackwell)

Simondon, Gilbert (1964), *L'Individu et sa Genèse Physico-Biologique* (Paris: Presses Universitaires de France)

Simons, Peter (2000), 'The Four Phases of Philosophy: Brentano's Theory and Austrian History', *The Monist* 83

Skolimowski, Henryk (1986), 'Quine, Ajdukiewicz, and the Predicament of 20th Century Philosophy', in L.E. Hahn and P.A. Schilpp (eds), *The Philosophy of W.V. Quine* (La Salle, Ill.: Open Court)

Skorupski, John (1984), 'Dummett's Frege', in Crispin Wright (ed.), *Frege: Tradition and Influence* (Oxford: Blackwell)

(1999), 'Irrealist Cognitivism', *Ratio* 12

Sluga, Hans (2004), 'Heidegger's Nietzsche', in Hubert L. Dreyfus and Mark A. Wrathall (eds), *A Companion to Heidegger* (Oxford: Blackwell)

Smart, J.J.C. (1984), *Ethics, Persuasion and Truth* (London: Routledge & Kegan Paul)

Smith, A.D. (2003), *Husserl and the Cartesian Meditations* (London: Routledge)

Smith, Daniel W. (2001), 'The Doctrine of Univocity: Deleuze's Ontology of Immanence', in Mary Bryden (ed.), *Deleuze and Religion* (London: Routledge)

(2005), 'Deleuze on Leibniz: Difference, Continuity, and the Calculus', in Stephen H. Daniel (ed.), *Continental Theory and Modern Philosophy* (Evanston, Ill.: Northwestern University Press)

(2007), 'Deleuze and the Question of Desire: Toward an Immanent Theory of Ethics', *Parrhesia* 2

Smith, David Woodruff (2007), *Husserl* (London: Routledge)

Smith, William (1889), 'Memoir of Fichte', in J.G. Fichte, *The Popular Works of J.G. Fichte*, trans. William Smith, Vol. 1 (London: Trübner)

Snowdon, Paul (2006), 'P.F. Strawson: *Individuals*', in *Central Works of Philosophy*, Vol. 5: *The Twentieth Century: Quine and After*, ed. John Shand (Chesham: Acumen)

Soames, Scott (2009), 'Ontology, Analyticity, and Meaning', in David J. Chalmers, David Manley, and Ryan Wasserman (eds), *Metametaphysics: New Essays on the Foundations of Ontology* (Oxford: Oxford University Press)

Sokolowski, Robert (2000), *Introduction to Phenomenology* (Cambridge: Cambridge University Press)

Solomon, Robert C. (1970), 'Sense and Essence: Frege and Husserl', *International Philosophical Quarterly* 10

(1985), 'Hegel's Epistemology', reprinted in Michael Inwood (ed.), *Hegel* (Oxford: Oxford University Press)

Sonderreger, Ruth (1997), 'A Critique of Pure Meaning: Wittgenstein and Derrida', *European Journal of Philosophy* 5

Sotirin, Patty (2005), 'Becoming-Woman', in Charles J. Stivale (ed.), *Gilles Deleuze: Key Concepts* (Chesham: Acumen)

Spinoza, Benedictus de (1985), *The Collected Works of Spinoza*, Vol. 1, ed. and trans. Edwin Curley (Princeton, N.J.: Princeton University Press)

(2002a), *Treatise on the Emendation of the Intellect and on the Way in Which It Is Best Directed to the True Knowledge of Things*, in *Spinoza: Complete Works*, ed. Michael L. Morgan and trans. Samuel Shirley (Indianapolis, Ind.: Hackett Publishing)

(2002b), *Short Treatise on God, Man, and His Well-Being*, in *Spinoza: Complete Works*, ed. Michael L. Morgan and trans. Samuel Shirley (Indianapolis, Ind.: Hackett Publishing)

(2002c), *Ethics*, in *Spinoza: Complete Works*, ed. Michael L. Morgan and trans. Samuel Shirley (Indianapolis, Ind.: Hackett Publishing)

(2002d), *Political Treatise*, in *Spinoza: Complete Works*, ed. Michael L. Morgan and trans. Samuel Shirley (Indianapolis, Ind.: Hackett Publishing)

(2002e), *The Letters*, in *Spinoza: Complete Works*, ed. Michael L. Morgan and trans. Samuel Shirley (Indianapolis, Ind.: Hackett Publishing)

Spivak, Gayatri Chakravorty (1976), 'Translator's Preface', in Jacques Derrida, *On Grammatology*, trans. Gayatri Chakravorty Spivak (Baltimore, Md.: Johns Hopkins University Press)

Sprigge, T.L.S. (1997), 'Spinoza and Indexicals', *Inquiry* 40

Stambaugh, Joan (1972), *Nietzsche's Thought of Eternal Return* (Baltimore, Md.: Johns Hopkins University Press)

Stanley, Jason, and Timothy Williamson (2001), 'Knowing How', *Journal of Philosophy* 98

Stenius, Erik (1964), *Wittgenstein's Tractatus: A Critical Exposition of Its Main Lines of Thought* (Oxford: Blackwell)

Stern, Robert (2002), *Hegel and the Phenomenology of Spirit* (London: Routledge)

(2006), 'Metaphysical Dogmatism, Humean Scepticism, Kantian Criticism', *Kantian Review* 11

(2009), 'Hegel's Idealism', reprinted in his *Hegelian Metaphysics* (Oxford: Oxford University Press)

Stich, Stephen (1983), *From Folk Psychology to Cognitive Science: The Case Against Belief* (Cambridge, Mass.: MIT Press)

Strawson, Galen (1992), *The Secret Connexion: Causation, Realism, and David Hume*, 2nd edn (Oxford: Oxford University Press)

(2000), 'David Hume: Objects and Power', in Rupert Read and Kenneth A. Richman (eds), *The New Hume Debate* (London: Routledge)

Strawson, P.F. (1959), *Individuals: An Essay in Descriptive Metaphysics* (London: Methuen)

(1966), *The Bounds of Sense: An Essay on Kant's Critique of Pure Reason* (London: Methuen)

(1976–1977), 'Scruton and Wright on Anti-Realism', *Proceedings of the Aristotelian Society* 77

(1992), *Analysis and Metaphysics: An Introduction to Philosophy* (Oxford: Oxford University Press)

(1993), 'On Referring', reprinted in A.W. Moore (ed.), *Meaning and Reference* (Oxford: Oxford University Press)

(2008), 'Freedom and Resentment', reprinted in his *Freedom and Resentment and Other Essays* (London: Routledge)

Stroud, Barry (1977), *Hume* (London: Routledge & Kegan Paul)

    (1984), *The Significance of Philosophical Scepticism* (Oxford: Oxford University Press)

    (2000), *The Quest for Reality: Subjectivism and the Metaphysics of Colour* (Oxford: Oxford University Press)

    (2004), 'Replies', *Philosophy and Phenomenological Research* 68

Sullivan, Peter M. (1996), 'The "Truth" in Solipsism, and Wittgenstein's Rejection of the A Priori', *European Journal of Philosophy* 4

    (2002), 'On Trying to Be Resolute: A Response to Kremer on the *Tractatus*', *European Journal of Philosophy* 10

    (2003), 'Ineffability and Nonsense', *Proceedings of the Aristotelian Society*, Suppl. Vol. 77

    (2004), 'What Is the *Tractatus* About?', in Max Kölbel and Bernhard Weiss (eds), *Wittgenstein's Lasting Significance* (London: Routledge)

    (2007), 'Dummett's Case for Constructivist Logicism', in R. E. Auxier and L.E. Hahn (eds), *The Philosophy of Michael Dummett* (Chicago and La Salle, Ill.: Open Court)

    (forthcoming), in Michael Potter and Peter M. Sullivan (eds), *The* Tractatus *and Its History* (Oxford: Oxford University Press)

Tanesini, Alessandra (1995), 'Nietzsche's Theory of Truth', *Australasian Journal of Philosophy* 73

Tanner, Michael (1994), *Nietzsche* (Oxford: Oxford University Press)

Taylor, Charles (1975), *Hegel* (Cambridge: Cambridge University Press)

Thorburn, William (1918), 'The Myth of Ockham's Razor', *Mind* 27

Turetzky, Philip (1998), *Time* (London: Routledge)

    (2005), 'Pictorial Depth: Intensity and Aesthetic Surface', *Axiomathes* 15

van Cleve, James (1998), 'Foundationalism, Epistemic Principles, and the Cartesian Circle', in John Cottingham (ed.), *Descartes* (Oxford: Oxford University Press)

van Fraassen, Bas (2002), *The Empirical Stance* (New Haven, Conn.: Yale University Press)

van Inwagen, Peter (1981), *An Essay on Free Will* (Oxford: Oxford University Press)

    (1998), 'Lewis, David Kellogg', in Edward Craig (ed.), *Routledge Encyclopedia of Philosophy*, Vol. 5 (London: Routledge)

Voltaire (1990), *Candide*, in his *Candide and Other Stories*, trans. Roger Pearson (Oxford: Oxford University Press)

von Wright, G.H. (1958), 'A Biographical Sketch', in Norman Malcolm, *Ludwig Wittgenstein: A Memoir* (Oxford: Oxford University Press)

Waismann, Friedrich (1959), 'How I See Philosophy', reprinted in A.J. Ayer (ed.), *Logical Positivism* (Glencoe, Ill.: Free Press)

    (1968), 'Analytic-Synthetic', reprinted in his *How I See Philosophy*, ed. Rom Harré (London: Macmillan)

Walker, Ralph C. S. (1989), *The Coherence Theory of Truth: Realism, Anti-Realism, Idealism* (London: Routledge)

Walsh, W.H. (1975), *Kant's Criticism of Metaphysics* (Edinburgh: Edinburgh University Press)

Warnock, G.J. (1957), 'Criticisms of Metaphysics', in D.F. Pears (ed.), *The Nature of Metaphysics* (London: Macmillan)

(1969), *English Philosophy Since 1900*, 2nd edn (Oxford: Oxford University Press)

Wartenberg, Thomas E. (1993), 'Hegel's Idealism: The Logic of Conceptuality', in Frederick C. Beiser (ed.), *The Cambridge Companion to Hegel* (Cambridge: Cambridge University Press)

Weber, Max (1946), 'Science as a Vocation', in his *From Max Weber: Essays in Sociology*, trans. and ed. H.H. Gerth and C. Wright Mills (Oxford: Oxford University Press)

White, Morton (1952), 'The Analytic and the Synthetic: An Untenable Dualism', reprinted in Leonard Linsky (ed.), *Semantics and the Philosophy of Language* (Urbana: University of Illinois Press)

Whitehead, Alfred North, and Bertrand Russell (1927), *Principia Mathematica* (Cambridge: Cambridge University Press)

Whorf, Benjamin Lee (1956), 'An American Indian Model of the Universe', reprinted in his *Language, Thought and Reality: Selected Writings of Benjamin Lee Whorf*, ed. J.B. Carroll (Cambridge, Mass.: MIT Press)

Wiggins, David (1984), 'The Sense and Reference of Predicates: A Running Repair to Frege's Doctrine and a Plea for the Copula', in Crispin Wright (ed.), *Frege: Tradition and Influence* (Oxford: Blackwell)

(1988), '"The Concept of the Subject Contains the Concept of the Predicate"', in Judith Jarvis Thomson (ed.), *On Being and Saying: Essays for Richard Cartwright* (Cambridge, Mass.: MIT Press)

(1995), 'Categorical Requirements: Kant and Hume on the Idea of Duty', in Rosalind Hursthouse, Gavin Lawrence, and Warren Quinn (eds), *Virtues and Reasons: Philippa Foot and Moral Theory* (Oxford: Oxford University Press)

(1996), 'Sufficient Reason: A Principle in Diverse Guises, Both Ancient and Modern', in Simo Knuuttila and Ilkka Niiniluoto (eds), *Methods of Philosophy and the History of Philosophy, Acta Philosophica Fennica* 61

(2002), *Sameness and Substance Renewed* (Cambridge: Cambridge University Press)

(2004), 'Wittgenstein on Ethics and the Riddle of Life', *Philosophy* 79

(2007), 'Three Moments in the History of Definition or Analysis: Its Possibility, Its Aim or Aims, and Its Limit or Terminus', *Proceedings of the Aristotelian Society* 107

Williams, Bernard (1973a), 'Imagination and the Self', reprinted in his *Problems of the Self: Philosophical Papers 1956–1972* (Cambridge: Cambridge University Press)

(1973b), 'Are Persons Bodies?', reprinted in his *Problems of the Self: Philosophical Papers 1956–1972* (Cambridge: Cambridge University Press)

(1973c), 'Deciding to Believe', reprinted in his *Problems of the Self: Philosophical Papers 1956–1972* (Cambridge: Cambridge University Press)

(1978), *Descartes: The Project of Pure Enquiry* (Harmondsworth: Penguin)

(1981), 'Another Time, Another Place, Another Person', reprinted in his *Moral Luck: Philosophical Papers 1973–1980* (Cambridge: Cambridge University Press)

(1995a), 'Replies', in J.E.J. Altham and Ross Harrison (eds), *World, Mind, and Ethics: Essays on the Ethical Philosophy of Bernard Williams* (Cambridge: Cambridge University Press)

(1995b), 'Which Slopes Are Slippery?', reprinted in his *Making Sense of Humanity and Other Philosophical Papers 1982–1993* (Cambridge: Cambridge University Press)

(2002), *Truth and Truthfulness: An Essay in Genealogy* (Princeton, N.J.: Princeton University Press)

(2006a), 'The Women of Trachis: Fictions, Pessimism, Ethics', reprinted in his *The Sense of the Past*, ed. Myles Burnyeat (Princeton, N.J.: Princeton University Press)

(2006b), *Plato: The Invention of Philosophy*, reprinted in his *The Sense of the Past*, ed. Myles Burnyeat (Princeton, N.J.: Princeton University Press)

(2006c), 'Descartes' Use of Scepticism', reprinted in his *The Sense of the Past*, ed. Myles Burnyeat (Princeton, N.J.: Princeton University Press)

(2006d), 'Descartes and the Historiography of Philosophy', reprinted in his *The Sense of the Past*, ed. Myles Burnyeat (Princeton, N.J.: Princeton University Press)

(2006e), 'Hume on Religion', reprinted in his *The Sense of the Past*, ed. Myles Burnyeat (Princeton, N.J.: Princeton University Press)

(2006f), 'Nietzsche's Minimalist Moral Psychology', reprinted in his *The Sense of the Past*, ed. Myles Burnyeat (Princeton, N.J.: Princeton University Press)

(2006g), 'Introduction to *The Gay Science*', reprinted in his *The Sense of the Past*, ed. Myles Burnyeat (Princeton, N.J.: Princeton University Press)

(2006h), '"There Are Many Kinds of Eyes"', reprinted in his *The Sense of the Past*, ed. Myles Burnyeat (Princeton, N.J.: Princeton University Press)

(2006i), 'Unbearable Suffering', reprinted in his *The Sense of the Past*, ed. Myles Burnyeat (Princeton, N.J.: Princeton University Press)

(2006j), 'An Essay on Collingwood', in his *The Sense of the Past*, ed. Myles Burnyeat (Princeton, N.J.: Princeton University Press)

(2006k), 'Wittgenstein and Idealism', reprinted in his *The Sense of the Past*, ed. Myles Burnyeat (Princeton, N.J.: Princeton University Press)

(2006l), 'Metaphysical Arguments', reprinted in his *Philosophy as a Humanistic Discipline*, ed. A.W. Moore (Princeton, N.J.: Princeton University Press)

(2006m), 'Philosophy as a Humanistic Discipline', reprinted in his *Philosophy as a Humanistic Discipline*, ed. A.W. Moore (Princeton, N.J.: Princeton University Press)

(2006n), 'What Might Philosophy Become?', in his *Philosophy as a Humanistic Discipline*, ed. A.W. Moore (Princeton, N.J.: Princeton University Press)

(2006o), *Ethics and the Limits of Philosophy* (London: Routledge)

Williams, James (2003), *Gilles Deleuze's Difference and Repetition: A Critical Introduction and Guide* (Edinburgh: Edinburgh University Press)

(2008), *Gilles Deleuze's Logic of Sense: A Critical Introduction and Guide* (Edinburgh: Edinburgh University Press)

Williamson, Timothy (1994a), *Vagueness* (London: Routledge)

(1994b), 'Never Say Never', *Topoi* 13

(2007), *The Philosophy of Philosophy* (Oxford: Blackwell)

Winch, Peter (1987), 'Language, Thought and World in Wittgenstein's *Tractatus*', in his *Trying to Make Sense* (Oxford: Blackwell)

Witherspoon, Edward (2002), 'Logic and the Inexpressible in Frege and Heidegger', *Journal of the History of Philosophy* 40

Wittgenstein, Ludwig (1929), 'Some Remarks on Logical Form', *Proceedings of the Aristotelian Society* Suppl. Vol. 9

(1961), *Tractatus Logico-Philosophicus*, trans. D.F. Pears and B.F. McGuiness (London: Routledge & Kegan Paul)

(1965), 'A Lecture on Ethics', *Philosophical Review* 74

(1967a), *Philosophical Investigations*, trans. G.E.M. Anscombe, 3rd edn (Oxford: Blackwell)

(1967b), 'Letter to Ficker', in Paul Engelmann, *Letters from Ludwig Wittgenstein, with a Memoir*, ed. B.F. McGuiness and trans. L. Furtmüller (Oxford: Blackwell)

(1967c), *Zettel*, ed. G.E.M. Anscombe and G.H. von Wright and trans. G.E.M. Anscombe (Oxford: Blackwell)

(1969), *The Blue Book*, in *The Blue and Brown Books: Preliminary Studies for the 'Philosophical Investigations'*, 2nd edn (Oxford: Blackwell)

(1974a), *Philosophical Grammar*, ed. Rush Rhees and trans. Anthony Kenny (Oxford: Blackwell)

(1974b), *On Certainty*, ed. G.E.M. Anscombe and G.H. von Wright and trans. Denis Paul and G.E.M. Anscombe, revised edn (Oxford: Blackwell)

(1975), *Philosophical Remarks*, ed. Rush Rhees and trans. Raymond Hargreaves and Roger White (Oxford: Blackwell)

(1978), *Remarks on the Foundations of Mathematics*, ed. G.H. von Wright, R. Rhees, and G.E.M. Anscombe and trans. G.E.M. Anscombe, 3rd edn (Oxford: Blackwell)

(1979a), *Notebooks: 1914–1916*, ed. G.H. von Wright and G.E.M. Anscombe and trans. G.E.M. Anscombe, 2nd edn (Oxford: Blackwell)

(1979b), *Wittgenstein and the Vienna Circle*, notes recorded by F. Waismann, ed. B.F. McGuiness, and trans. J. Schulte and B.F. McGuiness (Oxford: Basil Blackwell)

(1980a), *Culture and Value*, ed. G.H. von Wright and Heikki Nyman and trans. Peter Winch (Oxford: Blackwell)

(1980b), *Wittgenstein's Lectures – Cambridge – 1930–1932: From the Notes of John King and Desmund Lee*, ed. Desmund Lee (Oxford: Blackwell)

(1995), *Cambridge Letters: Correspondence with Russell, Keynes, Moore, Ramsey, and Sraffa*, ed. Brian McGuiness and G.H. von Wright (Oxford: Blackwell)

(2006), 'The Nature of Philosophy', including extracts from *The Big Typescript*, trans. Anthony Kenny, in his *The Wittgenstein Reader*, ed. Anthony Kenny, 2nd edn (Oxford: Blackwell)

Wittgenstein, Ludwig, and Friedrich Waismann (2003), *The Voices of Wittgenstein: The Vienna Circle*, ed. Gordon Baker and trans. Gordon Baker, Michael Mackert, John Connolly, and Vasilis Politis (London: Routledge)

Wood, Allen W. (1970), *Kant's Moral Religion* (Ithaca, N.Y.: Cornell University Press)

Wood, David (1988), '*Différance* and the Problem of Strategy', in David Wood and Robert Bernasconi (eds), *Derrida and Différance* (Evanston, Ill.: Northwestern University Press)

(2001), *The Deconstruction of Time*, 2nd edn (Evanston, Ill.: Northwestern University Press)

Wright, Crispin (1982), 'Strict Finitism', *Synthese* 51

(1983), *Frege's Conception of Numbers as Objects* (Aberdeen: Aberdeen University Press)

(1992), *Truth and Objectivity* (Cambridge, Mass.: Harvard University Press)

(1998), 'Why Frege Did Not Deserve His *Granum Salis*: A Note on the Paradox of "The Concept Horse" and the Ascription of *Bedeutungen* to Predicates', in Johannes L. Brandl and Peter M. Sullivan (eds) 'New Essays on the Philosophy of Michael Dummett', *Grazer Philosophische Studien 55*

(2001), 'The Philosophical Significance of Frege's Theorem', reprinted in Bob Hale and Crispin Wright (eds), *The Reason's Proper Study: Essays Towards a Neo-Fregean Philosophy of Mathematics* (Oxford: Oxford University Press)

(2002), 'What Could Antirealism About Ordinary Psychology Possibly Be?', *Philosophical Review* 111

Young, Julian (2002), *Heidegger's Later Philosophy* (Cambridge: Cambridge University Press)

Yovel, Yirmiyahu (1989), *Spinoza and Other Heretics: The Adventures of Immanence* (Princeton, N.J.: Princeton University Press)

Zabludowski, Andrzey (1989), 'On Quine's Indeterminacy Doctrine', *Philosophical Review* 98

Zimmerman, Dean W. (2004), 'Prologue: Metaphysics After the Twentieth Century', *Oxford Studies in Metaphysics* 1

Zöller, Günter (2007), 'From Transcendental Philosophy to *Wissenschaftslehre*: Fichte's Modification of Kant's Idealism', *European Journal of Philosophy* 15

Index